KENTUCKY STATE HOUSES.

KENTUCKY.

A HISTORY OF THE STATE,

EMBRACING

A CONCISE ACCOUNT OF THE ORIGIN AND DEVELOPMENT OF THE VIRGINIA COLONY; ITS
EXPANSION WESTWARD, AND THE SETTLEMENT OF THE FRONTIER BEYOND
THE ALLEGHANIES; THE ERECTION OF KENTUCKY AS AN
INDEPENDENT STATE, AND ITS SUBSEQUENT
DEVELOPMENT.

—BY—

W. H. PERRIN.   J. H. BATTLE.   G. C. KNIFFIN.

FOURTH EDITION.

ILLUSTRATED WITH NUMEROUS ENGRAVINGS.

LOUISVILLE, KY., CHICAGO, ILL.:
F. A. BATTEY AND COMPANY
1887.

This volume was reproduced from
an 1887 edition located in the
Library of the Filson Club,
Louisville, Kentucky

Please Direct all Correspondence & Orders to:

Southern Historical Press, Inc.
P.O. Box 1267
375 West Broad Street
Greenville, S.C. 29602-1267

Originally published: Chicago, 1887
Reprinted with new material by,
Southern Historical Press, Inc.
Greenville, S.C., 1979 & 1998
New Material Copyright © 1979 by
The Rev. Silas Emmett Lucas, Jr.
Easley, S.C.
All Rights Reserved.
ISBN # 0-89308-136-1
Printed in the United States of America

PREFACE.

THE purpose and design of this volume have been the presentation of the history of Kentucky in narrative form, its adaptation to the tastes and demands of the general reader, and, as far as consistent, to incorporate statistical facts for the benefit of those who would seek in its pages reference matter.

In the preparation of the work, the desire of the publishers has been to give to their patrons a history conscientiously prepared, and a volume faithfully executed in all its aspects. Much of the subject matter incorporated was submitted, before its publication, to those who were deemed critics upon the topics treated, in order to detect if possible any errors of statement that might inadvertently creep in. That perfection has been attained in *all* of our efforts we do not claim, but we do hold that a fair measure of accuracy and completeness has been reached, consistent with a work of this magnitude.

Those who are interested in the very exciting events which transpired in Kentucky during the period of the civil war, and in which her troops took part elsewhere, will find a fund of information between the covers of this book which has not heretofore been accessible to the general public, and much that has never before been published in any form. The difficulties to be overcome in collecting this material were almost insurmountable, owing to the fragmentary and chaotic condition of the documentary sources at command. Especially was this the case with that which had reference to the Confederates and their service.

Appendix B, which is almost wholly made up of statistical matter pertaining to army service, is taken largely from the State Adjutant-General's reports, and though possibly containing some inaccuracies in names and dates, has been corrected in some particulars, and is presented in as nearly a perfect form as possible.

THE PUBLISHERS

BIOGRAPHICAL SKETCHES.

(ILLUSTRATED ELSEWHERE.)

MILTON BARLOW was born at Flemingsburg, Fleming Co., Ky., February 6, 1818. The family to which he belongs is of French origin, having left France with the Huguenots, after the revocation of the edict of Nantes, and settled first in England, coming thence to America at an early period. His grandfather, William Henry Harris Barlow, resided at Lynchburg, Va., and immigrated to Kentucky from that State with the earliest settlers. He located near Millersburg, in Nicholas County, where he took up a large tract of land, and erected a block-house. He was surrounded by hostile savages, and his primitive dwelling was often used as a citadel of defense against their attacks. He married Elizabeth Kimbrough, daughter of another early settler in that locality, and had a family of seven children, of whom the sons were Samuel, William, James, Thomas H., John and Harrison. Betsey became the wife of Lawson Bell, and Sarah of his brother, Hosea Bell. Thomas H. Barlow was the father of Milton, and was born in the year 1787. He was reared upon his father's farm, and in early life enlisted in Johnson's regiment during the war of 1812–15, being present at the battle of the Thames. He subsequently engaged in farming; and being possessed of great mechanical ingenuity and skill turned his attention to the building of steam mills, and at Augusta, Ky., built a steamboat. He erected a steam mill at Cynthiana, Ky., and later established a foundry and machine shop at Lexington, where he chiefly manufactured saw-mill machinery and steam engines. He made the machinery for the Red River furnace, and in May, 1826, exhibited at Lexington a small locomotive which he had designed and made from his own model, without having seen one. About the year 1838 he built a steam mill in Lincoln County, which he operated for a time in conjunction with his son Milton, and later returned to Lexington, where he engaged successfully in the preparation of hemp for naval rope-making purposes—his son being also associated in this enterprise. Soon after he began work upon an instrument, afterward called a planetarium, which was an ingenious mechanical device, designed to illustrate, in a practical way, the motions of the heavenly bodies, and showing the relation which they sustained to each other at different seasons of the year, as well as to the sun and moon. After three years of study and experiment, assisted by Mr. Van Dalsem, Prof. Dodd, president of the university, and his son, to whom its mechanical construction and perfection was assigned, the instrument was completed, and pronounced a wonderful invention by those public educators of the country to whom it was shown. It was adopted by the United States Congress for West Point and Annapolis Academies, for which a complimentary prize of $4,000 was paid. New Orleans, Mississippi University, St. Louis and Washington Lee Universities and many other leading institutions of learning of this country were supplied with fine planetariums prior to the late war, which suspended the manufactory. In 1843 father and son conceived the idea of building a rifle-cannon, and after careful experiments completed it, and procured a patent on it in January, 1855. On August 30, 1856, an appropriation of $3,000 was made by Congress to furnish a gun to the Government which was tested, accepted, and the patent adopted for general use. Thomas H. Barlow died in Cincinnati near the close of the late civil war. He was pre-eminently a man of genius and great usefulness, and left the impress of his intellectual strength upon the men and institutions of his time. His wife was Keziah West, and his children, Milton, Samuel and Elizabeth. Milton Barlow at the age of twelve years was set to work in his father's shop. When about fourteen years of age he manufactured a low pressure steam engine with glass air pump and condenser for Rev. Benjamin O. Pears, who was the head of an excellent private school in Lexington, and by way of payment received $150 and three sessions of schooling. Upon the breaking out of the war between Texas and Mexico he enlisted under Gen. Gaines in Capt. Carter's company at Lexington, Ky. (for Fort Sabine), the expedition for the protection of our southwestern frontier; and upon the disbandment of his regiment returned home by way of New Orleans as a river engineer. He subsequently worked in the machine shop of Bridgeford & Hanson at Louisville, then engaged in milling in Lincoln County with his father, and finally manufactured silver-ware in Lexington for several years. He was the operative constructor of the planetarium, to which reference has been made, and prior to the opening of the war engaged in its manufacture at Lexington, disposing very readily of eighty-two of them in the United States. He exhibited it at the great Crystal Palace exhibition in New York in 1855. The breaking out of the civil war sadly disarranged all of his plans. Being opposed to both secession and coercion it was his intention to remain neutral, but having been placed under arrest by the Federal authorities in Lexington, and subjected to indignities, he espoused the cause of the South, and served in the Confederate Army, first under Gen. Abe Beauford, and later as captain of ordnance under Morgan. After the close of the war he resumed his residence in Kentucky. The planetarium was selected by the Kentucky Legislature as Kentucky's most suitable contribution to the International Exhibition at Paris, France, in 1867, contributing $1,500 to defray expenses, etc. During the exposition Mr. Barlow visited France, patented the planetarium and caused a manufactory to be established in Paris. At the close of the exhibition the planetarium was awarded the highest premium given to any illustrative apparatus. Thus Kentucky has furnished the world with the best illustrative astronomical apparatus. Returning to the United States Mr. Barlow located at Richmond, Ky., where he built a residence and large flouring-mill, which he is now successfully operating. He inherited his father's inventive genius, and has always been engaged in the conception or manufacture of some mechanical contrivance. He recently petitioned Congress to allow him to make a large gun for the Government coast-defense, to demonstrate the advantages of a new improvement he has designed, and which he thinks will prove efficacious against any ship that can be sent against us. Mr. Barlow was married on May 20, 1845, to Anastasia C., daughter of Lewis A. Thompson, of Lexington, Ky., and has had nine children, of whom seven are living, viz.: Margaret, Virginia, Carrie, Milton V., Richard A., Robert E. Lee and Florence Barlow.

ORMOND BEATTY, LL. D. In a history of Kentucky meant, in part at least, to contain notices or sketches of her distinguished and useful men, it would leave a blank which would astonish many, and be an injustice to a very learned and able man, to omit from its pages the name of President Beatty, a native of the State, well born and well raised, and who, from boyhood to old age, has been a beloved and honored teacher in her foremost institution of learning, the presidency of which he has recently resigned, at seventy-one years of age, on account of failing health. To make good the foregoing intimations in this attempted sketch will fill up the space allotted to the writer. The name of Beatty seems to indicate that the family were Scotch people; and one of the descendants of a late generation, whilst traveling in Scotland, ascertained that they were so and that the name, after the Scotch fashion, was orginally spelled Beattie. Those of them who came first to America settled in New York at Esopus, a point on the Hudson. About the year 1730, one of them, William Beatty, became a citizen of Frederick County, Md., where he owned land on which he settled and resided until his death. His son, William Beatty, Jr., who inherited the place, was born there on the 17th of January, 1739. In the year 1743, John Conrad Grosh and his family, German people from Mayence on the Rhine, settled five miles away from William Beatty, in Fredericktown, his eldest daughter, Mary, being then just four years old. In the year 1757, when they were each eighteen years old, these two, William Beatty, Jr., and Mary Dorathea Grosh, were married, too early, as it seems to the writer on some accounts, for they had sixteen children, and raised them all, twelve sons and four daughters. Three of the older sons distinguished themselves in the wars with England, and handsome notices of them can be found in the histories of the country. Young William Beatty, the eldest son of them, held a commission in the regular army and was killed in a charge at the head of his regiment, about the age of twenty-two, in the second battle of Camden; and Gen. Green, who belonged to the Southern Army, said of him, as Chief Justice Marshall has recorded with evident pride, in his life of Washington, that "he was an ornament to his profession." The writer heard some of his letters from the army read by one of his brothers with streaming eyes sixty years after their dates. Judge Adam Beatty, the twelfth child of this family, was the father of Dr. Beatty, the subject of this sketch. He was named after a brother of his mother, Adam Grosh. The second sister of Judge Beatty, Sophia, some years older than himself, had married Col. Nathaniel Rochester, a merchant of Hagerstown, Md., who subsequently founded the city of Rochester, N. Y., and left a large family there of most exemplary and accomplished sons and daughters. Judge Beatty in boyhood was a clerk in his store, having first, no doubt, been a helper along with his brothers in the cultivation of the farm. It is certain he was at work about something. Two elder brothers, Cornelius and Otho, had come to Kentucky and settled here, Cornelius at Lexington. Judge Beatty was born on the 10th of May, 1777, and it must have been when he was about grown that he made up his mind to come to Kentucky to study law and try his fortunes in this new land; and another branch of the family came to Kentucky at an early day and perhaps added to the allurements which brought Judge Beatty. Peter Grosh, the eldest brother of Mrs. Beatty, married Mary Charlton, whose children were three daughters and a son. They lost their mother before they were grown, and their home after her death was mainly the house of their aunt, Mrs. Beatty. The eldest of these sisters, Eleanor Grosh, married Thomas Hart of Kentucky. Sophia, the next, married Edward Porter Clay, a brother of the great senator. The other, Catherine, married John W. Hunt, of Fayette County, and their descendants of many names have always been among the foremost people of the commonwealth. No doubt accounts from all these went back to Maryland and had something to do with the hopes and schemes which brought Judge Beatty here, and about the beginning of the century he got to Lexington, where he became a clerk in the store of his brother, Cornelius, and, at the same time, a law student in the office of Judge James Brown. As early as 1802 he had come to Washington, Mason County, and begun the practice of his profession, for there is a letter from his mother to him at that place now before the writer, dated May 7, 1803, and there are other evidences of the same date. July 2, 1804, he was married to Miss Sally Green, eldest daughter of Capt. John Green, also a Marylander, who came

with his family to Kentucky only a few years earlier than Judge Beatty came. It was in the year 1811, when he was thirty-four years of age, that he was appointed by Gov. Scott to his office of circuit judge of the district in which he lived. Soon afterward he moved to his farm near by, on which most of his children were born and where he lived the rest of his long life, a happy, useful, studious and distinguished man, and, for many of his last years, a religious man. His family consisted of five sons, who grew up with perhaps the one disadvantage of not having a sister in their midst; but they were not without the good influences of female care and watchfulness; for surely no family of boys ever owed more to the management and training of a mother. She put no pettish restraints on boyish playfulness and she often joined them in their merriment and mirth; but somehow or other, without temper and without severity, she had a way of keeping them from all manner of misconduct and apparently from even an inclination to it. All the good lessons of innocence and purity, of industry and manliness, were taught by mother and father; and they were permitted to live to see five noble intellects and noble characters of usefulness, influence and distinction developed as the result, in good part, no doubt, of those lessons of early life. It was a friendly, cordial, affectionate, hospitable home, where the best of people from far and near were visitors and friends; and the writer supposes that not one of those who belonged to it carried away when he left it the recollection of one scene in the family life there which deserved reproach. It was on this farm and at this home, that Dr. Beatty, as was said before, was well born and well raised. He had heredity to help him and the environment also of that home and its memories, which are no mean aids, it must be admitted, in the case of a boy who is making his start; but they are a long distance away from the point he has reached, as could be easily shown by a capable pen, without exaggeration or the least departure from the honest truth. He was born on the 13th of August, 1815, and is the fourth son in his father's family. His chief preparation for college was at the old Franklin Academy in the town of Washington, when Mr. David V. Rannells was the teacher, to and from which he used to walk a distance of two and a half miles every school day without much concern for weather. Riding to school and staying at home in ugly weather had not then become the fashion. The way to Centre College in those days was a rough stage ride, on a dirt road, of two days; and the University of Ohio, at Athens, was more accessible; and the question was the choice between the two. There was a young schoolmate, however, who was starting to Athens, and the two trunks were packed for the latter place. Some mere accident, it is now forgotten what, perhaps low water in the river, changed the arrangement and changed with it every step in Dr. Beatty's subsequent life, made up of a few years as student and of fifty years as professor and president at Centre College. Ten thousand chances and more to one, without that accident, that the life of this honored and most useful man would have been as little like his actual life, as if he had been a different being. The writer has heard him tell the story with serious tone, as if he felt, as another has said, that there is a power above ourselves "which shapes our ends." In 1832 he entered the Freshman class in Centre College; but before the session was out he was put in the class above, with which he graduated in 1835, his classmates being Thomas Walker Fry, William W. Hill, John Montgomery, William N. Todd and Samuel H. Woodson. Rev. John C. Young had recently been made the young president of the college, when there was a lack both of professors and students. It was to aid in supplying the former want, that Dr. Young gave notice to Mr. Beatty, during the last year of his course, that he had chosen him to join the faculty, when he quit the class—a repetition of the very thing which happened in the case of his eldest brother, William Rochester Beatty, in the time of Dr. Holly, at Transylvania University. Dr. Young's offer, after consultation, was accepted, though the other was declined. A born lawyer, in that case, chose another profession. After spending a year with old Dr. Silliman at Yale, Dr. Beatty returned to Danville and became professor of chemistry and natural philosophy. This was in the year 1836, when he was just twenty-one years old. Very profound studies, as every student knows, belong to that department; but notwithstanding the youth of the teacher, the student who failed to master them had nobody to blame but himself. He kept this place eleven years until 1847, when the professor of mathematics resigned and when also they could find a professor of chemistry and natural science, but nobody for mathematics, except Dr. Beatty, and, accordingly, he was made professor of mathematics; and if there was a puzzle in that science, almost the whole of which is a puzzle to most men even of ability, which he could not solve, it is the belief of the writer that

nobody ever found it out. It was this chair that he always liked the most. In 1852 there was a reversal of the trouble—a mathematician could then be found and not a man for chemistry and natural philosophy except, again, Prof. Beatty, and he took once more his original chair. This remained his place for the next twenty years, when in 1872 he became president and the teacher of metaphysics and political science, etc., where nobody discovered deficiencies any more than they had been discovered elsewhere in his other places.

The truth is, as all his students know, he trod with firm step as teacher almost the whole curriculum, just as it lay before him in boyhood, when he was only learning the route. It was a good accident which carried Dr. Beatty to Danville—good for himself, good for Centre College and for the multitude of students who have been educated there in the last fifty years. His own life has been a placid and happy one, only disturbed by the deaths which have occurred in his family. The college has had his long and useful services and the students are wiser and better men on account of his wise instruction and friendly counsel, for which they are spreading his fame all over the land—both by what they are saying in praise of him and by what, as gentlemen and scholars, they are exhibiting in their own lives of the advantages of education; and it cannot be inappropriate to add here expressions about him recently made by two of the distinguished alumni of the college. At the meeting of the alumni at Danville, June, 1885, Hon. William C. P. Breckinridge delivered the address and said concerning Dr. Beatty: "I am chary of laudation to the living or of eulogy to the present, but it would do violence to myself and to my brethren, present and absent, if I failed to note that this closes the half century since Ormond Beatty received his degree of Bachelor of Arts, and in full health, 'his eye not dim,' nor 'his natural force abated,' he fills with conscientious dutifulness and singular accuracy the position he has so long and so ably occupied. May it be many years before some brother alumnus shall, in the presence of another assembly, speak of his completed labors and finished life. May I be pardoned for saying that such a life in the midst of such a community, through so many years, given to such labors with such success, is a rare fortune—fruitful labors in recurring years brought added esteem and accumulated confidence; a life where the sower lived to see so many harvests; a career like unto a tropical orange tree, where golden fruit, ripening orange and fragrant blossom give the reward of toil, the certainty of success and the fair promise of abundance. Such a life and such a career are indeed enviable and are only to the laborious, the dutiful and the able.'' Dr. Beatty had tendered his resignation to the trustees to take effect at the close of the session in the summer of 1886, and it had been resolved by a number of the alumni, that, at their meeting this summer, some public and general expression of their regard for him should be made, but this was prevented by severe affliction in his family. The address, however, which was meant for the occasion, was delivered by the Hon. John F. Phillips of Missouri and a few sentences of it, which are to the point here, are as follows: ''There doubtless have been and are men your superiors in specialties, but I trust you will take no offense at what your known modesty may deem excessive laudation, when I speak my honest convictions in saying, that I much question whether there lives to-day a man of letters who has exhibited such versatility of learning with so much of completeness in different branches of scholarship as yourself. Whether in the laboratory expounding the natural sciences in physics and chemistry, or as president, unfolding mental science and metaphysics, or in polemics, touching political economy, statecraft, the problems of government and current political history, you have adorned every chair and proved a foeman worthy of any man's steel, and, Doctor, a number of the alumni of Centre College have raised a fund of $1,000 for the purpose of constituting 'the Ormond Beatty Prize.' One object of its creation is to produce among the young who shall matriculate at this college a generous rivalry in those noble contests where mind meets mind in the struggle for intellectual supremacy. It is but a small token of their esteem for you. It originated in a desire, if possible, to connect the more inseparably your name with the most pleasing struggles and triumphs of college life. In the name of its generous donors I now commit it to your charge.'' Let nobody conclude, the writer begs, from what has been said or from what has been omitted, that this wonderfully clear-headed teacher has been the mere reflector of other men's thoughts. That would be the very opposite of the truth. You might strip him of all that he has gotten from other men and there would be much more of him left than was taken away. He has always stood on his own feet, as much apart from mere authority as any teacher to be found, with capacity as great to reject what

ought not to be learned as to acquire what deserved to be stored away; and, when he became a dissenter from authority as he often did, his reasons were given with a clearness and force which will never be forgotten by any sensible student who heard them. These traits were most distinctly personal and characteristic. Dr. Beatty has besides remarkable talents as a speaker and debater, which have often been felt and acknowledged by many able men who have encountered him in the discussions of almost all conceivable subjects of human thought in the famous old club at Danville, where the celebrated Joshua F. Bell used to say, he ''had heard speeches from Dr. Beatty, any one of which, if made in the United States Senate, would have won a national reputation in a single week.'' Within a few days a very able man, who is a great speaker, himself, and was once a member of that club, was heard to say that Dr. Beatty is the greatest debater he ever heard. But justice to others, as well as the truth itself, requires it to be said that to Dr. Young more than any man besides must the success of Centre College be attributed, and they require it to be said also that many scholarly and able men beside Dr. Beatty, who have been in the faculty from time to time, have contributed their shares to the work which has been done; and there is one only reason why no mention has been made of others, and that is, that this is simply an attempted sketch of Dr. Beatty. In conclusion it should, perhaps, be said that the degree of A. M. was given Dr. Beatty by his own college in 1847 and the degree of LL. D. by Princeton College, in 1868, but these at most do not signify much, though it should be remembered that the latter came from Princeton; and came, as the writer feels sure, unsought, to a man who never sought anything but to do his duty. If that can be said of anybody, it can as well be said of Dr. Beatty.

LINDSAY HUGHES BLANTON, D. D., chancellor of Central University, Ky., was born in Cumberland County, Va., January 29, 1832, and is the second son of Joseph and Susan (Walker) Blanton. Joseph Blanton was born in Cumberland County, Va., in 1805. He was educated in Virginia and became a large and prosperous planter. He was an active Whig before the war, but afterward affiliated with the Democratic party. He died in 1881. He was a son of David Blanton, a native of Caroline County, Va., and of English extraction and died when yet a young man. He had married Lucy Johns, a native of Cumberland County, Va.

She was an intelligent and well informed lady and lived to be over ninety years old. Her ancestors came from England in the early settlement of Virginia. Susan (Walker) Blanton was born in Cumberland County, Va., in 1814, and was a daughter of John W. Walker, who married Susan Berryman. John Walker was a substantial planter and died young, leaving a son and a daughter. His father was William Walker, a native of Virginia, who distinguished himself under Gen. George Washington, in the war of Independence. He is the great-grandfather also of Judge Thomas H. Hines, of Kentucky, and was of Scotch extraction.

Dr. Blanton was educated at Hampden Sidney College, Virginia, from which institution he was graduated in the class of 1853. His theological training was received at the Union Theological Seminary and at Danville Theological Seminary, from which latter institution he was graduated in 1857. He was soon after licensed to preach, and ordained and installed as pastor of the Presbyterian Church of Versailles, Ky., in 1858, where he continued in the performance of successful pastoral work until the fall of 1861, when, owing to his warm sympathy for the South in the prevailing civil contest between the States, he resigned his pastorate and returned to Virginia and was settled as pastor of the church in Salem, Roanoke County, and continued such until 1868. In the spring of 1863 the Doctor entered the army and became chaplain of the Fifty-fourth Virginia Regiment of Infantry, serving under Gen. S. B. Buckner, in his East Tennessee campaign. The next year he joined the Twenty-sixth Battalion of Gen. Echols' brigade and went through the great campaign of 1864, under Gen. John C. Breckinridge, first in the valley and then with Gen. Lee in his struggle with Grant, his battalion taking a prominent part in the bloody battle of Cold Harbor. In the fall of 1868 he returned to Kentucky and was installed as pastor of the Paris Presbyterian Church, and continued in that relation until July, 1880, when he was chosen chancellor of Central University, and removed to Richmond, Madison County.

It is due to Dr. Blanton to say that he brought to the administration of the affairs of Central University a degree of energy, skill, and executive ability that have resulted in placing that institution on a sound footing and in a most favorable state of development as an institution for the higher education of young men. The number of students in attendance has increased from forty in 1880 to nearly 200 in 1887, and the amount of money raised during that period for permanent endowment, and other purposes, aggregates $180,000. The Doctor is known and respected throughout the State as a man of intense earnestness in his chosen work of building up the university, and his success is due not less to his wide reputation for integrity and his high Christian character, than to the energy and executive capacity which he has manifested in the development of its interests. As an educator of youth he stands in the foremost rank in the State; and to his success as a pastor the prosperity of the churches over which he presided as pastor, bear ample evidence.

In October, 1857, he was united in marriage to Lizzie M. Irvine, of Boyle County, Ky., a daughter of Abraham D. and Mary P. (Irvine) Irvine, of Fayette County. They are of Scotch-Irish descent and their ancestors came to America in the same vessel with the McDowells. To the Doctor and Mrs. Blanton have been born six children: Mary, the wife of E. M. Dickson, Esq., a prominent young lawyer of Paris, Ky.; Irvine, also an attorney at Cynthiana, Ky.; Rutherford, Edgar, Katie and Harry.

GEN. JEREMIAH TILFORD BOYLE was born in Mercer (now Boyle) County, Ky., in May, 1818, and was the son of Chief Justice John Boyle, so long recognized as one of the leading jurists of the State. His mother was a Miss Tilford, a name well known in Kentucky. He was educated with great care, and completed his course at the College of New Jersey, Princeton, from which well known institution he was graduated. Subsequent to that time he attended the law department of Transylvania University, Lexington, Ky., whence he was also graduated in due course of time. He at first located in the practice of his profession at Harrodsburg, but after the county of Boyle was set off and Danville became the county seat, he removed to that place, where he engaged successfully in practice until 1861. He was appointed commonwealth's attorney, but resigned that position in order to attend to his private practice. He attained distinction at the bar, and was recognized as an eloquent advocate and an excellent counselor. Some years after removing to Danville he married a daughter of Hon. Simeon Anderson, of Garrard County, and subsequently engaged in business with his brother-in-law, William C. Anderson, of Danville, who at one time represented his district in Congress. In the great contest preparatory to the election of delegates to frame a new constitution for the State in 1849, Gen. Boyle advocated with great zeal the emancipation of the slaves, and both by his pen and eloquence before the people, proved himself one of the ablest champions of that cause in the State. When the civil war commenced, he gave his support to the cause of the Union, and raised a regiment for service. For meritorious conduct in the field, in 1862 he was promoted to brigadier-general, and was soon after placed in command of the department of Kentucky, assuming the direction of military affairs in the State. This position, peculiarly trying to a native Kentuckian, owing to his love of justice and great magnanimity of character, he discharged with singular faithfulness and met the approval of the Government and of those in the State who appreciated the motives of his action. He participated in the battle of Shiloh, commanding a brigade in Nelson's division. After having served with distinction for several years in the department of Kentucky, he resigned, being actuated by the unpleasant nature of the duties which his command imposed upon him. He was a man of untiring energy, and everything calculated to promote the material prosperity of the State found in him an able and willing advocate. He was the first person to urge the construction of street railways in Louisville, and, perhaps, owing to him that city now possesses its excellent system of roads. He was president of and organized the original company, and under his direction the first street railroad was built in that city, and that at a time when almost insurmountable difficulties surrounded the undertaking. Soon after the close of the civil war, Gen. Boyle took hold of the Edgefield, Henderson & Nashville Railroad, which had been dragging along with great difficulty for several years, and with his usual zeal imparted life to the enterprise. He visited Europe to negotiate with the French stockholders of the road, and so successful was he that he was able to prosecute the work with great rapidity to its completion. He subsequently devoted himself with great vigor to the inauguration of the narrow-gauge system in Kentucky, and by his presentation of the subject gained the favorable attention of the public. He was a man of great firmness of character, engaged with enthusiasm in whatever he undertook, and seldom failed in his purpose. He had good administrative ability, was generous and charitable to a fault, assisting unsparingly those in need. In his private life he was strongly attached to the domestic circle, and was a consistent professor of Christianity. He died in Louisville,

Ky., July 28, 1871, leaving a wife and seven children. His eldest son, Col. Wm. O. Boyle, known as the "Boy Major," served with distinction in the war, and fell at the head of his brigade at the battle of Marion, Tenn., December 18, 1865. He was the most youthful officer of his rank in the Federal Army.

CHARLES CALDWELL. The name of Caldwell is an honorable one in American annals. No family made a brighter record for patriotism and bravery during the war of the Revolution and in the trying pioneer times, when the States were coming into shape on new soil. From Rhode Island to Florida and as far west as Texas, this family extends to-day, growing out of the parent stock described in this sketch. Stanch defenders of Presbyterianism they have been friends of education, influential in politics and useful members of society. The earliest record of the Caldwell family relates to three brothers, John, Alexander and Oliver, who were seamen on the Mediterranean in the latter part of the fourteenth century under two men named Barbarossa. The influence of the latter was ended by the governor of Aran, after about twenty years, and those connected with them scattered over the world. The three brothers returned to Toulon, in France, where they had been born, and settled near by, at Mount Arid. Earning the enmity of Francis I of France, after his escape from imprisonment under Charles V, of Germany, the brothers were again forced to change their location. Going to Scotland they purchased, near Solway Firth, the estate of a bishop named Douglass, with the consent of James I, on condition that the said brothers, John, Alexander and Oliver, late of Mount Arid, should have their estate known as "Cauldwell," and when the king should require they should each send a son with twenty men of sound limbs to aid in. the wars of the king. An heirloom is a cup, from which it. is seen that the estate took its name from a watering-place. The cup represents a chieftain and twenty mounted men, all armed, and a fire burning on a hill over the words "Mount Arid," and a vessel surrounded by high waves. Joseph, John Alexander, Daniel, David and Andrew, of Cauldwell, went with Oliver Cromwell (whose grandmother was Ann of Cauldwell) to Ireland, of which he was the lord governor. After his promotion to the protectorate of England they remained in his interest in Ireland until the restoration of Charles II, when John, David and Andrew fled to America. Joseph died in Ireland and Daniel continued there, but several of their children immigrated to America, settling on James River, Va., and elsewhere. Another account renders it improbable that the last John, mentioned above, came to America. His son, John Caldwell (as the name had come to be spelled), married Margaret Phillips in County Derry, Ireland, where several children were born to them. December 10, 1727, they landed at Newcastle, Del., going thence to Lancaster County, Penn., and about 1742 in Lunenburg (now Charlotte) County, Va. Here they were joined by relatives, forming what was known as the "Caldwell Settlement" for many years. John Caldwell was the first justice of the peace, and his son, William, the first militia officer commissioned by George II for that section. He died and was buried by the side of his wife in 1750. Their children were William, Thomas,, David, Margaret, John, Robert and James. Each of these men contributed some things to American history. James Caldwell, D. D., the seventh child, one of the founders of Princeton College, was murdered by British soldiers at Elizabethtown, N. J., and his descendants received, by way of pensions, clerkships at Washington for many years. Two of his sons led in founding the Liberia colonization scheme, and gave name to Caldwell, Liberia. Martha, daughter of William Caldwell, became the mother of John Caldwell Calhoun, the statesman. The whole family was distinguished for patriotism during the war of the Revolution. One son, John, died lieutenant-governor; was buried at Frankfort, and honored with a monument at public expense. He gave name to Caldwell County, of which he was an early settler. Samuel was a major-general in the war of 1812, and the first clerk of Logan County court. Both were members of the Legislature frequently, as was Robert, who presided in the House when the famous resolutions of 1798 were adopted. The latter's daughter, Eliza, became the wife of O. H. Browning, Lincoln's Secretary of the Interior. Mary, daughter of Robert[6], married Dr. R. C. Palmer, David[3] Caldwell was buried in the old churchyard in Lunenburg County, and his widow with her children settled at the point marked "Caldwell's Station" (near Danville) on Filson's map of Kentucky of 1784. One of the sons was John, who married Dicey Mann, having descendants David, William Beverly, Polly and Phœbe. Robert[6] moved from Virginia in 1781 and settled where William L. Caldwell now resides, near Danville. He took up several thousand acres of land at that point and was identified with the pioneer life and early settlement of what was then Mercer County. He married Mary Logan and had a large family of children, who have occupied various positions of responsibility and trust in Kentucky. He led a plain and unostentatious life; was early identified with the Presbyterian Church at its first development in his locality and many of the early religious meetings of that body were held in his primitive, yet substantial dwelling. This ancient building, which was probably erected soon after his first settlement, is still standing on the farm of his grandson, William L. Caldwell, and is now used as a barn. It was a large building constructed of hewn logs, sealed with cherry plank sawed by hand and joined by handmade nails. Robert Caldwell died in 1806, and his remains were interred upon the farm where he had passed the greater part of his industrious life. William Caldwell, one of his sons, married a Miss Wickliffe, a sister of Gov. Wickliffe; was an extensive farmer, and in his business and social relations commanded the respect and confidence of a large circle of friends. He had but two children, Lydia, who married a Mr. McCord of Washington County, and the late Charles Caldwell of Boyle County. The latter, whose name appears at the head of this sketch, received a good English education in his youth, and upon attaining manhood married Elizabeth, daughter of Jeremiah Clemens of Danville, and shortly after settled on the farm where his grandson, Jeremiah C. Caldwell, now resides. He was one of the most prominent and successful farmers Boyle County has ever had, and became widely known as one of the largest and most extensive cattle raisers and cattle feeders for the markets of the East. He also speculated extensively in pork, at one time buying and packing large quantities. He was a man of decidedly methodical and systematic turn of mind, industrious, frugal and thrifty, of undoubted integrity and uprightness of character, an elder in the Danville Presbyterian Church, a trustee of Centre College, and a prompt and liberal supporter of all worthy evangelical and charitable objects. He died in the possession of a large estate accumulated by the exercise of these virtues, which all admire but few emulate, and by the provision of his will left liberal bequests to the Caldwell Female College of Danville, and the Theological Seminary of that place. His only son, Jeremiah Caldwell, married Margaret Wilson of Bardstown, and spent his life in agricultural pursuits on his father's farm. He had two children: Charles, who died in boyhood, and Jeremiah C. Caldwell who passed away at the age of twelve years. The larger portion of the estate of Charles Caldwell was devised to his grandson, Jeremiah C. Caldwell. He received a thorough English education at Centre College, Danville, but being designed by his grandfather to engage in farming operations, did not pursue the entire curriculum. He was early inured to a life of industry, and under the careful and judicious guardianship of William Logan Caldwell developed such a stability of character and such a decided capacity for the intelligent transaction of business, that the trustees of his grandfather's estate put him in possession of it nine years before they were compelled to do so, and he is to-day one of the largest and most successful farmers in Boyle County, a large handler of cattle for the Eastern markets and a prominent business man. He has inherited many of the characteristics of his grandfather, takes a lively interest in church and educational matters, and is the president of the Farmers' National Bank of Danville. He occupies his grandfather's farm, and is the seventh in line of descent from John Caldwell, who immigrated to this country in 1727. The line of descent is as follows: John, William, Robert, William Charles, Jeremiah, Jeremiah C. Caldwell. The latter married Annie Belle, daughter of Judge Fontaine T. Fox of Danville, and has four children: Charles Wickliffe, Eliza Hunton, Jeremiah Clemens and Fontaine Fox Caldwell. William Logan Caldwell is the fifth in line of descent from John Caldwell, whose emigration to this country together with the full genealogy of the family is described in the preceding sketch. His grandfather was Robert Caldwell, and his father James, the son of Robert[6]. The story of the early settlement of the latter on the place now occupied by the subject of this sketch, has already been told. James Caldwell was the youngest son of Robert and led an active and industrious career as a farmer on the old place. He was a man of strong convictions, of original and forceful ideas, an uncompromising follower of Henry Clay, and an advocate of the gradual emancipation of the slave. He was a devout man and a useful member and elder of the Cumberland Presbyterian Church near Danville, of which he was a liberal supporter. He died in February, 1850. He was married three times, first to Mary, daughter of Gov. Slaughter, of whom were born three sons and one daughter, who have now all passed away. For his second wife he married Phœbe, daughter of John and Elizabeth Henderson and a representative of an old Virginia family, by whom he had two sons, Rev. Robert H. Caldwell, a Presbyterian clergyman of Boyle County, and William Logan Caldwell. His third wife was Phœbe Caldwell, a distant relative of his family, who died without issue. William Caldwell, to whom this sketch is chiefly dedicated, was born on the ancestral place where he now resides, March 13, 1827. He received a good English education, and at the age of sixteen was placed in charge of his father's farm. Upon the death of the latter in 1850 he inherited the family homestead and has since devoted all his energies to its cultivation and improvement. He is a man of high character, of generous impulses and unswerving rectitude, and it can be truthfully said of him that no man in Boyle County is more worthy of the esteem of his fellows, nor enjoys in a higher degree their confidence and respect. He has been the executor of many trusts, which he administered with fidelity and satisfaction; has led a simple, blameless life, carefully avoided public station and undue notoriety and confined himself strictly to the legitimate phases of agricultural life. As a farmer he is both successful and progressive, and is recognized as one of the leading breeders of "jacks" and "jennets" in the United States. He is also an extensive breeder of high class cattle and hogs and of thorough stock in general. He is a member of the board of directors of the Central Kentucky Stock Association and sends a monthly report of the condition of the farming districts of the State to the Department of Agriculture at Washington. He is an elder in the Cumberland Presbyterian Church of Boyle County, a director in the Boyle National Bank at Danville, a commissioner of the State Deaf and Dumb Asylum at the same place, and president of several turnpike companies. Politically he was formerly an old line Whig, but now acts with the Democratic party. During the civil war he was true to the Union cause, and even when surrounded by the officers and troops of the South, boldly proclaimed his fidelity to the general constitution of our country and his faith in the ultimate triumph of the national arms. He was married, in November, 1847, to Ellen B., daughter of Eli Crumbaugh, of Caldwell County, Ky., and has had nine children, of whom eight survive: James B., who occupies a farm adjoining his father's; Robert C., a practicing physician at Bloomfield, Ky.; Nannie C., who is ardently engaged in home missionary work and travels extensively; William L., Jr., who resides with his father; Ella, widow of Dr. R. C. Palmer, Jr.; Maria, who resides at home; Obadiah B., a student in Centre College, and Lucy E., a student in Caldwell College.

COL. WILLIAM H. CAPERTON

was born on King's branch of Muddy Creek, in Madison County, Ky., in March, 1798. He was of the best French and Virginia stock. His ancestors on both the paternal and maternal sides were distinguished in the colonial and Revolutionary periods of American history, and afterward in the border wars, with the Indians of Kentucky. When he was about ten years old his father removed to the State of Tennessee, and during the second war with Great Britain, though only sixteen years old, he volunteered as a soldier, and in the Creek campaign, under Jackson, was found in the line of his duty, participating in the battles of Horse Shoe and Talladega. On the restoration of peace he removed to the county of his birth, and studied law with his uncle, Archibald Woods, Esq., and was admitted to the bar of the Madison Circuit Court in the year 1818. Col. Caperton had no advantage of a collegiate course, or of the instruction of a law school, but he studied the elementary books, and his strong common sense and popular manners gave him business at once. From the date of his admission to the bar until a few months before his death, he was connected with the most important cases in the circuit in which he practiced, and was often called to a distance, where the fame of his legal abilities and his splendid forensic powers as an advocate, had gone. It is believed in one branch of the profession, the department of criminal law, for success in which the highest intellectual abilities are demanded, he had few equals in the State; both as an advocate and prosecutor he was alike eminent. Those who heard him in the case of the Commonwealth vs. Baker, in Clay; vs. Davidson, in Rockcastle; vs. Barnes, in Madison; vs. Shelby in Fayette, in all of which he was matched against the first men in Kentucky, will remember the terrible power with which he lashed crime and vindicated public justice; and his arguments in behalf of many charged with similar offenses, easily recalled, attest the power of his eloquence, his pathos, and his logic in wresting his clients from the stern exactions of the law.

But it was not in this sphere alone that Col. Caperton acquired reputation. In causes involving the validity of wills, in the preparation of chancery causes, in which the most careful labor was requisite, he was not less successful. In all, he was ready, able, logical, and more so than almost any other man whom the writer can recall. He was felicitous in the application of an apparently exhaustless fund of wit and anecdotes. Among the members of the bar, he was always a favorite, with kind words for the young and struggling members of the profession, and genial courtesy for all.

In the year 1828 Col. Caperton was induced to serve the people in the Legislature, and was among the able men of that body; the peer of the proudest, and most distinguished. He was in his political opinions always conservative and patriotic, indoctrinated in the political opinions of Washington, Madison and Jay, and throughout his life, the ardent political and personal friend of Henry Clay. His labors on the stump in 1840 for Harrison, in 1844 for Clay, and in 1848 for Taylor, were effective, and widely known all over the State. They were wholly disinterested, too, for he sought no office. It was the earnest wish of his friends, to give him the nomination for governor of the State, which he remonstrated against; but, unsolicited by him, the office of United States district attorney was in 1850 conferred on him by President Taylor, accepted by him, and its duties discharged with fidelity, and ability. Upon the election of Mr. Pierce being known, he tendered his resignation of that office, and till his death sought no other, but in private life made himself the life of every social party in which he moved, and at his home was the kindest of husbands and fathers.

We may add that through the struggles connected with the great attempt to overturn the Government of the country, he was the steadfast friend of the Union, the Constitution, and the laws. During Jackson's campaign, he was sent out with some friendly Indians as scouts. About dark one evening in a swamp, where they had stopped to go into camp for the night, while getting some dry bark from a fallen tree to make the camp fire, he was bitten by a large rattle-snake, he at once informed the Indians and they rapidly scattered in the swamp, and soon returned with some leaves, and told him to chew them, swallow the juice, and apply the pulp to the bitten part, which he at once did, and although suffering greatly with pain, and his swollen limb, the next morning he was able to resume the march and soon got well. He never did know the kind of leaves the Indians used, but that it stopped the effects of the deadly poison and saved his life, he well knew.

During the same campaign, he was given by some Indians what they called a "mad stone;" it was about the size of a large chestnut, of a bluish color, rather soft and porous. He kept it up to a short time before his death, when it was in some unaccountable manner lost; its virtues, if it had any, were never tested. He was present at the surrender of Pensacola to Jackson, and saw the Spanish flag hauled down, and the American flag run up, and take its place.

When not fully grown he commenced to learn the stone-mason's business with John Parish, and his brother, Westly Parish. He worked only a few days, then threw down his hammer, and said "this business don't suit me," and went at once to read law with his uncle, Archie Woods. Nothing afforded Col. Caperton more real pleasure than an out-door life, free from business cares, confinement of a law office, or professional engagements, enjoying the beauties of nature; and the wilder and more solitary the scene, the more it was appreciated and enjoyed by him.

On one occasion, after a great and excited criminal trial, lasting many days, and after he had made one of those powerful and eloquent speeches, for which he was so famous, full of rare eloquence, and falling like a great trip hammer crushing everything in its way, entrancing judge, jury, audience and bar— he said to a friend he was going to the far off wild mountains hunting with some friends, and he wanted to get to some place, for the time being, where civilization was for the time blotted out, where no house-dog could be heard to bark, chicken crow, nor the sound of the axe in the forest heard, but wanted to enjoy nature in its silent wildness, listening to the wild notes of the mountain birds, the solemn caw of the raven, the howl of the wolf at night, and see and enjoy the wild mountain scenery, and gaze upon its beautiful waters, pure and crystal. This was his nature; he was created so by his Maker, God, and he enjoyed it above all earthly honors. He was a fine rifle shot at game, and fond of hunting deer in the prime of life, by nature and pratice a splendid woodsman, and could not be lost in the forest. Deer in the mountains were plenty then, and, in the fall, when the white frosts came, and the leaves changed to a redden hue and began to fall, it was his pleasure every fall to go to the mountains "deer hunting," still hunting, or stalking, as it is called in some countries, with such friends as Col. David Irvine, Col. William Rodes, William J. Walker, Judge Daniel Breck, Col.

William Holloway, John W. Walker, of Garrard County, and others, and camp out in the dark forest, near some pure running water, creek or branch. At night, around the camp fire, each would graphically tell of the day's hunt, tell jokes, spin yarns, and make themselves pleasant and agreeable to each other, and after a royal supper, frequently on a fallen log, of fresh venison, bear meat, wild turkey, hot coffee in tin cups and "Johnny cake," they would lie down on their blankets, with their saddles for pillows, and have that sweet sleep and rest unknown in this day of luxury and ease; these were all marked men of their day, all dead now, but had sense enough while living to have some enjoyment and pleasure in their own way, free from the business cares and worry of active life. Upon their return from their mountain hunt, a round of gaieties and pleasure commenced. At their different homes they would all meet, and with other invited friends have "venison suppers," having a whole saddle of venison cooked and placed at the head of the table, and again talk over their hunt, tell jokes, and enjoy themselves greatly. Col. Caperton, in the latter part of his life, when the wild deer in the mountains could no longer be found, went twice each year, spring and fall, to the mountain streams, fishing with his friends Holloway, John W. Parks, William W. Smith (the latter yet living), James Boggs and others, and they often caught very large pike, salmon and bass, and out of the fishing season he would often, on rainy days, join his friend Boggs, and ride on horseback over the fields, in the eastern part of the county, netting partridges, those fine birds then being plenty in the county.

He never cared for money, but always made enough by his profession to gratify every reasonable want of himself and family. He lived in a princely and lavish style, and entertained relatives and friends royally. To his friends he was kind and true, never refusing a favor asked, great or small, and never did any human being knowingly a wrong. To his wife and children, it is doubtful whether any man that ever lived was more kind, affectionate and devoted. He absolutely worshiped them, providing for their every want or even desire without a thought of the word "no," and it gratified him and made him more happy to do it. When any of his family were sick he turned himself into a nurse, remaining by them in their sick bed, calling in the most skillful medical aid he could get. He had a powerful constitution and frame—six feet high, straight as an Indian, and could stand any kind of hardship or exposure without fear of danger. In his family he was simply one of them, and more like a child with them than a great intellectual giant that he was. He never was sick or had anything the matter with him until his last illness, and on his death bed his great brain and intellect was as clear and powerful as ever. He did not have an unsound tooth in his head, and could, and frequently did, crack hickory nuts with his teeth, without injury to them, for the children. Col. Caperton wrote perhaps the best and most accurate account of the battle between Capt. James Estill and a band of Wyandotte Indians in March, 1784, near Mt. Sterling, Ky., called the battle of "Little Mountain," and by some "Estill's defeat," in which Capt. Estill was killed in trying to save the life of one of his men, Adam Caperton, who was desperately wounded by a rifle ball through the head, and was about to be scalped by a large Indian chief, and died on the battle field. Adam Caperton was a near kinsman of Col. Caperton, and Capt. Estill was the grandfather of Col. Caperton's wife. The account of the battle, as written by him, was published in "Cist's Magazine," at Cincinnati, Ohio. Col. Durrett, an eminent lawyer of Louisville, Ky., has now one of the copies of the magazine, believed to be the only one now in existence. Col. Caperton, in his account of the battle, obtained the exact facts from men in the fight: Col. Irvine, Proctor Cradlebaugh, and the colored man, Monk, who was taken prisoner and carried off by the Indians before the battle, and from others engaged in it. His descriptive powers were vivid and great; in conversation, anecdote, genuine wit and humor, he was unequaled. His laughter was wonderful, and once heard could never be forgotten. It was clear, loud and ringing, and musical as a silver bell, and spread joy all around and put all in a good humor. He was always exceedingly polite, bland and kind to all, and considerate of the feelings of all, even the most humble, even to his own servants, who actually loved him, and they would get up at midnight at any time cheerfully to do what he wanted, without murmur or complaint.

He was a man of peace, and never trampled rudely upon the rights or feelings of others, but knew no fear. Once aroused or mistreated, or any member of his family, and his anger and fearlessness were like those of the wild, untamed lion.

He was a great reader of the Bible, but was never a member of any church, but his respect for religion and religious people was well known. His wife was a member of the

Reformed or Christian Church. His dwelling-house was always open to the ministers of the different churches.

During his last visit to Richmond the great Alex. Campbell was his guest, and the blind and eloquent minister and good man, Jacob Creath, often made Col. Caperton's house his home while here, and many others. In the great religious debate at Lexington, Ky., between Alex. Campbell and Nathan L. Rice, he was chosen as one of the moderators to preside at that debate. He accepted and presided until the end, the debate lasting many days.

On the return of Gen. Cassius M. Clay from the Mexican war (then Capt. Clay) Col. Caperton was chosen by the citizens of the county to welcome him in a speech for and on their behalf, which he did at the old Methodist Church in Richmond, Kentucky, in a masterly and eloquent manner to an immense audience, civil and military.

In the celebrated duel between Gen. D. S. Goodloe and Col. C. I. Field, of Mississippi, fought on Drowning Creek, just over the border line, in Estill County, Col. Caperton was chosen by Goodloe, who was his relative, as one of his seconds, and he so acted and was present on that eventful occasion. The contemporaries of Col. Caperton at the bar and on the bench were among Kentucky's great men. The great judge, Wm. Goodloe, was his kinsman by blood, and they were devotedly attached to each other. Maj. Squire Turner, Judge Daniel Breck, John Speed Smith, Richard Runyon, Hon. C. F. Burnam of Madison, all of the Richmond bar, with whom Col. Caperton daily associated and had professional contest with, and many others equally distinguished throughout the State were among his associates.

When Col. Caperton came to the bar there was not in all this region where he lived and practiced law a turnpike or railroad, but simply and only old-fashioned dirt or mud roads, and the lawyers of that day traveled from court to court on horseback to the different counties in which they practiced, carrying their "saddle bags" with them, and in the winter riding with their leggings on.

They attended the court of appeals at Frankfort, the capital of the State, and went there on horseback on a mud road, as well as to other near towns: Winchester, Lancaster, Mt. Vernon, Irvine, etc., and it generally took them a whole day to make the trip to Frankfort; it required two days to get there from Richmond.

Col. Caperton was very fond of so attending the mountain courts; he was very fond of the people who lived in the mountains, and they were equally as fond of and proud of him. He frequently went to the Perry and Letcher Courts, high up on the head waters of the Kentucky River near the Virginia line, and enjoyed his trips there greatly.

He was always responsive to the calls of those who needed aid, in times of sickness and distress. When that fearful scourge, Asiatic cholera, broke out in his town in 1833, and again in 1849, he went from house to house, among all classes, white and black, waiting on the sick, closing the eyes of the dying, and attending to the decent burial of the dead.

The father of Col. Caperton was named William Caperton. He came from Virginia at an early day in the history of the country, and married Miss Lucy Woods, daughter of Archibald Woods, Sr., about the year 1800, and settled on the farm owned by the late Dr. Thos. S. Moberly, on Muddy Creek, in Madison County, Ky. He had ten children —eight sons and two daughters, as follows: Archibald, Hugh, Thomas Shelton, William Harris, Green, John, Milton T., Andrew Woods, Hulda and Susan. Hulda married her cousin, Andrew Woods, and Susan married Wallace Wilson; they are all dead but one, Milton T. Caperton, now an aged and venerable Baptist preacher, living near San Antonio, Tex.

Wm. Caperton, Col. Caperton's father, at an early day, with a large number of his relatives and neighbors—the Millers, Woods, Harrises, Estills, Kavanaughs and others— moved from Madison County, Ky., to Williamson County, Middle Tenn., and settled on Bean's Creek, Col. Caperton going there with his father and the rest of the family. From there, as the family grew up, they scattered out through the South, over north Alabama, Mississippi, Louisiana, Arkansas and Texas.

John Caperton, a brother of Col. Caperton, died during the late war in Mississippi; his son, Dr. A. C. Caperton, now resides in Louisville, Ky., with his interesting and charming family. He was a brave officer, soldier in the Confederate Army, and is now a Baptist minister of eminence throughout the State, a fine speaker and orator; he is also editor of the *Baptist Recorder*, published in Louisville, Ky.

A great deal of pains, and great care, has been taken to ascertain the true history of the Caperton family, and it has been ascertained, with certainty, that the first man of that name, who came to this country, was a Frenchman; his name was John Caperton, he came from France, landed in New York City, afterward went to Virginia, and there married Miss Polly Thompson, in Monroe County, Va.

He had three sons, Adam, Hugh and William. Adam was killed in battle at "Little Mountain," near the present site of Mt. Sterling, in March, 1784, at the time Capt. Estill had the battle with the Indians there; he was the grandfather of Maj. John Caperton, now of Louisville, Ky. Hugh was a man of prominence and ability, and was elected several times to the Legislature in Virginia; the other son, William, was Col. Caperton's father. A number of the family still reside in Virginia, and are highly respectable, honorable people, some of them highly distinguished in the councils of the Nation. The Hon. Allen T. Caperton was a member of the United States Senate from Virginia a number of years, and died in Washington City, while a member of the Senate a few years since.

The history of the Caperton name and family, by those who have carefully and vigilantly made it a study (and it has been done by at least one of the family and name), is highly honorable, and will bear the closest scrutiny in all countries, and in all climes. No man, bearing the name, was ever known or heard of as a rogue, nor of a woman bearing the name, or blood, that was unchaste. They are a rare and peculiar race of people, of great intelligence, orators of the first class, many of them. Courtly in manners, kind and affectionate, polite and affable to all, true reliable friends, but once mistreat or injure them, or rudely trample on their feelings or rights and their whole nature instantly changes; they at once become reckless and dangerous, knowing no fear, regardless of all consequences of their acts, and become bloodthirsty, like the wild, untamed tiger, not even apparent or immediate death at the hands of an antagonist checking them for one moment in their struggle of self defense, or to disable, or slay their assailant.

The Capertons, in all their generations, have been men of great physical and moral courage. It is believed now by those who have studied, and know the family history, that the true and correct way to spell and pronounce the name, is Caper-*Ton*.

Col. Caperton, in early youth, was united in marriage to Miss Eliza Estill, a daughter of James Estill, a wealthy and prosperous farmer of Madison County, Ky., and a granddaughter of Capt. James Estill, who fell at the battle of Little Mountain in March, 1784.

Mrs. Caperton had two brothers and two sisters; one of her brothers, Mr. R. R. Estill, still lives at the venerable age of four score years at his beautiful home in Georgetown, Ky., and with him resides his widowed sister, Mrs. Mary (Estill) Holmes, formerly of Louisiana. Another brother of Mrs. Caperton was Gen. James M. Estill, who died many years ago in California; and another sister, Maria, was married to A. W. Goodloe, Esq., a prominent citizen of Madison County, and long the acting sheriff there. He and his wife both died in Arkansas, where he had removed to engage in cotton planting. These family relations united Col. Caperton, directly and collaterally, to a very large number of the most prominent and distinguished people in the Southwest and East, and by all whom his fame was valued as a large part of the family wealth and distinction.

Col. Caperton had three children: Woods Caperton, Mary P. Caperton and James W. Caperton. Woods grew to manhood and studied law but had no taste for its practice and never practiced but little law. He was a brilliant young man, a fine natural orator, was endowed naturally with splendid genius, and was a most rare and captivating conversationalist and very affectionate and devoted to his family and friends. He never married, but had a large number of warm personal friends and admirers.

In the prime of his manhood and youth he was shot down and murdered in the streets of Richmond, Ky., by that cold-blooded murderer, Frank Searcy, the day after the presidential election in 1860, when Mr. Lincoln was elected president. His father and brother were both absent at the time from the county, attending the Clark and Estill Circuit Courts. Searcy was indicted for murder for that crime, but the case never came to a trial; it was continued from time to time until the war broke out, and during that period there were scarcely any trials had in the courts in Kentucky. After the war Searcy procured a pardon from Gov. Bramlette, who at that time granted pardons freely for crimes and public offenses.

Not long after Searcy received his pardon he murdered Anderson, and shortly thereafter he shot down and murdered Bergin in the streets of Richmond, Ky., on a county court day when the streets were thronged with people. For the latter cold-blooded murder he was taken out of jail in Richmond by the "Kuklux" at midnight and hung on a locust tree in the courthouse yard, where his body hung nearly all of the next day and was gazed upon by thousands who turned away satisfied that justice had at last fallen upon the bloody fiend in human form, and that he would commit no more murders. The entire people approved of his just, though terrible death, and knew the bloody monster could do them no more harm, and felt relieved and at peace once more.

Woods Caperton rests by the side of his distinguished father. His sister, Mary P. Caperton, was a woman of splendid sense and a well balanced mind. Her womanly charms and graces were many and rare. In person she was of splendid form; she was a true and splendid woman in every respect—kind to all and popular with all; she made lasting friends wherever she was; she was a pure, Christian woman, devoted and affectionate, calm and submissive to adversity, sorrow and affliction She married Leonidas B. Talbott, better known as Lee Talbott, a brother of the Hon. Albert G. Talbott, formerly a member of Congress from Kentucky. She died a number of years ago, in Lexington, Ky., leaving an only child, a son, Wm. C. Talbott, named after his grandfather, Col. Caperton. She was a member of the Methodist Church and truly devoted to her church and religious faith, and died as a true Christian woman in the faith of her adoption.

Her only child and son, Wm. C. Talbott, was twice married; the first time to Miss Zerelda Baxter, a highly worthy and handsome daughter of Milo Baxter, a highly respected farmer of Madison County, Ky. She survived but a short time after her marriage without leaving children. Subsequently he married Miss Annie French, the only child and daughter of Dr. Robert French, an eminent physician and farmer, of Madison County, Ky.

Mrs. Annie French Talbott is a splendid woman and wife in every respect, intelligent, domestic and affectionate, and fulfills all the duties of a wife, mother, neighbor, friend to the poor and humble, black and white; her kindness of heart is well known and highly appreciated. They have an only child, a beautiful, bright, intelligent and affectionate daughter, Miss Clyde Talbott, now about seven years old, of sweet disposition and temper, and, young as she is, kind, tender in her feelings, and considerate of the feelings and wants of others, and with her playmates sharing her little gifts freely and equally with all. Her father and mother are very proud and fond of her, and watch her growth and intellectual training with vigilant, watchful care and love.

Her father, Wm. C. Talbott, was during the late war sent by his grandfather, Col. Caperton, to the United States Naval Academy, then at Annapolis, Md. Subsequently the school was removed to Newport, R. I., where he remained several years and became a midshipman, and had several cruises in the Mediterranean in the United States naval training ships, and on board United States revenue war vessels. He finally resigned his position in the United States naval service, came home, and engaged in other business pursuits, all of which were honorably, faithfully and intelligently performed. His mother died when he was a child, and his grandfather, Col. Caperton, brought him home with him to Richmond, Ky., from Lexington, Ky., and reared and educated him and made him one of the family, the full equal of and the same in all respects as his other children. He is very affectionate and kind and devoted to his wife and child; no want or desire of either is ever uncared for. He is a kind neighbor and true friend, and of the highest order of intelligence and very popular, and greatly liked by all who know him. His latchstring is always out, and his hospitality well known and greatly appreciated. His house is a welcome home, always open to his friends, and none, whether known or not, no matter how poor, humble or destitute, are ever turned away, but are well entertained, and willingly so, too.

When his grandfather, Col. Caperton, died, his uncle, Col. J. W. Caperton took charge of and raised him and finished his education, and he made that his home until his first marriage. He now resides with his wife and child on a farm, a beautiful home near the Red House Depot, on the Kentucky Central Railroad, in Madison County, Ky.

Col. Caperton's only living child now is Col. James W. Caperton, of Richmond, Ky., who stands in the front rank of his profession as a member of the bar, and who is the president of the First National Bank of Richmond, Ky., and who has filled many honorable public stations, in which his integrity, capacity for business affairs and high intelligence have been signally displayed. Not the least creditable to him of his many excellent characteristics is the unswerving devotion he retains for his father's memory, and to make his example a beacon light for his own life. It is doubtful whether any father and son were ever more devotedly attached to each other. They were of the same disposition in many respects—fond of out-door life, fishing and hunting in the mountains, and never were separated in those enchanting, healthy sports and cessation from business cares, after his son became old enough to go with him. They slept side by side in camp and always hunted together, never separating but a short distance in the mountain forest, always in easy call of each other by an agreed signal, the solemn, melancholy hoot of the owl. And during the cholera they visited the sick and the dying together. The unerring rifles of both, in their mountain hunts, always kept the camp well supplied with deer and their fishing-rods the frying-pan with fine pike, salmon and bass. They were partners in the practice of law from the time the son came to the bar until the father's death, and always resided together. After the death of Col Caperton his son and the Hon. Curtis F. Burnam formed a partnership in the practice of law, and so practiced a number of years in the courts of Kentucky and before the departments of Washington City, D. C.

Col. Caperton, in his last illness, lasting several months, was attended unceasingly night and day by his son, and he died in the arms of his son, whose heart was nearly crushed to see his great father die. As priceless relics of his father and of his life he has kept and yet does and preserves and watches with great care his deer rifle, powder-horn, tomahawk, large hunting-knife and leather belt in which they were worn, fishing tackle, rods, reels, gaff-hook and other articles used by him when hunting or fishing, and also his partridge net.

Col. Caperton died at his residence on Main Street, in Richmond, Ky., surrounded by his distressed family and friends, on the 4th of July, 1862, just before the battle at Richmond, Ky., aged sixty-four years. He was buried with civil and military honors in the beautiful cemetery there, a large concourse of people, relatives and friends turning out to honor the great lawyer. His funeral was preached and his life and character presented in a true and masterly manner by the Rev. Edmund H. Burnam, then pastor of the old Baptist Church in Richmond. His widow survived him only a few years and quietly passed away. She was buried by the side of her distinguished husband, her grave covered with beautiful fresh flowers, gathered and placed by the gentle hands of kind friends and relatives.

CENTRAL UNIVERSITY. The rise of this young and vigorous institution to its present commanding position within little more than a decade of corporate existence may be traced to the confluence of two movements each of which was made in the interest of higher education.

The unhappy rupture of the synod of Kentucky occasioned by ecclesiastical issues growing out of the action of the Northern Church during the great civil war, left the southern branch of the broken synod without an educational institution, Centre College being in possession of those who themselves submitted to and enforced upon others the divisive measures enacted by successive General Assemblies during that trying period. In November, 1870, a conference of committees representing the two synods was held to "confer in reference to some adjustment of the difficulties touching the property of Centre College." It was earnestly hoped that this conference would lead to a termination of the litigation pending in the civil courts and to a mutual recognition of the joint property rights of the two bodies as the heirs of the original synod.

But the conference only disclosed the impossibility of an adjustment and convinced thoughtful men of the futility of further efforts to secure recognition of any property rights in Centre College. Wearied with litigation and deprecating the strife it engendered, the Southern Synod at its next meeting in November, 1871, determined to create an institution of its own—one worthy of the principles for which it had suffered. A resolution introduced by Dr. Stuart Robinson was passed, looking to the immediate endowment and equipment of a college.

In May following another movement arose, more popular and widespread in its character, and of far greater momentum.

Men of intelligence, wealth and culture, the friends and allies of the synod throughout the State, felt that the time had come for an institution of higher order and on broader foundations. In response to a call for a convention to be held in Lexington on the 7th of May, 1872, a large number assembled and a permanent association was organized which addressed a memorial to the synod soon to convene in the same city urging the immediate establishment of a university and pledging the earnest co-operation of the association in the enterprise. The appeal met a generous response from the synod; and a plan of organization was effected which adjusted the mutual relations of synod and the association in the government of the institution.

The scheme met with great popular favor, securing as it did the safeguards for conservative and Christian education and at the same time avoiding the evils attendant upon exclusive church or state control.

So thoroughly had popular interest been aroused that of the $500,000 proposed endowment $200,000 was soon subscribed. A charter was procured which vested in the donors of the endowment, and such others as they might associate with themselves, the ownership and control of the institution.

This association, known as the "Alumni Association of Central University," fills its own vacancies and elects its own successors from the alumni of the institution and its liberal benefactors, thus forever keeping the university under the control of those who feel the deepest interest in its welfare.

Its government and the management of its funds are entrusted to the chancellor and fifteen curators, two-thirds of whom, under the charter, must be members of the Alumni Association. Thus incorporated it sprang at once into popular favor. Efforts to secure its location aroused much competition. Anchorage, Bardstown, Danville, Paris and Richmond all made strenuous efforts and generous offers, and much difficulty was at first experienced in reaching a decision. Richmond, was finally selected, and events have justified the wisdom of the choice. Richmond, with a population of 4,000, is the county seat of Madison, one of the largest and wealthiest counties in the State, a portion of the famous blue-grass region and full of historical interest. With an altitude that secures immunity from malarial influences, a picturesque and inviting landscape, a community refined and hospitable and deeply interested in education and morals, thus giving a wholesome environment to the students, the location cannot be excelled by any community. A large and commodious building was erected in the center of the spacious grounds and four comfortable residences for professors on the east side of the campus.

The university opened on the 22d of September, 1874, with a goodly number of students. Three faculties were organized, with Rev. John W. Pratt, president of the faculty of the college of arts; E. D. Foree, president of the faculty of the college of medicine, and Hon. C. F. Burnam, president of the faculty of law.

Rev. R. L. Breck, D. D., a man of commanding ability and large influence, and who had been prominently associated with the enterprise from the beginning, was the first chancellor. Dr. Breck was supported by an able board of curators and trustees, prominent among whom was the lamented S. P. Walters of Richmond, whose recent death all the friends of the university so deeply deplore

Dr. Pratt, an attractive pulpit orator and a ripe scholar, was supported by an able corps of professors, each a specialist in his own department. The university prospered for several years; but its opening was contemporaneous with a great financial depression. This soon brought its administration into great embarrassment. It was difficult to collect subscriptions, and it soon became evident to those in charge, that the working force could not be maintained with the funds then in possession. In 1879 Dr. Pratt resigned and returned to the pulpit. A year later Dr. Breck resigned, somewhat broken in health, and removed to California, preaching at Berkeley several years, where his health improved. It is needless to say that at this time the friends of the enterprise so full of promise in its inception were disheartened.

There were but few students in attendance, and the income from other sources was small. The board of curators determined, however, to go forward. The Rev. Dr. J. V. Logan was made president of the faculty, and Profs. Barbour and Willson were retained in their respective chairs. Soon after this the suggestion came from Col. Bennett H. Young that a vigorous effort should at once be made to place the institution on a firmer basis, and urged that the office of chancellor, left vacant by the resignation of Dr. Breck, should be filled, calling attention at the same time to the Rev. L. H. Blanton, D. D., then pastor of a large and prosperous church at Paris, Ky. The board took prompt action, and Dr. Blanton was duly elected, and having accepted the office entered promptly upon his duties.

Dr. Blanton was known to have peculiar fitness for the position, and he has more than fulfilled the hopes of his friends. Comprehensive in his views, sagacious in his plans, tenacious in his purposes, lofty in his aims, he possesses unusual executive ability. He has lifted the institution out of its financial embarrassment and restored the fullest confidence in its future. He took hold of the work with all the energy of his nature and soon generous contributions began to flow in. The faculty was enlarged by the establishment of new chairs; a beautiful "memorial hall" was erected on the grounds, accommodating fifty students, and an elegant chancellor's residence—thus, with the main building and four professors' houses, making the most desirable property for an institution in the State. Recently he has added an additional $100,000 to the endowment, the contribution of a few individuals, and accomplished within thirty days. Of this sum, Hon. W. H. McBrayer gave $30,000; Orville Ford, Esq., $20,000; A. J. Alexander, $10,-

000; D. C. Collins, Esq., $10,000; Mrs. Mary R. Kinkead, $10,000; Mrs. Mary J. Lyons, $5,000; Mr. John McClintock, $5,000, and Mrs. Anna W. Walters, $4,000. The patronage has increased from year to year, the standard of scholarship has been steadily raised, until now it stands abreast of any similar institution in the country, and is justly regarded as an ornament to the commonwealth. The number of students in attendance upon its various schools for the last scholastic year was 239, representing sixteen States. Dr. J. V. Logan still holds the position of president of the faculty. His administration has been wise, efficient and accompanied by the best results in government and discipline. As professor of ethics and evidences he has no superior, possessing rare gifts and acquirements for this department. At present the faculty of instruction in the college of philosophy, letters and science consists of the following gentlemen: L. H. Blanton, D. D., chancellor; J. V. Logan, D. D., president of the faculty, synod's professor of ethics and evidences, and professor of psychology and logic; L. G. Barbour, M. A., D. D., professor of mathematics and astronomy; W. M. Willson, M. A., professor of Greek language and literature; James Lewis Howe, Ph. D., F. C. S., professor of chemistry and geology; J. T. Akers, Ph. D., professor of English and modern languages; E. R. Carichoff, M. A., professor of Latin language and literature; * * * professor of the Bible and Christian evidences; A. Wilkes Smith, D. D. S., M. D., lecturer in physiology; W. N. Ewing, B. A., adjunct professor of mathematics and English; C. G. Crooks, B. A., tutor in Hebrew; W. G. Cleland, assistant in chemical laboratory; A. Henry, B. A. registrar; Prof. Willson, librarian; Prof. Howe, secretary of the faculty.

The College of Medicine.—Contemporaneously with the opening of these schools at Richmond the college of medicine was opened at Louisville under the name of the "Hospital College of Medicine," and composed of some of the ablest medical practitioners of the city, E. D. Foree, M. D., being president of the faculty.

The object in establishing a medical department was to make every branch of the healing art part of the regular curriculum; to teach every branch by practical illustration and demonstration as far as the most recent discoveries in science would permit; to so arrange the courses of study that no student whose preliminary education did not enable him to comprehend the technology and qualify him to manipulate instruments of precision in the laboratories, could hold a place in the classes; to establish written examinations on all the branches taught before admitting the candidate to the doctorate. In this way the Hospital College of Medicine aims to take a leading position in the elevation of the standard of medical education. Its work has gone on in an unostentatious manner, but it has, through its alumni, indicated the wisdom of those who created it and dictated its policy. Its clinical instruction has covered all the legitimate specialties in practical medicine and surgery. The present faculty consists of the following gentlemen: Wm. H. Bolling, M. D., professor of obstetrics and diseases of women, president of the faculty; John A. Larrabee, M. D., professor of materia medica and therapeutics and clinical lecturer on diseases of children; Dudley S. Reynolds, M. D., professor of general pathology, hygiene and diseases of the eye and ear; Frank C. Wilson, M. D., professor of the principles and practice of medicine and clinical medicine, treasurer of the faculty; A. M. Cartledge, M. D., professor of the principles and practice of surgery and clinical surgery, secretary of the faculty; Samuel G. Dabney, M. D., professor of physiology and clinical lecturer on diseases of eye, ear and throat; C. Skinner, M. D., professor of descriptive surgical and comparative anatomy and clinical lecturer on gynæcology; Jas. Lewis Howe, M. D., Ph. D., F. C. S., professor of medical chemistry and toxicology, scientist to the Polytechnic Society of Kentucky; Wm. R. Kinney, Esq., lecturer on medical jurisprudence; Geo. F. Martin, M. D., demonstrator of anatomy; John F. Barbour, M. D., clinical lecturer on nervous diseases; T. Hunt Stucky, M. D., assistant to the chair of surgery and lecturer on surgical pathology and surgical dressings; Peter Guntermann, M. D., adjunct professor of principles and practice of medicine, and clinical medicine; T. D. Finck, M. D., assistant in pathology and hygiene; Thos. S. Bullock, M. D., clinical lecturer on gynæcology; John Oldham, M. D., assistant in ophthalmology and otology; J. H. Larrabee, M. D., assistant to the clinic for diseases of children; Austin D. Smith, M. D., assistant in pathology and histology. James Hines Morgan, clerk. College Building, Chestnut, near Preston Street, opposite City Hospital.

College of Dentistry.—In 1886 the board of curators established in the city of Louisville the "Louisville College of Dentistry." Suitable buildings were erected for the accommodation of the new department in connection with the Hospital College of Medicine. The following gentlemen compose the faculty: A. Wilkes Smith, M. D., D. D. S., professor of oral and dental surgery and operative dentistry, dean of faculty; Charles G. Edwards, D. D. S., professor of prosthetic and clinical dentistry; A. M. Cartledge, M. D., professor of surgery; Dudley S. Reynolds, M. D., professor of pathology and hygiene; Frank C. Wilson, M. D., professor of principles and practice of medicine; Samuel G. Dabney, M. D., professor of physiology and histology; John A. Larrabee, M. D., professor of materia medica and therapeutics; C. Skinner, M. D., professor of anatomy; James Lewis Howe, M. D., Ph. D., F. C. S., professor of medical chemistry and toxicology, scientist to the Polytechnic Society of Kentucky. Demonstrators: H. B. Tileston, D. D. S., demonstrator of operative dentistry; John H. Baldwin, D. D. S., demonstrator of prosthetic dentistry; George F. Martin, M. D., demonstrator of anatomy.

MORRIS EVANS, the subject of this sketch, was born at Louisville, Ky., August 28, 1828. His paternal ancestry were English, Welsh and Irish. His great-grandparents settled in Maryland. His grandfather was wounded in the patriot army in the Revolution. With his family he moved to Kentucky in May, 1799, and died the following spring. There were three children—two sons, one of whom died unmarried, and a daughter. John Chesire, the father of our subject, was born April 10, 1798. He married, September 27, 1821, a Miss Hall, of English descent. The Hall family were Virginians who came to Kentucky in 1790. The family was a very large one. The wife of J. C. Evans was born in Kentucky. The exact time of her birth was lost, as the Bible containing the family record was burned, and a renewal of the record was delayed until several dates were lost. Immediately after marriage they moved to Louisville, then a small village, where they remained until during the war between the States. They then removed to Chicago, where John C. Evans died December 24, 1872. His wife survived him until July 4, 1884, when she died in Bullitt County, Ky., having returned after the death of her husband to the neighborhood of her old home. Morris, the fourth in a family of seven sons, was educated in the schools of Louisville. After leaving school he studied civil engineering for some years. In 1848 he was licensed as a preacher in the Southern Methodist Church, and became a member of the Louisville Annual Conference. In 1851 he was appointed a missionary to California. The trip was made from New Orleans by steamer to the mouth of Chagres

River, then by boats and donkey to Panama, and thence by steamer to San 'Francisco. For thirteen years he devoted himself to his special work in that golden State. While the great mass of the people were devoted to money getting; while the State was being formed; while almost everything pertaining to social organization was in a chaotic state, he was consecrated to the one purpose of his mission. The mere presence of a man consecrated to the cultivation of the nobler impulses of man's nature is a benediction; the energetic efforts of well balanced and well educated young men must have been weighty factors in the evolution of order and good society out of the heterogeneous masses who thronged that State in its earlier days. During his stay there he filled successfully all the posts of honor and responsibility open to the members of his conference. In the establishing and managing of a church organ; in devising plans for the establishing and organizing of a college and such other church enterprises, he was always conspicuous. At an early day, finding the city of Sonora with a considerable number of children and no school facilities, he took on him, in addition to his pastoral work, the duty of teaching school. To manage those untrained Californians, who had the mastery at their homes, was no child's play. Yet the children soon became fond of the school and made rapid progress in their studies. Mr. Evans was married at San Jose May 12, 1858, to Miss Helen Lee Younger, who is nearly related to the Lee and Custis families of Virginia. As the fruit of this marriage is an only child, Harry Asbury Evans, born at San Jose May 18, 1862. During the war Mr. Evans determined to return to "the States" and find a home in Texas. While visiting his parents in Chicago, Lee surrendered, and the South was placed in such a condition as made it undesirable for a stranger with a family. The result was that Mr. Evans came back to Kentucky. He began his new career here as an agent for an oil company of Chicago. As oil was not found in the section in which he operated, he went to Somerset and again became a teacher. Abundant success attended this effort, and he was called to Stanford as a teacher of mathematics in the academy at that place. But the pressure on him to rejoin the annual conference was such that he gave up the ferule and resumed his work as a member of the Kentucky annual conference. He remained in this regular pastoral work until earnest and persistent persuasion of the friends of the Millersburg Female College induced him to assume the control of this institute. The one year there was a most gratifying success, and those directly interested in it endeavored to gain his consent to buy and manage that school. This he declined to do. The trustees of Garrard Female College sent for him to come and look at their school, and finally induced him to take charge of it. This school, with magnificent property, a new and handsomely furnished building, had to be organized and built up. Taking charge of it with loving zeal the work was pressed and success experienced. A complete laboratory has been purchased, a museum is being established which already contains most of those things needed for purpose of instruction, together with many rare specimens of nature's handiwork. Located in the blue-grass region, in a place absolutely healthy, surrounded by a liberal and intelligent community, under proper management there must be a growing school of the very best grade. Several years since the Kentucky Military Institute, by the unsolicited action of its large and able faculty, conferred upon Mr. Evans the degree of D. D. This was an expression from competent judges of the mental and literary attainments of Dr. Evans, which his numerous friends recognized as a just tribute. Dr. Evans thinks for himself and forms his own opinions. The result has been that he is frequently deemed seriously heterodox by the more conservative. Mild in manner, uncompromising in his devotion to the principle of right, with good ability as an organizer, he has always commanded the respect of the community in which he has lived, and been successful in his undertakings. He has published a tractate entitled "The Bible Doctrine of Hell," which treats exhaustively of its topic. He has in preparation a work on psychology and another on ethics. In both of these the process is strictly scientific, and the subject presented in a form that will probably earn him the reputation of being heterodox here as elsewhere. The Doctor is unquestionably in a field where his mental endowment, learning and training can be most usefully and successfully employed. With his conscientiousness no imperfect work will be allowed in his school. Incompetence in the teacher is to him well nigh criminal. Surrounded by his family and an able faculty, he is devoting all of his energies to the accomplishment of his life work, trying to develop himself and all those coming within the range of his influence.

FONTAINE TALBOT FOX. Among the old jurists and lawyers of Kentucky, who still abide with us, connecting links, as it were, between the early jurisprudence of the State and the better formulated and more progressive legal science of the present, none occupy a more conspicuous place in the eyes of his many friends than Judge Fontaine T. Fox, whose name heads this sketch. Born in Madison County, Ky., on the 28th of January, 1803, he enjoyed but meager opportunities for obtaining an education, reading Latin as far as Horace for five months at Richmond under the tutorship of John Ryan, and for six months under Samuel Wilson, and finally closing his course of academical instruction at Forrest Academy, Jessamine County. His father having removed to Pulaski County while his son was still of tender years, the latter, upon completing his education, began the study of law in that county in 1822, in the office of Charles Cunningham, and in the following year was admitted to the bar and at once began the practice of his profession at Somerset. He soon earned a reputation for himself as a careful and successful practitioner, and from 1823 to 1884 occupied the front rank among the able members of the profession in his judicial district, acquiring an extensive and remunerative practice. In 1829 he was appointed commonwealth's attorney for the Eighth Judicial District, and held that position for four years. In 1840 he removed to Lincoln County and was again appointed to the same office in 1844, resigning the position after two years. In 1849 he located at Danville and in 1862 was elected circuit judge for the Eighth Judicial District and re-elected to the same responsible position in 1868, holding it for twelve years, on both occasions being elected without opposition. During the twelve years of his service on the bench, its decisions were always rendered with promptness and great clearness; his judicial mind rapidly grasped the real questions involved and the law that governed them. No one wearing the ermine ever enjoyed a more enviable reputation for uprightness and impartiality, or was more considerate of all who came before him. If he had a lean or bias it was toward the ignorant or poor, those whose circumstances appealed to his kind nature. In politics Judge Fox was originally an old line Whig, but upon the breaking up of that organization, identified himself with the Democratic party, with which he afterward acted. In 1836 he was elected on the Whig ticket to the lower branch of the State Legislature in the Democratic county of Pulaski and in 1840 was chosen to represent Pulaski and Lincoln

Counties in the State Senate, where he served four years. Judge Fox is of Scotch-Irish extraction and throughout a long professional and political career has manifested many of the strong characteristics of that race. His grandfather, Samuel Fox, came from Virginia with the early colonists of Kentucky and settled in Madison County, where he pursued the occupation of a farmer, living to the extraordinary age of ninety-eight years. He married Rhoda, daughter of Richard and Lucy Pickering, and had a large family of children, consisting of ten sons and three daughters. His son, William Fox, father of Judge Fox, removed to Pulaski County in early manhood and for a period of about fifty-five years held the office of county and circuit court clerk in that county. During all that time he was recognized as one of the leaders in the county, was a man of great influence and unquestioned integrity and one whose advice and counsel were sought by all. He married Sophie Irvine, and his children were Amanda, who married Bourne Goggin; Jane, who married Dr. John Caldwell, and Elizabeth, who married John Fitzpatrick; Sophie, who married J. S. Kindrick; Fontaine T.; William and Samuel Fox. He died in 1855. The personal attributes of Judge Fox may be briefly described. He is a man of decided convictions, yet not one who is given to forcing his opinions upon others; was always considerate of the feelings and reputation of others, and it may be truly said that he was "no man's enemy." During the civil war he was a strong advocate of the Union and firmly supported the views and policy of the representatives of the National Government. His legal attainments were of the highest order, and, together with a natural uprightness of mind, combined what may be called an almost intuitive perception of those scientific and philosophical principles which underlie the system of modern jurisprudence. As an advocate and in the social circle he was genial, bright and witty, always had at his command a fund of anecdotes that were pointed and highly entertaining. He is a man of great natural suavity of manner, generous and polite, gallant in the extreme to members of the opposite sex, given to hospitality, and one who has always occupied a warm place in the popular heart, enjoying to the highest degree the confidence and esteem of the people, further attested by the fact that several years after he had declined to run for office, many votes were cast for him as judge without his knowledge or consent. At the ripe age of eighty-four, he has, of ccurse, retired from the active business of life, and resides in Danville. By his side still sits she whom he married on January 16, 1830, as Eliza Jane Hunton, daughter of Thomas Hunton of Lincoln County, Ky., who is the mother of his large family and has ever been a faithful wife and devoted Christian mother. Both are members of the First Presbyterian Church of Danville. The children who attained years of maturity are Thomas H., by profession a lawyer, now farming in Montgomery County, Ky.; William McKee (deceased), who lived at Somerset, Ky., practiced law in Pulaski and adjoining counties; Peter C. (deceased), who practiced law at Louisville; Fontaine T. Fox, Jr., now practicing law at Louisville; Samuel I., a practicing physician at Plantersville, Tex.; Felix G., a lawyer at Kansas City, Mo.; Sophie Irvine, who married Andrew M. Sea of Kansas City; John O. (deceased), who was a civil engineer at Danville; Annie Belle, wife of Jeremiah C. Caldwell of Danville, and Charles C. Fox, a lawyer at Danville and now somewhat interested in farming pursuits. Since the above sketch was put in type the sad intelligence has reached us of the death of the subject at midnight, April 6, 1887. Space only permits us to give the following extract in relation to his demise, from a leading Danville journal: "In the death of the venerable Fontaine T. Fox, there passes from the scene the last remaining, and by no means the least considerable among the imposing figures of that Kentucky, which was glorified in the Senate by Clay, Crittenden and Breckinridge, and at the bar by Rowan, Hardin and Bell. Judge Fox lacked the aggressive ambition to attain great place in public life, and as a politician was not a success. But his genius was brilliant and undisputed. A man of large affections and of captivating manners, he possessed, along with the most striking legal talents and learning, and an exalted character, the gift of charm, and was universally loved in his home. His standing before the courts, when in active practice, and as a jurist, when on the bench, was second to none. He dies full of years and honors, leaving a large progeny to inherit his virtues and his fame."

GENERAL SPEED S. FRY was born September 9, 1817, five miles west of Danville, on a farm known as "Spring house." He was the eighth of seven sons and six daughters, eleven of whom lived to be grown, born to Thomas W. and Elizabeth Julia (Smith) Fry. Thomas W. Fry was born in Albemarle County, Va., was brought to Kentucky when thirteen by his grandfather, afterward became a substantial farmer in Mercer (now Boyle) County, and owned about 1,200 acres, and many slaves. In 1836 he removed to Crawfordsville, Ind., and engaged in the milling business till his death in 1837, at the age of fifty-three years. His widow and family remained in Crawfordsville till her death in 1848. Thomas W. was a son of Joshua Fry, who was born in Albemarle County, Va., married Peachy Walker, immigrated with his family to Mercer County, Ky., about 1783, and was highly educated, and one of the most celebrated teachers in Kentucky. He taught without compensation, including several years in Centre College, also taught a large school in Garrard County without pay. He owned large farms in Garrard, Lincoln and Mercer (now Boyle) Counties, also a large tract near Louisville; was also a large owner in slave property; was a strong and active Whig, and died in 1836 at the age of seventy-five years; was of English and German extraction. Eliza J. (Smith) Fry, the mother of Gen. S. S. Fry, was born in Mercer (now Boyle) County, Ky., and was a daughter of John Smith, and sister of Hon. John Speed Smith of Madison County, Ky. John Smith was born in Virginia, where he married a Miss Speed. He was of English descent and one of the early pioneers of Kentucky. Gen. Fry received his early training in the common schools on Salt River, under Duncan Robinson, subsequently under his grandfather; entered Centre College, and after completing the sophomore year entered Wabash College, at Crawfordsville, Ind., in 1838, and graduated in 1840. Shortly after he returned to Kentucky, and commenced the study of law under his uncle, John Speed Smith, of Madison County; received his license in 1843, and entered into practice in Danville. The law not being congenial to his taste he engaged in mercantile pursuits until 1846, when, at the call for troops for the Mexican war, he organized a company of which he was elected captain, and was attached to the Second Kentucky Regiment under Col. McKee. He participated in the battle of Buena Vista, where his company had the honor of firing the last guns. Gen. Fry after his return re-entered the mercantile business. On November 7, 1847, he was united in marriage to Mildred T. Smith of Jefferson County, Ky., a native of Shelby County. One daughter was born to this union: Mildred S. Turner, of Bowling Green. Gen. Fry's wife died in June, 1849. He married his second wife, Cynthia A. Hope, in 1851, to whom three sons were born: Frank W., Thomas J. and Speed S. The two younger are in business in Kansas City. He lost his second wife August 31, 1884. In 1851, under the provisions of the new constitution, he was solicited to run for county judge, to which he was elected for a term of four years, was continuously re-elected, and held the office until the breaking out of the late war. He immediately and earnestly espoused the cause of the National Government, and set to work organizing a home guard. In April, 1881, he enrolled 100 young men, and succeeded in arming and maintaining the organization as "Home Guards" until President Lincoln called upon the State for troops. He received authority from Gen. Nelson to raise a regiment, and August 6, 1861, with a handful of recruits, opened "Camp Dick Robinson" in Garrard County; recruiting was slow, but on October 9, 1861, his regiment, the Fourth Kentucky Volunteer Infantry, was mustered into service by Gen. George H. Thomas. In September, 1865, Gen. Fry was mustered out of the service, carrying with him the honors of being a brave and good soldier and commander. In 1866 he was the Republican candidate in his district for Congress. For some time he was engaged in collecting claims against the Government. In April, 1869, he was appointed supervisor of internal revenue for his district, which office he held until the consolidation of the district in 1872. Gen. Fry was a strong Whig, and emancipationist before the war; since he has identified himself with the Republicans. In religious belief he is a Presbyterian, and has for several years been a ruling elder of that church.

OLIVER PERRY HILL, M. D., is a lineal descendant, in the fourth generation of Thomas Hill, one of the early settlers at Cartwright Creek and an emigrant from Virginia at a period when but few permanent settlements had been established in the State. Thomas Hill immigrated to this country from England and first settled in St. Mary's County, Md., where about the year 1754 he married Rebecca Miles, who bore him a family of seven children—three sons and four daughters. At the beginning of the year 1787 he and his brother-in-law, Philip Miles, arranged to remove their families to Kentucky, and while en route down the Ohio River, in boats, to Louisville in March of that year, they were fired upon with fatal effect by hostile savages, who lined the banks. A negro slave of Thomas Hill, as well as several horses, were killed, and he himself severely wounded in the thighs. They reached Louisville in safety, however, and soon after went to Bardstown, where, owing to the severity of his wounds, Hill remained some time. In the spring of 1789, he removed to Cartwright's creek, where he purchased land and entered upon the life of a farmer. He was very zealous in the Catholic faith, and one of the chief promoters of the strong Catholic colony which afterward centered in that locality. His death occurred in 1820, at the ripe age of ninety-seven years, and his descendants are numerously represented in the South and West. Among the children of Thomas Hill was a son, William, who left the paternal roof at an early age and located in Garrard County. He was a believer in the Protestant religion, and a teacher by profession, a vocation which he successfully pursued for many years in Kentucky. Upon the breaking out of the war with England in 1812, he volunteered his services in behalf of the Nation and served in the brigade of Gen. Jennings. He participated in the battle on Lake Erie under Commodore Perry, and later was taken ill with dysentery and died, his remains being interred at Put-In-Bay. His wife was Nancy Mayfield, of Garrard County, Ky., and his children, John; George; Isaac, who died young; Martha, who married Archibald Woods; Mary, who married John Sullivan; Elizabeth, who married William Young; Nancy, who became the wife of David Gabbard, and Jane, who was married to Luda Martin. John Hill, the eldest of this family, located in the northern part of Garrard County, near the Kentucky River, and during his lifetime became a successful and representative farmer. He married Malinda Pollard, daughter of Absalom Pollard, a Revolutionary soldier and one of the earliest settlers from Virginia to locate in Garrard County. He was related to the well known family of that name in Virginia. But two children were born to that union: Oliver Perry Hill and his brother William who was an artisan by vocation, and died in Butler County, Ky. Dr. Oliver Perry Hill was born in Garrard County, March 2, 1814, and was named in honor of the great naval captain, under whom his grandfather had fought on Lake Erie. His early educational advantages were naturally limited to the common schools of his day, and he assisted his father in working upon the farm until he had reached the age of nearly twenty years. He then began the study of medicine under Dr. William Pawling, of Lexington, and subsequently attended lectures at Transylvania University, at that place; from which institution he was graduated with the degree of M. D. in March,

1838. From that time until 1840 he practiced his profession near his birthplace in the north end of the county, but in the latter year located at Lancaster, where he has been in active practice since, a period of about forty-seven years. During all that time Dr. Hill has been recognized as an intelligent and skillful practitioner, and has been in the enjoyment of a large and lucrative practice, performing in the meanwhile the full duty of a useful and respected citizen. His first political vote was cast in 1836 for the candidates of the Democratic party, Van Buren and Johnson, and with that party he has always since acted, though never aspiring to political position. During the late civil war he was a consistent Union man and gave what support he could to the measures and policy of the National Government. From 1853 to 1855 Dr. Hill traveled extensively in the western country, crossing the plains on horseback, and extended his observations not only as far as the Pacific Ocean, but through Oregon and California down into Mexico and through several of the Central American States and the West Indies. He resumed his practice in 1855. He is of a naturally studious tendency of mind, and being possessed of a remarkably retentive memory, has added greatly to his store of knowledge, being able to repeat almost whole books from memory without special effort. He is particularly fond of the study of the languages, and has mastered, without a teacher, French, German and Spanish, possessing a large library in these languages on general subjects. In religion he is liberal; he believes in one God from whom all things in the universe have emanated. He believes in a future state of rewards and punishments. He believes in the immortality of the soul. He believes there is more or less good in all religions, as all are founded on Bibles claiming to be of divine origin, as all religions and all nations seem to be equally favored by God. He believes, if the Bible be true, that it teaches that all evil as well as all good comes from God, for His greatest prophet so declares—see Isaiah xlv, 7—and the Bible so declares in many places.

GEN. EDWARD H. HOBSON was born July 11, 1825, in Greensburg (this State), and is a son of William and Lucy A. (Kertly) Hobson. The former, William Hobson, was born in Virginia, in January, 1788. The precise date of his birth was not known to him and he adopted the 8th of January as his birthday, because on that day the great battle was fought at New Orleans. His mother and father died when he was quite young, and his father having been in indigent circumstances, he (William) was placed in the guardianship of his uncle, Jonathan Patteson, who removed to Green County, Ky., in 1796, bringing William with him. He learned the saddler's trade, and as his time permitted studied the common educational branches, but was not able to remain in school. He went to Nashville, but returned, and in October, 1808, located permanently in Greensburg, and went into business on his own account. When the war of 1812 broke out he enlisted in a company raised by Warner Elmore, and joined the First Regiment, Kentucky Volunteer Dragoons, under Col. James Simral. His regiment was attached to Gen. Harrison's army in the Northwest, and soon after arriving there Mr. Hobson was made second lieutenant of his company, and later was unanimously elected first lieutenant, and distinguished himself at the battle of Massisinna, Ohio. After the war he married and reared a large family. Upon the establishment of a bank at Greensburg, in 1818, he was elected a director, and for forty years he was a member of the board of village trustees of Greensburg, and much of the time was president. His father was William Hobson, and his mother a Miss Patteson. Gen. Hobson, whose name heads this sketch, has rendered his State distinguished services. He is one of the self-made men, and has carved out his own position. His early education was obtained in Greensburg. He was offered a classical education, but preferred engaging in business that he might assist his father, who had become somewhat involved. When but fourteen years old he made a trip to the South driving hogs; walked the entire distance to Selma, Ala.; returned by way of New Orleans to Smithland, and walked thence through the deep snow. He learned the saddler's trade, which he followed for ten years, earning money and assisting his father. At the age of twenty he embarked in the grocery business in which he was successful, and finally changed it to a general store. In 1846 he enlisted as a private, and assisted in recruiting Company A, of the Second Kentucky Infantry, for the Mexican war. He was elected second lieutenant of the company, and shortly before the battle of Beuna Vista, was promoted to first lieutenant. He participated in that hard-fought battle, and commanded the left wing of his company as sharpshooters and skirmishers. Upon being discharged from the army he resumed his mercantile business in Greensburg. He became a director in the Bank of Greensburg and in 1859 was elected its president, which position he held until December, 1861, discharging his duties with fidelity. He was major in the State Guards before the civil war, and his battalion comprised five companies. In 1861, when Fort Sumter was fired upon, Gen. Hobson's patriotism was aroused, and he resolved to render all the assistance in his power to the Union cause and began recruiting a regiment. Previous to this he received an order from Gen. Buckner to go into camp with his battalion of State Guards, an order he refused to obey. In August, 1861, he was handed a colonel's commission, and invited by Gen. Nelson to report at Camp Nelson. Shortly after he received the appointment of colonel from the war department at Washington. He immediately proceeded to raise the Thirteenth Infantry. It was reported that the Confederates intended to seize the Bank of Greensburg and its contents, and Gen. Hobson determined to thwart their intentions by removing the funds (then amounting to $140,-000) for safety to Louisville. Although he had but about 100 men recruited for his regiment, with these as escort he moved with the funds to Campbellsville, then with five men as escort to Louisville, where he arrived with them in safety, receiving great praise from the bank officials at Louisville for his promptness and forethought. While at Louisville he drew twenty guns for his regiment, and returned and established his camp at Greensburg, which was further south than any Federal camp then in Kentucky. Afterward he went into Camp "Andrew Johnson," at Campbellsville, into camp then at Tebbs' Bend (Camp Hobson), and here the Thirteenth, Twenty-first and Twenty-seventh Regiments were mustered into service. While recruiting Gen. Hobson had several skirmishes with the enemy, the first blood being shed at Cyrus Hutchison's in a skirmish with a detachment of Hardee's men. Gen. Hobson distinguished himself at Shiloh, his gallant conduct there being the means for his nomination for a brigadier-general, but he did not receive the merited promotion until in March, 1863. He was in the siege of Corinth, and afterward was in the memorable chase of Bragg to Louisville, and participated in the engagements at Mount Washington, Perryville, Crab Orchard, and at Mount Vernon. At the latter place with two regiments, the Fifty-ninth Ohio and the Thirteenth Kentucky, he was ordered to advance into Clay County; on the expedition he captured 150 men. He then joined Gen. Thomas and proceeded south. When near Nashville he was ordered by Gen. Rosecrans

to take the Thirteenth, Twenty-sixth and Twenty-seventh Regiments, and return to Munfordville to recruit and rest, and discipline other regiments that would report to him, and protect the Green River bridge. He remained here from November, 1862, to June, 1863, and while stationed here received his commission as brigadier-general, to take rank from the 29th of November, 1862. He was ordered to report to Gen. Hartsuff, at Lexington, and was placed in control of the Kentucky Central division of the department. With reluctance he accepted the trust, believing that, with his almost perfect knowledge of the country, he could render better service further south. He was soon ordered to return to Munfordville, and then to Columbia, and then report to Gen. Juda, at Bowling Green, who ordered him to Glasgow, and thence to Tompkinsville. While here he developed Gen. Morgan's (John H.) position, and was ordered to Marrow Bone, and directed to hold the place at all hazards; there on the 2d of July, 1863, skirmished and repulsed part of Morgan's command. He was arranging to attack Morgan on the 3d of July, when he received orders from Gen. Juda, who was twelve miles in his rear, to stop his preparations. This order of Gen. Juda afforded Gen. Morgan an opportunity to move toward the Ohio River to his doom. Gens. Hobson and Shackelford were ordered to advance after Morgan had a start of fifteen hours; the former proceeded by way of Greensburg, where he was to form a junction with Gen. Juda, but the latter not having arrived, Hobson pushed on to Campbellsville, where he was joined by Shackelford, and together they moved to Lebanon. At Lebanon Gen. Hobson received orders from Gen. Burnside to assume command of the pursuing force, including Gen. Shackelford's, Col. Wolford's and his own troops, and pursue and capture Morgan. With 2,500 men under his command, he pushed on after Morgan, and from the time he left Lebanon was in the saddle twenty-one days and nights successively. When within fifteen miles of Brandenburg, where Morgan crossed the Ohio River, he was overtaken by an orderly with orders from Gen. Juda, but disregarding Gen. Juda's orders, he directed the orderly to fall into ranks, which he did. With an advance guard of fourteen men and two pieces of artillery, Gen. Hobson came up with Gen. Morgan in Ohio, near Buffington Island, attacked and defeated him in battle, capturing and killing many of his men. He does not claim the honor of capturing Morgan, according that honor to one of his junior officers, Maj.

Rue, of the Ninth Kentucky Cavalry. The General and his men gave the ladies of Ohio and Indiana great credit for their smiles and cheers, and particularly for their excellent provender. Many amusing incidents occurred while passing through the States north of the Ohio River. In southern Indiana a Knight of the Golden Circle rode up to Hobson with "How do you do, Gen. Morgan, am glad to see you. We are waiting for Gen. Hobson. with 100 men with whom we intend to annoy and bushwhack him as much as possible." He was finally informed that he was then talking to Gen. Hobson, and was handed over to an Indiana officer to be treated as he deserved. After the capture of Gen. Morgan, Gen. Juda, who had come up the river on boats, assumed command of the Federal forces under protest from Gen. Hobson. But orders were soon received from Gen. Burnside to turn everything over to Gen. Hobson and not to interfere with him in any way. It is confidently believed that, had Hobson been in command from the first, Gen. Morgan never could have crossed the Ohio River. After the Ohio raid Gen. Burnside, in acknowledgment of his distinguished services, placed Gen. Hobson in command of the entire cavalry force, for the expedition against Knoxville, Tenn., but the long fatiguing march, in pursuit of Morgan, had prostrated him, and it was two months before he was again able for active duty, and hence, did not participate in the Knoxville campaign. His next service was the annihilation of Col. Johnson, in western Kentucky, after which he reported to Gen. Burbridge and accompanied that officer on his fruitless expedition against the salt works in Virginia. In the retreat from that place after the battle (the command having been turned over to him on the field, and in front of the enemy by Gens. Burbridge and McClain) Gen. Hobson successfully conducted it, the two senior officers (Burbridge and McClain) going in advance to avoid capture. The whole honor of saving the army from total destruction belongs solely to Gen. Hobson. During the retreat they were attacked several times by the enemy, and a negro regiment stampeded, being led in the rout by its officers. Gen. Hobson caught the Major's horse by the bridle and threatened to shoot him if he did not stand and endeavor to rally his men. The act had a salutary effect on the regiment. Gen. Hobson was a gallant officer, brave, but not rash; cool and determined in the midst of danger, and always at his post when there was work to do. He was well liked by his men, and very popular in the army. After the close of the war

he returned home and again resumed the mercantile business. In 1869 he was appointed collector of internal revenue for the Fourth District, which position he held until 1874. Since then he has been a director and president of the Cumberland & Ohio Railroad. He is also extensively engaged in farming and the lumber business, and is looked upon as one of the most enterprising and progressive men in southern Kentucky. Gen. Hobson married Katie Adair, a daughter of Alexander and Elizabeth (Monroe) Adair. They have had six children born to them: William A., Anna M. Penick, Atwood M. (deceased), John A., Edwena and Bettie K. His wife died in 1872. Gen. Hobson is a prominent and zealous Mason, and was Deputy Grand Master of Masons for the State when the war broke out. He is also a member of the G. A. R. In 1866 Gen. Hobson was strongly and urgently solicited, by the Union party of Kentucky, to make the race for clerk of the court of appeals. Very much against his wishes he reluctantly consented, saying that he knew, owing to the political situation at that time in Kentucky, that he would be sacrificed; that he was an ardent supporter of the Thirteenth Amendment to the Federal Constitution, which measure in time would become popular, but his strong and urgent advocacy of the amendment would be the cause of his defeat, which proved to be correct. Since the war Gen. Hobson has been an ardent Union man, and stanch Republican; has several times been tendered the nomination for Congress in the Fourth Congressional District of Kentucky, but owing to the nature of his private business was compelled to decline the nomination. He was always a great admirer and earnest friend of Gen. Grant, and was a delegate to the Chicago Convention when Grant was proposed for a third term, and was one of the famous 306 who voted for Grant until his defeat in the convention by Gen. Garfield.

HON. SILVESTER JOHNSON was born October 15, 1813, in Nelson County, and is one of nine children, viz.: Charles, Nancy, William, Thomas, John, Elizabeth, the subject, Ellen and Catherine, born to John and Dorothy (Miles) Johnson, natives of St. Mary's County, Md. They came to Nelson County in 1798, and settled near where New Hope now stands. He married for his second wife, Henrietta, a daughter of John B. Hill, by whom he had four children: Priscilla, Hillery, Mary and Sally. The family was of the Roman Catholic faith. Mr. Johnson became a substantial farmer in the county, and died in 1833, at the age of fifty-six years. The subject of this sketch, Silvester Johnson, was brought up on a farm, and received a good English education, finishing off with two years at St. Mary's College, in Marion County. He taught school during the summer months and flatboated during the winter, a business that had been begun by his uncle. Mr. Johnson was but eighteen years old when he commenced the battle of life on his own account. He flatboated and merchandised until 1843, when he retired from boating and acted as deputy sheriff for several years, but continued the mercantile business, and in 1853 was elected sheriff, serving one term; afterward acted as deputy sheriff up to 1857. In 1859 he was elected to the Legislature. He has since been solicited several times to offer for the same office but has always declined. He has drifted into the banking business, which he has successfully carried on for sixteen years. He owns considerable property in New Haven, where he has lived for the last fifty-one years, and is reported to be worth from $300,000 to $400,000, and has given away to charitable purposes $100,000. He still continues to give liberally; for several years he has been clothing the children of St. Thomas' Orphan Asylum. In 1873 he built a parochial schoolhouse in New Haven, at a cost of $6,000 and donated it to the Roman Catholic Church. He established two free Catholic schools and pays out of his own funds the teachers for both white and colored schools. He gave about $20,000 to a new Roman Catholic Church erected in New Haven at a total cost of $30,000. Mr. Johnson was married in August, 1835, to Mildred, a daughter of Charles and Susan (Howard) Boone, who came from Maryland in 1798, and settled in this county. Mrs. Johnson was born in February, 1816, and died July 29, 1875. She was a most excellent lady, noted for her charitable qualities. Mr. Johnson was originally a Whig and gave his first vote for Henry Clay for President. At the dissolution of the Whig party in 1855, and the springing up of the Know-nothing party, he joined the Democratic party, and has voted with it ever since without ever scratching the ticket. He has been a member of the Democratic committee for Nelson County for the last thirty years.

ALEXANDER ROBERTSON McKEE, M. D., was born on the 4th of February, 1816, near Lancaster, Garrard Co., Ky. He was the third son of Hon. Samuel McKee, who was a prominent and successful lawyer and politician during the early history of the State. Dr. McKee received a collegiate education at Centre College, Danville, Ky., and subsequently took his degree in medicine at the University of Pennsylvania with the class of 1839. Soon thereafter he located at Richmond, Madison Co., Ky., and formed a partnership for the practice of his profession with his cousin, the late Dr. William R. Letcher. He at once acquired a large and lucrative practice and commanded the universal respect and confidence of the community. During the time he resided in Madison County he was elected and served for many years as a director of the Northern Bank of Kentucky, as a member of the board of trustees of the town of Richmond, and as an elder in the Presbyterian Church. In 1857 Dr. McKee removed to Clay County, Mo., where he remained only two years. Returning to Kentucky in the spring of 1859 he located at Danville, where he resumed the practice of his profession, and resided at that place until his death on the 13th of February, 1886. Dr. McKee was engaged as an active and honorable practitioner of medicine for forty-seven years, commencing in 1839, and ending a few days before his death in 1886. He was a diligent student of medicine, thoroughly devoted to his profession, and was recognized by the medical profession and the community at large as a thoroughly qualified and conscientious practitioner. He acquired wide reputation as a safe and successful physician. Few men in any profession have, for so many years, retained their practice as Dr. McKee. Until four days before his death in the seventy-first year of his age he was engaged in the successful practice of his profession. He was remarkably successful as a general practitioner, but was known as specially successful as an accoucheur. It is known that out of over 1,600 obstetrical cases that he attended during his professional career, only one case resulted in the death of the mother. Dr. McKee was one of the organizers of the Boyle County Medical Society, also of the district society, and was frequently elected president of each. He was also a member of the Kentucky State Medical Society. He was a man of great physical as well as moral courage. He never failed, or even hesitated, in the discharge of what he considered to be his duty. No danger or personal inconvenience ever deterred him, or caused him to falter. This feature of his character was well illustrated by his conduct during the winter of 1862, after the battle of Perryville, where he had under his professional care as many as 1,200 sick and wounded Union and Confederate soldiers, many of whom had contagious and infectious diseases. To these he gave as careful and as faithful attention as he did to his nearest friends and patients suffering from ordinary diseases. He was a man of great firmness and determination. When once he had made up his mind, or come to a conclusion about any matter, no amount of threats or persuasion could induce him to abandon his position. No consideration of personal gain or popularity seemed to have the slightest influence with him; justice and right seemed to be the main considerations with him, let the consequences be what they would. He was a true and steadfast friend, a wise counselor, a public-spirited citizen, a skillful physician, and an upright and honest man, beloved and respected by the entire community. Dr. McKee's father, Hon. Samuel McKee, was a noted man in his day. Born in Rockbridge County, Va., October 13, 1774, he removed with his father, Col. Wm. McKee, to Garrard County, Ky., about the year 1800. He was a member of Congress from 1806 to 1816, succeeding Judge John Boyle in that office. He was circuit judge for a number of years, and an officer in the war of 1812. As a lawyer he commanded a very large practice, and as an orator he had few equals. He seldom ever had any opposition for any office to which he aspired. He was so popular in his own county that the largest number of votes ever cast against him in that county was six. He was repeatedly elected a member of the Kentucky Legislature, was a member of the first board of trustees of Centre College, and at the time of his death in 1826 was serving by appointment of President Monroe as president of the first commission to clear the Ohio and Mississippi Rivers of obstructions. Dr. McKee had only two brothers, Col. Wm. R. McKee, who graduated at the military academy at West Point in 1829 and was subsequently colonel of the Second Kentucky Regiment in the war with Mexico, and lost his life at the head of his regiment at the same time with Lieut.-Col. Henry Clay, Jr., at Buena Vista. His other brother, Judge George R. McKee, one of the most distinguished and successful lawyers of the State, still resides in Covington. Dr. McKee's only sister, Jane Logan McKee, was married to Dr. Benjamin F. Duncan, of Garrard County. She died at the old "McKee" homestead near Lancaster in 1873. Dr. McKee's grandfather, Col. Wm. McKee of Scotch-Irish descent, was a captain in the Revolutionary war for six years; a member of the convention that drafted the first constitution of the State of Virginia; a member of the Virginia Convention that adopted the Constitution of the United States; was high sheriff of Rockbridge County, Va.; removed to Kentucky about the year 1800, and settled upon Gilbert's Creek near Lancaster. Col. McKee's first wife was his cousin, Mariam McKee, and his second wife was also his cousin, being at the time of their marriage the widow of Col. Joseph Daviess, and was the mother by her first husband of Col. Joseph Hamilton Daviess, who was killed at the battle of Tippecanoe. Dr. McKee's mother was Martha Robertson, daughter of Alexander Robertson, the first sheriff of Mercer County; member of the first county court for Lincoln County; delegate to the Virginia Convention called to ratify the Federal constitution; member of Virginia Legislature until 1789; voted with all the Kentucky delegates, except Humphrey Marshall, against the adoption of the Federal constitution. Dr. McKee's mother was a sister of the late Chief Justice George Robertson and also of Mrs. ex-Gov. Robt. P. Letcher. Dr. McKee was married in September, 1842, to Mary Ashby, daughter of Dr. M. Q. Ashby, of Richmond, Ky. They were blessed with six children: Samuel, Ashby, George, Logan, Alexander and Margaret Logan McKee. George R. died in infancy, and Ashby, a young man of rare promise, died in the twenty-eighth year of his age, in Louisville, Ky. The remaining children are yet living. Mrs. McKee's family, the Ashbys, were also very prominent and bore a conspicuous part in the early history of Virginia and Kentucky. Mrs. McKee's father, Dr. M. Q. Ashby of Mt. Sterling, Ky., was a prominent physician for many years at Richmond and Lexington, Ky., and was one of the wealthiest and most influential men of central Kentucky. Her grandfather, Capt. Nathaniel Ashby, was a captain in the Revolutionary war; also in the war of 1812; served under Gen. Morgan throughout the war of the Revolution and was at the surrender of Cornwallis at Yorktown. Her great-grandfather, Capt. John Ashby, was an aid on George Washington's staff at Braddock's defeat in 1754; was also an officer in the Revolutionary war with his son, Capt. Nathaniel Ashby. Ashby's Gap, in Virginia, is named for Capt. John Ashby; and Gen. Turner Ashby, of "Black Horse" cavalry fame, is of the same family, being a second cousin of Mrs. McKee.

JAMES HARRISON MOORE, M. D. The original ancestor of the numerous and influential Southern family represented by the subject of this sketch, was Thomas Moore, who came from the vicinity of Liverpool and Bristol, England, at an early period and settled on the bank of the Nomonee River in

Westmoreland County, Va., where he began as one of the pioneers of that section, living in peace and friendship with the native Indian tribes by whom he was surrounded. He left two sons, William and Thomas, to whom he devised his estate. Thomas died on his portion of the old farm, leaving two sons, Thomas and James, who disposed of the property and moved to North Carolina, where they are now numerously represented by descendants. William Moore, son of the pioneer, married Sarah Lawson, and passed his life on his patrimonial estate. He also left two sons, Elijah and Vincent. The latter married and raised a family of children in Northumberland County, Va., where he died. Elijah, at the age of nineteen, married Judith Harrison, of Northumberland County, Va., and had three sons: Lawson, George and William. Shortly after the birth of his last son the father was killed by lightning at the early age of twenty-six years. He was a large, powerful man, of great perseverance and energy, and his sudden death was deeply regretted. His wife survived him eighteen months, leaving the three sons mentioned, who were placed under the guardianship of Christopher Collins, a merchant in Westmoreland County, who proved an efficient and trustworthy protector and guide, and whose noble traits of character were ever cherished by his wards. Lawson Moore, the eldest of the sons, married in 1794, Elizabeth Rochester, a representative of an old and prominent Virginia family, and four years later, 1798, moved with his family to Kentucky. He purchased a large tract of land near Danville, Boyle Co., Ky., and there passed his life engaged in farming pursuits. July 26, 1815, death deprived him of his wife, and January 22, 1817, he married her sister, Jane Murray Rochester, whom he survived some years. Lawson Moore was upward of six feet in height, large frame and commanding presence, a man of strong native intellect, well versed in history and abreast with the spirit of the age. Having a large family of sons and daughters, he fully appreciated the benefits of education and was one of the active workers in aid of erecting Centre College. He had a large family of children. By his first marriage were born Sally, who married Elijah Harlan; Betsy Lawson, who married Gen. William Moore, of Tennessee; Elijah, a lawyer by profession, residing at Little Rock, Ark., for a number of years and ending his career as a banker and general investor at St. Louis; John Rochester, a physician prominent in his profession, who practiced successively at Danville, Ky., New Orleans, La.,

Louisville, Ky., and died at Bowling Green, Ky.; Nancy Jordan, who married Archibald Yell, afterward governor of Arkansas, who fell at Buena Vista during the Mexican war, with McKee Hardin and the son of Henry Clay; George, a clergyman of the Presbyterian Church, who died in Mississippi, engaged in cotton planting; Jane, who married Rev. Robert McAfee, of the Presbyterian Church, and died at Columbus, Mo.; William, who was educated at West Point, settled in Texas where he was active in the war of independence and died at Moore's Bluff, on Trinity River; Lawson, who engaged in planting in Mississippi; Sophia, who married James F. McCaleb, a large cotton planter of Adams County, Miss., and died there, and Artemisia, who became the wife of Rev. John L. Sloan, of Tennessee. By his second marriage Lawson Moore had five sons, of whom Joseph Lapsley died during boyhood. Christopher Collins Moore was educated at Centre College, Danville, was a successful merchant at Harrodsburg for many years, and finally located on a farm near Danville, where he led a successful career and closed his days; he was for many years president of the First National Bank of Harrodsburg. Thomas Rochester Moore was born and educated at Danville and engaged in farming in Mercer County, owning the old Capt. Chaplin farm. Charles O. Moore was educated at Centre College, studied law and devoted his life to farming on the old ancestral estate near Danville; his widow and two sons now occupy the place. James Harrison Moore, second son of Lawson Moore by his later marriage, was born on the old farm near Danville, October 3, 1819. Here he passed his boyhood, receiving an excellent English education and subsequently entering Centre College, where he enjoyed the benefits of a classical course. He subsequently commenced the study of medicine under Drs. Joseph Weisiger and John Fleece of Danville, and matriculated at Transylvania Medical College, Lexington, from which institution he was graduated with the degree of M. D. in 1841. He located in Warren County, Miss., soon after, where he successfully practiced his profession for five years. There he met and married Mrs. Mary S. Foster, daughter of Daniel T. Messinger, of Berkshire County, Mass., and soon afterward returned to his native county. He first located at Harrodsburg, where he practiced for awhile and then joined his brother, Collins Moore, in trade, as Moore & Moore. Several years later (1851) he purchased the Maj. William Hoard farm, a portion of the old Capt. Chaplin farm near Harrodsburg, and entered upon the life of a farmer and breeder of thoroughbred Durham cattle, and horses. This is his present residence. In addition to this he also owns a large plantation on Deer Creek, Miss., where he is extensively engaged in cotton raising. Dr. Moore has been closely identified with the business and social life of his section for many years and is recognized as a useful and thoroughly trustworthy citizen. He was one of the organizers of the Mercer County National Bank of Harrodsburg, and is president of that institution. He is also an elder in the Southern Presbyterian Church of Harrodsburg, and interested in other local enterprises. In 1856 he passed from the Whig to the Democratic party with which he is at present identified. Though opposed to the secession of the States, the ties of interest and kinship which bound him to the South caused him to sympathize with that section during the civil war. His two sons are Hon. Daniel L. Moore, late State senator from the capital district of Kentucky, and Bacon Rochester Moore, a lawyer by profession, engaged in planting in the South.

DANIEL LAWSON MOORE was born at Harrodsburg, Ky., January 31, 1847. He is the elder of the two sons of Dr. James H. Moore and of Mary (Messenger) Moore, his wife, and a representative of an old and influential family of the South, whose origin and history are set forth in detail in the sketch of Dr. Moore, contained in this volume. He received his preparatory educational training under a private tutor, and finally entered Centre College, Danville, as a student, where he continued for three years. He then began the study of law in the office of Phil. B. Thompson, of Harrodsburg, and in due course of time was licensed to practice at the bar. He never entered upon the practice of his profession, however, preferring to labor in what he considered the more profitable financial fields of agriculture and stock raising. For five years he engaged in cotton planting in Mississippi; and on November 15, 1870, married Henrietta, only child of Judge William H. McBrayer, of Lawrenceburg, Ky. In 1881 he was elected on the Democratic ticket to represent the Twentieth, or Capitol District, in the State Senate of Kentucky, performing the duties of the office in an intelligent and capable manner, and eliciting the commendation of his constituents. In 1882 he was deprived by death of his accomplished wife, whose early demise caused many deep feelings of sorrow. Soon after, leaving his three children, May, Wallace and McBrayer, in the pleasant home of their grandparents,

he visited the distant West, where he met with the exciting scenes of frontier life, and found fortunate investments. He established a large ranch in Colorado, in the fertile foothills of the Rocky Mountains, and entered into the business of raising cattle and horses, importing some of the best blood of Kentucky to his ranch. He has met with great success in this line, and is recognized as one of the leading stock-raisers of Colorado. Half of each year is spent in the management of his business in that State, and the remainder is devoted to his manufacturing and farming interests in Kentucky; and to planting in Mississippi. Few men have more friends, or retain them better than Senator Moore. While not lacking in force and individuality of character, he possesses a genial and companionable nature, which draws friends to him, and inspires them with respect for him. He is liberal and generous to a fault, a representative of true Bourbon Democracy, of strict integrity, and thorough honesty of purpose and deed. As a business man he has by his success in other fields reflected great credit upon his native State of Kentucky.

DR. CHARLES HARVEY SPILMAN, of Harrodsburg, is one of the oldest and best known of Kentucky's early physicians, and for a period of fifty-two years has devoted himself assiduously to the practice of his profession. He was born in Garrard County, Ky., May 20, 1805, of English parentage. His father was Benjamin Spilman and his mother Nancy R., daughter of James Rice, of Virginia, and cousin of Parson Rice, a pioneer preacher of Kentucky, and of Rev. Nathaniel L. Rice, D. D., of Danville. He is a lineal descendant of Henricus Spelmannus, the original ancestor of the family, who was knighted in England and came to America at an early day. Dr. Spilman received a thorough classical education at Centre College, Danville, then under the presidency of Gideon Blackburn, and subsequently pursued his medical studies at Transylvania University, Lexington, Ky., from which institution he was graduated with the degree of M. D., March 1, 1835. While in attendance at the university he enjoyed the benefits of private instruction under Dr. Benjamin W. Dudley, then one of the most distinguished surgeons of the West. Previous to his graduation he spent several years, from 1832 to 1835, at Yazoo City, Miss., in the practice of his profession on a special license issued after examination by the Eastern Medical Board. April 9, 1835, he married Miss Mary Duryea Skillman, a native of Freehold, N. J., and a representative of one of the oldest and most prominent families of that commonwealth, and in May of the following year located in practice at Nicholasville, Jessamine Co., Ky., in which county he remained for a period of fifteen years. In January, 1850, he removed to Harrodsburg, Ky., where he is still, at the ripe age of eighty-two years, engaged in practice. Dr. Spilman has never limited his efforts to any special branch of medical science, but has always been a general practitioner. He was elected a member of the American Medical Association in 1850, and, on several occasions has been a delegate to the annual conventions of that body. He became a member of the Kentucky State Medical Society in 1851 and served as its president from 1854 to 1856. During the winter of 1854, by appointment of that society, he addressed the Legislature of the State on the "Relations and Reciprocal Obligations of Medicine and the State," the object being to get an appropriation to cover the expense of publishing the proceedings of the State society. Dr. Spilman is also a member of the Central Kentucky Medical Association and served as its first president in 1872. He has also frequently acted as president at the sessions of the Mercer County Medical Society. He never has taken any active part in politics, although at first a Whig and then a Republican. During the civil war he continued his work, oftentimes amid scenes of carnage and bloodshed, administered alike to those who wore the blue and those who wore the gray, and being earnestly in sympathy with the Union cause. While much of Dr. Spilman's time has necessarily been taken up in the laborious pursuit of an extensive general practice he has still found time to enrich the literature of the profession by many able contributions on various topics of interest, and for many years wrote for publication in the current periodicals of the day an average of two essays each month. Among the topics embraced in these contributions mention may be made of the following: "Report on Indigenous Botany," contained in the transactions of the Kentucky State Medical Society for 1852; "Suits for Malpractice," in the *Medical News*, Louisville, in 1856; "Blood-letting Then and Now," in the *Medical and Surgical Reporter*, 1868; "Metastatic Diversion of Labor," *ibid.*, 1867; "Boldness and Timidity in Practice Contrasted," *Repertory*, Cincinnati, 1868; "Blood-letting as a Therapeutic Agent," *Richmond and Louisville Medical Journal*,

1869; "Myelitis Spinalis," *Medical and Surgical Reporter*, 1870; "A Popular Physiological Fallacy," *Repertory*, Cincinnati, 1870; "Patent Medicines and Quack Remedies," *ibid.*, 1871; "Therapeutic Action of Mercury," *Richmond and Louisville Medical Journal*, 1873; "Embolism," *ibid.*, 1874, and "Pudendal Hernia," *ibid.*, 1875. A careful examination of these subjects will demonstrate, even to the unprofessional reader, how earnest, energetic and industrious Dr. Spilman must have been in his profession and how comprehensive and thorough his study and investigation. Dr. Spilman is one of the oldest residents of Mercer County and aside from his professional relations to that community has always performed the full duty of a useful and honored citizen and done all that he could to promote the spiritual and moral welfare of the section in which he has spent his life. He is an elder in the Assembly Presbyterian Church of Harrodsburg, enjoys the confidence and respect of the citizens of that place, and is regarded as an upright and valuable member of the community. Though he has long passed the allotted limitation of life of which the Psalmist sung, he is still well preserved in the possession of all his faculties and mentally alert and active. Much of his leisure time has been devoted to music, of which he is an ardent lover, and in singing of which he has always excelled. Of his large family of children but few now survive. John T. was a practicing lawyer at Harrodsburg during his lifetime; Abraham T. was a clergyman of the Presbyterian Church, and officiated at Paint Lick, Garrard County; Benjamin is a photographer at Harrodsburg, and his daughter, Mary Frances, became the wife of Clarence Anderson, of Hopkinsville, Ky.; his daughter, Elizabeth A. Spilman, married William Alexander and left two daughters and a son, who, together with a son of his deceased son, John T. Spilman, now reside with their grandfather.

GEORGE WINSTON WELSH was born in Lincoln County, Ky., September 9, 1809. His grandfather on the paternal side was James Welsh, a native of the North of Ireland, who married a representative of the prominent (Scotch) Douglass family and immigrated to this country at a period somewhat antedating the Revolutionary war. He established himself in the neighborhood of Harrisburg, Penn., where he passed his days in the peaceful pursuit of agriculture. He had a large family of children all of whom removed to Kentucky early in life and became identified with the pioneer growth and development of that now prosperous State. Thomas, Joseph and John located at Stanford, Lincoln County, about 1790 and engaged in mercantile pursuits. James, about the same period, settled at Lexington, whence he removed to Jefferson County, where he died ; Edward passed his life at Lexington engaged in teaching ; William became a tanner and resided in Barren County and Andrew engaged in farming operations in Jefferson County. Two daughters married ; one into the Darby family and the other the Guthrie family and also became identified with the early settlement of Kentucky. Of these sons, John was the father of the subject of this sketch ; for his first wife he married Sarah, daughter of William Withers, who ended his days near the mouth of Salt River. Of this union were born two daughters ; Sarah, who married John Merrifield of Bloomfield, Ky., and Nancy, who became the wife, first of William Stewart of Bedford, Penn., and secondly of Asa Combs of Nelson County, Ky. For his second wife John Welsh espoused Pamelia, daughter of George Lee, of Lincoln County, Ky., and a member of one of the pioneer families of that section. It is related of this lady that she used to take her turn standing guard in the blockhouse that formed the citadel of safety against Indian attacks in her younger days. The result of this marriage was five children, of whom four attained years of maturity, viz. : Joseph, who died in Georgia ; Elizabeth, widow of James Nichols and mother of Joseph W. Nichols, cashier of the Farmers and Drovers Bank of Louisville; George Winston; and John Welsh, who has been dead for many years. The father of this family, having pursued the occupation of a merchant and latterly a farmer in Lincoln County, finally removed to Hardin County, where he died in 1823 at the age of fifty-four, surviving his wife ten years. The opening years of the life of George Winston Welsh were passed in Lincoln County and upon the removal of his parents to Hardin County he accompanied them. His opportunities for obtaining an education in that undeveloped country were at that time very limited, his entire book training having been received within the short period of eighteen months. After the death of his father, in 1823, he returned to Lincoln County and soon after engaged in the business of a cabinet-maker, a vocation which he abandoned soon after and opened a general country store in that county. In the spring of 1832 he went on horseback to Palmyra, Mo., where he engaged in trade for a time, passing the winter of that year in Tallahassee,

Fla., whither he also went on horseback. Soon after he began farming in Illinois where he remained until 1836, when, being unable to outgrow the attachments and memories of his native county, he returned and opened a store at Hustonville, Ky. There he remained in trade until February, 1852, when he transferred his enterprises to Danville, Ky., where he has continued in active business since. Mr. Welsh has now attained the ripe age of seventy-eight years but is still in possession of all his faculties. For a period of fifty years past no citizen in this locality has been so closely identified with the moral, religious, commercial and material growth of this section nor more uniformly enjoyed the respect and confidence of his friends and associates. Politically he was originally a Henry Clay Whig, and has remained faithful to the traditions and principles of that party and of its natural successor, the Republican party, throughout a long life. During the trying period of the civil war, which was so closely associated with his section and State, he remained true to the Union cause and murmured not, though the issue of the Emancipation Proclamation deprived him of much of what he had been taught to believe was his rightful property. He never aspired to public position and has uniformly declined many flattering offers of preferment in that direction. With the business life of Danville no man has been more intimately identified for forty years and many of the worthy institutions and business enterprises of that place were either conceived and founded by him or received from him the most liberal encouragement and support. He was the chief organizer of the First National Bank of Danville in 1865 and president of that institution for fifteen years. He was one of the organizers of the Farmers National Bank of Danville in 1879 and is at present holding the office of vice-president. For a quarter of a century he has been a member of the board of directors of Centre College, Danville, and of the Theological Seminary, and is the president of the board of directors of the female college in that place, of which he was one of the founders in 1859 and of which he has been a liberal patron since. It was largely through his energy and activity that the right of way was obtained for the Cincinnati Southern Railroad through to Danville, which has done so much for the social and material development of that town, and it is not too much to say that Mr. Welsh has always lent liberal encouragement to all movements of a progressive and elevating character in his locality and in a generous and unostentatious way assisted them all. Now, in the

48

evening of life, it is deemed but fitting and right that some permanent record should be made of his life-work and character on behalf of his family and numerous friends. Mr. Welsh was married in November, 1834, to Mary, daughter of Capt. James Breath, of Madison County, Ill., formerly of New York. The golden wedding of the couple was fitly celebrated in 1884 and they are still in the enjoyment of a happy married life. Of the eleven children born to them, seven reached mature years: Elizabeth, wife of Camillus W. Metcalf, of Atlanta, Ga.; Adeline, wife of G. E. Wiseman of Danville, Ky.; George W., Jr., for ten years a merchant in Danville and now cashier of the Farmers National Bank of that place; John Edward, engaged in mining in Colorado; Mary Louise (deceased), who became the wife of John Greenway of Lexington, Ky.; James B., engaged in mercantile life at Kansas City, Mo., and William L. Welsh who is in trade at Danville, Ky.

JOHN AUGUSTUS WILLIAMS, A. M., LL. D., president of the Daughters College Harrodsburg, Ky., was born September 21, 1824, in Bourbon County, Ky. His father was Dr. Charles E. Williams, a native of Montgomery County, a physician of high standing, a man of scholarly attainments, who for many years was associated with his son in the management of the affairs of Daughters College, and who finally passed away in 1881 to the enjoyment of still higher scenes and associations. The mother of Prof. Williams was Arabella Dodge, daughter of one of the early merchants and manufacturers of Lexington, Ky. The Williams family is of Welsh extraction. Raleigh Williams, grandfather of Prof. Williams, immigrated to Kentucky from Virginia with the early settlers of the former State. Prof. Williams passed the opening years of his life at Paris, Bourbon County, where his earliest instruction was received, and at the age of fifteen, entered Bacon College, then located at Georgetown as a student. While in attendance at that institution it was removed to Harrodsburg, and subsequently became known as the Kentucky University, from which our subject graduated in 1843, under the presidency of Dr. James Shannon. He subsequently received the degree of A. M. from his *alma mater*, and later, that of LL. D., from the Masonic University at La Grange, Ky. After leaving college he entered on the study of law with a view of adopting that profession, but was prevented from accomplishing that purpose by the development of a very decided taste for teaching and the discovery of serious needs in the educational system of the State. In 1848 he took charge of what was called Prospect Hill Seminary, a boarding school for young ladies and gentlemen near Mount Sterling, an institution which became very prosperous under his management, and in which he obtained considerable distinction from his original methods and superior talents as a teacher. He soon after established a female college at North Middleton, in Bourbon County, known as Bourbon Institute, in which he aimed to carry into full effect his advanced plans of education. In 1851 he was urged to and did establish his institution at Columbia, Mo., the seat of Missouri University. A liberal charter was granted by the State, and under the designation of Christian College it was formally organized in the spring of that year. His conduct of the school brought it into popular notice and universal popularity, filling it to overflowing with young ladies of the best families in the State. He presided over that institution until 1856, when ill health and a desire to return and labor in his native State, induced him to resign. In that year he purchased, in connection with his father, the property at Harrodsburg, upon which is situated the celebrated Greenville Magnesian Springs, and established the Daughters College, now one of the most successful institutions of its kind in the State. The name was given to the school to express the two fundamental ideas of its educational system—that it was both a school that should be collegiate in its curriculum and methods, combined with a home that should meet the social and domestic wants of girls away from their parents. The success that attended the opening of the school in 1856 has been almost uninterrupted to the present time—a period of nearly thirty-one years. The war of the States cut off for a while some of its most distant patronage; but pupils continued to come even during that period, sometimes with military passes in their hands. Not a day was lost during the four years of strife, though the sound of distant artillery sometimes mingled with the voices of the faithful teachers in the class-rooms. In 1865 President Williams was appointed to the chair of moral and mental philosophy in Kentucky University, and afterward to the presidency of the State College, and then to that of the College of Arts at Lexington. The two former positions he accepted and filled, but declined the latter; yet during his temporary absence Daughters College, though limited in the number of its students, continued to prosper under the skillful management of able assistants. In 1868 Prof. Williams resigned his position in the university at Lexington, and returned to his beloved pupils at Harrodsburg. Soon its halls were filled. Students again flocked in from Kentucky and the surrounding States. Since that time it has gone on quietly in its career of usefulness; and, without any special effort to obtain patronage, it has always been full. It now has 150 students enrolled, representing fifteen States. It is assumed, in the system of education at this college, that every student is to become a teacher and trainer of youth, either in the capacity of mother, or in that of a professional teacher. The effect of this policy is to give to the school a decidedly normal character, evinced by the fact that so large a number of good teachers are annually graduated therefrom. From time to time, departures from the usual routine and customs of schools have been made as the experience of the faculty suggested. It has consequently been recognized as the pioneer in many of the reforms that now characterize our best female schools. The abolition of the rote methods of study and recitation, and the discontinuance of all public parades, rostrum performances and exhibitions of young lady students, were early insisted on; and papers adverse to these and other customs have been kept for years before the people in the annual catalogues of the college. Public sentiment, especially in Kentucky, has at last begun to array itself against many of these things; and other institutions are beginning to modify or to discontinue them altogether.

The life of Dr. John Aug. Williams has been a busy one, yet the wear and tear that attend the ofttimes routine labor of a popular educator, has made no strong impression upon his physical resources. He is still well preserved, ardently in love with his responsible and high calling, and actively engaged in solving the great problem of higher education in Kentucky. He was one of the original movers in the organization of the State Teachers' Association, has contributed extensively to various literary and religious periodicals, and delivered many addresses. His life of "Elder John Smith" is a well-known and standard volume. His most important work, however, will be the one on "Christian Ethics," now in course of preparation. He has also occasionally been induced to occupy the pulpit of various churches, both in and out of his own denomination. He is a man of fine tastes, has a great fondness for poetry, literature and art; of genial and attractive presence, kindly nature and greatly esteemed and respected by his associates and pupils, as well as by the community at large. He was married in 1848 to Miss Mary L. Hathaway, daughter of Philip Hathaway of Montgomery County, Ky., a representative of one of the early pioneer families from Virginia, and a lady of great excellence of heart and mind. Three sons born of the union are now living, viz.: Aug. E. Williams, professor of music in the college; Bowman Guy Williams, bookkeeper in same, and Lee Price Williams, a young student of medicine.

Sketches of Book Patrons.

BENJAMIN F. ABELL was born in 1827 and is a son of John H. Abell and Teresa (Beaven) Abell. John H. was the son of Barton Abell and was born on the Rolling Fork in 1792. His life was devoted to the pursuits of agriculture and terminated in the year 1878. His family, consisting of ten children, six of whom are deceased, were Lewis A., John B., George, Edward, Charles, Benjamin F., Alfred, Henrietta Ann, Susan E. and Elizabeth T. Abell. The mother died in 1851. The Abell family were closely identified with the early history of the county and also with the Catholic Church. Benjamin F. was educated in St. Mary's College, in Marion County, and is a practical farmer of Lebanon precinct, and is closely allied with the progressive enterprises of his native county of Marion. His farm, comprising 200 acres, is near the city of Lebanon.

JAMES C. ADAMS was born November 21, 1845, in Garrard County, Ky., and is a son of Wesley and Elizabeth (Davison) Adams, to whom three sons and three daughters were born, five of whom were reared. Wesley Adams was born in Virginia, in 1815, and brought to Kentucky when a boy. He died in 1852. His parents lived and died in Virginia. Mrs. Elizabeth Adams was born in Garrard County and is a daughter of Abner and Martha (Grashaw) Davison, both natives of Virginia and early settlers of Garrard County, Ky. Mr. Davison was a substantial and prosperous farmer. He was born in 1797, was of English descent, served for many years as justice of his country, in religion was a Baptist, and died in 1837. James C. Adams was the third child in order of birth, was reared a farmer and received an education such as the country afforded in his day. At twenty-one he began life on his own account, having worked for his mother from the time he was fifteen years old. He was united in marriage to Nancy Hockaday, a daughter of James S. and Sumyra (Shearer) Hockaday, natives of Madison County. Mr. Hockaday was a farmer and owner of slave property, had raised four sons and three daughters, was a member of Christian Church, in politics a Democrat. He died in April, 1885, aged sixty-seven. He was a son of James and Elizabeth (Fox) Hockaday, natives of Madison County. The issue from this marriage of Mr. Adams was six children, namely: William W., James W., Robert L., Leslie C., Stella H. and Nannie L. Mr. and Mrs. Adams are members of the Christian Church. Mr. Adams located in Madison County when he became of age. In 1875 he purchased 227 acres one mile south of Harris Station. In 1883 his residence was destroyed by fire, when he located where he now resides, one mile north of Silver Creek, on seventy-three acres. He is also possessor of two other tracts of 105 and 12 acres, owning in all 417 acres, all of which he accumulated by his own industry. In politics he is a Democrat and cast the first presidential vote for Seymour.

DR. EDWARD ALCORN was born August 10, 1843, in Lincoln County, and studied medicine under Drs. David J. Alcorn and George Hunn, and has devoted himself to the practice of that profession, in which he has been successful. He was married in 1871 to Annie K. Givens, and has a family of four children, viz.: Lucy, Mattie W., Anna K. and Amanda Alcorn. He is a resident of Hustonville, Lincoln County, where he enjoys an extensive practice. The family were first represented in Lincoln County by James Alcorn, one of the pioneer settlers, who probably came from Virginia. Dr. David J. Alcorn, father of our subject and son of James Alcorn, was born in Kentucky in 1812, was a prominent pioneer physician and also an extensive farmer. He married Lucy J. Masterson, of Lincoln County, and reared a family of six children, viz.: Mary M., Edward, Rachel B. (Given) deceased, Chloe H. (Hunn) and Lucien C. Alcorn, of Danville, Ky. Dr. David J. Alcorn died in 1865, at the age of fifty-three years.

ROBERT M. ALEXANDER, was born August 18, 1831. His father, Joseph Alexander, was born in Henry County, Va., July 30, 1780; he was a man of good business education and a good business man. He was married in Henry County, Va., on March 7,

1807, to Miss Ann C. Bouldin, of Charlotte County, Va., and to them were born four children: Fayette W., Ann Clark, Sarah Martin (Baker), and Hugh Nelson, of whom only Ann Clark (Baker) is now living. Mrs. Alexander departed this life aged about thirty, and is buried in Henry County, Va. The second marriage of Joseph Alexander occurred in Charlotte County, Va., December 10, 1818, to Miss Sarah Bouldin, a daughter of Thomas and Lucy Bouldin, of whom Thomas Bouldin emigrated from England and settled in Maryland, but afterward married in Virginia and lived in Charlotte County. He received a land grant from George II, and cultivated this tract of several thousand acres, by slave labor, naming it "Golden Hill," a name which it still retains. He was a man of considerable wealth. In 1824 Joseph Alexander immigrated to Kentucky, and settled a tract of 400 acres in Cumberland County, which land he acquired by purchase. He turned his attention partly to agriculture, cultivating his farm by slave labor, and partly to the manufacture of tobacco, which he carried on at his home four miles northeast of Burkesville. He was elected sheriff of Cumberland County, under the provisions of the old constitution, by which the senior magistrate became sheriff, and for several years was master commissioner of the county. He also held the position of commissioner of common schools, and also that of assessor of the county, and in 1839 was elected on the Whig ticket to represent Cumberland County in the lower house of the Kentucky Legislature. He also held many other responsible positions, not of a public character; was guardian and administrator, and a man in whom the people of his county trusted. Seven children were born to his last marriage: Richard B., Milton J., Thomas Tyler; Martha B., wife of Rev. Martin Baker; Margaret, who died in infancy; Joseph H. M. and Dr. Robert M., of whom only Thomas Tyler and Dr. Alexander are living. Mrs. Alexander, who during life was a member of the Methodist Episcopal Church, died May 4, 1857, in the sixty-third year of her age. Joseph Alexander, who departed this life October 2, 1859, was a Whig in politics, a great admirer of Henry Clay, and an emancipationist, although he was a slave owner. He had lived in good easy circumstances during life, but on account of security, left only a small estate to his children. John Alexander was born in 1741, about four miles from Glasgow in Scotland, from which place he was brought by his father, John Alexander, to America, and to Henry County, Va., where he grew to manhood. His father became a prominent man in early Virginia politics. He was a member of the House of Burgesses of Virginia prior to the Revolution, and during the troubles and oppressions which brought about that event. He commanded a company of provincial troops in the struggle. His son John became a man of wealth in the county of Henry. He was married to a Miss Lucy Martin, of Virginia, by whom he became the father of nine children: Thomas, John M., Ingram, Robert, Reuben, Phillip, Susan (Porter), Odedience (Gerhart) and Elizabeth (Smith). He immigrated to Kentucky, and settled on Marrowbone Creek, Cumberland County, in 1811, where he lived in affluent circumstances, and died aged eighty-eight, in 1830. Dr. Robert M. Alexander, a native of Cumberland County, in boyhood received a common-school education in the neighborhood schools of Cumberland County, attending a high school in Alabama one five months' term. His education is the result of home study, and close application after he had left school. In 1852 he began the study of medicine, under the preceptorship of Dr. T. Q. Walker of Haskinsville, Green County, and in the fall of 1853 began attending the lectures at the University of Louisville, graduating there in the spring of 1855. He then began the practice of his profession, in partnership with Dr. J. H. Cheek, which he continued until 1861. At this time he became assistant surgeon of the Fifth Kentucky Cavalry (Federal service); but on account of ill health of his family was compelled to resign and return home. He then began the practice on his own account in Burkesville, which, with the exception of four years' residence in Louisville, he has continued since. In 1874 he removed to Louisville and remained until 1879, when, on account of failing health, he returned to Burksville, and re-entered the practice there. Dr. Alexander, on May 1, 1860, was united in marriage to Miss Ellen B. Alexander, a daughter of John M. Alexander, Jr., and Martha R. (Thurman) Alexander, the former a native of Virginia, the latter of Kentucky. John M. Alexander, a nephew of Joseph Alexander, was a son of Thomas Alexander, and Martha R. Thurman, was a daughter of William Thurman, who was a distant relative of Hon. Allen G. Thurman of Ohio, and came from the same county in Virginia. To Dr. and Mrs. Alexander have been born ten children: John J., who is secretary of the Golden City Placer Mining Company of New Mexico; Hortense C., Lavelle M., Robert A., and Mary C., who are living, and four sons and one daughter who died in infancy. Dr. Alexander has a lucrative practice in his profession, confined mostly to the practice of medicine, with not a great deal of surgical work. He is also one of the board of medical examiners for pensions, and besides his medical practice, owns a young orange grove of 600 trees in Orange County, Fla. The plantation contains eighty acres of very valuable land in the richest and most valuable part of the State and also several hundred acres of valuable land in northern Texas. Dr. and Mrs. Alexander are both members of the Presbyterian Church, of which Dr. Alexander has been a ruling elder since he became a member in 1866. He was a Whig in politics in *ante bellum* days but since has been a member of the national Republican party. In 1859 he was elected on "opposition party" ticket (opposed to Democracy), to represent the counties of Cumberland and Clinton in the lower house of the Kentucky Legislature, and he was present and took part in the deliberations of that body during one regular, and two extra sessions, in those times that "tried men's souls." With this exception he has never sought or held political position. In addition to the diploma which he received from the University of Louisville, he attended a five months' course of lectures at Jefferson College, Philadelphia, graduating there in the spring of 1863.

WILLIAM FAYETTE ALEXANDER, a son of Fayette Wood and Nancy Gertrude (King) Alexander, was born April 22, 1848. His father, Fayette W. Alexander, a prominent business man in Cumberland County, was born September 30, 1811, in Henry County, Va. He began mercantile business early in life, by clerking in a store of general merchandise in the town of Burkesville, where he had lived since 1824. Shortly after having arrived at years of maturity, he entered mercantile life on his own account, carrying a small stock of general merchandise in Burkesville. January 8, 1840, he was united in marriage to Miss Nancy Gertrude King, the second of ten children born to Milton and Susan (Wiles) King, both natives of Albemarle County, Va. Milton King, a son of John Edwards King, was born January 17, 1799, and was married in his sixteenth year to Miss Susan Wiles, who at the time of her marriage was in her fifteenth year. This marriage occurred in Burkesville, where they had both lived from early childhood, and was blessed by ten children: Sally Wiles King (wife of Josiah Har-

ris, a merchant of Adair County), Nancy Gertrude King (wife of Fayette W. Alexander), Sophia (wife of Almarine Alexander), John Q. A. King (elected lieutenant governor of Kentucky in 1863, and afterward a prominent member of the Paducah bar, who died in Denver, Col.), Ellen Hopkins (wife of Judge William F. Owsley), Mary Ann (wife of Clinton C. Alexander), Josephine Bonaparte (the second wife of Almarine Alexander), Susan Victoria (wife of Louis Sweet, a wholesale clothing merchant of New York City), Milton Wiles King (an attorney at law living in Missouri), and Burgess King (who died at about the age of twenty-one, in 1857, while attending medical lectures at Lexington, Ky.). Almarine and Clinton C. Alexander were merchants and lived in Sherman and Bonham, Tex., respectively. Of this family of children, five are now living, Nancy Gertrude, Mary Ann, Josephine B., Susan Victoria and Milton Wiles. Milton King began writing in his father's office (county and circuit court clerk) at about the age of seventeen, which he continued until he was appointed to fill the position previously occupied by his father. This was under the old constitution when the two offices were combined in one, and he held this position until the adoption of the new constitution, which made the office an elective one. He then retired to his farm, two miles north of Burkesville, known as Melmont, a name which it still bears, where he remained until 1857. He then removed to Paducah, Ky., where he died in August, 1872, leaving a comfortable estate, having been worth before the war about $30,000, most of which was lost as a result of the freeing of his slaves. He was a member of the Christian Church, and in politics was a Whig, being a sympathizer with the Confederacy during the late war, and Democratic after that event. His wife, who was also a member of the Christian Church, departed this life in 1839 in the thirty-ninth year of her age, the mother of the ten children above named. Milton King was married a second time, in Virginia, to Miss Martha Harris, who died at an old age, in Paducah, in 1873. Maj.-Gen. John Edwards King, great grandfather of William F. Alexander, was born December 21, 1757, and married Miss Sally Clifton, in Fayette County, Ky., and became the father of five children: William King (who emigrated to Arkansas), Valentine (who emigrated to Louisiana and reared a large family of children), Edwards (who died in Cumberland County, Ky.), Milton, and Rev. Alfred King (who was first a

prominent attorney of Cumberland and surrounding counties, and afterward a minister
of considerable celebrity in the Baptist
Church). He removed to Victoria, Tex., in
1859. John Edwards King was deputy to
the first clerk of Cumberland County, under
the old Constitution, and was the second
clerk of the county, which position he held
twenty years. He was a man in good circumstances, and prominent among the pioneers of Cumberland County. He was a
major-general of volunteers in the war of
1812, was in politics an "old line Whig,"
and died May 13, 1828. The King family
are of Scotch-English origin, and have been
among the most celebrated families of the
State. John Edward King's mother was a
Miss Edwards, a descendant of John Edwards,
who during the reign of George III received
a large land grant where the city of New
York now stands from his sovereign, which
tract he leased to different parties in the city
for the term of ninety-nine years. This lease
expired about 1873, but his descendants lost
the estate, $90,000,000. To the marriage of
Fayette W. and Nancy Gertrude Alexander
were born ten children: Preston Pope, who
died in Texas on September 15, 1873, in the
thirty-second year of his age ; Wickliffe
Bouldin, who died in his fourteenth year, at
Paducah, June 20, 1858; Mary Ellen, who
died at Harrodsburg, Ky., while attending
Daughters' College there, in 1860, aged fifteen years; William F.; Susan A., wife of
Dr. W. G. Hunter, of Burkesville; Sally A.,
wife of W. F. Owsley, Jr., of Burkesville;
Horace King, of Burkesville; Victoria M.,
who died in infancy; Charles Wickliffe, of
Burkesville, and Nancy A., wife of John H.
Ritchey, a merchant of Burkesville. Fayette
W. Alexander was during life a leading
merchant and business man of Burkesville,
who accumulated in his business career
$130,000. He, in partnership with William
F. Owsley, took charge of a branch of the
Bank of Louisville, of Louisville, Ky., which
they managed until 1864, during which time
F. W. Alexander was president of the institution. On January 7, 1864, he departed
this life in the fifty-third year of his age.
Mrs. Alexander, who is still living, is a member of the Christian Church, and in the sixty-
seventh year of her age (1886). William F.
Alexander, a native of Burkesville, attended
the schools of Cumberland County until 1866,
when he attended a ten months' term of the
Urania College, of Glasgow, Ky. He then
attended one term of ten months at the business college of New Haven, Conn., graduating in 1868. He began business when 19

years of age, in partnership with Maj. C. T.
Cheek, and they handled a line of general
merchandise, with a joint capital of $8,000.
This they continued three years, when Mr.
Alexander bought Mr. Cheek's interest in the
business and continued it on his own account
three years, when he sold out, and in 1875
embarked in the wholesale queensware business in Louisville, in partnership with Capt.
R. L. Boyd, under the firm name of Boyd &
Alexander. He remained in this business
two years, then returned to Burkesville, Ky.
He was united in marriage to Miss Georgia
H. Phelps, a daughter of Capt. A. J. Phelps
and Anna M. (Hooker) Phelps, the former of
Preble, N. Y., the latter of Brook County,
Va. To this marriage have been born three
children: Lillian Phelps, born June 23,
1873, died September 15, 1874, aged fourteen months; Lalla Preston, born May 20,
1879, and Addie Hooker, born October 25,
1885. Mr. and Mrs. Alexander are both
members of the Christian Church and Mr.
Alexander is Democratic in politics.

THE ALLEN FAMILY. James Allen,
Sr., the progenitor of the Kentucky branch
of that distinguished family, was of Scotch
descent; he immigrated to America, and the
then colony of Pennsylvania, from Ireland,
some time anterior to the Revolutionary war;
after spending some time in Pennsylvania he
went to the West Indies, but shortly after returned to America and settled in Rockbridge
County, Va. He immigrated to Kentucky in
1780, and located near Danville in the present county of Boyle, where he with another
pioneer, Mr. Daviess, the father of the distinguished Col. Joseph Hamilton Daviess,
made a settlement a few miles from the station, leaving the fort on account of the pro-
fanity of the garrison and others, as he was a
strict Presbyterian. He lived there three
years, then went to what is now Nelson
County, and made a settlement near where
the village of Bloomfield now stands. He
put up a small cabin and returned for his
family, but upon taking them to their new
home he found the Indians had burned his
cabin during his absence. Winter was at
hand, but endowed with the energy of the
frontiersman, he went to work, and with the
aid of his wife soon constructed another cabin. Here he lived until his death at the beginning of the century. His farm, known as
"Allendale," is still in possession of the descendants; his wife, Mary (Kelsey) Allen,
was a native Virginian, but died in Nelson
County, Ky., in May, 1808. They had five
children, three sons and two daughters; the
sons were John, Joseph and James; the first,

Col. John Allen, was one of the ablest lawyers of his day, the rival of Henry Clay in the court of appeals. He was a colonel in the war of 1812, and fell at the battle of the River Raisin. His name, as well as that of the family, is perpetuated in that of a county (see historical sketch of Allen County). Joseph Allen, the second eldest son, was a small boy when his parents came to Kentucky. He removed to Breckinridge County about the time it was created. In the organization of its legal machinery he was chosen county and circuit clerk of the new county. No other evidence of his official integrity is required than the fact that he held the office for a period of fifty-eight years. He served in the war of 1812, and was the father of Hon. Alfred Allen, a distinguished lawyer and politician. The two daughters of James Allen, Sr., were Sallie (who married Andrew Rowan, brother of the celebrated John Rowan), and Margaret (who married Joseph Huston) and became the mother of the well known Judge Eli and Maj. Huston, of Natchez, Miss. James Allen, the only other child of James Allen, Sr., was born March 26, 1779; one year later the family immigrated to Kentucky; he was reared in and has always remained a resident of Nelson County; in early life received a limited amount of schooling at Bardstown and vicinity, but acquired most of his education by reading and association with men of culture in the transaction of business. He served in a number of official capacities in his county—high sheriff, representative in the Legislature, and other minor offices; in the settlement of neighborhood difficulties he was almost invariably called upon to act as an arbitrator. During the latter part of his life he devoted his entire attention to the propagation of small fruits and flowers. A Whig in politics, he was a warm personal friend of Henry Clay. He died May 13, 1852, at the age of seventy-three years. In his last hours he made a request that a copy of the word of God should be made the pillow for his head, in his tomb. While not identified with any church yet he lived an upright, true and consistent Christian. March 25, 1802, Mary Read became his wife. To their union seven children were born: Joseph, Oliver, Eliza, Mary, Nancy, John and Amanda, of whom Oliver, Mary and Amanda are the surviving ones. Mary is the widow of Henry Rowland, and Amanda is the widow of Charles Q. Armstrong. To the union of the latter were born seven children, of whom five are now living: Kate, wife of Capt. John H. Leathers of Louisville; Anna E., wife of Rev. E. H. Pearce; Lillie, consort of Frank Offutt; John A., who married Jennie Moore, and Mattie, wife of S. F. Wilkinson.

PROF. JAMES LANE ALLEN was born December 31, 1821, in Fayette County, Ky.; is a son of John and Elizabeth (Payne) Allen. John Allen was of English descent, his ancestors having settled in Virginia, and afterward moved to Kentucky in the first settlement of the State. The mother of James Lane Allen was a daughter of Judge Henry and Anna (Lane) Payne, of Fayette County, Ky. Anna (Lane) Payne was a daughter of Gen. Lane of Virginia, a distinguished officer in the war for independence. James Lane Allen was educated at Transylvania University, from which he graduated in 1841, while Dr. Lewis Marshall was president. He then studied law under his half-brother, M. C. Johnson, at Lexington, and graduated in the law department at Transylvania University in the spring of 1843. He removed to St. Louis and practiced law nearly two years, and then went to Texas. The Mexican war breaking out about this time, he joined the United States forces and became a lieutenant under Capt. Ben. McCulloch, later Gen. McCulloch, the famous Texas ranger. He was engaged in the storming of Monterey, after the surrender of which he returned to Texas, and became one of the leading and prominent members of the first Legislature of the State, and was sent as a delegate to the National Democratic Convention at Baltimore which nominated Gen. Cass for President. After the death of his father, which occurred in Fayette County, Ky., in 1848, he returned to Lexington and resumed the practice of law and there resided until 1854, when he went to Europe and spent a year with a view of general improvement, and upon his return in 1855 was united in marriage to the eldest daughter of John and Cecily (DeGraffenreid) McCaw, of Lexington, and removed to Missouri, where he engaged in agricultural pursuits until 1863. The war being in progress, he was, owing to his Southern sympathies, imprisoned, and upon his release obliged to leave the State. He returned to Lexington, Ky., and after a short residence there went with his father inland to Canada, where he remained until the close of the war. In 1865 he taught in the female school at New Castle, Henry County, which was under the control of Z. F. Smith, and afterward taught in the school of Prof. Mullins, at Lexington. He was appointed cashier of the bank at Eminence, Ky., which position he resigned in 1868, and removed to Danville, where he still lives. While a resident of Eminence, he was brought out as a candidate for nomination for Congress, but was defeated in the convention by Hon. Boyd Winchester, after a sharp contest. He married his second wife, the eldest daughter of Hon. Joshua F. Bell, on November 7, 1867. He filled a professorship in one of the Danville male colleges, and being a member of the Christian Church he was, upon the urgent solicitation of many of the prominent members of the denomination, induced to devote himself to the ministry, which he did. In 1876, upon the burning of the Caldwell Female Institute, he was induced by friends to organize the institute now known as the Bell Female Seminary. His wife, who possesses a wealth of talent, aids as co-principal; she is the life and soul of the institution. She was very carefully educated by her father, who was a man of distinguished talent and ability, which she has inherited in full. Prof. Allen has two sons: John Mc-Caw, a physician in Chicago, and George J., commission merchant in Chicago.

BENJAMIN C. ALLIN was born May 6, 1808. His father, Thomas Allin, was born in Hanover County, Va., May 14, 1757. In the beginning of the Revolution, soon after the battle of Camden, he entered Gen. Greene's army as a private, but before his term of enlistment expired was promoted quartermaster and commissary. He participated in the memorable retreat of Gen. Greene from South Carolina into Virginia, participating in the battle of Guilford C. H. After his term expired he immigrated to St. Asaph's, Lincoln County, about 1781, where he was the deputy sheriff who opened the the first court there, among the first in Kentucky. He surveyed the land for the site of the present city of Lexington, receiving as a compensation for this and other services the ground where Newport now stands, which he subsequently lost in litigation. He was then appointed deputy clerk in Col. Greenup's office at Danville, Ky., afterward becoming the first county clerk, and circuit or quarterly session court clerk of Mercer after its organization. These offices he held until his resignation, about 1824, of the circuit clerkship, and a few years later of the county clerkship, his son Thomas Allin, Jr., receiving the latter appointment. Thomas Allin, besides being a member of the convention that formed the Virginia constitution, and the convention that formed the first Kentucky constitution, was the commander of a company of mounted infantry in the Indian campaign of Gen. Scott in Indiana. He was married on February 16, 1787, to Miss Mary Jouett, a daughter of John and Mourn-

ing Jouett, of Albemarle County, Va. This marriage was blessed by ten children: Nancy H., wife of Samuel Woodson, clerk of Hopkins County; William H., born April 9, 1791, died in Missouri; John J., born Jan ary 23, 1793; Thomas, Jr., born July 20, 1794; Charles W., born July 13, 1796; Polly J., wife of Don Carlos Dixon Grant, born January 20, 1800; Philip T., born May 5, 1801; Samuel W., born April 8, 1805, and Benjamin C., who alone of the family is living. Thomas Allin and wife were both members of the Christian Church. His death occurred June 26, 1833, his wife's June 28, same year, both of cholera. The Allin family is of Scotch-Irish origin. Benjamin C. Allin, a native of Mercer County, received as good an education as the schools afforded, and also received a fair estate from his father, but by security soon lost it all. He was married January 28, 1829, to Miss Susan Hart Warren, a daughter of John and Judith (Boswell) Warren. Mr. Allin immediately began an agricultural life, at the same time being deputy for his brothers, Philip T. Allin and Thomas Allin, in both county and circuit court clerks' offices. On the death of his brother in 1849, Mr. Allin received the appointment of circuit court clerk, and when the new constitution went into effect was, in 1850, elected to this position, being re-elected in 1856. In 1862 Mr. Allin was not allowed, on account of his political opinions, to be a candidate for circuit clerk, but in 1866 he was elected county court clerk of Mercer County, and has been re-elected every four years since. Mr. and Mrs. Allin are both members of the Christian Church, and they are the parents of twelve children: Mary Boswell, who died in infancy; George T., who died in infancy; Ben C., Jr.; Maria C., wife of D. N. Wilson; John W., who died in infancy; Philip T., clerk of the district court of Cleburn, Tex.; Bushrod W. Allin, circuit court clerk of Mercer County; William B., county attorney of Mercer County; Susan J., who died in 1864; Grant, who died in August, 1885; Mary A., wife of George W. Reichenberg, and Thomas Allin, who died in infancy. Bushrod W. Allin, born February 6, 1843, in Mercer County, was educated in the Harrodsburg schools, attending several years the Kentucky University. He was in the sophomore year in that college in 1862, when he enlisted in September in Company H of the Second Confederate Cavalry, a part of Gen. Morgan's command. Mr. Allin was afterward transferred to Company H, in the same regiment (Gen. Duke's), and participated in all of the battles and raids of that celebrated command, serving all the time as a private. He served in the cavalry service until the spring of 1865, when he returned home and became deputy county court clerk in 1866, which position he has filled ever since. In 1865, December 21, he married Miss Lucy Hawkins, a daughter of Benjamin Hawkins, of Woodford County. Ten children resulted from this union: G. Jouett, James C., Bush W., Jennie Hart, Benjamin C., Jr., John Warren, Margaret Pearl, Susan, Mary and William Poteet, all of whom are living. August, 1885, Mr. Allin was elected circuit court clerk on the Democrat ticket.

DR. HENRY C. ALLIN is the seventh of a family of fourteen children born to Thomas and Mary B. (Thompson) Allin. Thomas Allin, Sr., grandfather of the Doctor, was a native of Virginia and an early resident of Mercer County, Ky., of which he was clerk for fifty years, his sons, Thomas and Philip, serving as his deputies. He was a man of culture and fine business qualifications, and died in 1833, a victim of the dread scourge, cholera, so prevalent in Kentucky during that year. Thomas Allin, Jr., father of the Doctor, was born in Mercer County, where he lived all his life. He was deputy under his father for a number of years, and later was appointed to the clerk's office, which he continued to fill until the breaking out of the civil war. He was a successful business man, accumulating a handsome competency, and died in the year 1864. His wife, Mary B. Allin, was the daughter of Maj. George Thompson, one of the early settlers of Mercer County and one of its most successful farmers. His death occurred in 1833. Dr. Henry C. Allin was born on the 10th February, 1825, in Harrodsburg. He grew to manhood on the home farm, received a good education at Bacon College, Harrodsburg, and at the age of twenty-two began the study of medicine with Drs. Slavin and Jones, and afterward attended the Louisville University, from which institution he graduated in the spring of 1850. In September of that year he began the practice of his profession at the village of Mackville, where he has since resided. He was married May 4, 1852, to Naomi F. Pendleton, by whom he has three children—Mary, wife of Thomas J. Smith; Anna, wife of S. B. Thompson, and Maggie, widow of J. W. Jones. The Doctor has a large and lucrative practice in Washington and adjoining counties, and is one of the leading medical men of Mackville. He is a member of the Masonic fraternity, in politics votes with the Democratic party,

and, with his family, is a member of the Christian Church.

WALTER W. ANDERSON was born December 3, 1839, and is the elder of one son and one daughter born to Alfred Anderson and Nancy Hert, natives respectively of Goochland and Bedford Counties, Va. Alfred Anderson was born October 19, 1795, and came to Green County, Ky., with his parents in 1819. January 2 of the same year his father purchased 1,000 acres where Walter W. now resides, on Caney Fork, in Green County. Alfred served as magistrate for several terms; also served in both branches of the Legislature as a Democrat, and when the war broke out was the owner of about one hundred negroes, and he also freighted by flatboat to New Orleans. He was a son of Garland Anderson, who married a Miss Winston, of whom Alfred Anderson was the only child, and who died December 3, 1873. Garland married for his second wife a Miss Minor, to whom four children were born; the third wife was Sally Trabue. He was born August 6, 1769. He became a member of the Virginia Legislature, and when he came to Kentucky he purchased 1,000 acres of the finest lands in the country, of Major Blain, for $16,000. Walter W. Anderson received a good English education at Columbia, grew to manhood on the farm, and in the fall of 1861 enlisted in Company F, Fourth Kentucky Confederate Infantry, but after a service of a few months was discharged. August 24, 1862, he was united in marriage to Sallie A., a daughter of Thomas and Sallie (Hatcher) Miller, natives of Kentucky. Mr. Miller was a farmer and his parents were early pioneers of Green County. By this union seven children were born: Ann Mary, Eliza C. (deceased at eighteen); Sallie E., now Parrott, William Lee (deceased), Alfred M. (deceased), Thomas J. (deceased) and Guy W. His wife died March 15, 1879, a devoted member of the Baptist Church; she was of German descent. Mr. Anderson married for his second wife Mary Ruth, daughter of John and Emily (Owens) Wilson. Mr. Wilson was an extensive and substantial farmer; was born in Green County and died in February, 1884, aged sixty three. He was a son of Hugh Wilson and Mary Thomas, who came from Ireland and settled in Virginia, and after marriage in Kentucky. Mr. Anderson had born to him by this last marriage three children: Emma O., Clyde G. and Andrew J. His wife is a member of the Christian Church. He located in August, 1874, where he now resides, on the old homestead of 560 acres, in a high state of cultivation, with fine brick cottage and good out-buildings. He is also the possessor of three other farms, containing in all 650 acres, besides other interests. Mr. Anderson was formerly a member of the Grange. In politics he is a Democrat, and cast his first presidential vote for J. C. Breckinridge.

FRANKLIN ANDERSON was born September 22, 1851. His father, William Anderson, was also a native Kentuckian, born in 1821, and married Miss Millie Weatherford in 1844. She died in 1878, leaving eight children, all of whom are living: Letitia (Edrington), Paralee (Drye), Mary J. (Wilcher), Millie (McCain), Franklin, Pauline (Beeler), Lucinda (Coppage) and William. Millie Weatherford was born in 1820. She was a daughter of George and Millie Weatherford, both of whom were of English descent and natives of Virginia, and later, residents of Casey County, Ky. William Anderson was a farmer, and for many years resided on the farm where he died on the 18th of December, 1878, three days prior to the death of his wife on the 21st of the same month. Both were consistent members of the Christian Church and died in that faith. The father of William Anderson was a Virginian, who was among the first settlers of Casey County, Ky. Franklin Anderson was born in Casey County and reared on his father's farm, and during his boyhood received a fair education in the common schools of his native county; at the age of twenty-one he was free to follow his inclinations, and having a love for agricultural pursuits, remained at farming, with which in 1885 he connected the business of distilling brandy. He has met with some reverses in life, but through energy and perseverance, connected with business tact, he has steadily increased his gains. He is now the owner of a farm of 400 acres of fine farming land, lying on the waters of South Rolling Fork, in Marion County. He was married to Bettie Coppage on the 29th of October, 1872. To this union is born one daughter, Alta (February 7, 1876). Mrs. Bettie (Coppage) Anderson was born August 7, 1855. She is a daughter of Fielden and Sarah (Kemper) Coppage, the former of Marion County (died in 1858) and the latter of Montgomery County (living, aged sixty-six years). Mrs. Anderson is a life-long member of the Christian Church; Mr. Anderson, though not a member, is a patron of the church; his political views are Democratic; he takes a live interest in schools and public enterprises generally, and he has for some years held the office of school trustee.

CLIFTON R. ANDERSON was born April 21, 1856, in Danville, and is a son of William C. and Amelia (Rhodes) Anderson, to whom two children were born and reared: Lizzie and Clifton. William C. Anderson was born in Lancaster in 1826, was a graduate from Centre College, and read law with Gov. Owsley in Frankford. After being admitted to the bar he located in Danville, and became one of the most successful of his profession. He represented Boyle County in the Legislature one term, was elected to represent his district in Congress in 1858, and in 1861 was again elected to the Legislature; while at Frankford he died December, 1861, at the age of thirty-five years. He was a son of Simeon Anderson, who was born in Garrard County, was a prominent attorney and represented his county in the Legislature; also represented his district in Congress, and while in Washington died, and was buried in the National Cemetery. He was one of the most popular and influential men in the county, and was never defeated for an office when he entered the race. He married Amelia Owsley, a daughter of Gov. Owsley. Mrs. Amelia (Rhodes) Anderson, was born in Madison County, and is a daughter of Clifton and Amanda (Owsley) Rhodes, natives of Virginia, and early pioneers of Kentucky. Clifton Rhodes was a wealthy farmer, but moved to Danville and engaged in banking in the then Central Bank of Kentucky. He had previously represented Madison County in the Legislature. He died in December, 1878. Clifton Anderson was reared in Danville, and educated in Centre College, from which he graduated in 1875; he afterward taught one year, then carried on the grocery business for four years. Since he has been actively and largely engaged in milling, handling and shipping grain of all kinds. He is in politics a Democrat.

WILLIAM K. ARGO was born October 8, 1857, in Lowell, Garrard Co., Ky., and is a son of Robert M. and Martha M. (Hobbs) Argo, to whom two sons were born: Robert M. Argo was born near Nelsonville, Nelson Co., Ky., was a saddler by trade, was a semi-mute, and self educated; his wife was also a mute and educated at Danville Deaf and Dumb Institute; his father came from Delaware to Kentucky, was of Scotch and Welsh origin and married a Miss Kavanaugh in Madison County. The mother of our subject was a daughter of John and Nancy (White) Hobbs, of Hardin Co., Ky. William K. Argo was educated in a village school; at eighteen entered Centre College, from which he graduated in 1879, after which he entered the Deaf and Dumb Institute as a teacher. In the fall of 1884 he became its superintendent. He is a young man of high character and intellect.

JUDGE CHARLES THOMAS ARMSTRONG was born May 9, 1824, on the Harrod Faunt LeRoy tract of land, near Danville, and was reared to manhood in Mercer and Lincoln Counties. In 1849 he located in Perryville, where he acted as police judge for seven years, and in 1876 he purchased and located on the Col. Wade farm, on Chaplin Creek, two miles south of Perryville, Boyle Co., where he has since resided. His father, John Armstrong, a native of County Fermanagh, Ireland, was born near Enniskillen in 1783, immigrated with his parents in 1797 to the United States and located at Greencastle, Penn. In 1815 he removed to Saundersville, Fayette Co., Ky., where he had supervision of the woolen mills of Lewis Saunders for many years. He was a machinist, and a finished mechanic. His death occurred at Perryville in 1852. His father, Thomas Armstrong, was a country gentlemen in Ireland, and a Loyalist. He erected and conducted the woolen factory at Greencastle, Penn. He was a zealous Methodist, and John Wesley often visited his family in Ireland. His death occurred in 1807. His wife was Mary, daughter of John Williams of Lappan, Ireland, and their children were Sally, Catherine Jane (wife of James Campbell, of Westmoreland Co., Penn.), John, Eliza (wife of Samuel Williams of Chillicothe and Cincinnati, Ohio), Hugh, William (lieutenant in the regular army in the war of 1812; captain of the Sixth Infantry in 1821, and died at Pensacola, February 11, 1827, aged thirty-three years) and Ann (intermarried with Jacob Aid of Brown County, Ohio). In 1813 John married Miss Rebecca, daughter of Charles and Jane (Johnstone) Rule of Kingston, N. J. (died in 1852, aged sixty-three years), and from their union sprang William, Sarah J. (deceased), Charles Thomas and John (deceased). William lived for twenty years in Lexington, Ky., and died April 28, 1886, leaving four daughters, viz.: Ella, Josephine, Rose and Lilly—the last two twins. Judge Armstrong was first married May 8, 1845, to Miss Lucy, daughter of George and Mary (Brown) Huston of Lincoln County (born in 1825, died in 1851), and their one daughter is Mrs. Jennie Jelf of Nicholsville. August 1, 1853, the Judge espoused Miss Talitha W., daughter of James and Mary (Taylor) Green of Washington County (born January 31,

1832), and to them have been born William G. (deceased), Ludic (deceased), Nannie L., Lizzie, and Mary (deceased). In 1849 Judge Armstrong, in partnership with his brother William, built a flouring-mill and carding factory at Perryville, which he operated with marked success and profit until 1876, when his mill was destroyed by fire, entailing a loss of $12,000. At present he is engaged in farming, possessing 423 acres of superior land in a fine state of cultivation. He has for twenty years been an elder in the Presbyterian Church, and is superintendent of the Sunday-school. He is a strong advocate of temperance and prohibition, is a member of the Masonic fraternity, is an Ancient Odd Fellow, and in politics is a Democrat.

DR. THOMAS CAVIN ARMSTRONG was born November 17, 1828, in Fayette County, Ky., but in 1851 located at Bryantsville, Garrard County. His father, Andrew Hogue Armstrong, a native of Pennsylvania, removed in childhood, with his parents, to Kentucky, graduated at Transylvania University, located on a farm near Walnut Hill, Fayette County, was a slave-holder, a captain of militia, forty years an elder in the Presbyterian Church, and died February 22, 1852, at the age of sixty-two years. He was the son of Andrew Armstrong, a native of Ireland, a stanch Presbyterian, who immigrated to Pennsylvania on account of religious persecution, soon removed to North Elkhorn, Fayette Co., Ky., was a soldier in the war of 1812, and died at Terre Haute, Ind., about 1832, aged nearly ninety years. He married Ann Hogue, a Scotch lady, and their offspring were William, of Texas; Andrew H. and Ann (Cruft), of Terre Haute. Andrew H., who married Jane, daughter of Thomas and Elizabeth (Erwin) Cavin, of Fayette County (born March 4, 1792; died November 5, 1859), and from this union sprang Ann (Irvin and Lyle), William (deceased), Emeline (Browning), Dr. John A., LaFayette, James W., Thomas C., Jane (deceased), and DeWitt Clinton. Thomas C. married, June 11, 1852, Miss Sybelle, daughter of James and Sallie A. (Patton) Dunn, of Garrard County (born November 5, 1837), and to them have been born John A., Jane (Taylor), and DeWitt C. In 1848 our subject began the study of medicine with Drs. Letcher and Bell, of Lexington, and afterward with Dr. E. L. Dudley. He attended two courses of lectures at Transylvania University, Lexington, and graduated at the Kentucky School of Medicine, Louisville, in 1851, since which time he has been successfully engaged at Bryantsville in a lucrative practice. Dr. Armstrong is a member of the Methodist Episcopal Church South, and also a member of the K. of H. In politics he is a Democrat and a prohibitionist.

JAMES B. ATHERTON was born October 23, 1825, in Hardin, now La Rue County, the first of four sons and one daughter born to John S. and Maria (Beeler) Atherton. John S. Atherton was born in 1804 in La Rue County, was a farmer and slave-holder, and died in 1840. He was the son of Peter and Elizabeth (Whitehead) Atherton, who came to Kentucky from Virginia as early as 1790 or 1795, bringing twenty-five or thirty slaves. Peter Atherton was of English descent, was a Whig, was under Wayne in the Indian wars, served as magistrate, and died about 1844, aged seventy-two years. Mrs. Maria Atherton was born in Nelson County and was a daughter of John and Elizabeth (Weaver) Beeler. John was a son of Christopher Beeler, who was of German origin, was a farmer and came to Kentucky from Maryland. James B. Atherton was reared a farmer and at twenty-one years of age began business for himself. For three years he ran a carding machine, then resumed farming, and in 1865, entered in mercantile business, which he followed twelve years, and then went back to farming. During the late war he was three months in the Government employ watching bridges. He now lives retired at Nelsonville.

CHARLES T. ATKINSON, lawyer, is a native of Nelson County, Ky., and is the third of three children born to John and Lucinda (Ela) Atkinson, the father a native of New Jersey and the mother of New Hampshire. The grandfather of Charles T. was Joseph Atkinson, a native of New Jersey, and a son of Thomas Atkinson, whose father, Timothy Atkinson, came from England in colonial times and settled in Maryland. Joseph Atkinson was a farmer and a miller; spent all his life in his native State, and died early in the present century. Rev. John Atkinson was born in Flemington, N. J., September 30, 1797. He early in life united with the Methodist Episcopal Church, entered the ministry, August 14, 1814, when but seventeen years of age, and began preaching in New Jersey. He was assigned a circuit in the Northwest Territory in an early day and spent a number of years among the sparse settlements of the present States of Indiana, Ohio and Illinois. He came to Kentucky in 1837, and located in Oldham County, where he remained until 1839, at which time he moved to Bardstown, and about one year later founded the Bardstown Female Institute, with which he was connected for sixteen years. He retired from the active work of the ministry in 1839, but still preaches, and is probably the oldest minister of the Methodist Church now living in the United States, his period of service extending fom 1814 to 1886, a period of seventy-two years. He resides near Bardstown, and is widely and favorably known throughout the counties of central Kentucky. Lucinda (Ela) Atkinson was the daughter of Jacob Ela, a native of New Hampshire. She was born in that State and died in Nelson County, Ky., in 1863. John and Lucinda Atkinson reared a family of three children whose names are as follows: Mrs. Sarah Winans, Mrs. E. B. Newcomb and Charles T. Atkinson. Charles T. Atkinson was born in Bardstown, December 8, 1846. He received his early education in the schools of his town, which he attended until his seventeenth year, when, in 1864, he entered Toronto University, Canada, from which he graduated in 1868. After graduation he began teaching in Bardstown, which profession he followed two years. At the end of that time he began reading law with W. R. Grigsby, and E. E. McKay of Bardstown, under whose instructions he continued for a limited period. He engaged in the practice of his profession in 1871, since which time he has done a lucrative business in the courts of Nelson and other counties. Mr. Atkinson married, September 1, 1870, in Bardstown, Miss Odessa Robertson, daughter of Rev. G. W. and Sarah M. Robertson of Nelson County. The children born to this union are as follows: Alma, Florine and Allan Atkinson. Mr. Atkinson was elected county attorney in 1874 and held the position one term of four years. He is a Democrat in politics, and takes an active interest in the political issues of the county. Mrs. Atkinson is a member of the Bardstown Baptist Church.

SAMUEL AVRITT, attorney at law, was born in 1842, and is the third of eight children born to John and Elizabeth M. (Tucker) Avritt. His grandfather, John Avritt, came from Virginia in boyhood and settled in Marion County (then Washington), married a Virginia lady named Vaughn, and reared a large family of children, John Avritt, Jr., being among the younger. The latter with his wife, Elizabeth (Tucker), is still living and is an honored citizen of Marion County. The grandparents of Elizabeth Avritt, nee Tucker, came from Virginia to Kentucky in the pioneer days, the grandfather, John H. Tucker, being a minister, and both he and his wife were killed by Indians in Fort Tucker, Adair

County. John and Elizabeth Avritt reared a family of eight children, all of whom are living in Marion County. Samuel Avritt, a native of Marion County, was educated at St. Mary's College, and entered upon the study of law at the age of twenty-one under the tutorship of Gov. Proctor Knott; was admitted to practice in the year 1865, since which time he has been a member of the Lebanon bar, taking front rank as a lawyer. George C. Avritt, a younger brother of Samuel, is also a member of the Lebanon bar, having been in the practice since 1870. In 1868 Samuel Avritt married Miss Mary, daughter of J. G. Phillips, Sr., and has one daughter, Laura E. Avritt.

BENJAMIN W. BAILEY was born October 23, 1842, and is the third of five sons and four daughters, all of whom lived to be grown except one girl, born to Grief and Martha P. (Durham) Bailey, natives of Taylor County, Ky. Grief Bailey was a farmer and slave holder, and died in October, 1874. He was a son of Robert Bailey, who was born in Virginia, and when a child was brought to Kentucky by his parents. Mrs. Martha P. Bailey was a daughter of James & Patsey (Compton) Durham, who came from Virginia in the early settling of Kentucky, where James Durham was a justice for many years. Benjamin W. Bailey was born in Taylor County, and grew to manhood on a farm, receiving a liberal education. In October, 1869, he was united in marriage to Ellen N. Edwards, a daughter of Chapman and Jane (Mitchell) Edwards, who were born in Green County. Mr. Edwards was a farmer and trader, was a quartermaster in the Thirteenth Kentucky Volunteers, and died while in the service. He had served as sheriff of Green County several terms; was a son of Thomas Edwards, who married Agnes Hobson, both of whom came from Virginia in an early day. Thomas Edwards was a farmer and owner of slave property, also a miller by trade. Mr. and Mrs. Bailey had born to them five children—four living: Clarence, Willie Wood, Jennie P. and Baswell E. Mr. and Mrs. Bailey are members of the Baptist Church. After marriage Mr. Bailey located on a farm adjoining the place where he now resides, four miles north of Greensburg. His present farm contains 348 acres, on which he located in 1876, nearly all of which is cleared and in an excellent state of cultivation, well improved with good substantial buildings, all of which he has accumulated by his own industry. He turns his attention especially to cattle raising, and was a member of the Grange while in existence.

In politics he is a Democrat, and cast his first presidential vote for J. C. Breckinridge.

JAMES A. BAKER was born October 7, 1848. His father, Albert T. Baker, also a native of Cumberland County, was born October 24, 1821. November 5, 1844, he was married to Miss Mary A. Vaughan, a daughter of James and Abigail (Barger) Vaughan, the former of Virginia, the latter of Pennsylvania. This marriage was blessed by five children: Robert F., James A., Amanda (wife of E. Emmons), Bettie (wife of E. O. Grissom) and Louisa (wife of William M. Binns), of whom Robert died aged eight years. The first farm owned by Mr. Baker consisted of 100 acres, on Crocus Creek, where he lived (until 1870) twenty-five years. He next owned a farm of 200 acres, one and one-half miles northeast of the first, where he remained until 1876, selling out and removing to another farm, on Crocus Creek, of 325 acres, where he remained until 1881. At this time he removed to Burkesville, and at present lives with his son, J. A. Baker. James Baker, grandfather of James A. Baker, was born in Chesterfield County, Va., and was brought by his father to Cumberland County in 1806. He was married to Miss Nancy Robinson, and they became the parents of nine children: Robert, Albert T., Lucy Ann (wife of Hugh Mitchell), Samuel K., Caroline (wife of Charles Wells), Feminine, James M., George F., Elizabeth (wife of John Edwards), four of whom, Robert, Feminine, Elizabeth and Lucy Ann, are now dead. Every year, for eighteen years, he went to New Orleans, on a flatboat, by way of Cumberland, Ohio and Mississippi Rivers, 2,000 miles, and three times walked back through the wilderness. Mrs. Baker, in life a member of the Methodist Episcopal Church, died in 1846, aged about forty-two years. Mr. Baker next married Miss Susanna Grigsby, in Chesterfield County, Va. His death occurred in 1858; his wife's in 1855, and in life they were members of the Baptist and Christian Churches, respectively. Thomas Baker, of English origin, and great-grandfather of James A. Baker, was also a native of Chesterfield County, Va., and was married there to Miss Nannie Elliott. They were the parents of four sons and four daughters. The family immigrated to Cumberland County, Ky., in 1805, where, upon the death of his first wife, Thomas Baker married Miss Elizabeth Robinson. James A. Baker, a native of Cumberland County, in youth received a moderate business education, and, until twenty-one years of age, followed agricultural pursuits, remaining at home with his father. In 1870 he began selling goods in Amandaville by clerking, and in 1871 continued the same for his uncle in Burkesville, where he remained five years. In 1875 he began traveling for a wholesale notion and fancy goods firm in Louisville, which was his business until in December, 1885, when he bought out the stock of T. M. Grissom & Co., in Burkesville. The stock of $3,000 consists of groceries, queensware, hardware and tinware, and he has a thriving business and a good trade at Austin, Texas. February 8, 1882, he was united in marriage to Miss Cora Lee Cunningham, a daughter of James B. and Jenny (Parks) Cunningham, of Newbern, Dyer Co., Tenn. Mr. and Mrs. Baker have two little boys: Joseph Harrell and Robert Arthur. Mr. Baker is a member of the Baptist Church, and a Democrat in politics, while Mrs. Baker is a member of the Cumberland Presbyterian Church.

JAMES L. BALE was born September 15, 1827, and is a son of John and Dimey (Lewis) Bale, to whom six sons and six daughters were born and raised. John Bale was a native of Green County, born in 1801; was a farmer and miller, also a Baptist preacher, and died about 1843. He was a son of Jacob Bale, who came from New Jersey, was of Dutch descent, was one of the very first settlers of Green County, and erected one of the first mills in the county, on Brush Creek; he was an expert and skilled blacksmith, and in his early day made a great many axes of all kinds. Mrs. Dimey Bale was a daughter of Edward Lewis, who was an early settler of Green County, from Virginia; became an extensive farmer and large slaveholder, and served as justice, also sheriff of Green County, for many years. James L. Bale, who was the third in the order of birth, is a native of Green County, grew to manhood on the farm, and received a fair common English education. At the age of twenty-three he began life on his own account, and engaged in building flatboats and running a mill. In April, 1852, he was united in marriage to Mary E. McDonald, a daughter of Matthew and Tabitha (Gooch) McDonald, natives of Ireland and Green County, respectively. Mr. McDonald was brought to the United States when a child of seven years, became a miller, also carried on a farm, and was the owner of several slaves. He was a son of John McDonald, who came from Ireland with his family, and first settled in Kentucky, where he remained a few years, then moved to Missouri. Tabitha Gooch was a daughter of Thomas Gooch and Tabitha (Arthur) Gooch, both natives of Virginia, and were

the earliest pioneers of Green County, Ky. Mr. and Mrs. Bale had born to them eleven children, of whom they reared eight: Tabitha, Holland, Emily C. (deceased), Edward L., Lura M. (now Shields), Elizabeth F. (now Shields), Katie H. Young, Leona Leota Kann and Bennie P. After marriage Mr. Bale located on a farm in Hart County, Ky., of 120 acres; seven years later located on the hill near Osceola, where he owns two farms, one of 150 and another of 96 acres, which are well improved. He also owns 160 acres in Clark County, Kas., also a house in Appleton, Ky. He is a member of the Masonic fraternity, and was a member of the Grange. In politics he is a Democrat, and cast his first presidential vote for James K. Polk; he and wife are members of the Baptist Church.

WILLIAM J. BALE was born April 24, 1843, and is the youngest of six sons and six daughters born to John and Diana (Lewis) Bale, who were born in Green County. John Bale was a minister of the Baptist Church, also a farmer, and died in 1843, aged forty-eight years. He was a son of Jacob Bale, of Dutch descent, who was born in New Jersey, and, after his marriage, located in Green County, Ky., where he engaged in farming and blacksmithing. Mrs. Diana Bale was a daughter of Edward Lewis, of Virginia, who migrated to Kentucky in an early day, and located where William J. Bale now resides. He was the very first settler on Brush Creek, and fastened the shingles on his house with wooden pegs, and sawed his plank with a whip saw; was also a farmer and blacksmith; served as magistrate for many years, and then became sheriff of the county by being the oldest magistrate. William J. Bale was born in Green County, was raised on a farm, and at nineteen commenced farming for himself. He was married, in September, 1866, to Harriet Welden, a native of Hart County, and daughter of Isaac and Lucy (Gardner) Welden, natives, respectively, of Virginia and Hart County, Ky. Isaac Welden was a farmer, and of Irish descent. The issue by this union was seven children: Samuel W., Charles S., Wilshire, Wallace, Ossian T., Minnie J. and Lou. Mr. Bale located where he now resides, on 130 acres; he now owns 177 acres, mostly under cultivation, and this place his grandfather settled—the oldest farm of Brush Creek. Mr. Bale has served as assessor of taxes for twelve years. Mr. Bale started in life penniless, but by his industry and good management has succeeded in establishing a good home. He is an active Democrat, cast his first presidential vote for

McClellan, and he and wife are members of the United Baptist Church.

JOHN BARR, merchant and manufacturer, was born in Liverpool, England, February 5, 1843, and when yet an infant came with his parents, John and Bridget Barr, to the United States. His father was a merchant tailor, and located in Louisville, where he engaged in that calling, and where our subject was chiefly educated. When he was about twelve years old his parents died, and for the six years next following he was learning the trade of carriage-maker in McLean County. Just after the completion of his trade (1861) he entered the Federal Army as drum major of the Seventeenth Kentucky Regiment. He was wounded at the battle of Shiloh, in consequence of which he received his discharge in December, 1862. He then located in Lebanon, Marion County, his present home, where for several years he engaged as contractor and builder, and in 1879 became a member of the firm of Lanham & Barr, which still continues. Mr. Barr has served one term as mayor of Lebanon, and in 1883 was made the supreme secretary of the Catholic Knights for the United States. In 1866 he was married in Lebanon to Miss Marietta Mitchell, daughter of George Mitchell. She died in 1873, and in the year 1875 he was married to Miss Anna Johnson, who died in 1876. His present wife, to whom he was married in 1877, was Anna Mitchell, a younger sister of his former wife. As a result of this latter marriage he has four children, viz.: Thomas J., Joseph, John G. and Mary A. Barr.

JOEL T. BAUGHMAN was born March 4, 1825, in Lincoln (now Boyle) County, Ky., where he grew to manhood; in 1851 he removed to Lincoln County, and in 1866 to "Oakland Place," near the Frying Pan bend of Dicks River, Garrard County, where he now resides. His father, Henry Baughman, Jr., a native of Virginia, was born in 1776; he came to Kentucky in 1780; remained here two years with his family, then went back to the "Old Dominion" for his mother; he was a farmer and large slave owner; was assessor of property in Lincoln County, a Whig, and died in 1865. He was the son of Henry Baughman, of Virginia, who was murdered by Indians eight miles above Crab Orchard. This sad event happened when Henry Baughman, Jr., was on his return from Virginia with his mother, and had reached the fort above Crab Orchard, when the Indians opened fire, and Henry Baughman, Sr., was killed in his attempt to give his relatives a chance to escape. The chil-

dren born to Henry, Sr., were Nancy (Gilbreath), Ticia (Duncan), Polly (McGill), Jacob and John (both killed at St. Clair's defeat), and Henry, Jr. Henry, Jr., married Patience, daughter of William Owsley, of Lincoln County (born 1784, died 1843) and to them were born Hamilton, William O., Rebecca (Shanks), Jacob, John, Henry, Samuel O., Nancy (Dunn), Nudiget O., and Joel T. Joel T. Baughman was married July 19, 1849, to Miss Sallie, daughter of Isaac and Cyrena (Wooly) Dunn, of Garrard County, born February 20, 1833, and having no children of their own they have reared John T. Baughman, Cyrena M. Craig and Lizzie S. Dunn. Mr. Baughman is a farmer, owning 279 acres of well improved land. In 1884 he was elected superintendent of common schools of Garrard County, and in 1886 was re-elected to the same position for a term of four years. Mr. Baughman is a member of the Cumberland Presbyterian Church, and in politics is identified with the Democratic party. He lost ten valuable slaves as a result of the late war.

EDWARD BRISCOE BAXTER was born January 4, 1837. His grandfather, William Baxter, was born in Ireland from which country he came to America before the war of the Revolution. He was among the first that came to Kentucky, and located in what is now Washington County; was married to a Miss Mary Walker and reared a family of sons and daughters, among whom was William Baxter, Jr., the father of Ed. Briscoe. William was born in Washington County in 1784; as a farmer he was very successful and when quite a young man removed to Missouri, carrying with him his household possessions and slaves. He located in Howard County, where he remained some years, then returned to his native State—settled in Washington County, where he afterward married Miss Elizabeth, daughter of Edward and Margaret (Harbison) Briscoe, who were of English parentage and natives of Virginia. Elizabeth Baxter died in 1859. Of eight children born to her marriage with Mr. Baxter, four sons and two daughters, William A., Lafayette, James H., Elizabeth, Lucebra and Edward B. lived to be grown. William Baxter died in 1857, aged seventy-three years; his life was one of remarkable activity. Politically he was a Democrat and held the office of sheriff of a district which was co-extensive with what is now Marion County, and carried on the business of that office in connection with farming. He was a soldier in the war of 1812, and fought in the memorable battle of the Thames. Ed. Briscoe Baxter was a native of Marion County; was reared on his father's farm. He received a common-school training in early life and finished at Perryville Institute, where he studied mathematics and collateral science up to 1857, when he was called home upon the occasion of the death of his father; from that time until the beginning of the civil war he had charge of the home farm. His sympathies being with the Southern cause, he and two brothers went South, and soon after joined Morgan's command. He was captured at Springfield, Mo., and for a year was held a prisoner of war at Johnson's Island; his two brothers were captured with Morgan and his command while on the road into Ohio; they were held prisoners at Camp Douglas until the end of the war. Ed. B. Baxter returned home after the war and resumed farming, with which he connected the business of trading in stock —he has been uniformly successful and is now the proprietor of 400 acres of valuable farming and stock land, lying on the waters of Beech Fork Creek in Marion County. He was married on the 7th of October, 1874, to Miss Ellen, daughter of Walter and Mary (Durham) Gregory, of Boyle County. Ellen (Gregory) Baxter was born April 8, 1848; to her and Mr. Baxter are born three sons, Walker, George and Edward. She is a member of the Presbyterian Church. Mr. Baxter, though not a member of the church, holds to the Baptist faith. Politically he is a Democrat, but without political aspirations, though he is a worker in support of his party and principles, and is also a strong advocate and supporter of schools.

GEORGE W. BEALL was born December 17, 1825, and is a son of Washington and Mary (Carter) Beall, to whom four sons and three daughters were born, of whom George W. is the sixth. Washington Beall was born February 9, 1790, and was brought to Kentucky when a lad by his parents, who were large land and slave owners. He died in 1866. He was a son of Nathan Beall, who married Sarah Beall, both natives of Maryland, who with four sons and seven daughters immigrated to Kentucky in 1798—the only members of the Beall family known to have settled here. The Indian depredations in the interior caused Nathan to hesitate about going there, but he finally went to Jefferson (now Marion) County, and settled on Rolling Fork, where he entered 600 acres of bottom land, and was a large slave-holder for that day. George W. still has the grindstone which his grandfather brought with him, manufactured in 1780. The Bealls are of Irish origin, and were of the Church of England. Mrs. Mary Beall was born in Culpeper County, Va., and is a daughter of Joseph and Jennie (Shelton) Carter, who immigrated and settled on Rolling Fork between 1800 and 1810. Joseph Carter, who served in the war for independence, lived to be nearly one hundred years old, and had numerous grandchildren in the Confederate Army, and some in the Federal Army, George W. Beall was born in Marion County on the farm on which he now resides, on Rolling Fork, and received a good common English education. He was married in May, 1852, to Minerva F. Stiles, of Nelson County, a daughter of Lewis and Rebecca (Willett) Stiles, who were born respectively in New Jersey and Nelson County, Ky. Lewis Stiles migrated to Kentucky in 1809. He was a distiller, was also engaged in farming on Rolling Fork, served as justice and sheriff in Nelson County, and furnished a substitute in the war of 1812. He was a son of David and Elizabeth (Kitchell) Stiles of New Jersey, who migrated to Kentucky and settled on Rolling Fork in 1810, one year after the son, who had preceded to look for a location. David was a son of Joseph Stiles, who married a Miss Gardner. He was born in Vermont and was of German descent. Mr. and Mrs. Beall had born to them two children: Lizzie Laura (deceased) and Mattie. After his marriage Mr. Beall located on a farm of 290 acres, adjoining his birthplace. In 1872 he located on the old homestead of 285 acres, mostly cleared and improved with a fine frame residence. Mr. Beall is the owner of 2,000 acres on Rolling Fork, divided in several farms, with fine buildings. He has also been engaged in distilling nearly all his life. In 1865 he with two others built the largest distillery in the State, and ran it for six years, when he sold out to Newcomb, Buchanan & Co. Mr. Beall is also owner of twelve lots in Perry City, Kas., and four lots in Hodgenville, Ky. With the exception of 280 acres, he has accumulated his large fortune by his own industry and economy. He is a leading member of the Masonic fraternity; was a member of the Grange; in politics is a Democrat, and cast his first presidential vote for Lewis Cass in 1848; with his wife he is a member of the Methodist Episcopal Church South.

MRS. SARAH E. BEALMEAR was born October 1, 1812, in Bullitt County, Ky., where she was reared to womanhood, and on the twentieth anniversary of her birth was espoused in holy matrimony by the late and lamented Samuel C. Bealmear. Mrs. Bealmear's father was Benjamin Summers, a native of Pennsylvania, who removed to Kentucky in 1798; having married Verlinda Beckwith, their union was favored by the birth of John B., George W., Susan W. (Sanders), Rufus K., Martha, Theresa (Wilson), Beverly B., Benjamin F., Sarah E., Patsey A. (Fry) and Mary V. (Williams). In 1833 Mrs. Bealmear removed with her husband, and settled on Cox's Creek, Nelson County, where she has since resided. Mr. Bealmear was born March 6, 1811, and died September 19, 1883. He was an active member of the Presbyterian Church, and was greatly esteemed for his many noble qualities. He was candid, frank and sincere, and in his manly character shed a light around him, the effects of which will be as enduring as time. It has been remarked by one competent to judge correctly that his life was a reflection of the better qualities of our nature, and that his acts, unostentatious in character, were more for the approbation of his Creator than of man. By industry and a long line of frugality he amassed a handsome competency. In politics he was an old line Whig, and when his country was assailed he clung to the Union with unswerving fidelity. He left a fine farm of 500 acres of well improved and productive land.

DR. JOHN J. BEARD, a native of Green County, Ky., was born October 9, 1823. His father, Josiah Beard, a native of Shelby County, Tenn., and born about 1790, was a farmer and married Miss Demia Mann, a daughter of Moses and Frances Mann, both Virginians. Moses Mann came to Kentucky when it was an unbroken forest inhabited by Indians and wild beasts. When he arrived in Marion County he settled on 1,000 acres, where he built a fort of palisades and resided several years. His son, Asa, was killed by the Indians while fishing in the Rolling Fork River at night. His companion, Nathaniel Carpenter, who was fishing with him, was badly wounded and left for dead, having been scalped, but before day crawled up to the palisade fort and finally recovered from his injuries. Moses Mann then sold his farm and fort and removed to what is now Taylor County, where he settled on 2,000 acres near Mannsville, which was named for him. His age at his death was ninety-seven years, his wife's eighty-seven. Josiah Beard became the father of the following children: Moses, Samuel (who died in youth), Rebecca (Batsell), Frances (who married Thos. Sharp, now deceased), Robert, Elijah, James and Joseph, of whom Robert and Joseph are dead. The marriage of Josiah Beard occurred at Mannsville when

he was a young man. He and his wife were members of the Christian Church, and he never held any official position, except captain and major in the State militia. In his old age he divided his estate among his children, and was called from his earthly labors in 1866; his widow in 1882, in her ninety-first year. Samuel Beard, grandfather of Dr. Beard, was also a native of Tennessee, and a man of wealth. He commanded a company of Revolutionary veterans and served in the Southern Army. Dr. Beard's boyhood days were spent, when not in school, in agricultural pursuits, until, at eighteen years of age, he began the study of medicine under Dr. Benjamin Hamilton of Campbellsville, and in 1844 began the practice of his profession at Bradfordsville, Marion County, where he remained two years. In 1846 he removed to Adair County, where he continued the practice very successfully, remaining until the beginning of the civil war. Dr. Beard was a Southern sympathizer, and at that time a man in good circumstances, but on account of being molested by the Home Guards had to sell out, when he moved to Marion County. In 1868 he returned to Adair County and settled in Cane Valley on eighty acres of land which he has in a high state of cultivation and improvement. Dr. Beard was married August 26, 1846, to Miss Mary N., daughter of Richard W. and Elizabeth (Southerland) McWhorter, natives of Adair County. Richard McWhorter before the war was a slave owner, and possessed of a large landed estate, but lost most of it. His wife, Mrs. Elizabeth McWhorter, is still living, a member of the Baptist Church, in the seventy-second year of her age. Dr. and Mrs. Beard are the parents of three children: Frances (deceased wife of John · D. Foyle of Lebanon), Anna (wife of Selden Hatcher of Adair County), and Dr. J. C. Beard of Rowlett, Hart County. Dr. Beard is one of the oldest physicians in the county, and has always enjoyed a large and lucrative practice. He and Mrs. Beard are both members of the Christian Church, and Dr. Beard is also a member of the Masonic order, and politically a Democrat.

JAMES W. BEARD was born in Green County, Ky., August 17, 1831, and is the eighth in a family of nine children, born to Isaiah and Diodema (Mann) Beard, natives of Greenbrier and Culpeper Counties, Virginia. Josiah Beard was born February 24, 1790, and in 1798 came with his parents to Kentucky. The family, numbering seventeen, including servants, accomplished the entire journey over the mountains on pack-horses, and first halted for a short rest at Crab Orchard Lincoln County, where there was a settlement and a fort; thence journeyed to Carpenter's Station, in the same county, and from that place to a point on the Green River, two and a half miles below the mouth of Casey Creek, in what was then a part of Green, but is now Adair County. Here the father located several thousand acres of wild land, and improved several hundred, on which he resided for many years. He gave away from time to time large bodies to friends and acquaintances, to induce them to settle near him. He also built on the Green River, near his home, the first grist-mill in Adair County. In this wild country young Josiah grew to manhood, early becoming inured to the hardships and privations incident to pioneer life, soon acquiring great skill as a hunter and trapper. Wild game of all kinds abounded on every hill and in every valley, and the numerous streams were filled with excellent fish and frequented by every species of water fowl. Josiah was married at the age of twenty-two years, and soon after moved to what is now Taylor (but then Green) County, Ky., where his father-in-law gave him wild land near the present village of Mannsville. There he improved a farm on which he resided for many years. In 1836 he sold this farm and bought another near Columbia, Adair County, upon which he remained until 1856, when he retired from active business and made his home with his son, James W., until his death, February 25, 1866. For many years he was a major in the old State militia, and he and wife were members of the Christian Church. He was also an old and bright member of the Masonic fraternity, having held numerous official positions in his lodge, and was buried with the honors of his order. His father, Samuel Beard, was a veteran in the Revolution, and after he came to Kentucky became a noted hunter. Late in life he moved to Tennessee, and settled near Jackson, where his death occurred suddenly from heart disease. Mrs. Diodema (Mann) Beard was born October 4, 1792, and died May 19, 1882. Her father, Moses Mann, was also a native of Virginia and a Revolutionary veteran. In the latter part of the last century he came with his family to Kentucky, also accomplishing the entire journey on pack-horses, and first settled in what is now Marion County, on the Rolling Fork, where he entered wild land and improved a farm upon which he remained several years. While living on this place he was appointed a Government scout, and he and a man named Coppage were for

several years engaged in hunting and Indian fighting from Rolling Fork to the Cumberland River. Just before he engaged in hunting and Indian fighting, however. he had a son, a nephew and a hired man shot and scalped by the savages, while fishing on the Rolling Fork. Later his associate, Coppage, was also killed and scalped while on one of their expeditions. After these occurrences he swore vengeance on the red men, and pursued them with unerring rifle to the end. He was one of the most noted and successful hunters in the country, and paid for several thousand acres of land through his skill with the rifle. About 1806 or 1807 he moved to Green County, where he located some 6,000 or 7,000 acres of wild land on Robinson's Creek, improved a large farm and became quite wealthy. There he resided until his death in 1843. He was for several years extensively engaged in the manufacture of salt in connection with farming and stock raising. He and wife were life-long members of the Old School Presbyterian Church. James W. Beard received a good English education in youth at the common and select schools of the county, and at the Columbia Male and Female College. At the age of twenty-two years he bought a partially improved farm on Casey Creek, in Adair County, to which he has added from time to time, now owning 300 acres, well improved and in a good state of cultivation, and is engaged in farming and stock raising. He commenced to teach at the age of seventeen and so continued in connection with farming for some eighteen or twenty years. In 1869 he went to Texas, returning to Kentucky in 1871. He married, December 25, 1858, Miss Elizabeth M. McWhorter, a native of Adair County, born March 2, 1842. She is a daughter of Richard W. and Elizabeth M. (Southerland) McWhorter, natives of Casey County, Ky., and of Scotch and English descent respectively. To Mr. and Mrs. Beard the following children have been born: William H., Creed T., Mollie E. (wife of William B. Hendrickson), Shelton C., John M., Florence R., Virgil, Herschell, James O., Sallie B., Bertha and Eugene. Mr. and Mrs. Beard have been for years members of the Christian Church, in which he has officiated as ruling elder for many years. He is also a bright member of the Masonic fraternity, having been W. M. of his lodge for many years. He is an earnest advocate of the temperance cause, and politically a Democrat.

FRANCIS K. BEAVEN was born October 20, 1827, and is the third child of Charles and Cecily (Luckett) Beaven. He was reared on a farm, was educated at St. Mary's College, and at the age of twenty-three commenced life on his own account at farming and distilling, which latter he followed up to the beginning of the war, when distilling was stopped. In 1870 he was elected sheriff of Marion County and was re-elected for a second time, and made an efficient and popular officer. In 1881 he was appointed magistrate, and after serving the appointed time was elected. In August, 1878, he married Mary J. Smith, a daughter of Joseph and Ellen (Ballard) Clark, who were both born and reared in Marion County. Mr. Clark was a prosperous farmer and slave-holder, and died in May, 1878, at the age of sixty-five years. He was a son of Joseph Clark, who came from Maryland in a very early day and settled in Marion County. His wife, Mary Clark, lived to be one hundred and four years old. Mr. and Mrs. Beaven had born to them three children: Ella C., George B. and Elizabeth E. Mrs Beaven has three children living by her former husband: Kate Smith, Mary L. and George F. After marriage Mr. Beaven located where he now resides, in the western part of Marion County, on the line of Marion and Nelson Counties, on the headwaters of Pottenger's Creek, on 355 acres, 250 of which are under cultivation. He also owns another farm of 100 acres in the county, and a fine stallion called Gold Dust, some fine saddle stock, and also a fine Jack. Mr. and Mrs. Beaven are members of the Catholic Church.

CHARLES BEAVEN was born November 3, 1838, and is a son of Charles and Cecily (Luckett) Beaven, to whom nine sons and three daughters were born; seven sons and two daughters lived to be grown. Charles Beaven, Sr., was born November 2, 1796, east of St. Mary's and was one of the leading and substantial farmers, owning about 1,000 acres, and a large number of slaves. In his early days he sold goods, and died February 8, 1869. His parents, Edward and Ellen (Green) Beaven, both natives of Maryland, were among the first settlers in Kentucky, and came with his brother, Col. Charles Beaven, who acquired his title during the Revolution. The Beavens were all substantial farmers and slave-holders and of English origin. Mrs. Cecily (Luckett) Beaven, was born in the western part of Marion County, January 14, 1800, and died February 6, 1883. She was a daughter of Hezekiah and Elizabeth (Hamilton) Luckett, who came from Maryland with the first Catholic settlers of Marion County. Mr. Luckett was a substantial farmer and slave owner, and died in November, 1859; Charles

Beaven, Jr., was born within two miles of St. Mary's, Marion County; received his education at St. Mary's College, was reared a farmer and in October, 1861, enlisted in Company D, Tenth Kentucky Federal Infantry; was in all engagements in which the regiment participated, except Jonesboro, Ga., and Missionary Ridge, and received a wound in the shoulder at Chickamauga. He was discharged December, 1864, at Louisville, after which he returned to his home and engaged in farming, which he has followed ever since. He was united in marriage October 15, 1867, to Susan M., daughter of E. H. and Alathaise (Spalding) Mattingly, of Marion County. Mr. Beaven after his marriage located where he now resides, one mile south of St. Mary's Station, on 150 acres, but now owns 265, with a fine residence and outbuildings. Mr. and Mrs. Beaven are consistent members of the Roman Catholic Church.

CHARLES H. BENNETT was born in Wadsworth, Medina Co., Ohio, December 2, 1840, and is one of nine children born to Timothy S. and Rachael (Brown) Bennett, natives of Vermont and New York and of English origin. Timothy S. Bennett was born March 8, 1795, and received an excellent education in his native State. In 1812 he emigrated to Medina County, Ohio, where he was among the earliest pioneers. There he taught school for a time, and February 27, 1821, was married to Rachael Brown, who was born January 13, 1800. He entered wild land, and subsequently improved a farm upon which he remained until 1852, when he sold out, but soon after bought several other farms, one for each of his children, near Granger, same county. There Mrs. Rachael Bennett died March 13, 1875, and Timothy Bennett September 18, 1875. Both were life-long members of the Christian Church. He was also a bright member of the Masonic fraternity, having advanced to the thirty-second degree in the Scottish Rites, or Consistory. Mrs. Rachael (Brown) Bennett's father, Holland Brown, was also one of the early pioneers of Medina County, Ohio, and was a veteran in the war for independence, and in the war of 1812. Charles H. Bennett received a good common-school education in youth. He was employed on the home farm for his father until he attained his majority, after which his father deeded him the old homestead. Here he remained, engaged in agricultural pursuits and stock raising until 1883, when he sold out and moved to Campbellsville, Taylor Co., Ky., where he has since been engaged in the real estate business, buying and selling for other parties and also on his own account, having in the past three years bought and sold some fifty or sixty farms besides over 6,000 acres of timber land. By means of extensive advertising and his indomitable, untiring energy, he has secured a large immigration to Taylor County from Ohio, Indiana, Michigan, and Pennsylvania. For some fifteen months during the late civil war, 1862–63, he served as a teamster in the United States service between Louisville and Nashville. He has been twice married; first, January 9, 1865, to Miss Elizabeth Painter of Holmes County, Ohio, born in 1846. She was a daughter of John and Jane Painter. To this union were born one son and two daughters, two of whom are yet living, viz.: Wesley and Eudora. Mrs. Elizebeth Bennett's death occurred November 11, 1865. She was a devoted member of the Methodist Episcopal Church. Mr. Bennett was next married February 13, 1875, to Miss Sarah C. Watkins, a native of Wildsville, W. V., born in 1857. She is the daughter of Ephraim and Rachael (Nickels) Watkins. One son has blessed this union, Lyman. Both Mr. Bennett and wife are consistent members of the Christian Church. In politics he is a Republican.

JOHN BENNETT, attorney at law, Richmond, Ky.

HON. WILLIAM BERKELE was born January 1, 1826, in Hesse Darmstadt, removed with his parents to the United States in 1838, located at New Haven, Conn., where he grew to manhood, and in March, 1865, settled at Bryantsville, Garrard Co., Ky., where he has since resided. In 1862 he was appointed sutler of the Eleventh Connecticut Regiment while in North Carolina; came west with Gen. Burnside in 1863 as sutler at headquarters, and in the spring of the same year was appointed post sutler at Camp Nelson, where he remained until the close of the war. His father, Michael Berkele, was born October 23, 1795, and died at New Haven February 27, 1863. He married Loisa Wilhelmina Rushstien (born March 14, 1796), and from their union sprang Barbara (Shumaker), Josephine (Klose), William, Mary (Mairer), Margaret (Heinz), Louis H., Charles, John and Henry. William Berkele first married Rebecca, daughter of Albert Alling, of Orange, Conn., and to them were born Louisa, Nettie M. (Jean) and William A. In 1867 he married Mrs. Mary Campbell, daughter of Dr. Benjamin Mullins, of Garrard County, Ky. (born September 22, 1838), and their union has been favored by the birth of Daisey and Eugene (twins). In youth Mr. Berkele learned the tailor's trade,

which business he followed until the commencement of the war. Since the war he has been engaged in the mercantile business, two years at Nicholasville and ten years at Bryantsville with success. In 1883 he erected a new distillery on the Lexington and Danville pike, at Rocky Springs, three miles from Danville in Boyle County. Since 1868 he has been successfully engaged in distilling in Garrard and Boyle Counties, manufacturing the old style, hand-made sour mash whiskies, known as the Berkele and E. H. Chase & Co. brands. He is also a farmer, having 325 acres of well improved land, upon which he grazes cattle and sheep, stall feeding about 100 head annually. Mr. Berkele has served two terms in the Legislature of Kentucky; has been four times elected magistrate and a member of the court of claims of Garrard County; was a delegate in 1872 to the National Republican Convention and an alternate in 1880. He is a commissioner of the Deaf and Dumb Institution of the State and treasurer of the Danville, Lancaster and Nicholasville Turnpike. He is a Knight Templar and in politics is a Republican.

NICHOLAS T. BERRY (deceased), one of the most worthy men who have been connected with the history of Lebanon, was born in Nelson County, Ky., April 28, 1825, and was the son of John H. Berry, who came from Maryland to Kentucky in 1815. He settled at a point called Old Hope, in Nelson County; married Elizabeth Hagan and reared eight children, viz.: Ann (Hagan), Mary (Buckler), Fannie (McIlvoy), Edward C., Nicholas T., Jeremiah, William L. and Robert M. Berry. Nicholas T. Berry was reared in Nelson County, educated at Mount Merino College, in Breckinridge County, and at the age of nineteen came to Lebanon and became the first circuit court clerk of Marion County under the present constitution, and filled the office for a period of nine years. In 1860 he was admitted to the practice of law, having studied in the office of R. H. Rowntree for several years prior. For a long period of years Mr. Berry served the county as master commissioner, proving himself an efficient officer. He was married in 1855 to Miss Josephine Boucher, of Washington City, D. C., who died in 1856, leaving one child, Sam B. Berry, now of the Denver (Col.) bar. In 1858 Mr. Berry contracted a marriage with Nannie H. Phillips, who survives him. In the management of his financial affairs Mr. Berry was prudent and judicious and at his death left a handsome fortune. On the 20th of April, 1882, he fell dead from his horse, being the seventh of his family who have as suddenly died. He was an ardent and faithful member of the Catholic Church, and his grave is marked by a huge cross, twenty feet high, cut from solid granite, said to be the largest of its kind on this continent. Sam B. Berry, the only son of Nicholas T., born June 1, 1856, graduated valedictorian of his class at St. Mary's College, Kentucky, in 1876, studied law under Gov. J. Proctor Knott, came to the bar in 1877, and in 1879 was elected prosecuting attorney for the city of Lebanon, Ky., and served as elector on the Cleveland and Hendricks ticket, receiving a larger majority than any of his associate electors. He married, in 1879, Miss Maggie C. Booker, daughter of W. F. Booker, of Washington County. In the fall of 1886, he moved to Denver, Col., where he is engaged in the practice of his profession.

F. J. BIBB, M. D., was born September 30, 1838, where he now resides, three miles west of Greensburg, Ky. He is the fourth of four sons and two daughters born to Robert and Sarah (Durrett) Bibb, who were born in Louisa County, Va. They moved from Monroe County, Ky., to Green County about 1830. Robert Bibb drove stock in his early days to Richmond, Va., from Monroe County; was a lieutenant in the war of 1812, but was taken sick while on a march and at once was discharged from the service. He died January 24, 1882, aged eighty-nine. He was a son of James Bibb who married Nancy Walker. They emigrated from Virginia to Monroe County, Ky., in an early day, but his latter years were spent in Green County; he was an orderly sergeant in the war for independence; subsequently was a large farmer and slave owner and lived to be about one hundred years old. His father came from Ireland. Mrs. Sarah Bibb was a daughter of John and Patsey (Bibb) Durrett, who were both born in Louisa County, Va. They came to Kentucky in an early day and settled in Taylor County. He was a substantial farmer and was of Irish descent. The Doctor grew to manhood on a farm, received a good English education and taught two terms of school. In 1862 he commenced the study of medicine, graduated from the Kentucky Medical School in 1865, and in 1866 from the university; he located where he now resides on the old homestead, and has here practiced his profession ever since. In politics he is Democratic, but cast his first presidential vote for Fillmore.

REV. WILLIAM A. BLAIR, a native of Adair County and the fifth of the twelve children of William and Lucy (Hopkins) Blair, was born July 4, 1835. His father,

Rev. William Blair, born July 29, 1803, was a minister of the church of the United Brethren in Christ. His early education was limited, but after entering the ministry in his thirty-second year he was a close student and an extensive general reader, so much so that his style of delivery implied scholarship. He was first licensed to preach in Decatur, Ind., in 1837, on trial by the quarterly conference of his church, and in 1842 was regularly ordained in Franklin County, Ind. The last twenty years of his life he was presiding elder of the church work of the United Brethren in Christ in five counties—Russell, Adair, Metcalfe, Clinton and Wayne, part of Cumberland and part of Casey. Rev. William Blair was twice married, first to Miss Lucy Hopkins, a daughter of William Hopkins of Adair County, and his marriage was blessed by the birth of thirteen children: Elizabeth (who died in childhood), a second (unnamed, deceased), John, another (who died unnamed), Dicy Jane (wife of Sydney Helm), George W., William A., James B., Lucy Ellen (died in her nineteenth year), Elizabeth (wife of William H. Helm), Jesse K. Polk, Robert J., and one who died in infancy. Mrs. Blair, a member of the United Brethren in Christ. died September 17, 1873, in the sixty-sixth year of her age. In 1874 Mr. Blair married Mrs. Martha E. (Wheat) Grider, of Russell County, who was the widow of Frederick Grider, and who is at present wife of Henry Smith, of Casey County. January 7, 1878, Rev. William Blair departed this life, having been minister of the gospel about forty years. His father, Alexander Blair, was a farmer, though he also worked at shoemaking, and was a native of Virginia. He married Miss Elizabeth Breeding, and became the father of twelve children. Rev. William A. Blair received an ordinary English education in youth and was reared to farming. He was married, February 14, 1854, to Miss Mary Miranda Scott, a daughter of Thompson and Elizabeth (Peake) Scott, the former of Virginia, the latter of Metcalfe County, Ky. His marriage was blessed by four children: George Paschall (who died in childhood), Elizabeth Ellen (wife of E. H. Rosenbaum), Lucy Jane (wife of R. A. Blair) and Mary Frances. Mrs. Blair, who was a member of the United Brethren Church, died November 6, 1885, in the sixty-first year of her age. Mr. Blair has owned six different farms in Adair County at different times, and at present owns eighty acres of well improved and fertile land on Glen's Fork, worth $20 per acre. He has erected a comfortable farm residence, barns and stables, and all necessary farm improvements. Five years ago Mr. Blair was licensed to preach by the quarterly conference, and two years ago he was regularly ordained as a minister of the church of the United Brethren in Christ. James B. Blair, a brother of Rev. William A. Blair, was born January 31, 1838, in Adams County. His life-long vocation has been farming, and his marriage occurred October 4, 1864, to Miss Arminta, a daughter of Andrew and Ursula (Stotts) Wilson, natives of Adair County. Andrew Wilson was a son of John and Sally (Miller) Wilson, natives of the Old Dominion. There was an estate of $2,000,000 in litigation, which was compromised in 1883, which estate was originally the property of Samuel Miller, of Virginia, and the heirs of Sally Miller, who were parties in the suit, received nothing in the compromise. The marriage of Mr. and Mrs. Blair has been blessed by four children: Eldridge, Lucy Lillian, Ursula J. and Minnie. Mr. Blair has settled two different farms, the present place in 1873. This contains 170 acres of fertile land on Glen's Fork, with good buildings and general improvements, and he turns his attention principally to the raising of corn. Besides his home place he owns a part of a farm of 110 acres, and a part of a town lot in Glenville. He and wife are both members of the United Brethren in Christ.

WILLIAM BLAIR, M. D., a native of Russell County, Ky., was born September 24, 1841. His father, Burton Blair, who was born in North Carolina in 1813, was brought to Russell in infancy where he remained during life. He was a man in moderate circumstances, owning and cultivating his own farm. He married Miss Elizabeth Rippetoe, a daughter of William Rippetoe, whose wife before marriage was a Miss Elizabeth Vincent. The names of the children born to Burton and Elizabeth Blair are Emeline (wife of Matthew Y. Leach), Albert, William, Samantha (deceased wife of Christopher C. Lawless, Elizabeth (deceased wife of John Lovelace), Martha (wife of Robert Anderson), Nancy (wife of Rubin Lawless), Harrison, Sarah Jane (wife of John Crider), Amanda C. (died in infancy) and James T. The death of Burton Blair occurred July 9, 1875; his widow is still living in the sixty-eighth year of her age. James Blair, grandfather of Dr. Blair, was a native of North Carolina, a farmer, and immigrated to Russell County, where he resided the remainder of his life. He married Miss Nancy Day, of North Carolina. James Blair's father was a veteran of the American Revolution. Dr. Blair in

youth received a good common-school education, and is more than ordinarily well posted in literature. He also has an archæological cabinet and some geological specimens. His early life until twenty years years of age was spent on his father's farm, when, October 2, 1861, he enlisted in Company B, Thirteenth Kentucky Infantry (Federal volunteer service). He participated in the battles of Shiloh, Perryville, Hough's Ferry (Tenn.), Campbell's Station (Tenn.), the siege of Knoxville, Rocky Face Ridge and Resaca, where he was disabled from further service, though not discharged until January, 1865, when his company was dismissed from the service. As a result of the wound received at Resaca, the Doctor lost a part of the radius of his right fore-arm. When he returned home he commenced to attend school, and taught and attended alternately for four years. He then began to read medicine under Dr. J. M. Wolford of Russell County, and in the winter of 1874–75, attended a course of lectures at the University of Louisville, graduating in the spring of 1875. He then returned home and continued the practice of his profession which he had begun before he went to college. August 12, 1869, he married Miss Sarah A., daughter of Michael G. and Rachel (Grider) McKinley, both natives of Russell County. He has had born to him seven children: Laura A., Lawrence C., Melvin E., Viantha, Frosia E., Aletha M. and Belva E., all living. Dr. and Mrs. Blair are both members of the Separate Baptist Church. The Doctor settled at his present location, Glenville, Adair County, in 1869, and it at that time consisted of a house and seven acres; he has enlarged it to eighty-eight acres. Dr. Blair has a large and lucrative practice, besides which he cultivates his farm.

ELIJAH H. BLAND was born December 15, 1814, in Nelson County, seven miles north of Bardstown. He is the eleventh of five sons and nine daughters, all of whom lived to be grown, born to William and Sarah (Peak) Bland. William Bland was born in Prince William County, Va., in 1777. In 1784, with his parents, he landed at Louisville, and settled near Bloomfield, Nelson County, where he became a substantial farmer and slave owner. He was a soldier under Gen. Wayne through the Indiana and Ohio campaign. A brother, Osborn Bland, and wife, were taken prisoners by the Indians at the burned station on Simpson Creek, Nelson County; also, their son. He was bound, but his wife succeeded in slipping away, and was in the woods for seventeen days before she was found by some hunters; her husband returned after an absence of three years, and they reared a large and influential family. William Bland moved to Hardin County in 1831, and settled on Nolin Creek, where he remained until his death, at the age of about eighty-five. He was the son of John Bland, who married a Miss Osburn, natives of England and Ireland respectively, who immigrated to Virginia in colonial days. From Virginia they came down the Ohio River in flatboats, and landed at Louisville; thence proceeded inland to Nelson County, where he became an active and influential farmer. Mrs. Sarah (Peak) Bland was born near Frankfort, Ky.; she was a daughter of Daniel Peak, who married a Miss Holderman. He lived to be over ninety years old, and participated in several Indian wars in colonial times. Elijah H. Bland was reared on a farm, and received a plain English education. At the age of twenty-three he left home, went to Louisville and engaged in teaming, which proved to be a very lucrative business. Having accumulated considerable money, in 1837–38 he embarked in the hog trade, in which he lost half his capital. He then returned to the farm in Hardin County, and also rode sheriff for several years. In 1846 he entered the grocery and dry goods business in Louisville, which he followed for twenty-eight years, in which time he had accumulated a snug fortune; after which he became a contractor in Louisville on public wells and cisterns, speculated in bonds and stocks of various kinds, and lost considerable during the panic of 1873. At present he owns eight houses and lots in Louisville, 1,200 acres of land in Nelson County, and 300 acres in Richland County, Ill. He was married October 29, 1841, to Corrilla Willett, a daughter of Griffith and Rhoda (Stiles) Willett, natives of Nelson County and New Jersey and born in 1798 and 1800 respectively. Rhoda (Stiles) Willett is still living. Griffith was a moderate farmer, and died in 1875. He was a son of George Willett, who married and settled on Pottinger's Creek, near New Haven, in a very early day. Mr. and Mrs. Bland had born to them seven children: Stiles P., William M., George G. (all of whom are dead), Bell (now Rush), Annie C. (now Stiles), Dr. Joseph E. and Mattie M. (now Farnsworth). Mr. and Mrs. Bland are devoted members of the Christian Church, as also are all their children.

THOMAS J. BLEVINS was born June 29, 1851, in Green County, near the Taylor line. He is the fifth of six sons and four daughters, eight of whom lived to be grown, born to Gabriel and Mary E. (Mears) Blevins. Gabriel Blevins was born in April, 1817, in Green County, and with the exception of two or three years in Indiana, has constantly lived here, engaged in farming, although a mechanic. He represented Green and Taylor Counties in the Legislature in 1877–78, and has served as magistrate for twelve years. He is a son of Charles Blevins, who was born in 1790, in Green County, and was a minister of the United Baptist Church; also served as magistrate for sixteen years (was a teacher in his younger days), and was a substantial farmer and slave-holder. He married Sarah Roark, a native of Kentucky, by whom four sons and three daughters were reared, and died in 1884. He was a son of William Blevins, a native of Ireland, who married a Miss Skaggs; he first settled in South Carolina,. was a soldier under Gen. Marion in the war for independence, and was one of the earliest settlers of Green County, Ky. Mrs. Mary E. Blevins was born in September, 1817, in Green, now Taylor County, Ky.; she was a daughter of Moses Mears, a native of Taylor County, who married Eda Hamilton, a native of Tompkinsville, Ky. He died in 1873, aged seventy-six. He was a son of Thomas Mears, who was a soldier in the war of 1812, and was also engaged in many battles with the Indians in the early settlement of Green County. He was of Irish descent, and died just before the late civil war, at the advanced age of one hundred and five years. Mrs. Blevins first married Garrett Underwood, to whom one son was born. Thomas J. Blevins was born in Green County, and was reared on a farm. After he became old enough to support and educate himself he successfully taught for seven years in the common schools of the county. His first school was taught in a cabin, the door of which was not sufficient in height to admit a grown person erect. In 1874 he purchased his first farm of 100 acres, but now owns 200 acres, which he has procured by his own efforts, and has it substantially improved with good buildings. August 9, 1880, he married Margaret T.; a daughter of Farris Bennett, a native of Taylor County. This union is blessed with two bright children. Mr. Blevins now resides eight miles northwest of Greensburg, where he has constantly lived since his marriage. He and wife are members of the Baptist Church. In 1876 he commenced the study of law, and in 1877 received license to practice. In politics he is a Democrat, and cast his first presidential vote for Tilden.

EDWARD H. BOARMAN was born April 15, 1836, and is the fourth child of Felix and Nancy (Clements) Boarman, to whom five sons and one daughter have been born—all yet living. Felix Boarman, was born in Maryland, immigrated with his parents to Kentucky in 1812, was a farmer, and died October 22, 1881, aged seventy-six; he was a son of Roswell Boarman, who married a Miss Mc-Atee and early came to Kentucky from Maryland. He was a substantial farmer and slaveholder and died in May, 1850, aged about eighty-four years. His father, Capt. James Boarman, of Maryland of English descent, was a farmer, and in politics, Whig. Mrs. Nancy Boarman was born in Lincoln County, Ky., and was a daughter of John Clements, who married Polly Hocker, and these were among the first settlers of Lincoln County, Ky., and Marion County. He was a wealthy farmer and slave owner. Edward H. Boarman, a native of Marion County, was reared on a farm and married Percilla Bullock, December 27, 1857; to this union thirteen children have been born: Anna B.'(Spalding), Mary J. (Hughes), Francis N., Geo. W., James A., Felix L., Nancy E., John O., Samuel E., Mary A., Joseph Lee, Susan E. and Leonard E. After his marriage Mr. Boarman lived on his father's farm fifteen years, then near St. Mary's two years, then in New Market. In 1877 he located where he now resides near Raywick, on 227 acres—160 under cultivation. He also owns a farm of 105 acres near Loretta, and was interested in a good business for three years at Raywick; in politics is independent and cast his first presidential vote for Gen. Scott in 1852; he was an advocate of the Union, during the late conflict between the States, and has been superintendent of the poor for the past twelve years. He and wife are members of the Catholic Church.

JOSEPH S. BOGGS was born June 16, 1819, one and a half miles south of Richmond, Ky., and is a son of Joseph and Elizabeth (Plow) Boggs, parents of ten children, of whom four are still living. Joseph Boggs, Sr., was born in Delaware, January 2, 1761, and with a brother, Moses, came to Madison County, Ky., about 1805 or 1806, and settled on a tract of land given him by his uncle, Bén Robinson, who had purchased 640 acres from Daniel Boone. He married, September 8, 1807, after he came to Kentucky; was a farmer but would never hold a slave; was a Whig in politics and in religion a Presbyterian, and died July 13, 1843. He was a son of Robert and Margaret (Robinson) Boggs, who were of Scotch descent and settled in Delaware; they were the parents of seven sons—James, Robert, John, Moses, Benjamin, William and Joseph—and two daughters. Of the sons, William, Robert, Benjamin and John were soldiers in the Revolutionary war under Washington. When the army of Lord Cornwallis were retreating before Washington in the State of Delaware they happened to pass though Robert Boggs' yard. The old gentleman, observing beforehand the approach of the enemy, and expecting some great damage to be done to the property, mounted his horse and betook himself to a high hill, where he could witness the proceedings. The soldiers on arriving, being hungry, attacked some beehives that were stationed near by in order to get the honey; as might be expected the bees became angry, so did the soldiers and a hot fight ensued. The bees, however, being very skilled in war with the use of the sword, overcame their antagonists and drove them from the premises. Mr. Boggs, feeling now somewhat relieved, exclaimed "even my bees are patriotic." Mrs. Elizabeth (Plow) Boggs was a native of Pennsylvania and of German descent. She died February 13, 1870. Joseph S. Boggs was reared a farmer and was married March 11, 1841, to Miss Mary M., daughter of Philip and Susan (Mullins) Gilisbie; Philip was a Virginian, who early settled in Madison County, Ky., and was a pioneer mail carrier between this State and Virginia. He was killed in a duel by Thomas Cannady. Mrs. Joseph S. Boggs died in May, 1857, and on the first day of January, 1863, Mr. Boggs married Mary E., daughter of James N. and Hannah (Boggs) Turley of Madison County, and to this union have been born four children: Bettie, James T., Mary M. and Joseph S., Jr. The family are members of the Reformed Church. For forty-three years after his first marriage Mr. Boggs lived on Taylor's Fork of Silver Creek; then bought 133 acres of land one mile south of Richmond, which farm he has increased to 305 acres, improved with a fine brick residence. He makes stock breeding a specialty. His first presidential vote was for William H. Harrision, but since the late war he has affiliated with the Republicans. He was a strong Union man, and after the battle of Richmond took special pains to provide for the wounded Federal soldiers.

JAMES H. BOGGS was born July 9, 1836, one and one-half miles southeast of Richmond, Ky., and is a son of Edward C. and Elizabeth J. (Woods) Boggs, to whom one son and three daughters were born and three reared. Edward C. was born September 27, 1814, one mile and a half south of Richmond. He was a prosperous farmer and owned considerable slave property prior to the war. He was a strong Whig and a supporter of the Union. After the war he, however, affiliated with the Democratic party. He died March 27, 1878. He was a son of James Boggs, who was also born south of Richmond in 1793, served as a common soldier in the war of 1812, and participated in the battle of the Thames. He married Phoeba Cornelison, born nine miles south of Richmond, a daughter of Edward Cornelison, who was one of the pioneers of Madison County and was of Dutch descent. The issue of this union was one son and four daughters. James Boggs, above, was in turn a son of James Boggs, who was born on board a ship while his parents were on their way to America. Elizabeth J. (Woods) Boggs was born five miles south of Richmond, April 23, 1813, died September 23, 1886, and was a daughter of John Woods, who was born in Virginia in 1777. He had three brothers, Adam, William and Andrew, and was next to the youngest. He also had five sisters. He was a son of Michael Woods, who, with his family, about 1780, came to Kentucky and settled at Crab Orchard Station, and while there participated in all the struggles with the Indians. The male members of the family were all large and strong and several of their exploits in Indian attacks are mentioned in history. Michael Woods and Hannah Wallace, his wife, the great-grandparents of our subject, were born in Ireland. They first emigrated to Scotland about the middle of the last century; thence to America, and settled in Virginia about 1775. James H. Boggs was trained on a farm and received a fair English education. At the age of twenty-two he began life on his own account, trading and shipping stock, which he continued successfully until 1862, when he enlisted in Company F, Ninth Kentucky Confederate Cavalry, under Jno. H. Morgan. While on the Ohio raid he succeeded in cutting his way out three times. Finding that all escape was impossible, he relieved himself of all his arms and rode up in the rear of the Federal troops and surrendered. In October, 1863, he was sent to Camp Chase, then to Camp Douglas, from which he made his escape by jumping the fence; was captured, and for this act was thrown into a dungeon, from which, with all the others confined therein, he made his escape through a tunnel. He immediately proceeded to the interior of the State of Illinois and hired to work on a farm near Blooming-

ton and Decatur, remaining until the close of the war, in June, 1865, when he returned to Kentucky. In the meantime, in 1864, during the National Convention which nominated McClellan for President, he was one of about 7,000 who went to Chicago, armed and equipped, to assist in liberating Confederate prisoners. The scheme was detected, and the morning of the day before the attack was to be made on the guards, he, with about thirty others, was in a hotel office in Chicago, when soldiers appeared and arrested all but three, Mr. Boggs being one who escaped. Mr. Boggs married January 16, 1868, Mollie C. Pigg, daughter of Johnson and Nancy (Mize) Pigg, who were natives of Clark and Estill Counties. Johnson Pigg was a farmer and a son of Anderson Pigg, a native of Virginia, who married Polly Perry. The issue from this marriage of Mr. Boggs was eleven children, seven now living: Edgar C., Nannie M., Lillie M., James H., Willie H., Otis T. and Rollie B. Mr. Boggs and Mrs. Boggs are members of the Christian Church. After his marriage he resided two years on Muddy Creek, seven years on Silver Creek, and in January, 1880, located where he now resides, on 563 acres one and one-half miles southeast of Richmond. Mr. Boggs makes a specialty of breeding shorthorn cattle, Poland China and Berkshire hogs, and Southdown and Cotswold sheep. His first presidential vote was cast for Bell and Everett, but since the war he has been a Democrat.

GEORGE BOHON, a native of Wayne County, Ky., was born July 4, 1849. His father, William F. Bohon, a merchant in Wayne and Mercer Counties, was born in November, 1810, in Mercer County. He began the battle of life with no property, but by great industry and good financial management, left an estate of between $40,000 and $50,000. After leaving his father's house he entered mercantile business by clerking in a store of general merchandise in Wayne County. He soon embarked in the business on his own account, which he followed in Monticello fifteen years, when in 1856 he sold out and removed to Harrodsburg, and opened a store of general merchandise. His marriage occurred when he was about thirty years of age to Mrs. V. A. Hutchison, of Danville, Ky. To this marriage were born seven children: Dr. J. T. of Lincoln County; W. J., wholesale hats, of Louisville; H. C., cashier of First National Bank, Harrodsburg; Elizabeth H., wife of L. W. Hudson, an extensive farmer of Garrard County; George; Mattie B., wife of A. H. Peacock, a jeweler of Sherman, Tex., and Rane S., dry goods merchant, Decatur, Ill., all of whom are living. William F. Bohon, who during life was a faithful member of the Presbyterian Church, and a director in the old Commercial Bank, died in the sixty-third year of his age, in April, 1873. Jack Bohon, the grandfather of George Bohon, was a native of Culpeper County, Va., but was one of the first settlers in Mercer County, after whom Bohontown is named. He owned a large and valuable farm, and many slaves who were lost by the late war. He married a Miss Martha Lightfoot, by whom he had nine children: W. F., Reuben M., John, Lucy (Williams), M. M., Mildred (McAfee-Hudson), living in Frankfort; Martha (Fennell), J. W. and R. H. Jack Bohon departed this life in 1860. George Bohon received a good English education in Harrodsburg schools, and his boyhood was spent in his father's store. When he was in his twenty-first year, in 1869, he began traveling for a wholesale notion house of Louisville, which he continued five years. He then opened a livery business in Danville, Ky., operating two years on a capital of about $5,000. In 1876 he sold out, embarking in the grocery business, and two months later in the harness and agricultural implement business. In 1883 he purchased a half interest in the Mercer Grain & Coal Company, remaining one year, when he embarked in his present business, as dealer in buggies, wagons and agricultural implements, operating on $15,000 to $20,000, and doing an annual business of $30,000. Mr. Bohon, in December, 1871, married Miss Irene Saunders, a daughter of S. B. and Phœbe (Duncan) Saunders, of Jessamine County. Three children have been born to them: Minnie, Davis and Hanly, all living. Mr. and Mrs. Bohon are members of the Christian Church.

GEORGE D. BOLDRICK was born October 25, 1842. His father, James P. Boldrick, was born and reared in Ireland, coming thence to the United States in his early manhood. He was by trade a merchant tailor, for the prosecution of which he located in Danville, Boyle County, where he married Miss Mary Doneghy, a native of Boyle County, but of Irish parentage. Both James P. Boldrick and wife are deceased. Their children are Mary (widow of Lee Mitchell), Lucy (Cundiff), Sarah (Cundiff) and George D. Boldrick. The last named was born and educated in Danville, and made that his home until removing to Lebanon, Marion County, where, in 1868, he established a drug store, which business he conducted profitably until 1880, when he sold to C. F. McAfee. He then engaged in distilling under the firm name of Boldrick & Callaghan, which still continues. Mr. Boldrick married, in 1868, Miss Carrie Spalding. She died in March, 1875, leaving three children: Samuel, Ralph and Charles Boldrick. His present wife, to whom he was married in 1878, was Miss Kate Tobin, daughter of Lawrence Tobin, of Frankfort, Ky. They have three children, viz.: Mary, George and John Boldrick. Mr. Boldrick is a member of the Catholic Church and also of the C. K. of A.

DR. JOHN BRISCO BOLLING was born August 25, 1825, seven miles west of Danville, Ky., and he has always retained his residence in that part of Mercer now known as Boyle County. His father, Dread Bolling, a native of Albemarle County, Va., was brought in childhood by his parents, to Mercer County, Ky., where they located on Shawnee Run. He was a soldier in the war of 1812, a major in the militia, represented Mercer County in the Legislature six times as a Democrat, was a farmer and slave owner, and died in 1847, at the age of fifty-eight years. He was the son of William Bolling, a Virginian, a farmer and correct business man, who died in 1835, at the age of seventy-eight years. He married Mary White (cousin to Hon. Hugh L. White, of Tennessee), and from their union sprang Dread, Mary (Wilson), Knight, Glover and Howell. Dread was twice married, first to Miss Mary, daughter of Thomas Davis, of Mercer County (died in 1832), and to them were born Elizabeth (Greenwood), Nancy (Curry), Silas, John Brisco, and Jeremiah (deceased). William's second wife was Mary Kimberlain, of Washington County, and their offspring were Thomas M. (deceased), George (deceased), Mary E. (Dorsey), and Rachael (Bottom). John Brisco was first married in 1847, to Miss Susan, daughter of Dr. Nelson and Jane Crane, of Perryville (born in 1823, died April 10, 1876), but from this union there was no issue. May 15, 1877, he espoused Miss Lucy J., daughter of David and Lucy (Kirk) Cleaver of Lebanon, Ky. (born May 31, 1842). In 1843 Mr. Bolling commenced the study of medicine with Dr. Nelson Crane, and in 1850 graduated at the medical department of the University of Louisville, and since that time has been successfully engaged in the practice of his chosen profession at Perryville. After the disastrous battle of Perryville, Dr. Bolling, though entertaining Southern sentiments, was for several months employed by the General Government as surgeon in the hospitals in the vicinity, and received ample compensation for such service. Dr. Bolling is a member of the I. O. O. F., and of the Baptist Church; is a aggressive prohibitionist and a Democrat.

JOHN C. BONER is a son of William B. and Elizabeth (Cavins) Boner, and was born March 5, 1825. William B. Boner, a native of Fayette County, was in early life a brick mason, but in 1835 removed to Garrard County, where he became a successful farmer. In 1808 he [married Elizabeth, daughter of Thomas Cavins, who bore him a family of six boys and four girls. William B. was first a Whig in politics, but afterward became a Democrat, and he and wife were Presbyterians. John B. Boner, who was born near Walnut Hill, Fayette County, moved to Garrard County with his parents in 1835, was reared a farmer, and is now the owner of 300 acres of well cultivated land. He first married Miss Mary Kemper, and had born to him four sons: William, T. K., John Quincy and Edgar S. His second marriage was to Miss Georgie Ann Raines, and to this union were born Mary F., Margaret E., Joseph C., Thomas Cavins, James Alfred, Oliver P. Morton, George Welsh and Speed Fry. In politics Mr. Boner was until the late war a Whig, but has since been Republican; he is also a member of the I. O. O. F.

W. F. BOOKER, clerk of the Washington County Court, was born in Springfield, January 3, 1830. His grandfather, Samuel Booker, was a native of Virginia and a descendant of an old Welsh family, several members of which came to America in colonial times and became well known in the early history of the country. Samuel Booker served with distinction in the war of independence, and was a member of the celebrated cavalry commanded by "Light Horse Harry Lee." At the surrender of Lord Cornwallis he, with two others, was selected to carry the news to Philadelphia, the selection being made in compliment to their superior horsemanship. He came to Kentucky shortly after the war and settled near Springfield, Washington County, where he engaged in farming, which vocation he followed until his death in 1849. William B. Booker, son of the preceding and father of subject, was born in Prince Edward's County, Va., and grew to manhood in that State. He was educated at William and Mary College and came to Kentucky at the age of twenty-one and engaged in the practice of law at Springfield, which he continued successfully until his death in 1865. He was county clerk for a period of twenty years and represented the county in the Legislature during the years 1855 and 1857. His wife was Louisa Nantz, a daughter of Frederick Nantz, who came from Virginia in an early day in company with Gen. Matthew Walton, and, like the last-named gentleman, took an active part in the early development of the county. He was a Revolutionary soldier also, and died when the subject of this sketch was quite a small boy. Mrs. Booker was born in Prince Edward County, Va., and departed this life in Washington County, Ky., about the year 1838. Mr. and Mrs. Booker had, besides our immediate subject, the following children, namely: Paul, Martha, Harriet, Samuel, Henrietta Louisa, Dr. Thomas J. and Eliza Booker. W. F. Booker was reared in Springfield and educated in the schools of the town which he attended until his nineteenth year. He then began the study of law with his father, under whose instruction he continued for three years, obtaining license to practice in 1850. He was appointed deputy county clerk one year later and served in that capacity three years, when he engaged in agricultural pursuits, purchasing a farm of 170 acres near Springfield, upon which he has since resided. In September, 1869, he was elected county clerk, a position he has held by successive elections ever since. He has proved himself a judicious and painstaking official, and such is his popularity in the county that he has had opposition but twice—the first time defeating his competitor by 1,000 majority, and was successful over his second opponent by 1,600 majority. Mr. Booker was married, November 9, 1852, in Jefferson County, Ky., to Mary Philips, daughter of Jefferson and Nancy (Edelen) Philips, by whom he had four children, namely: Horace, Louisa, Maggie (wife of Samuel Berry) and Lizzie Booker. Mrs. Booker died on the 9th of October, 1872. Mr. Booker's second marriage was solemnized June 21, 1876, in Cincinnati, Ohio, with Miss Euphemia Bates, daughter of Thomas Bates, of that city. Mr. and Mrs. Booker are members of the Catholic Church and belong to the St. Rose congregation. On national questions Mr. Booker is a Democrat, but in local affairs is independent.

CHARLES F. BOSLEY (deceased) was a prominent and popular citizen of his native county of Washington, born September 23, 1814, the child of Gideon and Elizabeth (Fleece) Bosley. His paternal ancestors were of German descent, and came to Kentucky from Maryland in an early day. His father was a soldier in the war of 1812, and was one of the successful farmers of Washington County. He was reared on the farm, receiving a very ordinary education. Upon the death of his father he took charge of the farm, and the maintenance and support of the family devolved upon him. At the age of twenty-two he was united in marriage with Eudotia B. Barbour, a most estimable lady; she died after their union had continued for a period of about thirty years, and August 8, 1866, the nuptials of his marriage with Margaret Steger Baker were celebrated; to the latter union four children were born, of which three are now living: Charles F., now attending Vanderbilt University; Lizzie and Lillie. With the exception of four years spent in the mercantile business at Springfield, he followed farming continuously all his life, meeting with flattering success; he owned a large number of slaves. Mr. Bosley served as sheriff of Washington County for several terms during the trying times of the Rebellion and immediately subsequent, and proved an able, active, vigilant and efficient officer. He was a Christian and died October 23, 1882, a devout believer in the faith of the Methodist Episcopal Church.

DR. HENRY P. BOSLEY was born March 21, 1823, and is the seventh of seven sons and three daughters born to Gideon, Jr., and Elizabeth (Fleece) Bosley, natives of Lincoln County. Gideon Bosley was born July 9, 1784, was a farmer, and a soldier in the war of 1812, and died November 29, 1830, a member of the Methodist Episcopal Church. He was a son of Gideon Bosley, Sr., who married a Miss Cole of Baltimore, and later settled in Lincoln County, Ky., on the Stanford road, about five miles from Danville. Mrs. Elizabeth (Fleece) Bosley died in 1864, aged seventy-four. She was the daughter of John Fleece, who was born in Germany, served in the war for American independence, and married a Miss Withers of Fayette County, Ky. He died about 1835, aged eighty-five. Dr. Henry P. Bosley, a native of Washington County, was reared on the home farm until sixteen, when he entered Centre College, and at twenty began the study of medicine with Dr. Fleece. About 1846 he located at Danville, studied awhile with Drs. Fleece and Pawling, graduated from Transylvania University in 1848, practiced at Etna Furnace, Hart County, three years, then at Lebanon two years, and then settled in Danville, where he has a beautiful brick cottage. He relinquished his profession about fifteen years ago, having practiced irregularly in connection with the cultivation of his farm of 300 acres. April 3, 1860, he married Mrs. Sallie Walker, daughter of James G. and

Amelia J. (Kavanaugh) Denny, of Garrard County. Mrs. Bosley died February 4, 1879, and on the 27th of April, 1880, the Doctor married Miss A. L. Bosley, daughter of J. S. and Josephine (Lytle) Bosley. To this union have been born two children, Elizabeth Fleece and Harry P.

HON. WILLIAM O. BRADLEY was born March 18, 1847, near Lancaster, Ky., and is the youngest of eight children (two sons and six daughters), born to Robert M. and Ellen (Totten) Bradley. The former was born in Madison County in 1808, and was among the ablest lawyers in Kentucky. His father, Isaac Bradley (grandfather of our subject), came to the State in an early day, and settled in Madison County, but finally removed to Bath County, where he died. He was of Irish parentage, his father emigrating from Ireland to America prior to the Revolutionary war; a war in which he gallantly served to the close, being present at the surrender of Cornwallis at Yorktown. His wife was Margaret O'Connell, a relative of Daniel O'Connell, the great Irish agitator and patriot. Robert M. Bradley (subject's father) married Ellen Totten, a daughter of Joseph H. Totten, whose father lived in Culpeper County, Va., and served in the Revolutionary war. He came to Kentucky and settled in Garrard County; was a prominent farmer and died at the age of eighty years. William O. Bradley, the subject of this sketch, is one of the brilliant young lawyers of central Kentucky, and although he has but attained the zenith of manhood's prime, the vigor of his intellectual life, he has already filled the measure of a just ambition—not so much on account of the public positions he has held, for he has been always upon the wrong side of the political fence to meet with success, but by the respect and confidence he has inspired in all men, political friends or foes. When he was quite young Mr. Bradley's parents removed to Somerset, Ky., where they resided until the breaking out of the civil war. He then, although but fifteen years of age, quit school and entered the Union Army, first as a recruiting officer in Pulaski County, and afterward at Louisville as a private soldier. He remained in the army but a short time when he returned home and commenced reading law with his father. Under a special act of the Legislature he was admitted to the bar at eighteen years of age—the first special act of the kind ever passed in Kentucky, the law requiring a man to be twenty-one when admitted to the bar. Upon receiving his license to practice, he entered into partnership with his father at Lancaster. In 1870 was elected commonwealth's attorney for his district, and in 1872 was presidential elector on the Grant and Wilson ticket; also made the race that year as the Republican candidate for Congress but was defeated. In the winter of 1875 he received the entire vote of his party in the Legislature for United States senator, and in 1876 he again made the race for Congress on the Republican ticket, but was again defeated, receiving, however, nearly 3,000 more votes than ever before received by a candidate of his party in the district. In 1878 and 1882 he was again nominated for Congress but declined; in 1879 he was nominated for attorney-general of the State, but declined on account of ill health. He was delegate for the State at large in 1880 to the Republican National Convention at Chicago; seconded the nomination of Gen. Grant, and was one of the famous 306; he was chosen the same year for a member of the National Republican convention of Kentucky, and made a number of speeches in Indiana, Ohio and New York. In 1884 he was again delegate for the State at large to the Republican National Convention, and chairman of the Kentucky delegation, and made a speech against the proposition to curtail Southern representation. He was selected in 1885 by President Arthur, just before the close of his term, to institute proceedings against the Star route thieves, and retired from the prosecution because the attorney-general hampered him and would not allow an impartial trial and prosecution. Mr. Bradley is a man of fine executive ability, personal daring and unflinching adherence to his principles. Though not disposed to be aggressive in his habits, he is a man who would make his mark in any great social or political movement. He was married July 11, 1867, to Margaret Robertson Duncan, a daughter of Dr. B. F. and Jane L. (McKee) Duncan of Lancaster, and a grandniece of Hon. George Robertson, formerly chief justice of Kentucky. They have two children, George R. and Christine.

TIMOLEON AND TARLETON T. BRADSHAW, the former a native of Russell, the latter of Adair County, are the sons of Seath and Sarah G. (White) Bradshaw. Seath Bradshaw, born October 23, 1805, was a native of Burke County, N. C. He was the eighth of ten children, and when only five years of age was brought by his father to Russell County, Ky., and shortly afterward to Adair. He always owned his own farm, and part of the time cultivated it with slave labor, being worth at one time nearly $20,000. He departed this life March 9, 1873. He had married, in 1828, Miss Sarah G. White,

daughter of Thomas and Nancy (Abrell) White, natives of the Old Dominion. The names of the children born to Seath and Sarah Bradshaw are Octavia, wife of Aaron McClure; Casandra, wife of Charles F. Jones; Tarleton T.; Timoleon; Ann L., wife of J. G. White; Charlotta W.; and Millie E., wife of T. W. Montgomery, of whom all are living except Casandra. Mrs. Bradshaw died April 11, 1855, in the forty-eighth year of her age, and in life was a consistent member of the Methodist Episcopal Church. Seath Bradshaw, Sr., the grandfather of the gentlemen whose names head these lines, was a native of Virginia, from where he emigrated to North Carolina, and finally to Kentucky. He was married to Miss Ann Lowe, a native of Virginia, and the names of their children were William, Isaac, Isaiah, Elijah, Seath, Millie (Miller), Ann (Bradshaw), Mary (Wilson), and Charlotte (White). Of his sons, Isaac and Isaiah served in the war of 1812, and he himself was a Revolutionary veteran. Mrs. Bradshaw, his wife, was killed at the age of ninety-seven, being thrown from a horse. The Bradshaw family are of Irish origin, and sprang from one of two brothers who came from Ireland to America. William Bradshaw, the son of Seath Bradshaw, Sr., was a man of some celebrity in the history of the politics of this section, having served in the Senate of Kentucky. Tarleton T. Bradshaw, born April 2, 1832, was the third of Seath Bradshaw's children. He began life by farming with his father, and this has since been his vocation. He had no inheritance, but at present owns about 400 acres on the line of Russell and Adair Counties, of which 75 acres are in cultivation. He has never been married, but has kept house with his sister, Charlotta W. Bradshaw, a number of years. Mr. Bradshaw enlisted, October 4, 1861, in Company D, Fifth Kentucky Volunteer Cavalry, Federal service. He participated in many of the prominent battles without a wound or being taken prisoner. He was first sergeant of the company, and was mustered out of the service and received an honorable discharge at Louisville, May 17, 1865. Mr. Bradshaw has a fair library and is a great reader. He is a member of the Masonic order, and has been a life-long Democrat. Timoleon Bradshaw in youth received a good business education in the common schools of Adair County, and his occupation in life has been mostly in the line of merchandise. He was married to Miss Sally Wilson, a daughter of H. W. and Agnes A. (Johnston) Wilson, natives of Taylor County, and this marriage was blessed by the addition of four children: Betty C., Mary G., Effie T. and William E. He first sold goods at Russell Spring, but afterward and most of his life in Columbia, and does a flourishing trade in general merchandise. In connection with Mr. Bradshaw's business, Mrs. Bradshaw handles a finely selected stock of millinery, in which she does a thriving business. The stock is worth at least $6,000, including general merchandise and millinery. Mr. and Mrs. Bradshaw are both members of the Christian Church, and Mr. Bradshaw is one of the trustees of the Columbia Christian College. All of the children of Mr. and Mrs. Bradshaw are living except their eldest, Bettie C., who died July 25, 1883. She was born March 4, 1863. She was a bright, intelligent girl in her youth, and at the age of thirteen became a member of the Christian Church. Her education was very thorough, and was completed at the Columbia Christian College, where she graduated in June, 1881, and after graduation was connected with it as teacher of painting in the Art Department, which position she held until her death. She left a large number of friends who mourned her demise, among whom was Miss Delray Taylor, an associate teacher in the same institution, who followed in a few brief months.

JUDGE ROBERT J. BRECKINRIDGE was born September 14, 1835, in Baltimore, Md., and is the oldest son of Rev. Robert J. and Sophonisba (Preston) Breckinridge, who were born in Fayette and Washington Counties, Va., respectively, and reared a family of five sons and four daughters. Robert J. Breckinridge was born in April, 1800, and was one of the eminent ministers in the Presbyterian Church; was also a lawyer and served in the Kentucky Legislature, and also as superintendent of public instruction of the State; was one of the most active and prominent men of Kentucky, and died in December, 1871. He was a son of John and Mary (Cabell) Breckinridge, natives of Fincastle, Va., and near Lynchburg, Va., respectively. John Breckinridge was elected to the lower house of Virginia Legislature twice before he became of age—the first time was but nineteen years old—and while attending William and Mary's College was elected to Congress but would not accept the office because he was not of constitutional age, besides having business in Kentucky, where he settled about 1790, and moved his family in the spring of 1793. He served in the Kentucky Legislature, also in the United States Senate from Kentucky; was Attorney-general under Jefferson's administration, died in 1806 and was a son of John Breckinridge, who was a patriot in the war for independence. He married a Miss Preston, of Virginia. They were of Scotch-Irish extraction. Col. Robert J. Breckinridge left Baltimore with his parents in 1845 for Kentucky. Then the family moved to Pennsylvania, his father having accepted the presidency of Jefferson College, which he resigned in 1847 and returned to Lexington, Ky., and took charge of a church and was the founder of the present school system in Lexington. In 1854 they moved to Danville and the father accepted a professorship of the theological seminary. Robert J. received his education at Transylvania and Danville and the University of Virginia; graduated from the latter in 1852, after which he spent three years in the service of the United States coast survey. He resigned the position in 1854 and soon after began the study of law at Danville under Gen. Boyle and Hon. W. C. Anderson. In the spring of 1856 he graduated from the law department of Transylvania University and immediately entered the practice of his profession at Lexington with uniform good success. In July, 1861, he raised a company for the Confederate service, which company became the second of the Second Regiment at Camp Boone, which he established. This was the nucleus of the Orphan Brigade. In 1862 he was elected to the Confederate Congress and served one session. In the spring of 1863 resigned his seat and again entered the army as colonel of a cavalry regiment, which was composed of the fragments of several regiments; first reported to Gen. Marshall, afterward to Gen. Breckinridge. In February, 1865, was captured in Kentucky and retained as a prisoner at Louisville, Columbus, Ohio Penitentiary and Johnson's Island, until the close of the war; was released in June, 1865, and located on a farm in Lincoln County and practiced his profession; in 1874 located in Danville; in 1876 was elected common pleas judge; previous to 1874 he had gone to Louisville and practiced two years, when he returned to Danville; in 1869 made the race for the Kentucky Senate. The issue was the right of negroes to testify in court, he taking the grounds that they should. This was the first time the subject was discussed in a campaign in the State; upon this issue he was defeated by only twenty-five votes. Judge Breckinridge is an able lawyer, is a pleasant gentleman and possesses many of the admirable and brilliant qualities of his distinguished family. He was married March, 1856, to

Miss Kate Morrison, a daughter of M. B. and Kate (Taylor) Morrison; her father was a merchant in Lexington and died in 1862, aged sixty-two years. This union of our subject is blessed with two children: Robert J. and Morrison. Mr. and Mrs. Breckinridge are members of the Presbyterian Church. The Judge is a Democrat and cast his first presidential vote for James Buchanan.

REV. JAMES BREEDING, the oldest minister in Adair County, was born in that county in 1803. His father, George Breeding, a native of Virginia, was born in 1772, and when fourteen years of age was brought to Kentucky where Maysville now stands. When about sixteen years of age he was brought to Lincoln County, and 1802 came to Adair County, where a farm was bought and deeded to George Breeding, where the little village of Breeding's now stands. Here George remained during the rest of his life, engaged in agricultural pursuits and left an estate of about $7,000 in land and slaves mostly. He was married three times; first to Miss Margaret Cloyd, a daughter of James and Jane (Lapsley) Cloyd, of Lincoln County. To this marriage were born sixteen children, of whom all died in infancy except two—Peter, who died aged nine, and Rev. James Breeding. Mrs. Breeding, during life a consistent Christian and member of the Methodist Episcopal Church, departed this life February, 1840, in the sixtieth year of her age. George Breeding next married Mrs. Sally Black of Lincoln County, who, at the time of her death, was a member of the Methodist Episcopal Church, and left no children by her last marriage. The third marriage of George Breeding was to Mrs. Parthenia L. (Carter) Turk, a daughter of Benjamin Carter of Adair County. This marriage was blessed by the birth of two children: Mary Elizabeth and Rachel Jane, wife of R. D. Priestly, of Canton, Miss. At the time of her marriage Mrs. Breeding had five children by her first husband. She died a member of the Methodist Episcopal Church. George Breeding was called from the scene of his earthly labors May 29, 1859, leaving a large estate of 840 acres of land to his widow and her two children, having previously given his son James 450 acres. George Breeding, grandfather of James Breeding, was a Virginian and a farmer. He married Miss Rachael Cassiday, by whom he had seven children: Peter, John, George, James, Sally (Young) Elizabeth (Blair) and Levinia (Bird). He died in 1811 and his wife in 1821. The Breeding family is of Welsh origin, the Cass-

iday of Irish and the Cloyd also of Irish, which makes Rev. James Breeding three-fourths Irish and one-fourth Welsh. Rev. James Breeding in boyhood received a moderate education in the log schoolhouse of pioneer Kentucky, and remained at home until his marriage in his twenty-second year to Miss Elizabeth B. Patterson, a daughter of Richard and Martha (Barnett) Patterson, natives of South Carolina, who came to Madison County and later to Adair, where Elizabeth was born January 13, 1807. The marriage of James and Elizabeth Breeding has been blessed by the addition to their family of eleven children: Jane C., wife of John M. Nunn, of Missouri; Francis M., of Bowling Green, Ky.; George W.; Richard P.; John C., architect, of San Antonio, Tex.; David C. (deceased); Jackson E., dentist of San Antonio; Sarah Ann, deceased wife of R. A. Baker; Margaret Susan, deceased wife of Dr. C. W. Williams; James A., dentist in Glasgow, and Samuel K., a Methodist minister. Rev. Mr. Breeding, after marriage, settled on the 450 acres given him by his father, where he has farmed ever since. He built a large two-story frame residence and good out-buildings on his farm, and increased his 450 acres to 1,000 acres, but at present owns only 350 acres in the home tract. Besides farming he worked twenty years at wagon and cabinet work and house carpentering, and a great deal of the furniture in his house he made. On July 27, 1834, he was licensed to preach the gospel by the quarterly conference, and has never failed to preach on any Sunday that he was able to travel. Fifty-two years has his voice been heard proclaiming the "Glad Tidings," and in the course of his ministry he has married 250 couples and attended to the funeral obsequies of nearly 500 persons. All of his children have grown up to be useful and respected members of society and members of the Methodist Episcopal Church; one of them, Samuel, is an itinerant minister. Mr. Breeding voted for Gen. Jackson in 1824, and for sixty-two years has voted the straight Democratic ticket.

GEORGE A. BRICKEN, dealer in grain, seeds and implements, Lebanon, was born in Marion County May 16, 1841. His father, William M. Bricken, was born in Washington County in 1817. He married Miss Ellen Cunningham and two sons blessed this union, George A. and Samuel B. Ellen (Cunningham) Bricken is yet living, aged sixty-three years. She is a daughter of Robert and Nancy (Beale) Cunningham, who were of Scotch parentage and natives of Maryland

and came to Kentucky in 1796, and located near the site of the present city of Lebanon. Wm. M. Bricken was, during life, engaged chiefly in the grocery trade in connection with farming. He was the first assessor of property elected in the town of Lebanon; he died in 1865. He was a son of Wm G. Bricken, a native of Virginia born near Richmond, where he grew to manhood and married a Miss Hardwick; afterward (in 1797) he came to Kentucky and settled in Washington County, where he purchased land and engaged in farming, which vocation he followed until his death; he reared a family of three sons and five daughters, among whom was Wm. M., the youngest, and the father of our subject. They have been a remarkably long-lived family, two sons and one daughter having died upward of eighty years of age each. Those living are Mrs. E. R. Terrell, Mrs. Martha Johnson, Alexander, Mrs. Maria Spraggins, and Mrs. Mahala Wilkinson. George A. Bricken was reared on a farm and educated in the common schools, finishing at the Lebanon Institute under the tuition of W. T. Knott. In 1859 he engaged in trade with his father in the grocery business, and afterward in the shoe trade until 1870, when he engaged in agricultural pursuits on a farm of 150 acres, that he owned. In 1881 he connected with his farming operations the trade in seeds, grain and farming implements, in the town of Lebanon. June 11, 1867, he was united in marriage with Miss Elizabeth V. Johnson. Three sons and two daughters have blessed this union: Wm. M., Felix J., Rosella, Blanche, and George A. Mrs. Elizabeth Bricken was born in 1846. She is a daughter of Felix and Rosetta (Medley) Johnson; both were native Kentuckians of Irish descent, and residents of Washington County. Mrs. Bricken is a member of the Catholic Church. Mr. Bricken is not a member of the church but is a patron of church and school. His political views are Democratic.

ANDREW BRIGGS was born September 20, 1853. His father, Thomas H. Briggs, was born in Nelson County, September 16, 1823. His wife was Miss Elizabeth McMakin. Their family consisted of four sons: Peyton, Andrew, John and Alexander, and one daughter, Katie. He has since attaining manhood followed farming with uniform success and has held the office of magistrate of the county for over forty years. His father, Andrew Briggs, was a native of Edinburgh, Scotland. He came to the United States a short time after the Revolutionary war, and settled in Nelson County, of which county he became

one of its most successful and extensive farmers. He was a true and consistent member of the Methodist Episcopal Church and died at the age of sixty-four in the year 1857. He was twice married, first to Miss Nancy Robinson, by whom he was the father of nine children; his next marriage was to Miss Mary Ferguson; to their union five children were born. Two of his sons were members of the Confederate Army. Peyton McMakin, maternal grandfather of our subject, was a native Kentuckian, born in Oldham County in the year 1800; he also became a very extensive farmer of Nelson County, and owned a large number of slaves. He married a Miss Katie Bane and they reared a family of nine children; three of his sons fought on the Confederate side in the late war. In politics he was a stanch Democrat; was a member of the Methodist Church. He died in 1864. Andrew Briggs, a native of Nelson County, has all his life followed the pursuits of the farm. His early education was good, partially obtained at Lynnland College in Hardin County. His wife, whom he married September 19, 1878, was Miss Elizabeth Muir; they have only one child, a son named Elmo. Mr. Briggs devotes his entire attention to his vocation of farming and takes a great interest in anything which will be to the advantage of his co-workers in that field; he is an active member of the Nelson County Agricultural Association, in which he holds the position of director, and is the proprietor of a fine, well improved farm of 166 acres, situated on the Bardstown and Bloomfield pike, about two and one-half miles from the latter place. He and wife are members of the Presbyterian Church. His political views are Democratic.

GEORGE ROBERT BRIGHT was born August 28, 1833, near Bryantsville, Garrard Co., Ky., where he grew to manhood, and in 1872 he located in the Big Bend of Dick's River where he has since resided. His father, Thomas Bright, a native of Virginia, removed, in childhood, with his parents to Garrard County, Ky., where he was reared; was a farmer, a Whig, lost six slaves by the late war, and died May 11, 1867, aged seventy-five years. He was the son of James Bright, of Virginia, who located on Sugar Creek, Garrard County, Ky., about 1800; was a farmer and slave-holder, and died in 1840, at the age of eighty years. He married Margaret Smith, and their offspring were Margaret (Garvin), Betsy (Hoskins), James, John, William and Thomas. Thomas married Sophia Rochester, of Boyle County (died August 5, 1848), and to them were born

Elizabeth J. (Grimes), William H., Margaret (deceased), Thomas H. (deceased), Mary H. (Robinson), John R., Martha E. (Saunders), and George R.   George R. Bright has never married.   He is a farmer and owns 343 acres of productive and well improved land, in a high state of cultivation; has also an interest in another tract of 455 acres.   He is a Presbyterian, a Democrat and a prohibitionist.

JOSEPH S. BRONSTON was born March 15, 1854, in Richmond, Ky., and is a son of Thomas S. and Henrietta A. (Baker) Bronston, to whom four sons and six daughters were born, Joseph S. being the eldest. Thomas S. was born in Fayette and in his early manhood carried on farming, but afterward became a merchant. He also served as assistant secretary under Gov. McCreary's administration, after which he resumed mercantile pursuits till appointed revenue collector of the Eighth Kentucky District.   Joseph S. Bronston was reared and received his early training in Richmond; afterward he attended the Kentucky University and in 1873 entered the circuit clerk's office, served as deputy for two years, then entered the store with his father till 1876, when he made a trip to the West and in 1877 entered his father's office at Frankfort.   In October, 1879, he became editor of the Richmond *Herald* and held that position till 1883, when he began the study of law and received his license to practice in March, 1884.   In June of the same year he was elected police judge of Richmond and served two years.   He has been very successful in his practice and is making his mark as a lawyer.   November 5, 1884, he was united in marriage to Miss Catharine B. Douglas, of Cincinnati, Ohio.   She was born near Utica, N. Y., and is a daughter of Robert L. Douglas, who married a Miss Billings.   Mr. and Mrs. Bronston are members of the Christian Church.   He is a member of the Masonic fraternity of Richmond and in politics he is a Democrat.

ELIAS B. BROWN, second son of Stephen C. and Mary E. Brown, was born December 9, 1829.   He grew to manhood on his father's farm in the Pleasant Grove neighborhood, Washington County, and received his early education in the Pleasant Grove Academy, where he attended at intervals until his eighteenth year when he entered Center College at Danville, remaining for the year and making substantial progress in his various studies.   He chose agriculture for his life work, and at the age of twenty-one engaged in farming two miles east of Springfield, where he has resided since 1851.   His

farm, consisting of 355 acres of fine land, is one of the best stock farms in the county, and as a successful raiser of stock, Mr. Brown has few equals in this part of Kentucky.   Mr. Brown was married April 4, 1855, to Miss Mary E. Thompson, daughter of James and Nancy (Litsey) Thompson, of Washington County.   The children born to this marriage are the following: Jane D., wife of James Ewing; Nannie, wife of Newell McClosky; Stephen C. (deceased), William, James T., Elias B. (deceased), Lucy, Mary, Beverly, Jewett and Veola T. Brown.   Mr. Brown has never been an aspirant for official position and is conservative in politics, voting for the man, rather than party.   He and wife are active members of the Pleasant Grove Presbyterian Church, to which he has belonged since 1855, and in which he holds the position of elder.

WILLIAM R. BROWN, a prominent farmer of Nelson County, is a native Kentuckian, born on North Elkhorn Creek, in Woodford County in 1835.   His father, Jonathan Brown, was born in Fayette County, January 23, 1803, and married a Miss Elizabeth Beauchamp; they were married in 1826; their family consisted of seven sons and three daughters, five of whom are living, viz.: W. R., George W., Benjamin F., Catherine (wife of E. W. Dugan), and Mary E. (now Mrs. W. J. Crume). Elizabeth Beauchamp was born in 1811 and is yet living; she is a daughter of Jesse and Elizabeth Beauchamp, both natives of Maryland.   Jonathan Brown was a farmer and breeder of blooded horses.   In the year 1850 he moved to Nelson County and located near Bloomfield, of which place he continued to be a resident until his death, which occurred October 2, 1885.   He was a member of the Baptist Church for over fifty years, and died as he had lived—a devout believer in that faith.   He was a man of great energy and force of character, always upright in his dealings, and was esteemed and respected by all who knew him.   His father, James B. Brown, was a native of New Jersey, came to Kentucky in an early period of the history of the State and located in Fayette County, where he remained for some years, but afterward removed to the State of Indiana, where he ended his days.   William R. Brown has all his life followed the pursuits of the farm. His early education was such as could be obtained in the common schools.   He has been a versatile reader and his business abilities have matured by contact with the affairs of life; his farming operations have proved uniformly successful, and through energy, economy and industry he is now the proprietor of a farm of 300 acres of fine land lying in Nelson County. His wife, whom he married in 1858, was Miss Mary E. Tichenor. Their family consists of two sons, Jonathan and Charles W., and two daughters, Emma and Georgia; the last named died young. Mrs. Brown was born February 17, 1835; she is a daughter of Timothy and Emily (Neal) Tichenor, the former a native of Nelson County, Ky.; the latter was a granddaughter of Michael Neal, whose father was born in Ireland. Mrs. Brown is a member of the Baptist Church. Mr. Brown, though not a church member, holds to the Baptist faith. In politics he is a Democrat.

JAMES H. BROWN, born August 6, 1861, in Lancaster, Ky., is a son of A. B. and Zerelda (Jennings) Brown. A. B. Brown was born in Garrard County in 1832, and is a son of A. J. Brown, who married Nancy McKinzie. A. J. Brown was postmaster of Lancaster during Presidents Polk's and Pierce's administrations and was also a major of militia. He was a Democrat and was a delegate to the first Democratic convention held in Garrard County. He was a son of Abe J. Brown, a native of Virginia, who married Bettie Dolling and came to Garrard County about 1791, and entered over 1,000 acres of land about a mile east of Lancaster. Mrs. Zerelda Brown is a daughter of Samuel and Rosana (McDonald) Jennings, and a native of Garrard County. James H. Brown was reared on a farm, and after a preliminary education in the common schools, began the study of law with Denny & Tomlinson. In February, 1880, he was admitted to the bar of Lancaster, and in August, 1882, was elected county attorney and re-elected in 1886 as a Democrat, and is probably the youngest man ever elected to the office, and only one ever re-elected to that office in Garrard.

STEPHEN C. BROWNE (deceased). Prominent among the active citizens and successful business men of Washington County was Stephen C. Browne, a brief sketch of whom is herewith given from a notice which appeared upon the occasion of his death. "Stephen C. Browne was born near Petersburg, Va., September 9, 1798. William Browne and Elizabeth Cock, his parents, died a few years after his birth. He was left to the care of his maternal grandmother, with whom he came to Kentucky as early as 1804. He was educated at Hampden Sydney College, Virginia, under the care of his uncle, Samuel Booker, with whom he returned to Kentucky about the year 1815. He spent several years in the clerk's office at Springfield, transact-

ing the business of circuit clerk. The education obtained from these two sources rendered him one of the most ready, accurate, and most useful business men that the county has ever possessed. His intimate acquaintance with men and things of that day, both in Virginia and Kentucky, gave him a vast amount of biographical and traditional history that proved of great interest, and is not to be found in books. He was married to Miss Mary Eleanor Davison, daughter of Elias and Maria (Ball) Davison, by whom he had the following children: Mrs. Sarah J. Thompson, Mrs. Elizabeth Nichols, William D., Elias B., Thomas R., Stephen E., John H., Beverly B., Mrs. Susan Leachman, Mary E. and Mrs. Lucy Rogers. Mrs. Browne was born in Springfield, September 11, 1805, and died on the 3d of December, 1867. After a short absence in Union County Mr. Browne settled in Washington County as a farmer, where by success as a farmer and stock raiser, he showed himself second to no man in this part of the State. He was an elder in the Pleasant Grove (Presbyterian) Church from its foundation, and as elder, clerk of the sessions, and liberal contributor to the support of the gospel, his services were invaluable to that congregation. Few men did more for the church, the school, and for the moral advancement of the community, than Stephen C. Browne. He died at his residence, six miles north of Springfield, on the 15th of January, 1864, in the sixty-sixth year of his age."

THOMAS R. BROWNE was born September 9, 1831, and is the third son and fifth child of Stephen C. and Mary E. Browne. He passed his youth and early manhood on the paternal homestead, and received excellent educational advantages, attending the Pleasant Grove Academy until his fifteenth year, when he entered Centre College, which he attended for a period of three years, graduating in June, 1850. He then engaged in teaching, taking charge of Pleasant Grove Academy, Washington County, a position he retained for one year, establishing an enviable reputation as an instructor. In 1851 he engaged in farming on the beautiful farm which has since been his home, and which is one of the best improved places in the Pleasant Grove neighborhood. Mr. Browne, while giving a great deal of attention to farming, has made stock raising his principal business, and is one of the most successful breeders of shorthorn cattle and trotting horses in central Kentucky. While never aspiring to official position, he takes considerable interest in politics, voting with the Democratic party. He filled the office of county school commissioner for a period of six years, and did more for the cause of education during that time than any man who ever held the office. Mr. Browne has been twice married—the first time in January, 1853, to Miss Mary E. Rogers, daughter of Milton and Elizabeth Rogers, of Washington County. One child was born to this union—Lizzie C. Browne (deceased). Mrs. Browne died in May, 1856. On the 18th of April, 1860, Mr. Browne's second marriage was solemnized in Boyle County with Miss Ardie Meyer, daughter of A. D. and Elizabeth Meyer. To this marriage have been born three children: Irvin M. (deceased), Mary R. (wife of F. M. Martin), and Thomas R. Browne, Jr. Mr. and Mrs. Browne are active members of the Pleasant Grove Church.

REV. JOHN G. BRUCE was born April 5, 1810, in Pittsylvania County, Va., and in 1816 removed with his parents to Hillsboro, Ohio, where he grew to manhood. In October, 1830, at the old stone church in Cincinnati, he was licensed to preach, and in 1831 was received on trial in the Ohio Conference Methodist Episcopal Church. After the division in 1844 he was connected with the Methodist Episcopal Church South. During his itinerant career he filled the following appointments, viz.: Greenville Circuit, which had twenty-eight preaching places in four weeks; Strait Creek, Springfield, Troy, Madisonville, Lancaster, West Union, Charlestown, Va., two years; Marion, Ohio, two years; 1841 transferred to Kentucky, and stationed in Newport, Ky., two years; Danville, Flemingsburg, Georgetown, Lawrenceburg, Taylorsville, Cynthiana. He was then placed in charge as presiding elder of Harrodsburg District four years, Lexington District four years, again on Harrodsburg District four years, Maysville District one year, Lexington District two years. In 1865 Father Bruce became again connected with the Methodist Episcopal Church, and was placed in charge of the Lexington and Danville District, remaining four years; Louisville District four years, Nicholasville three years, Danville one year, Lexington District four years, Middleburg three years, and Danville one year. He has been prominently identified with the onward progress of Christianity from the commencement of his ministerial career. He has represented his church in her highest councils, and has extensive acquaintance among her leading men, and now, after an eventful life of labor for the welfare of others, with failing strength but undimmed faith he is quietly awaiting the Master's call to a brighter inheritance. His father, William L. Bruce, was born in Pittsylvania County, Va., in 1782, and died near Hillsboro, Ohio, in 1827. His parents were James and Tabitha (Musteen) Bruce, of Virginia. James Bruce was probably a Revolutionary soldier, and died about 1814. He was the son of James Bruce, of Virginia, who, with two brothers (William of North Carolina, and Ward Bruce, of Georgia), came from England. James Bruce, Sr.'s, sons were Frederick, Thomas, James and Anslem. William L. Bruce married Mary, daughter of John and Mary (Preston) Eads, of Virginia, born 1792, died 1825, and to them were born James, John G., Caroline R. (deceased), Mary W. (Winters), Thomas J., Christopher L., William E., and Julia C. (Morgan). September 4, 1834, subject espoused in marriage Miss Annie, daughter of Thomas and Rosalinda (Cobb) Ross, of Cincinnati, Ohio. She was born September 30, 1808, and after a faithful life devoted to her trusts, passed to her rest May 1, 1886. Having no children of their own this worthy family reared four orphan children: Maria (Ross) Eads, Minnie L. Powell, Mary B. Powell, and Lillie A. Powell. During the past twenty-one years Father Bruce's family have resided at their comfortable home, "Ingleside," three miles north of Danville, on the Danville and Pleasant Hill turnpike. Father Bruce was an old line Whig, an uncompromising Union man, and now affiliates with the Republican party.

OBADIAH BRUMFIELD was born April 1, 1833, on the place where he now resides, twelve and one-half miles west of Danville, Boyle County, on the Lebanon turnpike. He is the son of James Brumfield, who was also born on this place November 5, 1808, but lived some years with his parents in Daviess County, when he returned to Boyle County, where he is still living. He was at one time an extensive farmer, and on the old homestead conducted a large hotel for many years, having an immense patronage from travelers and drovers; he was, financially, a great sufferer by the war, and among other misfortunes sustained a loss of thirty slaves. He is a Union man, and is connected with the Cumberland Presbyterian Church. He is a son of Obadiah Brumfield, Sr., a native of Washington County, who was born in 1785, and died in 1836, and whose father was James Brumfield of Virginia. His children were William, Richard, James, Robert, Samuel, Obadiah, Sr., and Rachael (Yeager). Obadiah, Sr., married Nancy Crow, and their offspring are James, Jr., Ellen

(Crumbaugh), Samuel (deceased) and William. James, Jr., married Ruan C. Sherrill (born 1814 in Indiana), and from their union sprang Maria J. (Irvine), Obadiah and Samuel (deceased). November 25, 1867, Obadiah, our subject, was married to Miss Phœbe A., daughter of Gabriel S. and Lucinda (Moss) Caldwell (born November 24, 1843), and to them have been born Annie, Lucy, Ella, Sue, James, Joie and Caldwell. In youth Obadiah attended college one year at Lebanon, Tenn., and graduated at Centre College at Danville. He served five years as surveyor of Boyle County; was postmaster for many years, and was re-elected surveyor in the fall of 1885. He is now engaged in farming and stock raising, having a well arranged and productive farm of 200 acres. His Holstein cattle are of superior grade. He also owns 800 acres of timbered land in the knobs near by. He is an elder in the Cumberland Presbyterian Church, a member of the Masonic fraternity, and a Democrat. Mrs. Brumfield's father, Gabriel S. Caldwell, was born in 1811. He was a magistrate and member of the court of claims, served several terms as sheriff, and was twice elected to the Legislature as a Whig. He was for many years an elder in the Cumberland Presbyterian Church, and died May 11, 1885. He married Lucinda Moss (born 1813), and their union was favored by the birth of James, Susan (Fleece), Lucy A. (Wharton), Sallie (Kirk), Mary (Boone), Phœbe A. (Brumfield), John T. (deceased), Parmelia (Smith) and Lucinda (Grinstead).

H. P. BUCHANAN was born March 11, 1828, and is the second of two sons and five daughters born to Alexander and Nancy (Mitchem) Buchanan, who were natives of Augusta County, Va., and Adair County, respectively. Alex. Buchanan came to Kentucky between 1805 and 1810, was a millwright by trade and was a son of Alexander Buchanan, who, with his wife, immigrated from Ireland. Mrs. Nancy Buchanan was a daughter of Little Berren Mitchem, who was born in Virginia and was an early pioneer of Kentucky, a miller by trade, and who married Rachael Whalen, who came from Ireland. H. P. Buchanan, a native of Taylor County, received his early training on the farm. Received an ordinary education and at the age of eighteen started in life for himself at teaming, which he has followed more or less all his life. When he started the first thing he bought was a wagon. Having the wagon he found he could not use it without a team, which he went in debt for. At twenty-three he married Susan Hutchison, of Taylor

County, a daughter of Steward and Mary (Avery) Hutchinson. To this union were born the following children: Melvin A., Alice V. (now Hagan), Mary A. (now Hagan), Louisa C. (now Sherrill), Robert B., Lester S., Virgene B., and Jessie F. Mrs. Buchanan died in 1878, a member of the Presbyterian Church. For his second wife Mr. Buchanan married Sallie Moore, daughter of Thomas and Lizzie (Craddock) Moore. After his first marriage Mr. Buchanan located in Taylor County, but in 1875 settled in Green County, six miles southeast of Greensburg, where he owns and runs a saw and grist-mill, also owns and runs a farm of sixty acres. He was a Whig in ante bellum days, and cast his first presidential vote for Gen. Taylor; since the war he has been an active Republican. Mrs. Buchanan is a member of the Presbyterian Church.

MELVIN A. BUCHANAN was born August 28, 1852, and is the first child born to H. P. and Susan R. (Hutchison) Buchanan. Mr. Buchanan received a liberal English education; was married May 14, 1873, to Samantha A. Elder, who was born near Livingston, Tenn., and is a daughter of Rev. Q. D. and Winnie (Ledbetter) Elder, who were born in North Carolina and Tennessee, respectively. Rev. Elder is a Cumberland Presbyterian minister; after the war taught school in Burkesville College, Kentucky; thence to Taylor County, Ky., where he has been engaged in active ministerial life, also ran a farm all his life. Mr. Buchanan after marriage ran a mill in his native county of Taylor, for two years. In 1875 located where he now resides six miles southeast of Greensburg, and ran a mill for two years, and for three years engaged in farming; in 1882 entered mercantile business at the same point, in which he had success; made a race for assessor on the Republican ticket in 1882 and was elected by a majority of one, and received his certificate of election, but contest was made, and the ballots recounted, and he was counted out by four votes. Mr. and Mrs. Buchanan had born to them three children: Monta P. (deceased), Gracie A. (deceased), and Carl A. He and wife are members of the Cumberland Presbyterian Church, and in politics he is a Republican, having cast his first presidential vote for R. B. Hayes.

GEORGE H. BUCHANAN was born September 1, 1838, and is the fifth of five sons and two daughters, all living except one, born to Thomas G. and Janie (Caldwell) Buchanan, who were born in Green, now Taylor County, January, 1801, and September,

1802, respectively. Thomas G. Buchanan was a farmer and slave owner, and died in 1867; his widow in 1883. He was a son of John and Jane (Gants) Buchanan, who were born in Wythe and Botetourt Counties respectively. She came to Kentucky with her parents, Thomas and Mary (McAfee) Gants, in 1779 and located on Salt River. Thomas Gants was in the battle of Blue Lick, and escaped, but was killed by the Indians a few weeks after the battle in 1783. He was a man with a strong constitution and iron will, and of more than ordinary intelligence, of English extraction, went from New England to North Carolina, and thence moved to Virginia. John Buchanan was a farmer and stock trader, and did considerable freighting with wagons in an early day. He was born May 17, 1768, and came to Kentucky in 1782, and settled on Salt River, and in Greene County in April, 1800. He was under Gen. Logan against the Indians, was a robust and healthy man, and a consistent member of the Presbyterian Church. He had acquired considerable property, but his conscience would not permit him to hold slaves. He died September 20, 1834. He was a son of George and Margaret (McAfee) Buchanan, natives of Virginia and South Carolina, respectively. George Buchanan was a soldier of the war for independence, and settled on Salt River, four miles below Harrodsburg, in 1782. He was a farmer, but never would own slaves or allow his children to own any. He died in June, 1813, at the age of sixty-seven years. He was a son of James Buchanan, who emigrated from Scotland, and was a member of the Presbyterian Church, to which the family still cling. The Buchanans first settled in Green, three miles east of Campbellsville. Mrs. Thomas Buchanan was a daughter of James Caldwell who was a soldier in the war of 1812, and an early settler just east of Campbellsville; was born in Taylor County, Ky. G. H. Buchanan grew to manhood on a farm and received a good English education. At the age of twenty-two he engaged in the mercantile business with his brother, continued two years, after which he located on a farm of 360 acres on the banks of Green River, near Roachville. He lost the old residence by fire, but has rebuilt and now is the possessor of the finest modern residence in the county. In October, 1862, he was united in marriage to Sallie Shively, a daughter of John W. and Jane (Roach) Shively, who were born in Green County, but whose parents came from Virginia in an early day. Mr. and Mrs. Buchanan had born by their happy union five children, three now living:

Corae H., Emma S. and Hattie A. Mr. and Mrs. Buchanan are members, respectively, of the Presbyterian and Methodist Episcopal Churches. He was a member of the Grange, and in politics is a Democrat. His first presidential vote was for Bell, in 1860.

DR. E. F. BUCHANAN was born May 29, 1840, and is the fifth child of Thomas G. and Jane C. (Caldwell) Buchanan. He grew to manhood on a farm in his native county of Taylor, and received a good English education. At the age of twenty-two he taught in the common schools and commenced the study of medicine with Dr. Wm. B. Mourning, of Roachville. In 1865 he graduated from the University of Louisville and located at Roachville, Green County, where he has since been engaged in a lucrative and extensive practice. In September, 1865, he married J. A. Smoot of Green County, a native of Barren County. To this happy union eight children have been born, six living: Laura J., Mary W., Sallie G., Robert C., Mattie E. and J. Hubert. The Doctor and wife are members of the Presbyterian Church. He is also a member of the F. & A. M., and in politics is a Democrat, having cast his first presidential vote for Gen. Geo. B. McClellan. The Doctor also owns and manages a farm in connection with his medical practice.

BENJAMIN M. BURDETT was born on the 2d of December, 1837, and is a son of Nelson and America Letcher (Samuel) Burdett, the former a native of Garrard, and the latter of Franklin County. His father followed agricultural pursuits mainly, but was for a long time justice of the peace, and for twenty years sheriff of Garrard County. He was of German extraction, and a son of Joshua Burdett, who was a son of Frederick Burdett, a Virginian, and who early settled in Garrard County. Subject's grandfather, Reuben Samuel, was a pioneer from Virginia to central Kentucky. His wife (grandmother of subject) was a sister of Gov. R. P. Letcher of Kentucky, and cousin of Gov. John Letcher of Virginia. Benjamin M. Burdett, the subject of this sketch, was brought up on the farm until his twenty-sixth year, receiving, in the meantime, a liberal education at Georgetown College. In 1862 he began to read law at Lancaster, under the instruction of his brother, Joshua Burdett. In 1864 he was admitted to the bar, and at once entered upon the practice of his profession at Lancaster, where he has since continued with success and ability. Since the war he has affiliated with the Democratic party; during the war he was an uncompromising Union man; his first presidential vote was cast for

Bell and Everett in 1860. Mr. Burdett was married in November, 1867, to Belle Walton, daughter of John H. and Susan J. (Frazee) Walton of Mason County. They are members of the Christian Church; he is a member of I. O. O. F. Society.

COL. CHARLES H. BURNS was born on the 5th of November, 1839, and is a son of Alvin and Amanda (McClure) Burns. His father, who is now living in Carter County, Ky., at the age of seventy-six years, is a native of Bath County, Ky., and his mother, who is deceased, was born in Bath County, of Scotch ancestry. Charles H., born in Nicholas County, was educated in Nicholas and Fleming Counties, and in early manhood began merchandising in Flemingsburg. At the breaking out of the civil war (in 1861) he entered the Federal Army as fourth corporal, Company A, Tenth Kentucky Cavalry, was promoted and mustered in as second lieutenant of Company A, same regiment, then appointed adjutant-general of C. J. Walker's cavalry brigade. In April, 1862, he was promoted to the office of first lieutenant, with which commission he was mustered out. He participated in the battle of Richmond, Ky., against Scott's cavalry, Skinner's Bridge, and other engagements, following Kirby Smith on his raid through the State of Kentucky. After returning from the service he engaged for a time in teaching school, which he continued until 1874, when he was appointed United States store keeper, and removed to Lebanon. In 1881 he was promoted to the office of deputy collector of internal revenue, and served until the change in administration (1885). He is now paying considerable attention to the interests of his farm, and real estate business. He is a member of the Masonic order, and of the Presbyterian Church. Col. Burns was married in Lebanon, April 25, 1865, to Miss Sallie J., daughter of Benjamin Edmonds of Lebanon. Their children are Ella J., Amelia, Thomas E. and Benjamin E. Burns.

F. P. BURRUS was born and reared in Mercer County, and is a son of E. Burrus, also a native of Mercer County and born in 1785; his father was Nathaniel Burrus, born in Virginia and came to this State in 1784, where he lived until his death in 1855, at the advanced age of ninety-three years. He was a soldier in the Revolutionary war, for which service he drew a pension for many years prior to his death. F. P. Burrus was brought up on the farm and has successfully followed the business. He owns a farm of 400 acres of fine land well improved. He married Miss Lizzie Miller of Adair County. They have two children: J. G. and M. L. Burrus.

EDMUND BURRUS, the subject of this sketch, was born in Mercer County, May 7, 1823, and is a son of Edmund and Mary (Slaughter) Burrus; the former was a well-to-do farmer, and the latter was a woman of fine practical common sense. His paternal grandparents, Nathaniel and Mary (Threlkeld) Burrus, were natives of Virginia, and moved to Kentucky in an early day; his maternal grandparents were Jesse and Lucy (Thornton) Slaughter, also natives of Virginia, and removed to Kentucky early. Mr. Burrus was brought up on a farm, his educational advantages being such as the common schools afforded. At the age of twenty-three he accepted a clerkship in a store in Lawrenceburg, Anderson County, where he remained for two and one-half years, and then returned home. He was married November 10, 1857, to Miss Lucy A. Miller, daughter of Madison and Elizabeth D. Miller of Adair County. About a year after his marriage he removed to his present home, which is handsomely improved. In October, 1867, he and his wife united with the Salvisa Baptist Church, and were baptized by Rev. P. S. G. Watson. He has since been an active and exemplary member, and soon after his admission to the church was elected deacon; in 1869 he assisted in the organization of a Sunday-school, and although he lives two miles from the church he has never been absent on Sunday morning on account of inclement weather. This has been one of his greatest fields of usefulness. In August of same year he was elected clerk of the Baptist association, and was re-elected for eleven consecutive years; in 1882 he was elected moderator of the same body, and was re-elected four years successively, making not only one of its best clerks, but one of its best moderators. He has served two full terms as justice of the peace, and in 1885 was commissioned by the governor to fill out an unexpired term of the same office, and in 1886, was elected again for a full term. These positions were all unsolicited on his part. In politics he is a Democrat; as a citizen he is public-spirited, the best commendation a citizen can enjoy in his standing among his neighbors, whose esteem and confidence he enjoys. While not rich he has a fair competence, and dispenses his means with generous liberality to advance the cause of Christ and to alleviate the woes of suffering humanity. In the town of Salvisa may be seen a beautiful brick church building, which stands a memento of his faith, liberality and public spirit.

JUDGE ROBERT A. BURTON, deputy collector of internal revenue for the Fifth District of Kentucky, was born in 1834, and is the son of Capt. John A. and Louisana (Chandler) Burton. Robert Burton, the grandfather of our subject, came from Virginia a short while after the close of the Revolutionary war, and settled at or near the present site of Perryville. John A. Burton was born there in 1801; he married Miss Louisana Chandler, and reared five children; was a life-long Democrat, but a supporter of the administration during the late civil war. He died in 1874. Louisana Chandler was born in Kentucky in 1810, and died in 1878. She was a descendant of one of the pioneer families of what is now Marion County, being the daughter of Richard Chandler, who, according to the only surviving member of the family, was born in what is now Marion County in 1775, but four miles from the town of Lebanon. He married Isabella McNeal, who was born in 1782, in Fayette County, Ky. The issue of Richard and Isabella Chandler were Quinton M., Richard L., Edward G., Sallie, Maria, Louisana, Susan, Eusebia Ellen and Elizabeth, each of whom, except Sallie (who died in early life), married and reared families. The only one of this family now living is Maria, widow of Henry Nantz. John A. and Louisana Burton reared five children, viz.: Col. Richard C., Robert A., Isabella M. (Irven) deceased, Augusta C. (wife of Dr. W. O. Robards of Mercer County) and Eusebia Q. (wife of J. G. Phillips, Jr., of Lebanon, Ky.) Judge Burton was born, reared and educated in Perryville, Boyle County, and while he has turned his attention largely to agriculture, he has nevertheless been prominent among the public men of his district. In 1858 he was admitted to the bar, though he has never made the practice of law a profession. In 1859-60 he represented his county in the lower house of the Kentucky Legislature; served for three terms as judge of the Marion County Court, and in 1869 was elected to represent Marion, Taylor and Washington Counties in the Kentucky Senate. He was appointed to his present office in 1885. Judge Burton is a member of the Masonic fraternity, and in politics is an able advocate of the principles of Democracy. He was married May 17, 1860, to Miss Margaret Lowry, daughter of the Hon. James Lowry of Jessamine County, Ky. They have four children, John A., Mary A., Robert Lee and Marion C. Burton.

NIMROD I. BUSTER was born November 10, 1842, in Wayne County, Ky., where he was reared to manhood, and in 1876 removed to Boyle County, where he has since retained his residence. His father, Charles H. Buster, also a native of Wayne County and a member of the Christian Church, was a farmer, lost sixteen slaves by the late war and died in 1872, aged about fifty years. He was the son of Gen. Joshua Buster, of Virginia, who died in 1860. Charles H. married Emerine, daughter of Nimrod and Nancy (Cecil) Ingram, of Wayne County, of an old Virginia family, and their union resulted in the birth of one child, Nimrod I. March 30, 1865, Mr. Buster was united in marriage with Miss Sallie, daughter of Alexander and Sophronia (Oatts) Babbitt, of Wayne County, born 1847, and to them have been born Emma T., John S., Sophronia, Nimrod and Everett. In youth Mr. Buster attained a fair English education at Somerset College. He is a successful farmer, owning over 500 acres of very productive and finely improved land, and on which he raises wheat, hemp, tobacco and live stock. He is a member of the order of K. of H., and in politics he is a Democrat.

LIEUT. NATHAN G. BUTLER was born in Adair County, March 25, 1828, within 400 yards of where he now resides, and is the eldest of twelve children, eleven of whom are yet living, born to Champness and Amanda S. (Cheatham) Butler, the former a native of Adair County, Ky., and the latter of Virginia. They were of Welsh and Irish descent respectively. Champness Butler was born March 10, 1799; was engaged in agricultural pursuits all his life and died on the homestead where he was born (which he also owned after his father's death), June 9, 1867, in his sixty-eighth year. He and wife were devoted members of the Christian Church. His father, John Butler, the grandfather of our subject, was a native of Maryland, and was born in 1769. While yet a young man, during or soon after the Revolutionary war, he immigrated to Kentucky, first settling in the upper part of the State in the blue-grass country, where he was married. Soon after that event he moved to Adair County, then a part of Green, where he bought wild land, and improved the farm upon which he resided until his death, in 1839, in his seventieth year. During the war of 1812 he was the captain of a band of scouts on the frontier, and during the Black Hawk war commanded a company in the militia. Mrs. Amanda S. (Cheatham) Butler, was born May 1, 1805, and departed this life September 3, 1883. Her father, Edmund Cheatham, was born and reared in Virginia, where he was also married and engaged in agricultural pursuits. In 1808 he came to Kentucky, first settling in Cumberland County, but afterward removing to Adair County, where he resided until his death, in 1836, in his seventy-second year. He was a life-long and zealous member of the Methodist Episcopal Church. Lieut. Nathan G. Butler received his early education at the old field schools, but has since acquired a practical business education. He has always lived on or near the old home farm in Adair County, one-third of which he now owns, in addition to other lands amounting in the aggregate to nearly 200 acres, and is successfully engaged in farming and stock raising. In the fall of 1861 he helped to recruit Company B, Thirteenth Kentucky Volunteer Infantry (Federal), and at the organization of the company in the following October was elected first lieutenant and served as such until July 11, 1864, when he resigned on account of failing health. He participated in the battles of Shiloh, Perryville, the siege and battles of Knoxville, Resaca, Kenasaw Mountain, Atlanta and many other engagements. Lieut. Butler has been twice married; first, October 5, 1864, to Miss Myra S. Smith, a native of Adair County, born June 23, 1832. She was a daughter of Nathan and Charity (Callison) Smith. To this union were born two sons: Nathan C. and William R. (deceased). Mrs. Myra S. Butler died April 7, 1871, a devoted member of the Christian Church. Mr. Butler next married, November 9, 1875, Miss Susan Conover, also a native of Adair County, born July 12, 1835, a daughter of Peter T. and Joann (Rucker) Conover, who were of German and French descent respectively. One daughter has blessed this union, Mary Tildon. Mr. and Mrs. Butler are members of the Christian and Baptist Churches respectively. In politics he is a Democrat.

FREDERICK CABELL was born a twin, January 7, 1814, and is the tenth in order of birth of seven sons and four daughters, all of whom lived to be grown, born to Samuel J. and Susanah (Ewing) Cabell. Samuel J. Cabell was born in Nelson County, Va., and was a wealthy farmer and slave-holder; he came to Casey County, Ky., in 1808; lived one year in Boyle County, and in December, 1824, located on Blue Spring, branch of Caney Fork, Green County, on 410 acres of excellent land. He was very successful in life, and had accumulated an estate of $75,000

before his death in 1854, at the age of seventy-eight years. He was a son of John Cabell, who married a Miss Jordan, both of Virginia. His father who was a Dr. William Cabell came from England, his mother from Ireland. Frederick Cabell was born in Casey County and lived on a farm all his life. In February, 1836, he married Paulina E. Sprowl, a native of Madison County, Ky., and daughter of Oliver Sprowl, who married a Davis. To this marriage of Frederick Cabell five children were born: Mary D. Owsley (deceased); Susan J. (deceased); Samuel J. (deceased); Oliver (deceased), and Bettie (now Penick). Mrs. Cabell died in December, 1851, a consistent member of the Presbyterian Church, and Mr. Cabell married his second wife, Sophronia H. Lewis, in November, 1853; she was a native of Simpson County, Ky., and a daughter of John and Ann G. (Snoddy) Lewis, both natives of Virginia. To this second union six children were born: L. H.; John F.; Thomas H. (deceased); Carrie (deceased); William E. 'and Charles R. Mr. Cabell owned at one time 800 acres, well improved with a fine residence and other buildings; has given to his children till he now has but 550 acres; before the war he owned a large family of slaves. Mr. Cabell and wife are members of the Presbyterian Church, and formerly he was a member of the Grange.

REV. ROBERT HENDERSON CALDWELL was born May 17, 1825, at the head spring of Salt River, Boyle County, where he has always resided. He was educated at and is one one of the alumni of Center College, Danville. In 1846 he was licensed as a probationer by the Kentucky Presbytery of the Cumberland Presbyterian Church, at Sugar Ridge, Scott County, and in 1848 was ordained to the whole work of the ministry, since which time he has been actively engaged in his sacred calling. Besides other arduous labors, he has been pastor of the Caldwell Church in Boyle County over thirty years; Walnut Flat, Lincoln County, twenty-eight years; Hebron, Anderson County (in all) twenty years; he also served Bethel and Perryville five years at first. From 1867 until 1872 he conducted the Thornhill Boarding School at his residence, and he has acted as county superintendent of public schools of Boyle County for over twenty years. He has been twice married: first, on March 30, 1847, to Miss Rachel A., daughter of James and Sally (Givens) Harberson, of Boyle County. She was born in 1828, and departed this life in August, 1847. In December, 1849, he married Miss Lucy E., daughter of Abraham and Amelia T. (Moss) Irvine, of Boyle County, born October 1, 1828, and their union has been favored by the birth of Abraham I., Phebe J. (Starkey), James L., Amelia C. (Starkey), Ella, Logan W., Joseph W., Gabriel I., Robert T., Charles G., Maggie and Bessie. Mr. Caldwell has taken the council degrees in Masonry; is an Odd Fellow and a Good Templar; was a Union man during the late war, and in politics is independent.

DR. ROBERT C. CALDWELL was born July 22, 1851. (For full account of ancestors see sketch of William L. Caldwell.) In 1873 he graduated at Centre College, Danville, then entered the medical university of Louisville, Ky., and graduated at the Louisiana University of Medicine, at New Orleans, in 1876. For several years Dr. Caldwell has been located at Bloomfield, Nelson County, where he is now enjoying a successful and lucrative practice of his chosen profession. On June 18, 1879, subject was united in marriage with Miss Maggie, daughter of John and Emma (Ray) Bowman, of Bardstown, Ky., born January 13, 1857, and to them have been born William Logan, James Bowman, Robert Crumbaugh (deceased), and George Robertson. Dr. Caldwell is a Royal Arch Mason, and a member of the Old School Presbyterian Church, and in politics a Democrat.

WILLIAM J. CALLISON is the second of seven children born to James and Mary L. (Miller) Callison, and was born March 7, 1851. James Callison, a native of Adair County, was born in September, 1826, and his life-long occupation has been farming, in which he has been successful, owning and cultivating at present 300 and 400 acres of land. He was united in matrimony to Miss Louisa Miller, on March 3, 1847, the sixth of a family of eight children born to Nathan and Rachael (Vannoy) Miller, natives of Adair County. The names of the children born to the marriage are George L.; Annie V., wife of James Butler; Bruce M., Elizabeth R.; Mattie D., wife of T. T. Tupman; Mary L. and William J., all of whom except George L. are living. Mr. Callison and wife are both members of the Christian Church and are living at their farm near Columbia. Joseph Callison, grandfather of William J. Callison, was a farmer and in moderate circumstances, dying in 1830, in the sixtieth year of his age. He was a native of Virginia, and was a veteran of the war of 1812, and immigrated to Adair County, Ky., while yet a young man, in the early part of this century. He owned and cultivated his own farm of

about 500 acres, which he bought in the woods. His first marriage, about 1792, occurred in Virginia, to a Miss Dawson, and they were the parents of nine children: Josiah, Robert, Gilmer, William, Dawson, Charity (Smith), Susan (Stark), Polly (Browning), and Mary, of whom Robert alone is living. The second marriage, about 1825, was to Miss Elizabeth Miller, a native of Pennsylvania, and this marriage occurred in Adair County. They were the parents of five children: James; Margaret, wife of James A. Browning; Charles; Phœbe and Martha, wife of John D. Mourning, all of whom are living except Martha, who died in 1883. Joseph Callison departed this life in 1839, and his widow, who was born in 1794, died in 1865. William Callison received a good English education in the common schools of Adair County, of which he is a native, and the Presbyterian High School of Columbia. After leaving school in February, 1873, he began selling goods in a dry goods store in Columbia, which he continued until September of the same year, when he, in partnership with his brother, G. L. Callison, embarked in the grocery business. This they carried on successfully about one year, when they embarked in the drug business. This they carried on from 1874 until September 6, 1883, when G. L. Callison died, and W. J. Callison bought his interest in the business, which he has since carried on in his own name. January 1, 1874, he was united in marriage to Miss Laura E. Robinson, the third of four sons and four daughters born to William N. and Sallie C. (Stone) Robinson, natives of Adair County, Ky. Their home has been gladdened by four children: Montie S., Carry Lee, Lula Belle and James Robinson, all of whom are living. Mr. and Mrs. Callison are both members of the Columbia Christian Church, of which he is one of the deacons. Mr. Callison is also a Mason, and in politics is a stanch member of the Democratic party. He carries a large stock of drugs, and a stock of jewelry and patent medicines, books, and an assortment of general merchandise, which he values at $3,500. He enjoys a large trade and is one of the leading merchants of the county, and is also one of the firm of Blandford & Callison, dealers in commercial fertilizer, farmers' implements, machinery, etc., which was first to introduce into this county the Homestead Fertilizer and Deering Twine Binder. Their sales on fertilizer began in 1882 on a very small scale, selling from fifteen to twenty barrels per annum, but have increased to 1,500 to 2,000 barrels in 1885 and 1886, giving perfect satisfaction to the farmers by increasing their crop from fifty to one hundred per cent.

CHRISTOPHER C. CAMBRON was born January 23, 1824, and is the third of a family of eight children born to Charles and Margaret Cambron. In 1788 Harry Cambron, the grandfather of Christopher C., came from St. Mary's County, Md., and settled on Cartwright's Creek, near Springfield. He was accompanied by his father, whose name was Baptist Cambron. Harry Cambron had married a Miss Harberson in Maryland and reared a large family, Charles, the father of our subject, being the third child, born on the 5th of November, 1791. He married Margaret Montgomery, daughter of Basil Montgomery, and died January 10, 1881; his wife died on the 27th of June, 1863. They reared a family of eight children, seniority as follows: Stephen H., William C., Christopher C., Martha A. (McGill), Margaret I. (died in early womanhood), James R., Nicholas L., besides one who died in infancy. Christopher C. is the only surviving member of this family. He was born, reared and educated in Washington County, now Marion, and has devoted his life successfully to the pursuits of the farm, but removed to his city residence in Lebanon in 1882. He was married in Washington County, Ky., March 1, 1859, to Miss Marry C. Wrinn, daughter of Patrick and Julia A. Wrinn. The Cambron family were characterized for their adherence and devotion to the Roman Catholic Church.

WHITAKER HILL CAMPBELL was born July 7, 1805, on Shawanee Run, Mercer County, Ky., and in 1833 removed to Garrard County, where he has since resided. His father, James Campbell, a native of King and Queen County, Va., was a very early settler in Mercer County, Ky., was a carpenter and builder; constructed Gen. Adair's and many other residences; was also a farmer and one of the processioners for Mercer County; was also a farmer and lost twenty slaves by the late war; was a Whig and a Baptist and died in 1865 at the age of eighty-five years. He was the son of Whitaker Campbell of Virginia, who married Jane Hill, and their offspring were James, William, Mrs. Carlton, Benjamin and Mrs. Pendleton. James first married Polly, daughter of Joseph Lewis of Mercer County, and aunt of Joseph H. Lewis, one of the judges of the court of appeals; from their union sprang Whitaker H. and William P. His second wife was Catherine, daughter of Benjamin Bradshaw of Jessamine County, and their children were Jane (Bradshaw), Robert P., Hopy (Hill), Benjamin B., Ann P. (Key), Alexander, Catherine (Doneghy), Susan (Peyton) and Thomas C. February 14, 1828, Whitaker H. married Miss Pamelia H., daughter of Col. Edmund and Sarah (Bowman) Perkins, of Garrard County (born March 10, 1810), and to them were born Elizabeth (Barkley), Orpah (Van Meeter), Elias H. (wounded in Confederate Army), John L. (died in Union Army), James W., Benjamin P., Hiram B. and Rebecca (deceased). Mr. Campbell was many years engaged as an educator, and was principal of the Cane Run Academy while Samuel Taylor Glover late of St. Louis, Mo., was a teacher of mathematics in that institution. Mr. Campbell served fifteen years as magistrate and member of the court of claims of Garrard County. He is a member of the Methodist Episcopal Church, belonged to "the old court party," was an old line Whig, an uncompromising Union man, lost fifteen slaves by the late war, and is now a Republican; acted as agent for pensioners of the Revolution, and obtained bounty land for the soldiers of the war of 1812. Hiram Barkley Campbell was born near High Bridge, Garrard County, August 13, 1849, and in 1881 located at his present home, Mt. Ararat, near Bryantsville. October 13, 1881, he married Miss Nannie D., daughter of William and Elizabeth (Thomas) Burnside, of Garrard County (born April 19, 1856), and to them have been born Benjamin P., June 11, 1883 (died March 31, 1885), and William Burnside, February 16, 1886. Mr. Campbell is a farmer and trader, having 231 acres of grazing land in good condition. He is a class leader, and has been seventeen years recording steward in the Methodist Episcopal Church South; has been fifteen years a Good Templar and is superintendent of the Sunday-school.

FRANCIS M. CAMPBELL was born December 31, 1836. Nathaniel Campbell, his paternal grandfather, a native of Virginia, of Scotch descent, immigrated to Kentucky in the year 1813; prior to his removal to this State he served with distinction in the second war for independence, and was wounded. His first settlement in Kentucky was made in Shelbyville, where he followed the trade of house carpentering until 1819, when he removed to Washington County and died there three years later. George P. Campbell, father of Francis M. Campbell, was born June 10, 1806, being the eldest in a family of eight children. Upon his father's death he assumed the maintenance and support of his widowed mother and his younger brothers and sisters. They purchased a tract of land and he adopted the vocation of farming, which he always followed. July 23, 1829, he united in marriage with Miss Lucy Martin. Francis M., the fourth child born to their union, was reared on a farm in his native county of Washington, receiving a good English education. For thirteen years, commencing at the age of twenty, he was engaged in teaching the public schools in the vicinity. February 18, 1865, his marriage was solemnized with Miss Fannie Campbell were celebrated; to their union nine children have been born, of whom seven are now living: Arthur B., Idella, Lula B., Myrtie, Robert E., Theodore and Bessie. Since 1869 Mr. Campbell has farmed, and has been very successful, owning 400 acres situated on the Springfield and Perryville pike. He also takes great pride in raising fine horses, including many fine specimens of the Von Moltke variety. He is a member of the Baptist Church; his wife belongs to the Methodist Episcopal. In politics he is a Democrat, and in 1884 was elected sheriff, and is the nominee for re-election to that position.

L. D. CARDWELL, druggist, is a native of the city of Louisville, and was born February 1, 1854. His father, Capt. J. W. Cardwell, a native of Shelbyville, was born February 1, 1809, served an apprenticeship of one and a half years in a printing office, then moved to Harrodsburg and began clerking in a dry goods house, being one of the first dry goods clerks of the town. After a number of years he formed a co-partnership with his employer, Capt. Bull, and they did business on what is known among the old citizens of Harrodsburg as "Capt. Bull's Corner." At Capt. Bull's death Mr. Cardwell purchased his interest and continued the business on his own account, remaining in the trade in all twenty years in Harrodsburg. He was then elected cashier of the Harrodsburg Savings Institution, which position he held until the close of the late war. During that terrible time many financially good men of Harrodsburg failed, after having overdrawn their bank accounts. The directors of the institution were disposed to place the responsibility of the overdrafts on the cashier, and he very cheerfully surrendered his entire estate, of about $75,000, to pay the liabilities, his wife at the same time, against the advice of her friends, signing away her dowry in all his property. They lived in comparative poverty the balance of their days. Capt. Cardwell was a Union man during the war and held the position of provost-marshal, rendering himself very popular by his treatment of the people of Harrodsburg and vicinity. He had two sons in the Confederate Army, T. M. and James M., killed at the battle of Bulls Gap, Tennessee. Capt. Cardwell was also captain of a militia company. He was married to Miss Sophia Bledsoe Taylor, a daughter of John and Nancy (Lewis) Taylor, natives of Virginia. To this marriage were born thirteen children, seven of whom are living: James M.; Lulu, wife of Levi Walter, of Harrodsburg, and after his death wife of Dr. T. H. Reid, a physician of Harrodsburg and a member of the Legislature, now deceased; Sue, wife of B. L. Hardin, of Harrodsburg; Thomas, ex-postmaster of Harrodsburg; Samuel Creed, chief deputy in the internal revenue office of Lexington; Westley K., clerk for his brother, L. D.; Nannie, wife of John H. Lucas, attorney of Osceola, Mo., and Llewellyn D. Mrs. Cardwell lived fifteen years after her husband's failure, and was during life a member of the Methodist Episcopal Church. Her death occurred July 27, 1876, in the sixty-fifth year of her age. Capt. Cardwell, who, during life was a member of the Methodist Episcopal Church, and who subscribed liberally toward the church building in Harrodsburg, survived his wife's death until February 9, 1882. After his wife's death he lived with his son, L. D. Cardwell. L. D. Cardwell attended school until fourteen years of age, when his father's failure occurred, and then became a carpenter's apprentice, serving two and one-half years. His first mercantile venture was selling newspapers and periodicals, beginning in 1871 with a capital of $41. In January, 1873, he began learning the drug business with his brother-in-law, Dr. Reed, and in October, same year, attended the St. Louis School of Pharmacy until the March following. At the solicitation of the Rev. W. P. Harvey Mr. Cardwell returned to Harrodsburg and purchased a third interest in the drug store of William Payne & Co., in which at that time Mr. Harvey was a partner, and which, on account of a poisoning, was in disrepute. The new firm was Reed, Harvey & Co., and their business soon improved rapidly, but in 1878 Reed & Cardwell purchased the interest of Mr. Harvey. The firm of Reed & Cardwell continued in existence until Dr. Reed's death in 1880, when Mr. Cardwell purchased his interest from his widow. Mr. Cardwell has since carried on the business by himself. On May 21, 1884, he was married to Miss Stevia, a daughter of R. E. and Maggie (Hughes) Coleman, natives of Mercer County. They have had one child, Margaret Bledsoe, who died September 25, 1885, in the sixth month of its age. Mr. and Mrs.

Cardwell are members of the Assembly Presbyterian Church. Mr. Cardwell is carrying a stock of drugs, books, paints and oils, wall paper and picture frames, with a capital of $10,000. Besides this he is in partnership with his brother, W. K., in the furniture business with a capital of $5,000. Mr. Cardwell's drug sales last year were $27,000, and the sales in the furniture business were $15,-000. Mr. Cardwell for three years managed the *Mercer County Enterprise*, a weekly newspaper, the first newspaper ever published in Harrodsburg which was a financial success. He also owns ten residences known as "Cardwell's Square" and valued at $10,-000, besides owning and managing the Cardwell Opera House

COL. JOHN B. CARLILE, Sr., member of the firm of Carlile & Litsey, Lebanon, was born in Green County, Ky., on the 7th of August 1826. Both his grandfathers, James Carlile and John Brawner, were soldiers in the Revolutionary war, soon after which struggle they immigrated to Kentucky, settling in Green and Adair Counties, James Carlile coming from North Carolina and John Brawner from Virginia. To James and Elizabeth Carlile were born nine children, William B., the father of our subject, being one of the number. William B. was born in Green County in 1799; devoted his life to agriculture, besides serving for several years as sheriff of Green County. He married Mary Brawner and had a family of seven children, John B. being the second. The latter was reared on his father's farm, attending the common schools of his neighborhood until sixteen years old, when he entered the business house of Lewis & Shreve as store boy. Thus early in life he began his mercantile career, which has only been broken for the period during his military and public life. In 1861 he was commissioned lieutenant-colonel of the Thirteenth Kentucky Federal Infantry, serving until the spring of 1863, when loss of health necessitated his resignation, having shared until then the fortunes of his command. He represented Green County in the State Legislature during the sessions of 1864-65, and in the latter year removed to Lebanon, where he has since been in active business. He was married in Green County in October, 1864, to Miss Mary Lisle, a daughter of Thomas W. Lisle, who represented Green County in the Constitutional Convention of 1849.

DR. WILLIAM A. CARRY was born in Anderson County, Ky., August 30, 1854, and was a son of Jonathan Carry, a native of Madison County, and who died in Anderson County, March 25, 1886. Dr. Carry was brought up on a farm, and received a liberal education. Afterward he read medicine, and graduated from the Louisville Medical College, and moved to Mercer County in 1878, where he has since practiced his profession successfully. He married Miss Laura A. Miller, daughter of Robert Miller. Dr. Carry has always voted the Democratic ticket.

JAMES W. CARTER was born in Adair County, Ky., January 24, 1851, and is the ninth in a family of twelve children born to George W. and Polly A. (Rabern) Carter, the former of whom was a native of Russell and the latter a native of Pulaski County, Ky. They were of Irish and English descent respectively. George W. Carter was born in 1812, and received his education at Georgetown and Danville Academies. He commenced to teach at the age of seventeen and continued the same, most of the time in connection with agricultural pursuits, until 1878, when he retired from active business. He first bought a partially improved farm in his native county of Russell; from there he removed to Pulaski County, where he was married, and then removed to Adair County, where he bought the farm upon which he yet resides. He is and has been for a number of years a magistrate or justice of the peace of his district. From early life he has been a devoted and consistent member of the Baptist Church. He is also a member of the Masonic fraternity. His father, Thomas I. Carter, was a native of the "Old Dominion;" was a soldier in the war of 1812, and was killed in one of the early battles of the war. Mrs. Polly Ann (Rabern) Carter departed this life in 1867. She was a life-long member of the Methodist Episcopal Church. Her father, John Rabern, was also a native of Virginia, but while yet a young man removed to the wilderness of southern Kentucky, where he was afterward married to a Miss Rainwater. James W. Carter received a fair common-school education in youth, and was employed on the home farm until he was sixteen years old, when he left home and was afterward employed on a farm and in the live stock trade until 1871, after which he farmed on his own account for two years. He then engaged in the grocery trade at Haskinsville, Green County, continuing until the fall of 1873. He then removed to Lebanon, Ky., where he was engaged in the commission and grocery trade, both wholesale and retail, until 1875. He then engaged in the liquor trade at the same place, which he continued until 1880. He then engaged in the lumber trade and hotel business at Campbellsville, Ky., which he continued for three years, after which he took a tour through the Western States, returning to Taylor County, Ky., in 1884, where he has since been engaged in agricultural pursuits. In 1886 he was an independent candidate for the office of county assessor. Mr. Carter was married January 25, 1871, to Miss Martha E. Sublett, a native of Cass County, Mo., born September 16, 1856; she is a daughter of James A. and Elizabeth (Moore) Sublett, both natives of Taylor County, Ky., and of Irish and English descent respectively. Mr. and Mrs. Carter have been blessed with six children: John H. and an infant not named (both deceased), who were twins; Berry A. (deceased); Robert R., Minnie W. and Jesse A. Mrs. Carter is a devoted member of the Cumberland Presbyterian Church. Mr. Carter belongs to no church, but is a member of the Masonic fraternity, the I. O. O. F. and K. of H.; in politics he is a Republican.

DR. HENDERSON L. CARTWRIGHT was born November 12, in the year 1849, in Adair County, Ky., where he grew to manhood, and in 1883 he located at Junction City, Boyle County, where he has since resided. His father, Manson W. Cartwright, was born in 1803 in Russell County, where he served as magistrate and member of the court of claims, and in 1859 he removed to his present home in Adair County. He is a farmer, and lost five slaves as the result of the late war. He was the son of Joseph Cartwright, a native of Virginia, who removed to Kentucky when a young man (his father, Samuel, having preceded him) and died in 1849 at a great age. Samuel Cartwright, the first settler on Cartwright Creek, removed to Middle Tennessee previous to the year 1800. Joseph married Mary White, of Adair County, and their offspring were White, Nathan, John, Manson W., Hulda (Smith), Lucy (Judd), Frances (Grant) and Sallie. Manson W. married Catherine, daughter of Adam and Susan (Walker) Yeiser, of Adair County, born in 1813, and from their union sprang Dr. Henderson L., Mary S. (deceased), Dr. Walker F., Lucy M., Susan C., Cora H., Dr. Adam Y. and Dr. Thomas S. Dr. Henderson L. Cartwright has been twice married; first, July 8, 1875, to Miss Hulda J., daughter of George W. and Sallie (Nell) Breeding, of Adair County, born 1857, died 1882, and to them were born Estella and Manson W., Jr. He was next married, November 20, 1884, to Miss Effie H. Wood, of Rockford, Ill., born in 1860. The Doctor was favored with a liberal education, and in 1871 commenced the study of medicine with Dr.

U. L. Taylor, of Columbia, Ky., and having attended two full term courses of lectures, graduated in 1875 at the medical department of the University of Louisville, Ky. He first practiced at Breeding's, in Adair County, afterward at Pace's in Cumberland County, and in 1883 located at Junction City, in Boyle County, where he has since enjoyed a successful and lucrative practice. He is a member of the Christian Church, also of the Masonic fraternity, and is identified with the Democratic party.

CATHOLIC CHURCH IN CENTRAL KENTUCKY. The counties of Nelson, Washington and Marion (all originally Nelson County) may be considered the cradle of the Catholic Church in Kentucky. The first permanent settlements made by Catholics in the State were made in Nelson County, and the first Catholic congregation was organized in the same community. The first Catholic emigrants to Kentucky were William Coomes and Dr. George Hart. The date of their coming is in dispute among writers of Kentucky history, Mr. Collins placing it at 1775, and Mr. Webb, in his "Centenary of Catholicity in Kentucky" as "between the years of 1773 and 1785"—quite a "latitude of expression." These gentlemen first located at Harrodstown (now Harrodsburg), but in a very few years, being joined by other Catholic families, removed to Bardstown. Dr. Hart was an Irishman, young, buoyant, an ardent Catholic—like most of his race—and lived for many years an honored citizen of Nelson County. He is believed to have been the first physician to practice medicine in Kentucky. Mr. Coomes was originally from Maryland, but settled in Virginia, and from thence removed to Kentucky. While residing in Harrod's Station Mrs. Coomes opened a school, which was probably the first school taught in the State. The first priest who appeared in Kentucky was Rev. M. Whelan, about the year 1787, and was sent to minister to the Catholic families in Kentucky by Bishop Carroll of Baltimore. Father Whelan was an Irishman, and had been a chaplain in the French Navy, sent to assist us in our Revolutionary struggle. After remaining in the community until the spring of 1790 he returned to Maryland. He left no churches or chapels built in Kentucky as monuments to his zeal, but it is left on record that he was a faithful and conscientious priest, and labored earnestly for the advancement of his church. Six months later Rev. William de Rohan came, and under his administration the church of the Holy Cross, the first Catholic Church erected in the State, was built. It was erected in 1792, and the next year Rev. M. Barrieres became its pastor. He remained in the new charge but a few months, and was succeeded by Rev. Stephen Theodore Badin, who had accompanied him to Kentucky. This eminent Catholic divine, often mentioned as the "Apostle of Kentucky," labored in the State for more than thirty years, and after his long term of service, though worn down with exertion, he continued to work in the vineyard he has so long cultivated. "His adventures and hardships would fill a volume. Wherever there was sickness or spiritual destitution; wherever error or vice was to be eradicated and virtue inculcated; wherever youth was to be instructed and trained to religious observances; wherever, in a word, his spiritual ministrations were most needed, there he was sure to be found laboring, with all his native energy, for the good of his neighbor. Difficulties and dangers that would have appalled a heart less stout and resolute were set at naught by this untiring man. He traversed Kentucky on horseback hundreds of times on missionary work, spending nearly half his time in the saddle. Through rain and storm, through hail and snow; along the beaten path and through the trackless wilderness, by day and by night he might be seen going on his errand of mercy; often for years together, alone in the field, and always among the foremost to labor, even when subsequently joined by other zealous Catholic missionaries. He was intimate with the most distinguished men of Kentucky in the early times, and his politeness, learning, affability and wit made him always a welcome guest at their tables."*

Father Badin did not confine his ministrations to the church of the Holy Cross, though nominally its pastor all these years, but engaged in missionary work throughout the State. From 1797 to 1803 Rev. M. Fournier at intervals served the church, as did also Rev. Anthony Salmon. But the last two named did not long survive a life of exposure in a new country, and both died near the beginning of the present century. Father Badin went to Europe in 1819, and his place in Holy Cross Church was supplied by Rev. Anthony Ganihl, a Frenchman. He was a man of great learning and piety and a zealous worker in his church. His name does not appear in the records after 1841, and it is probable that he returned to his native France about that time. From the fall of 1822 to the spring of 1824 the church of the Holy Cross was in charge of Rev. Charles Nerinckx, superior of the Loretto community.

*Collins, Vol. I, p. 486.

In connection with the Catholic Church in Kentucky it will be of some interest to note the first Catholic settlements made in the State. "In the year 1785 'a league' of sixty families was formed in Maryland—all Catholics, and mostly residents of St. Mary's County—each of whom was pledged to immigrate to Kentucky within a specified time. Their purpose was to settle together, as well for mutual protection against the Indians, as with the view of securing to themselves, with the least possible delay, the advantages of a pastorate and a church. They were not all to emigrate at once, but as circumstances permitted. The tradition of this league is sufficiently general among old people, as well in Maryland as in Kentucky, to give to it certainty. Of the sixty families subscribing to the compact, twenty-five left Maryland early in 1785, and reached Kentucky before the end of the spring of the same year. * * * * They arrived in due time at Goodwin's Station (near the present town of Boston in Nelson County), the nearest fortified post to their pre-arranged and ultimate destination, the Pottinger's Creek lands. Leaving the women and children under the protection of the fort, the able-bodied men and youths of the party soon set out in quest of their future homes, the sites of which lay some twelve or fifteen miles southeast of the station. * * * * The names borne by these twenty-five families are not now all certainly known; but the principal among them was Basil Hayden, whose bond for his land, signed at Baltimore in 1785, is of record in the Nelson County clerk's office. On the face of this bond appears the name of Philmer (Philip) Lee, as Hayden's security. It is quite certain that Basil Hayden and Philip Lee were living on adjoining farms on Pottinger's Creek in the year 1786. Lee may be said to have been a man of method. While still in Maryland he was in the habit of keeping a record of passing events. From the entries in that record extending back to 1735, and continued after his removal to Kentucky, it appears that his neighbors in both States bore identical names. Among the names most frequently met with in Lee's diary are Lancaster, Coomes, Brown, Thompson, Smith, Rapier, Bullock, Cash, Hayden and Howard. Though there is little doubt that the list that follows does not include the names of all the Catholic settlers on Pottinger's Creek up to the year 1800, it is reasonably certain that the omissions are few in number, and not of special consequence. The first names given are thought to be, in part, those borne by the twenty-five families of the Maryland 'league,' to which reference has been made: Basil Hayden, Philip Lee, William Bald, Bernard Cissell, Charles Payne, William Brewer, Leonard Johnson, Henry McAtee, Joseph Clark, Stephen Elliott, James Mollihorne, Henry Norris, Ignatius Cissell, Ignatius Byrne, Randall Hagan, Ignatius Hagan, Jeremiah Brown, Robert Cissell, Ignatius Bowles, Hezekiah Luckett, Stanislaus Melton, Thomas Bowlin, John Baptist Dant, Philip Miles, Harry Hill, John Hutchins, Isaac Thawles, John Spalding, William Mahony, Henry Lucas, William Bowles, John Bowles, James Queen, Bernard Nally, James Stevens, Ignatius French, Washington Boone, Francis Bryan, Jeremiah Wathen, Thomas Mudd, Raphael R. Mudd, Walter Burch, Philip Mattingly, Joseph Spalding, James Dant, Joseph Dant, Urban Speaks, Joseph Edelin, Joseph Howe, Joseph Miles, Harry Miles, Monica Hagan, Rodolphus Norris, Francis Peak."[*]

This was the first actual Catholic settlement made in Kentucky, and was situated some twelve or fifteen miles from where Bardstown now stands. The next year (1786) the Hardin's Creek settlement was begun. It was about ten miles east of the Pottinger's Creek settlement, and was composed of settlers from the same region as those on Pottinger's Creek. The pioneers of this settlement are supposed to have been Col. Charles Beaven and Edward Beaven, brothers. Col. Charles Beaven had been an officer in the Revolutionary war, and soon returned to Maryland, but his brother remained in Kentucky, and numerous descendants throughout the State still perpetuate his name. Other early emigrants to the settlement were Matthew, Zachariah, Sylvester and Jeremiah Cissell, William, Leonard and Lucas Mattingly, John Lancaster, etc. The Cartwright's Creek settlement was begun in 1787 and was one of the most prosperous Catholic settlements in Kentucky. Cartwright's Creek is a tributary of the Beech Fork of Salt River, and the main settlement on it was about twenty miles from Bardstown. Among the early settlers here were the Hills, John Waller and Henry Cambron. The settlement near Bardstown was made about 1790, though there were several Catholic families living from one to five miles from Bardstown prior to that time. Among the first settlers were Capt. James Rapier and two grown-up sons. They settled a few miles southeast of Bardstown on the Beech Fork of Salt River, in a district known as "Poplar Neck." Others who came a little

later were Thomas Gwynn, Anthony Sanders and Nehemiah Webb. The Rolling Fork settlement dates back to 1788, and the pioneers were Clement and Ignatius Buckman, and Basil and John Raleigh. A little later, perhaps, came Robert Abell, a man of considerable local prominence. These were the five principal Catholic settlements in Kentucky at the time the State was admitted into the Union (1792), and were all in what was then Nelson County, and is now comprised in Nelson, Washington and Marion Counties. From these settlements have gone forth emigrants to form settlements in different parts of the State. They formed the nucleus from which has irradiated the great Catholic religion, that in the hundred years past has penetrated every corner of Kentucky.

Rev. Father Nerinckx, already mentioned as pastor of Holy Cross Church about 1822, came to Kentucky in 1805. Like Father Badin he spent much of his time in missionary work, and on horseback he traveled thousands of miles through the wilderness, exposed to all the dangers of the early period in Kentucky. He was a native of Belgium, and was compelled to leave Europe in consequence of the disturbances caused by the French Revolution. He was zealous in his faith and shrank from no labor, and was disheartened by no difficulties. During the twenty years of his labor in Kentucky he built no less than ten churches, and often labored on them with his own hands. For a number of years he had charge of six large congregations, besides several minor stations scattered over the State. In order to promote female piety he founded the Sisterhood of Loretto[*] in April, 1812. This institution still exists, and has spread into a number of other States. Within twelve years, the period from its organization to the death of its founder, the number of sisters who had devoted themselves to this manner of life had increased to over 100, and they had under their charge more than 250 girls, distributed through six different schools, besides many orphans whom they fed, clothed and educated gratuitously.

The old log church, built by Rev. Father Rohan in 1792, and the first Catholic Church in Kentucky, gave place in 1823 to a handsome brick structure, which was built under

[*]Centenary of Catholicity in Kentucky, pp. 27, 28.

[*]The objects of this establishment were: To enable those young ladies who intend to retire from the world, and to devote themselves wholly to prayer and the exercises of charity, to be useful to themselves and to others by diffusing the blessings of a Christian education among young persons of their own sex, especially among the daughters of the poor. They were also to receive and rear up orphan girls, who if left on the cold charities of the world might have gone to ruin themselves, and have become an occasion of ruin to others.—*Spalding.*

the supervision of Rev. Father Nerinckx. This indefatigable servant of God died April 12, 1824, while on a missionary tour to Missouri. After his death the church was served for a short time by Revs. Fathers Butler and O'Bryan, and in 1825 Rev. Robert Byrne was ordained pastor. For thirty-one years Father Bryne devoted himself to Holy Cross congregation, and one other congregation only four miles distant.

The second Catholic Church built in the State was perhaps that of St. Ann, which was erected about five miles west of Springfield, and was completed in 1799. Father Badin was its first pastor. In 1807 Fathers Wilson and Tuite, of the Dominican order, came to Nelson County. In a few months they were joined by Rev. Edward Fenwick, afterward bishop of Cincinnati, and a Mr. Young, afterward Father Dominie Young. During the fall they purchased a farm and residence, the present site of the convent of St. Rose, and it was not long until they commenced the construction of the church of St. Rose.

Such is a very brief glance at the introduction of Catholicism in Kentucky, and its growth and expansion in the central part of the State, notably in Nelson, Washington and Marion Counties. The space to which this sketch is limited precludes the entering into details of the Catholic Church and the different congregations that have been organized in these counties within the past century, and that may trace their antecedents back to Holy Cross—the first Catholic congregation organized in the State. The 100 or more churches, schools and colleges that dot the hills and plains of these counties are monuments to the zeal and energy of the early Catholic missionaries in the wilds of Kentucky.

So far the names of the priests have been given in the order of their coming up to and including that of Father Badin. It is impossible, however, in this brief sketch to follow them further in detail, and this synopsis of the Catholic Church history in Central Kentucky will conclude with brief mention of one or two eminent Catholic divines whose names cannot well be omitted.

Rev. Benedict Joseph Flaget is a name familiar to the Catholic world, and is held in the utmost veneration by the Catholic Church of Kentucky. For many years he exercised as widespread influence in Kentucky, perhaps, as any priest ever did in the State. He was born in France, November 8, 1764, and was left an orphan at the age of two years. A pious aunt took charge of him and superintended the rearing of him up in the church in which he was born. He was educated at the city of Clermont for the priesthood. He studied long and arduously, and passed through all the different courses of theology, and in due time was promoted to the priesthood. He was then sent by his superiors to the seminary of Nantes, where for two years he served as professor of dogmatic theology. A few years later the French Revolution broke out, and in 1792 Father Flaget came to America, stopping in Baltimore. The first duty to which he was assigned by Bishop Carroll, of Baltimore, was the post, Vincennes, then an important military station in the Northwest. After some two and a half years at Vincennes he was recalled to Baltimore by his superiors, and stationed at Georgetown College, where he remained about three years, and was then sent to Havana. In 1801 he was again recalled to Baltimore, and again charged with college duties. After spending some seven years thus he was appointed bishop of Bardstown, and on the 4th of November, 1810, as such was consecrated. It is useless to give the life and administration of Bishop Flaget in Kentucky—it is familiar to all Kentucky Catholics, and would be merely a repetition of well known history. Bishop Flaget died February 11, 1850, at the age of eighty-six years, and as bishop of Kentucky the fortieth.

Rev. Robert A. Abell was one of the remarkable men of Kentucky, and one of the eminent divines of the Catholic Church. He was born in that portion of Washington County now embraced in Marion, in 1792. His father dying when he was but ten years old, he was left to his mother's care. His early educational facilities were limited, but developing a wonderful faculty for learning, he attracted the attention of those who had him sent to the best schools, where, it is needless to say, he made rapid progress, and in August, 1818, he was ordained a priest by Bishop Flaget. His first mission embraced western Kentucky and a portion of Tennessee. Many anecdotes and incidents of interest could be related of Father Abell, but space will not allow. Kentucky born, for over half a century he fulfilled his calling among the Catholics of his native State. He died suddenly in Louisville, June 28, 1873, having been an ordained priest for fifty-five years. Rev. William Byrne was another faithful and zealous worker in the Catholic Church of Kentucky. He founded St. Mary's College in Marion County, and was a prominent educator as well as a zealous minister of his church. He was born in Wicklow

County, Ireland, about the year 1780, and at the age of twenty-five came to America. He was ordained to the priesthood in 1819, in St. Joseph's Cathedral at Bardstown. He was an indefatigable worker; whether for the salvation of souls, or for the education of the youth springing up around him, he labored zealously and earnestly. He died on the 5th of June, 1833, of cholera, at St. Mary's College. Rev. Martin John Spalding is another name dear to Kentucky Catholics. He was born in Washington County, now Marion County, May 23, 1810. His father was Richard Spalding, the eldest son of Benedict Spalding, one of the pioneer Catholics of Kentucky, who came from Maryland in 1790, and settled on the Rolling Fork, then in Nelson County. He received the most liberal education, graduating from St. Mary's College in 1826, after which, having determined to study for the priesthood, he went to Rome, where he entered the renowned college of the Propaganda. He spent four years at that venerable institution, leaving it "with a reputation already made and already enviable."—*Webb.* His first charge after returning to America was the cathedral and congregation of Bardstown. But it is needless to follow Dr. Spalding through all his long service to his church, and to note all the important positions he filled. He was consecrated coadjutor bishop in September, 1848, and fifteen years later, in 1863, upon the death of Archbishop Kenrick, which took place suddenly in Baltimore, he succeeded to that exalted position, and in June, 1864, received the papal rescript appointing him archbishop. An ecclesiastical honor was, perhaps, never more worthily bestowed. "In 1867 Archbishop Spalding was present in Rome at the eighteenth centenary celebration of the martyrdom of Sts. Peter and Paul, and again, in 1869 and 1870, he was of the number of the princes of the church assembled in the same city from all the nations in the world, as the council by which was declared the Catholic doctrine of Papal infallibility." —*Webb.* Archbishop Spalding died February 7, 1872, almost a quarter of a century after his consecration as bishop.

NOTE.—The foregoing sketch of the Catholic Church in Central Kentucky has been rather hastily compiled from "Centenary of Catholicity in Kentucky," an excellent work on the subject by Hon. Ben. J. Webb of Louisville, and from a sketch of the Catholic Church in Kentucky, written by Bishop Spalding for Collins' "History of Kentucky." The work of preparing a sketch of the Catholic Church for this special edition of the "History of Kentucky" was voluntarily assumed by a gentleman well qualified for the task, but who was ultimately forced to give the matter up on account of feeble health. This, coming as it did at a late day, necessitated this hasty compilation.—ED.

THOMAS W. CECIL was born August 2, 1826. His father, Sylvester Cecil, was a native of Marion (at the time of his birth Washington) County, and married Hedric Medley, by whom he had three children: Thomas W., Ignatius C. and Annie S. Augustine Cecil, paternal grandfather, was born in St. Mary's County, Md., where his marriage to Miss Frances Hammit took place; he came to Kentucky by way of the Ohio River on a flatboat, leaving the river at the place where Louisville now stands, when there were but two or three dwellings within what are now the city limits. He settled on Pottinger's Creek in Washington County, where he resided until his death. Ignatius Medley, maternal grandfather of T. W. Cecil, was also a native of St. Mary's County, Md.; in immigrating to Washington County, Ky., he came through Lexington, where for about three years he worked as a house carpenter, and laid the first tongue-and-groove floor ever put down in Lexington. Upon locating in Washington County he married Sarah, daughter of Harry Boone, and purchased a tract of land on Hardin's Creek known as the Rice Survey, upon which land he erected the first copper-still ever operated in Washington County. Both paternal and maternal ancestors were members of the Catholic Church, to which all their descendants belong. Sylvester Cecil died in 1833, comparatively a young man, of cholera; his wife had died the December previous, thus leaving their children orphans, who were reared by their grandparents, the Medleys. Thomas W., who was born on Hardin's Creek, Marion County, remained with them on the farm until he attained the age of twenty-three years, receiving a limited education. He has made farming his principal life occupation, but formerly distilled liquor. September 17, 1848, his marriage with Roselle Riney was solemnized and to their union nine children have been born, of which eight are living: Sarah E., wife of James Burns; Frances M., Elizabeth H., Mary F. (now Mrs. George Thompson), Mattie I., Clement S., Annie S. and Ignatius C.

GRANVILLE CECIL was born May 3, 1850, in Boyle County, Ky., and is the fifth of five sons and three daughters born to James G. and Sarah Ann (Buster) Cecil. James G. Cecil was born in Montgomery County, Va., September 20, 1803; when a lad of sixteen he came to Wayne County, Ky., and worked on a farm with his brother-in-law for six years; then entered mercantile business and stock trading, which he followed twenty-one years and made many trips through the country with stock to Pennsylvania and Maryland, and sold to farmers. In 1848 he located on a fine farm of 430 acres, six miles west of Danville, which he afterward raised to 900. He was one of the most successful farmers in Boyle County, and had accumulated a large property. He was presidemt of the Farmers National Bank of Danville from its organization to his death in June, 1881; was also a director of the Central National Bank, and was the wealthiest man in Boyle County at the time of his death. His first wife died in 1862; his second wife was Margaret St. Clair Pinkard, of Lexington, who is still living. He was a son of Samuel Cecil of Montgomery County, Va., who married an Ingram; they came to Wayne County, Ky., about 1820; in 1841 removed to Lewis County, Mo., where he died at the age of eighty-two years. He was a descendant of the Cecil family of Cecil County, Md., who came from England about the time Lord Baltimore colonized Maryland. Sarah Ann (Buster) Cecil was a daughter of Gen. Joshua A. Buster of Wayne County, Ky. He was one of the early pioneers of Wayne County, and was. a captain in the war of 1812; participated in the battle of New Orleans, afterward became general of militia, served as judge of his county, was also elected to both branches of the Legislature. He died at the age of seventy-nine years. Granville Cecil was reared on a farm, and received a good English education; spent one year at Centre College, Danville, and three years at the Kentucky University. January 23, 1872, he was married to Emma Talbott, daughter of Hon. A. G. Talbott, and three children have been born to them: James G., Bessie O. and Albert (deceased). In 1879 he located where he now resides on 322 acres, three miles north of Danville; his place is embellished with a beautiful residence. Mr. Cecil is a breeder of fine shorthorn cattle, also several families of fine trotting horses, the principal being the Hambletonian. At this writing he owns about 150 head of the finest trotting stock in the United States; is also breeder of Berkshire hogs and Southdown sheep. He has an interest in the several banks of Kentucky, also in all the turnpikes of the county, and is a director of the Agricultural Association. He was a leading member of the Grange when in existence, and in politics is Democratic.

JOHN HAWKINS CHAMPION was born September 30, 1820, in Jessamine County, Ky., where he grew to manhood; in 1849 he removed to Mercer County; in 1854 to Collin County, Tex., and in 1860 he returned to Mercer County, locating on the banks of the Kentucky River in Shaker Bend, where he has since resided. His father, Edmund Champion, a native of Pennsylvania, an early settler in Jessamine County, Ky., a mechanic, and a man of most remarkable genius, died of cholera in 1833 at the age of sixty-five years. He married Sarah Neal, of Pennsylvania, (died in 1852, aged about seventy years), and from their union sprang Thomas, Peter, James, Mary (Smart) and John H. John H. was married at the time of the battle of Perryville, October 8, 1862, to Miss Sarah, daughter of George and Lucy B. (Gordan) Munday, of Mercer County (born March 5, 1841,) and to them have been born James, George Edward, Reuben (deceased), Katie S., John Price and Thomas (deceased). Mr. Champion was engaged as a carpenter and builder with success for a period of thirty years. He is now a farmer, having 400 acres of productive land. He is a Royal Arch Mason and an Ancient Odd Fellow. In religion he is a Methodist, was formerly an old line Whig, but is now a Prohibitionist. He lost two slaves by the late war.

WILLIAM U. CHELF, justice of the peace, was born in Culpeper County, Va., September 25, 1830, and is the third in a family of six children born to William M. and Judia (Burke) Chelf, natives of Culpeper County, Va., and of English descent. William M. Chelf was born August 6, 1797; was educated and married in his native county and at an early age learned the fulling business, serving an apprenticeship of four years, after which he followed his trade for several years. In 1831 he came to Kentucky with his wife and family, acccmplishing his journey over the Blue Ridge and Cumberland Gap in a four-horse wagon. He first settled at Bradfordsville, Marion County, where he erected and operated a carding-mill which was driven by an old-fashioned tread-wheel. In 1837 he removed to what is now Taylor (then Green) County, and bought a farm on Robinson's Creek, some two miles above the present village of Mannsville. There he was engaged in the cabinet business in connection with farming until 1844, when he sold out and returned to Bradfordsville, where he again engaged in the carding business and also in grinding corn. This mill was also driven by a tread-wheel. In 1852 he brought in steam power and erected a flouring-mill; in 1858 he sold the mill and removed to Green River Knob, Casey County, where he bought a farm and engaged in agricultural pursuits in connection with the distilling business until 1863, when he sold a part of the farm, and later made his home with his children. His death occurred at the home of William U., at Rolla, Adair County, December 11, 1881. He and wife were members first of the Baptist and later of the Christian Church. He was also a bright member of the Masonic fraternity and was buried with the honors of the order. His father, Elias Chelf, was also a native of Virginia and was a soldier in the war of 1812. In 1832 he came to Kentucky and settled near Bradfordsville, where he resided until his death, in 1836, at the age of about eighty-five. He married Miss Katie Weaver, of Virginia. Mrs. Judia (Burke) Chelf was born July 19, 1807, and died November 7, 1881. Her father, William Burke, was a native of Virginia, where he was educated, married and engaged in agricultural pursuits all his life. The Burke family were for many generations among the first families of the old commonwealth, and also among her most wealthy planters. William U. Chelf received a good common-school education and in early life was employed in his father's carding-mill. At seventeen he commenced to learn the carpenter's trade, serving an apprenticeship of four years at Lexington, Ky. He then returned to Bradfordsville, where he followed his trade until 1856, when he engaged in the saw and grist-mill business in Marion County until 1860, when he removed to Ohio County, Ky., where he engaged in the same business and also at carding until November 1, 1861. He then enlisted in Company H, Third Kentucky Volunteer Cavalry (Federal), and served until July 25, 1862, when he was taken prisoner and paroled at Elkton, Tenn., while lying sick at the house of William W. Smith, where he was taken care of and kindly treated for sixteen days. He finally reached home, but was never again able to join his regiment, and was honorably discharged December 26, 1864. He participated in the battles of Shiloh and many other engagements. After the war he returned to Marion County, where he resumed the mill business and continued the same until 1869 when he moved to a farm near Loretto, same county, and engaged in farming, wagon-making and blacksmithing. In 1872 he went to Liberty, Casey County, where, for one year, he was engaged in the grist-mill and carding business. In 1873 he moved to Rolla, Adair County, where he has since resided, engaged in the saw and grist-mill business. Afterward he added the stave business and in 1882 opened a grocery store

and drug store, two years later adding dry goods and general merchandise. He also owns a good farm near the village. He was town marshal of Bradfordsville for two years, deputy sheriff of Marion County one year, and in 1875 was elected a magistrate for Casey Creek District, No. 7, Adair County, which office he now holds, having been twice re-elected. He was married, December 9, 1851, to Miss Delilah H. Gartin, a native of Marion County, Ky., born May 12, 1838. She is a daughter of Nathan H. and Adelia (Speed) Gartin, natives of Marion and Casey Counties, Ky., respectively, and of English descent. Two daughters have blessed this union: Susan M., now Mrs. J. W. Martin, and Sarah C., wife of J. W. Caskey. Mrs. Chelf is a member of the Christian Church. Mr. Chelf belongs to no church, but is a consistent Christian and holds to the doctrines of the Christian Church. He was made a Mason September 28, 1850, and has advanced to the R. A. degree. He has been W. M. of the lodges to which he was attached, several times. He is a Republican and recognized as a party leader.

WILLIAM P. CHELF was born in Taylor County, Ky., September 19, 1842, and is the third of six children born to William J. and Rhoda A. (Baley) Chelf, the former a native of Virginia and the latter of Marion County, Ky., both of English descent. William J. Chelf was born April 19, 1818, and at the age of eight years, in about 1826, came with his parents to Kentucky, first settling in Marion County, where the family remained for many years. There William J. grew to manhood, was married and soon after moved to Taylor County, where he remained about six years. He then moved to Adair County, where he bought a partially improved farm on Casey Creek, near Roley, upon which he remained until 1861, when he sold out and bought another farm some three miles further down the creek, upon which he resided until his death, May 26, 1879. For several years he was engaged in general merchandising in connection with farming, and also in buying and shipping tobacco to Louisville, which at that day had to be hauled all the way on wagons. For some three or four years he also operated and owned a tanyard in connection with his other business. He and wife were from early life members of the Christian Church, in which he was a ruling elder for many years. He was also a member of the Masonic fraternity. His father, Presley Chelf, was born and reared in Virginia, and was one of the early settlers in Marion County, Ky. Afterward he removed to Taylor County, remaining some ten years, and in his old age moved to Adair County, where his death occurred in his sixty-fifth year in 1855. Mrs. Rhoda A. (Baley) Chelf was born March 27, 1819. She is still living and resides on the old home farm where her husband died. Her father, Hezekiah Baley, was also born in Virginia, where he was educated and married, and soon after immigrated to Marion County, Ky., being among the early pioneers. Here he remained for many years. His death, however, occurred in Adair County, at the ripe old age of eighty-two or eighty-three years, in May, 1863, to which county he had removed only a short time before. William P. remained with his parents on the home farm until he attained his majority. In September, 1863, he enlisted in Company I, Thirteenth Kentucky Volunteer Cavalry (Federal), and served until the expiration of his term of service, being mustered out at Camp Nelson, Ky., in January, 1865. After his return from the army he farmed on rented lands for some five years. He then bought a partially improved farm of 125 acres on Casey Creek, in Adair County, and adjoining the old homestead, to which he has since added other lands, now owning a well improved farm of some 475 acres. Here he has ever since been extensively and successfully engaged in agricultural pursuits, and also in the live-stock trade, mainly in the buying and selling of mules. The farm is not only well improved but is also in a high state of cultivation. August 29, 1865, he married Miss Louisa Hendrickson, a native of Adair County, born October 27, 1846. She is a daughter of Felix and Mary A. (Monday) Hendrickson, both natives of Adair County, and of English descent. Nine children have blessed their union, viz.: Anna M. F., Sarah A., Perry A., Mary L., Felix J. and Laura E. (twins), Jake, Patrick and Melcenia B. (deceased). Mr. Chelf and wife are consistent members of the Christian Church. In politics he is a Democrat.

JUDGE JOHN C. CHENAULT was born on Muddy Creek, Madison County, April 21, 1855, and is the eldest of the five sons born to Robert and Josephine (Cavins) Chenault. Robert was a native of Madison County; was born in 1824; was a farmer and slaveholder, and the first of the Chenault family to cast a Democratic vote. He died in March, 1881, a member of the Baptist Church. His father, Cabell Chenault, was born in 1795 on the banks of the Kentucky River in Madison County; married Emily, daughter of Andrew Mitchell, of Henry County; had a family of ten children, of whom six sons and two daughters were reared, Robert being the eldest, and died in 1878, a member of the Baptist Church. David Chenault, his father, was born in Albemarle County, Va., September 30, 1771; came to Kentucky with his parents in 1786; married Nancy Tribble, daughter of Elder Andrew Tribble, of Madison County in 1793; joined the church in 1795 and soon afterward became a minister. He was an extensive farmer and accumulated a fortune of not less than $100,000. He was a magistrate for over twenty years, and died May 9, 1851, the father of ten children: Cabell, Harvey, David, Waller, Tandy, Anderson, John, Joicy, Sallie and Nancy. David Chenault was the son of William, who was born in Virginia; was of French parentage; served under Washington in the Revolution, came to Kentucky in 1786, and settled about three miles north of Richmond. Mrs. Josephine (Cavins) Chenault is a daughter of John and Polly (Pruett) Cavins, natives of Fayette County and descendants of Fayette's early settlers. John C. Chenault was reared on the home farm; received a fair education, and when of age purchased the necessary books and commenced the study of law. For two years he attended the law department of Central University, and was admitted to the bar in January, 1878. In January, 1880, he was appointed police judge of Richmond, and held the office until June, 1884. In August, 1884, he was elected to fill an unexpired term as county judge, and in 1886 elected to the office without opposition. In his first race he received the vote of John G. Fee, president of Berea College, who for the first time cast his vote for a Democrat. The Judge was married December 16, 1884, to Miss Elinor B., daughter of Otheniel and Sidney (Noland) Oldham, of Madison County. The Judge is a Free Mason and Odd Fellow and a member of the Baptist Church; his wife is a member of the Christian Church.

BENJAMIN F. CHEWNING was born January 29, 1844, and is the elder of the two sons of William T. and Barrilla (Ball) Chewning. William Chewning was born in 1799 in Rockbridge County, Va., and in 1807 settled near Greensburg, Ky. He was a boatman and horse trader in early days, later became a farmer, and died in 1881 in Taylor County. His father, Killis Chewning, of Virginia, was a soldier in the war for independence and came to Green County in 1807, and engaged in farming. Mrs. Barrilla Chewning was born in Green County, and was a daughter of Col. Robert and Anna (Webb) Ball. Col. Ball was one of the very early settlers of Green County; was one of the patriots of 1812; was a colonel at New Orleans; became one of the leading farmers of Green County, and owned about thirty slaves. He was born in 1776 and died in 1866. Benjamin F. Chewning was born in Taylor County; was reared on a farm and attended school until sixteen, when, in the fall of 1861, he enlisted in Company G, Thirteenth Kentucky Volunteers, and was in all general engagements with his regiment from the time it left home till its return. He was at Huff's Ferry, Knoxville, Perryville, several Georgia campaigns; was made an orderly during the siege of Atlanta, and was discharged with the regiment at Louisville. After his return he resumed farm life, and in January, 1865, was united in marriage to Sarah Ann, a daughter of Simeon L. and Martha (Mitchell) Cowherd, who were natives of Taylor and Green Counties respectively. Mr. Cowherd, a blacksmith, was a son of Simeon and Sally (Richardson) Cowherd, early pioneers of Green County. To this happy union four children were born: William S., Robert H., Anna M. and Alex. S. After his marriage Mr. Chewning located where he now resides, ten miles east of Greensburg, on 160 acres; he now owns 300 acres, 200 acres of which are cleared and in a good state of cultivation, with a fine orchard. He served as marshal in taking the census in 1870, and has also served as justice four years. He is a member of the F. & A. M. In politics is a Republican, and cast his first presidential vote for U. S. Grant. He and his wife are members of the Baptist Church.

LARKIN C. CHUMLEY was born in Pittsylvania County, Va., October 10, 1814, and was a son of John Chumley, a native of Virginia, who had three children, William, Colman and subject, who was the eldest. The family came originally from England. Mr. Chumley, the subject of this sketch, came to Kentucky when thirty-five years old, and settled in Mercer County. He married Miss Elizabeth Montgomery, a daughter of William Montgomery, by whom he had nine children, all living but one, as follows: William T., Mary A., Nancy P., Charlotte, Robert, John, James and Lucy. His wife died and he again married, this time to Martha Adams, by whom he had five children, viz.: Frank L., George C., Benjamin, Edward and Cordelia. Mr. Chumley, his wife and nine of the children belong to the Baptist Church.

GEN. CASSIUS M. CLAY was born October 19, 1810, in Madison County, Ky., where he now resides, and in the house he now occu-pies. He is a son of Gen. Green Clay and Sallie (Lewis) Clay, who were among the first white settlers of the neighborhood. The former, Gen. Green Clay, was a native of Powhatan County, Va., and was born in 1757 of English parentage. He came to Kentucky in early life, and, being a surveyor, he accumulated considerable lands. He represented the district of Kentucky in the Virginia Legislature and was a member of the Virginia Convention that ratified the Federal Constitution, in 1788. He was a member of the Constitutional Convention of Kentucky which formed the second State constitution, and which remained in force for over fifty years. In the war of 1812 he was made a brigadier-general and led 3,000 Kentucky soldiers to the relief of Gen. Harrison, then besieged at Fort Meigs by British and Indians. He cut his way through their lines, and by the accession of his strength to the fort forced the enemy to withdraw. He was left in command of the fort, which was soon after attacked by Gen. Proctor and Tecumseh, and was highly complimented by Gen. Harrison for his defense of the fort. After the close of the war he retired to his estate in Kentucky, where he died October 31, 1826. Gen. Cassius M. Clay, the subject of this sketch, received his education under private tutors at the Richmond Academy, Centre College, St. Joseph's College, Ky., and at Transylvania University, finishing off at Yale College, from which he graduated in 1832. He studied law and attended lectures in Transylvania, as an aid to political life, but never practiced and has always been a farmer, taking great interest in the breeding of fine stock. Outside of agricultural pursuits he has taken an active interest in politics, and served several terms in the State Legislature. He was a member of the Whig Convention that nominated Gen. Harrison for the presidency in 1840, and in 1844 he made a tour through the North, advocating the election to the presidency of his relative, Henry Clay. He served as a captain in the Mexican war and was captured at Encarnacion, in 1847, and held a prisoner for some time after the term of service of his regiment had expired. In 1861 he was made minister to Russia by President Lincoln, but recalled the next year and commissioned major-general of volunteers; was sent by Lincoln in August on a mission to sound the Legislature upon the emancipation proclamation. He spoke to both houses at Frankfort, and his speech, reported in the Cincinnati *Gazette*, was given to Lincoln and on the 22d of September, 1862, he issued his immortal proclamation of liberty, the greatest event since the birth of Christ. Succeeding Gen. Lew Wallace of Lexington, Ky., he marched at the head of his corps against the invading army of Gen. Kirby Smith, but was superceded by his superior officer, Gen. Wilson. In the spring of 1863 he was re-appointed Minister to Russia, a position he filled under Presidents Lincoln, Johnson and Grant until the fall of 1869, his service in Russia being of great benefit to the American Government. Gen. Clay was in slave times what was called an "Abolitionist" but a Jeffersonian and Henry Clay Emancipationist, and established a newspaper in Lexington—*The True American*—which advocated the principles of the Republican party, of which he was the father. (See page 500, general history.) He has been an elaborate writer, mainly upon great political subjects, and in 1848 Horace Greeley published a volume of Mr. Clay's speeches. Among his latest literary efforts is an extensive history of his own life. (See his "Memoirs" 1886). He was married in 1833 to Mary J. Warfield, a daughter of Dr. Elisha Warfield of Lexington. He has six children living, four of whom are married. At this time (1887) Gen. Clay is a candidate for the nomination for governor on the Republican ticket, but for success will yield the nomination to Wm. O. Bradley when he shows the most strength, if at all—preferring the triumph of principles to personal prowess. Gen. Clay in his speech before the Kentucky Legislature in August, 1862, by authority pledged Lincoln himself and the Republican party that if Kentucky, as she was doing, would stand by the Union and the Republican proclamation of freedom of all slaves in the Rebel States, by the war power—the slaves of Kentucky could not and would not be freed. In this view he was sustained by the unanimous resolutions of the Republican party in convention at Frankfort, Ky. (See *Commonwealth*, files of 1866.) When the slaves of Kentucky were liberated contrary to this pledge and for other reasons, set forth in his memoirs, he stood with the Democratic party till the army was by Hayes withdrawn from the South, and the autonomy of the States restored. Whilst acting with the opposition, he aided in repealing the laws against blacks sitting on juries; opposed, with J. C. Breckinridge, and destroyed, the Kuklux in Kentucky; aided the black school system, and, trying in vain to repeal that clause of the Kentucky constitution of 1849-50 which declares "the right of the master to the slave and the increase higher than all constitutions and laws," he returned

to his old party, and in 1884 made forty-one speeches in Illinois, Indiana, Ohio and New York in favor of Blaine for President. He declares that at no time in his life did he ever swerve the ninth part of a hair from the Republican principles—and that at all times he holds and has held principles higher than party allegiance. He is in vigorous health and may speak again for his gallant leader, James G. Blaine, for President in 1888.

WILLIAM WELLS CLEAVER, a prominent physician of Lebanon, Marion County, was born on the 15th of March, 1827. His grandfather, David Cleaver, came from New Jersey in the close of the eighteenth century and settled in what is now Marion, then Washington County, serving the same as high sheriff. He had a family of twelve children, the eldest of whom bore the name of his father, and was the father of Dr. W. W. Cleaver. David Cleaver, Jr., was born in 1804, and married Miss Lucy Kirk, daughter of James Kirk, of Virginia, who settled near Lebanon in 1792, and who lived to the age of ninety-nine years. David and Lucy (Kirk) Cleaver each lived to be quite old and died on the old Cleaver homestead near Lebanon. Of their twelve children eleven are now living and have families. Dr. W. W. Cleaver is the second of the family. He was reared on his father's farm, attending the common schools and Lebanon Academy. When eighteen years old he commenced the study of medicine under Dr. M. S. Shuck, and after thorough preparatory reading he entered the medical department of the Louisville University, from which he graduated in 1850. With slight exception he has been practicing at Lebanon since his graduation, and is pronounced a leader of his profession. In the early months of the late civil war he organized a company of soldiers for the Confederate Army, which was attached to the Eighth Kentucky Cavalry. This company he commanded at the battle of Perryville and elsewhere, and until he was appointed to the office of regimental surgeon. He was twice made a prisoner and for four months held in the Federal prison at Fort Delaware. Dr. Cleaver was married in Marion County, July 9, 1850, to Miss Joanna Grundy, daughter of Felix B. Grundy. The Doctor is a member of the State and Beech Fork Medical Associations, and of the Masonic fraternity, and enjoys the esteem of a large circle of friends.

PAUL C. CLEAVER, youngest son of David and Lucy Cleaver, was born near the town of Lebanon, Marion County, on the 12th of June, 1847. He was reared to the pursuits of the farm, to which he still adheres, being owner of 200 acres of land, forming a portion of the old "Cleaver homestead." He removed to Lebanon in 1873 and engaged in the livery business in 1877, which he continues in connection with his farming interests. Mr. Cleaver was married in Lebanon, Marion County, in .1872, to Miss Antoinette McBeath, daughter of George W. and Dorinda (Price) McBeath, of Adair County. Their children are David B., John M. (who died in infancy), Charles B., Lizzie, Rose, Harry H., Robert A., William G. and Stephen Gray.

WILLIAM CLEVLAND was born December 7, 1819, in Jessamine County, Ky. In 1834 he removed with his mother to Garrard County, and in 1856 located in the neck of Polly's Bend, Kentucky River, where he has since resided. His father, Zatthue Clevland, a native of Pennsylvania, was born April 7, 1780; removed when quite young with his parents to the vicinity of Abingdon, Va., and to Pulaski County, Ky., about 1805, and afterward to Jessamine County. He was a farmer and cooper by occupation, served as a soldier in the war of 1812, and died in 1825. His brothers were Adin, Morris and Eli. In 1803 he married Elizabeth Hand, of Abingdon, Va., born March 22, 1784, and to them were born James, Sarah (deceased), Nancy (Ramsey), Elizabeth (Yates), Clarinda (Beaty), John, Delitha (Temple), William, George and Mary A. (Beaty). William Clevland has never married, nor is he attached to any church. He is a farmer by profession, having 300 acres of land in a good state of cultivation. In politics he is a Democrat and a prohibitionist.

JAMES T. CLOSE was born April 28, 1832, where he now resides, on the waters of Brush Creek, and is the eldest of three sons and eight daughters, born to Grayson and Lethe (Bloid) Close. Grayson Close was born in 1809, between the waters of Brush Creek and Lynn Camp. In an early day he made several trips to New Orleans on flatboats; was a substantial farmer, was also a wagon-maker, was a member of the Baptist Church, and died in‵May, 1886. He was a son of John Close, of English descent, who first settled at the mouth of Beargrass, but thence moved to Green County in its early settlement. He was once offered a large tract of land where Louisville now stands for an ordinary horse. About 1825 he moved with his family to Menard County, Ill., where he became extensively engaged in farming. Mrs. Lethe Close was born in Green County, and is a daughter of Stephen Bloid, who

married Nancy McCubbins, both natives of Kentucky. Mr. Close was raised on a farm in his native county of Green, and received a limited English education. At twenty-one he started in life on his own account. March 28, 1861, he was united in marriage to Elizabeth Bale, a daughter of John and Demmie (Lewis) Bale. Mr. and Mrs. Close had born to them four children: R. T., C. L., John G. and Laura L. He and wife are members of the Separate Baptist Church. With the exception of a short time in Illinois, Mr. Close has always lived where he now resides. He first purchased fifty acres, but now owns 155 acres, 130 cleared and in a good state of cultivation. He also works at the carpenter's and blacksmith's trades. In politics he is independent, and cast his first presidential vote for James Buchanan.

THOMAS COAKLEY was born September 1, 1828, and is the sixth of the nine sons and one daughter born to Col. William and Margaret (Carter) Coakley, who were born in King George County, Va., in 1788 and 1791, respectively. Col. William Coakley served in the war of 1812, came to Kentucky in 1817, settled where Thomas Coakley was afterward born, six miles south of Greensburg, Green County, became a colonel of militia, was a slave-holder and farmer, and died in 1836, a member of the Baptist Church. His father, also a William Coakley, was of Irish descent, from the first family of the name that came to America. He was an inn-keeper and died about 1830, aged sixty-five. Mrs. Margaret Coakley was a daughter of George Carter, a carpenter, who married a Miss Smith, sister of Gov. William Smith, of Virginia. Thomas Coakley, after his mother's death in 1848, commenced farming and trading with the South. May 4, 1854, he married Elizabeth C. Hazlewood, a native of Hart County, and a daughter of Henry C. and Cassander W. (Moss) Hazlewood, natives respectively, of Dinwiddie County, Va., and Green County, Ky., and of English descent. By their union Mr. and Mrs. Coakley have had born to them eleven children: George H. (deceased), Emma C. (now Mrs. D. M. Williams), Sarah M. (Mrs. A. C. Webster), Willie J., Lee W., Cassander F., Mary E. (deceased), Florence E., Thomas E., Mattie S. and Eliza Ann. After his marriage Mr. Coakley settled twelve miles northwest of Greensburg on 100 acres of land, but now owns 500 acres, of which 350 are under cultivation and improved with a fine residence. He also owns an interest in several other tracts, all accumulated by his own industry. Mr. Coakley has been a Free Mason over thirty years, was a member of the Grange, with his wife is a member of the Methodist Episcopal Church South, and in politics is a Democrat, having cast his first presidential vote for Franklin Pierce. Col. William Coakley was the only one of his name that left Virginia for Kentucky.

SAMUEL D. COAKLEY, M. D., was born February 3, 1855, and is the third of four sons and one daughter born to George and Martha J. (Durham) Coakley. George Coakley was born on Pitman Creek in 1821, was a substantial and leading farmer and slave-holder. Mrs. Martha Coakley was born in Taylor County in 1828, and is a daughter of Samuel M. Durham. Dr. Coakley was born on Brush Creek, Green County, was reared on a farm, and became sufficiently advanced in the common schools to enable him to enter Centre College, Danville, at the age of eighteen years, two years later attending school at Canmer, Hart County. In the meantime he studied medicine and entered and graduated from the University of Louisville, medical department, in 1878, and located where he now resides, ten miles northwest of Greensburg, where he has had a successful and extensive practice. He is a member of the county board of health, and also runs a farm of 160 acres of fine land, which he has embellished with a fine residence and substantial outbuildings. He married September 18, 1878, Nancy V. Ingram, of Taylor County, a daughter of Walter W. and Bettie W. (Edwards) Ingram, natives of Adair and Green Counties respectively. To this happy union four children have been born: An infant and Ada (deceased), Walter G. and Bettie J. The Doctor and wife are members of the Baptist Church, and he is a strong advocate of the temperance cause.

S. T. COBB was born March 17, 1832, five miles east of Richmond, and is a son of Zena and Provy (Tevis) Cobb, to whom four sons were born: Jesse (deceased), Harvey, John (deceased) and S. T. Zena Cobb was born in 1796, in Virginia; was brought to Kentucky by his parents when yet a small lad, and afterward became one of the leading farmers of Madison County, where he remained until his death, August 29, 1878. He was a son of Samuel and Nancy Cobb, who were born in Virginia, and came to Madison County, Ky., as early as 1805, and settled north of Richmond. They reared a family of three sons, Zena, Parker and Samuel, and four daughters, Matilda, Frances, Nancy and Elizabeth, all of whom lived to rear families. Mrs. Provy Cobb was a daughter of Nathan-

iel and Nancy (Burgin) Tevis, who were pioneers of Madison County. S. T. Cobb was reared on the home farm, and January 2, 1852, was united in marriage to Nancy Peyton, a daughter of Guffey and Elizabeth (Moore) Peyton, who were both born in Madison County in 1795. Guffey Peyton was a farmer, and died in March, 1871; his wife in September, 1865. He was a son of Yelberton and Anna (Guffey) Peyton, natives of Virginia, who came to Madison County, Ky., as early as 1785 or 1791, and settled five miles south of Richmond, where they reared a family of four sons and five daughters. The Cobb and Peyton families were Whigs in politics. Mr. and Mrs. Cobb have five children: Zerilda Mitchell, Brutus W., Zena G., Amanda Terry and Durrett W. Mr. and Mrs. Cobb are members of the Christian Church. After their marriage they lived near where they were born until 1859, when they located where they now reside, five miles south of Richmond, on 125 acres, now increased to 370 acres. Mr. Cobb has devoted much time and attention to the raising of mules. He cast his first presidential vote for Fillmore, in 1856, but since the war has been a Democrat.

GARRETT COBERT is a son of David Cobert, who was born in New Jersey in 1780, and came to Kentucky with his parents in 1784. The family settled on a farm near Harrodsburg, where David passed the winter season in the manufacture of boots and shoes. In 1810 he married Mary, daughter of Lieut. Philip Morgan, and there were born to him five sons and three daughters. The grandfather of Garrett Cobert was also a native of New Jersey, was a tanner and farmer, and served seven years in the Revolutionary war. He died a member of the Presbyterian Church. Garrett Cobert was born in Mercer County, Ky., May 9, 1815, but moved to Garrard County in 1838 and settled on a garden plot of six acres, which he cultivates in summer, devoting the winter months to the making and repairing of shoes. In 1839 he married Miss Elizabeth Woods, who, with himself, is a member of the Baptist Church. Mr. Cobert is also an Odd Fellow.

JOSEPH COFFEY, Jr., cashier of the Bank of Columbia, was born in Christian County, Ky., January 6, 1833, the youngest of twelve children born to Joseph, Sr., and Jane (Graves) Coffey, the former a native of North Carolina and the latter of Fayette County, Ky., and of French and English descent respectively. Joseph Coffey, Sr., was born in 1784, and while a young man immigrated to Kentucky, settling first in what is now Russell County, where he married, and engaged in agricultural pursuits until 1831, when he moved to Christian County, and bought wild land, and improved a farm on which he resided until his death, in March, 1834. He was a veteran of the war of 1812 and he and wife were life-long members of the Missionary Baptist Church. Mrs. Jane Coffey departed this life in June, 1861, in her seventy-first year. Her father, Thomas Graves, was a native of Virginia, and in early manhood immigrated to Kentucky, first settling near Lexington, in Fayette County, where he improved a farm and remained for several years. Later, however, he moved to Russell County, where he resided until his death. He served as courier for Washington during the entire Revolutionary struggle. Joseph Coffey, Jr., at the age of seventeen left the home farm and settled in Columbia, where he accepted a position in a general store, continuing in the mercantile business as salesman and on his own account until 1871. In 1872 he accepted a position as clerk and assistant cashier in the Bank of Columbia, and in 1880 was elected cashier of the same, which position he still holds. Mr. Coffey has been twice married; first September 27, 1859, to Miss Mary E., daughter of James V. and Elizabeth (Lankford) Warden. She was born in Monticello, Wayne County, Ky., August 9, 1842, and died at her home in Columbia, November 23, 1861. She was a devoted member of the Methodist Episcopal Church South. Mr. Coffey next married, January 20, 1863, Miss Virginia R. Page, a native of Adair County, born June 16, 1843. She is a daughter of W. W. and Sophia (Brawner) Page, both natives of Virginia. Seven children have blessed this union as follows: Henry R. (deceased), William A., John B., Robert G., George, Sophia and Joseph. Mrs. Coffey is a member of the Presbyterian Church. Mr. Coffey politically is independent, and belongs to no church or secret order.

GEORGE D. COLEMAN was born near Fredericksburg, Va., May 10, 1818, and immigrated to Kentucky with his parents. His father, James Coleman, also born in Virginia, moved to Kentucky in 1822, and settled on a farm in the eastern part of Mercer County, near Cane Run Spring, near where the town of Bergen is now located, a station on the Cincinnati Southern Railroad; he then moved to the neighborhood of Gen. John Adair, Capt. Abram Chaplin and Gov. Slaughter, on a part of Capt. Chaplin's pre-emption survey; he lived there seven years, and then purchased 300 acres of the same land, on which he resided until his death, and attained quite a fortune. He married Miss Mary Penny, and became the father of the followieg children: Meridith R. (deceased), John L. (deceased), Robert E. (deceased), Basil W. (deceased), Maria (Dedman) deceased, James Henry, Littleton, Ferris (deceased), Sallie Ann (deceased), Mary (Dannell) deceased, George D., William L. (deceased), Thomas C. and Jane Amanda (Sorrell) deceased. Mr. Coleman and his son owned about 100 negroes. In principle he was a Whig, and died in Mercer County, Ky., at the age of sixty-eight years. There are still living two of the old slaves that Mr. James Coleman brought from Virginia, Hampton and Millie. Of about fifty whites who came to Kentucky soon after James Coleman, there are but few living; Persickles Scoot, William R. Daniel, Susan D. Coleman, Bushrod Coleman, Foster and George D. Coleman, all relatives. George D. Coleman is the owner of five acres of rich land, situated one mile from Harrodsburg, a part of his father's old homestead on the Lexington pike; the place is called Colmanville, and contains about twenty families, who all use water out of Mr. Coleman's cave. He is principally a stock dealer on commission. There are two remarkable caves on this piece of land; one, situated twenty steps from the house, is three miles in length eastwardly; the other is four miles in length extending under the town of Harrodsburg; this cave has the names of Daniel Boone and Col. Miller inscribed upon the rocks. There is also a log cabin standing near the house 100 years old. On the same grounds where the caves are, in 1842 was held the celebration of the settlement of Kentucky. Mr. Coleman was married to Miss Sarah M. Hahn in 1845, and to them the following children have been born: Willis L. (deceased), Anna E., Mary B., Thomas C., Laura L. and Sarah C. The grandfather of Mr. Coleman, Robert E. Coleman, is of Scotch-Irish descent, immigrated from Virginia to Kentucky in 1800, took up some land, returned to Virginia, came again to Kentucky about 1804, and settled near Fountain Blue, three miles from Harrodsburg. He married Catherine Robinson, and from their union sprang seven children: James, Patsy, Sallie, Thomas, Catherine, George and Mary. He died at the age of seventy years. Of his own family Mr. George D. Coleman relates: "My father made several trips over the mountains with a wagon, to move his father and others to Kentucky. We fixed and started my mother in a four-horse wagon after she was the mother of ten children. My brother Thomas was born two weeks after our arrival here; my nurse, uncle Hampton, a faithful old slave, packed me and brother Linsfield over the mountains. After the birth of Thomas, Hampton was sent to the woods to get a sugar-trough to rock him in. Thomas was named for old Dr. Thomas Clellan, pastor of Providence Church, near McAfee Station, where all our family lie buried except Henry, who sleeps at Little Union Church, in Nelson County, and Sallie Ann in Virginia. My old nurse is now about eighty years old, and is making a dollar a day at Harrodsburg, with a shovel and hoe. After my sister Jennie was born, my mother rode on horseback to Virginia, and after giving birth to her twelfth child rode back again. My brother Thomas had born to him eight children, of whom three sons are still living; he is worth $80,000, and his homestead, called 'Farview' comprises 800 acres of land, lately a part of Col. Slaughter's, part of Col. Thompson's and a part of Col. Prather's land, the last, the grandfather of his first wife. His second wife was a daughter of Abraham Jordan, son of Col. Jordan. The farms owned by my father and brother Thomas are considered the prettiest in Mercer County, and lie on the waters of Sunny Run, where old Gen. Ray, Indian fighter, lived and died."

ROBERT E. COLEMAN, the proprietor of the largest livery stable in Harrodsburg, is a native of Mercer County, and was born July 14, 1836. His father, James H. Coleman, was born in Spottsylvania County, Va., October 6, 1809, and when a boy twelve years of age was brought by his parents to Mercer County, where he spent most of his life. He was a successful business man, and acquired in the course of his business career a very good English education, being an expert penman, at his death, although he could not legibly write when twenty-one. He owned twenty-three slaves and a farm east of Harrodsburg of 300 acres, being worth before the war $20,000, but lost his property on account of sympathizing with the Confederacy. He was married October 8, 1833, to Miss Martha A., daughter of Henry and Linda (Linthacomb) Lewis, both Virginians. Linda Lewis was a daughter of Thomas Linthacomb, a Virginian of great wealth, who immigrated to Bardstown, Ky., where he died and is buried. To the marriage of James H. and Martha Coleman were born ten children: Robert E.; Rev. Thomas H., a

Baptist minister living near Georgetown, Ky.; Sally Ann, who died at St. Catherine's Academy at the age of thirteen; Elinda L., wife of James E. Conrad, deceased; Rev. James M., a Baptist minister living in Lincoln County; Simeon Burton, a farmer living near Bardstown, in Nelson County; Susan Elizabeth, wife of Mr. Simpson, and living in Bardstown; Burr H., a farmer in Nelson County; Ellen B., wife of Julius Bukey of Nelson County, and a daughter Sally, who died in infancy. Of these children, Sally Ann and Linda are now dead. James M. Coleman enlisted in Capt. Gabe Alexander's company, of Morgan's cavalry, but lost his health and resigned. He did not recover for several years after the war. James H. Coleman was a member of the Baptist Church, and departed this life January 23, 1876. Mrs. Coleman, who has been a member of the Baptist Church since sixteen years of age, is living with her daughter, Ellen, in Nelson County, in the sixty-ninth year of her age. James Coleman, grandfather of Robert Coleman, was a Virginian, owning his farm and slaves. He was married in Virginia to Miss Mary Penny, and all of their children, eleven in number, except one, were born in Virginia. Their names were Meredith R., a farmer and trader in the South in horses and mules; John L., a farmer and trader in horses; Bozell W., same occupation; Robert E., a slave trader; James H., Mary R. (Daniel), George D., Linsfield, Jane Amanda (Sorral), Maria (Dedman), and Thomas C., of whom George D. and Thomas C. are now living in Mercer County, and Thomas C. is in affluent circumstances. Their brother, Robert E. Coleman, began life with no property except a sow and pigs, and in 1833, when he was killed by his slaves and a white man, was worth $30,000. The negroes were hung, but the white man, because negro evidence was not valid in Kentucky courts, escaped punishment. James Coleman immigrated to Mercer County in 1820, and at his death owned a farm of 300 acres. The Coleman family are of English-Irish origin. Robert E. Coleman, subject of these lines, received a fair business education in youth, at country schools, attending Bacon College one five months' term. He left home at the age of nineteen, and began a life of agriculture, trading at the same time in horses in the South, both of which he engaged in for the first seven years. At the age of twenty, March 6, 1856, he was united in marriage to Miss Margaret A., daughter of Stephen and Mary C. (Alexander) Hughes, both Virginians and of English-Scotch origin. Stephen

Hughes, who was a veteran of the war of 1812, enlisting when only seventeen years of age, was a farmer and trader during life. Mr. Coleman carried on agriculture until 1874, and during this time traded extensively in blooded horses, and bred and raised them. By the panic in 1873 he lost very heavily, having nothing left when he embarked in the livery business in 1879. He owned three horses and two vehicles at that time, and no other earthly possessions, and now runs one of the largest livery stables in the State, the building being 260 feet long, and forty-two feet wide, in which he has horses and vehicles to the amount of $6,000. Mr. Coleman was the first man in Mercer County who sold a pair of horses as high as $1,200, and the first who sold a trotting horse as high as $2,000. Three times has he failed and begun on nothing, and during this time has not received a dollar that he did not earn. To Mr. and Mrs. Coleman have been born seven children: Stevana A., wife of L. D. Cardwell of Harrodsburg; Clara, wife of Edward Rosser, railroad contractor. To them was born one child, Robert E. Rosser, born November 11, 1882; Thomas H., Jr., a partner of R. E. Coleman in the livery business; Mamie, wife of John M. Moberly, a bookkeeper in Harrodsburg—have one child, a boy; James H., a farmer in Reeder, Kiowa County, Kas.; Roberta and Robert, twins, of whom Robert died aged four years. Mrs. Coleman is a member of the Baptist Church in Harrodsburg, and Mr. Coleman, who has always been Democratic in politics, is a member of no organization except the I. O. O. F. and K. of H. His son, Thomas H., Jr., was married in April, 1884, to Miss Dixie, a daughter of Henry Cohen, a trader who lives near Georgetown, Ky. To this marriage has been born one child, Rosser.

WILLIAM H. CONN was born July 24, 1853, and was reared a farmer. His father, J. T. Conn, was born March 10, 1822, in Garrard County, and has been twice married: first to Miss Lizzie Yakey, who became the mother of nine boys and two girls; and secondly, to Miss Virginia Barker, who also bore nine boys and two girls. J. T. Conn is the owner of 700 acres of good, productive land. In religion he is a Presbyterian and in politics a Democrat. The grandfather of William H. Conn was John Fields Conn, who was born in Washington County, Va., came to Kentucky in an early day, settled on a farm, married Elizabeth Faulkiner (who bore him five boys and five girls) and died in 1839, aged fifty-five years, a member of the Methodist Episcopal Church. William H.

Conn was born in Garrard County, has principally followed farming and in 1870 married Miss Penelope Pocahontas Barker, who has borne him the following children: J. P., Mary, Lillie W., William W., Mike Owsley, Lillie Price and Penelope Pocahontas Barker Conn. In religion Mr. Conn is a member of the Reformed Church, and in politics is a Democrat.

WILLIAM GRANT COOKE was born May 23, 1848, in Fayette County, Ky., removed in childhood with his parents to Mercer County, locating near Bergen, where he grew to manhood; in 1864 he went to Chicago, Ill., where he remained one year, when he returned to Mercer County and located northeast of Harrodsburg, where he has since resided. His father, William A. Cooke, a native of Surry County, N. C., was born December 12, 1821, removed with his parents to Tennessee, and in 1831 to Mercer County. Ky.; in 1843 to Fayette County, and in 1848 returned to Mercer. He was an active and public-spirited man, and prominent in public improvements. He was largely interested in breeding fine stock, and made a specialty of shorthorn cattle. He was an old line Whig in politics. His death occurred in Florida, March, 1873. He married Sarah A., a daughter of Squire and Nancy L. (Mosby) Grant, of Fayette County (born in 1823, died in 1860), and of their nine children two only are now living, viz.: Nannie (Bowman) and William G. October 1, 1872, William G. was married to Miss Anna, daughter of Warren O. and Rebecca E. (McConnell) Parker, of Fayette County, and to them have been born Rebecca, Grant, Anna L., Nellie and William H. D. Mr. Cooke's great-grandmother was a sister to Daniel Boone.

HUGH P. COOPER, attorney at law, of the Lebanon bar, is a son of Philip B. and Cordelia (Smith) Cooper. Philip B. was one of four children born to Basil P. and Mary (Quinley) Cooper, and was born in Baltimore, Md., in 1803. When about nineteen years old he came to Kentucky, and was here employed as a traveling salesman. He removed to Lebanon in 1838, and for a number of years was variously employed as trader and speculator, also filling the office of master commissioner of Marion County for a period of eight years. From Lebanon he removed to a farm on Rolling Fork, where he passed the remainder of his life, which terminated November 16, 1884. His wife, Cordelia Smith, was the daughter of Samuel and Cordelia (Hamilton) Smith, and was born in Marion County, Ky., in 1809. She died on the 3d of September, 1873. Their children are Benjamin J., Samuel S., Thomas J., Walter H., Hugh P., Mary E. (Craycroft), Josie E. (Kindred), deceased, and Elizabeth E. (Spalding). Hugh P. Cooper was born on the 25th of March, 1861, and was educated in Columbia College, Notre Dame, Ind., and St. Mary's College, graduating from the latter institution in 1881. In connection with his collegiate studies he pursued a thorough course of law study, and came to the bar in 1882. Though young in the legal profession, he enjoys an enviable local reputation, is the efficient attorney for the city of Lebanon, and bids fair to take a leading rank among the lawyers of Kentucky.

SAMUEL S. COOPER was born February 7, 1845, and is a son of Philip B. and Cordelia (Smith) Cooper, to whom six sons and four daughters were born, all of whom lived to be grown. P. B. Cooper was born in Maryland in 1803, came to Kentucky when a lad of ten years and was a farmer till grown, when he rode sheriff of Washington County ten years, after which he returned to farming and merchandising; was also engaged in distilling all his life, and about 1855 began on an extensive scale on Rolling Fork. He also traded in stock in his early life, driving hogs to Georgia. He died in November, 1884. His father settled in Nelson County, where he became a substantial farmer and slave-holder. P. B. Cooper located on Rolling Fork about 1840, and here Samuel S. Cooper was born and reared on a farm, and educated at St. Mary's College. When he arrived at maturity he commenced life for himself on a farm on Rolling Fork, trading in stock and driving South. He was, without solicitation, elected justice in 1882, which position he fills with marked ability, and with credit to himself. November 22, 1870, he married Susan, a daughter of William and Catharine (McAtee) Spalding, and by this union five children were born, but only two are now living, Catharine and Leenett. Mrs. Cooper's parents were natives of Marion County. Her father was a substantial farmer, and son of Thomas Spalding, who came from Maryland in an early day. Mrs. Cooper died November 15, 1878, a member of the Roman Catholic Church. Mr. Cooper married Catharine Hamilton February 6, 1882. She was a daughter of William and Ellen (McAtee) Hamilton, who were natives of Springfield and Marion Counties respectively. There were born by this second marriage two children—Nellie and Samuel P. After his marriage Mr. Cooper located where he now resides, on 150 acres of bottom lands on Rolling Fork. He also owns 140 acres of timber in the hills. His wife's grandfather, Walter Hamilton, married Dorothy Smith; both were born in Maryland and came to Kentucky as early as 1790, and were of English stock. Our subject is a Democrat, and cast his first vote for Gen. McClellan. He and wife are devoted members of the Catholic Church.

GEORGE B. COOPER, county clerk of Lincoln County, Ky., was born in Lincoln County in 1857, and is the fifth of a family of eleven children born to George B. Cooper and Susan F. (Burton) Cooper. The first representative of the Cooper family in Lincoln County was Joseph Cooper, who settled on the land which is now the site of Hustonville in the west part of the county. His wife was a Miss Blain, and their family consisted of George B., John M. and Mary Cooper. George B. Cooper, Sr., was born on the 3d of January, 1818, reared in Lincoln County and first married Martha Burton, who was a daughter of Archibald Burton, and who died leaving one child, Martha Cooper. His second wife, Susan F. Burton, was a younger sister of his former wife. By this union he had a family of eleven children as follows: Joseph, Mary, Annie, Bettie, George B., Mittie, John M., Rosa, Archie, Joseph and Jennie. It will be noticed that the eldest and tenth members of this family bore the same name, and a remarkable coincidence is the further fact that both were born on the same day of the same month, both died on the same day of same month, and at the same age, of the same disease. George B. Cooper, Sr., removed from Kentucky to Texas where he died May 14, 1880, and where his wife still lives. George B. Cooper, Jr., was married May 31, 1881, to Miss Amanda W. Cook, daughter of James M. and Lucy B. Cook of Lincoln County, Their children are Lucille and George E. Cooper. For a number of years Mr. Cooper has engaged in merchandising, but in August, 1886, was elected to the office which he is now acceptably filling. He is an honored member of the A. F. & A. M.

GARRET COOVERT is a son of David Coovert, who was born in New Jersey in 1780, and came to Kentucky with his parents in 1784. The family settled on a farm near Harrodsburg, where David passed the winter season in the manufacture of boots and shoes. In 1810 he married Mary, daughter of Lieut. Philip Morgan, and there were born to him five sons and three daughters. The grandfather of Garret Coovert was also a native of New Jersey, was a tanner and farmer, and served seven years in the Revolutionary war. He died a member of the Presbyterian Church. Garret Coovert was born in Mercer County, Ky., May 9, 1815, but moved to Garrard County in 1838 and settled on a garden plot of six acres, which he cultivates in summer, devoting the winter months to the making and repairing of shoes. In 1839 he married Miss Elizabeth Woods, who, with himself, is a member of the Baptist Church. Mr. Coovert is also an Odd Fellow.

URIAH COPPAGE. Prominent among the venerable citizens of Marion is the worthy gentleman whose name heads this sketch. He was born in what is now Washington County, April 19, 1813. His father, James Coppage, was a native of Virginia and was born April 5, 1763. He came with a brother, William, to Kentucky when a young man. The country where they settled, on Rolling Fork River, was an unbroken forest, and the Indians were very troublesome. The brother of James was shot by an Indian; he survived, however, and afterward removed to Missouri. James continued to reside in Kentucky, and married Nancy O'Bannon. They reared a family of eight children, of whom are living Uriah, and Rhoda, the widow of Stewart Tapscott, who resided in Casey County and was killed by a falling tree. Nancy (O'Bannon) Coppage died in 1841; her parents were of Irish parentage, natives of Virginia, came early to Kentucky, and settled on Rolling Fork River, in which stream the father of Nancy O'Bannon was drowned. Moses Coppage, the father of James, was an Englishman and a citizen of the Virginia colony. Uriah Coppage had but little school training, his education being almost entirely practical; his vocation through life has been that of a farmer; he has been uniformly successful in his business operations, and has resided all his life on the farm where he was born. He is the proprietor of 300 acres of farming land, has been a man of energy and perseverance, and has followed his vocation with the zeal that brings success, and now in his declining years is able to live in comfortable circumstances. His wife was a Miss Margaret Mann; they were married July 25, 1833, and are the parents of twelve children, eleven of whom are living, viz.: James, Elizabeth, Stephen, Joseph, Hardin, Lucinda, Ellen, Moses, Killis, Mollie and Maggie. Margaret Mann was born near the Kentucky River in 1815; her parents, Joseph and Elizabeth (Hill) Mann, were Virginians by birth and natives of Green County. Mr. and Mrs. Coppage are members of the Christian Church. His political views are Democratic.

KILLIS COPPAGE was born on the 22d of May, 1850; he grew to manhood on his father's farm, receiving a good common-school training in early life. He was married on the 21st of November, 1872, to Amanda Coppage; to them has been born one son, Oscar (January 9, 1876). He followed farming for some time, but later engaged in the lumber trade. His mills are situated on the waters of South Rolling Fork River, in the southwestern section of his native county of Marion, and he makes a success of his business. Politically he is a Democrat and holds the office of postmaster at Rush Branch, and is also agent for the L. E. & St. L. Railway Company. He and wife are members of the Christian Church. Mrs. Amanda Coppage is a daughter of Willis and Sarah (Steele) Coppage, of Adair County, Ky.

ANDERSON CORLEY was born on the 27th of August, 1815. His father, James Corley, was a native of Virginia, born in Culpeper County in 1775. He was married to a Miss Nancy Tyrrell and reared a family of eight sons and daughters, of which number Anderson Corley is the eighth. Anderson, William and America are the only survivors. James Corley worked at the trade of millwright in connection with that of bricklaying; late in life he engaged in farming, which he followed up to the time of his death. He was a son of William Corley, who was of Irish lineage and a native of Virginia. The later years of his life were passed in Wilson County, Tenn., and he died at the age of one hundred and five years. He was for many years a ruling elder in the Presbyterian Church, and was a veteran in the war of the Revolution. Anderson Corley, a native of Garrard County, was brought up amid the scenes and labors incident to farm life and received his early training in the common schools. At the age of fourteen began to learn the saddler's trade and continued in that business until 1861; after that time he was engaged in various kinds of businesses up to 1877, when he began farming, which he has continued up to the present time in conjunction with the sale of farm implements and machinery in the town of Lebanon, Marion County. He has been twice married; first in 1839 to Miss Elizabeth Aulby, daughter of Perry Aulby of Marion County. To this marriage were born thirteen children, three of whom lived to be grown, viz.: Sallie, John and James. Elizabeth Aulby died in 1876, aged forty years. In 1877 Mr. Corley married Ellen Cunningham, widow of W. M. Bricken. To this marriage is born one daughter, Cassella, born in 1878. Mr. and Mrs. Corley are members of the Presbyterian Church. Politically he is a Democrat, and is a member of the board of trustees of Lebanon.

THOMAS GESS COTTON was born October 31, 1818, in Fayette County, Ky. In 1838 he removed to Danville, Boyle County, and in 1848 located four miles west of that city on the Lebanon pike, where he has since resided. His father, George Cotton, born near Athens, Fayette County, was a farmer and miller, and died in 1822, while a comparatively young man. He was the son of Harry Cotton, of Maryland; a soldier in the Revolutionary war, a contemporary with Daniel Boone in Kentucky; a farmer and slave owner who died in 1823. His children were Susan (Hudson); Almede; Mrs. Capt. Finfch, of Covington; George and Mrs. Jones. George married Susan Gess of Fayette County (died in 1839, aged forty-two years), and from their union sprang Mary (Oldham), Thomas G. and George, Jr. On September 17, 1848, Thomas G. Cotton married Miss Lucy, daughter of Samuel and Mary (Templeman) Wilson, of Boyle County (born May 15, 1826), and to them have been born Susan (Collingsworth); John Templeman; Mary P. (Cowherd); Samuel Wilson; David and Robert (twins), both deceased; Minnie (deceased); Stella Lee (lately deceased); Lou W. and Belle I. For ten years Mr. Cotton conducted a merchant tailoring establishment with success in Danville. He is now engaged in farming, having 155 acres of land in fine condition. His family are members of the Cumberland Presbyterian Church, and in politics Mr. Cotton is a Democrat. He lost eighteen slaves by the late war. Lucy (Wilson) Cotton's father, Samuel Wilson, was born three miles west of Danville, January 15, 1786; was a soldier in the war of 1812, and died July 12, 1870. His father was the first settler in the vicinity of Danville, and his stone dwelling is now standing, with its old port-holes intact, constructed when Indians were numerous and dangerous. He was a Revolutionary soldier and an Indian fighter in Kentucky.

JAMES J. COURTS was born November 11, 1852, in Greensburg, received a good English education at Greensburg and Urania College, Glasgow, and learned the saddler's trade with his father. In 1872 he went to Iowa, was a telegraph operator, also a clerk in a hotel at Malvern, and afterward taught common schools in Kansas. After two years sojourn in the west he returned to Greensburg and engaged at his trade till January 13, 1874; until 1884 was engaged as traveling salesman through the South. On January 13, 1886, became associate editor of the Greensburg *Times*, and on February 9 took full charge as editor and proprietor. In 1879–80 he served as marshal of Greensburg. February 9, 1886, he was united in marriage to Miss Mercie C., a daughter of Rev. R. C. and Mercie (Cosson) Alexander, who are natives respectively of Christian and Pulaski Counties. Mr. Alexander is a minister of the Methodist Episcopal Church, and son of William Alexander, who was a colonel in the war of 1812; his parents came from Ireland. He married Mercie T. Emerson. James J. Courts is a son of Braxton E. and Eliza J. (Durham) Courts, to whom seven children were born and five reared: James J., John W. (now dead), Mary J., William E. (deceased), and Braxton E. B. E. Courts was born June 17, 1826, twelve miles east of Glasgow, and is the youngest child, and only son of three children born to Jesse W. and Mary J. (Price) Courts. Jesse W. Courts was born in Barren County; when a boy was a salesman in Glasgow, afterward merchant on Nobob Creek; in 1828 he went to St. Louis, where he worked at carpentering one year; later went to Hannibal, Mo., and while there lost his wife, after which his son was returned to Kentucky, while he himself continued his journey westward to the Rocky Mountains. He finally returned to Quincy, Ill., where he died of cholera, aged fifty-five years. He was a son of William and Clarissa (Winn) Courts, natives of Culpeper County, Va. They were married in Fayette County, Ky., to which county they immigrated early, and were also early settlers of Barren County. William, with three brothers, served during the Revolution, one on a man of war; the other two, with William, were early settlers of Kentucky. One, John Courts, built and ran a powder-mill in Barren County, but it blew up, and he then went to Hart County, where he built and ran its first powder-mill. The grandfather of B. E. Courts was a farmer and a manufacturer of linseed oil, and died in 1848 at the age of eighty-four years, at Edmonton, Metcalfe County. His father came from England; his mother was a Douglass and of Scotch-Irish origin. The mother of B. E. Courts was born in Barren County, a daughter of Daniel und Mary (Lewis) Price, natives of Richmond, Va., and early settlers of Barren County, Ky. He was a wheelwright, a farmer, a soldier in 1812, moved to Iowa during the Black Hawk war (B. E. Courts going with him), settled near Keokuk, and lived to be over ninety years old. B. E. Courts was taken to St. Louis, then to Belleville, Ill., and in 1844 returned to Edmonton, Metcalfe Co., Ky., where he learned the saddler's trade. In 1849 he located in Greensburg, where he has lived ever since, except six years in Elizabethtown and Lebanon. During the war he was engaged in the dry goods and grocery business for a brief period; in 1863 was appointed sheriff of the county and elected the same year by 900 majority, but did not serve on account of troubles; served seven years as United States store-keeper; in May, 1884, was appointed postmaster of Greensburg, and was removed in December, 1885. He has a farm of 270 acres in a good state of cultivation. In April, 1850, he married Eliza J., a daughter of John and Margaret (Shreve) Durham, and of English descent. B. E. Courts acted as quartermaster while the troops were being enlisted for the war in 1862–63.

A. K. COX, M. D., was born September 6, 1827. His father, Gabriel E. Cox, was a son of the renowned Indian fighter, Gen. James Cox, who was one of the first settlers of what is now Nelson County. He located on a small stream in the northern part of the county, which has since been known as Cox's Creek. He served with distinction in the war of 1812. He was a very extensive land owner, and was unable by reason of its plentifulness to appreciate its value, frequently bartering away quite large tracts of what is to-day the best of land for merely a nominal price. He died at the advanced age of seventy-seven years, October 5, 1845. He represented Nelson County in the Legislature in the years of 1802 and 1803. Gabriel E. Cox, father of Dr. A. K. Cox, was born October 27, 1793, at the home farm on Cox's Creek, where he grew to manhood. By profession he was a physician, acquiring his education at Jefferson Medical College, Philadelphia. Very soon after reaching home he married Miss Delia M. Tingle, and located and commenced the practice at Bardstown, where he continued until he was compelled to retire from active work on account of enfeebled health. He had a very large practice, in which he was highly successful. A member of the Methodist Episcopal Church, with which he was connected a great many years, he died a devout believer in that faith, February 27, 1853. Politically a Whig, he represented the county in the Legislature twice. Dr. A. K. Cox was born in Bardstown and remained at home until he attained his majority, when he commenced reading medicine with his father. In the winters of 1858–59–

60 he attended two courses of lectures at the Kentucky School of Medicine, of Louisville, graduating from that institution in the latter year. August 10, 1848, his marriage with Ellen E. Bowman was celebrated, and to their union one child was born, Mary D., now Mrs. H. Clay Brown, of Georgia. Mrs. Cox is a daughter of Wilson and Mary Bowman. Her father, Wilson Bowman, was born in Virginia, June 16, 1787. He grew to manhood in his native State, immigrated to Kentucky at an early day, locating in Cumberland County, whence he removed to Nelson County about 1827. His vocation was that of farming and speculating in lands, and was regarded by those with an opportunity of seeing his operations on the farm as a most systematic and enterprising farmer, being highly successful. He was the first importer of thorough-bred horses to county, and handled them with great pleasure and success. In politics a Whig, he always manifested a great interest in political affairs, but sought no personal preferment. He died July 10, 1858. Dr. Cox has practiced his profession about twenty-five years, meeting with most flattering success. He and wife are members of the Methodist Episcopal Church South, and the Doctor occasionally fills the pulpit. In politics he is a Democrat.

HARVEY P. COX, physician and surgeon, is a native of Taylorsville, Spencer Co., Ky., and the eighth of a family of fourteen children born to Shelby and Sarah (Tutt) Cox. Isaac S. Cox, the grandfather of our subject, was a native of Virginia; was born in 1782, and in an early day removed to Kentucky in company with his brothers, Jonathan, James, Gabriel, David and George, and made a settlement in Nelson County, on the creek which still bears the name of the family. These brothers were among the earliest permanent residents of Nelson County, and their descendants are to be found in various parts of the State. Shelby Cox was born in Nelson County in 1812, and was a cabinet-maker by occupation. He was married in 1837 to Miss Sarah A. Tutt, daughter of William Tutt, by whom he had fourteen children, of whom the following are living: Mrs. Kate Martin, Mrs. Emma Groves, Isaac S., Mrs. Anna B. Price, Harvey P., Mrs. Ida Wells, William T., James A. and Sarah T. Mr. Cox served in the United States Arsenal at St. Louis during the Mexican war, after which he removed to Taylorsville and was engaged in the milling business. He gave each of his children a collegiate education, and took great interest in religious matters, having been an active member of the Christian Church for many years. He died on the 17th of July, 1873. Harvey P. Cox was born February 29, 1852. He grew to manhood in Spencer County, and began the study of medicine in 1872 with Dr. J. W. Smith, of Taylorsville, under whose instruction he continued one year. He then entered the office of Dr. E. W. King, with whom he remained for a little more than a year, when he entered the medical department of the Louisville University, from which he graduated in March, 1876. After graduating he located in the village of Mackville, where he has since resided, practicing his profession in Washington and other counties. He was married December 11, 1877, to Miss Obie Wycoff, by whom he has two children, Ella B. and Emma M. Cox. Dr. Cox is a member of the Masonic fraternity, I. O. O. F., and in politics votes with the Democratic party. He is an active member of the Christian Church, as is also his wife, and belongs to the Mackville congregation.

JACOB C. COZATT was born May 22, 1817, near Harrodsburg, Mercer Co., Ky.; in 1837 he removed to Vermillion County, Ill., and in 1841 returned to Kentucky, locating eight and one-half miles west of Danville, on the Lebanon Turnpike, Boyle County, where he has since resided. His father, Jacob Cozatt, was born September 11, 1773, in Pennsylvania or New Jersey; removed in childhood with his parents to Kentucky, and with Barton W. Stone, Humphrey Marshall and others, withdrew from the Presbyterian Church and entered the old Christian Church, of which he became minister. He was a hatter and farmer in Mercer County, and died September 10, 1822. His father was killed by Indians at Boone's Station. His offspring were Francis, David, Jacob, Peter, Henry and Albert (twins). Jacob was married in 1799 to Margaret, daughter of Henry Comingore, of Mercer County (born March 15, 1783, died June 2, 1842), and from their union sprang Peter, Daniel, Elisha, Rachael (Terhune), Mary (Randolph), Henry, David, Ann (Davis), Jacob C., John and Abraham. September 26, 1837, Jacob C. Cozatt was married to Miss Emily, daughter of Henry and Jemima (Cleland) May, of Mercer County (born December 6, 1815), and to them have been born Margaret (Caldwell); Jemima (Sinkhorn); Mary (Bower); Charlotte L.; Henry C.; William T.; Susan (deceased), and John A. In youth Jacob C. had but limited opportunities for procuring an education, such as were afforded by the old field schoolhouse, having a long hole cut in the building

to admit the light; puncheon floor, a very large chimney, and oiled paper used for the window instead of glass. The school was disciplined on the basis of "no lickin' no larnin'," and the "loud school" system surpassed Bedlam for racket, as many yet living can testify. By application in after years he has become somewhat conversant with standard and current literature. He was employed as deputy assessor of Boyle County for four years. He is now farming, owning 130 acres of land in a good state of cultivation. He is a member of the Christian Church, also of the Masonic fraternity, and is a Prohibitionist. Since the above was placed in type, the melancholy intelligence has been received that Mr. Cozatt died October 27, 1886. He was without a known enemy.

ROBERT F. CRADDOCK was born August 10, 1837, and is a son of Creed H. and Eliza G. (Sandridge) Craddock, who had born to them four sons and seven daughters, eight of whom lived to be grown. Creed H. Craddock was of English descent, was born in Virginia, came to Kentucky and settled in Green County as early as 1820; was a substantial farmer and owner of slaves, served as magistrate for several years; in an early day flatboated out of Green River to New Orleans, and died in 1862, aged fifty-three years. Mrs. Eliza G. Craddock was a daughter of Pleasant and Elizabeth (Edwards) Sandridge, who emigrated from Virginia in an early day. The father was an extensive farmer and long served as magistrate and sheriff. Robert F. Craddock was raised on the farm in his native county of Green and attended the common schools, receiving a liberal English education. In October, 1861, he enlisted in Company H, Twenty-seventh Kentucky Infantry, and was in all the principal engagements in which the regiment participated. While at the siege of Knoxville his life was saved by a testament, which he carried in his pocket, receiving a musket ball. In April, 1865, he was discharged as a non-commissioned officer. After his return home he engaged in farm life for two years, when he embarked in the distilling business; two years later he engaged in the grocery business. Then, after two years, he was engaged in the dry goods business for six years, since when he has run a mill at Osceola. He is the owner of three small farms, containing in all 170 acres, and also owns an interest in a tannery, although he started even in life after his return from the army. In February, 1871, he was united in marriage to Miss Emma F. Gooch, a daughter of A. E. and Lydia C. (Gardner)

Gooch, and there have been born by this happy union two children: Edward L. and Chas. W. Mrs. Craddock died in 1876, and he married his second wife, Mrs. Nancy J. Whitlock, in February, 1877. She is a daughter of Edward Perry. Mr. Craddock is a member of the F. & A. M., was a member of the Grange; in politics he is an active Democrat, has been a member of the central committee since the war, and his first presidential vote was for John Bell; with his wife he is a member of the Methodist Episcopal Church.

REV. JAMES E. CROW was born November 29, 1814, in Pulaski County, Ky., where he grew to manhood. In 1841 he removed to Lincoln County and in 1844 located in the northwestern part of Garrard County, where he still resides. He is the son of Samuel Crow, whose offspring were Samuel, Thomas D., George, Sarah, Robert R., John T., James E., Polly (Pascal), William and Cyrus. James E. married Eleanor Robinson, of Boyle County, and their children are James T., Delitha (deceased), Samuel (killed in the Union Army), Jalila (Scott), Sarah (Spoonamore), Susan (Dickerson), Polly (Larrimore) and Rebecca (Mantz). Mr. Crow is a minister in the Christian Church, with which he has been connected for over forty years. He was an old line Whig and a Union man, but is now a Republican and a prohibitionist.

HAMILTON CROWDER (deceased). The gentleman whose name appears at the head of this sketch was born December 27, 1829, in Jessamine County, Ky., where he was reared to manhood. He resided for some time in Indiana, and located at Decatur, Ill. He served as a musician in the Federal Army during the late war, and died May 2, 1871. On the 19th of November, 1862, he was united in marriage with Miss Phoebe E. Caldwell of Boyle County (born December 30, 1835), and to them were born John, Joseph and Mary. Mrs. Crowder's father John Caldwell, of Boyle County, who was born in 1790; was a soldier in the war of 1812 and died August 4, 1873. He married Mary, daughter of David and Isabella (Caldwell) Knox, of Boyle County (born July 3, 1795, died September 6, 1879), and the result of their union was Isabella D. (Durham), George L., James A., Martha A. (Thompson), Mary J. (Lyons), David K., Thomas J., Samuel K. N., William A. and Phoebe E. (Crowder). John was the son of David Caldwell, a native of Virginia, and was a pioneer in Kentucky. He married Phoebe Mann, and their offspring were Josiah,

Thomas, Francis, Sally, David, James, Dicy (McAfee), William, Phoebe (Adams), John, Cary A., Betsey (Caldwell), Jackson and Samuel. Mrs. Crowder now owns and resides on a part of her father's old homestead, and also owns her grandfather Knox's homestead. David Knox, her grandfather, was born October 17, 1760, near Philadelphia, Penn. He married Isabella Caldwell (born in Charlotte County, Va., November 17, 1771), and their union resulted in the birth of William, George, Mary (Caldwell), Andrew, John, Robert, Davis, James, Samuel, Benjamin F. and David R. (See sketches of W. L. Caldwell and Mrs. Fannie Knox in this work.)

RICHARD CUMMINS was born in County Carlow, Ireland, May 8, 1830, and is a son of Arthur and Ellen (Whallen) Cummins, to whom four sons and seven daughters were born and reared. Richard Cummins came to the United States in 1848, and located in Rahway, N. J.; five years later he moved to Louisville and thence to Bullitt County, Ky., where he ran a distillery for two years; then moved to Decatur, Ill., where he again ran a distillery. In 1859 he returned to Kentucky and located at Raywick, where for five years he ran a distillery, after which he ran a saw-mill four years. In 1868 he located in the western part of Marion County on 300 acres of fine land, which he has improved with good substantial buildings, built and ran a distillery near New Hope and called it Coon Hollow Distillery, which he afterward sold and built a distillery near his residence and named it Coon Hollow Distillery, from which the station takes its name. In 1881 he sold to the Nelson County Distilling Company, after which he purchased and ran a distillery at Loretto, in the name of R. Cummins & Co. Mr. Cummins also turns his attention to shorthorn cattle and fine saddle stock. He was married October 1, 1861, to Emily J., a daughter of John and Mary (Simpson) Brady, who are natives of Maryland and were brought to Washington County, Ky., when children. The issue from this marriage of our subject was ten children: M. A., born September 5, 1862; Mary A., August 22, 1864 (deceased); Mary E., July 30, 1865; John A., March 5, 1869 (deceased); James P., February 2, 1871; Catherine W., May 3, 1872; Richard D., August 29, 1874; Elizabeth J., November 27, 1877; John R., May 27, 1880 (deceased), and Anna M., May 27, 1880. Mr. Cummins' parents came to the United States in 1855 and located in New Jersey and later in Louisville, Ky., where they remained during the rest of their days. In politics he is a Democrat and his first presidential vote was for Buchanan in 1856, and he and wife are devoted members of the Catholic Church.

THOMAS H. CURD, M. D., was born in Murray, Calloway Co., Ky., January 3, 1849, and is the third in a family of eight children born to James H. and Elizabeth L. (Frazer) Curd, the former a native of Wadesboro, Calloway County, and the latter of Columbia, Adair County. They are of Irish and Scotch-Irish descent respectively. James H. Curd was married in Adair County and immediately returned to Calloway, where he followed tailoring until about 1861, with the exception of a few years he engaged in merchandising at Murray. During a part of the time he was also engaged in agricultural pursuits in connection with his other business, on a farm of 360 acres, which he inherited from his father and still owns. For several years also he was jailer of Calloway County. In 1872 he moved to Adair County, where he bought another farm of 140 acres, one mile north of Columbia on the Campbellsville pike, upon which he now resides and is successfully cultivating. He belongs to no church or secret order, but Mrs. Curd has been from early life a devout member of the Old School Presbyterian Church. Dr. Curd received a good classical and scientific education in the schools of his native county and at the Columbia College. For the first two years after attaining his majority he was employed on the home farm, after which he was engaged as salesman in a drug store at Columbia for another two years. He was then elected marshal of the town of Columbia, and held that position for something over a year. He then commenced the study of medicine under the preceptorship of Dr. Melvin Rhoel, of Columbia, and in 1877 commenced his medical course at the medical department of the University of Louisville, graduating with distinguished honors in the spring of 1879. He has since practiced with success at Columbia, with the exception of fourteen months, when he was located at Camp Knox, Green County. Dr. Curd married December 17, 1884, Miss Mattie, daughter of William Moses, of Louisville, where she was born in 1860. The Doctor is a member of the Old School Presbyterian Church, and his wife of the Missionary Baptist Church; he is a member of the Masonic fraternity, and is a Democrat.

ROBERT B. CURRY dates his birth from May 30, 1826. His grandfather, William Curry, emigrated from Virginia in an early day, and settled on Chaplin River in Mercer County, where he accumulated a large landed estate. He was a successful farmer, and died many years ago. Robert Curry, father of Robert B., was born in Mercer County, about 1781, and was a farmer by occupation. He died in his native county in the year 1857. His wife, Mary (Wilham) Curry, was born in Mercer County, and departed this life about 1830 or 1831. They were the parents of the following children: Mrs. Hannah Whittinghill, William, Edward, Mrs. Sarah Stines, Mrs. Jane Yeast, Martha, Mrs. Artemisia Cunninghan, Robert B., James and John Curry. By a subsequent marriage with Miss Artemisia Hill Mr. Curry had a family of nine children. Robert B. Curry, a native of Mercer County, was reared to agricultural pursuits, and grew to manhood on his father's farm, nine miles west of Harrodsburg. He attended the country schools from the age of twelve until his twenty-first year, and acquired a fair English education for that day. He began farming for himself at the age of twenty-two, purchased a tract of land in his native county in 1853, and resided upon the same for a period of fourteen years. At the end of that time he disposed of his place and later purchased a second farm, which was his home until 1871, when he moved to Johnson County, Ind., where he lived for a short time. Returning to Kentucky he bought a farm in the northern part of Washington County, to which he at once removed and upon which he lived until his election to the office of county jailer in 1882, when he disposed of his farm and moved to Springfield, where he has since resided in the discharge of the duties of his office. Mr. Curry was married October 12, 1852, in Mercer County, to Sarah, daughter of Enoch and Frances Thomas, who has borne him the following children: Isaac, William, Thomas (deceased), James, Mary F. (wife of "Doc." Cummings), John, Sarah E. and George Ann (deceased). Mrs. Curry died November 2, 1865, at the age of thirty-two years. Mr. Curry was next married, November 13, 1870, to Mrs. Icylinda Salle, widow of George Salle, and daughter of James and Mournen (Ham) Philips, of Madison County. By her previous marriage Mrs. Curry had one child—Selena, wife of John Sutton. Mr. Curry belongs to the Masonic fraternity, and since 1858 has been an active member of the Christian Church. He is a Democrat in politics, and one of the most efficient jailers the county has ever had.

SAMUEL L. CURRY was born April 9, 1858, in Harrodsburg, Ky., and was the third of three sons and two daughters born to James A. and Elizabeth (Lewis) Curry. James A. Curry was born in Harrodsburg, Ky., January 23, 1829. He attended the schools of the town, but is principally self-educated. He learned the tailor's trade, but in 1855 entered the drug business at Harrodsburg. In 1878 he located in Danville, Ky., and in 1883 he moved to Lexington, Ky., to become a member of the wholesale grocery firm of Curry, Howard & Murray. He is a son of James Curry, who was born in Mercer County, Ky., March 25, 1797, and was a carpenter by trade. He married Catherine Stagg, and to them were born and reared five sons and one daughter. He was a soldier of 1812, and participated in the battle of New Orleans; his parents came from Virginia, and were among the early settlers of Mercer County. He died at his work-bench, plane in hand, December 22, 1877. Catherine Stagg was born in Pennsylvania, October 10, 1794; died at Harrodsburg, Ky., November 23, 1871. The mother of Samuel L. was a daughter of Thomas P. and Arethusa (Yantis) Lewis, natives of Kentucky, and parents of three children, all daughters. Samuel L. Curry was reared in Harrodsburg, educated at Centre College, Danville, graduated in the class of 1878 as A. B. He was immediately taken into the firm of J. A. Curry & Sons, and continued in the drug business until the dissolution of the firm in January, 1883. From Danville he went to Louisville, Ky., and, as member of firm of Curry & Dearing, engaged in the book and stationery business. His health failing he sold his interest in March, 1885, and a short while thereafter accepted a position with Curry, Howard & Murray, at Lexington, which he held until his death July 7, 1886. His life was one of singular purity; his every action directed by the nicest sense of honor. His death was peculiarly distressing. Overcome with heat while bathing, he went down within a few feet of his brother, who thought him only diving, and his body was not recovered until after two hours of diligent search.

J. W. DANT was born May 7, 1820, in Washington (now Marion) County, and is the oldest of four sons and four daughters born to John B. and Mary J. (Smith) Dant, who were born in what is now Marion County. John B. Dant was a farmer, died December, 1881, aged eighty-two years, and was a son of Joseph Dant, who married Malinda Shirkles and came from Maryland and settled near Loretto at an early day and engaged extensively in farming, owning a large family of slaves. He was a son of John B. Dant, who came from England and settled in Maryland; from thence migrated to Kentucky, where he remained till death. Joseph Dant died in 1833. Mrs. Mary J. Dant is a daughter of Samuel Smith, who came from Maryland in the early settling of Kentucky and became a substantial farmer of Washington County. J. W. Dant was reared on a farm, and received his early education by his early application till after twenty years of age. When twenty-two he commenced blacksmithing, at which he worked for fourteen years. He was married February 12, 1849, to Catherine Ballard, daughter of William P. and Mary (Greenwell) Ballard, natives respectively of Nelson and Marion Counties. William P. Ballard was born in January, 1810, and is still living; he is a farmer and tanner, and served as justice for twenty-five years. His first wife was a Miss Mary Greenwell; his second wife was Mrs. Tucker, nee Ford. Mr. and Mrs. J. W. Dant have had born to them ten children: Joseph Bernard, Thomas S., John P., James R., William W., Mary J., Francis L., Ellen S., George W. and Anna C. Mr. Dant located where he now resides in 1860 on 196 acres of land, which he has improved. He is now owner of 400 acres at Dant Station and two farms near Loretto of 329 acres. He has followed distilling since 1836 more or less, and now owns a distillery at Dant Station with a capacity of 220 bushels. Before he became of age he had been hired out for nine years, and has accumulated his property by industry and good management, hence he deserves much credit. In politics he is a Democrat, and cast his first presidential vote for James K. Polk. Mr. and Mrs. Dant are members of the Roman Catholic Church.

JAMES N. DAVIS was born January 20, 1807, in Hanover County, Va. His father, Peter Davis, was also a native of Hanover County and a life-long farmer and slaveholder. He brought his family to Kentucky in 1817, and settled on and owned about 230 acres on Butler's Creek, Adair County, where he farmed until the spring of 1821, when he died in the seventy-fifth year of his age. He had been a soldier in the army of Gen. Washington. He married Elizabeth, a daughter of Robin Page, who owned a large plantation, which he cultivated with slave labor in his native county of Albemarle, Va. The names of the children born to Peter and Elizabeth Davis were Polly (wife of John Breeding), Jenny (Snead), Judith (Walker), Elizabeth (Schuyler), John, Patsy (Callison), Lucy (Lage), Rebecca (Banks), Nancy

(Browning) and James N., the only living one of the family. Mrs. Davis died about the same time her husband did, and was in the sixty-sixth year of her age, a member of the Methodist Church. John Davis, grandfather of James N. Davis, was also a Virginian; he was a man of considerable wealth, a slave owner and a farmer. The life of James N. Davis has been spent in farming. In October, 1829, he was united in marriage to Miss Elizabeth, daughter of John and Frances Holman, of Virginia. The marriage was blessed with two children: Frances Henry Edrington and Elizabeth James, who died in childhood. Mrs. Davis in life was a member of the Baptist Church, first of the Methodist Episcopal Church, and died in 1844, in the thirty-sixth year of her age. Mr. Davis was next married, in 1847, to Miss Jane, daughter of Alexander and Nancy (Foster) McClure, natives of Virginia. Mr. Davis is a member of the Methodist Episcopal Church, while Mrs. Davis is a member of the Christian Church. The first farm owned by Mr. Davis was on Green River, and contained 112 acres. There he lived during the years 1850 and 1851, prior to which time he had rented and made many moves. In 1851 he purchased the farm of 112 acres on which he now lives, two miles from Cane Valley, Adair County. This is a fertile tract and is in a fair state of cultivation and improvement. Mr. Davis began life with no inheritance but a strong constitution and willing hands, and by his own industry has accumulated all that he possesses.

WILLIAM FLEMMING DAVIS was born December 25, 1838, near Camp Dick Robinson, Garrard Co., Ky., where he grew to manhood. In 1869 he located on the old Harrod-Fauntleroy place in Boyle County, where he has since resided. His father, Asael Davis, Jr., was born April 3, 1787, in Garrard County, was a farmer for many years, was a deacon in the Baptist Church, and died May 3, 1848. He was the son of Asael Davis, Sr., a native of Rockbridge County, Va., and an early pioneer and Indian fighter in Kentucky. His offspring were Solomon, Edmund, William, Benjamin, Susan (Baxter), Sarah (Baxter), Martha (Pierce), Margaret (Street), Mary (Irving), and Asael, Jr. Asael, Jr., first married a Miss Henderson, and their children were Joshua (deceased) and Barbara (Hawkins). He was next married September 11, 1823, to Sarah Balenger, daughter of Robert and Phœbe Tucker, of Lincoln County (born January 26, 1796, died 1862), and from their union sprang Asael B., James H., Elizabeth (Allen), Martha (Burnam), Robert L.,

George R., John M. and William F. In May, 1869, William Flemming Davis married Miss Hannah E., daughter of John W. and Martha (Smith) Poor, of Garrard County (born March 23, 1848), and to this union have been born John Allen, Ashley McKee and William Barnes. Mr. Davis is a farmer and trader in Boyle County, having 480 acres of productive land. He is a member of the Methodist Episcopal Church South, a member of the Masonic fraternity and of the K. of P., and is also an Ancient Odd Fellow, and a Democrat. His dwelling is the old Fauntleroy home, in which are many portholes made for defense in pioneer days. Near his dwelling are yet visible signs of James Harrod's cabin, and in the yard is the famous spring which attracted Harrod to the place. A few rods distant, near the boundary line between Mr. Davis and Judge Sumrall, stood Harrod's Station, by another spring. The fertility of this land is remarkable after a century of cultivation.

JOHN DAWSON was born December 25, 1826, and is the fourth of three sons and three daughters born to Ignatius and Elizabeth (Ice) Dawson. Ignatius was born near Holy Cross Church, became a substantial farmer and slave-owner, was an active Whig, and died about 1863, a member of the Roman Catholic Church. His father came from Scotland and settled in Nelson County as early as 1790, and followed farming. Mrs. Elizabeth Dawson was born eight miles north of New Haven, and was a daughter of Jessa Ice, who married a Mrs. Lee, the mother of the Lees who were among the wealthy and leading citizens of Bullitt County, Ky. The issue by Mr. Ice was five children. Mr. Ice was an early settler and substantial farmer of Nelson County John Dawson was born near New Haven, on a farm, and received a good English education. At the age of twenty-five he left his home, and was a superintendent of slaves for four years, when he commenced farming on his own account. He was united in marriage, in May, 1865, to Jennie Wilson, an adopted daughter of C. J. Wilson. She was born in Ireland, came with her father to the United States, and first located in New Orleans, where her parents died shortly after. She was then brought to Louisville by a Mrs. Hanes, and Maj. C. J. Wilson, of La Rue County, adopted her. Mr. and Mrs. Dawson are blessed with three bright children: Mary E. Russell, Nannie and James Lee. After his marriage Mr. Dawson located where he now resides, one-half mile east of New Haven, on 700 acres of fine land. He lost one of the finest houses in his community, but has rebuilt an elegant frame residence on the site of the former. Mr. Dawson started about even in life, and by his skill and excellent financial abilities has made life a success. He turns his attention principally to the cattle trade. Mr. Dawson was a Whig in early life, but since the war has affiliated with the Democrats.

NATHAN B. DEATHERAGE was born on the 17th of December, 1843, in Madison County, Ky., and is a son of Amos and Susan G. (Lipscomb) Deatherage to whom five sons and three daughters were born, of whom Nathan B. is the eldest now living. Amos Deatherage was born March 20, 1813, three miles north of Richmond; was an active and substantial farmer, the owner of a large family of slaves prior to the Rebellion and was an active Whig in his early days, but since the war has affiliated with the Democratic party. He is a member of the Christian Church and a son of Baird Deatherage, who was born in Madison County in 1790, and who became a large farmer and slave owner. He lived north of Richmond and married Sallie Phelps, who was born in Madison County in 1793, and is still living in good health. They reared a family of eight sons. Baird Deatherage died in 1870. His parents came from Virginia in the early settlement of Madison County. Susan J. (Lipscomb) Deatherage was a daughter of Nathan Lipscomb and Nancy Gentry, natives of South Carolina and Madison County respectively. He was a farmer and served as major of militia as early as 1800; was very prosperous, accumulating about 3,000 acres of fine blue-grass land and was active and public-spirited. Nathan B. Deatherage was reared on a farm and received a common English education. In September, 1862, he enlisted in Company B, Ninth Kentucky Confederate Cavalry Regiment, and was in all the engagements of the regiment and until captured in Ohio. He was a prisoner one month at Camp Chase, and nearly nineteen months at Camp Douglas. When exchanged he was sent to Richmond, Va., but was one day late in reaching that point for the exchange and was sworn not to take up arms; before another exchange was made, Gen. Lee had surrendered, after which Mr. Deatherage walked from Virginia to Mt. Sterling, Ky., returning to his home in Madison County, where he resumed his occupation of farming. In 1876 he was elected sheriff of Madison County; commenced the duties of his office in January, 1877, and was re-elected in 1878. After the expiration of his sec-

ond term he returned to his farm. In 1884 he made the race again, and was elected and re-elected in 1886. He was united in marriage November 10, 1865, to Mary A. Oldham, daughter of O. and Sydonia (Noland) Oldham. His wife died in July, 1869, a member of the Christian Church. He married his second wife, Mary E. Noland, September, 24, 1872. She is a daughter of Nathan and Margaret (Broaddus) Noland, who were both natives of Madison County. Mr. Noland was a substantial farmer and a son of Col. John and Ann (Black) Noland, natives of Kentucky and Virginia respectively. They were among the early settlers of Madison County and of Irish descent. Nathan Noland's parents were born respectively in New Jersey and Ireland. His mother's maiden name was White. In religion they were Baptists. Mr. Deatherage and wife are members of the Christian Church, and in politics he is an active Democrat.

SAMUEL P. DEBAUN was born December 18, 1831, and is a son of Joseph Debaun, a native of Mercer County, and born in 1808; he had nine children—eight sons and one daughter; he died January 7, 1857. Samuel P. Debaun was born in Mercer County, receiving a common school education, and was reared a farmer. Mr. Debaun enlisted in Eleventh Kentucky Cavalry (Federal), and was first lieutenant of Company C. He took an active part in the war, and participated in a number of battles and skirmishes, including the siege of Knoxville. He married Miss Katie Mays. She died and he afterward married Miss Ellen Philips, by whom he had two children, one of them, Ida, living. Mr. and Mrs. Debaun belong to the Christian Church, in which he was an elder. Mr. Debaun is deputy county court clerk of Mercer County and also notary public. He had one brother, John W., killed by lightning, and one, Pleasant M., a Federal soldier, died a prisoner of war at Andersonville, Ga.

DR. JOHN DEBO was born in Jefferson County, Ky., May 27, 1840; his parents, Horatio and Elizabeth (Porter) Debo, had seven children, of which he was the third born. Henry Debo, his paternal grandfather, was a native of Virginia, of French-German descent, a hatter by trade and an early settler in Kentucky, where he resided until he became advanced in years, when he removed to Johnson County, Ind., and lived the rest of his days with his son. Richard Porter, maternal grandfather of Dr. Debo, of English descent, was a native of Maryland, and one of the early settlers of Nelson County; he later removed to Jefferson County, of which he died a resident. Horatio Debo was born in Virginia and was but a child when his father brought him to Kentucky; he was reared a farmer but at about the age of eighteen was apprenticed to learn the carpenter's and joiner's trade at Louisville, and continued in that vocation until his death in 1854. Dr. John Debo received a good English academic education. In 1860 he commenced reading medicine with Dr. S. M. Hobbs, of Mount Washington, with whom he remained two years; he then served one year following as acting medical cadet at the Federal military hospital, Louisville. In 1863 he located and began practice at Texas. In the winter of 1867-68 he attended a course of lectures at the medical department of the University of Louisville, graduating from that institution in the spring of the latter year; he then resumed his practice at Texas, where he has since continued. In May, 1866, he was united in marriage with Miss Lucetta Barbour; they have one child—Bettie B. In politics he is an ardent Democrat, and he and wife are members of the Baptist Church.

PHIL. T. DEDMAN, D. D. S., is a native of Virginia, born in Washington, Rappahannock County, August 27, 1850; his father, Robert Dedman, was also a Virginian, born in 1781. He married Miss Elizabeth Timberlake, of Spottsylvania County, and to them were born ten sons and two daughters, of which number Phil. T. is the youngest. Five of this family are yet living: Annie M. (Duke), Wm. D., Samuel L., James O. and Phil. T. The mother died in 1854; the father, Robert, survived until 1870. He was, during the greater part of his life, a merchant of Fredericksburg. Va.; from there he removed to Rappahannock and carried on business until the beginning of the war in 1861, when he retired to a farm in Loudoun County near Leesburg, where he remained until his death. He was a member of the Presbyterian Church, and also of the Masonic fraternity, and held the office of postmaster for many years. His father of Scotch and English extraction. Phil. T. Dedman was reared in the town of Washington, Va., where he received a good common English education, and in 1867-68 was a student in Westminster College of Fulton, Missouri. He returned to Virginia, where he was two years in the merchandise trade with G. W. and W. H. Adams of Middleburg, after which he was in the same business with Henderson, Stone & Co., of Fulton, Mo., until 1872, when he came to Harrodsburg, Ky., and began the study of dentistry. He remained here two years, then after two years' residence in Springfield, Ky.,

in 1876 entered the Pennsylvania Dental College of Philadelphia, from which institution he graduated in 1877, and in the following year located in Lebanon, where he has for eight years been actively and successfully engaged in the practice of his profession. The Doctor is unmarried. He is a member of the Presbyterian Church, and vice-president of the State Dental Association; also a member of the Masonic fraternity, and a K. T., of Marion Commandery, No. 24; also a member of the I. O. O. F. Politically he is a Democrat, and takes a lively interest in political affairs.

SAMUEL DEMAREE was born July 30, 1816, in Jessamine County, Ky., but was brought up principally in Mercer County, and is a son of Peter Demaree, a native of Shelby County (this State), and born there in 1780. Samuel's grandfather, John D. Demaree, was a Revolutionary soldier, and a native of New Jersey. Samuel Demaree was brought up on the farm, and received but a common-school education. He owns a good farm of 213 acres, a little north of Salvisa. He has been three times married: first to Miss Frances Leathers, of Anderson County; second to Miss Louisa Forsten, of Woodford County, by whom he had one child, Annie B.; his third wife was Miss Racie L. Smith (also deceased). This marriage resulted in the birth of three children: Mary L., Rosella and Maggie L. Mr. Demaree is a member of the Methodist Church and of the Democratic party.

GEORGE DENNY was born January 3, 1825, in Garrard County, Ky., and is a son of George and Margaret (Miller) Denny, by whom one son and two daughters were reared. George Denny, Sr., was born September 16, 1774, in North Carolina, and was brought to Kentucky by his parents, who settled near Paint Lick as early as 1785. He became an extensive farmer and slave owner; was a Presbyterian, and in politics a Whig. His first wife was Sally Graham, to whom two sons and five daughters were born. He died in 1841, and was a son of Alex. Denny, who was twice married and reared a large family, from whom spring many of the families of Garrard and adjoining counties. He was one of the earliest pioneers of Garrard County; in 1810 he moved to Boone County, Mo. Margaret (Miller) Denny was born in Garrard County, October, 1784, in Paint Lick Fort, and died December, 1871; was a daughter of William and Nancy (Yancy) Miller. George Denny was reared on a farm. At the age of sixteen years took charge of the home farm. September, 1849, he was united in marriage to Elizabeth Faulkner, a daughter of John and Jane (Kavenaugh) Faulkner, natives respectively of Virginia and Franklin County, Tenn. John Faulkner was brought to the State at a very early date by his parents, and became one of the leading farmers of Garrard County. In 1810 he was elected to the Lower House, in 1812 was elected to the Senate, and served successively in that branch for twenty years; served in the Legislature longer than any other man in the State. He was one of the patriots in the war of 1812, serving as major under Jennings, and was afterward made general of militia. He died in 1838. Jane (Kavenaugh) Faulkner reared three daughters and one son by her first husband. Her second husband was John W. Walker, by whom four sons and one daughter were reared. She was a relative of Bishop Kavenaugh. Mr. Denny was elected to the State Senate in 1861, and declined a re-election. He was one of the principal men in organizing Lancaster National Bank; was elected its president in 1872, and held that position ten years; in 1886 was appointed master commissioner of Garrard Circuit Court. Mr. Denny also owns an interest in the Lancaster Flouring Mill. He is a leading member of the F. & A. M., and he and wife are members of the Presbyterian Church. In politics he is a Republican. Before the war he was a stanch Whig.

BEN P. DOOM was born February 13, 1840. His father, James M. Doom, was born January 8, 1813, in Bardstown, and married Sarah E. Phillips in 1838. To this marriage was born one son, Ben P., and one daughter, who died in infancy. Sarah E. (Phillips) Doom was born in 1822, and died in 1843. She was a daughter of David and Elizabeth (Maxwell) Phillips, of Washington County. The former was of Dutch parentage, the latter of Scotch extraction. Both were born in Kentucky. James M. Doom learned the tanner's trade of his father; this trade he followed up to the year of 1866, when he retired from active life, and since has resided with his son, Ben P. Benjamin Doom, the father of James M., was born in 1782, near Bardstown, and was the first white child born in what is now Nelson County, his father having come from Virginia and settled in Kentucky a short time after the advent of Boone into the State. He came with his family, in company with the Hevenhill family, and settled on the site of the present town of Bardstown. He was made a colonel of militia, was a man of commanding stature and of imposing appearance, and was one of the best militia officers of his day. He sank the first tanyard in Kentucky, and during life amassed a large fortune in lands and slaves, which he left to his children. One story in proof of his close attention to business will bear relating: On the day preceding his marriage he quit work at 4 o'clock, and, on the same evening, borrowed a pair of shoes and a pair of socks, and rode on horseback to his bride's residence near the mouth of Hardin's Creek; he was married on Sunday morning, and in the afternoon returned to his home on horseback, with his bride behind him, who prepared the breakfast for his hired help before 6 o'clock on Monday, then washed the socks, which the husband returned to the owner during the dinner hour. He reared a family of two sons and three daughters, among whom was James, the father of Ben P. Ben. P. Doom, a native of Nelson County, bereft of a mother's care when he was but two years of age, and from that time until he attained to the age of twenty-three, he resided with his father and other relatives. He received a good English education in the common schools of Nelson County, and in 1863 engaged with his father in the tanning business, at what is called the "Old Doom Tanyard," at Bardstown. After about seven years he abandoned the trade and turned his attention to agriculture. He married, February 14, 1865, Miss Mollie Murphy, of Nelson County. To this union have been born one son, James Murphy, and two daughters, Mamie R. and Sadie E. Mrs. Mollie (Murphy) Doom is the youngest daughter of Judge F. G. Murphy, of Nelson County; her mother was a Miss Mary May. Both parents were Kentuckians by birth, and of Irish and English descent, respectively. Mr. and Mrs. Doom, now residents of Lebanon, Marion County, are members of the Presbyterian Church. He is a patron of and for many years has been a trustee of schools. Politically he is a Democrat, and on the question of temperance is strictly a prohibitionist.

DR. WILLIAM M. DOORES, of Crab Orchard, Ky., was born in 1830 and is a son of French Doores, who came from Culpeper County, Va., to Kentucky in 1828, and located in Boyle County. He was by profession a teacher with which he combined agriculture. He married Sallie Fisher, of Boyle County, and died in 1873, and his wife ten years later. The parents of French Doores were James Doores, a native of England, and Jemimah Jett, a native of Wales. French and Sallie Doores reared four sons and three daughters, viz.: William M., Robert (deceased), Elizabeth F., Jeremiah F., James E., Nancy B. and Emily Doores (deceased). Jeremiah was a soldier in the Confederate Army, a member of Capt. John Garrett's company, and was killed in 1862 at Pleasant Hill, Mo. Dr. William M. Doores, a prominent physician of Lincoln County, is the eldest of this family and a resident of Crab Orchard. He was married, in 1851, to Miss Mary A., daughter of Thomas Thomas and Joanna Thomas, nee Masterson, of Cass County, Mo. They have had seven children, named as follows: Thomas H. (deceased), Joanna A., Ella F. (deceased), Sallie F., Mary B. (deceased), Annie L. and Leila A. Doores. Dr. Doores served as a soldier in the Confederate Army under Gen. Sterling Price and participated in the battles of Wilson Creek, Dry Wood, Lexington, Lone Jack, Helena (Ark.), Pea Ridge, Prairie Grove and many other engagements, and during his term of service was four times wounded. Since the war he has been a resident of Lincoln County and engaged in the practice of his profession.

MAJ. LEVEN M. DRYE was born September 14, 1843. His father, Matthias P. Drye, was born in Lincoln (now Casey) County, June 28, 1798. He was married to Kizzie Batsell in 1825. Of the eleven children born to this marriage five are now living, viz.: Jacob A., Catherine, Leven M., Nathan M., and Lou (Fidler). Kizzie Batsell was born in 1805, and is a daughter of Thomas and Kizzie (Nall) Batsell, of Nelson County; the former was of Irish, the latter of Scotch descent. She is yet living, aged eighty-one years. Matthias P. Drye was a farmer, was a man of some local prominence, a member and worker in the Christian Church, and held the office of magistrate for a number of years; his death occurred August 16, 1883. His father, George Drye, was a native of Germany, who came to America when a young man, and was a farmer by occupation: he married Anna Pfeifer, and reared a family of three sons and five daughters, among whom was Matthias, the father of our Leven M. George Drye died March 21, 1855, aged ninety-four; his wife, Anna, survived until October 19, of the same year; her age was ninety-eight. Leven M. Drye was born and reared on a farm in Marion County, and educated in the common school. In December, 1861, he left school and entered the Federal Army, enlisting in Company D, First Kentucky Cavalry, under Col. Wolford, and with that command participated in the engagements at Perryville, Munfordville and Mount Vernon. After the battle at Mount Vernon he was promoted for meritorious conduct on the field, and was commissioned lieutenant of Company G, Sixth Cavalry, and afterward to first lieutenant of the same company; next was made a captain, and in 1865 was promoted to the rank of major of the Sixth Cavalry. He participated in the engagements at Chickamauga, Mission Ridge, Ringgold, Franklin and Brentwood, and was discharged at the end of the war, September 6, 1865, after an active service of nearly four years. One brother, Jacob A., held the rank of major in the Confederate States Army; he now resides at Pilot Point, Tex. One brother, James, was a lieutenant in the Sixteenth Texas Cavalry of the Confederate States Army, served as aid to Gen. Pillow, afterward served in Kirby Smith's command, was wounded in the fight at Cotton Plant, Ark., and died of wounds at Austin on the 27th of August, 1862. One brother, Dr. John Drye, served in the Federal Army, first as captain of Company G, Sixth Cavalry, from which he was promoted to surgeon of the Sixth, and afterward to the surgeoncy of Croxton's brigade, with the rank of major. After the war he located in Louisville, Ky., where he practiced his profession until his death from cholera in 1873. Maj. L. M. Drye since the war has been engaged principally in farming and stock raising; he is now the proprietor of the Valley Home farm, an estate of 400 acres lying on the waters of south Rolling Fork in Marion County. In politics he is a Republican. In 1873 he received the appointment of Government storekeeper and gauger, and remained in the Government's employ for about twelve years. He was married December 24, 1868, to Miss Lou Dunn, and to this union have been born two sons and three daughters: Claudia, Minnie, Myrtle, Jim Blaine and Don Victor. Mrs. Lou Drye was born November 5, 1847. Her father, George Dunn, was a native of Maryland, born in 1804; her mother, Dicy (Scandlan) Dunn, was of Irish parentage, and was born in Kentucky in 1810. She died in 1864, the mother of twelve children, of which Mrs. Drye is the ninth. Mr. and Mrs. Drye are members of the Christian Church, in which Mr. Drye holds the office of treasurer. He is a member of the G. A. R., Hays Watkins Post, No. 21, Department of Kentucky; also a Royal Arch Mason, and a member of Proctor Knott Chapter.

JAMES DUDDERAR is of German origin, being a descendant of George P. Dudderar, who immigrated to the United States in 1722, and settled in Philadelphia where he reared a family. Conrad Dudderar was a son of George P. Dudderar, and in early manhood removed to Frederick, Md., where he married and reared a family of children, among whom was Samuel Dudderar. The latter had three children, viz.: Catherine, Conrad and William. With his family he removed to Kentucky about 1798, and settled in Lincoln County, after which were born in the latter place Samuel, Margaret, Elizabeth, John and Polly Ann Dudderar. Conrad, the eldest son of Samuel Dudderar, and father of our subject, was born in Maryland, and at the time of the removal of the family to Kentucky was five years old. Here he grew to maturity, and married Catherine Ruffner, and this union resulted in the birth of five children: James, Margaret, Samuel, Mary Ann and Catherine. James was born January 8, 1820. He married Lucy A. Dudderar in 1846; she died September 2, 1881, leaving no children. He was married to his present wife, Mary K. Dudderar, September 6, 1883, and their alliance has resulted in the birth of one daughter, Mary E. Dudderar, born in 1886. Mr. Dudderar has lived an active business life, devoted to merchandise and agriculture.

EDMUND W. DUGAN resides on the farm, where he was born on the 28th of April, 1816. His father, George Dugan, was born in Virginia, near the Maryland line, about the year 1775; he in company with his brother, Thomas, came to Kentucky when young and engaged in farming near Bardstown; he subsequently purchased land eight miles east of Bardstown on the old Bardstown and Lexington road; he resided there the remainder of his life, and died in 1836, possessed of an excellent farm of 600 acres, nearly all of which is still in the possession of his descendants. He married a Miss Elizabeth Rubell, a daughter of Isaac and Ann (Harnedd) Rubell, of Nelson County. Isaac Rubell was a veteran of the Revolutionary war and was among the earliest settlers of Nelson County. He died at his home, near Bardstown, in 1809. Elizabeth Dugan belonged to the Baptist Church, of which she died a devout member in 1852 at the age of sixty-eight years. Edmund W. Dugan, a native of Nelson County, was reared on the farm and remained with his parents as long as they lived; he received a good education in the common schools of the county, and inherited a portion of the home farm, which he has supplemented by subsequent purchases; he is now the owner of 600 acres of land, well improved and mostly under a high state of cultivation. He makes a specialty of raising fine stock, having some of the best grades in

the county. Mr. Dugan was in 1852 united in marriage to Miss Catherine Brown, who was born in 1833, a daughter of Jonathan and Elizabeth (Beauchamp) Brown, her parents being of English descent and natives of Bourbon and Fayette Counties respectively. To the union of Mr. and Mrs. Dugan eight children have been born, six of whom are now living: George, Jonathan, James, Anna E., Susan and Edmund N. Politically Mr. Dugan is a Democrat; he never takes an active part in political affairs, but never fails to vote his sentiments. He and wife are not members of any church but hold the Baptist faith.

JACOB DULWORTH, a native of Cumberland County, was born February 6, 1835. His father, James Dulworth, was born near Knoxville, and was a farmer in fair circumstances. He began the battle of life without a dollar, and when in his twenty-fifth year married Miss Elizabeth Gwinn Spears, a daughter of Benjamin and Naomi (Crabtree) Spears, the former of the Old Dominion, the latter of Kentucky. Benjamin Spears was the son of John Spears, a Revolutionary soldier. To James Dulworth and his wife were born six children: Benjamin, Jacob, Mathias, John, Abraham and Nancy M., wife of James R. Coe. John and Benjamin are now dead. Mathias Dulworth served as a private in the Fifth Kentucky Federal Cavalry, but on account of his health was not able to serve out his term of enlistment. James Dulworth was brought to Cumberland County by his parents. He owned about 600 acres of fine land in the southern part of the county worth about $6,000, and he gave his estate, with the exception of 200 acres, to his children. Mrs. Dulworth, who was a member of the Methodist Episcopal Church, departed this life in 1878, about sixty years of age. Mr. Dulworth afterward was married to Miss Ibby Williams, daughter of Richard and Elizabeth (Spears) Williams, natives of Cumberland County, Ky. Mr. and Mrs. Dulworth, both of whom are members of the Christian Church, still live at their home in Cumberland County. John Dulworth, grandfather of Jacob Dulworth, had emigrated from Germany to the United States, and settled in Tennessee, where he was a farmer. Benjamin Spears, maternal grandfather of Jacob Dulworth, was a native of the Old Dominion, and for sixty years he was a strict and consistent member of the Methodist Episcopal Church. Before his death he divided his estate, which was small, consisting of 200 acres of land and $1,000 in cash, among his three children, two of whom were daughters, and several years before his death lived with Jacob Dulworth. In youth Mr. Dulworth acquired a moderate English education in the common schools of his neighborhood, and remained at home working for his father until twenty-four years of age. He then, in 1858, emigrated to California, but after working unsuccessfully nearly two years, both in California and Vancouver's Island, returned home in 1859, and went into brandy distilling. Prior to emigrating he owned and ran three whisky distilleries. He quit distilling in 1860 and turned his attention to farming entirely. The first farm Mr. Dulworth owned was in Overton County, Tenn., and it consisted of 180 acres, and was worth $2,500. In 1870 he removed to Adair County, and purchased 200 acres of fine land on Green River, where he has since resided. November 6, 1860, he was united in marriage to Miss Hannah, daughter of Burrell and Jane (Smith) Willis, natives of Overton County, Tenn. Burrell Willis was a farmer, and the father of ten children, only two of whom were sons, John and Charles Willis. John Willis was a veteran of the Mexican war, and served as private in Gen. Scott's army. Charles Willis was a private in the Fifth Kentucky Cavalry, Federal Volunteer service, and served until his death in 1863. To Mr. and Mrs. Dulworth have been born nine children: Martha, wife of George A. Fease; James A., Joseph M., Leslie, William B., Rufus M., Jane N., Marietta and Rosa Belle, all of whom are living. Mr. Dulworth is a member of the Masonic order, and of the Democratic party. He began life with $640 in 1856, and is now worth $12,000, which is all the result of his own industry. His farm comprises 576 acres of fine land on both sides of Green River, some of which is worth $100 per acre, and he has 200 acres of this tract in cultivation. He first lived in a log house, but five years ago erected a frame two-story residence. Mr. Dulworth does a great deal of trading and has been very successful in it—especially in tobacco and mule trading. He has bought 25,000 pounds of tobacco this year, and now has on hand thirty-two young mules, which he bought when colts, and will sell when two years old.

JOHN C. DUNBAR was born in Clinton County, Ky., January 22, 1839, and is the third of eleven children born to Sydney S. and Letitia T. (Campbell) Dunbar, both of whom were born in what is now Russell, but was then a part of Cumberland County, Ky., and were of English and Scotch descent respectively. Sydney S. Dunbar was born March 8, 1808, and was a natural mathematician, and a splendid penman. In early manhood he taught school for several years, and also taught one term later in life. He also learned the tanner's trade and followed it for a time. He made his home with his mother until he was twenty-five or twenty-six years old, when he was married. Soon after he bought a farm on the Cumberland River, in Clinton County, Ky., upon which he remained until 1852, when he sold out and bought a farm near Columbia, in Adair County, upon which he has since resided. For many years he was a magistrate in Clinton County. He was from early life a member of the Christian Church. His father, Thomas Dunbar, was a veteran of the war of 1812, with the rank of colonel, commanding a regiment under Gen. Jackson at the battle of New Orleans. Afterward he was engaged in the struggle with Mexico for the independence of Texas, and was one of the only three persons who survived the terrible massacre of the Alamo, making good his escape only by his fleetness of foot. Mrs. Letitia T. (Campbell) Dunbar was born October 18, 1816, and departed this life July 14, 1862. Her father, John Campbell, was a native of Virginia, and was born in 1794. When but a child he came with his parents to what is now Russell County, Ky., where he remained engaged in agricultural pursuits all his life. John C. Dunbar remained with his parents on the old homestead until he was twenty-five years old, during which time he taught several terms of school. He and his brother, William P., then bought a farm together on the Green River, near Neatsville, in Adair County, upon which he remained until 1872, when he sold his interest in the place to his brother and bought the farm of 291 acres on Casey Creek, in the same county, upon which he has ever since resided, and where he is extensively and successfully engaged in farming and stock raising. He has also been for several years engaged to some extent in the live stock trade, mainly buying and selling mules. He was married, December 21, 1865, to Miss Mary J. Knifley, a native of Adair County, born October 18, 1845. Eight children have blessed their union, as follows: Millard Volney, Joseph Sydney (deceased), Pinckney L., Cyrus W., Charles (deceased), Sarah L., Perry H. and Omeira T. Both Mr. Dunbar and wife are members of the Christian Church, she having been a member since her fifteenth year. He is also a bright member of the Masonic fraternity, and has been treasurer of his lodge. In politics he is a Democrat.

FAYETTE DUNLAP, M. D., was born March 3, 1855, in Danville, and is a son of

Dr. Richard W. and Sarah (Bailey) Dunlap, who reared four sons and one daughter, of whom Fayette is the oldest. Richard W. Dunlap was born in Lexington, Ky., July 4, 1817. He was a graduate of Transylvania University, also from the University of Pennsylvania; was one of the leading physicians of Kentucky; was a member of the State Medical Society; was its president in 1879–80; was also a member of the American Medical Association and president of the State Board of Health. In 1832 he moved to Danville, Ky., where he had a large and extended practice. He died July 28, 1885. His father, George Dunlap, was born in Fayette County January 29, 1789, and was a prominent attorney of Lexington, where he had accumulated considerable property. He married Mary Downton, who was born in Fayette County in 1787, and died July 17, 1843, after which he retired from active life, and died at Danville June 5, 1851. He was a son of Col. William Dunlap, of Augusta County, Va., born in 1751, in Scotland. He married Rebecca Robertson, who was born in Augusta County, Va., in 1754. He immigrated to and was one of the earliest settlers of Fayette County, Ky.; settled on what is known as "Walnut Hill" farm. He was a son of —— Dunlap, a minister of the Church of England, who was born in Scotland. Mrs. Sarah (Bailey) Dunlap was born in Lincoln County June 12, 1830; she was a daughter of Carroll and America (Patton) Bailey, both born in Lincoln County, he in 1796, she May 12, 1802. He was a soldier under Gov. Isaac Shelby in 1812, was captured, but made his escape. Fayette Dunlap has the equipment he carried during the war. He was a civil engineer, served as sheriff and surveyor of his county, and raised a family of one son and eight daughters. In 1850 he was thrown from a horse and killed. His widow is still living, and in good health. He was a son of Elijah Bailey, who married a Miss Sarah Jackman, and who was born in Rockingham County, Va., was an early settler of Lincoln County, and became a large and extensive farmer. John Bailey, his father, was born in Richmond, Va., was an Episcopal minister, served in the Revolution, after which he received a grant of land in Lincoln County, Ky., on which he located at the close of the war. He was a son of Elijah Bailey, of English parentage. Dr. Fayette Dunlap was born and reared in Danville, and graduated from Centre College in 1874; was engaged in civil engineering for a short time, also as a drug clerk. In 1876 he commenced the study of medicine and surgery,

graduating from the medical department of the University of Louisiana in 1879, serving one year in the Charity Hospital of New Orleans and going through the yellow fever epidemic of 1878; also received the degree from the University of Pennsylvania in 1883, and progresses with his profession by attending lectures during winter months when convenient. He has had excellent success, and established a good lucrative practice. He is Democratic in politics. His brother, W. W. Dunlap, graduated from West Point. He entered the Confederate Army; was lieutenant-colonel of artillery in the army of the khedive of Egypt, from 1868 to 1876, and is now civil engineer in the mining region of Colorado.

WOODFORD G. DUNLAP was born March 26, 1860. He is a son of George W. Dunlap and Nancy E. Jennings, to whom eleven children were born: Eugenia (Potts), Mary D. (Denny), John J. (deceased), George W., Jr., Victor (deceased), Woodford G., Frank H. (deceased), Alfred V. (deceased), and Nannie (deceased), and two who died in infancy. George W. Dunlap, a lawyer and politician, was born in Fayette County, Ky., February 22, 1813, and was a son of George Dunlap, who was a native and farmer of Fayette County. He filled various official positions in this county and died in 1851; his parents came from Virginia and were of Scotch descent. Mary (Downton) Dunlap, wife of George Dunlap, was a daughter of Richard Downton, an early pioneer of Fayette County. George W. Dunlap graduated at Transylvania University, Lexington, in 1834; began the study of law, and, by teaching school, secured means to enable him to attend law school and graduated in 1837; located at Lancaster in 1838 and at once secured a good practice. In 1843 was appointed master commissioner of the Garrard Circuit Court and held the office until 1874; was elected to the Legislature in 1853; in May, 1861, was a member of the Border State Convention at Frankfort; in the same year was elected to Congress and served through the XXXVII Congress; was chairman of the committee on the navy department and member of the committee on finances. He had been a strong advocate of the Whig doctrine, but during his latter life was independent in politics. He educated his family by sending them to the best colleges of the country. His wife was a daughter of John Jennings, a farmer of Garrard County. She was also a granddaughter of William Jennings, an early pioneer of Garrard County. G. W. Dunlap died of paralysis of the heart June 6, 1880. Woodford G. Dunlap graduated at Centre College, Danville, in 1879. He then established and edited an independent paper called the *Lancaster Enterprise* for one year; afterward moved to Chicago, where he was engaged in managing a large printing establishment until 1884. He is now editor of the *Danville Tribune*, an influential Republican newspaper, published at Danville, Ky. In politics he is a Republican and bends all of his energies and talents toward the advancement of his party. He is considered to be one of the foremost Republican editors in the State. He was married to Ella B., daughter of Gen. W. J. Landram, on October 26, 1880. The issue from this union is two children: Eugenia P. and George W. His sister, Eugenia (Dunlap) Potts, is the authoress of a work called "Song of Lancaster," containing the early pioneer history and brought down to 1874. Her husband, Richard Potts, was a surgeon in the Confederate Army.

JOSEPH B. DUNN was born July 23, 1853, in Garrard County, Ky.; in 1855 removed with his parents to Ray County, Mo., and in 1864 returned to Garrard County, where he has since resided. His father, William Dunn, a native of Garrard County, was born in 1827, is a farmer, a Democrat, and a member of the Methodist Episcopal Church South. He is the son of Joshua Dunn, also a native of Garrard County, born June 8, 1798; is a farmer, and has represented his county in the Legislature; was an old-line Whig and a Union man, and is still living. He is the son of Augustine Dunn, a native of Maryland, whose brothers were William, Benjamin and John. He married Eleanor Aldrige, and their offspring were John, William, Joshua, James and Harriet (Byars). Joshua Dunn married Elizabeth Swope, and from their union sprang Margaret (Smith), Benjamin, Augustine, William, Jesse, Charles, Joshua, Wilson, Sarah (Gaines), Bettie (Gaines) and Eliza A. (Cook). William Dunn married Belle, daughter of William Burnside, of Garrard County, and to them were born Joseph B., Elizabeth, Joshua, Orpha (deceased), Cora A., Mattie B. (deceased) and Minnie C. Joseph B. Dunn engaged in teaching for some time. In politics he is a Democrat and a prohibitionist. During the present year (1886) he and his brother Joshua engaged in general merchandise and drug business at Bryantsville, Ky., and are meeting with encouraging success. Joshua Dunn was born May 18, 1857, in Ray County, Mo., was reared to manhood in Garrard County, Ky., clerked three years in a store, was two years in partnership with E. S. Ford, in Bryantsville, Ky., and is now in business with his brother, Joseph B. He taught school one term at Buena Vista, studied law two years at Lancaster, with Burdette & Hopper, and was admitted to the bar in 1879. He is a member of the Christian Church, and in politics is a Democrat and a prohibitionist.

GABRIEL DUVALL was born February 29, 1828, on the place where he now resides. In 1847 he enlisted in Company C (Captain Rowan Harding), Fourth Kentucky Infantry, and remained in the army until the close of the Mexican war. His father, Gabriel Duvall, Sr., was born in 1787, at Annapolis, Md., and in 1790 removed with his mother to Kentucky, where he died August 1, 1827. He was both a farmer and cooper. He was the son of Miles Duvall, a privateer in the Revolutionary war, and afterward a coast trader supposed to have been killed by pirates in 1787. He was the son of Hugh Duvall, a French Huguenot. The sons of Miles were Thomas, Senate, Jacob, John and Gabriel, Sr. Gabriel, Sr., married Mary Grable (born on the farm where subject now lives, in 1792, and died here in 1869), and to them were born Cyrus G., Joseph, Thomas, Gabriel and Louisana (Overall). On January 7, 1851, Gabriel Duvall, Jr., was married to Miss Rebecca, daughter of Andrew and Priscilla McCormick, of Nelson County, born October 14, 1833, and from this union there is no issue, but they have reared an adopted daughter, Sallie Duvall. Mr. Duvall has served as magistrate and member of the court of claims of Nelson County for four years. He is a farmer, having 240 acres of productive and well improved land in his native county of Nelson. He is an Ancient Odd Fellow, but is not connected by membership with any church. In politics he is independent.

JAMES H. EDELEN was born in 1833 and descends from one of the early families of Kentucky. His grandparents came from Maryland and settled in what is now Marion County, soon after which time the grandfather died. He left a large family, among whom was Leonard Edelen, the father of James H. Leonard was born in 1800, and was but three years old at the death of his father. He learned the trade of hatter, which he followed until his death, which occurred in 1865. He married Susan Bruce, of Lincoln County, and had a family of eight children, all now living except one. The children of Leonard and Susan Edelen are Sarah A. (McAfee), William B., Mary C.

(Williams), James H., Lucy R. (Riley), Leonard G., George T. and Robert H., the latter being dead. The mother died in 1855. James H. Edelen was born and reared in Lebanon, Marion County, where he established (1858) a drug business, in which line he continues. He was married, in 1855, to Miss Mary S. Lewis, daughter of Thomas Lewis, of Harrodsburg, Ky. Their union has been blessed with two children: Sallie, wife of J. R. Gilkeson, of Lebanon, and Thomas Lewis Edelen, a modest and talented young attorney of the Lebanon bar. Mr. Edelen and family are members of the Presbyterian Church.

LEONARD GRAVES EDELEN was born at Lebanon, Marion Co., Ky., February 20, 1839. In 1860 he removed to Boyle County and engaged in farming; in 1868 he located at Big South Fork, in Casey County, where he conducted a large tannery, but at a severe financial loss, until 1877, when he removed to Lebanon; and in 1881 he located near Alum Springs, in Boyle County, where he has since resided. His father, Leonard Edelen, son of Geo. Edelen, was born at Baltimore, Md., in June, 1800, and located at Lebanon with his parents in 1804; was a very successful manufacturer and dealer in hats, at which he amassed a comfortable estate; had his residence and business house on the same ground for more than forty years; was for many years a magistrate and a member of the court of claims of Marion County; was by all regarded as an upright man, and died on the day President Lincoln was assassinated, in 1865. His father, a Catholic, settled near Lebanon in 1804. His offspring were Robert, Benjamin, Leonard, James, Lucy (Hamilton), Mrs. Medley, Aletha (Hamilton), and Priscilla. Leonard Edelen married Susan, daughter of William Bruce, born in Virginia in 1799, moved to Lincoln, County, Ky., in an early day and died December 8, 1856, and their union resulted in the birth of Sarah (McAfee), William B., Catherine (Williams), James H., Lucy (Riley), Leonard G., Robert H. (deceased), and George T. July 17, 1860, Leonard G. Edelen espoused Miss Mary E., daughter of William L. and Julietta (Maxwell) Tarkington, of Boyle County, born March 30, 1844, and to them have been born William T. (deceased), Catherine B., Georgia M., James L. (deceased), and Allen S. For the past eleven years Mr. Edelen has been engaged as a commercial traveler as the general southwestern agent of C. Buell & Son, of Waterville, N. Y., having supervision of the territory south of the Ohio River. He is com-

fortably and pleasantly located on a small farm of well improved and productive land. His surroundings are agreeable and his hospitality generous. He is a member of the Southern Presbyterian Church, also of the K. of H. and a conservative Democrat.

DELOUVOIS L. EDRINGTON was born in Adair County, June 11, 1844, the fourth of twelve children born to Benjamin and Emily (Settle) Edrington, natives of Adair County and of English descent. Benjamin Edrington was born February 27, 1812, and taught several years in the common schools. He married, at about the age of twenty-three years, and soon after bought a partially improved farm near Cane Valley, Adair County, on which he resided two or three years, when he sold out and bought a farm on the Green River, in the same county, near Wagoner's Bend. After a few years he sold this place also and bought another near Columbia, remaining until about 1841, when he left the place and removed to Livingston County, Mo., where he remained some two years and then removed to his farm in Adair County. Here he remained until 1850, when he sold the farm and went back to Livingston County, Mo., settling on a farm he had bought some years before, engaged in agricultural pursuits and, for two years, also in general merchandise until 1863, when he sold out and moved to Plymouth, Hancock County, Ill., where he engaged in merchandising for nearly two years. In 1865 he returned to Adair County, Ky., and bought a farm near Cane Valley, upon which he resided until his death, May 23, 1880. His father, Thomas Edrington, was born in South Carolina, March 2, 1778. When a young man he came to Adair County and settled near Wagoner's Bend, where he bought over 1,000 acres of wild land, improved a farm upon which he resided until his death, April 16, 1859. Mrs. Emily (Settle) Edrington was born September 16, 1817, and died August 1, 1869. Her father, Benjamin Settle, was born in Virginia and was one of the pioneers of Adair County, Ky., owning a large farm some 2,000 acres on the Green River near Plum Point, upon which he resided until his death. Delouvois L. Edrington received a good common-school and academic education in youth, including a thorough Latin course. In June, 1861, he enlisted in Company E, First Missouri Volunteer Infantry (Confederate), and served until February, 1862, when he was taken prisoner at Springfield, Mo., and was soon after paroled and returned home. He participated in the battles of Carthage, Mo.; Wilson's Creek, Mo.; Dry Wood and Lexington, Mo. After his return from the army he farmed one year and in April, 1863, started for California in company with some fifty or sixty emigrants, who accomplished the entire journey across the plains with an ox team, arriving in California in September. From Sacramento he went to Virginia City, Nev., where he was engaged in mining for a short time; thence he went to Dayton, Nev., where he was employed as chemist for a quartz mining company for nearly one year and a half. He then went to San Francisco and from there returned to his father's home in Plymouth, Ill. In the fall of 1865 he went to St. Louis, Mo., where he took a regular commercial course. The next year he opened a general store at Cane Valley, where he remained two years longer. In 1870 he removed his stock to Rolla, where he continued the business for some five years. In 1875 he sold the stock and bought a farm of 140 acres on Casey Creek, on a part of which the village of Rolla has since been built. He has here been successfully engaged in stock raising and farming, and for a time made the culture of tobacco a specialty, but has recently given more attention to fine stock and corn. For several years he was deputy county clerk of Adair County and is at present postmaster at Rolla. He was married, December 24, 1869, to Miss Sallie F. McWhorter, a native of Adair County, born January 28, 1850. Three children have blessed their union, as follows: Afton C., born September 18, 1870; Emma E., born August 25, 1872, and Albert B., born March 7, 1876. Mr. and Mrs. Edrington have been for many years members of the Christian Church, in which he has officiated as a deacon for many years. He is also a bright member of the Masonic fraternity, having been Worthy Master of his lodge for several years, and at present is secretary. Politically he is a Democrat.

IDA EDWARDS, the subject of this sketch, is a daughter of Henry D. and Sallie C. (Payne) Edwards, parents of two daughters. Henry D. Edwards was born in Virginia, was brought to Marion County when a child and received his education at St. Mary's College. By self application and industry he became one of the finest scholars in his part of the county, and followed teaching for fifteen or twenty years. He was married December, 1849, after which he located on the banks of Rolling Fork, three and one-half miles west of Raywick, on a farm of 600 acres, one-half of which is under cultivation and improved with a large frame residence. He also owned many slaves and about 1,000 acres in La Rue County, which

he disposed of before his death, as well as other property. He lost his parents when a child, after which he labored hard at the carpenter's trade, having been reared by a Mr. McElroy, and began life penniless. He died December 4, 1883, aged ninety years. He was a son of Thomas Edwards, who married Elizabeth Dent, both natives of Virginia, and among the first settlers of Marion County. Thomas Edwards was a carpenter by trade and of English descent. Sallie C. (Payne) Edwards was born in Marion County, near Raywick, February 20, 1821. She was a daughter of Richard and Elizabeth (Carter) Payne, natives of Virginia, and among the first settlers of Marion County. Mr. Payne, of English origin, was a large farmer and slave-holder, and followed carpentering. He died July 2, 1837, at the age of fifty years.

WILLIAM O. EDWARDS was born April 9, 1851. He is a son of James F. and Martha (Walston) Edwards. The former was born in Marion County in 1813; his wife, Martha, whom he married in 1844, died in 1862, at the age of forty years; she was the mother of three sons and four daughters, William O. being the third child. James Edwards, after the death of his first wife, married Miss Eliza Bottom. She died in 1882, and two years later he married Mrs. Elizabeth Dye, who is yet (1886) living. Josiah Edwards, the father of James F., was a native of St. Mary's County, Md. While he was yet a lad his father (who was also named Josiah) removed from Maryland and located in Marion County. His family consisted of eight children: Elkamah, Josiah, John, Stouton, Joseph, Hezekiah, Henry and Ann (Sharp). William O. Edwards, a native of Boyle County, from his tenth to his eighteenth year was a student in Harmonia College at Perryville, Ky. After leaving school he chose the profession of teaching, which he followed for eleven years, and since 1880 has been engaged in farming. He is an official member of the Methodist Episcopal Church South. His wife, Fannie L., whom he married June 19, 1879, is a daughter of Nathan W. and Keziah (Brand) Pipes, the former of Scotch descent and a native of Boyle County, Ky., the latter of Scotch-German descent and born in Bourbon County. The grandfather of Nathan W. was John Pipes, of South Carolina. He came to Kentucky in 1800, and afterward married a Miss Mary Morris. They reared a family of three sons and seven daughters, one of whom was Nathaniel, the father of Nathan W. The latter is yet living, and is one of the "solid" farmers of Marion County, in which county he has for many years been a magistrate. He is a member of the Christian Church. His wife, Keziah (Brand) Pipes, is a daughter of James and Catherine (Link) Brand, of Bourbon County, Ky. The great grandparents of Mrs. Fannie Edwards were Jacob Link and Elizabeth (Creagor) Link, the former born in 1762, the latter in 1769. . Both were natives of Frederick County, Md., and of German parents. They came to Kentucky in 1797 and settled in Bourbon County, where they reared a family of five sons and four daughters, among whom was Catherine Link, who married James Brand. He died in Washington County, Ky., in 1847. His widow survives, aged eighty-nine years. She resides in Marion County, and is the mother of nine children, of whom Mrs. Keziah Pipes is the sixth. Dr. Richard Brand, the father of James Brand, was a native of Maryland. He came to Kentucky, and located near Paris, in Bourbon County, in 1797. Mrs. Fannie Edwards, the wife of William O. Edwards, and her mother are members of the Methodist Episcopal Church South.

SAMUEL F. EMBRY was born in Madison County, Ky., in 1837, and is a son of Thomas H. and Cassandra (Fox) Embry. Thomas H. was also born in Madison County, and was a farmer and stock raiser, and was thrice married, first to Cassandra Fox, who bore him five sons and three daughters; his second marriage was with the widow Howard, and to this union one child was born; his third wife was the widow Kennedy, by whom he was the father of one son and one daughter. Samuel F. Embry was first a merchant at Richmond, Ky., which pursuit he followed twelve years, when he removed to Garrard County, and owns 200 acres of land near Lancaster, on which he now lives and is cultivating. He was married in 1871 to Miss Jennie Simpson, and their union has been blessed with two sons: Robert and William. Mr. Embry is a member of the Christian Church, and in politics is a Democrat.

JOHN JEFFERSON EPPERSON, a son of William Epperson, was born November 23, 1823. William Epperson, a native of Charlottesville, Albemarle County, Va., was born about 1772. He was a house carpenter and a fine mechanic, also a millwright. He was married to Miss Elizabeth, daughter of Francis Montgomery, who was a wealthy man and a slave owner ïn Virginia, and after he came to Kentucky, owned 2,000 acres of land in Adair County and many slaves. He was the father of three daughters and five sons, all of whom were in fine financial circumstances. In 1804 William Epperson came

with his father-in-law to Adair County, Ky., and became the owner of 1,000 acres of land. He built a mill on Russell Creek in 1819—to grind wheat and corn—which mill is still standing and being run regularly. He built a saw-mill also on Russell Creek in 1834. Although he owned a large body of land, he turned his entire attention to milling, having his farm cultivated by his sons and his slaves. His estate at his death, August 27, 1852, was worth $18,000, and his religious faith was first with the Baptist Church, afterward with the Christian Church. His wife, whose death occurred February 24, 1842, in the sixty-second year of her age, was also first a Baptist and afterward a member of the Christian Church. John Epperson, grandfather of John J. Epperson, was also a Virginian, whose remains lie buried in Lincoln County, Ky., with those of his wife. The Epperson family are of English origin. John J. Epperson, a native of Adair County, worked for his father until nineteen years of age. December 22, 1842, he married Miss Elizabeth, daughter of Samuel and Sarah (Hurt) Morris, the former a native of New Jersey, the latter of Virginia. He received a tract of 130 acres from his father, only a part of which was cleared, and on which there were no buildings. He now has 246 acres in the home farm, and owns 200 acres in two other tracts. His farm of 246 acres is a part of the limestone belt of country, a very fertile tract, and is situated on Russell Creek. To Mr. and Mrs. Epperson have been born seven children: Patrick Henry, Mary Priscilla, wife of W. H. Bryan; Charles Francis, Thomas Jefferson, Sarah Elizabeth, wife of Junius B. Montgomery; Virgil McKnight and Albert. Charles Francis Epperson was married to Miss Josephine Rowe, and they are the parents of two sons; Thomas J. Epperson is married to Miss Ann Mariah Rice, and they are the parents of two daughters; Mary P. Bryan lives in Prairie City, Iowa, the mother of two sons and a daughter— her oldest son is now dead; Sarah E. Montgomery lives in Adair County, the mother of one son; Patrick Henry Epperson enlisted in Company A, Third Kentucky Infantry, Federal service, in 1861, and after participating in one skirmish, took the measles at Lexington which so seriously injured his health that he was dismissed from the service in June, 1862, and received an honorable discharge. Although he had been a remarkably stout and robust young man before he entered the service, after he returned home, his health declined so rapidly that his death occurred August 31, 1862, after an illness of six weeks, of consumption, the result of measles. He was born March 27, 1844. J. J. Epperson has been, since the war, Democratic in politics, but before that event was a Whig.

DR. WILLIAM R. EVANS, a native of Mecklenburg County, Va., was born September 11, 1826, and is a son of Ludwell and Jane B. (Hardy) Evans, who came to Nicholas County, Ky., the same year. In 1833 they moved to Mercer County, where Ludwell Evans died in 1874, aged eighty-three years, his wife having died several years previously, aged sixty-three. Ludwell and his wife were of Welsh and English descent, respectively. At the age of fifteen William R. Evans, having completed the courses commonly taught in the schools in the neighborhood of father's farm, entered Bacon College at Harrodsburg, Ky. Having pursued the curriculum course of that institution for two or three years, he began to read medicine with Drs. Scales and McBrayer of Harrodsburg. He was a graduate from the medical department of the University of Louisville in 1850 and the following year was appointed assistant demonstrator of anatomy for the same institution and as such, with slight intermissions, served until the spring of 1855, also acting as private assistant to S. D. Gross, professor of surgery. He followed his profession in the interior of the State for awhile, and in the winter of 1862, went to Philadelphia, and further pursued his studies under Prof. Samuel D. Gross. He resumed active practice at Louisville, but failing health led to his purchasing a farm in the vicinity of Danville, where he combined agriculture with his medical practice. The Doctor was a charter member of the State Medical Society, is a member of the Boyle County Association, and has served repeatedly as delegate to the American Medical Association. He was married, October 18, 1855, to Mary J. Lee Forsythe, of Mercer County, daughter of Andrew and Narcissa (McAfee) Forsythe (see sketch of the Forsythe family elsewhere). Four children have been born to the Doctor and his wife, viz.: Jennie Lee (now Mrs. J. S. Robinson), William L., Mary R. (now Mrs. C. T. Worthington) and Andrew F. The family are members of the Christian Church. In 1876 Dr. Evans removed to the city of Danville, his present place of residence, in order to avail himself of its superior educational advantages for his children.

G. W. EVANS was born June 7, 1827, and is a son of Joseph and Nancy (Hite) Evans, the former a native of Virginia, who came to Kentucky when young. His marriage with Miss Hite resulted in the birth of ten sons and three daughters. With Mrs. Evans, he was a member of the Christian Church and in politics was a Democrat. He has been a farmer all his life and died at the age of sixty-five years. George W. Evans was born in Garrard County, where he owns, resides upon and cultivates a farm of 145 acres. He is a member of the Christian Church, is a Democrat in politics, and is yet unmarried.

WALTER M. EVANS, Esq., was born July 22, 1828. His father, John Evans, was born in 1800, near Bloomfield, was a wagonwright by vocation, and died of cholera in 1833. He was the son of James Evans, a Virginian, and a pioneer of Kentucky. John Evans espoused in marriage Mary, daughter of Zach. Wilkinson, of Nelson County. She was born in 1802, and died of cholera at the time of her husband's death. From their union sprang Albert, John L., Melissa (Forman), Walter M., Redman and Rebecca (Blackmore). On May 10, 1853, Walter M. was united in the bonds of matrimony to Miss Sarah L., daughter of Andrew and Nancy (McCormick) Oliphant, of Nelson County (born in Washington County, Ohio April 24, 1834), and to them have been born Dr. Andrew H., Willie P. (deceased), M. Fannie, Walter Lee, Ewing Oliphant, Edward Spencer and Nancy McCormick. In 1882 Walter M. Evans was elected magistrate and member of the court of claims of Nelson, his native county, and has always taken an active interest in public improvements, especially in thoroughly turnpiking the county roads. Having been left on orphan in early childhood, he had a hard time in youth; he was hard pressed and taxed for the profits of others, by severe labor and unremitting toil. By his own exertions he obtained a limited education, and, appreciating its advantages, is endeavoring to furnish better facilities for his children. Squire Evans is a farmer, owning 240 acres of productive and well improved land on Cox's Creek. In religion he is a Baptist and in politics a Democrat.

WM. F. EVANS was born January 31, 1831, in Pulaski County, Ky., a son of Josiah and Keziah (Ford) Evans, to whom three sons and three daughters were born: Paulina, John H., Ellen, Elizabeth, Geo. W. and William F. Josiah Evans was born in North Carolina, and when a child of three years was brought by his parents to Pulaski County, Ky., where he grew to manhood and became an extensive farmer and slave owner. He served as sheriff for twenty years and died in 1836 at the age of forty-nine. He was a son of John Evans, who was born and reared in North Carolina, was a captain in the war of 1812, and was engaged in the battle of New Orleans. His ancestors came from Wales. Mrs. Keziah (Ford) Evans was born in Culpeper County, Va., a daughter of Zachariah Ford, who came to Pulaski County about 1815, and was an extensive farmer and slaveholder on the Cumberland River. William F. Evans was raised on a farm and educated in the Western Military Institute, and taught for a short time. When a child of ten years with his mother he went to Missouri and lived in the first house ever built in St. Joseph; five years later returned to Lincoln County, Ky. In 1866 he located on 400 acres of fine land one mile west of Danville, and also owns 310 in Lincoln County. He has dealt largely in stock, principally cattle, of which he is a large feeder. In July, 1852, he was united in marriage to Josephine Graham, daughter of R. W. and Susan A. (Owsley) Graham. To this union two children have been born: Rob. G. and Jennie (now the wife of M. J. Farris). Mr. Evans and wife are members of the Baptist Church. His first presidential vote was cast for Gen. Scott, but he is now a Democrat.

JOHN B. EVANS, M. D., was born September 18, 1836. His father, Dr. Isaac G. Evans, was a native of Nelson County, was educated in Virginia, and afterward taught school and studied medicine, and for many years practiced in connection with agricultural pursuits in Nelson County. He was a member of the Methodist Episcopal Church, and was one of the most efficient Sunday-school workers in that portion of the State. He married Miss Sallie, a daughter of John Bartley of Mercer County, Ky. They were the parents of five sons and five daughters, eight of whom are now living, Dr. John B. being the eldest; after him Samuel P., James E., Rhoda, Elijah, Augusta, Mary B., and William. Dr. I. G. Evans was born March 9, 1806, and died January 28, 1875. His father, Edward Evans, was of English parentage, and a native of Virginia. He came to Kentucky among the early settlers of Nelson County, and located near Bardstown, where he died in 1840, aged upward of ninety years. Dr. John B. Evans, a native of Nelson County, finished his literary course of school training in the Bardstown High School, and soon after began to read medicine with Dr. William Hickman of Bardstown, and graduated from the Medical University of Louisville in 1860, after which he was for one year an assistant in the State Dispensary at Louisville. He then located in Mar-

ion County, where he practiced his profession one year, and in 1862 joined the Confederate States Army as a private soldier in Capt. Logan's company of Col. Grigsby's command, which was attached to the First Confederate States Cavalry under Gen. Wheeler. He was soon after commissioned surgeon of the command with the rank of major, and in that capacity served until his capture at Bridgeport, Ala., during Wheeler's raid into Tennessee. He accompanied Joe E. Johnston through Georgia to Atlanta, then was with Gen. Wheeler's command again until after the battles of Savannah and Smithville, after which he was attached to the escort of President Davis and cabinet until the fall of the Confederacy and the capture of its President. James Evans, a brother of Dr. John B. served through the war in the command of Gen. John A. Morgan. After the war the Doctor returned to his home in Marion County, where he has for more than a quarter of a century followed successfully the practice of his profession, in connection with the superintendency of the working of a farm that he owns. He was married, October 24, 1867, to Mary E., daughter of Moses and Susan (Simpson) Beard. To this union have been born two sons, William and Samuel; and five daughters, Susan, Sallie, Lizzie, Cordelia and Rhoda. Mrs. Mary E. (Beard) Evans was born October 17, 1846. Her parents were of Irish lineage and natives of Kentucky. The Doctor and his wife are members of the Methodist Church, in which he holds the office of steward, and superintendent of Sunday-school. He is a Royal Arch Mason of J. L. Rawlings Chapter, No. 122, and his political views are Democratic. He is a patron of church and school, especially of the Sunday-school, in which he is a most willing and untiring worker.

G. W. EVANS, M. D., was born February 5, 1843, in Clark County, Ky., and is a son of Dr. Peter and Lettie (Quisenbury) Evans, to whom three sons and one daughter were born: James E., Peter E., Mary and G. W. Dr. Peter Evans was born in Clark County in October, 1808; his wife in September, 1814, in the same county. The Doctor practiced his profession over fifty-five years, perhaps longer than any man ever practiced in the State, and died in 1884. He was a son of Peter Evans, who was born in Culpeper County, Va.; came to Kentucky about 1785, and became a wealthy farmer and owner of a large family of slaves. He married a Mrs. Baker, whose maiden name was Combs. She had given birth to two children by her first husband, and had five sons and one daughter by her second. Mr. Evans died in 1845, and was in turn a son of Peter Evans, who was born in Scotland, and who came to America before the war for independence, in which he took part as captain. The family still have possession of his equipage. He settled in Culpeper County, Va., and became a prosperous planter. The Evans family were all stanch Whigs up to 1860. They held to the Methodist Episcopal faith, but Dr. Peter Evans became a Baptist. Mrs. Lettie (Quisenbury) Evans was a daughter of Rev. James Quisenbury, who was a Baptist minister, and who had married two women, each giving him birth to twelve children, making him father of twenty-four children. He was of French descent, and was an early settler in Clark County. Dr. G. W. Evans was raised on a farm, and received but a common-school education. At nineteen he began the study of medicine with his father, and in 1865 graduated from Jefferson Medical College, Penn. He served in the United States service at Fortress Monroe for five months, and then came to Madison County and located at White Hall, where he established a large and lucrative practice. In 1881 he located in Richmond and continued his practice. The Doctor is a member of State and county medical associations, and is also president of the board of examiners for the United States Pension Department. He was united in marriage, May 30, 1867, to Nannie Chenault, of Madison County, daughter of Waller and Talitha (Harris) Chenault. To this union nine children were born: Waller (deceased); George; Lettie (deceased); Peter (deceased); Miller (deceased); Leslie; Joseph; Overton and Mary. The Doctor and wife are members of the Baptist Church; and he is a member of the F. & A. M. His first presidential vote was for Seymour.

JOHN OWSLEY EVANS was born September 18, 1854, in Lincoln County, Ky., and in 1879 removed to Boyle County, where he has since resided. His father, George W. Evans, was born and reared in Pulaski County, Ky.; was an extensive farmer; lost thirty slaves by the late war, and is now living in Lincoln County. He is the son of Josiah Evans, a native of Virginia, who was a farmer, also sheriff of Pulaski County, and who married Keziah Crawford, of Wayne County, their offspring being John; Paulina (Smith); Ellen (Gillmore); George W.; William F. and Elizabeth (Farris). After his death his widow married Mr. Beaty, and their children were Joseph and Jennie (Gillmore). George W. Evans married Mary, daughter of John and Jennie (Shanks) Owsley, of

Lincoln County, and from their union sprang John O., Ellen (Hutchings), Henry W., Mattie (James), George W., Jr., and Jennie. June 21, 1875, John O. Evans married Ellen, daughter of Joseph and Martha (Owsley) McAlister, of Lincoln County (born in March, 1856), and to them have been born Annie May and Harry Moore. Mr. Evans was engaged in merchandising in Standford; he is now a farmer and stock trader, and owns 150 acres of productive and well improved land. In church relations he is a Baptist, and in politics is identified with the Democratic party.

J. C. FALES, professor in Centre College at Danville, was born December 30, 1836, in Thomaston, Me., and is a son of B. and Nancy (King) Fales, who were natives of Maine and Nantucket Island, respectively, and to whom two sons and two daughters were born. Prof. Fales' father was an attorney, served as judge in Maine and was a descendant of James Fales, who came from Chester, England, in 1700. The Professor grew up in his native village, where he enjoyed the privileges of the common schools and academy; received his collegiate education in New England. In 1858 he removed to Lebanon, Ky., where he was employed in teaching for ten years, and then was engaged in New Albany until 1872, when he was elected to the chair of natural sciences in Centre College at Danville, which he has ably filled. The Professor was married to Miss Cleland, of Lebanon, Ky., in 1862. She was a daughter of Rev. T. H. Cleland, D. D., and she died in 1869. The Professor's second marriage was in 1876 to Amanda C. Helm, of Danville, a daughter of Joseph Helm. The issue from this marriage was Elizabeth A. and Margaret C. Fales.

JOSIAH E. FARRIS, farmer and miller of Stanford Precinct in Lincoln County, was born in 1844 and is the son of William and Elizabeth (Evans) Farris. His grandparents, William and Susan Ann (Owsley) Farris, came to Lincoln County, Ky., in an early day and reared a family of seven children, viz.: Henry, Cyrus W., E. B. Farris, James W., John, Susan (Gilmore) and William Farris. The last-named was born in Lincoln County, where he grew to maturity and married Elizabeth Evans. He conducted a hotel business for many years in Crab Orchard, after which he removed to Somerset, in Pulaski County, where he died in 1850. His wife was a daughter of Josiah and Keziah Evans, and who died soon after the death of her husband. They left a family of three sons: Henry Clay, Josiah E. and Maurice

Farris, all of whom are living. Josiah E. was chiefly reared in Pulaski County, Ky., returning to Lincoln County in his young manhood, and has engaged in agricultural pursuits with which he combined the milling business, being the proprietor of the Buffalo mills, near Stanford. He married in 1867 Miss Alice, daughter of Robert G. and Susan A. Graham, of Lincoln County. They have been blessed with three children, viz.: Elizabeth, Robert G. and Maurice J. Farris.

ELIJAH P. FAULCONER was born, February 22, 1844, near Lexington, Ky., where he was reared until sixteen years of age, when he removed with his parents to Boyle County, locating four miles and a half north of Danville, where he has since resided. His father, Joseph Faulconer, a native of Virginia, was born in 1801, and removed with his parents in boyhood to Fayette County, Ky., where he engaged in farming. By the late war he lost twenty-five slaves. He died February 25, 1880. He was the son of Nelson Faulconer, of Virginia, who died of cholera in 1833, leaving a family consisting of Joseph, Ann (Barton) and Susan (Offutt). Joseph Faulconer espoused Julia Nichols, of Woodford County (born 1808, died 1879), and to them were born Fannie (Dolan), Thomas (deceased), Margaret (Taylor), Henry (deceased), Mary (Spears), Joseph, Nannie (McCarley) and Elijah P. October 27, 1875, Elijah P. was united in marriage to Miss Effie C., daughter of Pleasant J. and Julia F. (Hill) Potter, of Bowling Green, Ky., (born February 28, 1852,) and their union has been blessed by the birth of three children, viz.: Pleasant Joseph, William Elijah and Pearl Potter. Mr. Faulconer obtained an education at the Kentucky University at Harrodsburg, Bethel College in Scott County and Transylvania University at Lexington. He is a farmer and is engaged in raising trotting horses, jacks and the purest grade of Berkshire hogs. He owns about thirty head of trotting breed horses, and receives trotting stock from distant parts for purposes of propagation. He owns 300 acres of very productive and well improved land, which he successfully cultivates in hemp, corn, wheat, barley and other crops, having raised 82,000 pounds of hemp last year. Mr. Faulconer is a member of the Christian Church, and in politics is identified with the Democratic party. He is also a member of the Masonic fraternity.

ARMSTEAD M. FELAND is a representative of one of the pioneer families of Kentucky. His grandfather, James Feland, came to Kentucky from Virginia at a very early day, and in company with the family

of a Mr. Robison, consisting of the parents and four small children. On their journey Robison was killed by Indians, and Mr. Feland took upon himself the care and protection of the family. The youngest of these four children was a daughter named Isabella, who, when about sixteen years old, proved her gratitude to her former benefactor by becoming his wife. Mr. Feland, for a short time, was a resident of the Harrod's Station, but after the danger from Indian depredations had subsided, he settled a tract of land about three miles north from the site of Logan's Fort, being the land now occupied and owned by A. M. Feland. James Feland became an extensive farmer and land owner, and died in 1819. He reared three sons: Thomas, James and William; the wife, Isabella, dying soon after the birth of the latter. James Feland, the second of these sons, and father of our subject, was born on the above named farm in 1793; married Sallie Milner, daughter of Armstead Milner, who was a neighboring farmer. Sallie Milner was born in 1796 in Lincoln County, and died in 1883. James and Sallie Feland had but two children: Isabella (deceased wife of W. M. Hay) and A. M. Feland. James served as a soldier in the war of 1812, under Dick Johnson, and participated in the battle of the Thames, where he was severely wounded. He died in Lincoln County in 1828. A. M. Feland was born in 1820, and has devoted his life to farming and stock raising, in which he has been successful. He is in politics a Democrat, but has not been in public life, save a service of three years as sheriff of Lincoln County. Mr. Feland has five sons: William B., a miner of Colorado; Albert, a farmer; F. R., a lawyer and an editor at Lawrenceburg, Ky.; Dr. John Morgan, at Bath County, Ky., and A. M., aged seven, at home. Mr. Feland is an honored member of the Masonic fraternity.

REV. DAVID FENNESSY, C. R., president of St. Mary's College and one of the leading educators of Kentucky, was born November 1, 1841, in Clonmel, Ireland, a son of David and Catherine (Ryan) Fennessy, who emigrated and settled in Ontario, Canada, in 1842. David Fennessy was a clerk in a flouring-mill in Ireland, and after his settlement in Canada became a farmer. He had ten children born to him. He died in Guelph, Canada, in March, 1876, at the ripe age of eighty-three years, after which his wife came to St. Mary's, Marion Co., Ky., where she died July 16, 1878, at seventy-nine years of age. David Fennessy, Sr., was a son of John Fennessy, a blacksmith in Ireland. Catherine (Ryan) Fennessy was a daughter of William Ryan, of Ireland. Rev. David Fennessy was reared on a farm till ten years of age; from 1851 to 1857 lived in the town of Guelph, where he received his early education. In September, 1850, entered St. Michael's College, Clover Hill, Toronto, Canada, from which he graduated in June, 1861; he then commenced theological studies at Grand Seminary, Montreal, and Assumption College, near that city, after which he attended St. Jerome's College, Ontario; here he entered the congregation of the Resurrection, and was ordained priest April 25, 1867. He remained in the latter college as a teacher till in July, 1869, when he went to Rome and studied for two years. In August, 1871, he was sent to St. Mary's College, Marion County, as vice-president. In December, 1873, at the resignation of Father Elena, D. D., as president, Rev. David Fennessy became president of the college.

JOHN FENTON was born July 17, 1819, in New York City, where he was reared. In 1840 he removed to Louisville, Ky., engaging in boot and shoemaking, and in 1844 located in Nelson County, where he engaged in merchandising, and as toll-gate keeper on the L. & B. pike. In 1859 he removed to Bates County, Mo., where he engaged in farming, and where he now owns 225 acres of well improved and productive land. In 1861 he enlisted in the Sixth Kentucky Federal Cavalry, and served as quartermaster sergent for nearly one year, when he was discharged on account of his eyesight. His father, John Fenton, Sr., a native of New York City, was a soldier in the war of 1812, and died in 1834, aged fifty-five years. He was the son of Peter Fenton, a native of Scotland and a Revolutionary soldier. His children were David, Robert, John (who served with their father in the Revolution), Frederick, Peter, Andrew and George. All seven sons served with their father in the war of 1812. John, Sr., married Lucretia Truce of Albany, N. Y., and their offspring are Mary A. (Ringgold), David (a soldier in the Mexican war), John, Abigail (Smith), Robert, and Lucretia (married to William Bishop, who was killed in the late war). John Fenton has been thrice married; first, March 1, 1840, in Philadelphia, to Miss Mary A., daughter of John Hulfish, of Philadelphia (born in 1810, died in 1846), and to them were born David R., who served four years in the Federal Army, and Emma F. (Deacon). In 1846 Mr. Fenton moved to Louisville and shortly after to Nelson County,

where he engaged in merchandising. His second marriage was in 1848 to Miss Parmelia Ball, of Nelson County (died in 1856), and their children are John, James and Robert. Mr. Fenton's third marriage was February 2, 1858, to Miss Mary J., daughter of Griffin and Lutitia (Montgomery) Crumes, of Nelson County (born July 2, 1829), and to their union were born Philip C., Charles F. and George W. Mr. Fenton has been a Mason and an Odd Fellow, and in politics he is a Republican. Mrs. Emma F. Deacon was born October 21, 1847, and on her twenty-first birthday was married to Nathaniel W. Deacon, of Nelson County (born January 23, 1842, died February 16, 1882), and to them were born Minnie and Orvill Woods.

JESSE P. FIDLER was born in Marion County October 14, 1844. His father, Samuel Fidler, was born in Bullitt County in 1810. In 1838 he married Minerva, daughter of John and Mary (Forsythe) Lawrence, the former a Virginian, and the latter a native of Maryland. To Samuel Fidler and his wife Minerva were born eight children: James M., William H., Jesse P., Napoleon F., Nannie E. (Johnston), John F., Newton F. and Mollie F. Mrs. Fidler is living, aged sixty-six years. Samuel Fidler was during his lifetime engaged in farming, merchandise and lumber trade; he died in 1861. His father, Samuel Fidler, Sr., was a resident of Bullitt County, where he died in 1812; his wife was a Miss Susan Fidler. After the death of her husband, Samuel, she married William Richeson, of Boyle County. John Lawrence, the maternal grandfather of Jesse P., was a farmer and trader. He came from Virginia and settled near Stanford, Ky., at an early period of the State's history. Jesse P. Fidler was educated in the common schools of his native county, and at the age of seventeen entered the Federal Army, enlisting in Company K of the Sixth Kentucky Volunteer Cavalry. He rose through merit to the rank of first lieutenant, and served as regimental commissary to the Sixth Cavalry until July 20, 1865. With his command he participated in many engagements, most notably those of Big Harpeth, Brentwood, and the fight with Bragg's troops on Cumberland Mountain on the 4th of July, 1863. He was also on the Wilson raid, fought Jackson at Tuscaloosa, and assisted in the capture of that town; afterward was in the engagement with Gen. Pillow at Sipsey Swamp on Blackwater River, and next at Chickamauga; was frequently engaged against Gen. Wheeler's forces in Broomtown Valley. James M., a brother of

Jesse P., held the rank of first lieutenant in the Tenth Kentucky Infantry. He was promoted to a captaincy and was provost-marshal of the Fourth Congressional District of Kentucky. He was an active Republican, and died October, 1875. William H., another brother, held the rank of major in the Sixth Kentucky Cavalry, for which regiment he recruited a company. He was captured near the Tombigbee River after being cut off from his command while fighting Gen. Pillow. He attempted to reach the Federal lines, but the enemy pursued and caught him with bloodhounds. He remained a prisoner for a short time, when he was exchanged at Vicksburg. He was soon after put in command of a number of paroled prisoners, and with 1,800 others was drowned in the Sultana disaster on April 27, 1865. Jesse P. Fidler after the war engaged in farming in Marion County, which he has followed successfully up to the present time, with the exception of the years 1867–85, which he spent in the United States revenue department as storekeeper and gauger. He was married on the 11th of November, 1873, to Miss Lou Drye, of Marion County, daughter of Matthew and Kizzie (Batsell) Drye. To this marriage were born three children, all of whom died in infancy. Mr. and Mrs. Fidler are members of the church, she of the Christian, while the captain holds the Baptist faith. Politically he is a Republican, and takes a lively interest in the politics of the day.

WILLIAM M. FIELDS was born November 10, 1815, about one mile northwest of Danville, Ky. He is a son of Henry and Susan (Ripperdam) Fields, to whom six sons and four daughters were born: Sarah C., Mary, Susan R., Eliza A., William M., Liberty B., Henry R., Frederick, Smith M. and John, who died in infancy. Henry, the father of William M., was born in Boyle County in 1790; his wife in 1788. He became an extensive farmer and stock raiser, and owned a large family of slaves. In politics he was a Whig, in religion a Presbyterian; died in 1844, and was a son of William Fields, who was born in Armagh, Ireland, in 1746. He was at the wharf when the captain of a ship, that was about to sail for America, asked him if he wished to go; he stepped aboard the ship, and when he landed in Philadelphia the captain took him to a hatter where he received employment. Thence he removed to Virginia, where he formed the acquaintance of Daniel Boone, and with whom he came to Kentucky and entered 1,400 acres of land, northwest of Danville, where he re-

mained until his death. He planted and raised the first corn ever raised in central Kentucky, perhaps in the State. He had many encounters with the Indians; was in the battle of Blue Lick, also battle of Pickaway, Ohio; was with Gen. Clarke in Ohio, occupied for several years the fort at Harrodsburg, Ky. He married a Mrs. Wright, whose husband had been killed by Indians; her maiden name was Mary Miller. To this second marriage were born five children: James, Daniel, Henry, John and Mary. William, in turn, was a son of Daniel Fields, of Ireland. After William came to America he never returned or even heard from his parents. The mother of William M. lived to be seventy-four years old, and was a daughter of Frederick and Sarah (Chiticks) Ripperdam, who were born in Germany, immigrated and settled first in Pennsylvania or Maryland, and were among the earliest settlers of Kentucky, first to Boonesboro Fort, where one child was born; they had several encounters with the Indians. One trip winter came on, and the party remained in the mountains till spring, when they proceeded on their journey. They left Fort Boonesboro, and located in what is now Boyle County, about 1782. He and brother had a bloody encounter with the Indians, when his brother fell, and a desperate fight ensued over the body, in which he came out victor. He was said to be very fleet on foot, and died about 1825, aged about eighty-five years; his wife was a few years his senior. They were Presbyterians in religion. William M. was reared on a farm, and received a good English education; at the age of seventeen entered a store as salesman; at the age of twenty he purchased a stock of goods and commenced business on his own account. In 1854 traded for a hotel which he kept until it burned down in 1860, when he re-entered the goods business. In April, 1836, he was united in marriage to Ann Thorn, a daughter of William and Anna (Gorthorp) Thorn, who immigrated from Yorkshire, England, in 1816, and settled in Lexington with a brother. William Thorn was a manufacturer both in England and the United States, and later in life located in Boyle County, Ky. The issue of this union of William M. was twelve children: Henry R., Elizabeth D. Joffrian, Susan R. Joffrian (two latter live in Louisiana), L. B., William M., Jr., John (deceased), Theodore T., Anna F., Carrie B., Alice, Ralph and Everiste (deceased). Mr. and Mrs. Fields were members of the Methodist Episcopal Church. She died in 1875. He was formerly a member of the I. O. O. F.; cast his first presidential vote for Gen. Harrison. Since the war he has been a Democrat. His sons, L. B. and William M., are breeders of fine running and trotting stock, and also continue the mercantile business.

JOSHUA M. FIELDS was born July 20, 1823, in the house where he now resides in Mercer (now Boyle) County. His father, James Fields, a native of Mercer County, was born in 1783, was a soldier under Gen. Hopkins in the war of 1812, was a farmer and lost ten slaves as a result of the late war, and died in 1865. He was the son of William Fields, a native of Ireland, who learned the hatter's trade in Philadelphia, was a soldier in the Revolutionary war, a real pioneer and Indian fighter in Kentucky, a member of Capt. Harrod's company, a farmer and slave owner, settled the place where Joshua M. now lives, and died about 1835. He married a Mrs. Wright, and their offspring were James, Daniel, Henry, and Mrs. William Childs. James married Sarah, daughter of Frederick Ripperdam, of Mercer County (born in 1781, in the fort at Boonesboro, died in 1863) and to them were born William, Mary (deceased), Jeremiah (deceased), James, Joshua M., Frederick R., Jemima (deceased) and Jefferson (deceased). Joshua M. Fields has never taken upon himself the responsibilities of matrimony, and is enjoying a comfortable and quiet life. He is a farmer, owning 265 acres of fine land, in a high state of cultivation. He was formerly an old line Whig, but is now a Democrat. The maternal grandfather of Mr. Fields, Frederick Ripperdam, while in Capt. Harrod's company, had a horse shot from under him, by an Indian in battle. His children were Catherine (Shaw), John, Martha (Bragsdale), Esther (Wingate), Abram, Sarah (Fields), Susan (Fields), Mary (Wigham) and Frederick.

W. D. FINNELL was born in Woodford County, Ky., May 16, 1838, and is a son of J. W. Finnell, a native of Culpeper County, Va., who ran away from home when but fourteen years of age; came to this State, settling in Woodford County, and was twice married, and had seven children born to him, six of whom are living. W. D. Finnell was brought up on the farm; his father removed to Mercer County in 1844, and bought the farm where our subject now lives. Mr. Finnell was married in 1859 to Miss Sallie E. Irvin, by whom he has four children, viz.: Lula H., born October 13, 1861; Lida Pearl, born May 27, 1867; Leonta Dudley, born in October, 1870, and Charles H., born July, 1874. Mr. Finnell was brought up in the Democratic faith, but has taken an active part with the Granger movement.

ALBERT T. FISH was born February 18, 1859, in Rockcastle County, Ky., and is a son of A. T. and Samantha (Haley) Fish, to whom five sons and six daughters were born, and who were also born in Rockcastle County, near Mt. Vernon. The father was a son of Jesse and Eveline (Anderson) Fish, natives of Garrard and Lincoln Counties, respectively. Jesse Fish was born in 1796 and served as surveyor and judge of Rockcastle County, whence he had moved with his parents when a lad. He reared four sons and one daughter by his first marriage. His second wife was Mrs. Mary Butner, whose maiden name was Hubbard. The issue of this second marriage was one son. She had born by her former husband four sons and one daughter. Jesse Fish died in September, 1883, and was a son of Thomas Fish, who married a Givins. They came from Virginia as early as 1790, and settled in Garrard County, afterward in Rockcastle County. They reared a family of seven sons and three daughters. Thomas Fish was of English origin, in politics a Whig, and died at the ripe age of eighty-five. Mrs. Samantha Fish was a daughter of John and Matilda (Lankford) Haley, who were early settlers of Rockcastle County, and reared a large family of children. Mr. Haley was a substantial farmer and slave owner, served as a common soldier in the war of 1812 and died early in life. His widow still survives him. Albert T. Fish was reared on a farm and received such an education as the common schools of his neighborhood afforded, sufficient to enable him to teach in the common schools of Rockcastle. When he arrived at maturity he engaged in the mercantile business at Berea, where he has been successfully engaged ever since. He has the largest and most extensive business in Berea, and by his energies and industry he has made life a success. In February, 1880, he was united in marriage to Jennie Galloway, a daughter of Frank and Arminta (Kerly) Galloway, natives of Madison County. The issue from this happy union was two children, Addie and Grover C. Mrs. Fish is a member of the Reformed Church. Mr. Fish is a member of the F. & A. M., and in politics is a Democrat.

RICHARD McKENNEY FISHER was born July 16, 1848, three miles east of Danville, Boyle County; in 1849 was taken by his parents to Danville, where he grew to manhood, and in 1879 located two miles west of that city, where he has since resided. His father, Issachar P. Fisher, was born near Danville, September 5, 1806, was a farmer and stock breeder, a magistrate and member of the court of claims of Boyle County, a Presbyterian, lost forty slaves by the late war, and died September 21, 1878. He was the son of Stephen Fisher, who, in turn, was the son of Stephen Fisher, a native of Culpeper County, Va., an early settler in Kentucky, a farmer and slave owner; the younger Stephen married a Miss Bryant; their offspring were Franklin, Albert, Richard, William, Issachar P., Susan (McKinney), Maria (Pope), Mrs. Harlan and Mrs. Barbee. Issachar P.'s first wife was Miss Ann E. Shanks, and their daughter Sarah married Dr. F. T. Taylor, a native of Boyle County, but now a resident of Bastrop, La. His second wife was Virginia A., daughter of James McKenney of Lexington, Ky. (died August 26, 1877, at the age of sixty-one years), and from their union sprang Anna (Read), Virginia (deceased), Caroline (deceased), and the subject of this sketch. On October 13, 1874, Richard McKenney Fisher was married to Miss Bettie, daughter of Jacob K. and Mary J. (Garnett) Bishop of Boyle County, and to them have been born Virginia M., Mary G., Anna R. and Garnett P. Mr. Fisher is a farmer and stock breeder, owns 200 acres of productive land, well improved, and has now on hand of pure blood recorded stock, fifty head of shorthorn cattle, and seventy head of Southdown sheep. His grandfather exhibited fine imported cattle at Lexington as early as 1827, and Issachar P. imported shorthorns to Kentucky as early as 1839. Mr. Fisher is a Knight Templar, and a Democrat. Mrs. Fisher is a member of the Presbyterian Church.

THOMAS D. FLOYD was born March 20, 1824, on the place where he now lives, on Dick's River, five miles east of Danville, Boyle County. In 1852 he removed to Garrard County, and in 1866 returned to his old home in Boyle County, where he has since resided. His father, Christopher Floyd, was born in 1790 near the Forks. Church in Garrard County; was a farmer, a school-teacher, a Whig, an elder in the Christian Church, and a Union man; lost twenty slaves as the result of the late war, and died in 1866. He was the son of John Floyd, born near Chesapeake Bay, Va., removed to Garrard County, Ky., when a young man, was a farmer, a large slave-holder, a Baptist and a Whig, and died about 1840, aged eighty-eight years. He married Sarah Singleton of Garrard County, and their offspring were Thomas, Davis and Christopher. Christopher married Elizabeth, daughter of Peter and Sarah

(Davis) Belles, of Boyle County, born in 1800, died October 16, 1873, and their union resulted in the birth of Mary J. (Byers), Thomas D., John B., Marion, Robert and Henry. January 23, 1849, Thomas D. Floyd was married to Miss Mary J., daughter of John and Fanny (Rorerty) Swope, of Garrard County, born July 2, 1828, died May 13, 1882, and to them were born William H., James B. and Fannie E. Thomas D.'s maternal grandfather, Peter Belles, built a mill where the Danville and Lexington pike crosses Dick's River, previous to the year 1800. His father had constructed a mill on the same site, nearly twenty years before. It was the first mill on the river except Horine's, built above. In 1875 Thomas D. and his brother constructed the present substantial stone dam, using 103 barrels of cement on the work. He operated the water mill seventeen years with success. He now owns a sawmill, with which he has done an extensive lumber business, but is especially engaged in farming, owning 283 acres of well improved land, in a good state of cultivation. He has for twelve years been a Deacon in the Christian Church. He was a Union man and lost two slaves by the late war.

EBENEZER A. FOGLE was born August 22, 1817. His father, Robert H. Fogle, of Maryland, was born in 1788, near Fredericktown, and came to Kentucky when four years old with his parents, who settled in Nelson County. He was twice married; his first wife was a Miss Rachael Shuttlesworth, of Washington County, Ky. She died in 1830, leaving the following children: Joseph McD., Ebenezer A., Sallie A., Mary D. His second wife, to whom he was married in 1831, was a Miss Sallie Newbolt. Their children are John N., Rachael J. and Maria C. Sallie Newbolt was born October 3, 1796, and died February 1, 1860. She was a daughter of John Newbolt, of Shepardsville, Ky. Robert Fogle was a saddler and plied that trade in Lebanon for many years. He built the first house in the town of Lebanon, and was the first postmaster at that place, and was a member of its first board of trustees. Later in life he turned his attention to farming, and cultivated 170 acres that he owned near Owensboro. After the war of 1861 he removed to Lebanon, where he died February 17, 1884. He was a son of Adam and Sallie Fogle, the former German and the latter English. They came from Maryland in 1792, landed at Maysville, and soon after located in Nelson County, where Adam purchased land and engaged in farming, in connection with the distilling business, the distilling of that day being the only way of utilizing the corn product of the country. Adam Fogle reared a family of nine children, among whom was Robert H., the father of Ebenezer A. Ebenezer A. Fogle, a native of Lebanon, Marion County, resided there with his parents until attaining to the age of thirteen years, then for six years he worked on a farm, then taught school for one year before his marriage, which occurred December 27, 1838. His wife was a Miss Sallie F. Withrow, and to them were born four sons and six daughters. Those living are Elizabeth, Hope (Floyd), Nancy J., Rachael (Helm), Mary A. (Penick), Catherine (Glazebrook), and Maud, wife of Dr. Jennings, of Louisville. Sallie F. (Withrow) Fogle was born December 5, 1822. She is a daughter of William and Nancy Withrow, the former a native of Maryland, and the latter of Kentucky. Ebenezer A. Fogle, after his marriage, sold goods for some time at New Market, in Marion County. In 1840 he purchased land and farmed in connection with teaching school, and accumulated a landed estate of nearly 600 acres. Mr. and Mrs. Fogle are members of the Methodist Episcopal Church, in which he holds the office of trustee. Politically he was an old line Whig, but later a Democrat. He held the office of magistrate in Marion County for twelve years in succession, and was also assessor of property for Marion County for twelve years.

HON. JAMES M. FOGLE (deceased), one of the brightest legal luminaries of his day, was born in Lebanon, Ky., in 1820. He received his literary education at St. Mary's College, studied law with Rowan Hardin, and came to the bar at the age of twenty. In 1841 he formed a law partnership with R. H. Rowntree, which continued until his death in 1871. Mr. Fogle was an able advocate, and one of the finest orators of the Kentucky bar. He served as elector for Pierce in the year 1852, and served as presidential elector again in 1856, also represented Marion County in the State Legislature during the session of 1855–56. In May, 1846, he was married to Miss Mary, daughter of John W. Davis, of Mercer County, Ky. She died in 1859, leaving four children, viz.: John D., William P., Martha B. (Grundy), and Betty P. (Allen). His second marriage was to Miss Melissa Lawrence, who died in 1871. This union resulted in the birth of two children, both of whom died in childhood. John D. Fogle, the eldest of the sons of James M. and Mary Fogle, and one of the ablest lawyers of the present bar of Lebanon, Ky., was

born in 1847, educated at St. Mary's College, and having decided on the profession of law, entered the law office of Rowntree & Fogle, with whom he performed the usual preparatory reading. He then pursued his legal study in the Harvard University of Cambridge, Mass., and was admitted to practice in January, 1868, since which date he has been a member of the Lebanon bar. From 1868 to 1872 he served as school commissioner of his county; in 1876 was assistant elector for the State at large on the Tilden and Hendricks ticket, and in 1881 was elected to the State Senate to represent the Fifteenth Senatorial District, serving acceptably for four years. In 1866 he married Miss Fannie Beard, daughter of Dr. J. J. Beard, of Adair County. She died in 1884. Mary Fogle is their only child.

SQUIRE DANIEL FORD was born November 20, 1815, on Kentucky River, Garrard County, where he was reared to manhood; in 1836 he removed to Jessamine County, and in 1864 to Bryantsville, his present place of residence. His father, Timothy Ford, a native of Goochland County, Va., was born, September, 16, 1773; removed to Garrard County, Ky., about 1800; was a teacher, a farmer, and a slave owner, an old line Whig, a Baptist, and died November, 29, 1839. He was the son of Reuben Ford, of Virginia, born August 19, 1742, a prominent Baptist minister, and a leader in securing liberty to the Baptist denomination in Virginia, a wealthy planter and slave owner who died October 6, 1823. He was the son of William Ford. Reuben Ford married Mary Bowles, in 1770, and their offspring were Reuben, Elizabeth, Timothy, Polly (Hughs), William A., Benjamin B., Daniel, and Sally G. (Henly and Mobley). Timothy Ford married in 1793, Betsy W., daughter of Rev. William Webber (born May 21, 1876, died, August 7, 1844), and from this union sprang Reuben, William W., John B., Polly W. (England and Reynolds) Fanny B. (Smith), Eliza (Ryan), Timothy, Benjamin B., Susan B. (deceased), Daniel, and Lewis T. Daniel was first married, January, 2, 1838, to Miss Sallie Jewell, who died in 1839. On August 20, 1840, he espoused Miss Sarah H., daughter of Joseph and Martha (Overstreet) Boughn, of Jessamine County (born July 3, 1820), and to them have been born Edward S., Cordelia H. (Combs) and Josephine L. (Jennings). Mr. Ford was engaged for twenty-five years as a carpenter and builder, and eighteen years in mercantile pursuits, with encouraging success. He is now engaged in the undertaking business. He is a member of the Methodist Episcopal Church South, and in politics a Prohibitionist. He has served as magistrate and member of the court of claims of Garrard County for eight years.

THE FORSYTHE FAMILY. The first representative of this family in Kentucky, as far as ascertainable, was Matthew Forsythe, who was born in South Carolina March 5, 1769, and who came to this State with Gov. Adair, just after the surrender of Cornwallis, and settled on the farm now owned by James Forsythe in Mercer County. He served four years in the war of 1812, was in several expeditions against the Indians, and afterward devoted his time to farming and stock raising in Mercer County. About 1790 he married Jane McAfee, daughter of Robert McAfee, and to them were born Robert, Andrew, John, William, Samuel, James, Sallie, and Julia (Buford). Robert Forsythe, the eldest of these, was a soldier in the war of 1812, and afterward retired to farm life. In 1827 he married Cozzie Cardwell, and from this union sprang Jane (Alverson), Sallie (Blackwood), now deceased; Mary (McAfee), also deceased; Lucy (Crockett), Lizzie (Mullins), James M, Robert, and John L. the father of these children died in 1865, and his son Robert now owns the farm on which he was born, five miles north of Harrodsburg, and which contains 312 acres of productive land. Robert has been three times married, first in November, 1865, to Miss Pattie Trible, who gave birth to one child who died in infancy. His second marriage was in December, 1873, to Miss Sallie, daughter of S. W. Given, and to this union were born Lillie and Given. The third marriage was with Miss Lulie, daughter of Kinelus Ammellman. James M. Forsythe, Sr., was born January 18, 1809, on his present farm, four miles north of Harrodsburg, which farm consists of 460 acres of as good land as there is in Mercer County, and where he gives especial attention to stock raising, Mr. Forsythe first married Miss Lizzie M. Washbourn, a granddaughter of Judge Washbourn, and had born to him Jane (Curry), deceased, and Belle (Ralston). In 1853 Mr. Forsythe took for his second wife Mary Irvin, who has borne one child, Sam Forsythe. J. M. Forsythe, Jr., was born on the old homestead, known as Fountain Spring, January 6, 1826, and is the owner of 600 acres of fine land, devoting much attention to the rearing of race horses. He married Miss Katie Alexandra, and is the father of Howard, Cardwell, Fred, Naomi,

and little Jim. John L. Forsythe was born August 6, 1845, and was married in 1869 to Miss Sallie Woods, who has borne him six children : Nannie, Edgar, Walter, Russell, Mary and Cozzie. Mr. Forsythe resides on 425 acres of well improved land, belonging to his son Samuel, one mile from his birthplace, and is an extensive dealer in live stock. The Forsythe family are of Irish and Scotch extraction, are members of the Presbyterian Church, and in politics are Democratic.

M. LEANDER FORSYTHE, A. M., M. D., was born December 19, 1840. His father, Andrew Forsythe, was born in Mercer County, December 24, 1795. In 1820 he purchased on credit 190 acres of land, ten miles north of Harrodsburg, near Salvisa, but at his death left an estate of three farms, aggregating 590 acres, and worth $40,000, all of which he accumulated by his own management. He was married, in 1830, to Miss N. W. McAfee, a daughter of George and Anna (Hamilton) McAfee, both natives of Kentucky. Andrew Forsythe and his wife were distantly related, both being descendants of the celebrated McAfee family. To this marriage were born eight children: Mary J., wife of Dr. W. R. Evans, of Danville, Ky.; Robert B., a farmer, living near Pleasant Hill, Mo.; George M. and William S. (twins), the latter a farmer living near Paris, Mo., the former a farmer of Mercer County; M. Leander; Joseph, deceased, a farmer of Mercer County; Annie, wife of William Mayes, a farmer of Washington County, and Willette, deceased wife of Ed V. Ferguson, merchant of Harrodsburg. Andrew Forsythe, at his death, was a member of the Presbyterian Church, and departed this life August 13, 1886. His wife, who was a lifelong member of the Presbyterian Church, died in April, 1875, in the sixty-ninth year of her age. Matthew Forsythe, grandfather of M. Leander, was born in Ireland, immigrated to South Carolina, and came to Kentucky with Gen. Adair, and settled in Mercer County, where he was married to Miss Jane McAfee, daughter of Robert McAfee, and sister to Gen. Robert McAfee. His children were Robert, Andrew, John, William, Sally, James and Julia (Buford). Dr. Forsythe attended in youth the schools of his native county of Mercer, afterward a high school at Frankfort, and in the autumn of 1860 entered the junior class in Centre College, of Danville, Ky., graduating there in June, 1862, with the degree of A. M. He immediately began the study of medicine under Dr. Evans, now of Danville. In 1863 he attended his first course of lectures in Brooklyn, N. Y., and graduated at Jefferson College, Philadelphia, in March, 1864. In the summer of 1864 he began practice in Harrison County, Ky., which he continued five years, removing to Harrodsburg in 1869, where, with the exception of four years' residence in Mississippi (1873–77), he has since resided, and practiced medicine and surgery. Dr. Forsythe owns and has managed a plantation in Jefferson County, Miss. June 27, 1871, he married Miss Elizabeth Griffing, daughter of J. D. and Elizabeth (Pearson) Griffing, the former a native of Jefferson County, Miss., the latter of Harrodsburg, Ky. Their marriage has been blessed with four children: Levinia Bush, Andrew Dunbar, Louise Tweed and Willette. Mr. and Mrs. Forsythe are members of the Presbyterian Church.

GEORGE S. FULTON is a native of Nelson County, Ky., and the third of a family of six children born to Samuel S. and Margaret (Anderson) Fulton, the father of Pennsylvania, and the mother of Jessamine County, Ky. Samuel S. Fulton was born in Washington County, Penn., March 8, 1814, and grew to manhood in his native State. He was educated in Washington College, and early in life engaged in teaching, a profession in which he acquired considerable distinction, and which he followed many years. He came to Kentucky in 1838, and settled in Jefferson County, where he followed his profession until 1840, when he moved to Spencer County, and there resided until 1848. He then returned to Jefferson County; two years later moved to Nelson County, and located on a farm near the town of Bloomfield, where he resided until his death, which occurred February 12, 1880. Mrs. Margaret Fulton was the daughter of John Anderson, an early resident of Nelson County. He was a captain in the war of 1812, and for a number of years sold goods at Bloomfield, dying in that town some time prior to the year 1833. Mrs. Fulton was born October 29, 1816, and died June 19, 1819. Mr. and Mrs. Fulton are the parents of six children, whose names are as follows: Mrs. Mary McClaskey, George S., Eugene (deceased), J. A. (present judge of the Nelson County Court), Samuel and W. A. Fulton. George S. Fulton was born in Taylorville, Spencer County, April 27, 1847. He grew to manhood near Bloomfield, Nelson County, and was reared on a farm, receiving his early education in the schools of the town, which he attended until his seventeenth year. In 1866 he entered the Forest Home Academy, Jefferson County, which institution he attended one year, completing the prescribed course in that time. He received material assistance in his school work from his father, who instructed him in the classics and higher mathematics, so that the year spent in the academy was comparatively an easy one. After quitting school he engaged in teaching in Nelson County, and later in the county of Washington, where he had charge of the Covington Institute, at Springfield, for one year. He began reading law in 1868, and in 1869 entered the law department of the Louisville University, from which he graduated in 1872; began the practice of his profession at Bardstown in 1873, and since that time has been actively engaged in the courts of Nelson and adjoining counties, having a large and lucrative business at the present time. Mr. Fulton has been a very active and painstaking lawyer, and occupies a prominent place in the legal fraternity of central Kentucky. He married, October 8, 1874, near Bardstown, Miss Kate R. Adams, daughter of Stephen G. and Elizabeth (Ray) Adams, of Daviess County. Two children have been born to this marriage: Eugene A. and Stephen G. Fulton, aged, respectively, ten and seven years. Mr. Fulton has never been an aspirant for official positions, but takes an active interest in politics, voting with the Democratic party. He is a member of the Presbyterian Church, with which he has been identified since 1867, and with his wife and family belongs to the Bardstown congregation.

MRS. ELIZABETH A. FUNK was born December 19, 1822, in Green County, Ky., where she was reared to womanhood. Her father, James Campbell, a native of Augusta County, Va., was an early settler in Green County, Ky., locating on the land now occupied by Campbellsville, so named in his honor. He died there about 1827. His brothers were Michael, David, Adam and Andrew. He first married Rebecca Turner, and their children were Andrew and John T. His second wife was Rachel Spears, of Virginia, and their offspring are Rebecca (Russell), Samuel, James, Mary J. (Van Cleve), Henry, Elizabeth A. (Funk) and Sarah (Moss). Elizabeth A. was married, in 1843, to Bartlett Eastland (died in 1852, aged thirty-five years), and to them was born one child, Maria (Gregory). In 1858 she was married to James Burnett, and their union was favored by the birth of one daughter, Mrs. Ella Hoover. In 1879 she was joined in marriage to Jacob Funk, of Jessamine County, who died September 22, 1883, at the age of seventy-four years. Mrs. Funk is engaged in farming in Boyle County, having 177 acres of well improved and productive land. She is a member of the Christian Church.

MADISON B. FUNK was born November 22, 1838. His parents, John W. and Harriet (Bosley) Funk, had a family of five boys and three girls; James F., Sarah E., John H., Martha W., Madison B., Joseph, Charles P. and Harriet M.; of the five boys, Madison B. is the only surviving one, the rest, by a curious coincidence, have all died accidental deaths, except one, James F., who died of pneumonia. William Funk, paternal grandfather, was of. German descent, and a very early settler in Kentucky; he located on the farm now owned by Thomas Cregor in Washington County, on which he continued to reside until his death. He became, for his day, an extensive farmer and slave owner. Gideon Bosley was the maternal grandfather. (See sketch of C. F. Bosley.) John W. Funk was born at the Funk homestead July 14, 1795; he grew to manhood there and was early inured to the hardships which attended farm life in those days. His marriage to Miss Bosley occurred March 16, 1826. Anterior to the year 1838 he was engaged in various pursuits, among which were teaming, milling, and farming; in that year he purchased a tract of land and thenceforward gave his undivided attention to farming until his death. Madison B. Funk was born in Washington County, and continued a resident of the homestead until the year 1872. September 21, 1871, he was united in marriage to Miss Willie A. Sharpe, by whom he is the father of five children: William H., Emma L. and Enna (twins, Enna dying in infancy), Hattie B. and Jane B., who were born respectively as follows: July 2, 1872, June 28, 1875, October 9, 1877, and May 12, 1884. Anterior to the year 1878 Mr. Funk was engaged in farming and milling; at that time he disposed of his landed interests and embarked in milling exclusively, which he continued until 1884, when he purchased a farm, his ill health not permitting him to remain in the milling business longer. From a business point of view Mr. Funk has been successful; he is the owner of 350 acres of land, 250 in Washington County, on which he lives, and 100 in Marion County. He and wife are members of the Methodist Episcopal Church. He belongs to the K. of H. fraternity, and votes with the Democratic party.

JOHN T. GADDIE was born May 25, 1842, and is the first in a family of seven sons and four daughters, all yet living, born to Bartholomew S. and Sarah A. (Handley) Gaddie. Bartholomew S. Gaddie, a native of Green, now Taylor County, was born December 15, 1803; he was a farmer and slaveholder, and a lover of and trader in horses; with his wife he is still living and is still a very active man. His father, Benjamin Gaddie, a Virginian of English descent, married Susan Crues; he came to Hart County, Ky., as early as 1790, but afterward moved to Green County, where he engaged in farming. Mrs. Sarah A. Gaddie was born in Marion County, a daughter of William and Jane (McColgan) Handley, natives respectively of Marion and Green Counties. John T. Gaddie, a native of Green, now Taylor County, was reared a farmer, received a good common and high school education, and in the fall of 1862 enlisted in the Forty-eighth Tennessee Infantry, but was discharged sooh after, on account of ill health. March 7, 1867, he married Miss Cris A. Stiles, of Nelson County, and daughter of Charles and Ann (Willett) Stiles, natives respectively of New Jersey and Kentucky. To Mr. and Mrs. Gaddie have been born eight children: Charles B., Robert P. (deceased), Robert D., John L., Lewis F., Joseph H., Ira C. and George T. After marriage Mr. Gaddie settled on his present farm of 130 acres at New Haven, Nelson County; he also owns 140 acres of timber land in LaRue County. He is a member of the F. & A. M., and, with his wife, of the Methodist Episcopal Church South. In politics he is a Democrat, and cast his first presidential vote for Seymour.

DR. NATHAN GAITHER was born in Rowan County, N. C., in 1788, and was the youngest son of Nicholas and Margaret (Watkins) Gaither. Nicholas Gaither was a major of State troops' and commanded a battalion at the battle of King's Mountain, and was several times a member of the North Carolina Legislature. Nathan Gaither immigrated to Kentucky about 1808, and received a fair English education at Bardstown College. He afterward studied medicine with his cousin, Dr. Edward Gaither, in Springfield, Ky., and attended lectures at the famous Philadelphia School of Medicine when such professors as Dr. Physic and Benjamin Rush were members of its faculty; and with the late Dr. Overton, of Tennessee, was one of the eighteen who volunteered, in the interest of science, to undergo the test of Jenner's discovery of kine-pox vaccination and variola innoculation, to discover the justice of its claim to be an antidote for small-pox. In 1812 he was surgeon to Col. Barbee's regiment of Kentucky volunteers in the war with Great Britain. Upon his return to Kentucky he permanently located in Columbia, Adair County, and was many times elected to the Legislature from that county. In 1817 he married Martha Morrison, of Madison County, the daughter of a Revolutionary soldier. She had three brothers in the war of 1812–15, in the military, and one brother, a surgeon in the navy (who died from the effects of wounds received in the fight between the "Constitution" and "Guerriere"). Dr. Nathan Gaither was, in 1829, elected to Congress, and re-elected in 1829. Andrew Stevenson was speaker, and he was at each session appointed upon the committee of ways and means, of which George McDuffie, of South Carolina, was chairman. During his first term a report from the committee was made by a majority favoring the United States Bank charter. Mark Alexander, of Virginia, and Nathan Gaither, of Kentucky, made a minority report, opposing the charter. In 1829 James K. Polk, of Tennessee, was elected and added to the committee, which again reported in favor of chartering the United States Bank, when Polk, Alexander and Gaither made another minority report, and the bill having passed, Jackson's famous veto message placed the seal of his approval upon the course of these old time Democrats. From this time forward Dr. Gaither, burdened with the payment of security debts (the universal misfortune of the gentleman politician), and the cares of a growing family, devoted himself to the practice of his profession. Although always actively engaged, and eminently successful as a practitioner, he was always sorely in need of money. When it is known that in a practice of more than fifty years he warranted only two men and sued only three, it may be seen how negligent he was of financial affairs. As he facetiously remarked to one of his more discreet business friends who upbraided him for not more closely collecting: "By George, my dear sir, it is bad enough to work a man off with a cathartic without afterward making him disgorge with a law-suit emetic." Apropos of his old-fashioned sayings, a few are reported: In his first race for Congress, in 1825, he was defeated by Judge Richard A. Buckner, of Greene County. He was passing through Crocus, in Cumberland County, notoriously a Whig county, and was hailed by Col. Bob Elliott. What Confederate of Morgan's command lives who does not remember Elliott's distillery, near the "Irish Bottom?" In those times the usual dose for fever and ague was

a heavy dose of calomel and work it off with rhubarb and jalap. Col. Elliott was a great Whig, a profound admirer of Judge Buckner, who was one of the profoundest lawyers and one of the most able men Kentucky ever produced. Thinking to humble Dr. Gaither, "Hallo, Doctor," said Elliott, "you don't know me?" "Why, certainly, Col. Elliott," returned the Doctor; "I met you in Burkesville and was introduced to you by my friend, Judge Buckner." This rather mollified Elliott, but who ever heard of a hotel-keeper, a distiller or a barkeeper who, when surrounded by his satellites, would not undertake to down the man who opposed his candidate? Elliott, thinking to abash Dr. Gaither, and at the same time show his power over the crowd of voters who were employed by him as laborers in a very ill-attended tobacco field, sarcastically said: "Well, Doctor, you want to doctor our laws against a judge as you doctor our people in the line of business. Now, what prescription would you make for this sickly tobacco patch?" Dr. Gaither, who was then in the prime of life, and was a splendid specimen of human architecture, responded immediately: "I prescribe a heavy dose of bull-tongue plows, and work it off with weeding-hoes." Elliott was always afterward his warm friend, and, as before stated, he was elected, Judge Buckner, after a short canvass, refusing to stand against him. When upbraided by some of his friends for his strict adherence to the granted powers of the constitution and the non-exercise of doubtful rights, his answer always was: "Progress without honesty is the rogues' march." When urged by some of his friends to advocate some new measure as a matter of policy, his universal answer was, in language more forcible than pious: " Policy is a — rascally virtue." These, a few of his sayings, are taught to this day by his old friends to their children in his old district. He never asked a man for his political support, and threatened to cane a man for asking him for money to be used in his election as late as the year 1847—in which year he was elected to the convention from Adair County as delegate to assist in framing our present constitution. In 1855, when out of 1,400 voters there were estimated to be 1,000 sworn Know-nothings, he was elected by nearly 500 majority. He was nominated by the Democrats for speaker, but was of course defeated, the Know-nothings being largely in the majority. He died August 12, 1862, from paralysis—his last remark to his old-time friend and medical partner, Dr. Samuel B. Field: "I have out-lived the liberties of my country and it is time for me to die." His eldest son, Edgar B. Gaither, was born in 1818. Having of-ten heard his father speak of Col. Richard M. Johnson, with whom his father had served in the late British war, and afterward in Congress, when "Old Tecumseh" was senator, young Gaither, without his father's knowledge, wrote to Col. Johnson, who was then Vice-President, asking to be appointed cadet to West Point. In response to his letter came his commission. He graduated in 1839, and served until 1841 as second lieu-tenant in the First Dragoons. He then re-signed, studied law with Hon. Thos. B. Monroe in Frankfort, and being licensed, practiced his profession in Burkesville until 1846. War against Mexico having been de-clared, he raised a company of volunteers in Adair County, but his command was not ac-cepted, the regiment being filled. He was subsequently appointed captain, under the Ten Regiment bill, in the Third Dragoons, and participated with his command in all the fights from the National Bridge until the City of Mexico was captured, and returned with the army when peace was restored. He was specially complimented in general orders for gallant conduct upon many occa-sions. Returning from Mexico, he practiced law for a time in Washington City in part-nership with Col. Theodore O'Hara. He was connected with Lopez in the inception of the Cuban expedition, and his widow now has a handsome portrait presented by the unfortunate Cuban patriot to Capt. Gaither in 1850. Capt. Gaither was mar-ried to Miss Emily R. Hutchison, of Mercer County. In the same year he was elected to the Legislature from Adair County, and in 1851 was elected commonwealth's attorney. He died while holding this office, September 25, 1855. He was a man of brilliant ca-pacity, thorough accomplishments, strict in-tegrity and dauntless courage. No man of his age ever died in Kentucky more uni-versally mourned. Dr. W. N. Gaither, the second son, was a successful prac-titioner of medicine in southern Kentucky and Harrodsburg until, within a few years past, his loss of health has compelled him to abandon his chosen calling. He is still vig-orous in mind, but never having sought political preferment he is only known and loved by the limited circle of his personal acquaintances. The daughters of Dr. Gaither, Margaret, Kate and Mattie, have been dead many years, and all died unmarried. George B. Gaither, the third son, entered as a private

in his brother's company, at the age of six-teen, and died in 1849 from disease contracted in Mexico. Dr. Gaither's experience as a soldier, caused him to seriously object to his son's entering the army at his tender age, but he was forced to yield his reluctant consent by reason of the boy's stubborn determination. George was stalwart, finely formed, and physically a well-developed man, being six feet two inches high. Capt. Gaither, like all West Pointers, was something of a martinet, and when his brother was enlisted and sworn in—the last man in the company—he remarked to George in a stern manner: "From this time forth, remember, I am no longer your brother. You are private and I am Capt. Gaither." George drew himself proudly to his full height, gave a military salute, and responded: "Capt. Gaither, it will be time enough to refuse when I ask a favor from you." Nat. Gaither, the only remaining son, except Dr. W. N. Gaither, is residing at Harrodsburg, practicing law. He has filled several offices, having been common school commissioner, county attorney, mem-ber of the Legislature, and secretary of State. Edgar H. Gaither, son of Capt. E. B. Gaither, is also a lawyer at Harrodsburg. He was cadet midshipman at Annapolis and resigned to study law, is master commissioner of the Mercer Circuit Court, and has thrice been elected city attorney in the Republican town of Harrodsburg, and is chairman of the Democratic County Committee of Mercer. Nat. Gaither, son of Dr. W. N. Gaither, lives at Hopkinsville, and is a prosperous business man. He served with Morgan in the Con-federate Army, and was for twelve years circuit court clerk of Christian County.

CHARLES WEBB GAITSKILL was born June 5, 1848, on the waters of Stoner Creek, Clark County. In 1884 removed to Lexing-ton, and May 1, 1886, located near Harrods-burg Junction, Mercer County, where he now resides. In September, 1864, he enlisted in Capt. Bedford's cavalry; was with Breckin-ridge, and acted as courier at the battle of the Salt Works, and surrendered with Col. Giltner at Mt. Sterling, Ky., May 2, 1865. His father, John Gaitskill, a native of Clark County, was born in 1817, and lived and died at the place of his birth. He was a quiet and successful farmer and stock raiser; lost seven slaves by the late war; was an old line Whig, and died in May, 1879. He was the son of Silas Gaitskill, a native of Culpeper County, Va., who removed to Kentucky in an early day; was a farmer and slave-holder, and died about 1843. He married Jonietta Butler, and their offspring were Henry; John; Joseph (deceased); Edward (drowned); Martha (Hedges); Nancy (Thompson); Louisa (Suddeth and Daniel), and Marietta (Prewitt). John Gaitskill married Frances V., daughter of Maj. Webb W. and Cinthey (Hedges) Branham, of Bourbon County (born November 26, 1827), and from their union sprang Charles W.; Katie (deceased); Silas H.; Jonietta (Rodgers); Strother S.; Mary W. (Burgin); James E. and Lula (Willis). Charles W. has been twice married, first, October 25, 1870, to Miss Sue F., daughter of Jeremiah and Nancy (Preston) White, of Montgomery County (born August 21, 1844, died January 8, 1882), and to them were born Fannie V., Nannie W. and John W. He was next married, October 18, 1882, to Miss Nannie, daughter of Daniel W. and Rebecca R. (Dunlap) Jones, of Danville (born May 22, 1850). Mr. Gaitskill is a farmer, having 221 acres of highly improved and well watered land, and yielding an abundance of fruit. The farm is known as the Davis place, and the mansion is almost palatial. In 1884 Mr. Gaitskill engaged in the foundry business with R. D. Williams at Lexington, where he spends his winters, his summers being passed on the farm. He is a member of the Christian Church, and in politics a Democrat.

SQUIRE JOSEPH E. GARDINER was born June 17, 1823, in the house where he now resides. His father, Theodore Gardiner, a native of St. Mary's County, Md., removed with his parents to Nelson County, Ky., in 1788, where he died in 1850, at the age of sixty-two years. He was the son of Clement Gardiner, of Maryland; a devout Catholic, who brought eighty slaves to Kentucky, where he died in 1820, aged seventy years. He was a direct descendant of Richard Gardiner, who landed with the first company on Plymouth Rock. Theodore espoused Elizabeth, daughter of Capt. James Rapier, Nelson County (died in 1848, aged sixty-two years), and their union was blessed by the birth of Matilda (O'Bryant); Christina (Heady); Louisa (Walker); William H.; Rosella (Adams); Joseph E.; Eliza A. (deceased), and Nancy Mills. On February 14, 1855, Joseph E. Gardiner, born in Nelson County, was united in marriage with Martha, daughter of Clem N. and Plagia (Leak) Buckman, of Union County (born August 23, 1833), and to them have been born Clement R.; Ida L. (Head); William G.; Arabella; Plagia and Elizabeth (twins, both deceased); Joseph E., John I. (deceased); Francis B.; Mattie B. and Harry T. Joseph E., Sr., served as deputy sheriff and constable for twelve years, and acted as magistrate and

member of the court of claims of Nelson County from 1855 to 1882. He was at one time colonel of the State militia. He is a farmer, having 340 acres of productive land in a good state of cultivation. He has ever been a zealous Catholic; in politics is a Democrat, but opposed secession in the lates truggle, through which he lost eight slaves.

WILLIAM GIBSON (deceased) was a leading and representative citizen of Madison County, and was born April 7, 1833, in Ireland. When but three years old he was brought to the United States by his parents, Stephen and Ann Gibson, who settled in Clay County, Ky. At the age of nineteen or twenty he went to California, where he made considerable money in handling cattle. He returned to Kentucky and soon after married Miss Ellen V. Bates, a daughter of Dr. S. W. and Sarah (Hogan) Bates. After marriage Mr. Gibson returned to California, where he remained but one year. In 1870 he located in Somerset where he entered the mercantile business with a brother. There he superintended the building of the courthouse. In the spring of 1875 he purchased and located on 210 acres immediately south of Richmond adjoining the grounds of the Central University. This land he improved with a fine residence. Mr. Gibson started in life penniless, but by his energy and perseverance has made life a success, accumulating and leaving a fine estate. He was an excellent and good business man and was a member of the F. & A. M. Mr. and Mrs Gibson had born to bless their union one son, John Gibson. They were members of the Christian Church. Mr. Gibson died November 29, 1884. In politics he was a Democrat.

FRANKLIN GOODE was born in Adair County, June 29, 1833, and is the second of seven children, five of whom are yet living, born to Edmond and Louisa (Caskey) Goode, both natives of Adair County and of Irish descent. Edmond Goode was born in 1807 and was married soon after attaining his majority; he soon after bought lands, on which there was very little improvement, on the waters of Casey Creek, near Rolla, in Adair County. Here he improved a farm, to which he afterward added other lands—on a part of which the village of Rolla was afterward built—upon which he remained many years. Later he sold this place and again bought wild lands some two miles further west in the same county, and afterward improved the farm upon which he resided until his death in 1855. Both he and wife were from early life members of the United Baptist Church, in which church he was for many years a ruling elder. His father, Fleming Goode, was a native of Virginia. When a small boy, about the time of the Revolutionary war, he came with his parents to Kentucky, the family first locating in what is now Boyle County. There he grew to manhood, soon becoming an extensive and expert hunter and trapper, killing large numbers of deer, bear and other wild game. He was married in Casey County and finally settled in what is now Adair County. He had a son who served in the war of 1812 under Gen. Jackson, and also in the Florida war. His father, John Goode, was born in the south of Ireland, but when a young man immigrated to the colony of Virginia. Mrs. Louisa (Caskey) Goode was born in 1807 and died in 1850. Her father, Robert A. Caskey, was born either in Virginia or in what is now Adair County, Ky. He was married in Adair County and engaged in agricultural pursuits all his life. He was for many years a constable, a magistrate and was sheriff under the old constitution. Franklin Goode is a man of wide and varied general information, having been an extensive, close and careful reader all his life. He remained with his parents on the home farm until he attained his majority, after which he farmed on rented lands and was employed as a laborer for some six years. He then bought a farm, on which there was a very slight improvement, on the waters of Casey Creek, in Adair County, where he remained only two years. In the spring of 1861 he bought a partially improved farm of 150 acres, on the. northwest or McCluer's Fork of Casey Creek, some two and one-half miles north of Rolla, upon which he yet resides. He continued to add to his real possessions from time to time, now owning well improved farms aggregating some 600 acres. He is extensively and successfully engaged in farming and stock raising, and has given some attention to the breeding of fine cattle. He was married November 9, 1854, to Miss Elgeline E. Christeson, a native of Casey County, Ky., born August 22, 1835. She is a daughter of Thomas and Susan (Stephens) Christeson, natives of Boyle and Casey Counties, Ky., respectively, and of English descent. Two sons have blessed their union, viz.: Deroy and Emmit E. Both Mr. Goode and wife have been from early life members of the Christian Church. In politics he is a Democrat, and although he has never been an office-seeker, he is universally recognized as a party leader in his part of the county.

THOMAS J. GOODE was born in Casey County, Ky., March 11, 1844, and is the eldest of five children born to Alfred and Mary (Ward) Goode, natives, respectively, of Lincoln and Casey Counties, Ky., and of Irish and English descent. Alfred Goode was born April 3, 1799, and while yet a young man, removed to Casey County, where he was afterward married and where he bought wild land on the waters of Casey Creek and improved a farm, upon which he resided for some forty odd years, when he removed to Marion County, Ky., where he bought another farm, upon which he resided until his death, August 10, 1876. For many years he was a captain in the old State militia, and during the civil war was first a captain and afterward colonel of one of the Kentucky Home Guard Regiments. He was also constable in Casey County for a number of years. He and wife were life-long members of the Catholic Church. His father, Fleming Goode, was a native of Virginia. While yet a young man he came to Kentucky, first settling in Lincoln County, where he was married, but soon after removing to Adair County. Mrs. Mary (Ward) Goode was born in 1818 and died August 10, 1863. Her father, Thomas Ward, was a native of Maryland and was also one of the pioneers of what is now Casey County, Ky. Thomas J. Goode has always resided on the old homestead of 250 acres, where he was born, on the waters of Casey Creek, in Casey County, Ky., and is extensively and successfully engaged in farming and stock raising. He enlisted, July 25, 1861, in Company A, First Kentucky Volunteer Cavalry (Federal service). After about eight months he was detailed for special service and served as orderly at regimental, brigade and division headquarters until the expiration of his term of service, being mustered out at Camp Nelson, Ky., December 31, 1864. He participated in all the battles in which his regiment was engaged, viz.: Wild Cat, Ky.; Mill Springs, Ky.; Lebanon, Tenn.; Horse Cave, Ky.; Perryville, Ky.; Dutton Hill, Ky.; the pursuit of Morgan through Kentucky, Indiana and Ohio (being present at Morgan's surrender); Sweet Water, E. Tenn.; Philadelphia, E. Tenn.; the siege of Knoxville, Bean Station, E. Tenn.; Dandridge, Tenn.; Resaca, Kenesaw Mountain, Lost Mountain, Atlanta, Ga.; and in the Stoneman Raid, being one of the few who cut their way out and escaped. He was also engaged in many other lesser battles and skirmishes. He was married February 17, 1865, to Miss Nannie Wethington, a native of Adair County and born February 19, 1843. She is a daughter of William and Mary A. (Carico) Wethington, natives of Adair and Casey Counties, Ky., respectively, and of English descent. Eight children have blessed their union, viz.: Silas F., Mary E., Jerome, Margaret B., Susan A., Nannie J., Clarie and Thomas McClosky. Mr. Goode, his wife and family, are devoted members of the Catholic Church. In politics he is a Republican and is one of the enterprising and successful young farmers of the county.

THOMAS WESTON GORE was born September 29, 1819, one mile east of Danville, was raised in Boyle County where he remained until 1868, when he removed to Nicholasville, Jessamine County, and with his brother, James, engaged in keeping hotel, remaining one year. January 1, 1869, they removed to Henderson, taking charge of the Hancock House, which they occupied over a year, when they took charge of the American House in Evansville, Ind., remaining there one year, when they returned to Kentucky and kept hotel in Shelby City one year, and in 1878 located at Junction City, Boyle County, where they have since been engaged in managing the Gore House, which they built and own. The father of T. W. Gore was Christian Gore, a native of Reisterstown, Baltimore Co., Md., where he was born April 11, 1788, removed to Mercer County, Ky., in 1811 and located six miles west of Harrodsburg on Glenn's Creek, on a survey of 1,000 acres of land purchased by his father. He was a blacksmith, was long a chairman of the board of trustees of Danville, was many years a steward in the Methodist Episcopal Church and was an uncompromising Union man. Latterly he was largely engaged in dealing in stock with success and died September 2, 1861, at Millporth's, Ohio, while absent with a drove of mules, but was buried in Danville, Ky. He was the son of Jacob Gore, a native of Baltimore County, Md., a Revolutionary soldier, a farmer, who died in Maryland. His father was the son of Michael Gore, of Baltimore County, an extensive land and mill owner, and he was the son of Christian Gore, an officer in the Prussian Army, noted for a single-handed conflict with three French soldiers in which he was victorious, and afterward one of the first settlers in Lehigh Valley, Penn. Michael Gore's children were Andrew, Christian, Jacob, George, John, Philip (sheriff of Baltimore County) and Samuel. The two latter were wealthy bachelors. Andrew was an early settler and reared a large family near Maysville, Ky. Jacob's children were Jacob, Christian and Andrew. His wife, Elizabeth (Weston) Gore, was the mother of the two latter. Andrew

settled at Harrodsburg and raised a family. Jacob, Sr., settled at Fredericksburg, Va., and was a noted Methodist at that place. Christian married Catherine, daughter of Michael Haines, of Mercer County (born in Baltimore County, Md., died in 1821) and to them were born James, November 5, 1812; Sarah (deceased) and Thomas W. James married a Miss Casey in 1847, who died childless. In religion Thomas W. Gore is a member of the Methodist Episcopal Church, and in politics is a Republican.

CHARLES PEYTON GRAHAM was born November 18, 1818. His father, Peyton R. Graham, was born near Harrod's Landing Run, Mercer County, where he was reared; was a farmer and slave-holder, and died in 1823, at the age of thirty-five years. He was the son of Samuel M. Graham, a native of Culpeper County, Va., and a pioneer near Lexington, Ky., where he lost his lands by an adverse claim; after which he purchased land of Maj. Hugh McGary, on Kentucky River, in Mercer County, where he was a farmer and slave owner, and died previous to 1800. His offspring were James; Jane (Shaw); Polly (Hamilton) and Peyton R. Peyton R. married Ann, daughter of Charles Spillman, of Garrard County (born November 23, 1783, died July 17, 1863), and from their union sprang James S.; Elizabeth Armstrong; Sarah (Williamson); Charles P. and Mary Crooks. Charles P. first married, 1840, Miss Elizabeth, daughter of Jonathan Nichols (born in Park County, Ind., in 1820; died March 8, 1876), and to them were born Belle (McEwen); Anna E. (Risk); John J.; Mary (Robinson); Minnie (McAfee); Charles S.; George W. (deceased); Loutie; Bess and William S. February 14, 1878, Mr. Graham married Miss Sallie, daughter of James and Permelia (Shepherd) Burnett, of Shelby County (born January 23, 1840), and their children are Alice (deceased) and Burnett. Mr. Graham is a farmer and stock raiser, having 276 acres of productive land well improved in McAfee Precinct, in his native county of Mercer. He is a Presbyterian and an Ancient Odd Fellow, and in politics is Republican.

E. J. GRAHAM, M. D., was born January 6, 1840, and is a son of Robert and Elizabeth (Young) Graham, to whom three sons and two daughters were born. Robert Graham was a native of Green County, Ky., born in October, 1804; was a millwright, also a farmer, and died in March, 1868. His wife was born June 14, 1813, and died in July, 1883. Dr. Graham was also born in Green County. At twelve years of age he was sent to New Albany, Ind., to receive his education and learn a trade; spent four years in school, then returned to his native county of Green, and remained on the farm till September, 1861, when he enlisted in Company H, Thirteenth Kentucky Volunteers, was made orderly of his company and was mustered in as first lieutenant. He was in the battle of Shiloh and Bragg's raid through Kentucky, but on account of ill health resigned in July, 1863; after his return home commenced the study of medicine with Dr. T. P. Hodges; graduated from the medical department of the University of Louisville in 1866 and located in the western part of Green County, where he has had an extensive and lucrative practice. He is president of the Green River Medical Association, which position he has filled three years in succession. He located where he now resides in November, 1885, on 250 acres, which is well improved, and embellished with a substantial frame residence. He was first married in August, 1865, to Elizabeth, a daughter of Stewart and Elizabeth (Jones) Sutherland. In February, 1868, he married his second wife, Nancy Bale, a daughter of John and Dimmie (Lewis) Bale. From this marriage sprang six children: John R., Edward Y., James H., Rutha C., Alberta and William M. The Doctor's wife is a member of the Baptist Church. The Doctor is a leading and influential member of the Masonic fraternity and also of the I. O. O. F. He is one of the members of the board of examining surgeons, and in politics is an active and uncompromising Republican.

DR. JAMES W. GRANT was born July 13, 1830, in Washington County, Va., and is the son of Hugh M. and Matilda (Nordyke) Grant, natives of Washington County, Va. Hugh M. Grant was born February 14, 1805; his wife was four years younger. He was a man with only an ordinary education, which he had succeeded in getting by self-application, and later in life learned dentistry. He was reared on a farm and lived there until after his wife's death in 1832; in 1833 he went to Cahaba, Ala., where he met and married Mrs. Caroline C. Cummings, whose maiden name was McCord; he then went to Selma, Ala. About 1845 he lost his second wife and returned to Virginia, where he married his third wife, Sophia M. Price. The children by this last marriage were three sons and six daughters. He was a Presbyterian in religion; at the time of his death was living in Fincastle, Va. Hugh M. Grant was a son of James and Janet (McGinnis) Grant. James Grant was born in Lenoir County, N. C., in 1777; his wife was born in Washington County, Va. He reared a family of eight sons and two daughters; was a farmer of Virginia, to which State he had moved when a young man. His religion was Presbyterian and in politics he was a Whig. He died in 1847; his parents came from the highlands of Scotland. He had an uncle, John Grant, who had a dream that he would die in ten years, which came true. Janet McGinnis was a daughter of Archibald McGinnis, who was born and reared in Ireland. He immigrated to America with Mary Scott and her parents, marrying her and settling in Virginia, where they reared a family. Archibald McGinnis was the younger son of an Irish gentleman, and therefore not entitled to patrimony. He determined to leave the "auld counthry" and seek his fortune in the New World. After having paid his passage, at the moment of his embarking at Cork, his oldest brother, Hugh McGinnis, who had not before learned of his intentions, followed him to the wharf and offered him a half of his estate, whose castle could be seen in the distance, if he would return. But Archibald McGinnis cared more for Mary Scott, who was on board, than for his brother or Irish lands. They came from County Down, Ireland. Matilda (Nordyke) Grant was a daughter of Bennajah and Jane (Foley) Nordyke, natives respectively of New Jersey and Virginia. Mr. Nordyke was a soldier in the Revolutionary war, and with his family came to Lincoln County, Ky., about 1838, and settled at Crab Orchard, where he died about 1862, aged ninety-eight years. His ancestors came from Holland; he was a Baptist, and in politics a Whig. Dr. J. W. Grant was reared on a farm, attended Emory and Henry College two years, after which he began the study of dentistry. After an experience of four years he attended dental college in Baltimore; in 1854 received his diploma; located in Holly Springs, Miss., the following year; four months later located in Crab Orchard, Ky.; in October, 1857, located in Lancaster, where he has lived and practiced his profession ever since, securing a large and extended practice. December 23, 1858, he married Emily P. Graham, daughter of Benjamin and Nancy (Price) Graham, natives of Garrard County. Nancy (Price) Graham was the daughter of Col. William Price of Garrard County, and Lucy (Jennings) Price, who was of the noted Jennings ancestry, descended from Humphrey Jennings, a titled English nobleman of royal lineage. Mr. Graham was an attorney; he enlisted in the Mexican war, was quartermaster with rank of major, and was killed by guerrillas. Dr. Grant and wife have been blessed with six children: Ida May, Lucy Jennings, Nannie, Hugh McKee, Nellie (deceased), and Lilla Dale Price. The Doctor is a devoted member of the Presbyterian Church; the wife, of the Christian Church. He is a leading member of the Masonic fraternity; cast his first presidential vote for Gen. Scott; since the war has affiliated with the Democratic party.

WILL H. GRANT was born January 25, 1839, in Spencer County, Ky., and in early childhood removed with his parents across the Nelson County line, and has always resided in the vicinity of his birthplace. His father, Posey D. Grant, a native of Prince William County, Va., was born November 4, 1814, and in 1818 removed with his mother to Kentucky, lived the life of a farmer, lost sixteen slaves by the late war, and died July 21, 1885. Posey D. Grant was the son of William Grant (great-grandfather of our subject), of Virginia, a soldier in the war of 1812, a relative of the Stuart family, and a great-uncle to George Grant. Posey D. Grant, grandfather of Will H. Grant, died in Virginia. Posey D. Grant, father of Will H. Grant, married Sophia, daughter of Baz and Margaret (Osborne) Thurman of Spencer County (born February 27, 1815), and from their union sprang Elizabeth (Davis), Margaret A. (Thurman), William H., and Mary M. (deceased). September 29, 1868, William H. Grant was married to Miss Elizabeth S., daughter of Adkinson H. and Finetta (Miller) Beeler of Nelson County (born December 22, 1843), and their union has been favored by the birth of Posey B., Vaughan, Drummond B., Mary M. and Elizabeth D. In youth Mr. Grant obtained a fair English education at the schools of the country, and by application has become well versed in the standard and current literature of the day. He is a farmer, owning 150 acres of highly cultivated land at High Grove, Nelson County, on the L. & B. pike, on which is situated his residence, the old stone Barclay tavern, erected seventy years ago. Mr. Grant has a herd of fine Jersey cattle, with which he is greatly interested. He is also engaged in the manufacture of crab cider, having 800 crab trees on his farm. In religion he is a Baptist, and in politics a Democrat.

ANDREW J. GRAVES was born a few hundred yards from where he now lives, July 27, 1816. His parents, Thomas and Sarah (Lawson) Graves, had six children, of whom Andrew J. was the next eldest. Will-

iam Graves, paternal grandfather, was a native of Virginia, and gallantly served in the war for our national independence. In 1789 he came to Kentucky, reached the fort at the forks of the Kentucky River, where he halted for about two years, when he settled in Washington County, about two miles southeast of Mackville, where he laid a land warrant for 300 acres, on which he continued to reside until his death; he reared a family of eleven children, and while not a wealthy citizen was one universally respected and highly esteemed. John Lawson, subject's maternal grandfather, came from Virginia to Kentucky in 1797, settled in Washington County, resided there several years, then moved to Bloomfield, Nelson County, where he died in his eighty-ninth year and was given a military burial, he having served in the Revolutionary war. Thomas Graves, father of our subject, was born January 15, 1790, during the residence of his parents in the fort at the forks of the Kentucky River. He was reared on the farm; in 1811 married and moved to a house of his own where he lived the rest of his days. Nancy, Andrew J. (our subject), Susan, Louisa, Caroline and Adaline were the children born to his marriage. He died in 1855. Andrew J. Graves was reared on the old homestead and has always lived there. September 14, 1858, his marriage with Jestine (Bottom) Cull was solemnized. Mrs. Graves is a member of the Christian Church, and in politics Mr. Graves is a Democrat.

SQUIRE ARCHIE GRAY was born February 10, 1820, in Mercer (now Boyle) County, Ky., where he grew to manhood. In 1850 he removed to Marion County, and in 1857 returned to Boyle where he has since resided. His father, James Gray, was born December 29, 1788, near Prince Edwards C. H., Va., removed in childhood with his parents to Mercer County, Ky., and located at the head of Doctor's Fork; was a farmer and slave owner; an elder in the Christian Church; a Whig, and died in 1856. He was the son of John Gray, a native of Virginia, an early settler in Kentucky, a Revolutionary soldier, a Presbyterian, and died about 1835, aged seventy-five years. John Gray married Lucy Jones, of Virginia, and their offspring were James, John, Archie, Sr., Charles, Jane (Sandifer), Polly (Huberry), Lucy (Webster), Patsey (Kinley), and Nancy (Pipes). James Gray married Elizabeth Gray, and the result of their union was Robert, John, William, Archie, Charles, Mary (Richeson), Lucy (Kelsie), Sarah (Bolling) and Nancy (Holland). Archie Gray was

married, February 2, 1843, to Miss Martha
A., daughter of Isaac and Nancy (Stone)
Montgomery, of Boyle County, (born May 31,
1820), and to them have been born Isaac M.,
Nancy E. (Harmon), and Sallie K. (Wade).
In August, 1885, Mr. Gray was elected
magistrate, and member of the court of claims,
of Boyle County, which position he now retains. He is a farmer and stock raiser and
owns over 300 acres of land, one half of which
is well improved and in a good state of cultivation, and a portion of which he has distributed among his children. He is a member of the Masonic fraternity; of the Good
Templars, and is an active member of the
Christian Church. He was formerly an old
line Whig, but is now a Democrat. As a result of the late war, he lost seven slaves.

SIDNEY GREEN was born in May, 1830,
being the tenth in a family of twelve children born to James and Mary (Taylor) Green.
William Green was his paternal and Leou-
ard Taylor his maternal grandfather; the
former was a native of Virginia and immigrated to Kentucky in an early day; the latter
was also one of the pioneer settlers of this
State, and a very extensive farmer and slave
owner for his time. James Green was born
in Virginia and was almost grown before the
family had left that State. He was married
in 1810, and in 1835 became a resident of
Washington County, and continued to live
there until his death, February 11, 1869. He
was a true and consistent member of the
Baptist Church, and died a devout believer
in its hopes. Sidney Green was born in
Madison County, but reared in Washington
County, where he now resides. He remained
with his parents until he attained the age of
thirty years, receiving a good English education. In October, 1860, he was married to
Miss Kate Kimberlin, by whom he is the
father of eight children: Lina (wife of Samuel Moore of Sherman, Tex.), Clifton,
Mamie, Lilly, James, Sidney, Kate and William. Mr. Green has always made farming his
vocation, and has been very successful. In
politics he has always been an ardent Democrat, and was honored with a nomination and
election to the office of sheriff of Washington
County, for two terms.

F. M. GREEN was born October 30, 1841,
in Madison County, and is a son of Irvine T.
and Nancy (Phelps) Green, of Madison County. Irvine T. Green was born in 1812 in
Madison County. He was a son of James
Green, who was also born in Madison County;
married Mary Taylor, of Washington County,
reared a family of seven sons and five daughters, was a substantial farmer three miles

west of Richmond, and died in 1867, aged
eighty-one years. His father, William
Green, came from South Carolina and located
west of Richmond as early as 1785, being
one of the earliest pioneers. Nancy (Phelps)
Green was a daughter of Philip Phelps, a
farmer of the county, a son of John Phelps,
an early pioneer who was killed by the Indians. F. M. Green, the first of two sons,
received his education in the Kentucky University, from which he graduated in 1862.
He also graduated in the Harvard Law
School in 1864. In 1864 he entered a law
office in Richmond, and read and practiced
his profession until 1871, when he, with
Judge W. C. Miller purchased the *Kentucky
Register*, became the editor, and in 1872 became the sole proprietor and editor. The
paper was established in 1866, by B. H.
Brown. Mr. Green has made this one of the
best papers in Kentucky, with a circulation
of 1,200. The *Kentucky Register* is Democratic, modern and progressive, conscientious,
liberal and fair in advocating its principles,
always with the people for justice and right,
and opposed to extreme measures.

G. W. GREENE, editor and proprietor of
the Washington County *Leader*, was born in
Washington County, February 22, 1859, and
is the second son of Charles and Julia (Mc-
Intire) Greene, both parents natives of Kentucky. Frank Greene, subject's grandfather,
was a native of Ireland. He came to the
United States many years ago and settled at
Louisville, where he engaged in the cabinet-
making business, which he carried on until
his death, a number of years before subject's
birth. He was a skillful workman, and did a
thriving business for many years. Charles
Greene was born in Bardstown, Ky., in 1823,
and is still living, his present home being
Springfield. He is an architect and builder,
and came to Springfield about the year 1855.
Subject's maternal grandfather, John McIntire, was born in Washington County, Ky.,
and is a son of Thomas McIntire, who came
from Maryland with the earliest pioneer settlers of central Kentucky. John McIntire
is still living in his native county, and is a
man of considerable local prominence, having
served as county court judge for a period
of twelve years. Julia Greene, wife of Charles
Greene, was born in Washington County, and
died in 1859. She was the mother of but
two children, named, John and G. W. Greene,
both of whom reside in Springfield. G. W.
Greene was reared in Louisville, and was educated in the public schools of the city and
Cecilian College, the latter of which he attended two years. At the age of sixteen he

entered the publishing house of John P. Morton to learn the printer's trade, and remained with him two and one-half years, at the end of which time he entered the *Courier-Journal* office, where he remained one year. Mr. Greene has traveled extensively over the South and West, and has worked on a number of the leading papers in Illinois, Kentucky, Tennessee, Missouri and Ohio, among which may be mentioned the Chicago *Inter-Ocean*, Cincinnati *Enquirer*, *Commercial-Gazette*, *Globe-Democrat*, Nashville *American*, Memphis *Appeal* and *Avalanche*, and others. He came to Springfield in 1884, and engaged as compositor on the Washington *Leader*, and on May 14 of the following year became editor and proprietor. The *Leader* is a flourishing local sheet, Democratic in politics, has a circulation of 800, and under Mr. Greene's management has become quite successful. Mr. Greene was married November 11, 1885, to Miss Annie Shader, daughter of J. A. and Emma (McAhan) Shader, of Springfield. Mr. and Mrs. Greene are members of the Catholic Church.

H. J. GREENWELL. The Bardstown Male and Female Institute was originally established by the Methodist Episcopal Church in about 1845. Later John Atkinson purchased a controlling interest and continued the school until 1865, when it had become so demoralized by the war that the stock fell greatly, and about that time it was purchased by the Baptist Church, under which management it has since continued. It had suffered severely by the devastation incident to war; in fact, the building was occupied by Federal troops as a hospital for a year; subsequently, up to 1876, considerable difficulty was experienced in getting a satisfactory head to the establishment, but at that time H. J. Greenwell became its principal, who has since, by dint of extraordinary exertion, coupled with his ability as an educator, gradually rebuilt the school to its former permanent and extensive usefulness. Its board of trustees are of the prominent and influential citizens of the vicinity, and its corps of teachers are all eminently qualified for the positions which they occupy. Mr. Hilory J. Greenwell, its principal, is a native Kentuckian, born in Nelson County, in 1840. His parents, John and Mary (Greenwell) Greenwell, were also native Kentuckians, whose parents in turn were natives of Virginia, and emigrated in an early day. Prof. H. J. Greenwell was educated at Georgetown College, Kentucky, and graduated from that institution in 1873; anterior in date to that he studied law, and was admitted to practice; immediately subsequent he engaged in teaching for five years previous to entering college. After graduation he resumed his profession of teaching, which he has since continued. In 1874 Miss Ida Bondurant became his wife, and to their union four children have been born, viz.: Wilton R., John W., Basil M. and Charles L. His wife is a very fine artist and an excellent educator, her works of art having taken premiums whenever exhibited.

THOMAS N. GREER, the next eldest child of James and Elizabeth (Milton) Greer, was born October 5, 1825, in Nelson County. Samuel Greer, his paternal grandfather, was a native of Ireland, and there grew to manhood. When he came to the United States he first located in Pennsylvania, where he lived for a number of years, and where his marriage to Miss Rebecca Howard occurred. In 1783 he came to Kentucky, passing through Pittsburgh and down the Ohio River to the falls, where he landed, and after a short stop proceeded to the interior and settled in Nelson County of which he continued a resident until his death, which occurred about 1819, at an advanced age. Richard Milton, subject's maternal grandfather, was a native of the "Old Dominion," and came to Kentucky when a youth, locating in Nelson County, and remaining a resident until a few years anterior to his death, when he removed to Shelby County, near Mount Eden, where he died at the age of seventy-nine years, in 1851. James Greer, father of Thomas N., was born September 7, 1797. In 1822 he was united in marriage to Miss Elizabeth Milton, by whom he became the father of the following-named children: Milton, Thomas N., Sarah (deceased), Harriet H. (deceased), William B., Samuel H., Cornelia A., Richard J. and Elizabeth (deceased). His vocation was farming and he was a member of the Methodist Episcopal Church, with which he had been connected for over thirty years. He died July 11, 1871. Thomas N. Greer remained at home and assisted his parents on the farm until he attained the age of twenty-six years. March 1, 1855, he married Miss Sarah L. Foster, and to their union eight children have been born, of whom six are now living: James F., who married Virginia Lee; Anna D., Harriet H. (wife of Hezekiah Wigington), Bertha, Walter and Margaret F. In his vocation of farming Mr. Greer has been highly successful and owns about 500 acres of well improved land. He and wife and three children are members of the Methodist Episcopal Church South, and one of the children is a member of the Baptist Church. In politics he has always been a Democrat.

RICHARD J. GREER, the next youngest child of the family of James and Elizabeth (Milton) Greer, was born on the farm where he now resides, February 9, 1842. He was reared on the homestead farm and received a good common education in the schools of his native county of Nelson. October 23, 1873, his marriage with Miss Kate W. Watts was solemnized, and to their union seven children have been born, of which these four are now living: Mattie W., Minnie L., Bessie C. and Richard J. Our subject has always followed farming with uniform success, and is the proprietor of a fine, well improved farm of over 248 acres, situated on the Bardstown and Bloomfield pike. He and wife are members of the Methodist Episcopal Church. In politics he is a Democrat.

DR. STEPHEN HANNA GROOMS was born July 2, 1838, in Elkton, Todd Co., Ky. His father, Dr. Hiram Butler Grooms, a native of Culpeper County, Va., was reared in Scott County, Ky. He practiced medicine at Vevay, Ind., then at Hickman, Ky., and about 1838 located at Elkton, where he practiced until his death, October 6, 1857, at the age of fifty-seven years. His brother, Col. Horatio, a soldier in the war of 1812, burnt the barn on the battle-field at River Raisin, and was lieutenant-colonel from Kentucky, in the Mexican war. Thornton and Charles were also his brothers, and Elizabeth (Goul), his sister. Hiram B. married Nancy Hanna, of Allensville (probably born in Mercer County, died December 20, 1856, aged fifty-seven years); daughter of Stephen Hanna, Sr., native of Pennsylvania, and a soldier in the Revolutionary war; Elizabeth Forman, a native of Virginia, was Stephen Hanna, Sr.'s wife. From the union of Hiram B. and Nancy Grooms sprang Stephen H., who was married September 18, 1867, to Miss Virginia A., daughter of Fielding and Adelaide (Halliard) Bush, of Clark County, born February 20, 1847, and to them have been born Horace Bass (deceased), Walter Bush (deceased), Stephen Madison and Forrest B. In 1857 Stephen H. commenced the study of medicine with Dr. McReynolds of Elkton, and graduated in 1859 at Jefferson Medical College, Philadelphia, practiced first at Elkton, and to some extent at his present location on the pike, two miles south of Pleasant Hill, Mercer County, to which he came in 1869. The Doctor is also engaged in farming, having 150 acres of land in a high state of cultivation. He is a Royal Arch Mason and an Ancient Odd Fellow; is a member of the Christian Church and a Democrat.

ANDREW JANUARY GRUNDY was born in Maysville, Ky., October 18, 1842. His father, Rev. Dr. R. C. Grundy, was born in Washington County, Ky., in 1807. He officiated as pastor of the First Presbyterian Church at Maysville for twenty-one years, afterward in the second church of Memphis, Tenn., for seven years, and for several years he had charge of the Central Church of Cincinnati, Ohio, where he ended his labors in 1865. He was thrice married, first to Miss Hannah M. Camfield of Morristown, N. J.; to this marriage was born one daughter, Elizabeth, now deceased. In 1838 he married Sarah A. January, of Maysville, Ky. To this union was born one son, Andrew J., and one daughter, Sarah, who died in infancy. His third marriage was with a Miss Kemper of Cincinnati, Ohio; her father was a Virginian, and one of the early settlers of the "Ohio Country." To this third marriage were born five children: James, Robert, Frank, William and Nellie. Samuel Grundy, the father of Rev. Dr. R. C. Grundy, was a native of Washington County, Ky. He was an extensive farmer and a large landed proprietor, and a part of the estate left by him is now owned by Andrew J. Grundy. The father of Samuel was a native of England. Felix Grundy, a brother of Samuel, was one of the most successful criminal lawyers of his day. He removed to the State of Tennessee, where he soon took a high rank in his profession. He was a member of President Monroe's cabinet, and also served in both houses of the National Congress. Andrew January Grundy's maternal grandfather, Andrew McConnell January, was born in 1794; his ancestors were Huguenots, who left France at the time of the revocation of the edict of Nantes by Louis XIV in the year 1685. Andrew McConnell was born in Jessamine County; his wife, Sarah, a descendant of the Houstons of Fayette County, Ky. He removed some time after his marriage to Maysville, in Mason County, where he engaged in the commercial business, and afterward purchased the Maysville cotton-mills, and built up a business under the firm name of January & Wood, which name it retains to this day. His death occurred in 1877. Andrew January Grundy was educated in Maysville Male and Female Seminary, and in Centre College at Danville, Ky., and in 1863 took a position as teacher in the seminary. He was also principal of the high school at Maysville for four years. In 1868 he engaged in the book trade in Terre Haute, Ind.; after two years entered the Terre Haute High School, and was principal of that institution for some years. In 1871 he was married to Miss Willie J. Mc-Elroy: they are the parents of seven children, five of whom are living: John A., Sarah J., Bessie R., Hattie C. and Mary L. Mrs. Willie (McElroy) Grundy was born February 7, 1851, and is a daughter of John McElroy of Marion County. Mr. Grundy, in 1872, abandoned teaching, and returned to his country seat, Mount Aire, near the town of Lebanon, Marion County, where he owns 600 acres of valuable land; his attention is now given to the raising of stock. Mr. and Mrs. Grundy are members of the First Presbyterian Church of Lebanon, in which he is a ruling elder; he is also a member of the board of directors of the Danville Theological Seminary. Politically he is a Republican, but declines all offices with which politics have any connection. His many hundreds of volumes constitute one of the most valuable private libraries in the State, and he is liberal with his means in support of schools and colleges, more especially of his *alma mater*, Centre College.

ED C. HAGAN was born January 8, 1824, and is a son of Sidney and Nancy (Cecil) Hagan, who had born to them three sons and five daughters. Sidney Hagan was born in 1800, one mile east of New Hope, was reared a farmer and had 700 acres of land; he was also a large holder of slave property; was a clerk in his young days, also carried on distilling for forty years. He has lived in Marion County since 1823, and served several times as magistrate. He was a son of Clem Hagan and Millie (Miles) Hagan, who were natives of Maryland and Virginia respectively, and were among the first settlers on Pottinger's Creek. Clem Hagan was a farmer and distiller, and when but a small boy he lost his parents, who were of Irish descent. Mrs. Nancy Hagan was a daughter of James and Susan Hammett, who were natives of Cecil County, Md., and raised a family of eight children. Ed C. Hagan, who was born in the west part of Marion County, was raised on a farm and received a fair English education; he spent one year in St. Mary's College, taught in the common schools a few terms, and commenced the battle of life for himself at the age of eighteen years. September 2, 1861, he enlisted in Company B, Ninth Kentucky Confederate Infantry, participated in the battles of Shiloh and Stone River, and in fact was in all engagements in which the regiment took part except Baton Rouge. At the battle of Jonesboro, Ga., he lost his right arm, was captured and sent to the hospital, where he remained for eight months;

was at Camp Chase for four months, when he was released at the close of the war in June, 1865. He then turned to his home and engaged in stock trading two years, then engaged in general farming for seven years. In 1874 he commenced selling goods, which he continued four years, after which he returned to farming. In November, 1884, he returned to the dry goods business at New Hope where he is now engaged; he was also engaged for four years in distilling. October 7, 1879, he married Anna Parolee Barry, daughter of Dr. J. J. and Frances Felicia Barry of New Haven, Ky. Dr. Barry was born in County Cork, Ireland, came to Kentucky at the age of sixteen, graduated in medicine in Louisville, was the author of several religious and scientific works; understood seven different languages, lived and died a member of the Roman Catholic Church. Mrs. Barry was the daughter of the Rev. Samuel Jesse of Shelby County, Ky., and is a convert to the Catholic Church, her parents were born in Virginia. To Mr. Hagan's marriage four children were born: Joseph S. (deceased), Frank Miles, Augustine Bradford (deceased), and John Sidney. Mr. and Mrs. Hagan are members of the Roman Catholic Church. Mr. Hagan cast his first presidential vote for James Buchanan.

RICHARD HAMILTON (deceased), son of Alexander and Harriett (Edelen) Hamilton, was born in Washington County, Ky., December 29, 1811. His grandfather, Thomas Hamilton, was a native of Maryland, and one of the earliest pioneers of Washington County. He settled about five and one-half miles northwest of Springfield and was a resident of his adopted county until his death, which occurred many years ago. Alexander Hamilton was born in Maryland, but was brought to Kentucky when a small boy, and passed the remainder of his life in Washington County. He was a successful farmer, accumulated a large estate, and died in 1878 at the advanced age of ninety-one years. His wife, Harriett Hamilton, was born in Kentucky and died a number of years ago. She was the mother of six children, only one of whom is now living, Thomas G. Hamilton. Richard Hamilton was reared a farmer, and received a good education in the country schools and St. Mary's College. He began life as a teacher, which profession he followed a short time near Fredericktown, and later was elected magistrate, which position he held for several years. He was deputy sheriff under his father for some time, and later was elected sheriff. He acquired the reputation of being one of the most skillful business men in the county, and his services were constantly in demand, settling estates, etc. He engaged in farming in 1869 near Fredericktown village, which vocation he followed until his death, February 20, 1883. He was married August 1, 1876, to Mrs. Sallie J. Thompson, widow of John C. Thompson, and daughter of Stith and Catherine (McIlvoy) Thompson, by whom he had three children: A. Richard, Mary S. and S. Thomas. Mrs. Sallie J. Hamilton was born August 14, 1841, and is the fourth of a family of seven children. Her father, Stith Thompson, was the son of John Thompson. He was born November 5, 1805, and is still living in Washington, his native county. Catherine (McIlvoy) Thompson, daughter of Alexander and Magdalen McIlvoy, was born in Ireland on the 15th of August, 1811. Her parents came to America in 1818, and settled near the village of Mackville, Washington County, where the father died in 1863, at the age of ninety-three years. The mother died in 1846. The children of Stith and Catherine Thompson were the following: Alexander, William R., John M., Sallie J., Maggie, Rosa, and Daniel M. Thompson. Sallie J. Thompson was married February 10, 1867, to John C. Thompson, by whom she had three children, namely: Peter J., Simeon A. and John C., all living. John C. Thompson, Sr., son of Thomas and Susan (Blanford) Thompson, was born in Washington County on the 25th of March, 1825. He was a farmer by occupation, a successful trader, and resided nearly all his life near the village of Fredericktown. He was twice married, the first time on the 22d of October, 1861, to Miss Maggie Thompson, by whom he had two children: Alexander and Thomas. Mrs. Maggie Thompson died April 19, 1866, aged twenty-two years. His second marriage to Sallie J. Thompson, sister of former wife, has already been alluded to.

JAMES L. HAMILTON was born April 20, 1843, and is the second of five sons and seven daughters, all of whom were reared, born to Benjamin A. and Ann Margaret (Mayes) Hamilton, natives of Virginia. Benj. A. Hamilton immigrated to Green County with his parents about 1821 and settled on Pitman Creek, and became an extensive farmer and large land-holder. He was a son of Leonard and Martha (Chaudoin) Hamilton. Leonard was a carpenter and farmer, a patriot and soldier of 1812, settled on Pitman Creek in 1821, was of Scotch-Irish origin. Mrs. Ann M. Hamilton was a daughter of James Mayes, who was of English descent, born in Virginia, and settled in Green County about 1810. James L. Hamilton, born in Taylor County, was reared on a farm until seventeen years old, and received a common English education. In October, 1861, he enlisted in Company E, Thirteenth Kentucky Volunteers, and was in all the engagements in which his regiment took part. His first battle was Shiloh. He was discharged with his regiment January, 1865, and after his return home resumed farm life till 1878, when he made the race for jailer; was elected and still holds the office. He has been a resident of Green County since a child of one year. January 28, 1869, he was united in marriage to Nancy E. Hagan, a daughter of H. T. and Mary Jane (Smith) Hagan, natives of Brownstown, Ind., and Virginia, respectively. Mr. Hagan in his early day was a wool carder; when yet a young man he settled in Green County, Ky., and during and since the war has been a merchant at Rolling Ridge, Green County; was of Irish descent. Mary Jane (Smith) Hagan is a daughter of John Smith, who was a farmer and early settler in Taylor County. Mr. and Mrs. Hamilton have had born to them two children: Lela G. and Ulysses Grant. He is now an active Republican, but cast his first vote for Geo. B. McClellan.

WILLIAM H. HAMILTON, the only merchant in the village of Breeding's and a native of Metcalfe County, was born November 2, 1857. His father, William Hamilton, also a native of Metcalfe and a life-long farmer, was born June 1, 1829. In 1853 he married Miss Melissa F. Kinnaird, a daughter of Harrison and Isaphena (Patterson) Kinnaird, the former a Kentuckian, the latter a Virginian. Their marriage was blessed by the birth of one child—William H. (subject). He owns and cultivates a well improved, fertile farm of 125 acres, on which he has placed a log and frame residence and good general improvements. Mr. and Mrs. Hamilton are both members of the Cumberland Presbyterian Church. Harrison Kinnaird was a Virginia farmer, and the son of David and Polly Kinnaird. William Hamilton, grandfather of William H., a native of the Old Dominion and a farmer, immigrated to Metcalfe County in early life, where he entered 150 acres of the forest, erected a log cabin of the pioneer style of architecture, and began the life of a Kentucky farmer. He married Miss Butler, of Virginia—which marriage occurred in Kentucky—and to them were born six children, by name John, Edward, Susan, wife of Samuel Marrs; William, Benjamin and Elizabeth, wife of John Price—of whom only William and Susan are now living. The death of William Hamilton occurred in his seventy-fourth year, and that of his wife in the seventy-first year of her age, and in life they were members of the Cumberland Presbyterian Church. William H. Hamilton in youth received a good English education in the three-months schools of Metcalfe County and in the high school of Edmonton, where he attended one session of ten months. His early life, until seventeen years of age, was spent in agricultural pursuits, and at the age of eighteen taught one school of three months. He then began selling goods for J. H. Kinnaird, of Red Lick, which he continued thirty months. In 1880 he embarked in the general merchandising business in Breeding's, with a capital of $1,100. He has since continued the business very successfully, and now does a very large business, with a flourishing trade of $20,000 per annum sales. His stock, which consists of groceries, dry goods, hardware, drugs, and a general line of merchandise, is valued at $6,000, and besides the merchandising business he buys tobacco—this year to the extent of 125,000 pounds. Mr. Hamilton was united in marriage in July, 1880, to Miss Theo K. Woodward, a daughter of Julius and Mary J. (Marrs) Woodward, natives of Metcalfe County, and their marriage has been blessed by one child—Gilford Etrick, born in June, 1881. Mrs. Hamilton is a member of the Baptist Church, while Mr. Hamilton, who is not a member of any church, believes in the doctrines of Presbyterianism. He is politically a member of the Democratic party. He owns a small farm of 125 acres near Breeding's, and his estate is worth about $8,000.

SQUIRE JOHN W. HAMNER was born December 6, 1815, in Mercer (now Boyle) County, Ky.; in 1816 was taken by his parents to Hardin County; in 1820 to Bartholomew County, Ind., and in 1829 was brought to Boyle County, Ky., where he has since resided. His father, William Hamner, a native of Mecklenburg County, Va., removed with his parents in an early day to Boyle County, Ky., and located two and one-half miles south of Perryville. He assisted in laying off the town of Columbus, Ind., was a magistrate there and a Methodist class leader, having preaching at his house. He was accidentally killed by a falling limb, June 10, 1822. He was the son of Henry Hamner, a Virginian and a Revolutionary soldier; a Methodist in Kentucky, and at his house Cartwright, Linsey, Stevenson, Akers, Bascomb and others preached. He passed away at a great age about 1842. He married Sarah Decker, and from their union sprang Polly (Cole), Nancy (Day), William, James, Lucy (Clarkston), Rev. Henry, Sarah (Mitchell), Elizabeth (Minor), Jesse and Rebecca (Bilbo). William married first, Rebecca, daughter of John Day, of Boyle County (died about 1826), and their offspring are James B., Frances E. (Blackketter), Henry L., John W., William M., Edmund D. and Sarah A. (Hopkins). By a second marriage, Martha J. (Owsley) was born. October 12, 1847, John W. Hamner was married to Miss Sarah Pitman, daughter of Giles and Jemima (Mozee) Andrews, of Lincoln County (born in 1822), and to them have been born two daughters: Sarah Frances and Rachel Ann (twins). Mr. Hamner served as magistrate and member of the court of claims of Boyle County four years. For many years he followed stone cutting as a profession, but is now engaged in farming. In religion he is a Methodist. He was formerly an old line Whig and a Union man, but now affiliates with the Democratic party. He lost fourteen slaves as the result of the late war.

WILLIAM E. HANCOCK was born November 29, 1838. His father, J. P. Hancock, was born March 27, 1813, in Adair County. He began the battle of life with no inheritance, and was married first to Miss Emma, daughter of Richard Cundiff, a native of Adair County and a wealthy farmer. By this marriage J. P. Hancock became the father of six children: Mary E. (Stone), W. E., Richard, George W., T. T. and Hannah J., of whom W. E., Mary E. and T. T. are living. Richard Hancock enlisted in 1861 in Company A, Third Kentucky Infantry (Federal Volunteer service) and served eighteen months as fifer, during which time he contracted the consumption, of which he died in 1862. Geo. Hancock enlisted in Company C, Thirteenth Kentucky Infantry, Federal Volunteer service, and was killed in a skirmish in Louisville, in the fall of 1864. Mrs. Hancock was in life a member of the Christian Church, and died in 1848, in her fortieth year. The second marriage of J. P. Hancock was to Miss Elizabeth, daughter of Tandy Bailey, a native of Adair County and a farmer. Mrs. Elizabeth (Bailey) Hancock was also a member of the Christian Church, and lived only about five years after marriage, dying about 1856. Mr. Hancock's third marriage was to Miss Elizabeth, daughter of Elijah and Julia (Bomer) Cravens, and they are the parents of four children, Nancy Bell, Oliver P., Sally (who died in infancy) and Benjamin C. J. B. Hancock owns a farm of 130 acres, where he has lived during the past thirty-four years. He and wife are both members of the Christian Church, and he is

Republican in politics. William Hancock, grandfather of William E. Hancock, was a native of the Old Dominion, a veteran of the American Revolution, and one of the pioneer settlers of Adair County. He was married to a Mrs. Mary Emerson, and they were the parents of three children: J. P., O. H. and Nancy. He had been married before and had three children by this first marriage: Simon, Elizabeth (Cheatham) and William. William E. Hancock, a native of Adair County, remained at home until twenty-two years of age, when, on December 9, 1863, he was married to Miss Celestia B., a daughter of Elijah and Julia (Bomer) Cravens, also natives of Adair County. Elijah Cravens was a carpenter, in his latter days a farmer, and died July 17, 1873, in the seventy-fourth year of his age. His widow, a member of the Christian Church, died August 4, 1879, in the seventy-eighth year of her age. Mr. and Mrs. Hancock have been blessed by four children: Elijah P., Julia E., Edward F. and Sally F., all living. The first tract of land that Mr. Hancock owned was fifteen acres, which he purchased from his father. The next was a tract of seventy-six acres near Cane Valley, which he enlarged to 152 acres, which was his home eight years. December 17, 1884, he removed to his present location on 210 acres of well improved and fertile land, on which is a good two-story frame residence, good barns and stables. He values the place at $2,250. All of this is the result of Mr. Hancock's own labor and management, as he began without a dollar. In November, 1861, Mr. Hancock enlisted in Company C, Thirteenth Kentucky Volunteer Infantry, Federal service, and was orderly sergeant until captured in August, 1863, by Morgan. He was exchanged in April, 1864, after which he served as private until January, 1865, when he received an honorable discharge. He participated in the battles of Shiloh, Corinth, Hough's Ferry (Tenn.), Knoxville and Atlanta. While on duty at Louisville, a short time before he was mustered out of the service, he received a gunshot wound in the right knee, for which he draws a pension. Theodore T. Hancock, a brother of William E., enlisted in 1863, in Company L, Thirteenth Kentucky Cavalry, Federal Volunteer service, and served until January, 1865, when he received an honorable discharge. Mr. and Mrs. Hancock are both members of the Christian Church, and Mr. Hancock in politics is a Republican.

JUNIUS HANCOCK was born June 2, 1851, in Adair County, and is the second in a family of three children—two sons and one daughter—born to John and Martha J. (Miller)

Hancock, both natives of Adair County, and of Irish and Holland descent, respectively. John Hancock was born October 27, 1824, and is the ninth of ten children, born to Wm. and Alsie (Settles) Hancock. September 4, 1847, he married Miss Martha J., the fourth child and second daughter of Nathan and Rachel (Vannoy) Miller's family of ten children. Her family were originally from the "Old Dominion" and were among the early pioneers of Adair County. Mr. Hancock and wife are yet living and reside about four miles northeast of Columbia on the old homestead, where Mr. Hancock was born and where he has all his life been successfully engaged in agricultural pursuits. He and wife are, and have been from early life, devoted members of the Christian Church, in which church he has officiated for many years both as deacon and ruling elder. His father, William Hancock, was born in Virginia, June 1, 1782. Junius Hancock received a good common-school and academic education in youth, although his early life was spent on the old home farm. After attaining his majority he commenced the study of law under the preceptorship of Maj. T. C. Winfrey, of Columbia. He was admitted to the bar in August, 1873, and commenced the practice of the profession at Columbia, continuing until August, 1874, when he was elected clerk of the Adair County Circuit Court on the Democratic ticket, and was re-elected on an independent ticket in 1880, and is still the incumbent of the office, being now a candidate on the Republican ticket for the responsible position of county judge. Mr. Hancock was married December 29, 1875, to Miss Mollie J., youngest daughter of the three children of George W. and Elizabeth V. (Watson) Damron, both natives of Adair County. Four children have blessed their union, as follows: William F., Mason W., Samuel N. and Bettie D. Both Mr. Hancock and wife are members of the Christian Church, in which church he has officiated as deacon for several years. In politics he was formerly a Democrat but is now identified with the Republican party, and is one of the enterprising and successful professional and business men of the town and county.

JOHN G. HANDY (deceased) was born April 2, 1801, in Scott County, Ky., where he was reared to manhood, and early turned his attention to construction and building, at which he rose to considerable eminence, erecting many of the finest buildings in the central portion of the State. He was preeminently a self-made man and his successful career was largely due to his untiring energy and well known integrity. In his later life he engaged in farming, and was long a magistrate and a member of the court of claims of Mercer County. Democratic in politics, he sustained a loss of thirty slaves as a result of the late war. As a Christian he united with the church under the ministrations of Rev. Barton W. Stone and remained a consistent member until his death, which occurred March 19, 1867. Firm in his convictions, he was a man of marked decision of character. On October 30, 1825, he was united in marriage to Miss Mary, daughter of Benjamin and Jane (Minter) Watkins, of Woodford County, (born October 30, 1802, died August 6, 1877,) and their union was favored by the birth of William A., Martha J. (deceased), Benjamin W. (deceased), Walter W., George N. and Mary E. (McElroy).

George Nuckols Handy was born August 12, 1840, in Woodford County; in 1842 removed with his parents to Mercer County, locating on the old Gabriel Slaughter farm, and in 1870 settled on "Adair Place," three miles east of Harrodsburg, where he has since resided. June, 1861, he enlisted in Capt. McNairy's Company, Tennessee Confederate Cavalry, with whom he remained until after the evacuation of Nashville, when he united with Capt. Phil B. Thomson's company, Kentucky Cavalry, and after the battle of Shiloh entered Company E, Second Kentucky Confederate Cavalry, colonel, Basil Duke. He was captured in 1863 in Mercer County, and remained a prisoner of war at Camps Chase and Douglas, until near the close of the contest. August 19, 1882, he was united in marriage to Miss Mary H., daughter of Dr. David S. and Amelia (Handy) McGaughey, of Morristown, Shelby Co., Ind. (born March 31, 1843), and to them has been born one daughter, Georgie, September 3, 1884. Hr. Handy is a farmer, having 362 acres of well improved land. This place was formerly the home of Gen. John A. Adair, and here his body reposed until removed by the State and placed among the remains of other eminent men of the commonwealth.

SMITH HANSFORD was born October 30, 1839. His father, John S. Hansford, was born in Lincoln County in November, 1800, and was a farmer and merchant. In 1824 he was married to Miss Harriet, daughter of William and Martha Bain (Owsley) Farris, of Lincoln County. William Farris was a farmer and breeder of blooded stock, being among the first Kentuckians who turned their attention to fine stock. His wife was a daughter of Gov. Owsley. John S. Hansford sold goods at Crab Orchard and in Keene, but lost all his slaves and other property during the late war. In 1868 he removed to Harrodsburg and purchased a hotel, which he ran under the name of the Hansford House. He was elder of the Christian Church, and died in November, 1874. Mrs. Hansford, who was also a member of the Christian Church, died in 1876 in the seventy-second year of her age. The names of their children are W. T. (deceased); Susan M., first married to Elder Richard Swift, of the Christian Church and professor in the college in Georgetown, and after his death married to Daniel Lyne who is also dead; Emma, wife of H. P. Middleton, of Lincoln County, and Smith. Of this family Smith and Susan M. are living. Thomas Hansford, grandfather of Smith Hansford, was born in Virginia, near Abington. He was married to Miss Margaret Beatty, and they immigrated to Lincoln County, Ky., when it was a wilderness. They reared a family of ten children, of whom the only survivors, Margaret (Stevenson) and Lucinda (Stevenson), are living in Harrodsburg. Thomas Hansford was a farmer, and a minister of the Baptist Church the early part of his life. He and his wife died and are buried in Lincoln County. The Hansford family are purely of English origin and there is but the one family in Kentucky. Smith Hansford was educated in the schools of Lincoln, his native county, and began selling goods for his father before he reached his majority. In 1862 he enlisted in Company B, Sixth Kentucky Confederate Cavalry, a part of Gen. Morgan's celebrated command. He was captured at Buffington Island on Morgan's raid through Ohio and confined in prison at Camp Douglas, from which he, with four others, escaped by digging a tunnel, which took them two weeks. He was arrested while on his way back to the army at Maysville, Ky., and a guard placed over him at the Lee House, but he and a comrade who was under arrest gave the guard the slip, and subsequently joined Gen. Duke in Virginia. Mr. Hansford was surrendered and paroled at Gen. Lee's surrender. On March 6, 1866, he was married in Harrodsburg to Miss Elizabeth A., daughter of John K. Wilson, of Harrodsburg. John K. Wilson's father, John Wilson, was an officer in the Continental Army during the American Revolution and underwent a most severe term of confinement in the Dartmore prison. Mr. Hansford came to Harrodsburg in 1868 and entered the dry goods business with James C. Wilson. At this time Mr. Hansford had less than $1,000. The firm of Hansford & Wilson sold out their business to W. T. Curry, and one year after this Hansford and Tribble purchased the business of W. T. Curry and continued business together about six months, when Mr. Hansford purchased his partner's interest in the business and was alone the succeeding five years. In 1874 Mr. H. C. Bohon purchased an interest in the business, and the firm of Bohon & Hansford did a thriving business until 1884. Mr. Bohon became cashier of the First National Bank and sold his interest in the business to Hansford, Curry & Co., who still conduct it. To the marriage of Mr. and Mrs. Hansford have been born three children: Hattie May, Emma Bird and Maurice Farris, all living. Mrs. Hansford, a member of the Christian Church, died on January 14, 1883, in the fortieth year of her age. On April 15, 1886, Mr. Hansford was married to Miss Cornelia Oldham, of Mt. Sterling.

JUDGE CHARLES A. HARDIN was born May 8, 1836. He is the eldest son of the late Parker C. Hardin, by his second wife, whose maiden name was Caroline Watkins. Judge Hardin, on his mother's side, is a lineal descendant of Bartholomew Depew, the French Huguenot, and the ancestral tree is yet preserved in the family. His mother was a very pious woman, and possessed an excellent judgment and a good education. Charles A. Hardin received his preparatory education in the schools of Columbia, in his native county of Adair, after which he spent five years in Centre College, graduating there in 1856. His contemporaries at college were W. C. P. Breckinridge, Boyd Winchester, William Leroy Delaney, John Young Brown and James B. McCreary, either with whom he was personally associated, either in the classroom or the halls of the literary societies. He then spent a year reading law in the office of his father, obtained license to practice in 1857, and started west to recruit his health. In 1858 Mr. Hardin settled in Georgetown, Mo., and entered into a law partnership with John F. Phillips, with whom he had spent four years at college. A year later he married Miss Jennie, daughter of Col. Ebenezer Magoffin, who resided near Georgetown. At the begining of the war, Mr. Hardin enlisted under Gen. Price, and was in active service in the Confederate Army, until failing health again interfered with his plans, and he was obliged to return home. In the winter of 1862 he was captured by Gen. Smith, and subjected to severe imprisonment for refusing to join the home guards. After his parole he returned to Kentucky and settled in Harrodsburg, in the spring of 1863, where he immediately entered the practice of law. He devoted himself to the practice of his profession, and never entered the arena of politics until 1876, when he was candidate for the nomination of his party to Congress. Judge Durham received the nomination, and Mr. Hardin was not again a candidate for office until 1880, when he was nominated for circuit judge of the Eighteenth Judicial District of Kentucky. He only became a candidate after the earnest solicitation of a large number of citizens, and when he acceded to their wishes he entered the race with a determination to win, which he did after an exciting canvass. Judge Hardin has been a Democrat throughout his life, and has been a member of the Christian Church since his fifteenth year. He has a strong liking for domestic life, and spends much time with his family, which consists of himself, wife and three sons, of whom, E. M., the eldest was formerly publisher of the *Harrodsburg Observer*. He enjoys excellent health, is five feet ten inches in hight, weighs 160 pounds, and has dark hair and eyes. Judge Hardin's legal practice has ever been large, and his clients belong to that class of people who select an attorney on account of his ability and honesty, rather than for any other quality. He is justly proud of the memory of his father, and claims to be indebted to him for the training which has given him success in life. Hon. P. W. Hardin, attorney-general of Kentucky, is his brother, and was the junior member of his law firm in Harrodsburg, Ky., at the time of his election.

AARON HARDING. The father of Aaron Harding was born in 1756, in the Monongahela country, in Pennsylvania, near the Virginia line; was a soldier in and many years afterward was pensioned as a survivor of the Revolutionary war; was a soldier in some of the Indian wars and was severely wounded in battle. He removed to a farm near Campbellsville, Ky., about 1787, and here Aaron Harding was born February 23, 1805. The latter spent his boyhood on the farm. At the age of eighteen he had a long and extremely painful attack of white swelling, which lasted for years, and lamed him for life. The stern, self-reliant character of the man, is well illustrated by an incident which occurred during this illness. The treatment of his physician consisted of local applications and internal remedies, and did not in his judgment meet the requirements of the case. Having procured a keen penknife, with his own hand he cut his leg to the bone, opened a long wound, and then called the family to his assistance. The treatment was trying and dangerous, but effective, as his convalescence dated from this time. Every interval of freedom from suffering from this disease was improved by earnest study and judicious reading, and he came forth from the sick room, having added greatly to the stock of knowledge he had acquired in the common schools in boyhood. As soon as he could walk on crutches he began teaching school, and at the same time to study law. He afterward completed his studies while residing with his brother-in-law, Mordecai Hardin, of Washington County, Ky., and was licensed in 1833. He immediately began to practice at Greensburg, in his native county, the bar there being celebrated for its able lawyers. He continued to study with the most earnest diligence, acquiring the art of shorthand writing, so that notes of his reading might be copiously and rapidly taken. Almost at once he acquired the reputation of a laborious, painstaking lawyer, thoroughly versed in the principles of the law, and a master of the intricate system of pleadings then in vogue. He was county attorney for Green County, from October, 1837, to October, 1839, at once distinguishing himself as an earnest and forcible speaker. He was elected to the Legislature in 1840, after a notable canvass defeating Hon. Wm. T. Willis, who was most justly regarded as one of the most talented and popular men of his day. His career in the Legislature attracted marked attention, and was highly commended by the press and people. He resumed the practice of the law, traveling over a large circuit, uninterruptedly, during a period of twenty years, being employed in most of the important litigation of that section. In the long series of legal battles he built up for himself a reputation as a lawyer that any man might have been proud of. In 1861 he earnestly opposed secession, believing a division of the Union would be destructive to commerce, result in continual complications and mutual hatreds, would compel the maintenance of hostile standing armies, and that bloody and interminable conflicts would result, that the South could not succeed, but that success itself would be disastrous. He urged his people to turn away from extreme counsels on both sides, and while condemning the Southern leaders he most vigorously fought, the extremists of the North, viewing, with bitterness and pain, the unhappy condition of the South in the years succeeding the war. He was elected to Congress in 1861 by a majority vote of 7,875, he receiving 10,344

votes, and his opponent 2,469. The State was then redistricted, many new counties being exchanged for the old ones in his district, but he was again elected in 1863 by a majority of 7,927, he receiving 10,435 votes, and his opponent 2,508 votes. In 1865 he was again elected by a majority of 5,785, receiving 9,437 votes, and his opponent 3,652 votes. He was a candidate for the United States Senate in 1867, being for a week during the balloting the leading candidate, and lacking but few votes of an election. While in Congress he acted with the Democrats, making an enviable record. He now removed to Danville, and resumed the practice of the law. It was impossible for him to be otherwise than thorough in all he undertook, and the eager interest in his business was, after a few years, too much for his delicate constitution. He was after a few years stricken with paralysis, and after a few years more died in Georgetown, December 24, 1875. He was through life a most earnest and consistent member of the Baptist Church, never failing to let his Christian light shine in every walk in life. He was twice married; first to Margaret Campbell, from whose father Campellsville received its name. Five children survived them, viz.: Mrs. McDonald, wife of Rev. Dr. McDonald, of Atlanta, Ga.; John Harding, of Henry County, Ky.; Mrs. James H. Gentry; Samuel and Robert Harding, of Danville. His second wife, who was Miss Sallie Callendar, also survives him.

ROBERT HARDING was born February 12, 1852, in Green County, Ky., and is a son of Aaron and Margaret (Campbell) Harding, who had born to them five children: Mattie, John, Samuel, Sallie and Robert. (See sketch of Samuel Harding above.) Robert Harding lived in Greensburg until ten years old, and was raised partly in Washington, D. C., while his father was in Congress. He graduated in the class of 1873 from Centre College, and in 1874 began the study of law in Danville, with his brother. In the same year he was licensed to practice. In 1878 he was elected county attorney, and re-elected in 1882. He was married October 22, 1879, to Maggie B. Robinson, daughter of Richard M. and Margaret (Hoskins) Robinson. Mr. Robinson was a native of Fayette and his wife of Garrard County. Richard M. Robinson died at the age of fifty-one. Camp Dick Robinson, the first Union camp south of the Ohio River, was located on his beautiful farm; here Gen. Nelson was buried. Mr. Harding and wife are members of the Baptist Church. In alluding to the nuptials of Mr. and Mrs. Harding a local paper contained an elaborate notice from which the following is extracted: "Both of the contracting parties have been well and favorably known in this community since their earliest youth, and both have been general favorites in society. The bride is the youngest daughter of Mrs. M. P. Robinson, widow of the late Richard Robinson, for whom Camp Dick Robinson took its name. She is well known throughout central Kentucky as one of the most beautiful young ladies of the State, and an acknowledged belle. Her cultured mind, and lovely and amiable disposition, her bewitching and gentle manners always caused her to be admired and beloved by all who knew her. The groom, Mr. Robert Harding, is the youngest son of the late Aaron Harding, and now holds the office of county attorney for Boyle County. He is a young lawyer of ability and rare promise. Trinity Church was elaborately and beautifully decorated with rare and exquisite natural flowers and evergreens. An hour before the appointed time for the ceremony to take place, the church was filled to overflowing, aisles, lobby, door and windows being filled with eager spectators. The following young ladies and gentlemen were the attendants: Miss Sallie Harding and Mr. Richard Dunlap; Miss Sallie Brown, of Nicholasville, and Wm. Robinson; Miss Annie Shelby and Robert Evans; Miss Annie Lee and Jas. Gentry. Immediately after the ceremony the bridal party and a large number of invited guests repaired to 'Camp Dick,' the home of the bride, where they were hospitably and elegantly entertained."

DAVID HARDING was born October 30, 1844, and is a son of Stephen and Charlotte (Cleaver) Harding. Stephen Harding was a substantial farmer and slave owner, and a son of John C. and Susan (Fisher) Harding, of English descent, who came from Virginia in the early settlement of Kentucky, were substantial slave owners and died at an advanced age. David Harding was born in Marion County, as were also his parents, and was reared on a farm. He received a liberal common education, and at twenty-one commenced active life for himself. He was married in February, 1871, to Mary E., a daughter of Wayne and America (Dodson) Ferguson, both of Harding County. Wayne Ferguson was a farmer and hotel-keeper in Bradsfordville, Marion, to which county he moved about 1857. He served as captain in the Sixth Kentucky Federal Regiment, and lives in Lebanon, to which place he moved in 1870. Mr. and Mrs. Harding have had born to them two children: Candacy L. and Benjamin David.

After his marriage Mr. Harding located where he now resides on 300 acres formerly his father's. The farm is well improved, and in a good state of cultivation, containing considerable Rolling Fork bottom. He also owns several tracts of timber land. Mr Harding in politics is a Democrat, and he and wife are members of the Baptist Church.

DR. WILLIAM BAUGHMAN HARLAN was born July 1, 1828, on the Hanging Fork of Dick's River, five miles southeast of Danville, Boyle County; in 1848 he removed to Buchanan County, Mo.; in 1853 he returned to Kentucky, and with his brother Jacob purchased Crab Orchard Springs, which they managed two years, when he returned to Boyle County where he has since resided. His father was Henry Harlan (see sketch of J. W. Harlan). Dr. William B. was first married April 3, 1855, to Miss Sarah E., daughter of Samuel O. and Mary (Porter) Middleton of Lincoln County (born July 7, 1837, died January 27, 1862) and their children are Samuel, Jacob and Henry Miller. He was next married June 2, 1862, to Miss Eliza O., sister to his first wife (born March 28, 1842), and to them have been born Sarah E. (Bright), Mary A. (deceased), Martha (Hutchings), Almira, Rhoda, William, Thomas J., Eliza and Robert J. (deceased). Dr. Harlan commenced the study of medicine in 1849, with Dr. T. W. Jackson, of Danville, and graduated at the Louisville University in 1853. He has practiced at Danville, Crab Orchard, and his present location in Boyle, where he has met with success. He is a member of the Baptist Church, and was formerly an old line Whig, but is now a Democrat. He lost twenty slaves by the late war.

JEHU WELLINGTON HARLAN was born September 30, 1856, in Boyle County, where he has always resided. His father, Jacob Harlan, was born May 1, 1818, five miles southeast of Danville, where he was reared. In 1843 he removed to Buchanan County, Mo., and in 1847 returned to Boyle County, Ky. In 1853 he purchased Crab Orchard Springs, and in 1855 he purchased the ancestral homestead where he now resides, consisting of 250 acres of productive land in a good state of cultivation. He was an old line Whig, a Union man, and lost sixteen slaves by the late war. In religion he is a reformer. He is the son of Henry Harlan, born in 1790 four miles east of Danville, who furnished a substitute in the war of 1812, was a farmer and slaveholder, a Whig, a Christian, and died in 1855. He was the son of George Harlan, a native of North Carolina, who traded a negro woman for 300 acres of good land, where he settled in (now) Boyle County, Ky., was a pioneer, a Christian, and died in 1836. He married Catherine Pope, and their offspring were Jacob, Henry, George, Jeremiah (who was lost sight of), James, Joseph, Benjamin, John, Mary (Fleece), and Susan (McGee). Henry married Elizabeth, daughter of Robert and Nancy T. (Thomas) Bryan, of Boyle County (born in 1800, died in 1840), and the result of their union was Catherine (Carter), Jacob, Robert, George, James P., William B., Jeremiah, Mary (Bentley and Neal), John, Martha (Simpson), Henry, Paulina (Armstrong), and Elizabeth (Streit). Jacob Harlan first married in 1842, Miss Atlanta B., daughter of Jehu and Clarissa (Black) Harlan, of Salt River, Boyle County, (born in 1823, died October 8, 1856), and from their union sprang Mary C. (Bruce), Clarissa (Dunn), Maria I. (Baughman) and J. W. In 1857 he married Mrs. Louisa T. Roberts, daughter of James Center, of Lincoln County (born in 1825), and they have been favored with one daughter, Carrie M. (Bruce). On May 11, 1880, J. W. Harlan was married to Miss Annie S., daughter of George W. and Susan (Streit) Harlan of Cooper County, Mo. (born May 11, 1859), and to them have been born one daughter, Susie Lee, and a son, George Wellington Harlan. Mrs. Atlanta B. Harlan was a daughter of Jehu, the son of James Harlan, of Harlan Station. George, Sr., and James were cousins of Maj. Silas Harlan, who was slain at the battle of Blue Lick. J. W. Harlan is a farmer, having 300 acres of well improved land, and is a Baptist and a Democrat.

JAMES L. HARLAN was born December 26, 1828, where he now resides, two miles west of Danville, and son of Elijah and Sallie (Moore) Harlan, to whom two sons and eight daughters were born and reared, James L. being the eighth. Elijah Harlan was born at Harlan Station on Salt River, Boyle County, Ky. He served as sergeant in the war of 1812, Shelby's campaign. In 1812 he located where James L. now resides, on 350 acres, which he cleared and improved; built a stone house in the same year, which is still standing and occupied by James L. He died November 26, 1843, aged fifty-two years, and was a son of James Harlan, who married Mary Caldwell, both natives of Virginia; located in Mercer, now Boyle County, as early as 1780 or 1785, where Harlan Station now stands; remained here until his death in 1836. James Harlan, with seven sons, participated in Shelby's campaign; each

of these seven sons sent a son to the Mexican war, and the latter had sons in the late civil war. The Harlan family sprang from two brothers who came from Wales and settled in Pennsylvania, and from those spring all the known Harlans. Many of the early families participated in the war for independence. Sallie (Moore) Harlan was born in Boyle County and was a daughter of Lawson Moore, who came from Virginia as early as 1785, settled about one mile west of Danville, and who married Jane Rochester, daughter of Col. John Rochester, one of the earliest settlers and merchants of Danville, Ky. James L. was reared where he now resides, and received a good English education. In June, 1846, he enlisted for the Mexican war in Capt. S. S. Fry's company, Second Kentucky, participated in the battles of Buena Vista and Monterey. After his return resumed farming and trading, which he has successfully followed all his life, and now owns 225 acres. April 5, 1855, he was married to Lettie Maxwell, of Marion County, daughter of Joseph and Eunice (Stiles) Maxwell, of Marion County, Ky. Mr. and Mrs. Harlan had born, to bless their union, ten children: Jennie M., Eunice (now McCord), Julia (now Starks), Elijah, James L. (deceased), Joseph M., Hugh Lee, John M., Charles M., Walter Scott. Mr. and Mrs. Harlan are devoted members of the Presbyterian Church. He is an F. & A. M., was a member of the Grange. Mr. Harlan is one of the largest men in the county and is known as Big Jim Harlan. In politics he is a Democrat; prior to 1860 was a stanch Whig.

JOHN BRADFORD HARMON was born July 22, 1822, on the place where he now resides, in Mercer (now Boyle) County. His father, Peter Harmon, a native of Pennsylvania, was born in 1782, removed with his parents to Mercer County, Ky.; resided on this place as a farmer; was a member of the Cumberland Presbyterian Church, a Democrat, and died in 1852. He was the son of Michael Harmon, who established a tanyard on this place, and who married Margaret Trump (both born in Germany); their offspring were Barbara (Roberson), Katie (Henry), Margaret (Pipes), Michael, Jr., Jacob, John and Peter. Peter first married Abigail Pipes, and from their union sprang Michael, Lucinda (Butler), Samuel, Thomas J., Nathaniel, Catherine (Montgomery), William D. and John B. His second wife was Mrs. Jane Gray, sister to first wife, and their children were Rice and Minerva J. (Russell). February 18, 1847, John B. Harmon married Miss Catherine J., daughter of Isaac and Nancy (Stone) Montgomery, of Boyle County, born December 16, 1824, and to them have been born William T., Nancy A. (Williams), George D., Elias A., and John C. B. In youth Mr. Harmon enjoyed only such facilities for obtaining an education, as were afforded by the common schools of the vicinity, but by improving his opportunities has become familiar with much of the current literature of the day. He is a farmer and owner of 320 acres of land, in a good state of cultivation. He is a Cumberland Presbyterian, a Granger and a Democrat. Mrs. Harmon's mother, Nancy Stone, was born in a fort on Clark's Run.

ELDER MARION F. HARMON was born November 25, 1861. His father, C. W. Harmon, was born in Adair County when it was a portion of Green, January 19, 1836. His life-long occupation has been in the line of agriculture, and he is a man of limited education, but acquired sufficient to teach in the pioneer schools. He was married, March, 1861, to Miss Louisa Smith, the fifth of a family of seven children, three of whom were daughters, born to Zachariah and Sallie (Puryear) Smith, natives of Virginia, and among the earliest settlers of Taylor County. Only two of Zachariah Smith's children are now living, John W. and Samuel F., both of whom reside in Taylor County. Two of his sons, James and William, were in the Federal service during the late war, and the former was killed at the battle of Perryville, Ky.; the latter died in the Andersonville prison. C. W. Harmon in 1861 moved to Adair County, near Neetsville, and was a renter until 1870, when he bought a farm six miles south of that place, where he resided until the spring of 1886, when he sold out. He now lives about two and a half miles from Columbia. He and wife are both members of the Christian Church, and parents of eleven children: Zachariah; Sarah C., wife of Benjamin Montgomery, now residing in Bates County, Mo.; Nancy M.; Mary L.; Ulysses S.; Martha S.; Ida E.; Montie C. and Marion F., who is the eldest; the others not mentioned died in infancy. Rollin Harmon, the grandfather of Marion F., was a native of Marion County, Ky., but his father's family originally emigrated from North Carolina. He was married to Miss Casander White, a native of what is now Adair County, and they were the parents of four children: John, Marion, Creed W. and Benjamin N. He next married Miss Gunter, of Marion County, and they were the parents of three children: Archibald, Sophronia and Casander. Rollin Harmon was a farmer, and also navigated the Green River as a raftsman. He was a man of great personal bravery, and lived to an advanced age, always in moderate circumstances. Elder Harmon, a native of Adair County, had the advantage of attending the common schools of his neighborhood until sixteen years of age. In the autumn of 1878 he entered the primary department of the Columbia Christian College. Every cent of the money necessary to pay tuition, buy books and clothing and pay living expenses, was earned by him while attending school by extra work out of school. This was the case the first year, but the other four years he taught in the country schools of Adair, and attended college the remainder of the session. While attending college he became acquainted with Miss Mary S. Squires, the youngest of six children, two of whom were daughters, born to Winfield and Sally M. (Montgomery) Squires, both natives of Adair County. Winfield Squires was a son of John and Lockie (Jones) Squires, both natives of Kentucky. Sally M. Montgomery was the third of a family of five children, two of whom were daughters, born to Francis and Lockie (Hurt) Montgomery, both native Virginians. The marriage of Mr. and Mrs. Harmon occurred October 12, 1882, before his graduation, and their home has been gladdened by the addition of a bright little girl, Lena Burkley, born October 28, 1883. June 5, 1883, Elder Harmon graduated from Columbia College with the degree of Bachelor of Sciences (B. S.), but in April, 1883, was ordained to preach the gospel by Elder John W. Sweeney. His first sermon was preached in 1881, and since then he has entered into the life work of the ministry. In the years of 1884 and 1885, he was one of the faculty of Columbia College, and now has the entire management of that institution. In October, 1885, he established the Columbia *Herald*, a weekly newspaper, Republican in politics, which he ran successfully three months, but which he sold out to take charge of Columbia College. He now has charge of the Egypt Christian Church in Adair County, and this is his third year in the ministerial work in connection with that congregation.

HON. JOHN D. HARRIS was born December 29, 1829, three miles south of Richmond, Ky., and is the son and the only child of William and Malinda (Duncan) Harris. The former, William Harris, was born in East Madison County, May 16, 1805, and was a son of John and Margaret (Maupin) Harris, natives of Albemarle County, Va., who came to Kentucky about the year 1790. He (John Harris) acted as associate judge, assisted in laying off the town of Richmond, and was a man of more than ordinary prominence. He was born March 14, 1765, and his wife, Margaret Maupin, February 1, 1767. They were married June 23, 1785, and to them were born nine children, as follows: Robert, born October 27, 1786; Christopher, born April 1, 1788; Overton, born November 24, 1789; Betsey, born September 30, 1791; James, born May 1, 1794; John M., born December 30, 1795; Frances M., born March 26, 1802; William, born May 16, 1805; Susanna W., born May 10, 1808. Robert married Jane Ellison; Christopher married Sarah Wallace (his second wife was Elizabeth Berry); Overton married Polly Woods; James married Minerva Harris; John M. died in early manhood, unmarried; William married Malinda Duncan; Betsey married Anderson Woods; Frances M. married James Miller; Susanna W. married William Duncan. Christopher Harris, the father of John Harris, married, for his first wife, Mary Dabney. Their issue was as follows: Sallie, Robert, Tyre, Dabney, Christopher and Mourning. His second wife was Nancy McCord, who bore children as follows: John, Jane, Benjamin, Nancy, William, Barney, Overton and Isabel. William Harris, the father of subject, was a man of considerable local prominence. He represented Madison County in the Lower House of the Legislature in 1850, and for twenty years held the office of school commissioner. He was a wealthy farmer, enterprising and progressive, and a public-spirited citizen. He died October 25, 1872. His wife, Malinda Duncan, was a daughter of John and Lucy (White) Duncan, one of a family of six children, as follows: Malinda, Elizabeth (Taylor), Emily (Goodloe), John A., Lou Ann (Hart), and Olivia (Gregory). Hon. John D. Harris, the subject of this sketch, was liberally educated. Receiving a preparatory course in the schools of his county, he entered Bethany College, Virginia, from which he graduated in 1847. He read law one year with Judge William C. Goodloe, but never entered into practice, preferring the older occupation—that of a farmer. He was married, September 20, 1849, to Nancy White, a daughter of Valentine M. and Jane (Gentry) White; she was one of a family of four children—three sons and one daughter. Her father, V. M. White, died in 1833, and her mother married James Blythe, by whom she had two daughters. Mr. and Mrs. Harris have had born to them four children, viz.: William V., who died at six years of age; John D., a bright and promising young man,

who died at the age of seventeen, and Pattie (Stone) and Mary P. Mr. Harris gave his children the advantages of the best schools and colleges in the country, and their education, in consequence, is of the most liberal. He began farming after his marriage, and is, to-day, one of the most prominent and wealthy farmers of the State. He owns about 2,500 acres of fine land, well improved, and in which are included the homestead of his father and that of his wife's father. He commenced farming with about 500 acres, and by good management and proper investments has been successful, and accumulated considerable wealth. He makes a specialty of shorthorn cattle, and is one of the leading as well as one of the largest stock traders in the county. He has never cared to enter into the excitement of public life, and the positions he has held have, in a great measure, sought him, his inclinations drawing him to quiet home life; he takes an active interest in the prosperity of his country, and is liberal in fostering its improvements, mentally and physically, to speak figuratively. He has been president for some years of the Madison Female Institute, and is popular among his neighbors, and universally esteemed by all who know him. He was elected to the State Senate in 1885, and is still a member (January, 1887) of that body, and one of its most active and energetic workers. He is a prominent and formidable candidate at the present time for nomination as governor of the commonwealth on the Democratic ticket, with strong chances in favor of his ultimate success.

R. W. HASELWOOD, M. D., was born April 11, 1839, and is a son of Richard and Nancy (Cowherd) Haselwood, to whom three sons and six daughters were born, six of whom lived to be grown. Richard Haselwood was born in Virginia, and July 25, 1797, when nearly grown, came to Green County, Ky., with his parents. In early life he was a carpenter, and made the first two panel doors ever used in Greensburg, and received for the work $50. In later years he followed farming and died in June, 1859. He was a son of Clifford Haselwood, who married a Miss Towler, both of Virginia, and early settlers of Kentucky at a time when land was offered at Lexington for $1.25 per acre; but they settled in Green County, where the father died soon after. He was of English origin. Mrs. Nancy Haselwood was born in Virginia, March 17, 1807, and was a daughter of Maj. James Cowherd, who was also one of the early settlers of Green County, Ky., now Taylor

County. He was a large farmer and slave-holder; was also a great hunter. The name Cowherd is said to have originated from the finding of a boy by some cowboys. The boy, it is supposed, had been captured by Indians and afterward was lost and found, hence the name. Dr. R. W. Haselwood, who was the eighth child, was born on a farm four miles south of Greensburg. At the age of eighteen he commenced the study of medicine with Dr. B. T. Marshall and later attended the Kentucky School of Medicine of Louisville, from which he graduated in March, 1860, and located in Greensburg. March 15, 1860, he was united in marriage to Emma J. Rickets, of Lebanon, a daughter of Moses and Elizabeth M. (McAfee) Rickets. Moses Rickets was born in Marion County in 1809, where he became a leading merchant. In 1862, when Gen. Morgan was making one of his raids through Kentucky, Moses Rickets was with the Home Guards, who were trying to defend the town against the enemy. In the fight that ensued Mr. Rickets was killed. Dr. Haselwood and wife had born to them ten children: Jane H., who married a Haselwood; Mary E., Susan L., Richard M., Emma McAfee, William H., Alfred H., George M., Lovelace and Thomas P. The Doctor and wife are members of the Methodist Episcopal Church South. In November, 1863, the Doctor enlisted as assistant surgeon in the Thirty-seventh Kentucky Mounted Infantry; was wounded at Salina, Tenn., in the left hand, but never lost a day from sickness while in the service and was discharged in December, 1864. Afterward he resided in Louisville one year; thence removed to New Market, Marion County. In December, 1868, he located where he now resides on 286 acres of good land, eight miles northeast of Greensburg, on the Taylor County line. He has a large and extensive practice and makes a specialty of piles and fistula. In politics he is a Democrat and cast his first presidential vote for John C. Breckenridge.

GEORGE W. HASELWOOD was born April 21, 1842, and is the youngest in the family of two sons and four daughters, born to Henry C. and Cassandre W. (Moss) Haselwood. Henry C. Haselwood was born in Dinwiddie County, Va., came to Kentucky when about ten years old and died in November, 1843, aged thirty-seven years. Cliff Haselwood, his father, married Phœbe J. Cousins in Virginia and came to Kentucky about 1814. Mrs. Cassandre W. Haselwood was born in Barren County in 1810, and was a daughter of Frederick and Mary (Coats) Moss, natives of Virginia, who early came to Kentucky, first settling in Boyle County, thence moving to Green. Frederick's father, David Moss, married Catherine Price, served during the Revolution and died on his way to Kentucky. George W. Haselwood was born in Hart County, was reared a farmer and married, in March, 1866, Luella S. Ford, of Taylor County, a daughter of Thomas and Emily J. (Thurman) Ford. Thomas J. Ford was born in Virginia in February, 1804, and was a farmer and slave owner, and died in November, 1873. He was a son of William Ford, who married Elizabeth Harris, of Virginia, and was of Scotch descent. Mr. Haselwood located, where he now resides, in Green County, on 200 acres of land, of which 150 are in cultivation, and three-fifths of it he has acquired by his own industry. He is a member of the Masonic fraternity and with his wife belongs to the Methodist Episcopal Church South.

JAMES WEATHERS HAWKINS was born December 22, 1815, in Woodford County, Ky., where he grew to manhood. In 1850 he removed to Salt Spring, Mercer County; in 1860 to Harrodsburg, and in 1865 to Mundy's Landing, where he has since resided. His father, James Hawkins, a native of Jessamine County, was a farmer and slave-holder, a Whig, a captain of militia, and died in 1824. He was the son of John Hawkins, a native of Virginia, an early settler in Jessamine County, a representative in the Legislature, a farmer and slave-owner, and was drowned in the Kentucky River, near Brooklyn, in 1824. His wife was a Miss Weathers, and their offspring were James, John, Thomas, Allen, William, George, Hannah (Smith), Katie (Singleton), Sally (Haydon), Patsy (Overstreet), Betsy (Overstreet), Nancy (Ashford) and Polly (Reed). James married Barilla, daughter of Thomas Ashford, of Woodford County. (She and her husband died at the same time from the effects of bleeding by a physician for fever.) Their children were Nancy (Talbott), Senate A. and James W. James W. first married, in 1837, Miss Emily, daughter of John and Caroline (Milton) Watkins (died in 1838). John Watkins, was a half brother to Henry Clay. J. W. Hawkins was next married, February 8, 1844, to Miss Sarah, daughter of Hezekiah and Sarah (Singleton) Elgin, of Fayette County (born November 22, 1826), and to them have been born James E. (deceased), John T. (murdered at Courtland, Ala.), William H. (murdered at Harrodsburg), Sallie B. (Reed), James E., Matilda A. (Nooe) and Charles M. (deceased). Mr.

Hawkins has been engaged in mercantile pursuits for more than forty years, and owns a farm of 100 acres of good land. He was formerly an old line Whig, but now acts with the Democratic party. He once was a colonel of militia and lost nineteen slaves by the late war, worth $20,000.

DR. J. E. HAWKINS was born August 21, 1852. His father, Col. J. W. Hawkins, was born in Woodford County, Ky., had been a merchant principally, settled in Harrodsburg in 1860, and in 1862 and 1863 served as deputy sheriff of Mercer County; was assassinated on the night of September 30, 1886, aged seventy years. About 1844 he married Miss Sarah E. Elgin, who bore him seven children: J. E., J. T. (assassinated in Alabama), W. H. (assassinated in Harrodsburg, Ky.), Sallie Bell (Reed), James Elgin, Lena and Charles (deceased). Dr. J. E. Hawkins was educated first at Bacon College and then at St. Mary's College, and in 1871 and 1872 attended a medical college. He completed his professional course in the Louisville Medical College in 1872, and in 1880 settled in Bohon, in his native county of Mercer, where his skill has secured him a lucrative practice.

JUDGE D. R. HAYS. The paternal ancestors of Judge D. R. Hays were natives of Scotland, his grandfather, William Hays, coming from that country to the United States and settling in Washington County, Ky., between the years 1785 and 1790. He made a home near Springfield, was a farmer and for a number of years was a minister of the Methodist Episcopal Church. He later moved to Hardin County, where he died. Subject's maternal grandfather was David Burchum, a native of one of the Eastern States. He came to Kentucky four years after the Hays family, settled near Springfield and died in Hardin County. William Hays, father of Judge Hays, was born in Maryland and was eighteen months of age when his parents came to Kentucky and settled at Harrod's Station, near Harrodsburg; at seven years of age his parents moved to Washington County, where he grew to manhood, was a successful farmer and business man and departed this life in 1866. His wife, Eleanor (Burchum) Hays, was born in Maryland and died in Washington County in 1863. Thirteen children were born to William and Eleanor Hays, to wit: Mrs. Mary Lewis, Mrs. Rebecca Short, Mrs. Nancy Ray, Hercules, Mrs. Sallie Shaunty, John J., Alfred B., Teneriffe, Cyrus W., William H., D. R., Ellen and James B. Hays. Judge Hays grew to manhood in Washington County and was educated in the country schools, which he attended until his eighteenth year. He remained at home until twenty-two and then commenced life for himself as clerk in a mercantile house at Chaplin Town, Nelson County, serving a short time, and later effected a copartnership with J. B. Marshall in the goods business, which was continued about eighteen months. He afterward sold goods with J. I. Lyle for one year, then returned to Washington County and engaged in farming, purchasing a farm a few years later near Willisburg, upon which he resided seventeen years. He next purchased his present beautiful place of 400 acres—Locust Hill Farm—six miles north of Springfield, in the Pleasant Grove neighborhood, where he has since resided. Mr. Hays was elected judge of the Washington County Court in 1870, and held the position four years, and was elected president of the First National Bank of Springfield in 1880, an office he at present holds. He is a Democrat in politics, but originally voted with the Whig party, his first vote having been cast for Henry Clay. He was married on the 12th of June, 1849, in Nelson County, to Miss Mary McMakin, daughter of Peyton and Catherine (Bayne) McMakin, by whom he had three children: Catherine E. (wife of B. L. Litsey), Mary E. (died at sixteen months of age) and William P. Hays. Mr. and Mrs. Hays are active members of the Willisburg Christian Church.

FRANCIS M. HEAD was born July 29, 1842, the second of two sons and four daughters, three of whom are now living, born to Richard and Ann C. (Meadley) Head. Richard Head was born near New Hope, and his children were all born at the same place. He was a good, substantial farmer and slaveholder; was also a distiller and owned the largest distillery in his part of the country in his day. He died in 1858 at the age of forty seven. He was a son of Francis Head, who married a Willett, both natives of Nelson County, born on Pottinger's Creek. Francis Head died at the age of about eighty years. His parents were of Scotch descent, came from Maryland, and were among the very first settlers on Pottinger's Creek. Mrs. Ann C. Head was born in the west part of Marion County, and is a daughter of Ignatius Meadley, who came from Maryland in the early settling of Kentucky, located on Hardin's Creek, Marion County, was an extensive farmer and distiller, a large slave owner and died about 1852, aged seventy-five. Francis M. Head, who was born near New Hope, received a liberal English education at St. Mary's College and Cecilian College, and at eighteen began farming on his own account; two years later he entered mercantile business at New Hope, and followed it constantly until April, 1886. In the meantime he ran a distillery for twelve years, commencing in 1872; he also owns 100 acres south of New Hope, in Marion County; he was appointed postmaster at close of the war, which office he held till 1884. He was married December 1, 1870, to Mary E. Bryant, of Marion County, a daughter of Ben. S. and Allie (Spalding) Bryant, natives of Nelson and Marion Counties respectively. Mr. Bryant was a farmer, and his parents came from Maryland. His father, William Bryant, was a soldier in the war of 1812, and died in 1884 at the ripe age of ninety-two years. Mr. and Mrs. Head had born to them seven children: Mary Regina, Marion Joseph, Robert Vincent, Joseph Mary, Joseph Regmon, Frank Paul, Mary Lizzie, all members of the Roman Catholic Church. Mr. Head once lost about $8,000 by the blowing up of a distillery, but has made life a success financially. In politics he is an active Democrat.

VICTOR E. HEAD, a popular druggist of Lebanon and one of the substantial business men, was born in 1863, in Nelson County, Ky. Both his parents, William Head and Rosalia (Spalding) Head, were natives of Nelson County; the father was born in 1808, followed the pursuits of the farm, and died in 1879; his widow is a resident of Nelson County. They had a family of twelve children, of whom Victor E. is the youngest, and of whom eleven are still living. Victor E. was reared on the farm and educated in the Cecilian College, of Hardin County, under Prof. H. A. Cecil. In the spring of 1884 he purchased an interest in the drug business of H. D. Rodman, and in May, 1885, bought the entire stock, and is now doing a thriving business. Mr. Head is an honored member of the Catholic Church, and is held in universal esteem.

HAMILTON ATCHISON HEADLY was born July 20, 1826, in Fayette County. In 1879 he removed to Boyle County, locating on the Harrodsburg pike, four miles northwest of Danville, where he still resides. His father, James Headly, Jr., a native of Maryland, at the age of seven years removed with his parents to Fayette County, Ky., was a successful farmer, but lost about ten slaves by the late war, and died April 22, 1884, at the age of ninety-two years. He was the son of James Headly, Sr., a native of Ireland, who died about 1850, aged eighty years. He married Elizabeth Patterson, of Maryland,

and their offspring were Polly (Shivry), James, Jr., William, Elizabeth (Elmore), Samuel, John, Rebecca (Dunn), Francis, Marshall, Nancy (Farra) and Alexander. James, Jr., married Melinda, daughter of Hamilton Atchinson, of Fayette County, (died in 1841 at the age of forty years), and to them were born Hamilton A., George, James and William. November 25, 1847, Hamilton A. Headly was married to Miss Sallie A., daughter of Aaron and Sallie (Neet), Farra, of Jessamine County (born August 26, 1827), and their union resulted in the birth of George A. and James Hamilton, both deceased. In youth Mr. Headly enjoyed good educational advantages and is a reading man. He is a successful farmer, owning 385 acres of first-class blue-grass land, well improved and in a high state of cultivation, on which he grows wheat, hemp, corn and hay; he also raises stock. He makes mules a specialty, and breeds some thoroughbred horses. He is a member of the Christian Church, and in politics is a Democrat.

DR. JOHN HEALY was born in Galway, Ireland, and a son of James and Winifred (O'Brian) Healy, to whom three sons and three daughters were born. The Doctor came to the United States in November, 1853, and landed in Philadelphia where he had two brothers living, who had preceded him about four years. The Doctor had commenced the study of medicine while in Ireland; while employed as salesman by his brother, he continued the study in his leisure moments. In 1855 he migrated to Washington County, Ky., where he finished his studies, returned to Philadelphia, and graduated from Jefferson Medical College in the spring of 1858, after which he located at Chicago, Ky. In 1862 he located where he now resides, in Raywick, where he has successfully practiced his profession ever since. He was a strong Union man during the war, and acted as local surgeon, and has been examining surgeon since the war. The Doctor owns several houses and lots in Raywick. August 6, 1878, he married Julia G., a daughter of Dr. John J. and Felecia (Jesse) Barry. Dr. Barry was the leading physician of New Haven, Ky., and was post surgeon for a time during the war. He was also a writer for scientific and medical journals and is the author of " Medico Christian Embryology," and a "Life of Christopher Columbus;" was one of the most intellectual and best informed men of his county, and was highly respected. He was born in County Cork, Ireland, in 1808, and died at New

Haven, Ky., in 1880. His wife, a daughter of Rev. Samuel Jesse, of Shelby County, Ky., who was a Baptist minister, was born in the Shenandoah Valley, Va., and married Catherine George, of Maryland. He was one of the first pioneers of Kentucky. Dr. Healy and wife are consistent members of the Catholic Church, and in politics he is Democratic. Mrs. Julia Barry Healy inherits her father's taste for literature. She contributes to various publications in the United States and in Canada. For several years prior to her marriage she edited the *Orphans' Garland*, the official organ of the diocese of Louisville. She is also a clever musician and linguist.

M. C. HEATH, M. D., a leading physician of Richmond, was born March 26, 1845, in Lancaster County, S. C., and is a son of Moses C. and Mary (Morrow) Heath, who were born in South Carolina in 1806 and 1809 respectively, and had a family of eleven sons and four daughters, twelve of whom were reared. Moses C. Heath was a leading cotton planter, and died in 1866; his wife is still living in good health. He, in turn, was a son of Moses C. Heath, who married a Miss Chapel, both natives of Virginia, and of English descent. The family were all planters as far as known. The Doctor was reared on a plantation and received a good English education. In 1862 he enlisted in Company I, Seventeenth South Carolina Infantry, and in Gen. N. G. Even's command; was in the Jackson (Miss.) campaign, Bermuda Hundred, and Petersburg, Va.; also in the battle of Five Forks, and at the surrender at Appomattox. After the surrender he returned to South Carolina where he remained two years; then he went to Georgia; in 1868 he located in Lexington, Ky., and commenced the study of medicine with Dr. Sweeny. He attended his first course of lectures in Louisville, and graduated from Bellevue, New York City, in 1871, and immediately located in Camilla, Ga. In 1874 he located in Richmond, Ky., where he has continued to practice with success. He is one of the active members of the State Medical Association, also of the Madison County Association. He was united in marriage in December, 1873, to Mary Emery, a daughter of Zalton and Martha (Fostes) Emery. The issue to this marriage was seven children, four living: Nannie C., Flora H., Moses C. and J. J. The Doctor and wife are members of the Presbyterian and Christian Churches. The Doctor is a member of the F. & A. M., and in politics is a Democrat.

WILLIAM WALKER HENDERSON was born May 12, 1818, ten miles west of Danville, and has all his life been a resident of Boyle County. His father, James Henderson, also a native of Boyle County, was a soldier in the war of 1812, and died in 1819. He was the son of John Henderson, a Virginian, who came to Kentucky during the Revolutionary war, was an Indian fighter, constructed port-holes in his dwelling for defense, and at times with his wife alternately kept watch while the other secured rest in sleep. He married Elizabeth Mann of Virginia, and their offspring were Nancy (Magill), Polly (Caldwell), Dycie (Johnson), Phœbe (Caldwell), Elizabeth (Pritchett), James, Esther (Duncan), Sarah (Parkes), Ann (Rice), Peggy (Robinson), Priscilla (Gordon), John and Louisa. James Henderson married Mary, daughter of Philip Walker of Boyle County (died in 1876), and to them were born William W. and Albert E. After the death of her husband, Mrs. Henderson married Thomas Davis, and their union resulted in the birth of Thomas, Susan (Mitchell), Matilda J. (Ellis), Frances (Green), Hester A. (Green) and Martha (Ellis). In January, 1864, W. W. Henderson was married to Mrs. Jane Harlan, daughter of Ludwell Evans of Boyle County, but to their union there has been no issue. In youth Mr. Henderson served an apprenticeship at the tailor's bench, and with an even start with the world, by industry, frugality, and careful attention to his own business, he has amassed a comfortable competency, and is now classed among the wealthy men of Boyle County, although he lost five slaves by the late war. He is a farmer and trader, and owns 340 acres of very productive land. His fine blue grass farm is now almost wholly devoted to grazing. He is taking an active interest in the education of several children. In politics he is identified with the Democratic party.

JEFF HENRY, of Scotch and Welsh descent, was born February 26, 1849, in Cedar County, Mo., and is the fourth of four sons and four daughters, all of whom lived to be grown, born to James L. and Margaret (Brownlee) Henry. J. L. Henry was born February 22, 1811, four miles north of Greensburg, Ky., and was a farmer; in 1837 he with his family moved to Cedar County, Mo., where he became the owner of 4,400 acres, also owned a large slave property, and became the first county judge; and after Dade was stricken off became its first county judge, and held the position for twenty years, up to the breaking out of the war. In 1861 he went to Sherman, Tex., with his negroes. In 1863 his family joined him. After the war he located in Cane Hill, Ark., where he educated his family. (He had a son, C. M. Henry, who became a brigadier-general in the Confederate Army.) He died in 1871, but his family continued to remain in Arkansas. He was a son of Bellfield and Elizabeth (Kirtley) Henry, both of Virginia. They immigrated to Green County, Ky., about 1800, where Bellfield Henry became an extensive farmer, served as sheriff, and died in 1850. Mrs. Margaret Henry was born in Green County, Ky., and was a daughter of Charles and Elizabeth (Allen) Brownlee, who came from Virginia in the early settling of Green County. Charles Brownlee was a captain in the war of 1812; flatboated considerably in early days to New Orleans, and was an extensive farmer and trader. He was a son of Gen. Wm. Brownlee of Virginia, who received his title in the war of 1812; after the war he received a large land grant, and was a very early settler of Green County. Jeff Henry was reared on a farm; up to the war he was educated at the common schools, and after the war at Cane Hill, Mo. In November, 1871, he located in Greensburg, Ky., where he has been engaged in the practice of law ever since. He had commenced the study under instruction of Gen. Reagan, now of Texas, procured his license soon after locating in Greensburg, was elected county attorney in 1874, and held the office two terms. December 12, 1872, he was united in marriage to Josie L. Tery, a daughter of Joseph and Sarah (Tebbs) Tery, who were natives of Adair (now Metcalfe) and Green Counties respectively. Mr. and Mrs. Henry have had born to them one child, Claudia M. Mrs. Henry is a member of the Presbyterian Church, and in politics Mr. Henry is an active and influential Democrat, and cast his first presidential vote for Tilden.

HENRY J. HENSON, a farmer, was born November 1, 1836, in Casey County. His father, Joseph S. Henson, was a farmer, born in Pulaski County, February 2, 1814. He was married at the age of eighteen to Miss Maria, daughter of Henry and Mary B. (Phœbyhouse) Baker, natives of North Carolina. To this marriage were born eleven children: John W., H. J., Robert, Elizabeth (wife of Stephen Evans), Mary (wife of Simpson Evans), Amanda (wife of William Evans), George, Serilda (wife of James Rexrhod), David, Nanny (wife of R. Pitts), and an infant that died unnamed. Joseph Henson was never in any war, but was a member of the State Guards under command of Capt. Edmund Goode, and during Morgan's raid through Casey County he received a very severe gunshot wound in the head. Mrs. Henson, a member of the Methodist Episcopal Church, departed this life in February, 1881, in the sixty-second year of her age. Mr. Henson now owns 150 acres of his original farm which he has rented out, and now lives with his son, H. J. Henson. Joseph Henson, grandfather of H. J., born in Amherst County, Va., was a carpenter most of his life, and a No. 1 mechanic, who followed his trade until too old to do hard work, when he turned his attention to farming in Pulaski County, on about 150 acres. He moved to Casey County, where he carried on a farm of about 200 acres until his death in 1841, in his seventy-fourth year. The maiden name of his wife was Jemima Evans, a Virginian, and they were the parents of nine children: Elisha, Nancy (Vest), Elizabeth (Meeks), John, Robert, Polly (Raborn), Melinda (Murphy, Malson and Newman), James and Joseph, of whom James, Joseph, Melinda and Polly are living. Elisha Henson was a soldier in Gen. Scott's army in the war of 1812. Henry J. Henson remained at home until twenty-one years of age, when, in possession of only a horse, he began the battle of life on his own account. March 16, 1858, he married Miss Catherine, daughter of William and Mary (Reynolds) Holliday, natives of Adair County. To this marriage were born four children: William J., James H., Anna, and H. C. who died in infancy. Mrs. Henson departed this life March 13, 1865, aged twenty-eight years. The second marriage of Mr. Henson was May 23, 1866, to Miss Mary, daughter of John and Martha (Reynolds) Tupman, natives of Adair County. To this marriage have been born ten children: Charles L., Mattie Ocilla, Rosa L. and Retta F. (twins), Ellen M., John T., Samuel T., Elizabeth, Truman K., and an infant that died unnamed. Mr. and Mrs. Henson are both members of the Methodist Episcopal Church and Mr. Henson is a member of the Democratic party and of the Masonic order. Mr. Henson, in 1871, purchased 230 acres of improved land in Adair County, on Green River, very fertile. He has since built on and improved this farm and added to it until he now owns 400 in a high state of cultivation and improvement, and worth about $8,000. He has 220 acres in cultivation, and in addition to farming buys tobacco—this year to the extent of 80,000 pounds—and has bought mules and sold them in the South during the past twenty years. His estate, worth $10,000, has been all acquired by his own industry, economy and good management.

A. G. HERNDON was born in Virginia July 13, 1808, and was a son of George and Elizabeth Herndon. His mother's maiden name was Elizabeth Zachery. His father was also born in Virginia, and came to Kentucky about 1815 and settled on a farm in Madison County, but later moved to Missouri, where he farmed the remainder of his life. He and wife were members of the Baptist Church, and in politics he was a Whig. There were born to him seven sons and four daughters. A. G. Herndon came to Kentucky with his father and was reared to farming, and now owns 557 acres of good land in Garrard County near Lancaster, on which he now resides. His wife's maiden name was Nancy B. Pollard and he became the father of three children: Lucie Anderson, Betty Anderson and Nancy Jane Herndon, who died aged three years and four months. Mr. and Mrs. Herndon are members of the Christian Church, and in politics he is a Democrat.

WILLIAM HERNDON was born in Estill County, Ky., January 10, 1843, the son of Elijah and Ann P. (Crothwait) Herndon. Elijah Herndon was born in Winchester, Ky., in 1811, was married in 1835; moved to Estill County at the age of twenty-six; engaged in the grocery trade, and also followed milling for ten years; he served six years as sheriff of Estill County, and in 1862 was elected clerk of the Estill Circuit Court, which office he held also for six years. He died in Kansas, in 1876. Mrs. Ann P. Herndon was born in Cynthiana, Harrison Co., Ky., and was a relative of President Madison. By her marriage to Mr. Herndon she became the mother of four sons and two daughters, all of whom were reared to maturity. William Herndon's grandfather was born in Charlotte County, Va., came to Kentucky in 1800, settled in Winchester, married Catherine Winn, and reared five children. William Herndon was not classically educated; he began the study of law in Estill County under Col. S. M. Barnes; he received his license to practice in 1868, but then entered the revenue service, in which he remained until 1877, when he resigned his position, engaged in practice at Lancaster, Ky., and in August, 1886, was elected commonwealth's attorney of the Eighth Judicial District, for a term of six years. July 3, 1873, he married Miss Helen, daughter of William H. Kinnard, cashier of the Lancaster National Bank. To this marriage have been born five children: Horace K., William L., Ben D., Lewis and Annie C. Mr. Herndon is a member of the Presbyterian Church, of the Masonic fraternity, of the G. A. R. and is a Republican.

THOMAS J. HERRING was born October 28, 1836. His father, Terrell Herring, was born in Virginia in 1788, and came to Kentucky in 1804 and settled on Dick's River, in Garrard County. In 1817 he married Miss Nancy Pollard, who was born on the waters of Sugar Creek in 1798, and to this union were born five boys and four girls. Thomas J. Herring, a native of Garrard County, in 1875 married Miss Nicy Floyd, who has borne four children: Patty, Maggie (deceased), Sallie and Lee. Mr. Herring owns and cultivates 343 acres of land, and he and a brother own and operate a distillery having a capacity of forty gallons per day. Mr. Herring is a Free Mason, and Mrs. Herring is a member of the Baptist Church.

OLIVER P. HIESTAN, M. D., was born in what is now Taylor (then Green) County, Ky., January 15, 1827, and is one of a family of nine children born to Jacob and Evy (Landis) Hiestan, the former of whom was a native of Pennsylvania, and the latter of Virginia, both of German descent. Jacob Hiestan was born in 1787, and received an ordinary English education at the common schools of his native State. He very materially added, however, to his early training by his own exertions and diligent application to study after attaining to manhood's years, and was all his life a consistent, close and careful reader, being well informed not only on the current topics of the time, but also in both ancient and modern history. When a young man he removed to Virginia, where he was married and soon after that event came to "the dark and bloody ground," settling near Campbellsville in what is now Taylor County, where he established a tanyard, having learned the tanner's trade in early life, and continued to follow the business for many years. Afterward he bought a farm near Campbellsville where he was extensively and successfully engaged in farming, stock raising and the distilling business until his death, in 1848. For many years he was a colonel in the old State militia. He belonged to no church, but was a bright member of the Masonic fraternity. He was a man of great energy, and by honesty, integrity and industry, amassed a handsome fortune. His father was from Germany, and spelled the name Hiestand, and so it was spelled and is still spelled by all his relations and by all his sons, except Jacob and his descendants, who dropped the final d. Mrs. Evy (Landis) Hiestan was born in 1788, and departed this life in 1849. She was a life-long member of the Missionary Baptist Church. Her father, Abraham Landis, was a native of old Virginia, where, most of his life, he was successfully engaged in agricultural pursuits. In his old age, however, he removed to Green County, where his death occurred on the Green River at the ripe old age of seventy-one. Dr. Oliver P. Hiestan received an excellent common school and academic education in youth. He remained on the home farm until he was twenty-two years of age, when he commenced the study of medicine under the preceptorship of Dr. Jas. A. Shuttlesworth, of Campbellsville, Ky., and afterward under the preceptorship of Dr. L. J. Frazee, of Louisville, Ky. He graduated with high honors at the Kentucky School of Medicine of Louisville, in the clsss of 1851, after which he practiced his profession to some extent at Campbellsville until the spring of 1854, when he removed to Texas, locating at Kentuckytown, Grayson County, where he continued to practice until the fall of 1857, when, in consequence of the loss of his eyesight, he returned to Louisville, Ky., where he was treated by Dr. Samuel D. Gross for a time; thence he went to Cincinnati, Ohio, where, for about nine months, he was treated by Drs. Talliaferro, Potter and Williams, who gave him some little relief, after which he went to Boston, Mass., and was treated by Dr. Dicks, who succeeded in restoring him to partial, though very imperfect sight. In 1860 he returned to Grayson County, Tex., and resumed the practice of his profession with the most gratifying and unvarying success, although unable to distinguish the most intimate acquaintance five steps away, or to read the coarsest print. In July, 1866, he came to Kentucky again and located in the western part of Casey County, near the Adair line, where he has continued to practice his profession with his usual abundant and unvarying success. He is also quite successfully and extensively engaged in farming and stock raising, owning three farms, aggregating some 450 acres. The home farm is well improved, one of the best in the neighborhood, and is in a high state of cultivation. Although he has sustained numerous and severe reverses by which, and in the almost fruitless search for sight, he lost or expended his entire fortune, being thus compelled, though nearly blind, to begin the battle of life anew without a dollar, yet, by his indomitable energy and persistent industry he has not only carved out for himself a place at the head and front of his profession, but has also acquired a handsome property. Though unable to recognize his most intimate friends a few steps away he yet rides almost constantly through the woods and brush and

over a rough and hilly country in the discharge of his professional and other duties, and although unable to read even the coarsest print, yet, through the assistance of his family, and especially by the aid of his estimable wife, who finds time from her household cares to read to him, and who is by the way an accomplished lady, a most excellent reader, and a thorough scholar, he keeps fully up, not only with his professional reading, but also with the current literature of the day. The Doctor married, July 8, 1860, Miss Maria J. Mercer, a native of Taylor County, Ky., born June 18, 1840. She is a daughter of James O. and Rosalinda (Eades) Mercer, natives of Kentucky. The father of James O. was Joseph Mercer, and the father of Joseph was John Mercer, of Scottish descent. Mrs. Rosalinda Eades was of English descent. Eight children have blessed this union: Evy (now Mrs. Hezekiah Lainhart), Thornton, Morgan, Araminta, Perry, Jacob, Etsel and Maria. In politics the Doctor is a Democrat, and one of the most successful, prominent and influential professional and business men in the county and district.

HON. CLEMENT S. HILL. Among the old Catholic families that at an early period in the history of the State became identified with its pioneer history and development, none have occupied a more conspicuous and honorable place than the one represented by the subject of this sketch. About the middle of the last century Thomas Hill, a member of an old English Catholic family, immigrated to America and settled in St. Mary's County, Md., where, about the year 1754, he married Rebecca Miles, a representative of another family of similar faith, who bore him a family of seven children—three sons and four daughters. At the beginning of the year 1787, he, with his brother-in-law, Philip Miles, living up to that time near Leonardtown, St. Mary's Co., Md., arranged to remove their families to Kentucky. Their proposed journey was begun in February, and toward the end of March, on the very day they expected to land above the falls of the Ohio, their boat was fired on by the Indians. A negro slave of Thomas Hill was killed, besides several horses, and he himself was seriously wounded by the passage of an ounce ball through both of his thighs. This happened about eighteen miles above Louisville. The boat was soon carried by the current beyond reach of the savages' guns and before night its living freight of men, women and children was safely housed in that town. Soon after the entire party went to Bardstown, where they remained a year, and Thomas Hill, owing to the severity of his wounds, for a much longer time. In March, 1788, Philip Miles and Harry Hill, son of Thomas Hill, purchased lands in the Pottinger's Creek settlement, to which they removed immediately and upon which they passed the remainder of their days. Thomas Hill, after recovering from his wounds, moved from Bardstown to Cartwright's Creek, in the spring of 1789, where he soon purchased land and entered upon the life of a farmer. He was very zealous in the Catholic faith and was one of the chief promoters of the strong Catholic colony which afterward centered in that locality; and was chiefly instrumental in erecting the first house of worship there. He labored also to provide for his children every facility for culture that was within his means, and especially to found them securely in the Catholic faith, and to present to them reasonable motives for its constant and systematic practice. His death occurred in 1820, at the ripe age of ninety-seven years, and his descendants are numerously distributed through the South and West. Clement Hill, the youngest son of Thomas Hill, remained with his parents until after his majority, when he married, in 1798, Mary Hamilton, a daughter of Thomas Hamilton, whose cousin Leonard was the maternal grandfather of the late Most Rev. M. J. Spalding, bishop of Louisville and archbishop of Baltimore. In the year 1803 he removed to and opened a farm lying within two miles of the site of the present town of Lebanon, where he lived to the date of his death, December 13, 1832. He was a man of exemplary faith and piety, true to the tenets of his church, and of unquestioned integrity in all the relations of life. He was the father of seventeen children born of one wife. Clement S. Hill, son of Clement, to whom this sketch is chiefly dedicated, was born on the old homestead near Lebanon, on the 13th of February, 1813. He received a thorough education at St. Mary's College, Lebanon, when that institution was still controlled by its founder, Rev. Wm. Byrne. He afterward taught school in different parts of the State, and subsequently pursued the study of law under the late Benjamin Chapeze, of Bardstown, a lawyer of great ability and a man of singular worth and purity of character, and in the fall of 1837 was admitted to practice at the bar. He located at Lebanon, and, being possessed of an analytic mind and of rare gifts as a speaker, soon secured a lucrative practice and full recognition of his legal acquirements at the hands of the leading lawyers of the State,

among whom he soon occupied the front rank. He continued in active practice, adding constantly to his reputation as a successful practitioner down to 1885, when, feeling the effects of years of close professional study and of active work as an advocate, he relaxed his energies and made way for younger men. As a general practitioner Mr. Hill has had few superiors at the Kentucky bar. To an unexampled skill as a pleader, he had the added qualities of a strong advocate and an exceeding aptitude in the taking of proof and the establishment of his case. Politically Mr. Hill was formerly a Henry Clay Whig, but since the dissolution of the Whig party has acted more or less with political independence. He was a strong Union man during the late civil war, and was authorized by the Government to raise a regiment for the national defense, but was prevented by failing health from taking the field. In 1839 he was elected on local issues to the lower branch of the State Legislature, and in 1853 was elected on the Whig ticket to represent the Fifth District in Congress, serving the full term at Washington. In his religious belief he is a firm and ardent supporter of the Catholic faith. Since 1846 he has resided on his farm about two miles from Lebanon, coming to the county seat each day to attend to his professional business. He was married November 24, 1840, to Miss Alathair, daughter of Joseph Spalding, of Marion County, who became the mother of twelve children. Of these four only attained years of maturity: Ann Mary, Clement J. (who died a farmer and left seven children), John B. (who died at the age of twenty-four) and Susan (wife of H. W. Rives, a native of Mississippi practicing law at Lebanon).

COL. THOMAS P. HILL, the gentleman whose name heads this sketch, was born in Lincoln County, Ky., in the year 1828. He is a son of Thos. P. Hill and Louisa (Peyton) Hill, both parents representing pioneer families. He received a thorough literary education in the St. Mary's College of Marion County, Ky., and began the study of the law while quite young. He enjoyed the benefits of an able legal instructor in the person of the Hon. John Kincaid, then living in Lincoln County, and he made such progress in his study that at the age of nineteen he was admitted to practice. For a period of nearly forty years Col. Hill has been in the active practice of his profession and for many years has occupied the front rank in the Kentucky bar. Besides being an able jurist he is one of the best advocates in the State and as an orator has few superiors in central Kentucky. He has tenaciously adhered to the practice of his profession, and though an ardent Democrat, has studiously avoided the political arena. He has been twice married: first to Miss Maria A. Peyton, and next to his present wife, Frances Fowler.

WILLIAM S. B. HILL was born August 13, 1837, and is a son of Dr. James A. and Elizabeth (Medley) Hill, to whom seven sons and three daughters were born, nine of whom lived to be grown. Dr. James Hill was born five miles southwest of Bardstown, on Beech Fork, August 12, 1804; was a farmer and merchant, made thirteen trips to New Orleans on flatboats, and was south during the cholera scourge of 1833; was a passenger on the steamer "Helen McGregor," that blew up, but with two brothers escaped unhurt. After he quit flatboating he engaged in merchandising at New Haven and Bardstown for four years; about 1840 he commenced the study and practice of medicine, which he followed until his death in 1865 at Danville, to which point he had gone during the war for better protection. He had served as magistrate for a few years in Nelson. He was a son of Joseph and Jane (Atkinson) Hill, born in Pennsylvania near the Virginia line. Joseph Hill's parents came from Ireland. The family settled on Beech Fork, Nelson County, as early as 1790, and were substantial farmers and slave-holders. Joseph served as justice for several years, was a man with a strong constitution, stout and robust, and was very quick to resent insult. He reared a family of five sons and three daughters, and died about 1825, at the age of about sixty. Mrs. Elizabeth Hill was a daughter of John L. and Ann (Atwood) Medley, of Baltimore, Md., of English descent, and among the early settlers of the north part of Nelson County, to which point they brought about fifty slaves from Maryland. William S. B. Hill was born in Bardstown; at eleven years of age he with his parents removed to the country; at the breaking out of the war he took sides with the South, and September 18, 1861, enlisted in Company H, Sixth Kentucky Volunteers, and was in all the engagements in which the regiment participated, except two at Baton Rouge and Atlanta; he was taken a prisoner at Jonesboro, Ga., in September, 1864; twenty days later was exchanged, and remained with his brigade till the close of the war, but was never wounded. After his return home he taught for awhile, then engaged in agricultural pursuits. In 1871 he went to Tennessee, and engaged in the cotton trade for four years, then returned and taught school a short time; was elected as deputy and appointed deputy sheriff; was elected sheriff two terms, which position he filled with credit to himself, and satisfaction to the people. In October, 1883, he went into the store of Mr. Miller as salesman. He was married April 17, 1860, to Louisa Magruder, a daughter of Ezekiel and Nancy (Miller) Magruder; to this union two children were born: Frank A. and Henry V. His wife died in 1867, a Baptist. He married his second wife, Mrs. N. A. Harned, in February, 1868; she was a daughter of James and Eliza (Johnson) Holsclaw. Four children are the issue of this second marriage: Ella E., Ida G., Blanche and Mary V. His wife had two children by her former husband: John D. and Cassie E. Allen. Her first husband was wounded at Shiloh, of which wound he died. She is a member of the Baptist Church, and Mr. Hill is an active Democrat, having cast his first presidential vote for Stephen A. Douglas.

DR. WILLIAM L. HOCKADAY was born June 16, 1843, where he now resides six miles south of Richmond, Ky., and is a son of James S. and Surmira (Shearer) Hockaday, to whom two sons and four daughters were born. James S. Hockaday was born September 5, 1816, on the farm now occupied by the Doctor. He was an active and prosperous farmer and owned considerable slave property, possessed two farms, containing in all about 700 acres, and died April 1, 1885. His father, James Hockaday, was born in Virginia and settled in Madison County, Ky., as early as 1790, and was married to Elizabeth Fox of Madison County. He reared a family of four sons and six daughters. He settled on the farm owned by the Doctor and built the house on which he resides in an early day, and it is still a good comfortable residence. Mrs. Surmira Hockaday was born May 29, 1821, in Madison County, and was a daughter of William and Nancy (Fowler) Shearer, who reared a family of five sons and one daughter. The Doctor began the study of medicine at Richmond, but graduated at Jefferson Medical College in 1866, and has remained on his farm and practiced ever since. He was married June 30, 1868, to Miss Louisa D. Wood, daughter of Starling and Louisa (Collins) Wood, who are natives of Madison County. The Doctor and wife had born to bless their union four children: Lawson S., Walter, Mary V. and James S. Mrs. Hockaday died February 23, 1886, a member of the Christian Church. The Doctor is the possessor of his grandfather's homestead of 470 acres, which is in a good state of cultivation. Before the war he was owner of slave property. He is a member of the F. & A. M. and in politics a Democrat.

DR. SAMUEL G. HOCKER, farmer, and retired physician of Turnersville, Lincoln Co., Ky., descends from one of the oldest families of that county. About 1780, two brothers of the name, with their families, came from Virginia, and settled in Lincoln County; for protection from the Indians they first located about McKinney's Station. But little can be learned of the immediate families of these brothers; one of them had a son, Samuel, who married Polly Hocker, and settled on the land now owned by G. Carter, one mile south of Turnersville. They had but two children, Tilman Hocker and Lucinda, who married Burton McKinney. Tilman Hocker was the father of Dr. Samuel Hocker, and was born in Lincoln County in 1800; was reared on the farm without the advantages of schooling, other than of the most primary character. By reading he stored his mind with useful knowledge on the current topics of the day. He early attached himself to the Presbyterian Church, occupying the office of elder for many years prior to his death and which position his son, S. G. Hocker, now holds. He married Lucinda Carter, daughter of Jesse and Frances Carter. She was born in 1804. Tilman Hocker died in Hustonville, Lincoln Co., Ky., in the year 1869, and his wife died in 1881. Their family consisted of Frances, Ann, Jesse, Samuel, Eliza, Samuel G., Mary C. (Settle), Charles R. and Richard R. Hocker. Samuel G. Hocker, the only living member of this family, was born in 1831; was educated in Stanford, where he also studied medicine. He then entered the College of Physicians and Surgeons of New York, where he graduated in 1852. He practiced successfully in Lincoln County until 1872, when he retired from the profession to devote himself to agriculture. In 1852 he married Miss Matilda Helm of Lincoln County; she died in 1878, leaving one son, Jesse Hocker, now of Texas. His present wife was Miss Lizzie Fair, daughter of William and Naomi (Jones) Fair, and is the third of a family of seven children born to those parents. William Fair was a native of Lincoln County, born in 1806; was a son of James and Elizabeth (May) Fair, and died in 1883. Dr. Hocker is a member of the Presbyterian Church. Two children, Mary F. and William R., are the results of his last marriage.

DR. THOMAS P. HODGES (deceased) was a native of Kentucky, and was one of the intelligent and substantial citizens of Green County. His parents came from Virginia in the early settlement of this State. He

was a graduate from one of the medical institutions of Louisville and commenced practice in 1855, which was extensive and successful till his death. In July, 1857, he was united in marriage to Catharine Carter, a daughter of James T. and Ann (Ramsey) Carter, who were natives of Virginia, and came to Kentucky when children, and settled in Hart and Jefferson Counties respectively. James T. Carter was a farmer and was a patriot and soldier of 1812 under Gen. Harrison. His final location was in Green County, where he became one of its solid and substantial farmers, and served as sheriff of the county several years. He was a son of Daniel Carter, a farmer. Dr. Hodges' final location was on 400 acres five miles northwest of Greensburg, where his family now reside. He reared but two children: James C. and Mattie (now Hobson). The Doctor died in 1872, aged forty-four. He was a devoted and leading member of the Methodist Episcopal Church, and a member of the Masonic fraternity, and as a man who commanded the respect of all who knew him. His son, James C. Hodges, was born in September, 1861; is well educated, and has the care of the family and homestead.

REV. JOSEPH A. HOGARTY, rector of St. Dominic's Church, Springfield, is a native of Lexington, Ky., and the youngest of a family of six children born to Martin and Mary (Fraser) Hogarty, the father a native of Mayo, and the mother of Belfast, Ireland. The father of Martin Hogarty was William Hogarty, who died in Ireland in the year 1849. Martin Hogarty was a stone-cutter by trade, and in early life became a very skillful workman. He immigrated to America in 1851, and located in Cincinnati, where he worked at his trade until about 1857, at which time he moved to Lexington, Ky., for the purpose of assisting in the construction of the Henry Clay monument, and there remained until his death in 1880 at the age of sixty-four years. Mary (Fraser) Hogarty, subject's mother, was a daughter of an officer in the English Army, and was born July 28, 1816. She is still living, making her home in Union County, Ky. The following are the names of the children of Martin and Mary Hogarty: Alexander; Rev. William Hogarty, pastor of the Church of the Sacred Heart, Union County; Mary, deceased; Martin, deceased; Michæl, and the subject of this sketch. Rev. Joseph Hogarty was born January 9, 1860, and spent the first thirteen years of his life in Lexington. In 1873 he entered St. Joseph's College at Bardstown, which institution he attended seven years, taking a thorough course and graduating in June, 1880. After graduating he entered the Preston Park Seminary at Louisville, where he pursued his theological studies, completing the same in June, 1883, at which time he was ordained priest, and assigned to duty at the cathedral, where he served in the capacity of assistant for nearly a year. In October, 1884, he was transferred to Springfield, as assistant to Rev. A. McHenry, rector of St. Dominic's Church, in which capacity he remained until June, 1885, when he was placed in charge of the congregation, a position he still retains. Father Hogarty is a young man of fine abilities, a close student and a polished speaker. He is untiring in his labors to advance the interest of his congregation, and is a deservedly popular pastor. St. Dominic, numbering about 100 families, is an offshoot of the St. Rose congregation, and was established a number of years ago under the auspices of the Dominican order, Father Hogarty being its second secular pastor.

W. A. HOLMAN was born October 2, 1832. His educational facilities were meager, and he early began business for himself. He learned the trade of a carpenter, which he has followed ever since. He was married in 1864 to Miss Priscilla A. Sharp. They are both members of the Southern Presbyterian Church. Mr. Holman is a native of Mercer County and of English ancestry, his grandfather having been born in London, and stolen when a child and brought to the United States.

CREED HOOD was born March 2, 1837. His grandfather, Jesse Hood, was married in North Carolina to Miss Jarvis, and about 1798 they immigrated to Adair County, where Jesse Hood purchased 1,000 acres at $4 per acre. He also brought a good number of slaves with him. He was a farmer and dealer in tobacco, which he would load on flatboats and carry to New Orleans. On one of his trips, about 1818, he was taken ill and died near Louisville, where he is now buried, and a large amount of money he had on his person, the proceeds of the sale of a boatload of tobacco, was never recovered. Some of the slaves were sold to finish paying for the land, but his children, Patsy (Murray), Martha (Sharp), Eliphalet, John, Joel, Napoleon and Jesse inherited a small estate. His sons, John, Joel, Napoleon and Jesse enlisted and served as privates in the Mexican war, and the first three died in Mexico. Jesse Hood served in the late war, dying in the service. Eliphalet Hood, father of Creed Hood, was born in 1801, in Adair County,

and married to Miss Kalista, daughter of Joseph and Fanny (Bondurant) Taylor, both Virginians, who came to Kentucky when their daughter Kalista was only six years old. Eliphalet Hood was the father of ten children: Jesse, Thomas, Joseph, Creed, Sarah Ann (Kelly), William, Elizabeth (Young), Robert, John and Louellen, of whom Thomas, John, Robert, William and Louellen are now deceased. Thomas and Joseph enlisted in the Federal service, and Thomas Hood was killed at Chickamauga. Eliphalet Hood died in 1872, and his widow on May 22, 1885, in the seventy-sixth year of her age. Creed Hood, a native of Adair County, remained at home working for his father until his nineteenth year, when he began life on his own account. His occupation has always been farming, and he was worth at the outbreak of the civil war about $1,000. In June, 1861, he enlisted in Company A, First Kentucky Confederate Cavalry, and after participating in several skirmishes, he was honorably discharged in Chattanooga in June, 1862. He then returned to Kentucky, and in October, 1862, at Hopkinsville, he enlisted in Company H, Second Kentucky Cavalry, a part of Gen. Morgan's celebrated command. He was captured in May, 1863, at home while on a furlough, and confined at Camp Douglas twenty-one months, but was exchanged in February, 1865, in Virginia. After traveling to the salt works in West Virginia by rail, he came the rest of the way to Adair County afoot. He arrived barefooted and bareheaded, and went to work on his father's farm. The first crop he made was stolen or destroyed by Federal troops, but by industry and economy he has accumulated some property. He was united in marriage, December 25, 1876, to Miss Fanny, daughter of Francis and Jane (Mason) Clemons, of Russell County, and there have been born to him five children: Allie M.; Melvin, who died in childhood; Dollie, who died in infancy; Walter A. and Myrtie Valeria. Twelve years ago Mr. Hood purchased the farm of 120 acres formerly owned by his father, since which he has bought 150 acres additional near Cane Valley. During the past ten years Mr. Hood has, besides farming, traded in mules, selling them in the South. Mr. and Mrs. Hood are both members of the Mt. Pleasant congregation of the Christian Church, and Mr. Hood in politics has been a life-long Democrat.

JAMES W. HOPPER, editor and manager of the *Standard and Times* of Lebanon, was born November 28, 1839, in Nicholas County, Ky., and is the son of

John and Lucy A. (Campbell) Hopper. Subject received an academical education in Millersburg, Bourbon County, and on the 4th of July, 1859, graduated from Bethany College, W. Va., where, in addition to his pursuing his literary studies, he edited a college paper. Soon after his graduation he began the study of law, and was admitted to the bar in 1862, but did not engage in the practice of his profession until five years later, devoting himself chiefly to teaching. In 1867 he established a practice in Lebanon, and in the following year was elected to the office of county attorney of Marion County, serving until 1874. He began his editorial work on the Lebanon *Clarion* in the meantime, and in 1870 inaugurated the *Standard*, which was consolidated with the *Times* in 1881, since which time he has virtually surrendered the law practice to devote himself exclusively to journalistic labor. He is Grand Master of Masons for the State of Kentucky, and Past Grand Master of the Grand Council of the Royal and Select Masters of the same State. Mr. Hopper was married in Texas in 1872 to Miss Isabella Johnson, who died in 1875, leaving two children: Lee M. and Annie L. Hopper.

THOMAS HUDGIN was born April 14, 1853, in Hart County, Ky. He is the fourth of two sons and two daughters born to Hugh and Martha (Vaughan) Hudgin. Hugh Hudgin was also born in Hart County, was a substantial farmer and merchant, enlisted in the Thirteenth Kentucky Volunteers, and served nine months, when he was discharged. He died October 22, 1880, aged sixty-four. He was a son of Payton Hudgin, who was born in Virginia, migrated to Lincoln County, Ky., in an early day, and there married Elizabeth Sweeney, becoming an early settler of Green County, Ky. He was a son of John Hudgin, who was of English descent. Mrs. Martha Hudgin was born in Green County, and is a daughter of William and Ellen (Skeggs) Vaughan, natives of Kentucky. William Skeggs was a substantial farmer, served as magistrate, and was one of the earliest pioneers of Green County. Thomas Hudgin was reared on a farm and received but a plain field education. When in his teens he made a trip to Illinois, where he worked one summer. He was married June 8, 1879, to Susan A. Rogers, of Hart County, a daughter of Allen and Mahalah (Dickens) Rogers, natives respectively of Lincoln and Marion Counties. Allen Rogers was a farmer and son of John Rogers, who was of Irish origin and one of the early set-

tlers of Lincoln County. Mr. and Mrs. Hudgin have had four children born to them: Daisey, Maud, Ethel and Emery B. After marriage Mr. Hudgin located in Green County, and engaged in the dry goods business, which he has followed with success for seven years. In the spring of 1885, he located where he now resides on 233 acres in the northwestern part of Green County; 180 acres are in cultivation, and in good condition. In politics he is a Republican, and cast his first presidential vote for Garfield.

DRURY HUDSON was born March 5, 1823, and is the fifth in a family of three sons and four daughters, all of whom lived to be grown, but is now the only survivor. His parents were Pleasant and Margaret (Vance) Hudson. Pleasant Hudson was born in Pittsylvania County, Va., and came to Kentucky with his parents in 1808, became a substantial farmer of Green County, was an active Democrat, and died October 17, 1843, at the age of fifty-two. He was a son of John P. Hudson, who was born in South Carolina, but when a young man immigrated to Virginia, where he married a Miss Witcher, by whom two sons and two daughters were born, all of whom lived to a ripe old age, some to be nearly a hundred years old. His second wife was Joyce Fears, who was the grandmother of Drury Hudson; she was born in Virginia, and gave birth to five sons and three daughters. John P. Hudson, a Revolutionary soldier, was a blacksmith and wagon-maker, and also carried on a farm in Kentucky, to which State he came through the wilderness by wagon. He died in Green County, at the age of eighty-five years. Mrs. Margaret Hudson was born in Kentucky, and is a daughter of William and Fanny (Wooldridge) Vance, born, respectively, in Maryland and Kentucky. William Vance, one of the pioneers of Green County, became a substantial farmer. He reared a large family, and died in 1832, over eighty years of age; his wife survived him a few years. Drury Hudson was born in Green County, and was reared on a farm near Greensburg. From the age of sixteen he hired out till twenty-three, as a farm hand, but, during this time, flatboated some to New Orleans, and in the winter taught in common schools for two years. In the meantime he commenced the study of law. In April, 1850, he commenced selling goods six miles west of Greensburg, which business he followed for nearly five years. March 8, 1855, he married Bettie J., daughter of Fielding and Eliza (Gum) Vaughan, who were both natives of Green County. Fielding Vaughan was a farmer and slave owner, was a trader south for thirty years, and represented Green County in the Legislature two terms. Mr. Hudson and wife had born to them two children: Helen (born January 8, 1856, married W. H. Sandidge; died six months later) and Fielding L. (born September 7, 1862). Mr. Hudson, after his marriage, moved to Kansas, then to Liberty, Clay Co., Mo., where he remained till in August, 1856, when he returned to Green County, Ky., where he has resided ever since. He engaged in merchandising up to September, 1861, when he entered the Confederate Army as a guide for a time; then he became a purchasing agent in the commissary department. He was with Maj. Proctor at Rome, Ga., surrendered at Atlanta, and returned to Green County, where he has been quietly engaged in the practice of law ever since. He served as county attorney one term before the war, and has served as county surveyor, the first under the new constitution, for two terms. He has always taken an active interest in county affairs and in politics; has been a member of the F. & A. M. Lodge, No. 54, and also an active member of Chapter No. 36. He and wife are devoted members of the Methodist Episcopal Church South, and in politics he is an active Democrat, and cast his first presidential vote for James K. Polk, in 1844.

THOMAS ELBRIDGE HUDSON was born November 17, 1824, in Fleming County, Ky; in infancy removed with his mother to Pickaway County, Ohio, where he grew to manhood, and in 1848 located on the extreme point between Dick's and Kentucky Rivers, in Garrard County, Ky., where he has since resided. His father, John Hudson, was born and reared in Garrard County, but removed when a young man to Fleming County. He was the son of Benjamin Hudson, who was born in Virginia November 12, 1762, was an early settler in Garrard County, Ky., was a Revolutionary soldier for six months, was a farmer and slave owner, and died near Lancaster October 1, 1832. Jemima Berry, wife of Benjamin Hudson, was born in Culpeper County, Va., January 10, 1763, and died January 4, 1845. John Hudson married Eliza Ritchie (born in Fleming County, died February 13, 1870), and from their union sprang Thomas E., John and William. Thomas E. married in 1846 Margaret, daughter of William and Jeriah (Hudson) Downing, of Bryantsville, Ky., and to them have been born John, Mary C., James S., Elizabeth, Thomas D., Eliza (Back), Abraham L., Horace G. and Fannie. Mr. Hudson is a farmer by occupation, own-

ing 750 acres of productive land. In 1869 he purchased this farm on credit, for nearly $18,000, and paid for it out of its proceeds in six years. The farm is situated in plain view of High Bridge, and was first entered by Jonathan Jenkins, whose son-in-law, William Downing, purchased the place. Mr. Hudson was married to Mr. Downing's daughter, and the place has never been out of the hands of the descendants of the original patentee. Mr. Hudson has never been connected with any church or secret society. He was originally a Whig, and an uncompromising Union man, and is now Republican. He was one of the three in Garrard County, and the only one in his precinct, who voted for Lincoln in 1860. The children born to Benjamin and Jemima (Berry) Hudson were born as follows; Susannah, born in Virginia, October 16, 1786; Betsy, in Kentucky, July 26, 1788; William, April 13, 1790; Francis, November 3, 1791; Jeriah, June 29, 1793; Margaret, August 5, 1795; John, the father of Thomas E., February 9, 1797; David, November 3, 1798; Waller, July 28, 1800; Jesse Berry, April 3, 1802; Joshua, September 4, 1804; O. Deney, April 2, 1806, and Morgan, June 13, 1809. Waller Hudson was killed by the falling of a tree that he was chopping down April 4, 1821, in Garrard County, Ky. John Hudson, the father of Thomas E. Hudson, died in Fleming County, Ky., January 10, 1830.

L. W. HUDSON is a son of L. B. and Eliza (Schooler) Hudson, and was born December 8, 1846. The father, L. B. Hudson, was born in Garrard County in 1816; was graduated from the Transylvania Medical College; for thirty years practiced his profession at Lancaster, and is now leading a retired life on his farm at Bryantsville. In 1835 he married Eliza, daughter of Benjamin Schooler, and there were born to this union seven boys and two girls. The parents are members of the Christian Church, and in politics the father is a Democrat. L. W. Hudson, a native of Lancaster, Garrard County, resides at Camp Dick Robinson on 800 acres of as good land as there is in the county. His wife was a Miss Lizzie Bohon, daughter of Hon. William Fry Bohon, of Mercer County; his children are Florence (Knight), Scott, Banks, and Lynn W. Mr. and Mrs. Hudson are members of the Christian Church, and in politics Mr. Hudson is a Democrat.

WILLIAM HUFFMAN, M. D., was born December 21, 1828, on the line between Lincoln and Garrard Counties, and was a son of William and Elizabeth (Jackman) Huffman, to whom five sons and five daughters were born and reared, William being the youngest. William Huffman, Sr., was born in Garrard County, Ky.; he was a leading farmer and breeder of fine Rice horses; the only official position he ever held was that of justice. He died in 1867, aged eighty-two years, a member of the Christian Church; he was a stanch Whig. He was a son of Frederick Huffman who came from Virginia, and was among the first pioneers of Garrard County; his father, in turn, came from Germany. Elizabeth (Jackman) Huffman was born near Lancaster, Garrard County, and was a daughter of John Jackman, who moved his family on horseback over the mountains to Garrard County, and was one of the earliest pioneer farmers. Dr. William Huffman was reared on a farm until a lad of ten years, when his father moved to Stanford; here William attended school, and at the age of twenty commenced the study of medicine with a brother; graduated from the medical department of the University of Louisville in the spring of 1854, and commenced his practice in Stanford. In 1858 he attended the College of Physicians and Surgeons in New York; in the winter of 1865 attended a course of medical lectures in New York; is a member of the Central Kentucky Medical Association, of which he has served as president. The Doctor has a large and extended practice, and has been very successful in his profession, ranking among the leading physicians of the State. March, 1859, he was united in marriage to Kate Cook, of Lincoln County, daughter of Moses and Sallie (Robison) Cook, who were born in Lincoln and Garrard Counties, respectively. The Doctor and wife have had born to them six children, four living: Sallie (now Young), Lizzie, Fannie and Bruce. The Doctor and wife are members of the Christian Church. In politics he was a Whig until 1860; since then has affiliated with the Democratic party.

DR. JAMES R. HUGHES, one of the extensive farmers of Nelson County, was born in Washington County, Ky., July 8, 1821, of a family of seven children born to John Hughes, Jr., and Martha H. (Nantz) Hughes; he was next to the eldest. His paternal grandfather, Edward Hughes, was a native of Ireland, where he grew to manhood. He, in company with two brothers, came to the United States a short time subsequent to the Revolutionary war, coming immediately to Kentucky and settling near Danville, where he was united in marriage with Miss Letitia Reed, who was a sister of Thomas Reed (United States senator of Mississippi), grandaunt of Humphrey Marshall and aunt of James Birney. By her he was the father of fifteen children, fourteen of whom they reared to manhood and womanhood. By occupation he was a farmer, in which vocation he was very successful; but later in life he removed to Washington County. His parents educated him with a view of his entering the priesthood, but he digressed from the Catholic and united with the Presbyterian Church, of which he died an elder in 1833, a victim of the cholera, which was so prevalent that year. Frederick Nantz, maternal grandfather of J. R. Hughes, was born in Virginia, and served from the incipiency to the close of the Revolutionary war; he was a participant in the riots when the indignant colonists threw the tea overboard in Boston harbor. Before leaving his native State for Kentucky he married a Miss Harriet Watkins, by whom he became the father of eleven children; by a second marriage to Miss Cosby, he was the father of four children. Upon moving to Kentucky he settled in Washington County, where he continued to reside until his death. John Hughes, Jr., our subject's father, was born in March, 1797, and was, perhaps, during his short life, one of Washington County's most popular young men. At the age of fourteen he entered the county clerk's office as deputy under his uncle, John Reed. At nineteen years he was elected clerk pro tem. of both county and circuit, and upon attaining his majority, that election was confirmed without opposition, the county then embracing what are now Washington and Marion Counties. He died while an incumbent, in 1833, of cholera, and in his death the county lost an efficient, honest and obliging official.. James R. Hughes remained at home with his mother until he was nineteen years old; he received a good common education, attending Marion College for one year. In 1840 he commenced reading medicine with Drs. Linton & Polin; in 1842 and 1843 he took two respective courses of lectures at St. Louis, graduating in the latter year. He immediately located and began the practice at Springfield, where he continued until 1848, when he retired from the medical profession and began farming, in which vocation he has since continued and has been very successful, owning a farm of 1,043 acres well improved. In 1858 he removed to Missouri and remained there three years. June 10, 1843, he married Miss Susanna Davidson, who died March 25, 1846, leaving one son, Davidson Hughes. June 1, 1847, he married Mary R. McElroy, by whom he is the father of six living children:

Susanna, now widow of Dr. R. H. Gale; Sallie, wife of Dr. William Ray; James R.; Mamie; John L. and Bessie. Dr. Hughes and wife are members of the Presbyterian Church. In politics he is a Democrat.

M. D. HUGHES was born November 28, 1845, near Stanford, Lincoln Co., Ky., a son of Joseph N. and Amelia (Russell) Hughes, to whom six sons and three daughters were born, five of whom were raised, of which our subject is the fourth. J. N. Hughes was born in Lincoln County, Ky., and died January 6, 1869, aged fifty-four years. He was a leading farmer and trader; was a contractor for the Union Army, furnishing supplies. He had served as justice in his county; was a son of Gabriel Hughes, who was born in Culpeper County, Va.; was one of the pioneers of Lincoln County, Ky., where he became a large and influential farmer. He served as a common soldier in the war of 1812. His father came from Wales. Amelia (Russell) Hughes was born and raised in Lincoln County, daughter of Frank Russell, a native of Lincoln County, Ky. The most of his family settled in Hendricks and Lawrence Counties, Ind. M. D. Hughes was raised on a farm and received an academic education, after which he taught school in Stanford and vicinity for eight years. He then engaged in farming for a few years; in 1878 was appointed to a place in the revenue service, where he remained two years; in 1880 was an elector on the Hancock and Hendricks ticket; in 1876 was elected justice in Stanford and declined to serve; in 1883 established the *Central Kentucky News*, and succeeded in making one of the best county papers in the State, with a good circulation; September 30, 1886, sold the paper. February 9, 1869, he was united in marriage to Mattie, daughter of Robert and Polly (Salter) Elkin, natives of Shelby County. Robert Elkin moved to Garrard, thence to Lincoln; was a substantial farmer and a prominent officer in the Christian Church. He was a soldier in the war of 1812; was in the battle of Thames. He died of cancer in 1875; was of English descent. Mr. and Mrs. Hughes had born to them to bless their union three children: Robert Elkin, Frank Sanfley and May Z. He and wife are members of the Christian Church. He is a leading member of the I. O. O. F. and K. of H. In politics he is a Democrat.

JUDGE JOHN W. HUGHES, a native of Jessamine County, Ky., was born March 22, 1854. His father, William Calvin Hughes, was born in May, 1816, also in Jes-

samine County. He received a handsome estate from his father, and was married, in 1838, to Miss Eunice F. Davenport, a daughter of Maj. and Elizabeth (Williams) Davenport. Mr. Hughes remained in Jessamine County, engaged in farming and trading south in stock until in 1855, when he removed to Jackson County, Mo., remaining there until 1862, losing in the war there his entire estate. He then came to Mercer County, Ky., and at present is living on a farm one and a quarter miles from Harrodsburg, belonging to his son, Judge Hughes, having been an invalid since 1867. Mr. Hughes and wife are members of the Christian Church, and they are the parents of eight children: Leonidas (county treasurer of Saline County, Mo.), Mary J. (died in girlhood), Jefferson (died in childhood), Nannie E. (wife of Dr. T. T. Smith, deceased), Sallie S. (twin sister of Mrs. Dr. T. T. and wife of John N. Frost, of Jessamine County), Mattie H. (died in childhood), Judge John W. and Bettie W. (deceased wife of James Dugan, of Nelson County). Joseph Hughes, grandfather of Judge Hughes, was a veteran of the war of 1812, who emigrated from Virginia, and settled in Jessamine County. He was a farmer of wealth and a large slave owner. The Hughes family are of Scotch-Irish origin, one of whom, Col. James Hughes, represented the St. Joseph, Mo., district in the Lower House of Congress in 1872. Judge Hughes acquired his education by his own efforts, earning the money by herding and trading in cattle for and with his uncle, M. R. Hughes, of Independence, Mo., in western Missouri and Kansas. He attended the State University of Missouri four years, graduating in the scientific course June 28, 1874. He then entered the public schools of Kansas City, and was principal of one for two years, studying law while teaching. In April, 1879, he removed to Harrodsburg, Ky., and began teaching in the public schools, studying law in the meantime. In 1881 he received his license, and entered the practice on his own account. In 1882 he was elected police judge of Harrodsburg, and one year later superintendent of public schools, both of which offices he now holds. April 3, 1886, he received a majority of 504 votes in the primary election for nominees for the office of county judge of Mercer County, and was elected to that office without opposition on August 2, 1886. Judge Hughes was the first Democrat elected in Harrodsburg for police judge since the war, and has received the largest majorities in his races ever received by any one in Mercer County. He is a member of no organization except the I. O. O. F.

JACOB HUGUELY was born May 22, 1852. His father, John W. Huguely, a native of Madison County, born July 18, 1820, was a farmer, lost thirty-nine slaves by the late war, and is now living. He is the son of John Huguely, of Virginia, an early settler in Madison County, Ky., a farmer and slave owner, who died in 1820, at the age of about seventy years. His father was a German, of Jewish extraction. John married Rachel Green, of Virginia (died about 1842), and their offspring were Jacob, John W., Polly (Green) and Kittie (Leavell). In 1842 John W. married Miss Nancy, daughter of Cabell and Emily (Mitchell) Chenault, of Madison County(born in 1826, died January 21, 1874), and from their union sprang, John A., Cabell C., Emily (deceased) and Jacob. September 21, 1876, Jacob, who was born near Richmond, married Miss Fannie, daughter of William H. and Sarah (Taylor) Robinson, of Mercer County (born March 5, 1855), and to them have been born Nannie Chenault, William R., Jacob, Jr., and John C. Mr. Huguely is a farmer and stock dealer, owning 585 acres of land in a high state of cultivation; and he is turning his attention to the breeding of trotting horses. Mr. Huguely is a member of the Christian Church, and in politics is identified with the Democratic party. In 1856 he removed with his parents to Boyle County, and in 1878 located in Mercer County, on the Pleasant Hill pike, five miles from Danville, where he continues to reside.

HENRY A. HUMPHREY was born February 27, 1850. His father, William M. Humphrey, was also a native of Nelson County, born December 6, 1821. He married Sarah Briggs, and to their union ten children have been born, eight of whom are living: Henry A., Alice (Tucker), Robert A., Lydia E. (Tucker), John C., Simon L., Maggie F. and Emma E. William M. Humphrey has followed agricultural pursuits with great success. He is a member of the Methodist Episcopal Church, with which organization he united when quite young, and has been for forty-six years steward. He was a son of Simeon Humphrey, born in Nelson County, February 23, 1791. He died in 1867. By occupation a farmer, his farm of 200 acres, which was left to his children at his death, was a model of neatness and one of the best improved in the county. He was twice married, first in February, 1814, to Miss Nancy Elliston, of Washington County,

Ky. To this marriage two daughters were born, Mary A. (deceased) and Winnie A., (now Mrs. James Hutchins). His second marriage occurred in 1820, with Miss Lydia Benedict, by whom he was the father of twelve children: William M., George W., Amanda C., Joseph S., Miranda A., John A., Simeon L., Lydia A., Thomas F., Elizabeth L., Sarah F. and Charles M., of whom eight are now living. He, like most of his ancestors and descendants, was a member of the Methodist Episcopal Church. Henry A. Humphrey was born and reared on a farm in Nelson County, received such education as he could obtain by attending the schools of the vicinity during the winter months, and remained at home until he attained his majority. September 5, 1871, he married Miss Elizabeth Dugan. To this union one son and two daughters, Sallie W. and Harriet D., were born; the son died in infancy. Our subject after his marriage commenced farming, in which he has met with uniform success. He is the proprietor of 350 acres of well improved land, and in addition to his general farming, he devotes considerable attention to breeding and raising shorthorn cattle and Southdown sheep. He and wife and daughters are members of the Methodist Episcopal Church, in which Mr. Humphrey is steward. Politically he is a Democrat.

DR. GEORGE HUNN was born December 25, 1829, two miles north of Danville, eldest of two sons and one daughter born of Anthony and Theresa (Peach) Hunn. Anthony was born and raised in Saxony, Germany, but came to the United States when a young man. He was educated in Germany in the same institute in which Martin Luther was educated, but finished in Paris; became tutor for some years. He married for his first wife a Miss Wise, by whom four sons and one daughter were raised. He came to Kentucky about 1800, practiced his profession of medicine; published a paper in Engleman, on Hanging Fork, and also edited papers at other points; lived in Boyle and Lincoln Counties, then in Lancaster, Garrard County, where he died in October, 1834. Subject's mother came from Fauquier County, Va., about 1820 and settled in Lincoln County, Ky; she was a daughter of Daniel and Elizabeth (Gibson) Peach. Dr. George Hunn was partially raised on a farm, but at seventeen commenced the study of medicine with Dr. David J. Alcorn, of Lincoln County; attended the University of Louisville, from which he graduated in 1853 and located at Middleburg, Casey Co., Ky., where he practiced ten years; in 1860 he located at Hus-

56

tonville, Lincoln County, where he remained till 1880, then moved to Shelby City, Boyle County, where he has an extensive practice. He was married in October, 1852, to Emma C. Riffe, of Casey County, daughter of Geo. C. and Elizabeth (Anderson) Riffe, natives of Casey and Lincoln respectively. George C. Riffe was born in 1801 and died in 1875; his wife was daughter of Walter Anderson. Geo. C. Riffe was a son of Gen. Christopher Riffe, who was a soldier in Shelby's campaign. He first married Mary Spears and raised a large family; his second wife was Elizabeth Coffy, by whom he had three children. He was a farmer and represented Casey County in the Legislature. He had two sons who also represented the county. He built the first house ever built in Casey County, on Green River. Dr. Hunn had born to him four children: Anthony, Mary E. (now Simpson), Theresa (now Hood), and Susan. His wife died in December, 1861. In September, 1862, he married his present wife, Nellie Ann Bell, daughter of Wm. and Catharine (Hawkins) Bell, a native of Fayette County, Ky. Wm. Bell was a substantial farmer and slave owner, was born in 1808 and died in June, 1838; his widow married Rob Blaine. Wm. Bell was a son of David Bell, who married widow Tathan, whose maiden name was Nancy Holmes. The following children have been born to the Doctor's second marriage: Ann C., Wm. B., Rob. W., John T., Fannie B. and Edward A. The Doctor is a member of the F. & A. M., and of the R. O. Cowling and State Medical Associations.

WILLIAM DRAKE IRVIN was born June 16, 1829, near Walnut Hills, Fayette Co., Ky., and in 1832 removed with his mother to Jessamine County, where he was reared until 1846, when he entered Centre College, at Danville, from which he graduated in 1848. After reading two years in the office of Hon. Joshua F. Bell, in Danville, he spent one year at the law school at Balston Spa, N. Y. His father, John Glover Irvin, a farmer and tanner, and large slave-holder, died in March, 1832. He was the son of Robert Irvin, who was reared near the head of Salt River, five miles southwest of Danville, and in after years was sheriff of Fayette County, and whose father owned the first house having glass windows in Kentucky. Robert Irvin married Judith Glover, and their union was favored by the birth of John G., Mary (Praither), Sarah M. (Lyle) and Robert, Jr. John G. Irvin married Emeline, daughter of William and Nancy (Cunningham) Drake of Jessamine County (born November 29, 1805, now living near Mexico,

Mo., and from this union sprang one child, William Drake Irvin. After the death of her husband Mrs. Emeline Drake married Dr. William Henderson, of Concord, Mo., which union resulted in the birth of one son, Thomas C. Henderson. December 30, 1851, William Drake Irvin was united in marriage with Miss Corrilla, daughter of Andrew and Camilla (Brashear) Parker of Lexington (born July 1, 1832), and to them have been born William P., Emeline (deceased), Camilla (Young), John G., Alexander M., Robert O. (deceased), Mary, Charles M., Lela, Harry B., Clara H. (deceased) and Andrew T. In 1852 Mr. Irvin located three miles west of Danville, Boyle County, on the Perryville Turnpike, where he has since resided. He is a farmer and stock dealer, and owns ninety acres of productive land. Having been somewhat extensively engaged in buying and selling South, just before the commencement of the late war, he sold $10,000 worth of mules on credit, on the line of "Sherman's march to the sea," which he was unable to collect, and a whole venture proved a loss; he also lost about forty slaves by the late war, from all of which losses he has not recovered. In religion Mr. Irvin is a member of the Presbyterian Church. He is a member of the Masonic fraternity, and is an A. O. F. He was formerly an old line Whig, an uncompromising Union man, and now affiliates with the Democratic party. The place on which he resides is historical, and was, in the long, long ago, known as the old Rogers Tavern, and a part of his residence is more than 100 years old; batteries, also, on the retreat from the battle of Perryville, were planted on this farm. The aunt of Mrs. Irvin, Andrew Parker's sister Mary, married Robert S. Todd, and their daughter was Mrs. Abraham Lincoln, to whom Mrs. Irvin was first cousin.

ISAAC SHELBY IRVINE was born June 19, 1827, in Danville, Ky., and is the first of two sons and two daughters: David, Isaac S., Sarah and Elizabeth, born to David and Susan (McDowell) Irvine. David Irvine was born near Richmond in October, 1796. He was a prosperous farmer and about 1812 became county [and circuit clerk, which office he filled until the change in the constitution in 1812. He was an officer on Gen. Green Clay's staff in the war of 1812, and has also represented his county in the popular branch of the Legislature for several terms, also served in the Senate two terms. He was a strong and conscientious advocate of the Union in the recent great conflict and had considerable estates in Kentucky and Mississippi at his death in 1872. He was a son of Col. William Irvine, who was born in Roanoke County, Va.; came to Madison County, Ky., soon after Boone, participated in Estill's defeat, where he was badly wounded and carried home by Joe Proctor. William Irvine was one of the members of the State Constitutional Convention in 1799 and was the first county and circuit clerk of Madison, which offices he filled until his death about the beginning of the war of 1812. His son, Christopher, was appointed to fill the vacancy. Christopher shortly after raised a company and entered Gen. Green Clay's command, and at the battle of Fort Meigs was killed. David, the father of I. Shelby Irvine, was then appointed to fill the offices left vacant. The Irvine family filled the county and circuit clerks' office from the organization of the county up to the change of the constitution in 1852. William Irvine married Elizabeth Hockady, of Clark County, a daughter of William Hockady. To this happy union seven children were born and reared as follows: Christopher, David, Adam, Edmond, Albert, Patsie and Amelia. From these spring many of the most prominent and wealthy families of Kentucky. The Irvines were of Scotch-Irish descent and were all strong Whigs in politics. Susan (McDowell) Irvine was born in Danville and was a daughter of Dr. Ephraim McDowell, who was one of the most distinguished surgeons of his day. He had married Sarah Shelby, a daughter of Gov. Isaac Shelby. Isaac Shelby Irvine was reared in Danville, where he received his preliminary education; afterward attended Transylvania University and graduated from Bethany College, Va. in 1846, since which he has turned his attention to farming and has made a specialty of fine Jack stock. He has a beautiful farm three miles north of Richmond; also owns a large cotton plantation in Louisiana. He now resides in Richmond, where he has erected one of the finest residences in the county. In April, 1871, he was united in marriage to Betty Hood, a native of Carroll Parish, La., and daughter of Gooy and Ann (Chandler) Hood, who were natives of Marion County, Ky. There is no issue from this union. Mrs. Irvine is a member of the Episcopal Church. Mr. Irvine's first presidential vote was cast for Gen. Taylor, but since 1860 he has affiliated with the Democratic party.

ORIN J. ISHAM, an enterprising farmer of Mackville Precinct, Washington County, was born January 29, 1844, in the house in which he now lives, the third of a family of five children born to Henry and Margaret (McKittrick) Isham; he is the only one surviving. William Isham, his paternal grandfather, was a native of Boyle County, where he always resided. John McKittrick, his maternal grandfather, was a native of Virginia and was one of the earliest settlers in the vicinity of what is now the village of Mackville. He purchased a large tract of land, a portion of which was platted into a town, which was called after him. He was for that day an extensive farmer and slave owner, a man of considerable local prominence, and captain of the militia. He lived to an advanced age. Henry Isham was born in Boyle County in 1807, was there reared, and was united in marriage to Miss Ersley McDonald, by whom he was the father of five children. A short time after his removal to Washington County his wife died, and about one year subsequently he married Miss Margaret McKittrick, who has borne him five children: Gordon and Mary (both deceased), Orin J., Artimissia and Henrietta (the last two also deceased). He was a successful farmer and merchant, being engaged in the former vocation all his life and in the latter for over forty years. Death closed his active and useful life in October, 1884. Orin J. Isham was reared on the farm, receiving a good common education in the schools of the vicinity. In 1861 he enlisted in Company I, First Kentucky Cavalry, served ten months and was honorably discharged by reason of wound received at Lebanon, Tenn. At the age of twenty-two he entered his father's store as clerk; two years later he was given an interest in the business, but retired from the firm and formed a partnership with James Reid in the wholesale and retail grocery business at Louisville, in which he continued eighteen months; he then returned to Mackville and again entered into a partnership with his father, with whom he remained ten years. At the death of his mother in 1880 he inherited a portion of the estate left her by her parents, on which he commenced farming; in 1884 he came to the possession of the portion left his father, and now has a fine farm, well improved. March 12, 1868, his marriage to Tolitha Reid was solemnized, and their union has been blessed with this one child, Maggie. He and wife are members of the Presbyterian Church. In politics he is a Republican.

W. L. JARVIS was born March 6, 1865, and is a son of J. L. Jarvis, who was born in Shelby County in 1828, and removed to Mercer County and died here in 1876. He had five children, all of whom are living, subject being the second. The Jarvis family came originally from Ireland. W. L. Jarvis was born in Mercer County, was reared on a farm, and received a classical education, first attending school in Harrodsburg, and then at Danville in 1883. He has made farming a business, and owns 200 acres of land well improved. In politics Mr. Jarvis is a Democrat.

WILLIAM JENNINGS, M. D., was born June 10, 1827, in Lancaster, and is a son of John and Elizabeth May (Love) Jennings, to whom five children were born, four of whom were reared: Nancy E., William, James L. and John. The father, John Jennings, was born near Lancaster in 1800; was a general business man and in politics an active and influential Clay Whig. He died in 1833 while serving his county in the Legislature. He was a son of Gen. William Jennings, who was born in Fauquier County, Va., and who came to Garrard County, Ky., when a young man, and there married a Miss Ballinger, who bore him two sons and five daughters. She was the grandmother of Dr. William Jennings. After her death her husband married a Miss Marksberry. William Jennings acquired his title from having been a general of militia. He had served in St. Clair's campaign and also under Gen. Harrison in the war of 1812 as an officer. His sword used in the war of 1812 is now in the possession of Dr. Jennings. He also served as justice and afterward sheriff under the old constitution and died about 1832. He was a son of William Jennings, of Virginia, who was one of the patriots of the war for independence with six brothers. William Jennings had two sons. He was one of the first settlers of Garrard County, Ky., and was of English extraction. Elizabeth May (Love) Jennings, the mother of Dr. W. Jennings, was born in Knox County, Ky., in 1803. Dr. Jennings received a good English education in Lancaster and at fifteen entered a store as salesman, where he remained two years. He then began the study of medicine with Dr. Josiah Joplin of Mt. Vernon. In 1846 he entered Capt. Price's company, First Kentucky Cavalry, under Humphrey Marshall as corporal. He was in all the battles in which the regiment participated while in Mexico. After his return he resumed his studies and graduated from Louisville University in 1849; located in Lancaster, where he practiced his profession four years, meeting with success. He then located at Terrebonne Parish, La., and practiced two years. In 1855 he located at Richmond, Ky., where he continued the practice until 1862, when he enlisted and was made captain of Company

K of Gen. Morgan's regiment. In November, 1862, he was transferred to the medical department with the rank of major. He had charge of a hospital of Knoxville, until August, 1863, when the city was evacuated. He was in the battle of Chickamauga in charge of the field hospital of Buckner's corps. Afterward was appointed medical director of Buckner's corps; was chief surgeon of the division and medical director of the department of Southwest Virginia and East Tennessee until October, 1864, when he was ordered to Savannah; thence to Charleston, where he served until the city was evacuated. In April, 1865, he was paroled, when he returned to Richmond, Ky., and resumed practice. He located where he now resides eight miles north of Richmond, in October, 1882, on a beautiful farm of 240 acres, improved with a fine residence. In April, 1852, he married Lucy, daughter of Carey A. and Celia (Walker) Hawkins, who were both natives of Madison County. Mr. Hawkins was born in 1806, and became an extensive planter and trader. He served as deputy sheriff of Madison County eleven years, was a mail contractor and one of the most active citizens of the county. He died in 1876 and had reared two sons and two daughters. He was a son of Nicholas and Nancy A. (Robinson) Hawkins, natives of Albemarle County, Va. They reared a family of four sons and six daughters and were among the first settlers of Madison County. Nicholas Hawkins was a farmer. His wife's mother, Mrs. Nancy (Smith) Robinson, came from Virginia in an early day and located lands on Silver Creek, in all about 3,000 acres, after which she brought her family to Kentucky. Her husband was William Robinson. Nicholas Hawkins was a lieutenant in the war for independence and was at the surrender at Yorktown. Mrs. Jennings, the wife of Dr. Jennings, is in possession of a shot pouch, which her grandfather, Hawkins, carried through that war. The Hawkins and Robinson families were of English descent. The Doctor and wife had born to them four children: Carey H. (deceased), Ida V. (now Greenleaf), John M. (deceased) and Nickoleena H. (now Chenault). The Doctor and wife are members of the Christian Church, and he is a member of the F. & A. M. In politics he is a Democrat.

GEORGE W. JETER (deceased) was born in Amelia County, Va., October 4, 1810, and was the eldest of nine children born to Anderson and Sorrow S. (Allen) Jeter, a sketch of whom will be found below. In 1816 he was brought by his parents to Green County, Ky. Here he grew to manhood, and after attaining his majority learned the carpenter's trade, which he followed in connection with his live stock business for many years. At the live stock trade he was eminently successful for many years, driving large droves of hogs and other stock to Southern markets. In about 1854 he discontinued the live stock business and was afterward engaged in agricultural pursuits in connection with his trade until his death, August 10, 1874. He was first married in September, 1840, to Miss Susan S. Craddock, a native of Green County, Ky., born in 1819. She was a daughter of Robert Craddock, a native of the Old Dominion and one of the early pioneers of Green County. Mrs. Susan S. Jeter died in April, 1842, leaving no children. She was a consistent member of the Cumberland Presbyterian Church. Mr. Jeter was next married in 1845 to Miss Priscilla Hazelwood, a native of Green County. To this union were born five children: Daniel (deceased); Mary S., now Mrs. Jas. M. Durham; George R.; Robert H., and Lucy H. (deceased). Mrs. Priscilla's death occurred June 1, 1865. She was a life-long and devoted member of the Methodist Episcopal Church. Mr. Jeter's third marriage was in 1872, to Miss Maggie A. Shipp, also a native of Green County, and a daughter of Thomas Shipp, of what is now Taylor County. Mrs. Maggie A. is yet living, having again married, and resides in Illinois. Mr. George W. Jeter was a devoted member of the Christian Church, and a bright member of the Masonic fraternity, in which he took great interest, having advanced to the R. A. degree, and was buried with Masonic honors. George R. Jeter, the second son of George W. Jeter, received a fair common-school education in youth, to which he has since materially added by his own exertions. His early life was passed on his father's farm, but after attaining his majority he was employed as a salesman in a general store in Campbellsville for several years. For the past year, however, he has been clerk and business manager of the Border's Hotel in same city, and is resident agent for several insurance companies, as well as passenger agent for the O. & M. Railway. He is a member of the Masonic fraternity, having advanced to the R. A. degree, and is a young man of fine business qualifications.

CAPT. RODOPHIL E. JETER was born November 30, 1821, and is the sixth of nine children born to Anderson and Sorrow S. (Allen) Jeter, natives of Amelia and Cumberland Counties, Va., and of English and Irish descent, respectively. Anderson Jeter was born September 11, 1786, and his marriage occurred December 1, 1809. Upon the breaking out of the war of 1812, he recruited a camp of volunteers at Chinquapin Church, Amelia County, Va., of which camp he was commissioned captain, and after the battle at Norfolk, Va., was promoted to be major. Soon after the close of the war, in 1816, he removed with his family to Green County, Ky., and bought some 700 acres of land, upon which he resided until his death, November 20, 1842. He owned a large number of slaves in addition to his real estate; but suffered severe financial losses by endorsing too freely for his friends. For many years he was colonel in the old State militia. His father, Rodophil Jeter, Sr., was also born in Old Virginia, where he represented his county for six consecutive terms in the Legislature, and was a veteran in the Revolutionary war, attaining to the rank of colonel. Mrs. Sorrow S. (Allen) Jeter was born May 13, 1790, and departed this life in December, 1842. She was a member of the First Presbyterian Church, and afterward of the Baptist Church. Her father, John Allen, was also a native of the Old Commonwealth. Her maternal grandfather was the Hon. John Austin, who was one of the wealthiest planters in Virginia, and owned also some 14,000 acres of land in Clark County, Ky. Capt. Rodophil E. Jeter, a native of Green County, Ky., is a man of wide and varied information, having been an extensive, close and careful reader all his life. Until he was nearly twenty-one years old, when he was married, he lived on his father's farm. Soon after his marriage he commenced to learn cabinet-making and the carpenter's trade, serving an apprenticeship of three years. After this he followed his trades in Green County, until the breaking out of the late civil war. In April and May, 1861, he recruited and organized a camp of Home Guards of 130 men, under the "Armed Neutrality" act, procuring arms for his camp from Gen. Rousseau (then stationed at Jeffersonville, Ind.), by paying the freight on them himself. These were the first Union arms or "Lincoln guns," as they were called, ever suffered to come into Kentucky. He also furnished his men with drums and other equipments, and ammunition, at his own expense. The camp was recruited in the neighborhood of Cane Valley, in Adair County, at which place they were drilled. They did not go into camp, however, but remained at their homes, being called together when wanted by a signal. When Gen. Buckner invaded the State September, 1861, his camp was called together one night to escort the money from the Greensburg Bank to the Railway, from whence it was conveyed to Louisville. On the 23d of the same month he went into camp with his company at Greensburg, under the call of the State for troops for the United States service, and was mustered as Company C, of the Thirteenth Kentucky Volunteer Infantry, on the 31st of the following December, paying his own expenses from September to that date, with the exception of one month, when they were paid by the State. He served with his regiment until after the battle of Corinth, Miss., in 1862, when he resigned on account of disability caused by his horse falling with him while on a scout. He participated in the battle of Shiloh, as well as many other lesser engagements. After his return from the army he was appointed provost-marshal for Green, Taylor and Adair Counties, serving as such until the beginning of the draft in 1864, when his territory was restricted to Taylor County. In 1863 he was taken prisoner by Col. Scott, of the First Louisiana Cavalry, but was released on parole. After the war he was appointed general storekeeper for thirteen counties, in the internal revenue service, serving for three years, and was engaged in the hotel business at Campbellsville during a part of the same time. Afterward he engaged in the lumber and stave business at the same place, which he continued for several years. He was one of the leading men in securing the building of the Chesapeake & Ohio Railway, of which road he is now and has ever since been one of the directors. He has served as city marshal, city judge, magistrate and postmaster for a short time. Notwithstanding the fact that he lost a large number of slaves by the war, he is still a wealthy man, and for the past year has lived a retired life. Capt. Jeter was married January 6, 1842, to Miss Martha A. Chaudoin, a native of Green County, Ky., and born February 27, 1823. She is a daughter of Thomas G., and Martha (Penick) Chaudoin, natives of Virginia, and of French and English descent respectively. Four sons and two daughters blessed their union: Bettie B., now Mrs. Creed Haskins; Martha A., now Mrs. T. C. Cox; John J., and Thomas R., and two deceased. Both the captain and wife have been from early life members of the Methodist Episcopal Church, in which he has officiated as class-leader for many years. He is also a bright member of the Masonic fraternity, having advanced to the council degrees of R. & S. M., and having served as W. M. of his lodge and H. P. of the Chap-

ter. He is also a member of George H. Thomas Post, G. A. R., of Indianapolis. In politics he is a Republican.

ALEXANDER JOHNSON, proprietor of the Marion County Trotting Park, was born in Boyle County, Ky., March 24, 1843. His father, Alexander Johnson, Sr., was born in Botetourt County, Va., in 1795; when three years of age he was brought to Kentucky by his parents, who settled in Mercer (now Boyle) County, where he grew to manhood, and in 1826 married Ann Smith. To them were born five sons and two daughters: Jacob, John, William, Perry, Alexander, Hannah, wife of G. W. Wolford, and Elizabeth, wife of George Russell. Ann Smith was born in 1802 and died in 1873. She was a daughter of William Smith, of Lincoln County. Alexander Johnson, Sr., was a farmer and distiller during the early days. He and wife were noted for their unbounded hospitality and it is believed that he fed more people at his table than any other Kentuckian of his day. He was a man of remarkable strength and activity, and was one of five brothers whose aggregate avoirdupois was 1,180 pounds. The prevalent disease in this family was that of the heart, of which disease all died. Alexander was a man of some local prominence, and held several minor offices in his county. Though not a member of the church, his house was always a home for the circuit rider, who was sure of a hospitable welcome and good cheer. He died February 1, 1866. He was a son of Jacob Johnson, a native of Botetourt County, Va., who settled in Mercer County, Ky., in 1798, and who was a farmer and horseman and the first to introduce race horses into Kentucky. He reared a family of five sons and two daughters, among whom was Alexander, Sr., the father of our subject. Alexander, Jr., was reared to the business of horse training and at the age of sixteen went into the business on his own account and for twenty-seven years has been thus engaged. He is considered one of the most expert horsemen in the State. He began as proprietor of the Falkland training track and stables, on the old Johnson'farm in Boyle County; afterward removed to Danville and remained two years, and in 1883 located near Lebanon, in Marion County, and is now proprietor of the Marion County trotting park and track, which is one of the fastest tracks in Kentucky. His stables represent stock from six different States. Mr. Johnson was married November 14, 1865, to Phoebe A. Penn, and they are the parents of three sons: Thomas M., John J. and William Ru, and one daughter, Lucy Lee. Mrs.

Johnson is a daughter of Gabriel and Cynthia (Conder) Penn, of Casey County. The former was a Virginian and a grandson of William Penn. The latter was of Dutch parentage and a native of Kentucky. Mr. Johnson's political views are Democratic.

P. B. JOHNSON was born October 22, 1845, in Madison County, Ky., and is a son of William and Frances (Hooton) Johnson, to whom three sons and four daughters were born, and all raised except one son. William Johnson was born in 1811, and his wife in 1812, in Madison and Clark Counties respectively. He was a farmer; served as justice for twelve years; in religion was a Baptist and in politics a Democrat. He was a son of Maj. Johnson, who came from Virginia and settled ten miles east of Richmond. He reared a family of one son and five daughters. P. B. Johnson was reared on a farm and received a common education. At twenty-two he engaged in mercantile business at Berea, where he has been engaged ever since, and is also the possessor of 150 acres near Berea. He was united in marriage in July, 1873, to Maggie J. Merriman, of Bloomington, Ill., a native of Garrard County, Ky., and daughter of James B. and Sophia (Henderson) Merriman, who were natives of Garrard County. Mr. Merriman was a farmer who enlisted in Col. Faulkner's regiment and was killed in the battle of Wild Cat, Ky. Mr. Johnson has had born to him three children: James B. (deceased), Joseph E. and William B. Mr. Johnson was appointed postmaster at Berea in May, 1886. He is a member of the F. & A. M., in politics is a Democrat, and, with his wife, a member of the Presbyterian Church.

OLIVER H. P. JOHNSON was born January 1, 1850, in La Rue County, and is the first of four sons and three daughters born to Absalom and Ellen (Beeler) Johnson, natives of Nelson and La Rue Counties respectively. Absalom Johnson was a substantial farmer and slave owner, and died at the age of forty-four years. He was a son of William Johnson, who married Elizabeth Johnson, both natives of Maryland, and early pioneers of Nelson County, Ky., where William Johnson served as magistrate several terms. Mrs. Ellen Johnson was a daughter of Dorsey and Ellen (Hill) Beeler, early settlers of La Rue County. Dorsey Beeler was a progressive farmer and slave-holder, and was of Irish descent. Oliver H. P. Johnson received his education at Cecilian College, and at Bardstown; at the age of twenty-one commenced farming on his own account, and was married September 21, 1871, to Emma Beeler, a

daughter of Adkin and Margaret (Ross) Beeler, natives of Nelson County. Mr. and Mrs. Johnson had born to them one child, Hazard. Mrs. Johnson died in 1873, a member of the Baptist Church. December 8, 1874, Mr. Johnson married Ella Harned, a daughter of John and Kate (Lee) Harned, who were natives of Nelson and Hardin Counties. Mr. and Mrs. Johnson are members of the Baptist Church; he is also a Mason. He owns 400 acres of fine Rolling Fork bottom land, well improved, well adapted to the raising of corn and grass. He is a Democrat in politics, and cast his first presidential vote for Horace Greeley.

JAMES L. JOHNSTON, a leading farmer and prominent citizen of Adair County and a son of Thomas B. Johnston, was born in the county December 17, 1820. Thomas B. Johnston, born in 1774, in Nelson County, Va., immigrated to Adair County in 1812, where he bought a tract of 412 acres on Green River, which at that time was an unbroken wilderness. He cleared the forest and tilled the soil, was a slave owner and remained here eighteen years. He then purchased another place of 412 acres, the one at present owned by James L. Johnston, on which was a brick residence erected by the former owner. Here he lived and farmed very successfully, and became quite wealthy, until 1854, when his death occurred. He was a member of the Christian Church, and took great interest in politics, although he never would accept any political office. His wife's maiden name was Sally Dawson, a daughter of Capt. Ben and Mehala (Lyon) Dawson, one of the wealthy and prominent families in Virginia at this time. Capt. Ben Dawson was an officer in the Continental Army during the American Revolution, and served during the entire war. The University of Charlottesville was founded by William Dawson, a brother of Capt. Dawson, and a man of great wealth. The death of Mrs. Johnston, who was in life a member of the Baptist Church, occurred October 27, 1838, in the forty-fourth year of her age. Thomas B. Johnston began life with no inheritance but his native industry, and left an estate of $80,000. His father, Stephen Johnston, was also a Virginian, a man of classical culture, prominence, and considerable wealth. He lived in Nelson County, owned a large plantation and cultivated it with slave labor. He was the son of Stephen Johnston, Sr., who with his brother, Henry Johnston, emigrated from Scotland to America and settled in Virginia. Stephen Johnston was married to Agnes Waller, a sister of three celebrated Baptist ministers—

John, Edmund and George Waller—who were compelled to leave England on account of persecution consequent to their religious belief, and settled in the Old Dominion. The names of Stephen and Agnes Johnston's children were Thomas B., Henry Goodlow, Peter and Stephen. The names of Thomas B. Johnston's children were John Waller, William H., Thomas B., S. D. and James L., all of whom except John are living. James L. Johnston in youth was under the tuition of a classical scholar, Caleb H. Ricketts, for a number of years, and received a classical education, although he never graduated at any institution. He has been an extensive farmer, and before the war was worth $70,000 in slaves and real estate. He has also been an extensive and successful trader, and although he has always been a man whose ability and integrity were recognized by the community, he would never accept any public office, although frequently importuned to do so. He was united in marriage May 31, 1843, with Miss Diana Logan, the youngest of a family of seven children, three of whom were daughters, born to Matthew and Sally (Fleece) Logan, both native Kentuckians. Matthew Logan was a son of the celebrated Benjamin Logan, one of the earliest pioneers of the "dark and bloody ground." This marriage has been blessed by the addition of five children, by name: Mary Agnes, wife of Benjamin F. Hunter; Cornelia Minor, wife of Robert Conover; Mattie Sally, wife of H. K. Robertson; Dollie Elizabeth and Annie Maria, all of whom are living. Mr. and Mrs. Johnston and all of their children are members of the Hebron congregation of the Christian Church, of which Mr. Johnston is one of the elders. He owns in the home place 512 acres of fine land, well improved and in a high state of cultivation, on which is the old brick residence originally built by a Mr. Cayce, and twice remodeled since, and the 200-acre tract on Green River. His farm is one of the most valuable in Adair County, and his estate is worth $12,000. Mr. Johnston has been a life-long Democrat.

JAMES MILTON JONES was born December 19, 1817, on Hinckston Creek, Bath County, Ky., where he grew to manhood; in 1835 removed to Mount Sterling; in 1840 to Clark County, where he was deputy sheriff three years, during which time there was not a case of felony in that county. In 1844 he removed to Boyle County; in 1846 to his present place at Harrodsburg Junction; in 1849 to Pettus County, Mo., and in 1885 returned to his present home in Mercer County. His father, James R. Jones, a native of

Bath County, was born in 1784; was a soldier in the war of 1812 and was captured with Gen. Winchester. He was a farmer and slave-holder, a Whig, a Regular Baptist and died in 1849. He was the son of John Jones, who was born on Wataga River, North Carolina; was a soldier at the battle of King's Mountain in the Revolutionary war; a pioneer in Bath County, Ky., who died in 1847 at the age of ninety years. His brothers were Benjamin, Joseph, Franklin, Jesse and two others, whose names are not known. John Jones married Hannah Renfrew and their offspring were James R., Thomas T., John, David L., Elizabeth (Bridges), Lydia (Boyd) and Polly Jones. James R. first married Lydia, daughter of Nathaniel and Susan (Stone) Ralls, of Bath County (born in 1794, died in 1830), and from their union sprang John R., James M., Daniel R. and Hannah L. (Wilson). His second wife was Paulina M. (Nelson) and Thomas. James Milton Jones first married, in 1843, Miss Margaret P., daughter of John and Nancy Woods, of Mercer County (born May 5, 1822, died January 4, 1848), and to them were born John Sanford, who died a prisoner of war at Alton, Ill., and Daniel deceased. He was next married, October 16, 1849, to Mrs. Elizabeth H. Mitchell, daughter of Harvey and Sarah Woods, of Harrodsburg (born in 1821, died September 1, 1852), and their child was Elizabeth E. deceased. In 1859 he married Mrs. Minerva Hanson, nee Mason (born in 1826, died in 1876). October 31, 1876, he was married to Mrs. Narcissa Smith, daughter of Temple Burgin (born July 10, 1839). Mr. Jones clerked at Mount Sterling when a young man. He is now a farmer and stock raiser, having in fee 80 acres and control of 200 acres of fertile land. He lost 14 slaves as the result of the late war. He is a member of the Christian Church, also of the Masonic fraternity. He was formerly an old line Whig in politics, but now advocates native Americanism.

JOSEPH JONES was born January 5, 1820, where he now resides, five miles north of Richmond, and is a son of Jesse and Sallie (Newland) Jones, to whom three sons and five daughters were born and reared. Jesse Jones was born in Foxtown, Madison County, and was a prosperous farmer. He was a Whig in politics, in religion a Baptist and died in August, 1875. Joseph Jones, his father, came from Virginia in the early settling of Madison County. He was of Scotch-Irish origin, a plain farmer and owner of slave property. He married for his first wife a Miss Parks, of Estill County. By this marriage one child was born, Jonathan. After his wife's death Joseph located in Madison County, where he met and married Jennie Chenault, and to this last marriage were born eight children: Jessie, Waller, William, Richard, Elizabeth, Rebecca, Sallie and Mary. Mrs. Sallie (Newland) Jones was a daughter of Abraham Newland, who was of German parentage, and who came from Pennsylvania, was a pioneer of Madison County, became a prosperous farmer and was a slave owner. Joseph Jones was reared on a farm and received a common English education. At eighteen he entered a store as salesman for a short time, when he returned to the farm, on which he was engaged up to the breaking out of the war. At the close of the war he engaged in the whisky business in Cincinnati and New York City. He was very successful, but, being liberal and ready to assist others in business, he freely put his name to paper, and the consequence was he had nearly $100,000 security to pay. Failing, he returned to his farm of 450 acres, which was all he had remaining of 1,200 acres. He has since been engaged in farming, raising jack stock and Hambletonian horses. May 1, 1845, he married Nancy Phelps, a daughter of Samuel and Tabitha (Taylor) Phelps. The issue from this union was seven children, five of whom were reared: George W., Nannie, Tabitha and Sallie (triplets) and Joseph. Mr. and Mrs. Jones are members of the Christian Church. Mr. Jones cast his first presidential vote for Henry Clay and was an uncompromising Union man. Since the war he has been a stanch member of the Republican party.

WELCH JONES was born April 24, 1835. In 1861 he enlisted in Company E, First Kentucky Confederate Cavalry (colonel, Ben Hardin Helm), and in 1863 was captured in Mercer County, remaining a prisoner at Camp Chase and Rock Island until near the close of the war. His father, William C. Jones, a native of Mercer County, was born in 1808, was a farmer and slave-owner, a member of the Christian Church, a Whig and died in 1859. He was the son of David Jones, born in North Carolina, but brought by his parents, at the age of seven years, to Mercer County, Ky. He was early a magistrate and member of the court of claims and also high sheriff; was a member of the first constitutional convention, and died in 1855 at an advanced age. He married Susan, daughter of Capt. John Lillard, of Mercer County. She died in 1852, at the age of eighty-two years. To David Jones were born Christopher L.,

Patsy (Shy), Beriah M., Samuel M. and William C. William C. married Mary, daughter of William Owsley, of Lincoln County (born in 1818), and from their union sprang Welch, Bryant O., William C., Beriah M., Samuel H. and Lizzie C. (Jones). Welch married, December 15, 1872, Miss Amanda, daughter of Mason H. and Anna Owsley, of Platte County, Mo. (born December 29, 1843), and to them have been born Anna M., William M., Sarah C., Pearl A. and Mary. Mr. Jones, a native of Mercer County, is a farmer, and owns 102 acres of productive land near Harrodsburg. In politics he is identified with the Democratic party.

SQUIRE BRYANT OWSLEY JONES was born December 4, 1839. His father, William C. Jones, a native of Mercer County, was born in 1808, was always a resident of the county, a farmer and slave-holder, and died in 1858. He was the son of David Jones, a native of North Carolina, who removed to Kentucky in an early day, where he was a magistrate and high sheriff, a farmer and slave owner, a member of the Christian Church, a Whig, and died in 1854. He was the son of Robert Jones, whose offspring were Samuel, Robert, John, David and Mrs. Robinson. David married Susan, daughter of Capt. John Lillard, of Mercer County (died 1858, aged eighty-four years), and their children were Christopher L., Beriah, Samuel M., William C., Patsey (Shy) and Polly (Horine). William C. married Mary, daughter of William Owsley, of Lincoln County (born in 1817), and from their union sprang Welch, David M., Bryant O., William C., Elizabeth C. (Jones), Beriah M. and Samuel H. Bryant O. married, February 15, 1876, Miss Mary E., daughter of Wilkes and Martha (Farris) Morgan, of Anderson County (born April 29, 1851), and to them have been born Wilkes M., Mary E., Bryant R., Welch H. and Nannie B. Bryant O. Jones was elected magistrate and member of the court of claims, of Mercer County, in August 1866, which honorable position he now retains. He is a native of Mercer County, is a farmer, and owns 130 acres of productive land in McAfee Precinct. He is a member of the Christian Church, also a member of the Masonic fraternity, and in politics is a Democrat.

JAMES W. JONES was born in Adair County, November 12, 1839, and is the eldest of seven children born to Philip A. and Elizabeth V. (Humphries) Jones, the former a native of Taylor and the latter of Adair County, Ky. Both were of English descent. Philip A. Jones was born in June, 1818, and received his education at the primitive field schools of the Kentucky frontier. When a young man he moved to Adair County, where he was afterward married, and has ever since been engaged in agricultural pursuits. He and wife are members of the church—he of the Christian and she of the Methodist Episcopal Church South. His father, Thomas Jones, was a native of Virginia, and was one of the early settlers and prominent farmers of Taylor County, Ky. Mrs. Elizabeth V. (Humphries) Jones was born February 14, 1810, and departed this life in September, 1878. Her father, James Humphries, was also a native of Virginia, but when only a lad he ran away from home and engaged himself to drive a team for a man who was moving to Kentucky. He drove this team all the way over the mountains and through a wilderness, infested on every hand by wild and ferocious beasts, to Taylor County. Here he grew to manhood, was afterward married, and settled on the Green River, in Adair County. James W. Jones has been all his life engaged in agricultural pursuits, making for several years the culture of tobacco a specialty. October 12, 1861, he enlisted in Company C, Twenty-seventh Kentucky Volunteer Infantry (Federal service), and served with his regiment in all its marches and engagements until the close of the war, being mustered out at Louisville, Ky., in March, 1865. He participated in the battles of Stone River, Knoxville, Bean Station, Resaca, Kenesaw Mountain, Lost Mountain, Altona, the battles around Atlanta and many other lesser engagements. At Stone River he had two brothers and a brother-in-law killed, all of whom were near him in the action. He was married February 22, 1859, to Miss Susan A. Adams, a native of Taylor County, Ky., born October 20, 1843. She is a daughter of John and Eliza (Baley) Adams, both natives of Marion County, Ky., and of English descent. Eight children have blessed their union, viz.: Hezekiah B., Sarah E. (deceased), Geo. G., Eliza F., Susan M., Nancy E., John W. and James P. Both Mr. Jones and wife are members of the Christian Church. In politics he is a Republican. and is one of the respected citizens of the district and county. Mr. Jones' parents, Philip A. and Elizabeth V. (Humphries) Jones, were remarkably stout or heavy persons, each weighing over 300 pounds, and their joint weights aggregating 746 pounds.

JACOB JOSEPH was born in Prussia, July 5, 1854. His father, Abraham Joseph, was born in Gollub, Prussia, in 1822, was a cloth weaver, came to Cincinnati, Ohio, in 1865, and engaged in peddling through the country. Jacob's mother, Sarah E. Abraham, was born in Inawaratzlav, Prussia, in 1832, and became the mother of three boys and three girls. Both parents were members of the Jewish Church. Jacob Joseph came to America with his parents and for seven years was engaged in peddling, when he moved from Cincinnati to Lexington, Ky., and clerked in a clothing store six months; thence he went to Georgetown, Ky., and for five years clerked for Davis Brothers; in 1879 he moved to Lancaster and opened a large dry goods and clothing establishment, and now stands at the front in that trade. He married Miss Lizzie Forx of Eaton, Ohio, and has one child, Margaret Marie. Mr. Joseph is a Free Mason, and in June, 1886, was elected a member of the Lancaster City Council.

H. CLAY KAUFFMAN, an attorney of Lancaster, was born June 26, 1852, in Hustonville, Lincoln County, and is a son of Francis S. and Mary (Holmes) Kauffman, to whom three children were born, Alice, Minnie and H. Clay. Francis S. Kauffman was born in York County, Penn., from there went to Cook County, Ill., where he owns a large tract of land; thence to Lincoln County, Ky., about 1830, where he carried on a saddler business. He was a Clay Whig and took an active interest in politics; was an uncompromising Union man during the war. He served as postmaster at Hustonville for over thirty years, and died in 1882. He was actively engaged in raising troops for the Federal Army, was one of the leading citizens of his county, and was instrumental in holding many in his vicinity to the Union cause. His ancestors came from Germany and settled in York County, Penn. Mary (Holmes) Kauffman was born at Crab Orchard, Ky., and was a daughter of Samuel and Mary (Faulker) Holmes, who were early pioneers of Garrard and Lincoln Counties. He reared a large family and came from Virginia. H. Clay Kauffman received a good English education, attended Kentucky University at Lexington, graduating from the Commercial Department. In 1874 he located in Lancaster and began the practice of law with Burdett & Hopper, and was admitted to the bar April, 1875; afterward was elected county attorney in 1878, and served but one term; in 1881 he was appointed master commissioner of the circuit court of Garrard County and served until 1886. He was united in marriage December 30, 1879, to Emma Greenleaf. The issue of this union is three children: Louisa,

Alice L. and Frances. Mr. and Mrs. Kauffman are members of the Christian Church. He is a leading member of the F. & A. M., and cast his first presidential vote for Tilden. JOHN S. KELLEY, attorney at law, Bardstown, was born in Jefferson County, Ky., on the 1st of January, 1853, and is a son of Dailey and Sabina (Woodsmall) Kelley. Samuel Kelley, his grandfather, was one of the pioneers of Jefferson County, and a farmer by occupation. He was a soldier in the Indian war of 1811–12, held a major's commission and participated in the battle of Tippecanoe. Dailey Kelley was born in Jefferson County about 1827, and remained there until 1856, at which time he moved to Platte County, Mo., where he engaged in farming until 1861. In the latter year he went to Pike's Peak and engaged in mining, which business he carried on for a number of years in the different Territories; returned to Kentucky in 1884 and located at Bardstown, where he now resides. His wife, Sabina (Woodsmall) Kelley, was the daughter of John Woodsmall. She was born in Jefferson County and died in Platte County, Mo., in 1857. She was the mother of three children, viz.: John S. (subject); Annie, wife of C. Broaderson, and an infant (deceased). John S. Kelley was but three years old when his parents moved to Missouri, and after his mother's death, which occurred one year later, he was brought back to Kentucky and placed in charge of his grandfather, John Woodsmall, with whom he remained until his twelfth year. Later he lived in the family of an uncle, Charles W. Moore, for three years, and then with another relative, Samuel K. Baird, of Spencer County, with whom he remained until his sixteenth year. He attended the country schools of Jefferson and Spencer Counties until arriving at the above age, at which time he entered the mechanical department of the Kentucky University, which he attended from 1869 until 1871. He came to Nelson County in the latter year and engaged in teaching at High Grove, which profession he followed at intervals until his graduation from Forrest Hill Academy, in June, 1874. After graduating he followed the profession of teaching until 1876, at which time he began the study of law with G. G. Gilbert, of Taylorsville, and in the latter part of the same year entered the law department of the Louisville University, graduating from the same in 1877. In May, 1877, he located at Bardstown, and since that time has practiced his profession in the courts of Nelson and adjoining counties. He was elected county school commis-

sioner, October, 1880, and the same year was appointed master commissioner of the Nelson County Circuit Court, both of which positions he still holds. Mr. Kelley married, September 13, 1881, in Bardstown, Miss Mattie L. Ball, daughter of Capt. Joseph K. Ball, of Louisville. The children of this marriage are two in number: John J. (deceased), and Anna B. Kelley. Mr. Kelley takes an active interest in politics and votes with the Democratic party. Mrs. Kelley is a member of the Catholic Church, belonging to the St. Joseph's congregation of Bardstown.

JOHN SMITH KENNEY was born April 5, 1810, in Fayette County, Ky., where he lived on the old family homestead until 1855, when he located near Junction City, Boyle County, where he has since resided. His father, Matthew Kenney, Jr., was born January 22, 1776, near the fort, Augusta County, Va.; removed with his parents in 1792, to Fayette County, Ky.; was a soldier under Col. McMullen in the Indian war; while a young man superintended the Highland Salt Works, in Hopkins County, and was a farmer and also a slave-holder in Fayette County, where he died July 29, 1837. He was the son of Matthew Kenney, Sr., a native of County Tyrone, Ireland, where the family were mostly destroyed by the Papists, while he and his brother, Robert, and sisters, Agnes and Margaret, escaped in a Spanish ship to America and were sold in Philadelphia for their passage. He was a soldier in Braddock's war, and was also an intrepid patriot all through the Revolutionary war. He was a weaver, but located his homestead at the head of Boone's Creek, ten miles east of Lexington, Ky. Having a classical education, he taught school in his old age, and among his pupils, when boys, were Chilton Allen, Thomas Corwin, John Allen, Gov. Trimble, Chief Justice Robinson, of Kentucky, Garrett Davis and others. His father, Robert Kenney, of Dundee, Scotland, married a Miss Robinson, murdered as above. She was a sister of the grandfather of Judge George Robinson, of Kentucky. Matthew, Sr., married Elizabeth, daughter of James and Margaret (McCreary) Huston, of Greenbrier County, Va., came to Kentucky as above and died in Fayette County, May 5, 1821. Their children were James, Matthew, Jr., Rebecca (Givens), Robert P., Agnes (Lyle), Alexander (M. D.), Elizabeth (Montgomery), Sarah (deceased), William Mc. and Mary (deceased). Matthew, Jr., married Jane, daughter of John Smith, of Miller's Iron Works, Rockingham County, Va., and from their union sprang John S., Silas P., Sarah F.

(Campbell), William R., Joseph S. and Virginia (Sherer). John S. Kenney served six years as deputy sheriff of Fayette County under the old constitution. He was also executor of a number of estates and occupied many positions of trust. He is now engaged in farming, having 268 acres of land in a high state of cultivation. He also owns 112 acres of timber land. He lost eight of the best of servants during the late war, to whom he had often tendered their freedom, which was declined. He had habitually given them six per cent of the net income from the farm, and some of them were well prepared for emancipation. He was an old line Whig and an uncompromising Union man. Fortune has generously smiled on him, and he is now enjoying a contented and happy old age. He is not a church member, but a firm adherent of the tenets of Calvin. Mr. Kenney's maternal great-grandfather, James Huston, was a gunsmith in the Revolution and inspector of arms under Washington. He established Huston's Station, in Bourbon County, Ky.; was the friend of Daniel Boone, and an Indian fighter. He married Margaret, daughter of Col. John McCreary, of the Revolution, and their offspring were Robert C., John, Phœbe (Kenney), Elizabeth (Kenney), Patience (Kerr), Sarah (Boggs), Ephemia (McDowell), Hester and Jane, never married.

JOHN KINCAID was born in Mercer County, February 15, 1791. His father, Capt. James Kincaid, served in the Revolutionary war in the Virginia State line under Gen. George Rogers Clark, and in the thrilling campaigns of the "dark and bloody ground." His uncle, Capt. Joseph Kincaid, was killed at the battle of the Blue Licks, at the head of his company. His grandfather moved with the remainder of his family from Virginia, and settled near the town of Danville, Ky., in the year 1778. They were of Scotch descent, and were intense Presbyterians in their religious convictions. John Kincaid, when a young man, removed to the county of Lincoln, and taught school near the town of Stanford. While he was thus engaged, in the year 1815, Hon. Thomas B. Montgomery, then judge of the Lincoln Circuit Court, attracted by his intellectual powers, persuaded young Kincaid to study law, which he did in the office of Judge Montgomery, at the conclusion of his school in the latter part of the year. After procuring his license he practiced law at the Stanford bar for six years, representing the county in the State Legislature in the meantime. He was then appointed commonwealth's attorney by Gov. Slaughter for the district for which Thomas

B. Montgomery was judge. He held this position for about five years, and no similar office in Kentucky was ever filled with more ability than he brought to bear in the discharge of his official duties. This office he resigned to run for Congress, to which body he was elected, and served from 1829 to 1833, during the administration of President Jackson. He then returned to the county of Lincoln and resumed the practice of law, in which profession, it is safe to say, that he had few equals and no superiors in the State. In the forensic contests of that day with George Robertson, Ben Hardin, Squire Turner, James Harlan, Judge Richard Buckner, and Robert and Charles A. Wickliffe, John Kincaid was considered the peer of any of those distinguished men, and held front rank as a jurist. The conspicuous characteristics of his mind were strength and simplicity. He possessed great power in the analyzation of legal propositions, reducing them to their simplest elements, and letting daylight down into the bottom facts or principles of whatever he discussed. He was not what might be called an eloquent speaker. His mind gravitated irresistibly toward facts and principles. An original thinker, he had no use for books to furnish him with arguments, but used them simply to sustain himself in the positions already taken. He saw through the law of his case clearly, and could make others see without the aid of authorities. His manner of addressing court or jury was entirely natural. His voice was metallic and harsh, but this defect was lost sight of in the clearness of his statement and the resistless power of his logic. Awkward and slow without preparation, he was the most irresistible and powerful man in the argument of difficult legal propositions (after a thorough preparation) that central Kentucky has yet produced. It was almost impossible for the clearest legal mind to discover the exact line of separation between logic and sophistry in his arguments. He was by nature a modest man, but when convinced that his cause was just, his intellect and whole person seemed to be on fire and consumed whatever opposition existed in the minds of his audience. He died while on a visit to his daughter, Mrs. Joseph Weisiger, near Nashville, Tenn., February 7, 1873, and in his death one of the greatest legal lights that Kentucky ever produced was extinguished.

ABNER KING was born February 25, 1817, on the premises now in his possession, where he has always resided. His father, Abner King, Sr., a native of Stafford County, Va., was born in 1773, and removed with his parents to Kentucky in 1782; was a colonel of militia, a member of the Legislature, a surveyor, a zealous Baptist, and died March 4, 1834. He was the son of William King, a Virginian, who was a Revolutionary soldier, a member of the first constitutional convention of Kentucky, and died in 1832, at the age of ninety-four years. His father was Valentine King, a native of England, who married a Miss Edwards, of Wales, and died in Virginia, leaving four sons: William, Weathers, Valentine and John Edwards King. Abner, Sr., married Polly, daughter of Philip Webber, of Shelby County, and their union was favored by the birth of Jacyntha E. (Reddish), Thompson W., Sarah A. (Wells) and Abner. Abner King, Jr., a native of Nelson County, May 29, 1838, was married to Miss Nancy, daughter of Bernard and Betsey Stone, of Nelson County, born April 26, 1822, and to them were born Elizabeth (Wells), Albert D., Bernard S., Thompson, James B., Elmira (Wright) and William E. Mr. King is a farmer, owning about 950 acres of land highly improved. His children are all settled around him and are in a prosperous condition. He has for over fifty-nine years been a member and for over thirty years been moderator in the Baptist Church. In politics he is a Democrat.

JAMES B. KINNAIRD, M. D., physician of Lancaster, was born December 24, 1856, in Lancaster and is a son of Wm. H. and Pattie (McKee) Kinnaird to whom eleven children were born: Robert, Helen (Herndon), Margaret R. (Gill), Mariah (Kirby), James B., William, Elizabeth (Burnsides) Alex. McKee, Mary A. (Weisiger), Katie and Lillian. Wm. H. Kinnaird was born August 6, 1822, near Marietta, Ohio. In 1836 he came to Lancaster (where he had an uncle living engaged in the mercantile business) and entered his uncle's store as salesman till 1845, when he purchased an interest. In 1857 entered the Deposit Bank of Lancaster; in 1865 organized and opened Lancaster National Bank as cashier. He is one of the leading and most successful business men of Lancaster; is a Republican. He was a son of David and Jemima (Mail) Kinnaird, to whom two sons and three daughters were born, William H. being the eldest. David Kinnaird was born in Leslie, Scotland; came to the United States in 1818 and settled in Ohio; was a teacher in early life, later turned his attention to farming. He died in 1868, aged sixty-seven years, and was a son of Wm. Kinnaird, who died in Scotland at nearly one hundred years of age. Jemima (Mail) Kinnaird, grandmother of Dr. Kinniard, was

born in Greenbrier County, Va. Her first husband was a Mr. Richards. Pattie (McKee) Kinnaird, mother of the Doctor, was a daughter of David and Elizabeth (Letcher) McKee. The Doctor was reared in Lancaster, and graduated in Centre College, Danville, Ky. Began the study of physic in his last college year, with Dr. Mays. In the winter of 1880–81 he attended the College of Physicians and Surgeons. In the spring of 1882 he graduated at Bellevue Medical College; located at Lancaster, where he has succeeded in establishing an excellent practice. Took a post graduate course at New York polyclinics in 1886. The Doctor is a member of the State Medical Society and recorder of the Central Kentucky Medical Association. The Doctor has had marked success. In politics he is a Republican and cast his first presidential vote for James G. Blaine.

THE KIRK FAMILY. In 1790 James Kirk came from Virginia and settled on Cartwright's Creek, a short distance from the town of Lebanon, Marion County, the territory being then embraced in Nelson County, Ky. He there developed a farm, and reared his family, consisting of six sons and two daughters, named as follows: Edward, Dixon, John, Jesse, Travis, Robesson, Mary and Lucy. Dixon married Nancy Hoskins, a daughter of Rudolph Hoskins, of a Virginia family, who had settled in the same locality on Cartwright's Creek. Dixon Kirk was born in Virginia in 1790, and consequently was an infant when the family removed to Kentucky. He lived for a time in each of the counties of Washington, Marion, Adair and Grayson, but in 1856 removed to Missouri, where he died the same year, his wife having died in Grayson County, Ky., in 1836. They had a family of ten children, viz.: Mary J. (Lyon), Eliza A. (Landers), Susan M. (Murray), Martha C. (Martin), Elizabeth E. (Hoffman), James H., Joseph E., Daniel H. (who died in childhood), John T. and Paulina C. (Martin). James H. Kirk, the sixth of the above named, and one of the most prominent citizens of Lebanon, was born on the 29th of October, 1820, in Washington County; was reared on his father's farm, and in 1842 married Miss Rachel E., daughter of James and Nancy (Purdy) Blaine, and a native of Warren County, Ky. James H. Kirk was the proprietor of one of the early hotels, and erected the first livery stable in Lebanon; served from 1864 to 1868 as sheriff of Marion County, and since 1863 has been collector of the railroad tax in that county.

J. HENRY KIRK, the eldest son of James H. and Rachel E. Kirk, was born in 1843, in Marion County, educated in Lebanon, and has been chiefly engaged in agriculture. In 1868 he was elected to the office of sheriff of Marion County, serving one term, and is now the efficient deputy stamp collector for the Fifth District of Kentucky. He was married in 1868 to Miss Alice Bell Cowherd of Green County. She is the daughter of Frank Cowherd (deceased), and Judith F. Cowherd (nee Cox), now of Green County. An only son, James F. Kirk, died in infancy.

ROBERT E. KIRK, one of the principal business men of Lebanon, and cashier of the National Bank of Lebanon, is the youngest son of James H. and Rachel E. Kirk and was born July 11, 1847. He received a good English education in the schools of Lebanon, and on the 20th of September was married to Miss Grace Green, daughter of Charles Green, of Berkeley Springs, W. Va. Their three children are May, Grace and Alethia Kirk. Mr. Kirk is an honored member of the Masonic fraternity, and of the Second Presbyterian Church.

REV. JOSEPH KNIFLEY was born in what is now Taylor County, Ky., then (Green) County, December 10, 1809, and is the fourth of five children born to Philip and Sarah (Mourning) Knifley, who were of English and Irish descent respectively. Philip Knifley was born in Pennsylvania in 1777; while yet a young man he came to what is now the southeastern part of Taylor County, Ky., but was at that time a part of Green County. Here he bought wild land and subsequently improved a farm, upon which he resided until 1814, when he sold out and bought another farm in the north part of Adair County, on Casey Creek, upon which he remained until his death, in August, 1862. From early life he was a devoted member of the Cumberland Presbyterian Church. His father was most of his life engaged in agricultural pursuits in his native State of Pennsylvania. He was a veteran of the Revolutionary war and died in Green County, Ky., aged nearly a hundred years. Mrs. Sarah (Mourning) Knifley was born in Ireland in about 1784; while yet a child, however, she came with her parents to what is now Taylor County, Ky. Her death occurred about 1818 or 1819. She was a life-long member of the Separate Baptist Church. Her father, Roger Mourning, was one of the earliest settlers of Taylor County. Rev. Joseph Knifley was employed on the home farm until he attained his majority, when he bought a farm on Casey Creek, near Rolla in Adair County, upon which he remained until about 1838, when he sold out and rented lands for some two years. He then bought the farm of 260 acres, some three miles farther down Casey Creek, upon which he has since resided, and where he has been for many years extensively and successfully engaged in farming and stock raising. He has for several years taken considerable interest in breeding blooded stock, both horses and cattle. For many years in ante bellum days, he was a captain in the old State militia. Mr. Knifley has been twice married; first, February 16, 1832, to Miss Sallie Martin, a native of Adair County, born February 7, 1812. She was a daughter of James and Jemima (Butler) Martin, both natives of Adair County, and of English descent. Five children were the fruit of this union, viz.: Eliza J. (Bland), now the widow of Charles H. Jones; Nancy E. (deceased), married Mr. R. M. Tucker; William W., Mary J., now Mrs. J. C. Dunbar; and Philip H. Mrs. Sallie Knifley departed this life January 10, 1863, a devoted member of the Christian Church. Mr. Knifley was next married, October 26, 1865, to Miss Elizabeth H. Lainhart, a native of Casey County, Ky., born December 8, 1827. She is a daughter of Christopher and Rebecca (Hight) Lainhart, natives of Madison and Casey Counties, Ky., respectively, and of English descent. Both Mr. Knifley and wife are members of the Christian Church, in which church he has been a regularly ordained minister for nearly half a century. He is also an old and bright member of the Masonic fraternity, having been a member of the order for over thirty-five years, and has advanced to the Council degree of R. & S. M. In politics he is a Republican, and is one of the successful farmers as well as one of the most respected citizens of the county and district.

MRS. FANNIE KNOX was born February 1, 1841, in Springfield, Ky., and on December 22, 1863, was united in marriage to Mr. Thomas Davis Knox, with whom she removed to the old Knox homestead on Salt River, five miles west of Danville, Boyle County, where she has since resided. Her father, James C. Lyons, was born near Elizabethtown, Ky., March 7, 1816, removed to Springfield about 1832, was a druggist by profession, served long as a steward in the Methodist Church, and died April 16, 1862. He was the son of Joseph Lyons, a native of Vermont, who removed to Kentucky in youth, was a farmer, and died about 1820. His children were William, Joseph, David, James C., Martha (Woods), Anna (Miller), Rebecca (Floyd) and Mrs. Pearman. Thomas D. Knox was born May 19, 1842, was a farmer and a Presbyterian, and died November 24, 1883. To him and our subject were born six children, viz.: James Robert, Emma Davis, Mary Jane, Wallace Scott, Fannie Kate and Virginia Walker. Thomas D. was the son of Andrew W. Knox, who was born April 1, 1796, near Philadelphia, Penn., removed with his parents to Boyle County in 1801, was magistrate, major of the militia, and superintendent of schools, and died April 8, 1855. He was the son of Abner Knox, born March 12,1769, in Franklin County, Penn., settled the place where Mrs. Fannie Knox now lives, and died August 2, 1821. His father, Andrew, was born in county Antrim, Ireland, in 1728, immigrated to America in 1732, and was the son of David Knox, born in County Antrim, Ireland, in 1700. Andrew married Isabella White, of Philadelphia County, Penn., in 1755. Their children were Robert, David, Martha, James and John (twins), William, Abner, Mary and Andrew. Abner married Elizabeth Tagart, of Pennsylvania, born March 13, 1769, and had born to him the following children: Andrew W., Robert T., Maria (Wilson), David A. and William G. Andrew W. married Mary, daughter of James Davis, and their children were Jane M. (Walker), Robert T. and Thomas D. Mrs. Fannie Knox is farming the old Knox estate, consisting of 361 acres of productive and well improved land. She is a member of the Presbyterian Church.

JUDGE JOHN GLOVER KYLE was born April 2, 1840, at the ancestral home where he now resides, three and one-half miles south of Harrodsburg, Ky. His father, Andrew Galbraith Kyle, was born in 1796, in Washington County, Ky., removed with his parents to Mercer County in 1798; he was a farmer and slave-holder, president of the Savings Institution of Harrodsburg, a successful business man, was colonel of the State militia, an old line Whig, a Union man, and latterly a Republican; lost thirty slaves during the late war, and died September 8, 1872. He was the son of Rev. Thomas Kyle, a native of Pennsylvania, born in 1757, who once sat with Gen. Washington in the Masonic lodge, was a soldier several years in the Revolutionary war, and carried a sabre mark on his head, inflicted by a British officer. He studied medicine with Dr. Benjamin Rush, of Philadelphia, removed to Washington County, Ky., in 1790, was a dignified and very active local minister in the Methodist Episcopal Church for sixty-five years, and died at his residence, the present home of Judge Kyle, June 26, 1846. His offspring were John, Matthew, Andrew G., Jane (Sargeant) and Rebecca (Nourse). Andrew G. married Jane, daughter of John Glover, of Mercer County, late of Missouri (born August 29, 1809, died June 30, 1882), and from their union sprang John G. and Thomas A. November 24, 1869, John G. married Miss Marian, daughter of Dr. John L. and Patsy O. (Letcher) Smedley, of Mercer County, and to them have been born Overton G. (deceased), Jennie Fay, Andrew G. and William Riker. Judge Kyle attended at Transylvania University and Centre College, and graduated at the Louisville Law School in 1862. He practiced for several years in Mercer and adjoining counties, and frequently sat on the bench by the election of the bar in the absence of the judge. December 12, 1875, he received a paralytic stroke, from the effects of which he has not fully recovered. He is now engaged in farming, having 700 acres of well improved land, which he is grazing. He is a member of the I. O. O. F., and a Republican. He was chosen elector for the Ashland District during Gen. Grant's campaign for the presidency in 1868, and in 1874 was the Republican candidate in his district for circuit judge; he was defeated by only 211 votes, although the district was Democratic by several thousand majority.

DR. MILES LAHA, an active and energetic young physician, was born December 6, 1858, in La Rue County, Ky., near Buffalo, and is the eleventh of seven sons and five daughters, all of whom are still living, born to Daniel and Catherine (Hailey) Laha. Daniel Laha was born in Ireland in 1814; when a lad of twelve, with an uncle, he immigrated to Canada, then to the States, and lived in New England till 1825, when he located in Virginia, where he married, since which he has been engaged at farming. After the birth of the first child, he came to Kentucky, and settled near New Haven, Nelson County. One year later he located in La Rue County. Dr. Miles Laha remained on the home farm until the age of seventeen years, when he started in life for himself; at nineteen he attended school in Green and Taylor Counties; at twenty-one he commenced the study of medicine with Dr. S. D. Coakley; in the spring of 1883 he graduated from Central University of Medicine, Louisville; in June of the same year he located where he now resides, on Rolling Fork in Nelson County, where he has succeeded in building a good practice. He was married September 16, 1885, to Melissa J.

Ferrill of La Rue County, a daughter of Joel and Nancy (Cravens) Ferrill, the former a native of La Rue County, the latter of Nelson County. Joel Ferrill was a son of William Ferrill, who married Mary Killen, and was an early pioneer farmer. Dr. Laha cast his first presidential vote for Hancock.

ROBERT B. LANCASTER, farmer and distiller, was born in 1835, and is a son of Benjamin Lancaster and grandson of John Lancaster who came from Charles County, Md., to Kentucky, settling near the present village of Loretto, Marion County. John Lancaster had a large family; his son Benjamin was born in 1799 and passed his entire life in Marion County. He maried Ann Pottinger of one the oldest families of Nelson County and had a family of eight children, of whom five grew to maturity, viz.: Mary J., who died in 1844 in early womanhood, Samuel P., James M., Robert B. and Ann E. Lancaster, the last of whom died in 1868. The entire family were adherents of the Catholic religion. The father, Benjamin Lancaster, died in 1840 and the mother in 1881. Robert B. was born near Loretto, was but five years old when he removed with his widowed mother to Nelson County, and there grew to manhood, receiving a good English education in St. Joseph's College of Bardstown. He embarked in the mercantile business (1856) in Lebanon, but returned to Nelson County, pursuing the vocation of farming until he permanently located in Lebanon in 1874, since which time he has been variously employed in merchandising, farming, distilling and trading. In 1867 he married Miss Mary Teresa Abell, daughter of John and Jane (Spalding) Abell. She died January 6, 1879, leaving six children as follows: Mary J., Anna E., Joseph S., Benjamin H., John A., and Mary T. Lancaster. His present wife, to whom he was married in 1881, was Sallie Dougerty of Louisville. Their only issue is Robert B. Lancaster, Jr.

GEN. WILLIAM J. LANDRAM was born on the 11th of February, 1828, at Lancaster, Ky., where he has since resided. He is the eldest son of Lewis and Martha (George) Landram, the former a Virginian by birth, and a lawyer by profession. He came to Kentucky in the beginning of the century, when it was the frontier of civilization, locating in Scott County. Subsequently he removed to Lancaster, where the remainder of his life was spent, and where he died in 1873. He was a good lawyer, a sound reasoner, but not a gifted orator. He held various offices under the Government, and was particularly noted as a faithful and zealous Mason, and was elected, prior to the war, Grand Master of the State. Gen. Landram, the subject of this sketch, received a liberal education in the best private schools of his county, and in 1845 became deputy clerk for the county and circuit courts of Garrard County. In the Mexican war he enlisted as private in Company A of the First Kentucky Cavalry, Humphrey Marshall, colonel, and at the end of the first month was promoted to orderly sergeant; he participated in the battle of Buena Vista, where he was wounded. At the termination of this term of enlistment he returned home and resumed his place in the clerk's office, reading law during his leisure moments. In 1850 and 1851 he edited and published the "Garrard Banner," a political journal. In 1854 he was elected clerk of the circuit court of Garrard County, and was continually re-elected, and held the office until the commencement of the late civil war. In 1861 he entered the Government service at Camp Dick Robinson, and was commissioned colonel of the First Kentucky Cavalry, which position he soon resigned on account of his dislike to the cavalry service. Under orders from Gen. Sherman he took charge of the Government grounds at Harrodsburg, and in two months recruited the Nineteenth Kentucky Infantry Regiment, and was commissioned its colonel. He participated in the following battles: Chickasaw Bayou, Arkansas Post, Port Gibson, Champion Hills, Black River Bridge, siege of Vicksburg, and siege of Jackson. In these battles he commanded the Second Brigade, Fourth Division, Thirteenth Army Corps, composed of the Nineteenth Kentucky, Forty-eighth Ohio, Seventy-seventh, Ninety-seventh, One Hundred and Eighth, One Hundred and Thirtieth Illinois Regiments, and the Chicago Mercantile Battery. In the battle of Sabine Cross Roads, La., he commanded the Fourth Division, Thirteenth Army Corps. In 1865 he was promoted to brigadier-general of volunteers, and commanded the Baton Rouge district for some time. He had charge of the cavalry camp of instruction at New Orleans, and when the end of the war finally came he returned to his home at Lancaster. He was appointed collector of internal revenue for the Eighth Kentucky District by President Johnson, and held the position by successive appointments until in July, 1885. He then entered upon the practice of law at Lancaster. He was married, in 1848, to Sarah Walker, a daughter of William Walker, of Bath County. They have had nine children, six of whom are living, viz.: Walker, Mary (now Burnside), Addie (now McFarland), Ella (now Dunlap), Lewis and Katie. Gen. and Mrs. Landram are members of the Presbyterian Church. He is a Mason and an I. O. O. F. He cast his first presidential vote for Gen. Scott, and since the war has voted the Republican ticket. He was chairman of the Republican State Central Committee of Kentucky during the presidential campaign in 1876.

ETHELBERT B. LANGSFORD was born January 26, 1845, on the place where he now resides. His father, Daniel Langsford, a successful farmer and stock raiser, was a native of Nelson County, was born September 4, 1808, and died in 1876. He was the son of Nicholas, who left England when a lad, and located in Kentucky when a young man, where he died about 1832. Daniel Langsford was married, November 15, 1836, to Rebecca, daughter of David and Elizabeth (Stone) Stallard, of Nelson County, born August 18, 1821, and their offspring are Nicholas B., Sarah F. (Nichols), Ethelbert B., Anna U. (Stoner), Lizzie L. (Smith) Cathie B. and James H. On May 15, 1873, Ethelbert B. was married to Miss Mary L., daughter of Henry and Charlotte (Johnson) Harned, of Nelson County, born February 27, 1851, and to them have been born Walter, Earnest B., Lottie Ree and Daniel H. Mr. Langsford is a farmer, owning 350 acres of productive land in his native county of Nelson. He is a member of the Missionary Baptist Church, and votes the Democratic ticket.

WILSON N. LANKFORD was born December 18, 1828. His father was a Virginian, born in Albemarle County, in 1795. He married Jane Martin in 1815, and two years later, with his wife and one child, came to Kentucky and located in Washington, now Marion, County. Here he pursued the trades of wheelwright and carpenter, in connection with the working of a small farm that he owned. His wife, Jane, died in 1873, aged seventy-five years. She was the mother of twelve children: William, James, Oliver, Joseph, Mary, Eliza, Wilson, John, Samuel, Charles, Nancy and Thomas. The last named was a soldier in the war of the Rebellion, and served under Gen. Wolford. James Lankford died in 1882, at his home in Marion County. James Lankford, Sr., grandfather of Wilson N., was a Virginian by birth and of English and Irish parentage. Two of his sons served under Gen. Smith in the war of 1812. Wilson N. Lankford was reared on a farm in his native county of Marion, receiving such early school training as could be obtained in the common schools; he read

much in after life and stored his mind with useful knowledge. His vocation through life has been that of agriculture and stock trading. He began business without pecuniary aid, and has been successful. He is the proprietor of 160 acres of excellent farming land, which is well improved, he having lately completed a beautiful and commodious residence at a cost of upward of $1,000. On the 2d of March, 1854, he was married to Miss Rachael E., daughter of Joel and Frances P. (Crews) Spires of Marion County. To this marriage have been born eight children: Mary F., wife of Francis M. Pinkstaff of Lawrence County, Ill.; Martha J. (Isaacs); Sarah E. (Mouser), died in 1883; Joel T., Clem H., James I., Lilly B., and Daisy I. Mr. and Mrs. Lankford are life-long and consistent members of the Methodist Church. Politically Mr. Lankford is a Republican.

M. G. LEACHMAN was born December 18, 1837, and is the son of Harrison and Ellen M. (Childs) Leachman. His paternal ancestors were Virginians, his grandfather, Sampson Leachman, settling in Boyle County, Ky., where his death occurred many years ago. Harrison Leachman grew to manhood in Boyle County, and was a farmer. After his marriage he removed to Washington County, locating in the Pleasant Grove neighborhood, where he resided until his death in 1863. His wife, Ellen M. Leachman, was born in Boyle County, and died in Washington County in 1842 or 1843. The following are the names of their children: W. T., Elizabeth, M. G., Stephen and Harrison. M. G. Leachman was born and reared in Washington County, attended the country schools until his eighteenth year, and later entered the Georgetown College, where he remained two years. At the age of twenty he quit school, and, joining a company of fortune seekers, crossed the plains to California, in which State he remained five years, his employment in the meantime being mining and the lumber business, in the latter of which he was reasonably successful. He returned to Kentucky in December, 1864, and in January of the following year was married to Miss Sue D. Brown, daughter of Stephen C. and Mary E. Brown, of Washington County. Immediately after his marriage he moved to the beautiful farm which has since been his home, and is one of the progressive farmers of the Pleasant Grove neighborhood. He was elected representative from Washington County, in 1883, and took an active part in the deliberations of the Legislature in the sessions 1883 and 1884. He is a Dem-

57

ocrat in politics, and a member of the Baptist Church. Mrs. Leachman belongs to the Pleasant Grove Presbyterian Church. Mr. and Mrs. Leachman have one child living, Beverly B. Leachman, who was born March 4, 1867.

J. Y. LEAVELL was born March 21, 1817, in Garrard County. He received a liberal education, and became one of the leading farmers of Garrard. He accumulated considerable property, and assisted in organizing the First National Bank of Lancaster, and was its president from 1870 to 1872, afterward a director. In 1883 he removed to Mercer County, and in March, 1885, he was the first man to receive an appointment as storekeeper. He was a son of Benjamin and Isabella (Miller) Leavell, to whom five sons and five daughters were born and reared. Benjamin Leavell was born in Virginia in 1772; he settled in Garrard County in 1795, was a farmer and a slave owner; he was a son of Edward and Elizabeth (Hawkins) Leavell, who reared a family of five sons and four daughters. Edward Leavell was a soldier in the war for independence, and was an early pioneer of Garrard County. Isabella (Miller) Leavell was born in Fort Paint Lick, November, 1781; she was the first of four children born to William and Nancy (Yancy) Miller. William Miller was born in Virginia, in 1747. The Legislature of Virginia provided and requested Daniel Boone to mark a road or trail, from Virginia to Boonesborough, Ky. William Miller, with several others, was employed to mark a route for guiding emigrants over the mountains into the rich and fertile lands of Kentucky. This company of men worked unmolested until they reached the head waters of Silver Creek, when they were attacked by the Indians, and two of their party killed. When they reached the head waters of Taylor's Fork of Silver Creek, they were again attacked, and one more of their number killed. After completing the enterprise, William Miller returned to Virginia, and was married, January, 1781, and soon after started for his new home, which he had selected before returning to Virginia. He occupied Fort Paint Lick where all his children, four in number, were born. He was with Gen. Morgan on his northern campaign in 1794-95. He is supposed to be of Scotch-Irish parents.

JUDGE GEORGE F. LEE was born December 5, 1820, in Lincoln County, Ky., and was the fifth of six sons and five daughters, all living to be grown except three daughters, born to George and Lucy (Thompson) Lee. George Lee was born near Georgetown in 1792. In the same year his parents located in Montgomery settlement, Lincoln County, where he became an extensive farmer; he was drafted in the war of 1812, his youngest brother taking his place. In 1837 he located in Boyle County, where he lived until his death at the age of eighty-seven years. He was a son of George Lee and Elizabeth Shelton, both natives of Amherst County, Va. In the fall of 1791 George Lee, the eldest, emigrated and purchased lands near Georgetown, Ky. Not finding a good title to the lands he immediately moved to Lincoln County. He had viewed several locations previous to this and found titles bad, but Gov. Shelby offered to protect him in his purchase, which induced him to locate in Lincoln County. He was the owner of slaves which he brought from Virginia; raised a family of six sons and three daughters, and died in 1825, aged seventy-seven years. He was of English descent and embraced the Baptist faith. The mother of George F. Lee was born in Albemarle County, Va., in 1792, and was a daughter of Nelson A. Thompson, who married a Miss Carr. Nelson A. Thompson died in Virginia; his widow, with one son and six daughters, migrated to Lincoln County, Ky., as early as 1795; from these children sprang some of the most active and leading citizens of Kentucky. George F. was reared on a farm. At the age of twelve years he entered Centre College, from which he graduated in the class of 1839, after which he returned to the farm and handled stock. In 1845 he located in Lincoln, and married, March, 1846, Susan J. Miller, a daughter of Robert and Sallie (Murrell) Miller, who were natives of Madison and Lincoln Counties respectively. Robert Miller served as justice of the peace for many years, also as sheriff. He died in 1879, aged seventy-seven years, and was a son of Daniel Miller, who came from Virginia in an early day and settled in Madison County, Ky. Mr. and Mrs. Lee were blessed with seven children: Eugene W., George, Sarah Virginia, Lucy A., McElroy, Lizzie N. Rowland, Robert (deceased), and Frank N. Mr. and Mrs. Lee are members of the Presbyterian Church. In 1851 Mr. Lee located on a farm in Boyle County; in 1874 was elected county judge, and has held the office ever since; in 1855-56 he represented his county in the Legislature, but refused to run again. He cast his first presidential vote for Henry Clay, but since 1860 has affiliated with the Democratic party.

JOSIAH ELLIS LEE was born March 31, 1825, four miles north of Hustonville, Lincoln Co., Ky. In 1837 he removed with his parents to, and located on Salt Run, in Boyle County, where he remained until 1845, when he returned to Lincoln County, but in 1854 settled in Boyle County, where he has since resided. His father, George Lee, Jr., native of Scott County, Ky., was reared in Lincoln County, was an extensive farmer and trader, and died in 1878, at the age of eighty-seven years. He was the son of George Lee, Sr., who was born in Amherst County, Va., removed to Kentucky about 1792, engaged in farming, and died in 1825. George Lee, Sr., married Elizabeth Shelton of Virginia, and their union was favored by the birth of Ambrose, Richard Henry, William F., Abram, Francis Lightfoot, Emily (Welsh), and Parmelia (Montgomery). George Lee, Jr., married Lucy, daughter of Andrew and Emily (Kerr) Thompson, of Lincoln County, born in 1792, died in 1841, and from their union sprang Eliza (Dickson), Nelson T., Judge George F., Parmelia (deceased), Josiah E. Ambrose (deceased), Richard H., and James L. (deceased). Josiah E. was first married December 12, 1847, to Miss Elizabeth, daughter of Col. Robert and Sallie (Murrell) Miller, of Lincoln County, born in 1827, died in 1865, and to them were born Lucy (Bell), George M., James A., Josiah N., and Edmund S. On January 5, 1871, Mr. Lee married Miss Fannie, daughter of Hon. Joshua F., and Mary M. (Helm) Bell, of Danville, Ky., born July 31, 1840, and their union has resulted in the birth of two sons, viz.: Joshua Bell and Thomas Helm. By vocation Mr. Lee is a farmer, having 600 acres of productive land, besides an interest in the family homestead of 340 acres. He lost $20,000 in slaves, as a result of the late war. He is a member of the Southern Presbyterian Church, and in politics was formerly an old line Whig, but is now identified with the Democratic party.

ALBERT LEE. This name introduces a family whose history is contemporary with the first settlement of Marion County. Near the close of the eighteenth century, Samuel Lee came to Kentucky from St. Mary's County, Md., and settled near Rolling Fork in what was then Nelson County. He married Nancy Rapier, and his children were James, Samuel, Raymond, Richard, George, Charles and William, besides several daughters, thirteen in all, each of whom grew to maturity. The gentleman whose name introduces this sketch is the oldest descendant of this family now in Marion County, and is the son of James R. and Susan (Hayden) Lee, the latter being a representative of a family who early emigrated from Maryland. James R. Lee was born in Marion County, Ky., in 1811, and his wife, Susan, in 1813. He died in January, 1844, and she afterward married her present husband, Francis Ford, and resides in her native county. James R. and Susan Lee had a family of five children of whom Albert is the eldest. He was born September 14, 1834, was reared on the farm, to the pursuits of which he has devoted his life. In 1880 he was elected to the office of sheriff of Marion County, and re-elected in 1882, serving two full terms, but continues to reside on his farm near Lebanon. He was married, in 1856, to Miss Mary Abell, daughter of James and Eliza (Raley) Abell. Seven children have blessed their alliance: James R., Mary J. (deceased), Samuel, Emma, Robert E. (deceased), Marietta, and Joseph A. Lee. The family names, Lee, Hayden, Raley and Abell, are among the pioneers of the Rolling Fork settlement, and are all noted for their faithfulness to the Catholic Church.

SAMUEL M. LETCHER, M. D., was born September 10, 1841, in Lexington, Ky., and is a son of Dr. Samuel M. and Ellen (Robertson) Letcher, natives of Lancaster, Ky. Dr. Samuel M. Letcher, Sr., served as professor in the medical department of Transylvania University for several years. At the beginning of the war he was placed in charge of the United States medical hospital, which position he filled until his death, February 8, 1863, which was caused by performing an operation in the hospital. He raised a family of four sons and two daughters, and died at the age of fifty-eight years. His father, Gen. Benjamin Letcher, was born near Staunton, Va., and about 1795 was sent to Kentucky by the governor of Virginia to locate lands. He, himself, located about the same time in Lancaster, Ky., where he remained until his death. He served as clerk of county and circuit courts for many years, and in politics was a Whig. He and descendants were all stanch and strong advocates of the Union during the war. He was of Scotch-Irish origin and Presbyterian in religion. Mrs. Ellen (Robertson) Letcher was a daughter of Judge George Robertson. Dr. S. M. Letcher, the subject of this sketch, was reared in Lexington, and received his education in Transylvania University till he reached the junior year, when he entered the junior class at Princeton. In 1857 he was compelled to abandon his studies on account of ill health.

In May, 1861, he entered the United States service. December 6, 1861, he entered the Twenty-first Kentucky Regiment as a private; six days later he was detailed as a clerk at Gen. Thomas' headquarters, and June, 1862, was commissioned as captain of Company G, Twelfth Kentucky Infantry. After the battle at Perryville the colonel of the regiment was put in command at Lebanon, and Capt. Letcher was made post-adjutant. In May, 1863, he reported to Gen. Boyle, and was put on his staff as commissary of musters. In December, 1863, he was ordered to report to Gen. J. M. Schofield, stationed at Knoxville, Tenn., with whom he remained as commissary of musters till the close of the war. He was mustered out of the service in August, 1865, and returned to Kentucky and engaged in mercantile pursuits. In 1876 he graduated from the medical department of the University of Louisville, and immediately engaged in the practice of his profession at Lexington. In 1880 he located at Richmond, Ky., and has since taken a course of lectures in the University of New York. He is an active member of the State Medical Society, and ranks high in his profession. In politics he is a Democrat.

WILLIAM R. LETCHER was born July 31, 1845, in Richmond, Ky., and is the only child of Dr. William R. and Ann M. (White) Letcher. Dr. W. R. Letcher was born in Mercer County, Ky., June 8, 1794; was a soldier in the war of 1812, and was captured in Dudley's defeat. He received his medical training at Transylvania University, and settled at Richmond when quite young, and there practiced his profession all his life. For his good qualities he had been frequently solicited to accept office, but declined any tendered to him. He lost his wife November 26, 1845. He then married Mrs. Ann (Douglass) Chenault, the widow of Harvey Chenault. She gave birth to one son, James B., April 10, 1854; he died in February, 1881; the mother is still living. Dr. Letcher died in July, 1863. He was a son of Benjamin Letcher, who married a Miss Robertson, and a brother of Gov. Letcher, and his wife a sister of Chief Justice Robertson and of Gov. Letcher's wife. Benjamin Letcher reared a large family. The sons were William R., Dr. J. P., Dr. Samuel, Judge James H. and Dr. R. P. There were four daughters, but one now living. The Letchers came from Virginia, and were among the early pioneers of Mercer County, but later moved to Garrard County. Ann M. (White) Letcher was a daughter of Gen. Hugh White, of Clay County. William R. Letcher, our subject, was reared and educated in Richmond. In 1863 he entered the county clerk's office as assistant, and in September, 1866, he entered a dry goods store as bookkeeper and salesman. From 1868 to 1871 he was storekeeper and gauger. In January, 1871, he entered the First National Bank as bookkeeper, and afterward became cash teller, then cashier. He remained in the bank until November, 1885, when he resigned and has since turned his entire attention to the breeding of fine trotting horses—Wilkes stock—also thoroughbreds, which he has been engaged in more or less since 1875. He trains his horses on his own track, and owned and sold the famous Harry Wilkes, record 2:14¾. Mr. Letcher owns 100 acres near the city of Richmond, improved with one of the finest residences in the county, and upward of $20,000 have been expended on the farm to beautify it. He is also president of the Peacock Coal Company, Laurel County, Ky., and is a partner of W. R. Brasfield, of Lexington Combination Sales. Mr. Letcher was married December 22, 1868, to Hattie Walters, of Madison County, only daughter of Singleton P. and Minerva (Kikendall) Walters. Mr. Walters first started a private bank, which he had converted into the First National Bank in 1870; he became its president, which place he filled until his death, in February, 1885. He was a native of Estill County. The issue from the marriage of Mr. and Mrs. Letcher was six bright and beautiful daughters: Minnie W., Anna W., Sallie R., Mary C., Dovey B., and Hattie W. Mr. and Mrs. Letcher are members of the Presbyterian Church. He is also an active member of the A. F. & A. M., and is P. M. of the Richmond Lodge and P. H. P. of R. A. Chapter and P. C. of Richmond Commandery.

T. M. LEWIS, M. D., is the son of Robert and Maria (Patton) Lewis, of Virginia and Kentucky, respectively. The Doctor's paternal ancestors were natives of England, his grandfather, John F. P. Lewis, emigrating from that country to America in colonial times, and settling in Virginia, where he lived until 1790. In that year he came to Lincoln County, Ky., and settled on Hanging Fork, where he engaged in the practice of medicine, and was the first medical man in that county, and one of the earliest in the State. He was quite a successful man, and during his residence in Lincoln, accumulated a large estate. He was a surgeon in the American Army during the war of independence, and died in Kentucky many years ago. Robert T. Lewis was born in Virginia in

1784, and was but six years of age when brought to Kentucky. He grew to manhood in Lincoln County, was a soldier in the war of 1812, a farmer and a man of considerable prominence. He died in October, 1866. Maria Lewis, wife of Robert Lewis, was the daughter of Thomas Patton, one of the early residents of Green County. She was born near Danville, Boyle County, in 1801, and died in Lincoln County in 1870. The following are the names of the children born to Mr. and Mrs. Lewis: Sarah A., T. M. (subject), W. P., Thomas P., Robert T., Mahala, Maria D., Jaqueline A. and Lucy J., the first named and last three and subject being the only members of the family now living. Dr. Lewis was born near the town of Stanford, Lincoln County, January 2, 1831, and remained with his parents until his fourteenth year, when he began life for himself as a clerk in a mercantile house at the village of Hustonville, in which he served for two years; he then began the study of medicine with Dr. D. J. Alcorn, with whom he remained seven years, practicing with his preceptor at intervals. In 1853 he entered the Louisville University and attended several sessions, graduating in the year 1856. He located first at the village of Liberty, Casey County, where he practiced his profession for eighteen months, and then moved to Mill Springs, Wayne County, where he resided for six years, obtaining large practice. In 1866 he located near Danville, Boyle County, where he practiced until January, 1886, when he removed to Beechland, Washington County, his present location. Dr. Lewis has been a very successful physician. In addition to his profession he has given a great deal of attention to scientific studies and general literature, and is an ardent supporter of education. He is a member of the Christian Church, with which he has been identified since 1856, and is also a member of the Masonic fraternity and of the A. F. M. The Doctor was married February 9, 1858, in Lincoln County, to Miss Lizzie Alcorn, daughter of Alfred and Polly A. (Walker) Alcorn, of the same county. Seven children have been born to this marriage: Alfred Lewis, editor of the Somerset *Republican;* Robert T., Georgia M., Maggie, John L. and Lucian M., living, and Nancy E., deceased. Mrs. Lewis is a member of the Christian Church, and she and three children are members of the Danville congregation.

J. W. LEWIS, attorney at law, and son of William and Ann (Carlile) Lewis, was born in Kentucky, October 14, 1841. His grandfather, John Lewis, was a native of Pittsylvania County, Va., and a son of John Lewis, Sr., who came to America from Wales in the time of the colonies. Mr. Lewis' maternal ancestors came from North Carolina, and were among the earliest pioneers of Kentucky. His grandfather, William B. Carlile, was the son of James Carlile, whose father entered the ground upon which the city of Elizabethtown now stands. He was killed there many years ago, and his remains lie buried within the city limits. James Carlile was a Revolutionary soldier, and an early pioneer of Green County, settling on Meadow Creek, where he acquired a large property. William B. Carlile was born in Green County, was a farmer, served ten years as sheriff, and died October 10, 1868. William Lewis, subject's father, was born in Pittsylvania County, Va., came to Greensburg, Ky., at the age of twenty-one, and has since been a resident of Green County. He has been an active business man, and one of the leading merchants of his adopted town. His wife, Ann (Carlile) Lewis, was born in Green County about the year 1823, and is still living. Mr. and Mrs. Lewis reared a family of nine children, whose names are as follows: John W., Archie, Mrs. Elizabeth Baldwin, Thomas E. (died in 1882), Henry C., Mrs. Maria Tyler, Woodson, Hortense and James C. By a previous marriage with a Miss Groves, Mr. Lewis had one child, Mrs. Mary Buchanan. J. W. Lewis grew to manhood in his native county of Green, and attended the schools of Greensburg from the age of six years until seventeen. In 1858 he entered Centre College, Danville, which he attended four years, graduating in 1862. After graduating he began the study of law at Greensburg, and one year later, on the 3d of October, 1863, was admitted to the bar, receiving his licenses from Judges John E. Newman and F. T. Fox, Sr. He began the practice of his profession in Greensburg, where he remained until 1869, at which time he came to Springfield, Washington County, and effected a copartnership with R. J. Brown, Esq., which was continued until January, 1879. Since the latter year Mr. Lewis has been practicing by himself and at the present time stands at the head of the Washington County bar. He is an attorney of much more than ordinary talent, and has a lucrative practice in the courts of Washington and adjoining counties, his name appearing in connection with many of the most important suits entered for litigation. He was temporary chairman of the Republican State convention of April, 1880, and in June following was delegate to the national convention, when he cast thirty-six ballots for U. S. Grant, and was also delegate for the State at large in the national convention of 1884, and cast four ballots for Chester A. Arthur. Mr. Lewis was married June 20, 1877, in Marion County, to Elizabeth Philips, daughter of James G. and Laura (Castleman) Philips of Marion County. The fruit of their union is one child, Mary A. Lewis, born April 24, 1885. Mrs. Lewis is a member of the Springfield Presbyterian Church.

DR. WILLIAM M. LEWIS was born August 19, 1857, and is the fifth of three sons and three daughters born to Dr. Archibald S. and Anna Bell (Adair) Lewis. Dr. Archibald S. Lewis was born in Pittsylvania County, Va.; with two brothers on horseback came through the country in two weeks and settled about 1836 in Green County, where he has resided ever since. He was a salesman for a few years; also rode deputy sheriff for a few years. In 1871 he was elected to represent Green and Taylor Counties in the Legislature. Dr. A. S. Lewis acted as post surgeon during the war. He had commenced his practice in 1846. He was a son of John and Millie (Shelton) Lewis, of Virginia. John Lewis was a farmer and owner of a large family of slaves. He died in 1842, aged seventy years. Mrs. A. B. (Adair) Lewis was born in Courtland, Ala., and was a daughter of Maj. Alex and Katie (Monroe) Adair. Katie Monroe was a sister of Judge Thomas and Benjamin Monroe. Mr. and Mrs. Adair were natives of Kentucky, but moved to Alabama, where he was engaged in farming. He was a son of Gen. John Adair, who secured the appointment for him as marshal of the Territory of Florida under Jackson, where he died of yellow fever. Dr. W. M. Lewis was born in the village of Greensburg, where he received the foundation for a good English education; then entered Warren College, Bowling Green, where he finished his education. He commenced the study of medicine with his father. In 1877–78 he attended two courses of lectures in the University of Louisville. In 1879 he graduated from Bellevue Hospital, N. Y., and located and practiced his profession in Greensburg, meeting with the best of success ever since, except 1882 and three years in Kansas City. He is a member of the State Medical Association; also of the Tri-State Medical Society, composed of Kentucky, Indiana and Illinois. October 22, 1884, he was united in marriage to Mary Buckner, daughter of Robert W. and Sarah (Hazelwood) Buckner. Mr. Buck-

ner is a farmer and was a soldier in the Mexican war. The Doctor's wife is a member of the Methodist Episcopal Church.

THOMAS MADISON LILLARD was born December 5, 1815, in Madison County, where he lived until 1849, when he located on the Stanford pike, four and one-half miles southeast of Danville, Boyle County, where he has since resided. His father, Thomas Lillard, Jr., a native of Culpeper County, Va., removed to Madison County, Ky., in 1808; enlisted in the war of 1812, but was prevented by sickness from service; was a farmer and died March 3, 1816, aged about thirty-five years. He was the son of Thomas Lillard, Sr., who was a farmer and large slave owner in Culpeper County, and whose children were Benjamin, John and Thomas Jr. Thomas, Jr., married Deborah, daughter of Alexander Ryder, of Madison County (died in 1835, aged fifty-six years), and from their union sprang Christopher, Elizabeth (deceased), Matilda (deceased), Nancy (Morris) of Colorado, Catherine (Patterson) of Shelby County, Ill., and Thomas M. On October 23, 1848, Thomas M. Lillard was united in marriage with Mrs. Williams, nee Miss Mary, daughter of John and Elizabeth (Morrison) Bright, of Lincoln County, born March 3, 1823, and to them have born Elizabeth B., Erwin, Fannie (Robinson) of Belton, Mo.; John T., of Bloomington, Ill.; Henrietta, Mary T. (Adams, deceased), Maria (Hargis), of Belton, Mo.; Catherine (deceased), Thomas L., Nancy B. (Adams) of Louisville, Stonewall J. (deceased) and William H. From 1839 until 1848 Mr. Lillard spent his winters in Charleston, S. C., and summers in New York, dealing in live stock, in partnership with Walter Chenault, their business often reaching $300,000 per annum. Mr. Lillard is now engaged in farming, owning 490 acres of exceedingly well improved and very productive land, devoted mainly to grazing. From observations he concludes that the farmer in the blue-grass regions in Kentucky cannot better his condition in the same business elsewhere. In youth Mr. Lillard had an even start with the world, and by industry, frugality and careful attention to business has amassed an ample competency. With only a limited education, he has improved his opportunities by reading and is possessed of a valuable miscellaneous library. He has always been an emancipationist, though he lost eighteen slaves by the late war. He is a member of the Christian Church, and a Prohibitionist. He is remotely related to Rev. Joseph Lillard, who in 1793 preached the first Methodist sermon in Illinois.

CHARLES ALEXANDER LILLARD was born October 4, 1838, on the place where he now resides, on the Louisville Turnpike, four miles north of Harrodsburg, Ky., where he grew up manhood, and has always lived. His father, John Lee Lillard, also a native of Mercer County, was born May 9, 1797, and died August 21, 1842. He was the son of Joseph Lillard, who was born in Culpeper County, Va., in 1768; removed with his parents to Mercer County, Ky., as early as 1786; was among the first to receive license as a local preacher in the Methodist Episcopal Church in Kentucky; joined the western conference in 1790, and traveled two years; preached the first Methodist sermon, and organized the first class in Illinois in 1793. He contributed largely for the erection of "Joseph's Chapel," and a similar church at Salvisa, which later he dedicated. In 1852 he started on a journey to Missouri, and was never afterward heard of by his friends. He was the son of Capt. John Lillard, a native of Culpeper County, Va., who died in 1801, and who was the son of Benjamin Lillard, who immigrated from England or Wales, to Virginia, as early as 1730, and died at the age of one hundred and twenty years. The family was well represented in the Revolutionary war. Benjamin's children were Thomas, James, William, Moses, Benjamin and John. John married a Miss Pulliam, and their offspring were Thomas, Ephraim, Joseph, John, David, James, Susan (Jones), and Mrs. Childs. Joseph married a Miss Hughes, and from their union sprang John Lee, Rev. Asbury, Joseph (unmarried), Samuel (unmarried), Nancy (Rynerson), Sarah (Moore), Jemima (Smith), and Prudence (Armstrong). John Lee Lillard married Nancy Armstrong, and to them were born Joseph R., Mary (deceased), Elizabeth (McAfee), James (deceased), Charles A., and John L. Charles A. has remained unmarried. He obtained a common English education at the schools in the vicinity where he was reared, and by careful reading has become familiar with the history of the important events of the past. He is engaged in farming, and is possessor of 100 acres of good land. In politics Mr. Lillard is a Republican.

E. W. LILLARD was born January 1, 1862, in Anderson County, Ky., and is a son of Ephraim and Martha (McQuiddy) Lillard, to whom six sons and eight daughters were born, eleven now living, E. W. being the twelfth in order of birth. Ephraim Lillard was born in Lawrenceburg, Ky., about 1819. He is one of the leading farmers, and before the war owned considerable slave property. He is a devoted member of the Christian Church. He is a son of Ephraim Lillard, who was a large farmer and distiller; he reared a large family, from whom spring many families of that name in Kentucky. The latter, in turn, was a son of Capt. John Lillard, who was born in Culpeper County, Va., and married a Pulliam, removed to Mercer County, Ky., between 1782 and 1784, and settled on Salt River, near the line of Boyle, south of Harrodsburg. Capt. John was a son of Benjamin Lillard, who came from England or Wales as early as 1725; he also married a Miss Pulliam. Martha (McQuiddy) Lillard was born and reared in Kentucky. Her father came from Ireland, and was a pioneer farmer of Kentucky who married a Miss Perry. E. W. Lillard was reared on a farm, and received a common English education, which was finished at the Kentucky University. At the age of eighteen years he entered the drug business at Lawrenceburg, where he remained three years; then went to Richmond and engaged in the same business eighteen months. In January, 1885, he located in Lancaster, Ky., where he opened and operates one of the finest drug stores in the county. He has taken a course of pharmacy, which makes him a safe and competent druggist to deal with. He was united in marriage August 4, 1886, to Lula Stout, of La Rue County, daughter of John B. Stout, whose father was a Knickerbocker and who himself came from New York to Kentucky, and was one of the leading educators of the State. E. W. Lillard is a member of the Baptist Church; in politics is a Democrat. October 30, 1885, he was elected captain of Company G, Second Regiment, Kentucky State Guards. He served in this capacity during the years 1885–86, during which time he was placed in command of the troops at Greenwood mines; he resigned his commission soon after the withdrawal of the troops.

WILLIAM J. LISLE, lawyer of Lebanon, is a native of Green County, Ky., and descends from Scotch ancestry. His father, Thomas W. Lisle, was born in the same county in 1805, was a lawyer of acknowledged ability, and served as a member of the convention of 1849 that framed the present constitution of the State. He died on the 9th of January, 1858. The mother of William J. Lisle, who is still living, was Nancy J. C. Tate, whose grandfather, Captain Tate, was killed at the battle of Guilford Court House. William J. Lisle received a good English education, read law under Hon. Aaron Hardin, and in 1859 graduated from the law department of the Louisville University, since which time, with slight exception, he has been in the active practice of his profession. In 1861 he entered the Federal Army as an adjutant in the Tenth Kentucky Volunteer Infantry, was promoted to the position of captain of Company A in the spring of 1863, which commission he held until mustered out, having participated in the battles of Perryville, Shiloh, etc. From 1873 to 1877 he was a resident of the city of Louisville, during which time he was a member of its bar, and also secretary and treasurer of the Chesapeake & Ohio Railroad Company. In 1877 he formed his present law partnership with R. H. Rountree, the oldest practicing lawyer of Lebanon. In 1862 Mr. Lisle married Miss Ada McElroy, who died in 1877, leaving four children, viz.: Nettie, Elizabeth, Marion and William. In 1879 he contracted a marriage with his present wife, Mary (Mouring) Bevill, which union has been blessed with two children, Ada and Virginia Lisle.

B. L. LITSEY. Prominent among the early residents of Kentucky was Randolph Litsey, who immigrated from Maryland, prior to the beginning of the present century, and located near Springfield, where he engaged in farming and later in the distillery business. He was born about the year 1770, and died in September, 1849. His wife was Mary Gregory. She was the daughter of Richard Gregory, who early came to Washington County, and settled about seven miles northwest of Springfield, where he accumulated a large estate, and where his death occurred. Mrs. Litsey was born in Kentucky and died in Washington County about 1859. Mr. and Mrs. Litsey were the parents of eight children, all dead except one, Uriah Litsey, father of B. L. Uriah Litsey was born in Washington County, October 15, 1813, and is one of the oldest residents of the county, now living. At the age of twenty-seven he engaged in life upon his own responsibility, purchasing his present beautiful farm upon the Beech Fork, to which he moved in 1841. He was married October 7, 1841, to Eleanor J. Lewis, daughter of Berry and Mary Lewis of Washington County. Ten children were born to this marriage, the following of whom are living: Berry L., W. H., Uriah E., and Mrs. Mattie, wife of James Reed. Mr. Litsey was originally a Whig in politics, but at the dissolution of that party identified himself with the Democratic party, with

which he has since voted. He is a member of the Presbyterian Church, having joined in 1856. Berry L. Litsey was born August 3, 1842. He was reared on a farm and received a good English education in the common schools, besides attending several sessions at the Taylorville High Schools, where he acquired a knowledge of the classics. He commenced life for himself at the age of twenty-two, choosing agriculture as his vocation, being a successful farmer and stock raiser in Washington County. He purchased his home place in the Pleasant Grove neighborhood in 1878, but had previously resided near the Beech Fork, of which he became the possessor in 1868. Mr. Litsey's present farm, consisting of 220 acres of fertile land, in one of the most productive regions in central Kentucky, is a model of neatness, and his improvements are among the finest in Washington County. He owns in all 425 acres. Mr. Litsey was united in marriage February 3, 1870, with Miss Kate Hays, daughter of Judge D. R. and Mary (McMakin) Hays of Washington County. This union has been blessed with four children: Mary H., Nellie R., Katie B., and David R. Litsey. Mr. Litsey is a member of the Presbyterian Church, to which he has belonged since 1866, and is a deacon in the Pleasant Grove congregation. He is a Democrat in politics, and cast his first vote for George B. MacClellan. Mrs. Litsey is an active member of the Willisburg Christian Church.

BEATY LOGAN (deceased) was born August 1, 1788, on the Danville road five miles from Stanford, Ky. He removed to Marion County about 1810, returning to Lincoln County in 1832. He was a soldier in the war of 1812, with Gen. Hopkins, in the Northwest. He was a member of the Reformed Church; in politics a Democrat; a farmer, losing about thirty slaves as the result of the late war, and, dying August 13, 1872, was buried at Danville. He was the son of Capt. James Logan, who, a valiant soldier from beginning to end of the Revolutionary war, was with Gen. Greene in the South and afterward removed from Virginia to Kentucky in an early day and located near Stanford; was a relative and friend of Col. Benj. Logan, and was associated with him in many conflicts in pioneer days. Ready as he ever was to do battle for his country in all her conflicts for liberty and justice, he was noted as a peace-maker in the civil walks of life, and was greatly esteemed and generally sought as an arbiter among neighbors, securing them against litigation and its evil consequences. He was a member of the Presbyterian Church, in politics a Democrat, and lies buried at Stanford. He married Sarah Beaty, of Washington County, Va., and from their union sprang Robert, Matthew, Sally (Dawson), and Beaty. Beaty married Patsey, daughter of Martin Everheart, of Marion County (born November 17, 1796, died June 8, 1870), and to them were born John F., Sarah E. (Walters), Rose Ann (Ray), Matthew D., Elwiza (deceased), Allison E., Robert D., Victoria (Hunley) and Jennie (Prewitt). Matthew D. was born in Marion County, January 8, 1822, and enlisted in Capt. Doherty's company, Second Kentucky, Col. McKee's regiment, in the Mexican war. He commenced the study of medicine with Dr. Huffman, of Stanford, graduated in 1850 at the Jefferson Medical College at Philadelphia, and practiced at Lancaster, Ky., until the commencement of the late war. In 1861 he was elected captain of Company I, Forrest's cavalry; was captured at Fort Donelson and remained a prisoner of war at Johnson's Island seven months. He was exchanged at Pittsburg, Miss., reported to Breckinridge at Knoxville and organized an escort for that general; was assigned to Morgan's command and appointed major of Gano's regiment, in which he was early promoted to the lieutenant-colonelcy. He was captured in the famous Ohio raid, consigned to the pen at Columbus and exchanged before the close of the war at Charleston, S. C. Here he secured the release of a number of war prisoners of the One Hundred and Fifty-seventh New York on account of kind treatment of himself and others by officers of that regiment while prisoners. Col. Logan is still a consistent Democrat. Allison E. Logan was born May 4, 1826, in Marion County; early in the late war enlisted in Company A, Sixth Kentucky Confederate Cavalry under Col. Grigsby, Morgan's command; was captured on the Ohio raid; escaped from Camp Douglas by *permission* of the guard, constructed a raft and placed Gen. Morgan across the Tennessee River on his escape, for which service he declined a captain's commission and served in the last battle of the war. In politics he is a Democrat. Capt. Robert D. Logan was born January 20, 1829, in Marion County, Ky.; was captain of Company A, Sixth Regiment, Kentucky Confederate Cavalry, remaining in the service until the final surrender. He was captured on the Ohio raid but was exchanged at Hilton Head, S. C. He and his brothers formed a part of the escort of Jefferson Davis at his attempted escape. They with others proffered to conduct him

out of the United States, which offer he declined in words of tender sympathy. They each received a portion of the Confederate specie at its final distribution, which they retain as valued relics. From a part of it a very handsome silver fishing reel has been constructed, which is highly prized by the brothers. They are now engaged in farming, with marked success, all living together, happy, genial and intelligent gentlemen, whose hospitality is of a kind that still reminds the stranger of the "the old Kentucky home." None of them have ever married, and they all cling to the tenets of the Democratic party.

JOHN M. LOGAN was born February 25, 1852, in Garrard County, seven miles northeast of Lancaster, and is a son of Timothy and Sarah (Lear) Logan, natives of Garrard, and to whom five children were born: John M., E. A., Bettie, Amanda and Hugh. Timothy Logan was a farmer and slave owner; moved to northeast Mercer County in 1878; was a strong Union man, and opposed to secession, and an active advocate of Whig principles; since the war has affiliated with the Democratic party. In religion he is a Baptist, and his wife is a member of the Reformed Church. Timothy Logan was a son of Hugh Logan, who was born in Garrard County in 1790, was a farmer, and participated in the war of 1812. To his first marriage four sons and five daughters were born; his second wife was a widow Beazley—maiden name Adams—by whom one daughter was reared. In politics Hugh Logan was a Whig; his father, Timothy Logan, came from North Carolina in the early settlement of Kentucky, about 1778, was a great Indian fighter, and caused many a foe to bite the dust in his encounters with the savages. He was a farmer in the northeast part of Garrard County, was the only member of this branch of the Logan family who came to Kentucky and died at the age of ninety-six. The Logans are of Scotch-Irish extraction. Hugh Logan died in Decatur, Ill., in 1873. Sarah Lear Logan was a daughter of James and Sarah (Logan) Lear, to whom three sons and four daughters were born. John M. Logan, one of the leading business men of Lancaster, was reared on a farm, and received a common English education; at the age of seventeen he entered a dry goods store at Lancaster, as salesman, and remained till 1876, when he bought an interest in the store with W. H. Smith. Mr. Smith, afterward, in 1878, started a branch store at Hustonville, and J. M. Logan took charge of it. In 1880 they moved to Harrodsburg; in 1881 he sold his interest in both stores to W. H. Smith; in the same year he went to Cincinnati, and traveled for M. and L. S. Fechheimer & Co., for four years, then commenced traveling for Henry Geiershofer & Co. In November, 1884, he purchased R. W. Lillard's store, and in January, 1886, he took in J. B. Brewer as a partner, and they now do business in two rooms which are connected. They have one of the largest and best dry goods and clothing houses in Garrard County. Mr. Logan is still connected with a Philadelphia house, and is one of the best salesmen on the road. June 8, 1882, he was united in marriage to Lillia J. Smith, a daughter of W. H. and Bettie W. (Fox) Smith. Mr. Logan is the father of one child, William Fox Logan. He and wife are members of the Methodist Episcopal and Baptist Churches respectively. He is a leading and active member of the Masonic fraternity, and in politics is a Democrat.

FINIS E. LONG was born October 31, 1836, south of Hardinsburg, Breckinridge Co., Ky., and is the sixth of three sons and five daughters born to William C. and Elizabeth (Crutcher) Long. William C. Long was born in North Carolina, April 30, 1796, was a Presbyterian minister, settled in Ohio County, Ky., about 1820, and afterward moved to Missouri, where he lived five years. His first wife was Martha J. Dunlap, of Missouri; one child—a daughter—was born by this marriage. He moved from Missouri to Kentucky, continuing in the ministry. He married his second wife in Breckinridge County, November 23, 1824; then lived two years in Ohio County, when he finally located in Breckinridge County. He was a soldier of 1812, participated in the battle of New Orleans, and died March 28, 1842. His wife survives him and is living in Louisville, eighty-two years of age in August, 1886. William C. was a son of John Long, of English descent, who married Jane Lawler, natives of Maryland and South Carolina respectively. From South Carolina he moved to Tennessee, thence to Breckinridge County, Ky., was a substantial farmer and slave owner, raised a family of ten children, and died in 1842. Mrs. Elizabeth Long was born in Jessamine County, Ky., and was a daughter of James Crutcher, who was one of the early settlers; from there he moved to Hardin County, about 1810, where he was the owner of a tract of land near Cecilian Junction; was also a large slave owner; served as magistrate for many years, and was a soldier in the war for independence; he purchased his lands for 12½ cents per acre.

He died about 1835, at an advanced age, and was of German origin. Finis E. Long received a good academic education at Princeton, Ky., and Paris, Tenn.; he entered and worked in a planing-mill for a few years, when he again attended school for two years, after which he taught. At the age of twenty-four he engaged in the commission business in Owensboro; in the fall of 1860 he went to Louisville; April, 1861, he enlisted in Company A, First Kentucky Confederate Volunteers, was a sergeant and was captured at Dranesville in December, 1861. In the spring of 1862 he was elected captain of his company. About the close of the war was on his way home on furlough, but surrendered at Fort Donelson; after the final surrender of Lee he returned to Louisville, and became a leading contractor and builder. He has built nearly all of the buildings, including distillery and storehouses, at New Hope, at which place he located in 1880. He was united in marriage October 31, 1867, to Mary Rooney, a daughter of Peter Rooney and Sarah Ahull, natives of Belfast, Ireland, and Lexington, Ky., respectively. Mr. Rooney came to the United States when a young man and engaged in the mercantile business, first in Baltimore and then in Louisville. He died in 1856 at the age of eighty years. Mr. Long had born to him seven children: William C., Robert E., Allen D., Charles E., John W., Mary Ruter, deceased, and Elizabeth G. Mr. and Mrs. Long are members of the Presbyterian Church. Mr. Long owns 700 acres in Marion and LaRue Counties, on which he has a store eight miles south of New Hope; is also the owner of a good house and lot. Mr. Long, after being captured was held a prisoner about six months at Washington, D. C.; was among the first prisoners ever exchanged, after which he and Capt. Harvey raised a company at Richmond, Va.; after the Murfreesboro fight was commissioned captain. He served under Wheeler and Forrest. Mr. Long is an active member of F. & A. M., and also of the I. O. O. F. In politics he is a Democrat, and cast his first presidential vote for Bell in 1860.

LORETTO ACADEMY was established in 1824 by the Sisters of Loretto, under the auspices of the Right Rev. Benedict Joseph Flaget, then bishop of Bardstown, Ky., which see was transferred to Louisville, Ky., in 1841. This institution of learning is situated in Marion County, Ky., and is yet conducted by the same Sisters who comprised the "Loretto Literary and Benevolent Institution," and was incorporated December 29, 1829, by the Legislature of Kentucky with the Right Rev. Benedict Joseph Flaget as "moderator of the board of trustees during his natural life." Loretto Academy is two miles from Loretto Station on the Knoxville branch of the Louisville & Nashville Railroad. A conveyance of the institution meets the trains twice a day regularly and whenever informed by dispatch or letter, it meets extra trains. The place is healthy and beautiful. A new and large building is in course of erection with all the latest improvements and conveniences for the comfort of the young ladies. The Sisters of Loretto make teaching a specialty, and are most favorably known as educators. They conduct flourishing academies in many States of the Union, and especially in the West. They leave nothing undone to improve the pupils under their care in virtue and science and to fit them for their different walks in life.

EZEKIEL WILLIAM LYEN was born September 22, 1833, in the northwest portion of Mercer County, Ky., where he grew to manhood, and in 1873 located on the Lexington pike, three miles east of Harrodsburg, where he has since resided. In 1862 he enlisted in Company H, Second Kentucky Confederate Cavalry, and shortly after his enlistment he was promoted to a lieutenancy. He was captured in Anderson County, and remained a prisoner of war until near the close of the contest. His father, William Lyen, was born in Mercer County in 1809, where he was reared a farmer, and died in 1885. He was the son of Ezekiel Lyen, Sr., a native of Virginia, who died in Mercer County in 1839, aged about eighty years. His children were Stephen, John, David, William and Ezekiel (twins), Susan, Polly (Cawhorn) and Betsy (Conyer). William married Nancy, daughter of Joel Bickers, of Mercer County, born in 1818, died in 1880, and from their union sprang Ezekiel W., James T., Martha J. (James), Almira (Birdwhistle), John A. T., Joel, Phillip B. and Annie (Kennedy). Ezekiel W. Lyen was first married, in 1856, to Miss Susan F., daughter of Henry and Jane (Burrus) Bell, of Mercer County, born in 1836, died in 1861, and to them were born Cara B. and Mattie L. He was next married, February 3, 1868, to Miss Sue N., daughter of John and Sallie Holman, of Mercer County, born in 1843, but from this union there has been no issue. Mr. Lyen is a farmer, and owns 150 acres of very productive land, a part of the old Capt. Chaplaine homestead. In politics Mr. Lyen is a Democrat.

JAMES J. McAFEE was born February 23, 1824. His father, John McAfee, a native of Botetourt County, Va., was born October 20, 1775, removed in infancy, with his parents, to that portion of Kentucky now embraced in Mercer County, where he was reared, and in the war of 1812 furnished a substitute on account of sickness. He was a farmer and a slave-holder, a stanch Presbyterian, connected with the New Presbyterian Church, a Democrat, and died April 28, 1833. He was the son of Samuel McAfee, who with his brothers, Robert, William, George and James, came to Kentucky in 1773, made their surveys of lands on Salt River on a part of which James J. was born and now resides; he returned again in 1775, made improvements, and planted fruit tree seeds, and permanently located in 1779. With his family, in times of danger he lived in the fort at McAfee's Station; was active and aggressive as an Indian fighter, slew the Indian who killed his comrade at his side; owned 1,400 acres of land north of Harrodsburg, was the first magistrate in Kentucky, a prominent farmer and slave-holder, was one of the founders of the New Providence Church, and died June 8, 1807. He married a Miss McConsic, and their offspring were John, William, Samuel, Robert, Hannah (Daveiss), Mary (Moore), and Jane (Macgoffin), John first married Miss McCama, and their children were Samuel, Joseph, William, John, and Cynthia (Allen). His second wife was Mrs. Dicey Curry, daughter of David Caldwell, and from their union sprang Caldwell, Mary A. (Singleton, Williams, and King), James J., Phœbe E. (Thompson), and Francis M. James J. first married, 1845, Miss Elizabeth J., daughter of William and Priscilla (Armstrong) Adams, of Mercer County, who died June 17, 1847, and from their union there was one child, Elizabeth J., deceased. June 3, 1851, he was united in marriage with Elizabeth, daughter of Lee and Nancy Lillard, of Mercer County, who died November 3, 1858, aged twenty-seven years, and to them were born Joel P., deceased, and Nannie C. (Davis). He next married, in 1860, Mrs. Minerva J. Harris, daughter of Jonathan and Eliza (Hamilton) Nichols, of Bloomington, Ind., and their union has been favored by the birth of Monroe Harris, deceased, and Bettie H. (Hudson). Mr. McAfee was engaged for a period of six years in merchandising. He is now a farmer, owning 127 acres of well improved and productive land, in McAfee Precinct. He is a member of New Providence Presbyterian

Church, also an Ancient Odd Fellow, and a Democrat. The ancestors of the McAfee family were identified with the reforms of Oliver Cromwell; afterward removed to Ireland on account of the persecutions of the Covenanters, assisted in placing William of Orange on the throne, removed to Lancaster County, Penn., and thence to Virginia. Joseph, Samuel, William and John, sons of John, and grandsons of Samuel McAfee, about the year 1835, with their families, emigrated from Mercer County, Ky., to Marion County, Mo., and procured their lands at Congress price, which was $1.25 per acre. After partially improving their homes, and the settlement had become somewhat strengthened by the influx of immigration, they set about building a house of worship; they soon had a comfortable frame building erected, which they named New Providence, for the church they left in Kentucky. Joseph, Samuel and John were elected elders. Joseph, who married Priscilla, a granddaughter of the old pioneer, John Armstrong, educated two of his sons for the ministry; the oldest one, John Armstrong McAfee, was one of the founders, and president of Park College, ten miles from Kansas City, Mo., which has been in successful operation for a number of years.

JOSEPH McALISTER, deceased, was born in 1806, in Pulaski County, Ky. His father, who was of Scotch parentage, was Robert McAlister and was a native of Virginia, and a Baptist minister, the maiden name of his mother being Rachel McKenzie, who was also of Scotch ancestry. Robert and Rachel McAlister were the first representatives of the family in Kentucky, settling in Pulaski County in an early day. They reared to maturity a family of nine children, whose descendants are now numbered among the best citizens of the State. Joseph was reared to manhood under the influences of pioneer life, obtaining but a very indifferent education, but in the partial management of his father's affairs, being the eldest son, he acquired a good business training. He was placed upon his own resources, however, in early manhood and came to Lincoln County, a poor, but energetic young man. He first located near Crab Orchard. In time he came to wield an extensive influence in the business circles of Lincoln County, and though he made agriculture a specialty, he was also largely interested in banking, general trading and manufacture, and at his death left a vast estate. Mr. McAlister was a man of strong physical development, with which was combined an indomitable energy

and will power; public-spirited, he was originally a Henry Clay Whig, and later a Democrat, and supported the administration during the civil war. In religious tenets he was a Baptist and died in that faith in 1873. His wife, who still survives him, was Miss Martha Owsley, daughter of John Owsley of Lincoln County. They had a family of nine children; John McAlister of Texas; James W. McAlister, a banker of Missouri; Joseph H. McAlister, a farmer of Lincoln County; Robert McAlister, of Lincoln County; Ellen (Evans); George McAlister, a druggist of Stanford, Ky.; Annie (Johnson) deceased; Jennie (Hundley), and Mattie McAlister.

WILLIAM C. McCHORD, attorney at law, was born in Kentucky, July 3, 1850, and is the second son of Robert C. and Laura (Hynes) McChord, of Washington and Nelson Counties respectively. Subject's paternal grandfather was John McChord, a native of Maryland and of Scotch lineage. He came to Kentucky in an early day and settled near Springfield, where his death occurred many years ago. His wife, Lydia (Caldwell) McChord, was the daughter of William Caldwell, a man of considerable distinction in the early history of Washington County. Mrs. McChord was a woman of rare intelligence, and is remembered for her many excellent qualities. Robert C. McChord was born in Washington County, December 27, 1824, and is still living. He is a farmer, resides nine miles east of Springfield, and represented the county in the Legislature in the year 1854. Laura (Hynes) McChord was born in Nelson County, Ky., about the year 1824, and departed this life in 1879. Mr. and Mrs. McChord reared a family of eight children, whose names are as follows: A. H., William C., Robert C., John, Mary, Charles C., Lydia and Elizabeth McChord. William C. McChord was reared on a farm in his native county of Washington, and received his primary education in the country schools. He afterward attended Centre College at Danville, and at the age of seventeen entered the mercantile house of Philips & Co., at Lebanon, as clerk, in which capacity he continued two years. At the age of nineteen he severed his connection with the mercantile business, and sought employment on a farm, so that he could devote his leisure time to the study of law. He borrowed legal works of R. J. Brown of Springfield, and pursued his reading under many difficulties for two years, at the end of which time he accepted the position of deputy circuit clerk, under James P. Barbour, with whom he remained about two years. He was admitted to the bar in 1871, but did not engage in the active practice of his profession until three years later, at which time, August, 1874, he was elected county attorney of Washington County, a position he held for eight years. In September, 1874, he was also appointed master commissioner of the Washington County Circuit Court, in which capacity he continued for a period of six years. Mr. McChord has been a very successful lawyer, and his name appears in connection with the majority of important suits in Washington County. He was married January 14, 1875, in Springfield, to Miss Nannie McElroy, daughter of Charles R. and Mary (Shuck) McElroy, of Washington County. To their union have been born the following children: Charles M., Annie L. and William C. McChord. Mr. McChord is a member of the Masonic fraternity, belonging to Springfield Lodge, No. 50, Royal Arch Chapter No. 27, Springfield Council and Marion Commandery No. 27. With his wife he is a member of the Springfield Presbyterian Church.

CHARLES C. McCHORD, brother of the preceding, and sixth child of Robert and Laura McChord, was born in Washington County, December 3, 1859. He attended the common schools until his fourteenth year, at which time he entered Centre College, where he took a thorough course, graduating in 1878. After graduating he began the study of law at Lebanon, where he remained until 1879, when he moved to Springfield and entered the office of his brother, William C.McChord, under whose instruction he remained one year, at the end of which time, May, 1880, he was admitted to the bar, obtaining his license of Judge R. J. Breckinridge of Boyle County. Immediately after his admission to the bar, he engaged in the practice at Springfield, where he has since resided. He effected a copartnership with his brother in August, 1882, under the firm name of William C. and C. C. McChord, which still continues. He was nominated for county attorney of the Democratic ticket, December, 1885, and elected without opposition in August, 1886. Mr. McChord belongs to the Masonic fraternity, and is a stanch supporter of the Democratic party.

ROBERT C. McCHORD, M. D., was born November 1, 1851, and is the third of a family of eight children born to Robert C. and Laura (Hynes) McChord. Five generations of this family have been represented in Washington County, Ky. John McChord, grandfather of the subject, came in boyhood from Maryland, with his parents, who settled in that county. John married Lydia Caldwell of Boyle County, and reared a family of but two children: Robert C., Sr., and Lydia McChord, the others dying in youth. Robert McChord, Sr., was born December 25, 1824; married December 8, 1846, to Miss Laura Hynes, daughter of Abner Hynes, of Bardstown, Nelson County; she died in Lebanon, Ky., February 26, 1879. Robert C., Sr., is now living and an honored citizen of Washington County. Dr. Robert McChord received the advantages of a thorough literary education, attended the schools of Springfield, in his native county of Washington, and afterward the Centre College of Danville, Ky. He began the study of medicine at the age of twenty-one years; in 1873 entered the Louisville Medical College, graduating in 1875. He immediately established a practice in Lebanon, Marion Co., Ky., where he has since remained and where he enjoys an enviable reputation as a skillful physician. He is a member of the Beech Fork Medical Association, junior vice-president of the Kentucky Medical Society, and a member of the American Medical Association. Besides this he enjoys the distinction of being a surgeon for the Knoxville branch of the Louisville & Nashville Railroad Company, and president of the board of United States examining surgeons for pensions. He was married in 1880 to Lizzie L., daughter of Charles B. and Eliza L. Harrison, and has two sons, William C. and Charles McChord. Dr. McChord is a consistent member of the Presbyterian Church and a Mason of high rank.

JOHN McCLANE, deceased, a native of Fayette County, Ky., was born October 29, 1792, near Lexington, where he was reared to manhood. In 1832 he removed to Mercer, now Boyle County, locating five miles north of Danville, on the Harrodsburg Turnpike, where he resided until his death, which occurred April 15, 1883. He was a careful and successful farmer, having a fine body of land, consisting of 500 acres, which he managed with consummate skill. He was a member of the Christian Church, and was identified with the time-honored old line Whig party. Among his other losses resulting from the late war were ten slaves. His father, James McClane, a native of Virginia, was a soldier in the Revolutionary war, a pioneer in Woodford County, Ky., and died in 1804. His children were Mrs. Elizabeth Taylor, of Fayette County; Mrs. Mary Burns, of Columbus, Miss.; Dr. William McClane, of Tennessee, and John, our subject. On

December 3, 1816, John McClane espoused Miss Teresa, daughter of Lewis and Mary (Watkins) Knuckols, of Woodford County, (born August 3, 1801, and died August 8, 1842,) and to them were born Mary W. (May), Martha (Dunlap), George H., deceased; Eveline S. (Eastland); Robert A., deceased; Elizabeth, deceased; Catherine A., deceased; Louisa N., Amanda W. (Eastland), Eliza A., James L., deceased; Amelia, deceased, and Catherine E. Mr. McClane was a quiet and unobtrusive gentleman, who was esteemed most by those who knew him best.

WILLIAM B. McCLURE was born May 20, 1858, at Louisa, Lawrence Co., Ky., and is the second of three sons and one daughter born to Strather and Martha (Garrett) McClure, natives of Lawrence County, Ky., and Wayne County, W. Va. Strather McClure was a merchant and lumber trader. He died in 1876, aged forty-six. He was a son of William and Lue (Chapman) McClure. William McClure was born and reared in Botetourt County, Va., settled in Lawrence County, Ky., as early as 1785 or 1790, was an extensive farmer, raised a family of seven sons and eleven daughters, accumulated a large estate, educated his family in the best of schools, and died about 1860, aged ninety. The family is of Scotch descent. Mrs. Martha McClure was a daughter of Benjamin and Sarah Garrett, natives of West Virginia, who raised a family of three sons and eleven daughters; the three sons were in the Federal Army. William B. McClure was reared in Louisa, received his education in Louisa Academy, and taught in the common schools for four years. At eighteen he commenced the study of physic under Dr. G. W. Wroten, of Louisa; in the winter of 1879-80 he entered the Louisville Medical College, and graduated from the same in the spring of 1883, with honors. He located at Junction City, Boyle County, where he now has a large and lucrative practice. He is secretary of the R. O. Cowling Medical Society, also a member of the State and district medical associations. In politics he is a Republican and cast his first presidential vote for Gen. Garfield.

HON. JAMES BENNETT McCREARY was born July 8, 1838, in Madison County, Ky., and is a son of Dr. E. R. and Sabrina (Bennett) McCreary, also born in Madison County. Dr. E. R. McCreary was born in 1803; received his education in the best schools of Kentucky and his medical education at Jefferson College, Philadelphia. He entered practice at Richmond, Ky., where he had a large and lucrative practice.

He accumulated a large fortune, but in his latter years turned his attention to agricultural pursuits in his native county. He was a Democrat, earnest and active all of his life. He died in 1874, a respected and honored citizen. He was a son of James McCreary, who came from Virginia as early as 1785, and settled in Madison County. He was one of the patriots of 1812, and participated in Gen. Harrison's campaign. He married Mary Barr and the issue by this marriage was one son and one daughter. Dr. Charles McCreary, a brother of James McCreary, represented Ohio County in the Kentucky Legislature as early as 1809. From that time to the present the family has been one of the most active and prominent families of the State and its members have filled nearly all its offices from county clerk to that of governor, reflecting honor and credit upon their constituents. John McCreary, the great grandfather of Gov. McCreary, was born in Ireland, where he met Nancy Crawford, a daughter of a distinguished gentleman of Dublin. Their marriage being opposed they were married in the presence of a few friends and fled to America, landing in Baltimore in 1767, where five sons and four daughters were born. One son settled in Virginia, one in Pennsylvania, one in Indiana, and the other two south. From these spring many leading and influential families. At the age of eighteen James B. McCreary graduated with high honors from Centre College, Danville, Ky. He chose the law for his profession and, after a full course of reading, graduated from the law college of the University of Tennessee, at Lebanon, and was the valedictorian of the class of 1847. He at once opened an office in Richmond and entered upon practice, rose rapidly and became one of the ablest advocates at the bar. Although engaged in the practice of law, he has been more or less engaged in agricultural pursuits. He is the owner of large landed estates in Madison and Fayette Counties, Ky., and a large cotton plantation near Selma, Ala. At the beginning of the war, although deeply regretting the circumstances which brought about that unhappy conflict between the North and South, when forced to take sides he chose the South and assisted in raising a regiment for the Confederate service, of which he was elected major. Subsequently he became lieutenant-colonel of the Eleventh Kentucky Cavalry and continued in this position until the close of the war, serving with distinction under Gens. Bragg and Morgan in the West and toward the close of the war under Gen. Breckinridge, in Virginia. When the surrender came he accepted the result in good faith, returned to his home and resumed his former occupation. He married, June 12, 1867, Miss Katie Hughes, daughter of Thomas Hughes, of Fayette County, a prominent and leading agriculturist and owner of thoroughbred cattle and horses. The issue of this marriage was one son, Robert H. Mc-Creary. Prior to 1869, James B. McCreary had acted as delegate to a Democratic National Convention and was elected presidential elector and in the same year, although not aspiring to political position, he was elected without opposition to represent Madison County in the lower branch of the Kentucky Legislature and was twice re-elected. From the time of taking his seat in the Legislature, he developed a remarkable talent as a presiding officer, being often called during his first term to the speaker's chair *pro tem.* After serving his first term he was elected speaker in 1871, also in 1873, and during the entire four years no appeal was taken from his decisions. Such was his familiarity with all points and bearings of parliamentary law, and such his skill in the management of the legislative body over which he presided, that he received encomiums from old legislators and prominent men. Having served six years with distinction, gaining an enviable popularity over the State, he designed returning to the practice of his profession; but the Democratic Convention in May, 1875, nominated him as their candidate for governor and he made the race against a very popular Republican, Gen. John M. Harlin, and, after an active canvass, was elected by a large majority and received the largest vote ever cast for any candidate for any office in the State. The canvass was conducted throughout with marked ability, decorum and chivalrous courtesy on both sides, nothing growing out of the contest to disturb the friendly relations which had always existed between the candidates, and yet it is remembered as one of the most energetic contests ever made in the State. He performed the duties of governor of Kentucky with ability and conscientious devotion to the best interests of the commonwealth, unsurpassed by any of his predecessors, and was clear headed, comprehensive, just, conservative, yet liberal and far-sighted in all his views of public policy, constantly siding with the demands of genuine progress; blessed with a robust constitution and an iron will he was enabled to accomplish an amount of official work and could stand more mental and physical labor than any of his predecessors in office. Although an ex-Confederate and the first who had ever been elected governor of a State

which remained in the Union during the war, he has always favored restoration of fraternal feeling between the sections. In his inaugural address and his first biennial message to the General Assembly, he recommended the hearty participation of Kentucky in the centennial celebration and exposition at Philadelphia, not only as a means of bringing the vast resources of the State before the world, but also as a fitting occasion for the development of fraternal feeling between people of all sections. In his inaugural he said: "I wish to see the records of secession, coercion and reconstruction filed away forever and the people of the whole country earnestly advocating peace and reconciliation and all looking to the Constitution as a guarantee of our liberties and the safeguard of every citizen." Gov. McCreary's administration was one of the most popular of any the State has had. His people put him forward as their candidate for Congress in 1884, and he was elected by a large majority and re-elected in 1886. The fact that he was elected in 1884 by 1,836 majority and in 1886 by 3,346 majority is an excellent indication of his popularity.

EPHRAIM McDOWELL, M. D. Of Kentucky's citizens of the preceding generation many attained distinction in their respective pursuits, but it is doubtful if any of them "builded so deeply" the foundation of an enduring fame as did Dr. Ephraim Mc-Dowell, of Danville. While others wielded great power and rendered eminent services in their day and generation, Dr. McDowell inaugurated a work which continued to live and grow after the originator had passed from the scene of his labors. By his originality, skill and courage, he opened up a new departure in the science and practice of surgery, which has grown to be the crowning glory of that great and human art, thereby rescuing thousands of women from certain and painful death. By his own hand he demonstrated the practicability of the new work his genius had opened up, and published the results of his labors. The creation was complete in execution as well as in priority. He is recognized throughout the civilized world as the originator of a great department of surgical practice, and as a benefactor to his race. His name is familiar to students of medical science in every land and clime, forming, in the language of Fitz-Greene Halleck,

"One of the few, the immortal names
That were not born to die."

In every land the practitioner of surgery is utilizing the results of McDowell's work amid the most brilliant achievements of his art, and to the restoration of life and health. In the rapid progress of science other hands and minds have widened the scope and extended the application of his great operation, but this only adds to the grandeur of the original step, and lends additional luster to the fame of him who first led the way. With the exception of J. Marion Sims, a native of South Carolina, no physician on this continent has contributed such far-reaching and potential influences toward advancing and enriching the resources of surgical science. Indeed these two great American surgeons founded the modern science of gynecology (the treatment of diseases peculiar to women), which has brought to American medicine and American physicians so much of the renown and esteem in which they are regarded in all foreign countries. Since the early history of the commonwealth the medical profession of Kentucky has ranked alongside the most advanced of the entire country, and within her borders was established one of the oldest and most renowned of American medical schools. But great discoveries springing from that wonderful creative faculty which utilizes all previous research in conception, and combines skill, courage and intelligent penetration of undiscovered lines of thought in execution, are uncommon in all branches of science. To rend the veil which conceals the mysteries of science is allowed to comparatively few. Such privileges fell to the lot of Ephraim McDowell.

Dr. McDowell was born in Rockbridge County, Va., November 11, 1771. His ancestors came to Virginia from the northern part of Ireland, where they had gone from Scotland. His father, Samuel McDowell, was actively engaged in political life for a number of years in Virginia, and in 1782, having been appointed a land commissioner for Kentucky, removed to Danville. He was afterward judge of the district court of Kentucky. The maiden name of Dr. McDowell's mother was Sarah McClung. The early education of Ephraim McDowell was obtained at a classical school taught at Georgetown, and afterward at Bardstown, Ky. After finishing his course in this seminary he went to Staunton, Va., where he began the study of medicine in the office of Dr. Humphreys, of that place. In 1793-94 he attended medical lectures at the University of Edinburgh, Scotland. Among his instructors was John Bell, an able surgeon and gifted teacher of anatomy and surgery. It was the custom of this eminent Scotch surgeon to allude to those diseases for which McDowell's operation is the only possible relief, and to dwell at length upon the possibility of recovery following such a severe operation as would be necessary. There can be no doubt that the principles and suggestions of the teacher directed the attention of the pupil to the difficult task undertaken after his return to his home at Danville. Our British cousins, with characteristic assumption and conceit, have, at times, endeavored to detract from McDowell's fame by claiming that the conception of the operation of opening the abdomen and removing diseased ovaries originated with British surgeons. To any unprejudiced mind it is evident that greater credit is due McDowell for undertaking a feat, the dangers of which had been explained to him, and which his greatest teacher did not have the temerity to attempt, than had he, ignorant of the danger, stumbled upon so great an achievement. Indeed, the fact that Mr. John Bell so carefully instructed his pupil in the difficulties and perils of the task, conceding his own unwillingness to attempt its execution, renders McDowell's deliberate assumption of such an undertaking all the more creditable. In 1795 he returned to Danville, and at once entered upon the practice of his profession. He did not receive a diploma from the University of Edinburgh, not having studied there the requisite time to complete the course, and it was not until 1807 that he received any diploma, when the Medical Society of Philadelphia sent him its diploma. In 1823 the University of Maryland, unsolicited upon his part, conferred upon him the honorary degree of M. D. In a few years after beginning practice, McDowell established a wide reputation, and became known throughout all the Western and Southern States, as the first surgeon this side of Philadelphia. His practice extended in every direction, and persons came to him from the neighboring States for treatment. He made long journeys on horseback, sometimes hundreds of miles, to operate in such cases as could not come to him at Danville. He performed the most difficult operations known to the science of surgery in that day and with striking success. In the winter of 1809, when he had been practicing for fourteen years, he was summoned to visit a Mrs. Crawford, residing in Green County, Ky. He found her to be the subject of an ovarian tumor. He explained with fidelity the grave and hopeless nature of her disease if allowed to run its course, and also told her of the hazardous and experimental nature of an operation for removal of the tumor. At the same time he told her of his belief that such an operation could be successfully performed, and assured her of his willingness to undertake such a procedure. Mrs. Crawford was a woman of decision and courage, and promptly consented to submit to the operation. She came to Danville on horseback, and McDowell, with the assistance of his nephew, Dr. James McDowell, performed the operation, which was followed by prompt recovery. She returned to her home at the end of twenty-five days in perfect health, and enjoyed good health until her death at the ripe age of seventy-eight years. Seven years thereafter, when he had successfully operated in two additional cases, he made a careful report of the same, which was published in a Philadelphia medical journal. He operated altogether in thirteen cases, of which number eight patients recovered. When we remember that this surgeon was, at that time, living on the border of western civilization, remote from a hospital or medical college where skilled assistants could be had, without instruments especially adapted for the purpose; without chloroform, ether, or other protection from pain; performing an untried operation of fearful magnitude, appreciating the responsibility as well as the danger to his patient, and the peril of his reputation and standing, then we appreciate and admire both his courage and his skill, Dr. McDowell was nearly six feet tall and of commanding presence. He was kind-hearted, amiable, and readily approached by the world. He was of cheerful nature and full of good humor. In his professional work he was earnest, affable and dignified, but like men of genuine ability, he was unassuming, blending in an agreeable way due self-respect with perfect freedom from egotism and self-assumption. It is said that an easiness to the extent of familiarity existed between him and his fellow-citizens. As a citizen he was charitable and public-spirited. He was active in the foundation of Centre College at Danville, and one of its original incorporators. He was an Episcopalian, and the site of the present edifice, Trinity Church, in Danville, was a contribution from him. In 1802 he married Sarah, a daughter of Gov. Isaac Shelby, with whom he lived happily, and raised a family of two sons and four daughters, only three of whom survived him. His wife was his survivor by ten years. While in the full vigor of life, and in the midst of his professional labor, at the age of fifty-nine years, he died on the 20th of June, 1830, after a brief illness. His remains were laid to rest in the family burying-ground at "Travelers' Rest," the estate of the Shelby family, six miles south of Danville. In 1873,

long after the great work he began had been extended in its beneficent results to the afflicted of every country and his great services as a pioneer were acknowledged, the late Dr. John Davies Jackson, of Danville, inaugurated an effort to suitably mark his resting place. The matter was brought to the attention of the Kentucky State Medical Society, and Dr. Jackson was made chairman of a committee to endeavor to accomplish the worthy purpose. Dr. Jackson's death occurring in 1875, the society appointed the writer of this sketch to his place at the head of the committee, and the work was continued. By the subscriptions of members of the State society with several voluntary subscriptions from eminent surgeons in Philadelphia and New York, a sum was raised, with which a neat granite shaft was erected to the memory of McDowell. The remains of himself and wife were removed from the old neglected family burying-ground on the Shelby farm, and re-interred in Danville. The citizens of Danville donated the beautiful square of ground, which was beautified and improved to receive and retain the remains of Kentucky's greatest surgeon, and one of the world's greatest benefactors. In the center of "McDowell Park" rest the remains of McDowell; beside them lie those of his devoted and accomplished wife, and above, the neat and tasteful monument tells the visitor of the eminent service rendered humanity and science by him who rests beneath. The erection of this monument to the memory of McDowell was made the occasion by the Kentucky State Medical Society to publicly recognize his great scientific achievements. This was appropriately done May 17, 1879, during the session of the State Medical Society in Danville. The memorial oration was delivered by the late Prof. Samuel D. Gross, M. D., then acknowledged the most eminent surgeon in America. In addition to the members of the society and a large and cultivated audience from all parts of the State, the governor, secretary of State and other officials of the State, as well as many eminent surgeons from various parts of the Union were present. Prof. Gross' memorial oration with the other addresses and proceedings incident to the occasion were published in a handsome volume by the society, and copies furnished leading physicians and the various medical libraries of this country and Europe.

NICHOLAS McDOWELL was born February 6, 1834, and is a son of Samuel and Martha (Hawkins) McDowell, to whom five sons were born: Joseph, Charles, Nicholas, Samuel and William; three now living.

Samuel McDowell, the father, was born June 22, 1795, two miles east of Danville, and was educated at Centre College; was a farmer and slave-holder; was captain of militia; was a member of the Presbyterian Church, and in politics was a Whig; he died August 7, 1854. He was a son of Col. Joseph McDowell, who was born Rockbridge County, Va., September 13, 1768, and migrated to Kentucky in the first settling of the State; participated in Shelby's campaign as colonel of a regiment. He was a farmer and slave-holder; was an elder in the Presbyterian Church; married Sallie Irvine, September, 1794, and reared a family of four sons and seven daughters. He was a Whig in politics, and died at the age of eighty-seven years. He was a son of Samuel McDowell, who was born in Rockbridge County, Va., October 9, 1735; married Mary McClung January 17, 1754, and to whom eight sons and four daughters were born (the sons were John, James, William, Samuel, Joseph, Ephraim, Caleb and Andrew). He represented his people (Augusta County) in the colonial convention in Richmond, and was a distinguished and active leader in the war for independence. After the war he migrated to Kentucky, and died near Danville, September 15, 1817. His fourth son, Samuel, was the father of eleven children, and had a son named Abram Irvin McDowell, the father of Gen. Irvin McDowell. Ephraim McDowell, the sixth son of Samuel McDowell, became one of the most distinguished surgeons of his day, and his monument ornaments the park in Danville. This monument was erected by the State Medical Society through the instrumentality of Dr. McMurtry. Dr. McDowell received his education in medicine and surgery in Edinburgh, Scotland, and was, perhaps, one of the greatest surgeons America ever produced. He was the first to perform the operation of ovariotomy, but, while in Edinburgh, Scotland, was denounced as a butcher. Samuel McDowell was a son John McDowell, who married Magdaline Wood, who in turn was a son of Ephraim McDowell, who participated in the battle of Londonderry. He reared four children: John, James, Mary and Margaret. He emigrated from Scotland to Rockbridge County, Va., prior to 1700. Mrs. Martha (Hawkins) McDowell was a daughter of Nicholas Hawkins, who came from Rockbridge County, Va., and settled in Madison County, Ky., in early days. He was a soldier in the war of 1812, and became a large and extensive farmer and slave owner. Nicholas McDowell was brought up on

a farm in his native county of Boyle, and received his education in Centre College, from which he graduated in 1854. He then began the study of medicine, and took one course of lectures at Louisville University. After his father's death he abandoned the medical profession and engaged in farming near Danville, but in 1882 located in the village. He has also been engaged in mercantile business. May 1, 1860, he was united in marriage to Lizzie McElroy, of Washington County, a daughter of Anthony and Anna G. (Rice) McElroy, natives respectively of Washington County, Ky., and Virginia. Five children, Annie, Nicholas, Jr., Sue, Sallie and Bessie, have been born to Mr. and Mrs. McDowell, who are members of the Presbyterian Church. Mr. McDowell cast his first presidential vote for Fillmore, but since the war he has affiliated with the Democrats.

PAUL IRVIN McELROY resides on the farm where he was born on the 9th of October, 1822. His father, William E. McElroy, was born in Campbell County, Va., February 9, 1776, and came to Kentucky with his father's family in 1789. William E. McElroy married Miss Kittie Cleland in 1804. She died ten years later, leaving five children: Maria J., Eliza K., Phillip E., Harriet P., and Margaret I., the last named, now aged seventy-five years, being the only survivor. William E. McElroy married his second wife, Mary Kirk, of Marion County, in 1821; to this marriage were born the following children: Paul I., Robert L., Cecil F., Lucy (Ray), William T., of Louisville; Dr. James F., of Bowling Green; Samuel R., of Little Rock, Ark.; Keturah J. (Hubbard), and Sarah; the last named died in infancy. Mary (Kirk) McElroy died in 1865, aged sixty-nine; she was a daughter of James Kirk, a Virginian, and one of the early settlers of Washington County, Ky. William E. McElroy in early life followed the trade of a carpenter and builder; later he engaged in agriculture and stock raising; he died in 1874 at the advanced age of ninety-nine years. His father, Samuel McElroy, who came to Kentucky in 1789, settled in Washington County, where he pursued the vocation of farming up to the time of his death in the year 1807. He was of Scotch and Irish descent; was a veteran in the war of the Revolution, and a member of the Presbyterian Church, in which he was for many years a ruling elder. Paul I.'s maternal grandfather, James Kirk, was also a soldier in the war of the Revolution; he was of English parentage, and died at the age of ninety-seven. Paul I. McElroy was reared on a farm, and educated in the common schools of his native county of Marion, and finished at Lebanon in 1839, when he engaged in farming and stock-raising, which he has continued up to the present time. He is now the proprietor of the "Valley Home" farm, a fine estate of 350 acres, lying one mile north of the town of Lebanon. He was married October 17, 1865, to Miss Susan McElroy, a daughter of Hon. Hiram McElroy of Union County, Ky. She was a member of the Presbyterian Church, and departed this life in 1884, leaving four children: Mary L., Paul I., Jennie F. and Proctor K. Mr. McElroy is a ruling elder in the Presbyterian Church, of which he has been a life-long member. The McElroys have, for 200 years, been prominent as rulers and workers in the church. Mr. McElroy is a Democrat. He is president of the Lebanon & St. Rose Turnpike Company, but has persistently refused all offices in which politics held a place. As a patron of schools he has done much for the improvement of the school system in his county.

GEORGE W. McELROY is a son of Abram McElroy and Eliza N. Skiles, the former a native of Marion, and the latter of Warren County. They were married in the latter county, but settled in Marion County, where they resided until their death. Abram McElroy engaged in merchandising in Lebanon, and died in 1883, his wife having died in 1850. They had but two children—George W., and Clarence U. McElroy, now of Warren County. George W. was born March 1, 1846, was chiefly reared in Lebanon, and graduated from Centre College at Danville, Ky., in 1868, since which time he has been engaged in the pursuits of the farm. He was married in Lebanon in September 1881, to Miss Lucy Cleaver, daughter of Dr. W. W. Cleaver, and has two children, Grundy and William C. McElroy, the former born February 22, 1883, and the latter July 12, 1884. Mr. and Mrs. McElroy are members of the First Presbyterian Church of Lebanon.

JAMES B. McFERRAN was born September 17, 1841, in Boyle County, Ky., and is the third of six sons and four daughters born to James M. and Ruth (Brown) McFerran. James M. McFerran was born November 26, 1809, two miles south of Danville; was a large farmer and trader in stock; served as justice for twenty-four years, and represented his county one term in the lower house of the Kentucky Legislature, and died September 17, 1884. He was a son of James McFerran, who was born in Ireland, July 16, 1757, and came to the United States with his parents when a lad of four years, and settled in Botetourt County, Va.; when a young man about eighteen or twenty, he migrated, and located four miles south of Danville and became a substantial farmer and slave owner. He married Elizabeth Young, of Lincoln County, and died in 1835, aged seventy-eight years. He was the son of Martin McFerran, who came to Virginia from Ireland with his three sons, John, James and Martin, before the war for independence. His religion was Presbyterian. Mrs. Ruth (Brown) McFerran was born in Franklin County, Ky., in 1811, a daughter of Scott and Lucy (Monday) Brown, of Scotch descent. She died September 26, 1885. Scott Brown was a large farmer, and served as magistrate and sheriff of Franklin County. James B. McFerran graduated from Centre College in the class of 1862; was a trader until 1867, when he began the study of law. In the winter of 1867–68 he attended the law school at Louisville, and was soon after admitted to the bar at Danville, where he had an excellent practice. He has served as master commissioner four years, and also represented his county in the Kentucky Legislature in 1873–74. In 1883 he located on a farm of 200 acres, two miles south of Danville. He was married May 17, 1876, to Miss Mattie Davis, daughter of James H. and Mattie (Alexander) Davis, the former a native of Garrard, and the latter a native of Mercer County, Ky. James H. Davis located in Boyle County about 1852, and became a leading farmer and breeder of shorthorns. He had the reputation of having the finest herd of shorthorns in the State, realizing fabulous prices, but paying as high as $5,000 for a single bull. He was well known all over the United States as one of the best breeders of shorthorn cattle. He was a son of Asel and Sarah (Tucker) Davis, from Virginia. Mr. and Mrs. McFerran have one bright daughter to bless their home. In politics he is a Democrat, and is now engaged in the practice of his profession at Danville.

JAMES McGARVEY was born June 24, 1819, in County Derry, Ireland. In 1842 he immigrated to the United States, landing at New York. March 12, 1843, he landed at Lexington, Ky., and October, 1858, located near Pleasant Hill, Mercer County, where he has since resided. His father, Stephen McGarvey, a native of County Tyrone, Ireland, was born about 1783, was a farmer and died in 1866. He was the son of James McGarvey, Sr., of Tyrone County, a quiet old farmer, who died about 1825. He was the son of Hugh. James, Sr., married Bridget Shearon, and their offspring were Hugh, James, Stephen and Ellen. Stephen married Mary Sweeny, born in 1788, died in 1867, and their children are John, Ellen (O'Harran), Peter, James and Susan (Sharry). October 25, 1842, James McGarvey was married to Miss Rosana, daughter of John and Mary (Breen) Hagan, of Derry County, born 1825, and to them have been born Peter, deceased; John, a priest, who died of yellow fever at Memphis, August 26, 1878; Mary, deceased; James; Stephen; Peter; Bridget, deceased; Eliza, deceased; Francis, Mary (True) and Lena. Mr. McGarvey was engaged in contracting on turnpikes for many years; is now a farmer, owning 205 acres of well improved and productive land in good condition and in a high state of cultivation. He is a Catholic and a Democrat.

GRANVILLE B. McGEE was born November 25, 1829. His father, Jacob McGee, born in Wayne County, Ky., in 1806, was a farmer and was married in 1824 to Miss Sarah Jones, a daughter of Landy and Lucy (Farrow) Jones, both born near Richmond, Va. To this marriage were born five children: Julia Ann, wife of William Eston; Elizabeth, who died in infancy; Granville B.; Jane, wife of Henry Lawhon, and Jacob. Jacob, father of Granville B. and Jacob, died in 1834; his wife is still living in the seventy-eighth year of her age (1886). John McGee, grandfather of Granville and Jacob McGee, was also a native Virginian, who came in a very early period of Kentucky's colonization to Wayne County, Ky., where he lived all his life, and after his death his widow, Miss Elizabeth Cox before marriage, moved with the family of ten children to Fentress County, Tenn. The names of his children are Robert, William, Samuel, John, Jacob, James, Hannah, wife of Samuel Hinds; Jane, wife of John Martin; Polly, wife of David Cox, and Rachael, wife of John Moss, of whom Mrs. Rachael Moss alone is living. The great-grandfather of Granville B. McGee, with his wife, came from old Ireland and settled in Virginia, where he lived and died. Landy Jones, maternal grandfather of Mr. McGee, was a man of wealth in Virginia, but by unsuccessful trading lost most of his property, and on the death of his wife returned to the Old Dominion. His son, Meriweather L. Jones, a maternal uncle of Granville B. McGee, was a Baptist minister of great notoriety in Virginia, and the Jones family are of English origin. Granville B. Mc-

Gee, a native of Cumberland County, Ky., was four years old when his father died. His early training was all in the direction of agriculture, and he was hired a great part of the time to do farm work at 25 and 30 cents per day. The two sons left Mrs. Sarah McGee had the care of the family, and the partners in youth and adversity have continued to be partners in prosperity. At the age of thirty-three Mr. McGee was married to Miss Margaret Dixon, a daughter of William J. and Elizabeth (Neely) Dixon, of Cumberland County, Ky., and in six short weeks after marriage death entered his new home and took from him his wife. She was in the eighteenth year of her age. On May 3, 1871, Mr. McGee was married to Miss Ellen Martin, a daughter of Nelson and Mary J. (Hickey) Martin, natives of Warren County, Ky. This marriage has been blessed by six children: Jacob, William, Frank, Robert, Mary Bowman and James L., of whom Frank and William are now dead. Until 1865 Mr. McGee and his brother Jacob farmed in partnership, but since that time have been engaged in farming and general merchandising in Burkesville, Ky., together, with considerable success. In October, 1885, they admitted into the business John Q. Alexander, and the style of the firm is McGee Brothers & Co., with a capital of $15,000, and they do a thriving business of $30,000 worth of sales per annum. Mr. and Mrs. Granville B. McGee are both members of the Christian Church. In addition to merchandising, McGee Bros. & Co. own four valuable farms in Cumberland County, Ky., aggregating 1,225 acres. Jacob McGee, in October, 1856, was married to Miss Nancy Johnson, a daughter of James L. and —— (Wilson) Johnson, natives of Adair County, Ky., and there were born to them five children: John Q., James, Mary T., wife of John Q. Alexander, and two who died in infancy. Mrs. McGee, who was a member of the Christian Church in life, died in 1866. In 1867 Mr. Jacob McGee married Mrs. Sarah (Williams) Baker, and they are the parents of seven children: Elva, Leslie, Curtis, Charles, Jacob, Hattie and Effie. Mr. and Mrs. Jacob McGee are both members of the Christian Church.

HENRY McKENNA was born January 9, 1819, in Draperstown, County Derry, Ireland, and in 1837 immigrated to the United States, landing in Philadelphia, where he remained one year. In August, 1838, he removed to Kentucky and was engaged in hard labor around Lexington for many years. Husbanding his wages, he was enabled in time to contract on pike work, at which he met with some encouragement. In 1851 he located in Fairfield, and was for six years engaged in the construction of turnpikes, as a contractor. In 1855 he was also interested in a steam flouring-mill, which was not very profitable. He commenced distilling whisky in 1857, extending the business from time to time, manufacturing at first from 150 to 300 barrels per annum. The business proving lucrative he enlarged the capacity of the distillery, until from 500 to 600 barrels are now made annually. In addition to other business, he owns and has conducted a valuable farm of 380 acres of productive land, near which stands his palatial residence, a model of symmetry and utility. What is most remarkable during his labors of the past forty-four years, he has been almost a confirmed invalid. He has three times visited the Fatherland since he came to the land of his adoption. He is the son of Daniel McKenna, who died in 1839, at the age of forty-eight years; Daniel's father was Teague McKenna. Henry McKenna was married at Lexington, Ky., on November 9, 1847, to Miss Bettie, daughter of Patrick and Ann (Conway) Goodwin, of Lexington (born 1819, near Draperstown, County Derry, Ireland, died July 10, 1880), and their union was favored by the birth of Daniel, Henry J. (deceased), Anna (deceased), Mary, James, Peter (deceased) and Stafford. Mr. McKenna was reared and still clings to the faith of the Catholic Church, and in politics is a Democrat.

REV. JAMES PRESSLEY McMILLAN, of Burkesville, Ky., is of Irish descent. On his mother's side his great grandfather, James Huie, was born in Ulster Province sometime before the middle of the last century. Coming to this country, he served in the Revolutionary War, and died in 1828, leaving two sons, Joseph and Robert. Robert was the father of six sons and two daughters. His elder daughter, Sallie Huie, who was also his eldest child born in 1805, is the mother of J. P. McMillan. The great grandfather, James, and also his two sons, Joseph and Robert, with their wives and many descendants, lie in the same graveyard near Morrow's Station, Clayton Co., Georgia. Robert, the grandfather, and several of his sons, now all dead, except two, were ruling elders in the Presbyterian Church; and all their descendants still adhere to the faith of their fathers; and J. P. McMillan is not excepted from this statement. Turning now to his paternal ancestry, we find his great grandfather, Daniel McMillan, in Ul-

ster Province, Ireland, before the middle of the 18th century. His sons were Peter and Sam and Archy and James and John—all of whom except the last came to this country; and of those coming, all except Peter, who was a minister of the gospel, served in the Revolutionary War. James, the fourth one of these sons, and grandfather of J. P. Mc-Millan, distinguished himself at one time by a daring escape from British imprisonment. Buried, with his wife, his grave is found in Jackson Co., Georgia. His sons were James and George and Sam. His second son, George, was born in 1805 in Jackson County, Ga., and was married in 1825 to Sallie Huie, already named, who was born the same year. They started in life without a dollar, but by industry, economy and thrift, they acquired a competence which increased and remained with them down to old age. They had seven children, viz.: Martha Elizabeth, Robert Huie, James Pressley, Joseph A., Mary Jane, George Washington and Margaret Ann,—all living, except Joseph, who died in infancy, and Martha E., who died in 1879. The three sisters married three brothers, all well-to-do farmers, the sons of John Orr of Acworth, Ga. Martha married Joseph Orr; Mary, David Orr; and Margaret, Linn Orr. Robert H. McMillan lives near Acworth, Georgia, with his children grown up, and growing up, around him to honor his unsullied name. George W., educated at Centre College, Ky., lives at the same place. He has but one child, Mary Lee, for many years a pupil, and now the principal teacher at Alexander College, Burkesville, Ky. James P. McMillan, the second son, left his home in 1849. He spent four years in the academies of Georgia. Thence he came to Danville, Ky., where he spent three years in Centre College—and three more in the Theological Seminary, finishing his course in 1859. Thence he spent nine years in Shelby Co., Ky., as pastor of Olivet Church. He was ordained in 1860; married in 1861; came to Burkesville in 1868 where he built up a church and founded Alexander College, in which work he has been assiduously employed for nearly nineteen years. The college buildings cost $15,000; the endowment is about $7,000; and the institution is still rising on a solid foundation and extending in usefulness. Its young lady-boarders come from the entire Southern Country. Mrs. Hattie McMillan, the wife of J. P. McMillan, is the daughter of Lewis Beatty well known in Shelby Co., Ky. She was educated at the Stewart Female College in Shelbyville. Her mother's maiden name was Elizabeth

Fullinwider, descended from a long line of German Ancestry, firm in the faith of the Reformed Churches—in which faith some of her ancestry and near relatives were able ministers of the gospel. Mrs. McMillan's maternal grandmother was a Winter and a near relative to President Lincoln. J. P. and Hattie B. McMillan have only two children, Bessie Miller and Georgia Ray, aged twelve and seven years, both pupils of Alexander College and both preparing for usefulness in the work of teaching. The McMillan family for many generations back has been noted for its ministers of the gospel and office bearers in the Presbyterian Church.

DR. LOUIS S. McMURTRY, of Danville, who is widely known in the State as a skillful and accomplished physician, was born in Harrodsburg, Ky., September 14, 1850. His youth was spent in Garrard County until he was sixteen years of age, when he entered Centre College at Danville, from which institution he graduated in 1870. He at once entered the office of the late Dr. John D. Jackson, of Danville, as his pupil. He received the degree of M. D. from the University of Louisiana in New Orleans in March, 1873. He then spent a year in that city as assistant demonstrator of anatomy in the university, and was attached to the staff of the great Charity Hospital. In July, 1874, he began the practice of his profession in Danville, and quickly worked his way into the confidence of the community. He spent the winter of 1877–78 in New York City pursuing advanced studies in the medical schools and hospitals of that city. In 1882 he accepted the chair of anatomy, tendered him by the Kentucky School of Medicine in Louisville. The following year he discharged the duties of demonstrator of anatomy and lecturer on clinical surgery in the University of Louisville. He was at the same time associate editor of the Louisville Medical News. He discharged the duties of these exacting public positions most acceptably, but preferring the active duties of general practice, he resigned these positions and resumed his practice in Danville. In 1879 he married Miss Mary E. Ball, of Covington, Ky., who died a year later, leaving a daughter. Dr. McMurtry has made numerous and valuable contributions to medical literature upon practical subjects, mostly relating to surgery and gynecology. He has successfully performed some of the most difficult and heroic operations in surgery, among which may be mentioned the successful ligation of the subclavian artery for aneurism, ovariotomy, etc. He is a member of the Kentucky State Medical Society and of the American Medical Association; an honorary member of the New Orleans Medical and Surgical Association. Three years ago he was elected a fellow of the American Academy of Medicine at its annual meeting in Baltimore. He is thoroughly devoted to his profession, and is an earnest student of medical science. He is a man of broad, general culture, and a graceful and forcible writer.

CHARLES V. McWHORTER was born July 29, 1846, in Adair County, and is the ninth in a family of ten children born to Richard W. and Elizabeth M. (Southerland) McWhorter, natives of Casey County, Ky., and of Irish and English descent respectively. Richard W. McWhorter was born November 3, 1803. At his majority he was employed for a time in the salt works on the Green River, Casey County. He married, January 6, 1828, and for about two years after farmed on his father-in-law's farm in Casey County. In the spring of 1830 he bought wild land on Casey's Creek in Adair County, and improved a farm on which he resided until his death, September 10, 1878. In early life he learned the surveyor's art, which he followed for many years in Adair and adjoining counties, locating many of the important roads. He was a member first of the Separate Baptist and afterward of the Christian Church. He was also a member of the Masonic fraternity. His father, John McWhorter, was a native of Virginia and a veteran of the Revolution. He was married in his native State and soon afterward came to Kentucky, settling in Casey County. He was a member of the United Baptist Church. His father was a native of the North of Ireland and about the middle of the last century with three brothers came to the colony of Virginia. From these four brothers all of the name in the country have descended. Mrs. Elizabeth M. (Southerland) McWhorter was born May 31, 1810, is yet living, and resides with her son, Charles V., on the old homestead in Adair County. She has been a member of the Separate, but is now a member of the United Baptist Church. Her father, Owen Southerland, was also a native of Virginia, but at the age of fourteen or fifteen, about 1790, came with his parents to what is now Casey County, Ky. He and wife were members of the Separate Baptist Church. The Southerlands, of Virginia, are descended from a long line of English nobles. Charles V. McWhorter received only a limited education in youth; however, he has by his own exertions acquired a very good business education. He has always resided on the old farm, with the exception of two years when he was engaged in general merchandising at Rolla, Adair County, and two years when engaged in the live stock business in Texas. Here he is extensively and successfully engaged in farming and stock raising. The farm is an excellent one; is well improved and in a good state of cultivation. In March, 1865, he enlisted in Company B, First Kentucky Cavalry (State service), and served with his regiment in all its marches and engagements until October of the same year, when they were mustered out of service at Lebanon, Ky. The regiment was principally engaged in scouting and guerrilla warfare. Mr. McWhorter married, May 28, 1874, Miss Eliza G. Tucker, a native of Green County, Ky., born January 13, 1855. She is a daughter of Robert M. and Nancy E. (Knifley) Tucker, natives of Taylor and Adair Counties, respectively. To Mr. and Mrs. McWhorter seven children have been born: Ada A., Minnie I., Robert W. (deceased), Lucian A., Fannie L. (deceased), Nancy E. (deceased), and Beersheba. Mr. and Mrs. McWhorter are members of the Christian Church. In politics he is a Democrat and is one of the enterprising and successful farmers of the county.

BUFORD MAHAN was born June 1, 1829. His father, James V. Mahan, was a native of Virginia; was born in 1794, and was brought to Kentucky by his parents when he was four years of age. After attaining his majority he was married to Matilda Penick a daughter of Edward and Nancy Penick, of Marion County. To James V. Mahan and his wife, Matilda, were born the following children: Edward, William, Buford, James, Agnes (wife of Rev. S. W. Cheney, of Springfield, Ky.) and Nancy (Moore, now Penny) of Perryville, Ky., Mattie (the wife of H. C. Dunn) and Anna (the wife of Isaac Lewis.) The mother was a member of the Presbyterian Church, and died in that faith on the 16th of July, 1862. James V. Mahan was a farmer, and a worker in the Presbyterian Church, and it is said that few men of his day surpassed him in a knowledge of the doctrines of the church. He died at Perryville in 1873. His father, William Mahan, was of Scotch and Irish parentage; was born in Shippensburg, Penn., in 1760; moved to Virginia in 1782, and came to Kentucky in 1798, and located on what was known as the James Sanders survey on Muldrow's Hills in Green, now Taylor County. He was a minister in the Presbyterian Church and a teacher of the Latin, Greek and Hebrew languages. While yet a resident of Virginia he married a Miss Venable, and they reared a family of six children: William, Samuel, James, Elizabeth (Harbison), Jane (Foster), and Mary, wife of Judge Reade, of Indiana. Buford Mahan was born and reared on his father's farm near Bradfordsville, Marion County. He was educated in the common schools, finishing at Lebanon Male Seminary, under W. T. Knott; taught school for a short time, and at the age of twenty-one engaged in farming on his own account, but soon after connected with that occupation business of trading in stock. In later years he has sold goods for parties in Lebanon, Ky., where he is yet employed. He was married October 8, 1861, to Miss Harriet F. Crawford. Six children have been born to this union: James C., Sallie C., Emma, John R., Hugh D. and William H. Harriet (Crawford) Mahan was born in 1833. She is a daughter of John and Sallie Crawford, who were of Scotch and Irish parentage, and residents of Marion County, Ky. Mr. and Mrs. Mahan are consistent members of the Presbyterian Church, with which they united under the ministry of Rev. Thomas H. Cleland, of Lebanon, Ky. Mr. Mahan is a Republican, but liberal in his views, and casts his ballot for men rather than for party.

JOHN BEVERLY MANN was born June 12, 1851, on the place where he grew to manhood, and now resides in Mercer County, Ky. His father, James B. Mann, was born in 1807, on Salt River, three miles south of Harrodsburg, where he was reared. He was a farmer, a Whig, a Union man; for thirty years ruling elder in the Presbyterian Church, and died February 28, 1886. He was the son of Jackson Mann, a native of Virginia, who, when five years old, was brought by his parents to Kentucky, and was reared in Mercer County; was a ruling elder in the Presbyterian Church, which he joined in 1813, and was a farmer and slave owner. His father was Beverly Mann. Jackson Mann married Mary Adams and their offspring were Andrew, David, Sally (Davis), James B., Beverly, Eliza (Irvine), Jackson and Mary (Meyer.) James B. Mann married, in 1833, Miss Mary, daughter of Garrett and Rachel (Rynerson) Terhune, of Mercer County, born in 1814, and from their union sprang Thomas C., William J., Sallie F. (Brinton), Anna E. (wife of Gen. Cockrell, of Missouri), Jane M., Mollie (deceased), Kate (deceased), John B. and Alice (Meyer). October 13, 1874, John B. Mann married Miss Bettie F., daughter of James M. and Mary A. (Banta) Clarke, of Mercer County (born July 4, 1854), and to them have been born Owen R., Hugh J.,

Mattie Marie and Bessie C. Mr. Mann owns 256 acres of productive land, which is kept in a good state of cultivation. He is a deacon in the Southern Presbyterian Church, and in politics is a Democrat.

GEORGE D. MARSHALL, farmer and merchant, was born November 11, 1846, and is the third of seven children born to Josiah B. and Mahala J. (Dodson) Marshall. Josiah Marshall, paternal grandfather of our subject, was a native of Virginia and came to Kentucky and settled in Nelson County, where he died about 1843. He was one of the extensive and well-to-do farmers of the county. Jonathan Dodson, subject's maternal grandfather, was a native Kentuckian, born in the latter part of the eighteenth century. He commenced a farmer's life a poor boy and was highly successful, amassing quite a competency, and was a strict member of the Methodist Episcopal Church. He died about 1861. Josiah B. Marshall was born in Nelson County April 28, 1817, and died in May, 1885; he followed the pursuits of the farm until 1873, when he established a store at Stringtown, and carried on the mercantile business at that place in conjunction with his farming until his death. He was a man who had few or no enemies, and a host of friends; while not a member of any church, yet he was a firm believer in the Christian faith, and led a true, honorable and upright life. His son, Geo. D. Marshall, a native of Nelson County, remained at home and assisted his parents on the farm until he attained the age of seventeen years; he then entered, as a student, the Indiana State University, which he attended one year; the following year he was in attendance at St. Mary's College, after which he immediately engaged in teaching. November 11, 1868, his marriage with Annie McCrocklin was solemnized and to their union five children have been born, of which these three are living: Minnie G., Clyde O. and Walter E. In 1869 he embarked in the mercantile business in Carroll County, where he continued two years. He was then tendered and accepted the position of traveling salesman for V. Overall & Co., of Louisville; upon the termination of his year's contract with them he traveled for S. S. Clarke for one year. He then entered the store of his father at Stringtown. Upon the death of the latter he succeeded him in business, and also inherited a farm of 100 acres. He and family are members of the Methodist Episcopal Church. In politics he is a Democrat.

ROBERT H. MARTIN was born March 19, 1837, and is the youngest of eight children born to William and Matilda (Young) Martin, natives of Shelby and Garrard Counties, Ky., and of English and Irish descent respectively. William L. Martin was born about 1776, his parents being among the earliest pioneers of the "dark and bloody ground." In early life he learned the tailor's trade, which he followed all his life. While yet a young man he removed to Garrard County, Ky., where he was married; thence went to Burkesville, Cumberland County, where he remained only a few years. He then moved to Campbellsville, Taylor Co., Ky., where he resided until his death, in March, 1841. His father, William Martin, was a native of Virginia, and was one of the friends and associates of Daniel Boone. Mrs. Matilda Martin departed this life May 17, 1884, in her ninety-fifth year. Her father, Patrick Young, was born in Ireland, and at the age of twelve years came to the United States, first settling in Virginia, and thence removing to Garrard County, Ky. Robert H. Martin was born in what is now Taylor County, Ky., and has acquired an excellent practical business education. When he was only four years old he lost his father, and at the age of sixteen he was employed as a salesman in a dry goods store at Campbellsville, remaining until 1863, when he was appointed postmaster at the same place, and held that office until 1867, when he resigned that and again engaged in the dry goods business as a clerk, continuing the same until February,. 1877, when he was again appointed postmaster, and held the office until 1885, since which time he has been engaged in the grocery trade. He has also been engaged in the fire insurance business since 1868, and part of the time was police judge of Campbellsville. Mr. Martin was married November 17, 1864, to Miss Sophia S. Wheat, a native of Columbia, Adair Co., Ky., born January 30, 1844. She is a daughter of Eli and Elizabeth (Allen) Wheat. Three sons and four daughters have blessed this union; their names are as follows: Bettie (deceased), Anna A., Henry H., Willie (deceased), Mary K. Y., Robert T. and Matilda. Both Mr. Martin and wife are, and have been for many years members of the Methodist Episcopal Church, in which church he has held numerous official positions, and has been superintendent of the Sunday-school for the past fifteen years. He is also a bright member of the Masonic fraternity, having advanced to the council degree of R. & S. M., and has officiated for many years, both as W. M. of his lodge and H. P. of the chapter. In politics he is a Republican.

J. H. MATHENY was born May 18, 1831. His father, F. G. Matheny, a native of Bourbon County, and born February 9, 1808, was a dry goods merchant. He first hired to C. C. Chinn, a merchant of Harrodsburg, for his food and clothing in 1820, and in 1827, when in his nineteenth year, purchased a small stock of goods and embarked in business at Salvisa, in Mercer County. He was married in 1828, to Miss Mary E., a daughter of Maj. Samuel and Nancy (Tilford) McCoun. The McCoun family were in Mercer County during the Indian troubles, living in the fort at Harrodsburg, and Joseph McCoun, while a youth, was captured by the Indians and burned at the stake. Samuel McCoun was the son of John and Margaret McCoun, who emigrated from Virginia to Kentucky. Nancy (Tilford) McCoun was a niece of Maj. John Tilford; president of the Northern Bank of Lexington for thirty years. Samuel McCoun was adjutant for Gen. Andrew Jackson at the battle of New Orleans, and made a fortune flatboating on the Kentucky, Ohio and Mississippi Rivers. F. G. Matheny sold a line of general merchandise in Salvisa more than thirty years. Several years of this time he sold $100,000 worth of goods per annum. The late war swept nearly all of his accumulations away, but in 1863 he embarked in the dry goods business in Harrodsburg in a moderate way. The names of his children are Samuel M., of Louisville; J. H.; W. M., attorney and real estate agent of Dallas, Ark.; F. G., Jr., who left with Gen. Walker in the Nicaragua expedition and has not been heard from since; Dan W. artist, of Sedalia, Mo.; L. T., real estate agent in Chicago; Joseph Stiles, a graduate of Bacon College, who died in his twenty-first year, 1859; Nannie, who died in her seventeenth year; Elizabeth, wife of James Lowry, of Springfield, Mo., and Charles F., a farmer of Cherokee County, Kas. F. G. Matheny, who was a member of the Presbyterian Church, died in 1873, and his widow, who was totally blind the last twelve years of her life, and also a member of the Presbyterian Church, died in 1881, in her seventy-fourth year. Michael M. Matheny, grandfather of J. H. Matheny, emigrated from Harper's Ferry, Va., to Bourbon County, Ky., and shortly afterward moved to Mercer County. His marriage occurred in Virginia to Miss Rachael Ruby, and they were the parents of four sons: F. A., F. G., L. T. and A. M., who is living at Stephensport, Ky. Mr. Matheny, who was an old time tavern-keeper and a farmer, is buried with his wife in the northern part of the county.

The Matheny family are of Scotch-French origin. J. H. Matheny in boyhood received a commercial education, partly at Salvisa, in his native county of Mercer, but finished in a commercial school in Cincinnati. When in his eighth year he began selling goods under the instruction of his father, who was said to be the best salesman in the county. This has been his business since, and in 1854 he was admitted into his father's business as partner, which continued ten years. He then removed to Harrodsburg and formed a partnership in the dry goods business with Augustus Jones, continuing three years, and during the four years following did business again with his father. In 1874 Mr. Matheny formed a partnership with W. J. Poteet, which, under the firm name of Matheny & Poteet, still exists. On May 10, 1855, Mr. Matheny was married to Miss Sarah L., a daughter of Thomas and Ann E. (Ferguson) Broaddus, natives of Mercer County. She was a step-daughter of Col. John McAfee. To the marriage have been born four children: Mary I., wife of John Curry; Annie D., deceased wife of W. D. Powell; Henry Eugene, and Eddie H., who died in childhood. Mr. and Mrs. Matheny are both members of the Presbyterian Church.

DR. WM. E. MATTINGLY. Among the first comers to what is now Marion County, Ky., was Leonard Mattingly, who came from Maryland. Basil Mattingly, son of Leonard and grandfather of Dr. Wm. E., was reared to manhood in Kentucky, married Polly Hagen and reared a large family, from whom sprang many of the leading families of the county. Of their eight children but two are now living, viz.: Edward H. and Mrs. Mary Jane Spalding. Edward H., who is one of the most highly esteemed citizens of Marion County, was born here in 1818 and married Miss Alethia Spalding, daughter of Thomas and Susan (Abell) Spalding. The subject of this sketch is the eldest of their family of eight children. He was reared in Marion County and chiefly educated at St. Mary's College, in which institution he was afterward employed as a teacher. He began the study of medicine at the age of twenty-three, performing the usual preparatory reading with Drs. Cleaver and McElroy. In 1867 he entered the medical department of the Louisville University, from which he graduated in 1869. He then located in Lebanon, Ky., for the practice of his profession, and has built up a desirable practice, and surrounded himself with a host of friends. He is a member of the Beech Fork District Medical Association and of the Catholic Church.

BENJ. F. MATTINGLY was born October 11, 1828, and is a son of Benjamin and Susan (Graves) Mattingly. Benj. Mattingly was born near Lebanon, December 25, 1792. He was a substantial farmer, was a soldier of 1812 and was in Gen. Harrison's army. He was an active and prominent Democrat, died April 9, 1854, and was a son of John Mattingly, of Maryland, who married a Miss Fenwick and immigrated to Marion County and settled first near Lebanon, as early as 1790; later located on 100 acres one mile west of St. Mary's, which he partially improved and died in 1804, aged about forty years. He was a son of Leonard Mattingly, who married a Miss Hagen, both natives of Maryland. He came to Kentucky, settled and died, where Benjamin F. was born and now resides, in Loretto Precinct, Marion County. He had a large apple orchard and manufactured considerable cider and brandy, of which he was particularly fond, and made in large quantities for that early day. He was of English origin and his ancestors were supposed to have immigrated to Maryland during Lord Baltimore's reign. The first who came to America were mechanics, after which they turned their attention to plain farming, which has continued to be the occupation of successive generations. The mother of Benjamin F. was born near Roan's Knob, in Nelson County, Ky., 1794, and was a daughter of John and Susan (Noble) Graves, natives of Maryland and of English origin, who immigrated to Nelson County as early as 1790 and engaged in farming. Benjamin F. Mattingly, a native of Loretto Precinct, Marion County, was reared on a farm and received a liberal education at St. Mary's College; at the age of seventeen he commenced business on his own account at farming and distilling. In 1860, with his brother, he located and engaged quite extensively in distillery business at Louisville; in 1880 sold his interest to his brother and immediately erected another distillery with a capacity of 1,000 bushels. With the exception of four years' residence in Louisville Mr. Mattingly has resided all his life about one mile west of St. Mary's on 140 acres improved with a fine residence and an apple orchard of seventy-five acres of fine winter varieties, and he is of the fourth generation owning the old homestead. Mr. Mattingly also owns a number of other valuable farms in Marion County to the extent of 3,000 acres, all of which (excepting a small legacy) he has accumulated by his own energies and careful management. He also runs a saw and grist-mill. Mr. Mattingly is a liberal giver to any enterprise enhancing and advancing the interest of his community. August 9, 1864, he was united in marriage to Kate Willett, of Nelson County, a daughter of George and Catharine (Miles) Willett. To this union thirteen children were born: Agnes. Mary (deceased), Imelda, Francis X., Bernard (deceased), Benedict (deceased), Teresa, Anna Mary, Paul, Veronica, Margaret, Mary and Gertrude. Mr. and Mrs. Mattingly are consistent members of the Roman Catholic Church. In politics he is a Democrat.

GEORGE W. MAUPIN was born March 7, 1842, six miles south of Richmond, and is a son of George W. and Mary (Walker) Maupin, to whom seven children were born; six sons lived to be grown. George W. Maupin, Sr., married for his second wife Susan Haley, by whom four sons and three daughters were born. Mr. Maupin was born in 1807, four miles south of Richmond. He was a prosperous farmer, was the owner of a large family of slaves, traded extensively and was a great hunter. He represented his county one term in the Legislature, and died in 1868. He was a son of David Maupin, who was born in Albemarle County, Va., and who served as a common soldier in the war for independence and was at the surrender of Yorktown; he came to Madison County, Ky., as early as 1785, where he became a prosperous farmer. His second wife was Margaret McWilliams, who was the last Revolutionary pensioner in Madison County. She was the grandmother of George W., Jr. Mr. Maupin was in his day one of the best and most prosperous farmers in the county. His father came from France. The family held to the Christian or Campbellite faith and in politics were Democratic. Mrs. Mary Maupin was a daughter of William Walker, who married an Estill, who were among the first settlers of Kentucky. George W. Maupin, whose name heads this sketch, was reared on a farm and received a common-school education. In September, 1862, he enlisted in Capt. Terrill's company, Ninth Kentucky Confederate Regiment, and participated in all its principal engagements and many skirmishes. He was elected second lieutenant and resigned in 1863, on account of ill health. He returned to his home and resumed farming, which he continued successfully till 1886, when he was elected jailor of Madison County, which position he now fills. He was married March 18, 1873, to Fannie Stives, of Madison County, daughter of John W. and Mary (Ballard) Stives, natives of Madison County. Mr. Stives was a merchant. To this marriage have been born six children:

Jennings W., Horace, William, Mary P., (deceased), James McCreary (deceased), and Jessamine P. Mr. and Mrs. Maupin are members of the Christian Church. He is a member of the F. & A. M.; was a member of the Grange, and cast his first presidential vote for Gen. McClellan.

JAMES W. MAXEY (deceased) was born September 28, 1847, in Hart County, Ky., and was a son of David W. and Jane (Whitman) Maxey, natives of Kentucky. David W. Maxey was a substantial farmer and slave owner, was a strong and uncompromising Union man during the war, and for his pronounced Union sentiments was killed by guerrillas. James W. Maxey was reared on a farm till sixteen years of age, when he moved to Munfordsville and learned telegraphing. In 1868 he located in New Haven, as agent and operator for the Louisville & Nashville Railway. He also had an interest in a mercantile business, and served as postmaster seven or eight years before his death, which occurred November 16, 1882. He was the only son of four children. He was married, December 13, 1871, to Attie Miller, a daughter of Thos. H. and Susan B. (Vernon) Miller, natives of Nelson and Hardin County, Ky., respectively. Mr. Miller was a blacksmith and owner of about twenty slaves. He was born in 1819, and died in October, 1884. He was a son of Wm. Miller, who came from Pennsylvania, and was one of the earliest settlers of Nelson County; was a farmer and blacksmith, followed flatboating in an early day on the Rolling Fork and Ohio River, and was the owner of a family of slaves. He married Casandra Magruder. He was of German origin and his wife of Irish. Wm. Miller was a son of Jacob Miller. Susan B. Vernon was born in Hardin County, and a daughter of Richard and Frances (Bledsoe) Vernon, born respectively in Hardin and Scott Counties, Ky. Richard Vernon was an extensive farmer and slaveholder, served several terms as sheriff, and was a son of Anthony Vernon, who married Frances Quinn, both natives of Virginia, and among the first settlers of Hardin County, Ky. Mr. and Mrs. Maxey had born to them three children: Sue Hite, Eugenia Mattie, and James W. Mr. Maxey was one of the live, active and substantial business men of New Haven. He was strictly moral, highly respected by all who knew him, and was an active member of the F. & A. M. In politics he was an uncompromising Republican. Mrs. Maxey is an active and devoted member of the Baptist Church.

EUSEBIUS S. MAYES, farmer and stock dealer, was born August 6, 1835, being the eldest son in a family of four children born to Archibald S. and Harriet P. (McElroy) Mayes. His paternal grandfather, Robert Mayes, was born in Virginia, March 26, 1766; immigrated to Kentucky in 1808, and settled in what is now Taylor County; his marriage to Miss Margaret McClanahan occurred in his native State in 1790. In the county of his adoption he became quite an extensive farmer and slave owner. Archibald S., his son, was born near Staunton, Va., April 1, 1800, making him eight years of age when his parents came to Kentucky. He was reared on the farm, and early inured to the hardships which are incident to the settlement and clearing of a new country. October 9, 1828, he married Miss Harriet P. McElroy in Marion County. In early manhood he engaged in buying, trading in, and shipping stock, principally mules, in which business he continued almost all the rest of his life. In 1851 he purchased the farm in Washington County on which his widow and heirs now live. He was a consistent member of the Presbyterian Church, and died a firm believer in its hopes, October 27, 1883. Eusebius S. Mayes was born in Marion County, and made his home with his parents until the breaking out of the late civil war. October 9, 1858, he married Miss Mary L. Green. She died October 22, 1862, and of the three children born to their union none survive. December 18, 1866, he married Miss Mary A. Curry of Harrodsburg, Ky.; to their union eight children have been born, of whom seven are now living: Paulina, Kate, Mat, Mary, Eusebius, Annie and Archibald. Until the year 1862, Mr. Mayes lived with his parents; he then embarked in the mercantile business at Lebanon, in which he continued until 1874, when he engaged in buying and shipping cattle to the West, in which business he has since remained. He is a Democrat in politics; belongs to the Masonic and Knights of Honor fraternities, and he and wife are members of the Presbyterian Church.

MERCER GRAIN & COAL CO. (Tabler & Cogar) began business in Harrodsburg in 1879. The capital at that time was $20,000, and the company erected an elevator with a capacity of 20,000 bushels of grain, and leased the branch railroad to Harrodsburg Junction. They handled coal also, and did a large business from the beginning, the company being composed of Jno. B. Thompson, Jas. A. Tomlinson, J. H. Wilson and J. E. Cogar. They built another elevator in 1880, at a cost of $12,000, with a capacity of 70,000 bushels; and they handled 100,000 bushels of coal per annum, and 100,000 bushels of grain. The lease of the railroad expired in 1884, and the Mercer Grain & Coal Co. sold their elevators to Messrs. Tabler & Cogar at $18,000 cash. Dr. Tabler owns about 90 per cent of the railroad to Harrodsburg Junction, and runs it as his own private enterprise; but the elevators and coal business are run by Messrs. Tabler & Cogar. In 1884 they erected a large frame tobacco warehouse 160 feet long, 60 feet wide and 54 feet high, in which they do a large re-handling business, having handled this year 300 hogsheads. They have, also, this year handled 250,000 bushels of wheat, double the quantity handled in any preceding year, and their elevators, warehouse and other property invoices $32,500. They have invested in grain, coal and tobacco $100,000, and there is no business in the State outside of Louisville that compares with that of the Mercer Grain & Coal Co. They generally have in their employ twenty-two men.

J. E. COGAR was born in Jessamine County, Ky., September 19, 1836. His father, Thomas Cogar, who was a steamboat captain on the Kentucky and Ohio Rivers, was born in Rockingham County, Va., in 1797. He was a man of limited education and began life in moderate circumstances on the river. He was a pilot on the steamer "Ocean," the first boat that ever ran on the Kentucky River; after running pilot two years he became captain of the "John Drenom," which position he held two years. He began river life by learning to pilot flatboats, and several times after piloting a flatboat to New Orleans walked back home through the forest, then infested with Indians. He finally embarked in the commission business at "Cogar's Landing" on the Kentucky River, the place being named for him. He was married to Miss Ruth, a daughter of Jesse Ewing, of Jessamine County, and the marriage was blessed by seven children: M. H., who enlisted in the Ninth Missouri Infantry as private, and was killed at Vicksburg; T. M., steamboat pilot since 1844, on the Kentucky and Ohio Rivers; John S., a carpenter living in Jessamine County; Amanda T. (Edgerton), living at Highbridge, Ky.; Elizabeth (Robb), living in Nicholasville; Mary C., living also in Nicholasville, and Jesse E. Thomas Cogar represented the county of Jessamine two terms in the Legislature, being elected on the Democratic ticket; never was rich in life. He died in 1884, and his widow, a member of the Presbyterian Church, is still living in Jessamine County, in the eightieth year of her age. The Cogar family are of German and Irish origin. Jesse E. Cogar received a very limited education in the country schools of Jessamine County, and began life on his own account at the age of fifteen. His occupation at that time was in the commission business, and he was in business by himself at Cogar's Landing twenty-one years, making and losing a great deal of money alternately, but in 1876 removed to Shaker's Landing and resumed the commission business, removing the next year to Highbridge. His next move was to Harrodsburg. In 1869 Mr. Cogar was married to Miss Lucy A., a daughter of Draper Newton, a farmer of Mercer County. To Mr. and Mrs. Cogar has been born one child, D. N., who has been, since ten years of age doing a junk business. When he was thirteen years of age, an act of the Legislature was passed making him in law of age, and since that time he has accumulated an estate of $4,000. He is now sixteen years of age, and owns a part in and has charge of a saw-mill worth $9,600. He owns a one-third interest in the business.

MERCER NATIONAL BANK. This institution began business in June, 1881, in the room formerly occupied by McBrayer, Trapuale & Co., bankers, in the Commercial Hotel building. The capital (cash) was $60,000, but increase of business soon warranted the directors in increasing the capital stock to $100,000. Subscription books were accordingly opened for the purpose, and in a short time the capital stock had reached $140,000. After the first year's business, the bank purchased, from William Payne, a lot on the corner of Poplar and Main Streets, and erected a handsome two-story iron-front brick building, at a cost of $7,000. May 27, 1885, this building was destroyed by fire, and immediately a new, much handsomer, more commodious building was erected on the ruins of the old one, at a cost of $10,000. This is one of the handsomest buildings in Harrodsburg; is of brick, iron and stone, has two stories and is fire-proof, with all modern conveniences and appliances. It has a fire-proof vault, in which is a burglar-proof steel safe, with one of Hall's latest improved time-lock attachments. The bank issues semi-annual dividends to its stockholders, which have been, during the five years of its existence, 3 per cent at each issue, and such has been the financial success of the institution that its capital stock is very much in demand at 115. It is one of the safest banking institutions in this part of the State. The officers are J. H. Moore, president; R. H. Cecil, vice-president; J. K. Sumrall, attorney, and Robert C. Nuckols, cashier. The directors are J. K.

Sumrall, R. H. Cecil, J. M. Forsythe, J. L. Cassell, David Walter, J. H. Moore, W. E. Gill, Joseph Royers and H. C. Williams. Robert C. Nuckols, the cashier, is a native of Shelbyville, Ky., and was born January 7, 1852. His father, George W. Nuckols, was a practicing physician for fifty years in Shelby, and adjoining counties, living many years in Shelbyville. He was a native of Scott County, Ky., whence he moved to Shelby County, and his wife, Abigail (Butler) Nuckols, was born near Augusta, Me., and was married to Dr. Nuckols while on a visit to Shelbyville, Ky. They were the parents of four children: George, commercial traveler for Samuel Woodside & Co., of Cincinnati; Annie P., wife of G. Helm Hobbs, farmer, of Nelson County; Charles, who died in childhood, and Robert C. Dr. Nuckols was married in early life, prior to the marriage above mentioned to Miss Thustin, but had no children by her. The practice of Dr. Nuckols was very large and lucrative, but he only left a small estate. He died in 1864 in his seventy-fourth year, and in life was a member of the Christian Church. His wife, who was a member of the Christian Church, died in 1854 in the thirty-fourth year of her age. Robert C. Nuckols was educated in the schools of Shelbyville under the tuition of Prof. Dodd, and entered Georgetown College in the fall of 1868. In January, 1870, while in the sophomore year, he went into the Farmers' Bank as clerk, which position he held until June, 1881, when he accepted the position he now holds. On February 27, 1873, he was united in marriage to Miss Lydia S. Viley, a daughter of Jackson and Mary Lou (Peak) Viley of Scott County. Mrs. Nuckols is second cousin to John C. Breckinridge, and related also to the Johnstons. To the marriage of Mr. and Mrs. Nuckols have been born two children: Jackson Cecil, born August 14, 1878, and Mary Louise, born June 12, 1882. Mr. Nuckols is a member of the Christian Church, while his wife is a member of the Baptist Church.

W. T. MERRITT was born September 9, 1824. His grandfather, Richard Merritt, was born near Hanover, Va., but came to Kentucky about the time of the organization of the State, and was one of the pioneers of Lincoln County. His death occurred in Garrard County, when the subject of this sketch was a small boy. Subject's father was Peter Merritt; he was born in Virginia and was brought to Kentucky when a mere child. He grew to manhood in Garrard County, was a farmer, and died in 1875, aged about eighty-three years. His wife, Nancy Merritt, was the daughter of James Hoskins, who came to Kentucky from Virginia several years before the present century. He was one of the first settlers of Lincoln County, and a man of considerable prominence. Mrs. Merritt was born in Virginia, and died in Garrard County in 1867 or 1868. The following are the names of the children born to Peter and Nancy Merritt: Jeremiah, Zedekiah, Zachariah, Zephaniah, Nancy, Hezekiah, Elizabeth, W. T., Peter and Isaiah. W. T. Merritt was born in Garrard County, and spent his youth and early manhood on his father's farm, and received a fair education in such schools as the country then afforded. He engaged in farming at the age of twenty-one and continued the same for nine years, when he effected a copartnership with his brother, Zachariah Merritt, in the goods business, which was continued several years at Fitchport; the firm also did a good lumber and coal business. At the end of about seven or eight years W. T. Merritt withdrew from the firm, and emigrated to Newton County, Ind., where he resided one year. He returned to Kentucky in 1860, and in August, 1862, enlisted in Company B, Third Kentucky United States Infantry, with which he served fourteen months. He was elected first lieutenant of his company, and was with the regiment in several engagements. Resigning his commission in 1862, he returned to Kentucky and purchased a farm in Jessamine County, upon which he lived four years; in 1868 he purchased his present large farm of 760 acres seven miles north of Springfield, upon which he has since resided. He is an extensive stock raiser, and one of the leading citizens of his adopted county. He was originally a Whig in politics, and cast his first vote for Henry Clay at Paoli, Ind. He is now a Democrat. Mr. Merritt was married September 5, 1862, in Adair County, Ky., to Nancy T. Todd, daughter of William and Patsey (Bradshaw) Todd. The children of this marriage were seven in number, the following of whom are living: Eliza, wife of Alfred Dohoney; William P., Annie E., and Addie Merritt. Mrs. Merritt was born February 18, 1836, and is the second of a family of six children. Her father, William Todd, was the son of Robert and Jenny (Yates) Todd. Robert Todd was born in Pennsylvania, but early came to Kentucky and settled in Fayette County near Lexington. He afterward moved to Adair County, where his death occurred in 1729. He was an accomplished surveyor, and filled several official positions, at one time serving as county judge of Adair County. William Todd was a successful farmer, and died in Adair County, in

December, 1877, at the age of seventy-two years. Patsey (Bradshaw) Todd was born in the above county, and died in February, 1882, aged seventy-two years. Mr. and Mrs. Merritt are both active members of the Christian Church.

DR. JOHN M. MEYER was born December 1, 1817, in Barnwell District, South Carolina, where he was reared to manhood. In 1835 he entered Centre College, Danville, Ky., where he graduated in the regular course in 1840. He then commenced the study of medicine at Lexington with Dr. Benjamin W. Dudley, and graduated from the medical department of Transylvania University in 1843. He located in Boyle County, on the Perryville pike four miles west of Danville, where he has since enjoyed an extensive and lucrative practice. His father, Michael Meyer, was born in 1780, in Barnwell District, South Carolina, was a planter and slave-holder, and died about 1836, at the age of fifty-six years. His brothers were Jonathan and David. Their father was Davis Meyer, born in Pennsylvania and died at the age of ninety years. Michael married Miss Rebecca Jackson (thought to be related to Gen. Andrew Jackson), and from their union sprang Anslem D., James J., Dr. John M., Elizabeth (Marshall), Rebecca (Love), and Martha (Stallings). December 12, 1844, the Doctor was married to Miss Mary R., daughter of Samuel and Maria (Ball) McDowell, of Boyle County (born July 18, 1823, died July 1, 1885), and to them were born Joseph, Maria Ball (McGoodwin), Florence, Mary (Lyne), Oscar, Thornwell and Carolina. The Doctor owns and resides on a farm of 200 acres of well improved and productive land. He has a fine herd of thirty registered Jersey cattle, among them one that is classed as a twenty-pound cow. Dr. Meyer is an Ancient Odd Fellow. He has for thirty years been elder in the Presbyterian Church. He lost thirty-five slaves as a result of the late war. In politics he is a Democrat.

RICHARD C. MILBURN was born January 28, 1830. His father, Israel Milburn, was born in Marion County in 1801. He married Miss Margaret Thurman in 1822, and to them were born five sons and three daughters: William, John H., Israel, Thomas C., Richard C., Civilla (Curtsinger), Mary A. and Elizabeth. Israel Milburn died in 1831, and his widow subsequently married Shadrick Inman; she died in 1855, leaving by her second marriage three sons and one daughter. Israel Milburn was a stone-mason, and one of the best of his craft. He was a member of the Baptist Church, and a man of strict business principles and unbending integrity. He was a soldier in the war of 1812, and participated in the battle of New Orleans. His father, Robert Milburn, was a minister of the Methodist Episcopal Church, and proclaimed the gospel throughout Kentucky at a day when the Indians were numerous and troublesome, and when the settlers took firearms to church. Rev. Robert Milburn died some time in the first decade of the present century; his father, Hobart Milburn, was a native of Virginia and came to Kentucky prior to the war of the Revolution, in which he engaged. Richard C. Milburn received a common-school education in his native county of Marion, and remained on the home farm until he attained his majority. Having learned the blacksmith's trade, he carried on that business in Kentucky and later in Dallas, Tex., after which, in 1861, he returned to Kentucky and located at Haysville, in Marion County, where he remained for a few years, then removed to Springfield, and after three years returned to his present location in Precinct No. 2, where he purchased land in 1867 and carried on farming in connection with blacksmithing. His farm of 170 acres is well kept and improved and very productive. He was married, February 25, 1852, to Miss Elizabeth Brown. They are the parents of four sons and two daughters: Thomas, Frederick, Henry, William B., Sallie, wife of John Ware of Bradfordsville, and Minnie. Elizabeth (Brown) Milburn was born December 29, 1829. She is a daughter of Alexander and Margaret (Mouser) Brown, both natives of Kentucky. Mr. and Mrs. Milburn and all their family are consistent members of the Baptist Church in which Mr. Milburn has for thirty years held the office of deacon. He is a member of the Masonic fraternity, which he joined in 1854. His political views are Democratic.

WILLIAM B. MILBURN was born November 25, 1858, and is the youngest of four sons and two daughters born to the union of Richard C. and Elizabeth (Brown) Milburn. William B. Milburn received a good education in the schools of his native county of Marion, and in 1879 took up the profession of teaching, which he soon after abandoned as uncongenial with his tastes; he then returned to the trade of blacksmith, which trade he had learned with his father previous to his career as a teacher. He is yet in partnership with his brothers, and doing a successful and lucrative trade in blacksmithing and wagon and carriage making at Bradfordsville. February 28, 1883, he was united in marriage with Miss Celesta F. Ware. They are the parents of one daughter, Myrtie M., born January 5, 1884, and one son, Wm. R. R., born April 20, 1886. Celesta (Ware) Milburn was born September 2, 1861. She is a native of Pulaski County, Ky., and a daughter of Rice Ware and Sarah (Cooper) Ware, of English lineage and natives of Pulaski County. Rice Ware is yet living, aged forty-four years; the mother died January 26, 1883, aged thirty-seven years. She was a daughter of Levi Cooper, whose father, Malachi Cooper, was a Baptist minister who came to Kentucky in 1796. He was pastor of the church at Somerset for many years and was much devoted to his religious duties, and highly esteemed by his people. He was a persistent worker in the temperance cause, and was one of the strongest pro-slavery men of his day. He reared a family of three sons and five daughters, of whom was Sarah, the mother of Celesta (Ware) Milburn. Sarah was also the name of the grandmother of Malachi Cooper. Mr. and Mrs. Milburn are members of the Baptist Church. He is a member of the I. O. G. T. and a worker in the temperance cause. His political views are Democratic, and he takes an interest in political affairs. In 1883 he was elected marshal of the village of Bradfordsville, and in that capacity served one year.

EDWARD L. MILES, born August 15, 1825, is a son of Henry and Ann (McAtee) Miles. Henry Miles was born in Maryland, came to Nelson County, Ky., with the earliest Catholic settlers, and was wounded in a fight with the Indians in coming down the Ohio River. He was not a wealthy man at the start but left an estate of 1,000 acres at his death in 1839 at the age of sixty-nine years. His father, Philip Miles, was a native of Maryland, of Scotch-Irish descent, and married a Miss O'Brian. Mrs. Ann Miles was a daughter of George McAtee, who married a Miss Hamilton of Maryland, and both came to Nelson County, Ky., at an early day. Edward L. Miles was born where he still resides in Nelson County, was educated at St. Joseph's College, Bardstown, and graduated in 1846. In May, 1848, he married Anna Bradford, daughter of David and Amanda (Davis) Bradford. David Bradford was an attorney and for many years was superintendent of the mint at New Orleans. After his marriage Mr. Miles purchased a farm near Bardstown, but five years later removed to the old homestead; about 1857 he went to Louisiana and purchased an interest in a sugar plantation of 1,000 acres; at the close

of the late war he sold his interest in the land and returned to New Hope, Ky., and in the winter of 1867–68 built a distillery, starting with a capacity of 200 bushels, which had been increased in 1881 to 1,000 bushels. In 1871, however, he sold out to Tom Shirley. At present he owns 1,000 acres of farming land, and his residence is a fine brick erected by his father over seventy years ago, but recently remodeled and enlarged. Mr. and Mrs. Miles are members of the church of Rome.

THOMAS W. MILLER was born December 3, 1811, in Madison County, Ky., and is a son of Daniel Miller and Susana Miller, nee Woods. These parents removed from Virginia to Kentucky near the close of the last century, the former being a native of Albemarle County, where he was born in 1764, and the latter a native of Nelson County, Va. They settled on a farm eight miles from Richmond, Ky., where their lives were passed. Daniel Miller was a Jeffersonian Democrat. He was long known as Maj. Miller, a title derived from his official commission as a major of Kentucky militia. He served three terms in the Kentucky Legislature, from Madison County, and died in that county in 1841. They had ten children: Mary, Robert, John (who was killed at the battle of Richmond, Ky.), James, Elizabeth, Susan (Hume), Margaret (Shackelford), Malinda (Shackelford), Thomas W. and Christopher Miller. Thomas W. Miller, of Stanford, is the only surviving member of this family. He was married in Madison County, in 1841, to Miss Mary J. Hocker, a daughter of Col. Nicholas Hocker, and they were residents of Madison County until 1864, when they removed to Lincoln County. They reared but one child, S. Malinda, the wife of J. S. Owsley, of Lincoln County.

ROBERT MILLER was born November 7, 1823, two miles east of Richmond, and is a son of Robert and Sallie (Estill) Miller, to whom four sons and three daughters were born, five of whom were reared, Robert being the sixth in order of birth. Robert Miller, the father, was born March 1, 1775, in Albemarle County, Va., and was brought to Madison County, Ky., by his parents in 1784, and settled at Oldtown, four miles south of Richmond. He became an active and leading farmer, conducted a hotel in Richmond in early life and served in the Kentucky Senate two terms; in politics he was a Whig and in religion was originally a Baptist, but later united with the Christian Church. He died June 21, 1861. He was a son of John and Jane (Delaney) Miller, who were natives of Albemarle County, Va., and early pioneers of Kentucky. John Miller was a captain under Washington in the war of independence. He reared a large family, of which there were seven sons. He built the first house in Richmond, which was a hotel; he also was a farmer. In politics he was a Whig and in religion a Presbyterian, of Scotch-Irish descent. Mrs. Sallie (Estill) Miller died in February, 1863, aged eighty-four years. She was a daughter of Capt. James and Rachel (Wright) Estill, who were natives of Albemarle County, Va. Robert Miller, Jr., was married March 24, 1859, to Elizabeth Miller, daughter of Harrison J. and Patsie I. (Field) Miller, natives of Madison County. H. J. Miller was educated for an attorney, but turned his attention to agricultural pursuits. He reared a family of two sons and six daughters, and died in January, 1863, aged fifty-six years; his widow still survives him at the age of seventy years. He was a son of Dr. Al Miller, who was born in Rockingham County, Va., who came to Madison County when a young man, and was one of the pioneer physicians of Richmond. He married Elizabeth Barnett, daughter of Col. James Barnett, of Revolutionary fame, and an early pioneer farmer of Madison County. Dr. Miller died at the age of ninety-two years. His eldest son is still living aged eighty years. Robert Miller and wife had born to them four bright children: Sallie E., Pattie F., Harry J. and Bessie. Mr. and Mrs. Miller are members of the Presbyterian Church. Mr. Miller located where he now resides, two miles east of Richmond, in 1863, on 400 acres of fine land, and has been devoting much time to cattle and mules. His first presidential vote was cast for Henry Clay, but since 1860 he has affiliated with the Democratic party.

THOMAS J. MILLER was born December 5, 1827, and is a son of Jacob and Amanda (Shaw) Miller, to whom four sons and three daughters were born, six of whom lived to be grown. Jacob Miller was born in 1801, on Rolling Fork, Nelson County. In his early day he was a flatboatman, became a farmer and slave-holder, a stock raiser and distiller from 1816 to 1860, and is still living. He is a son of Jacob and Elizabeth (Masterson) Miller, natives of Pennsylvania, who, as early as 1790, in flatboats floated as far as Louisville, walked from there to Nelson County, and for a time lived in the fort at New Hope. Mr. Miller next settled on Rolling Fork, where he entered about 1,000 acres. He was a united Baptist of Dutch descent, and was blind for about thirty years

before his death in 1850, at the age of about eighty. Mrs. Amanda Miller was born in Nelson County; she lost her parents when a child and was reared by Thomas Lewis. Thomas J. Miller was reared on a farm, and at sixteen commenced working and trading for himself; at twenty-one he engaged as salesman for Miller & Bowman, at Raywick, and remained twenty-eight months, after which, with Dr. Mitchell, engaged in merchandising in Raywick for two years; he then ran alone for a few years, sold and entered into stock trading and shipping to New Orleans. In 1859 he purchased 730 acres at New Hope, and entered farming, but shortly after resumed the mercantile business; he now owns two farms of 500 acres each, also one on Rolling Fork, Marion County, of 370 acres; another on Salt Lick Creek, Marion and La Rue Counties, of 370; also another in Marion and La Rue, of 725, and one of 150, in La Rue; also holds an interest in several other farms, and has been more or less engaged in stock raising. He is a heavy lender of money, and was also engaged in the distilling business near New Hope, but his distillery was destroyed by fire in 1884. He was one of the principals in the start of the distillery now owned by Miles & Co. At present he is a notary. Mr. Miller was married in June, 1870, to Alice Humphrey, a daughter of Simon and Caroline (Head) Humphrey, who were natives of Nelson County. Mr. Humphrey, of German origin, was a farmer, and served as sheriff and deputy sheriff for eighteen or twenty years. Mr. and Mrs. Miller had born to them six children: Anna, Sadonie, Caroline, Mary Willie, Thomas J. and McKay. Mr. Miller is an active Democrat and cast his first presidential vote for Lewis Cass in 1848; with his wife he is an active member of the Baptist Church.

BENJAMIN H. MILLER, deceased, was born August 10, 1835, on Rolling Fork, in Nelson County, and a son of Jacob and Amanda (Shaw) Miller. B. H. Miller was united in marriage, April 9, 1868, to Julia Pottinger, of Nelson County, a daughter of Thomas J. and Vienna (Ramey) Pottinger, to whom three sons and three daughters were born. Thomas J. Pottinger was born July 29, 1820, in New Haven. He is a good substantial farmer, owned a large number of slaves when the war broke out, and is the sixth of seven sons and three daughters born to Samuel and Lucinda (Jameson) Pottinger. Samuel Pottinger was born in 1797, where T. J. Pottinger now resides, two miles northwest of New Hope, on Pottinger's Creek.

He owned all of the land from New Haven to New Hope, five miles east. In 1818 he laid out New Haven and built the first house, which was a warehouse. He also ran several distilleries and mills. He died in September, 1832. His father, Samuel Pottinger, of German descent, was born in Prince George County, Md., in 1747, immigrated to Kentucky about 1775 and settled on Pottinger's Creek, where he entered about 1,200 acres of land and built a fort, where he located, near New Hope close to a large spring, now owned by T. J. Pottinger. By this spring he built the first brick house ever built in Nelson County, which was in 1788. The house is now occupied by T. J. Pottinger and seems good for another century. He married Elizabeth Withrow, participated in some of the Indian wars, reared a family of three sons and three daughters, and died in 1830. Mr. and Mrs. Miller had born six children to bless their union: Ramey, Birdie, Vienna, Naomi, Attie and Ben Hardin; were active members of the Baptist Church. Mr. Miller, by his activity and energy, succeeded in leaving 1,200 acres of fine river land to his widow. He also owned an interest in a distillery near New Hope and owned other securities in considerable amount; was a member of the F. & A. M. and died April 29, 1881. His wife was educated at the Baptist Female College, Bardstown, from which she graduated in 1866. She now manages the farm, which is embellished with one of the finest brick residences in Nelson County.

WILLIAM H. MILLER was born in 1842 and is a native of Lincoln County, Ky. His father was James Miller, who was born in Madison County in 1800; came in his early manhood to Lincoln County, settling in the northern part, where he engaged in farming. James Miller married Miss Frances M. Harris and reared a family of nine children, of whom seven are living. He died in Lincoln County in 1869 and his wife died in 1880, at the age of seventy-eight years. William H. Miller is the youngest member of this family; was educated in the common schools of his county, and at Centre College, of Danville, Ky. But before completing the course at that institution he abandoned his studies to champion the cause of the Confederacy, and in 1862 he enlisted in Company B, of the Sixth Kentucky Cavalry, the fortunes of which command he shared until he was captured at Cheshire, Ohio, in 1863. In the following year he made his escape from the Federal prison at Chicago, Ill., and rejoined Gen. Morgan in Virginia, remaining until the fatal day that terminated

Gen. Morgan's life, at Greenville, Tenn., at which time Mr. Miller received a severe wound. He was discharged in 1865 and soon after returned to his Kentucky home, and having decided upon the profession of the law, he entered the office of Squire Turner, of Richmond, Ky., under whom he performed his preparatory reading. He was regularly admitted to practice in September, 1866, and soon after located at Stanford, in Lincoln County. In 1868 he was elected clerk of the circuit court, and during his incumbency, in connection with M. C. Saufley, edited the *Central Dispatch*. In 1873 he was appointed assistant clerk of the House of Representatives, and in 1874 was defeated for the office of circuit court clerk of Lincoln County. In politics Mr. Miller is a Democrat, and was presidential elector for the Eighth Congressional District of Kentucky in 1876, and has served his county as county attorney one term, being elected thereto in 1878. He is a member of the I. O. O. F. and of the A. F. & A. M. He was married in 1879 to Miss Catherine Portman, daughter of M. C. Portman, of Stanford, Ky.

WILLIAM H. MILLER was born October 22, 1852, in Madison County, Ky., and is the eighth of six sons and four daughters now living born to Christopher I. and Talitha (Harris) Miller. The eldest is Sarah W.; the second, Robert D., who entered the Confederate Army in 1862 and joined in with two companies of soldiers that were proceeding to Central Kentucky, when they were ambushed and routed on Pine Mountain; losing his horse, Robert D. made a safe retreat, temporarily, but seeing no chance of escape, surrendered; was paroled and soon exchanged and joined Morgan's command; was again captured on the Ohio raid and taken to Camp Morton; thence to Camp Douglas, escaping from a car on the road from Camp Morton to Camp Douglas. He called to see his parents, but finding it unsafe, he went to Minnesota, visited Idaho and Montana, and afterward located at Benton County, Ind. The third child was James C., who was also in Morgan's command and was captured on the Ohio raid; the fourth, John T.; the sixth is Christopher I., followed by Susan W., William H., Mary E. and Elizabeth F. The father of these children was born December 20, 1813, on Hickory Lick Creek, Madison County. He was a skillful blacksmith, a good farmer, and in politics a Democrat. He was the son of Daniel Miller, who was born in Albemarle County, Va., May 28, 1764, and who married Susan Woods of Nelson County, Va., No-

vember 28, 1792, and in a few years after he
moved to Madison County, Ky., and located
on Drowning Creek, where he lived until his
death, April 23, 1841. Daniel Miller and
wife had ten children: Polly; Robert; Gen.
John Miller, who was mortally wounded near
Mount Zion Church, Madison County, while
trying to rally a column of Union soldiers,
and whose remains lie in the Richmond Cemetery; James; Elizabeth; Susannah; Margaret; Malinda; Thomas W. and Christopher
I. Daniel Miller was a son of Robert Miller, who reared a family of three sons and
six daughters. The sons were John, Thomas
and Daniel. Robert Miller was a brother of
Col. John Miller, who immigrated to and located and built the first house in Richmond.
Robert Miller married Peggy Maupin, who
was of French parentage. Mrs. Talitha
(Harris) Miller was born March 17, 1815, on
Drowning Creek, Madison County. She died
January 2, 1882, and was the daughter of
Christopher (first judge of Madison County
Court) and Sallie (Wallace) Harris of Albemarle County, Va. Christopher Harris was
a son of John and Margaret (Maupin) Harris, natives of Virginia, who came to Kentucky as early as 1790, when Christopher
was a mere child. John Harris was a son of
Christopher Harris, a Baptist minister, who
married Miss McCord. William H. Miller
was reared on a farm and received only a
moderate English education. At the age of
eighteen he entered the county clerk's office
under George D. Shackelford in 1870. In
1872 he commenced riding deputy sheriff,
and one year later returned to county clerk's
office, where he remained until 1874, when
he entered the circuit clerk's office as deputy
and remained until April, 1879. He then
became a candidate for the office, and in
March, 1880, was appointed to fill an unexpired term. August of the same year he
was elected, and in 1886 re-elected. He
was married February 27, 1884, to Catherine
Oldham, a daughter of William K. and Catherine (Brown) Oldham, all natives of Madison County. William K. Oldham was a
farmer and a son of Hezekiah and Pollie
(Kavanaugh) Oldham, who were early pioneers of Madison County. Mr. and Mrs.
Miller are members of the regular Baptist
Church. He is a Democrat, politically.

NATHAN BRAXTON MILLER is the
son of James P. and Sarah A. (McClure)
Miller, natives of Russell County, and was
born at Millersville, Russell Co., Ky., February 13, 1860. James P. Miller, ex-
sheriff of Russell, was born March 19, 1826,
in Russell County, and was married, first to

Miss Louvenia Lester, a daughter of James
M. Lester, a native of Russell County, and
the marriage was blessed by two children:
William H. (deceased) and James O. (physician of Russell County). Mrs. Miller died
about 1858, and Mr. Miller's second marriage
was to Miss Sarah A. McClure, a daughter of
Nathan and Sallie (Kean) McClure, both natives of Russell County. Hon. Nathan McClure
was a member of the Kentucky Senate three
terms. The result of this second marriage
was the birth of eight children: Nathan B.
(the subject of this sketch), Louvenia (wife
of Dr. E. B. Kelsey), Dr. Samuel P., Bryan
S., Mary P., Sallie, Albert and Edward, all
of whom are living. Adam Miller, the grandfather of Nathan B. Miller, was an extensive
farmer and distiller, a man of considerable
wealth and a native of Russell County. He
was one of the most prominent men in his
day and was united in matrimony to Miss
Patience Whitson of Russell County, by
whom he had ten children. He lived to an
advanced age and left his family in fine circumstances. George Miller, the great grandfather of Nathan B., came from Germany and
came to Garrard County and settled near
Lancaster, Ky., in an early day, and later he
removed to Russell County, being among the
earliest settlers. The Miller family are of
Scotch-Dutch origin. James P. Miller is
still living in Russell County at Crocus, formerly Millersville, and is farming and selling merchandise. He was sheriff of Russell
County eighteen years. Nathan B. Miller,
a native of Russell County, but now a resident of Columbia, Adair County, attended
the common schools until eighteen years of
age, farming during the time school was not
in session. He attended the Columbia
Christian College in 1878 and 1881, and in
1880 attended the Burkesville Normal School,
also the normal school of Glasgow in 1883.
From there he obtained the appointment as
cadet to the United States Military Academy
at West Point; after attending eight months
he resigned; came home, and entered the
study of law under Hon. James Garnett, a
prominent lawyer of Columbia, Ky. He obtained his law license and was admitted to
the bar of Columbia, Adair County, November 20, 1884, since which time he has been
practicing his profession in the courts of
Adair and Russell Counties. He is a member of the Christian Church and is a stanch
member of the Democratic party. He was
married to Miss Ellen Kate Winfrey October
26, 1886. She is the daughter of the late
Maj. T. C. Winfrey, who was a prominent
lawyer of Kentucky

THOMAS R. MITCHELL was born July 24, 1842, on the farm where he now lives, near Camp Knox, in the southeast portion of Green County. He is the oldest of two sons and two daughters, viz.: Elizabeth C. (born May 5, 1844), Mary J. (born November 20, 1847, died February 18, 1863), and John A., Jr. (born June 11, 1850), born to John A., Sr., and Amelia E. (Coun) Mitchell, who were born respectively in the counties of Rockbridge and Washington, Va. John A. Mitchell was born December 23, 1801, was the second child and oldest son, and was brought by his parents, who immigrated in 1805, to the above mentioned place, and was reared in what was at that day but little more than a wilderness, where books, schools and church privileges were difficult to get. He did not have more than two years at school, but at an early age he became a fluent reader, and having a great admiration for such writers as Milton, Addison, Steele, Johnson and Pope, he became familiar with the English language, and could probably recite as many lines from their works as any man of his day, cultivating a taste for fine language which was natural to him in conversing or writing. He contributed largely to the support and portioning of his father's family of nine children. This accomplished, he was married to Amelia E. Coun, October 2, 1841, in Cumberland County, and succeeded his father at the homestead, and pursued the vocation of a farmer until infirmity overcame him. He survived his wife, who died February 1, 1863, some ten years. His father, Thomas Mitchell, was born on Buffalo Creek June 16, 1768, and was the youngest son, and was educated to law, but the death of his father changed his course in life and he returned to the farm. On February 12, 1799, he was married to Rachel Crawford, but he was soon seized with a desire to go to a new country. He sold his estate, and in company with his brother-in-law, Mr. Crawford, set out to cross the mountains with their teams for Kentucky, where they had bought 1,000 acres of land in the canebrake and heavy timber with which all the country was covered, which rendered it no small undertaking to open a farm and construct the necessary buildings and fences. Nothing short of great labor and indomitable energy could overcome such obstacles. He was a man of more than ordinary mental as well as physical capacity, and was considered the best informed historian of his time and section. His wife was born in Rockbridge County, Va., January 3, 1777,

and was the daughter of James and Catherine Crawford, and died December 23, 1842. He attained the age of eighty-six years, and died March 4, 1855. His father, John Mitchell, was born January 1, 1719, in the northern portion of Ireland, and was brought to America at two years of age. He married Margret Porter, who was born in 1733 and died in March, 1795. He died in November, 1789. He was the son of John Mitchell and Mary Boyd, who, as above stated, immigrated in 1721, and located in Lancaster County, Penn., but not being suited there, after about five years' residence removed to what was then Augusta County, Va., but was afterward formed into Rockbridge County, and located on Buffalo Creek, four miles from the natural bridge. His loyalty to the government of Great Britain he never renounced, but paid taxes to both it and the colonial government. Thomas R. Mitchell attained the years of manhood, attended the country schools until prevented by their close upon the breaking out of the war, which overturned all calculations, but through this period continued his labors on the farm until 1865, when he engaged in the business of dealer in leaf tobacco and also conducted a blacksmith shop, which in the following year were merged into general merchandising, and this he continued with the varying fortunes attending such vocation until 1872, when he resumed the tobacco business in connection with the farm, on which during this period he built comfortable buildings for a residence and business. On December 20, 1875, he was married to Mrs. H. Lewis Hutchison, of Owensboro, a daughter of Charles R. and Artitia (Howard) Moorman; the former was born in Breckenridge County, the latter in Daviess County. Mr. and Mrs. Mitchell have had four children born to them: Nellie, Mary, Thomas W. and Florence C. He and wife are members of the Presbyterian and Baptist Churches respectively. Mrs. Mitchell has one son by her former marriage, Richard W. Hutchison. Mr. Mitchell is a member of the Masonic fraternity, and in politics is a Republican.

THOMAS SHELTON MOBERLEY was born July 18, 1855, seven miles east of Richmond, and is a son of Dr. Thomas S. and Nancy (Lipscomb) Moberley, who had born to them three sons and two daughters, of whom Thomas S. is the only survivor. Dr. Thomas S. Moberley was born May 15, 1804, on the same farm on which his son Thomas S. was born. He graduated from the medical department of the Transylvania University, and was one of the most successful practitioners in Madison County. He was also one of the earliest engaged in the breeding of mules, which took the premium at the world's fair in Woodford County, and commanded the highest price of any ever raised in Madison County. He acquired a handsome fortune, and died December 14, 1884, a member of the Hardshell Baptist Church. His father, Richard Moberley, was born in Virginia, was a Baptist minister, and came to Kentucky with the Estill family. He married Elizabeth Woods, and reared one son and three daughters. Mrs. Nancy Moberley was born in Madison County, and was a daughter of Maj. Nathan Lipscomb, who was a native of Virginia, resided awhile in South Carolina, came to Madison County as early as 1795, married Nancy Gentry, daughter of John Gentry, and died in 1843. Thomas Shelton Moberley was reared on the home farm in his native county of Madison, was educated at Georgetown College and Central University, and was married, September 28, 1876, to Miss Ida M., daughter of Wiley R. and Letitia (Ross) Brasfield, natives of Kentucky and Ohio, respectively. Wiley R. Brasfield was a son of James E. Brasfield, of Clark County, Ky., who married Tabitha Moberley, and died in Springfield, Ill., November 23, 1883. To the marriage of Mr. Moberley and Miss Brasfield have been born four children, of whom two are living: Shelton Neville and Genevieve Elizabeth. After his marriage Mr. Moberley settled on 200 acres, three-quarters of a mile north of Richmond, and commenced the breeding of shorthorn cattle, and later Berkshire hogs. He now owns 368 acres just north of Richmond, and also another farm. Mr. Moberley is also a director in the Madison National Bank. With his wife he is a member of the Christian Church.

WILLIAM RANDOLPH MOCK was born July 20, 1843, on Cedar Grove Stock Farm, three and one-half miles north of Danville, Boyle Co., Ky., where he has always resided. His father, John J. Mock, was born on this place March 19, 1803, was a successful farmer, owned twenty-five slaves, and died March 19, 1862. He was the son of Randolph Mock, a native of Virginia, who removed in childhood, with his parents, to Georgia, became a carpenter, and at the age of nineteen years located on this place, where he engaged in farming, and died in 1853, aged eighty-six years. He married Sallie, daughter of Barnett Fisher, and to them were born Rosa (McKay), John J., Lewis M., Eliza (Saunders), Ann E. (Vanarsdall), Robert A., Ezekiel F., Sarah (Kalfus) and Will

iam R. John J. Mock married Ellen A., daughter of John and Harriet (Dunn) Byers, of Garrard County, born January 19, 1814, died January 19, 1881, and from their union sprang Sarah E. (Hewey), Henry C., Harriet A. (Nichols), John L., Mary E. (Rice), William Randolph, Jarrett T., Amanda (Offutt) and Joshua D. William Randolph Mock procured a common English education at the schools in the vicinity where he was reared, and is a reading man. He owns a half-interest in the old family homestead, consisting of over 500 acres of valuable and productive land, which is devoted to the breeding of fine trotting horses, on a somewhat extensive scale. In 1866 Mr. Mock commenced running the old "Mock Distillery," which has a capacity of fifty bushels of corn per day, and has met with fair success. He has kept up the reputation of the "old Mock whisky," the manufacture of which was established by his grandfather, and continued by his father. Mr. Mock has never married, is not connected with any church, and in politics is a Democrat.

ROBERT S. MONTAGUE was born in Harrodsburg, Ky., January 28, 1824. While an infant his parents moved to Elizabethtown, where he grew to manhood, removing in 1845 to Greensburg, and thence in 1857 to Carthage, Ill. In 1862 he returned to Kentucky, locating for twelve years in Campbellsville, and after one year in Bowling Green and two more at Greensburg, returned to Campbellsville, where he now resides. His father, James Montague, was a farmer, a native of Virginia, and of Norman-French descent, his ancestors having come during the conquest from England, whence the family is immediately descended. James Montague married, about 1805, Miss Elizabeth Edmonson, also a Virginian. To them were born Warner R., Samuel (deceased), Diana (Davis), James, Lucy (Hodgen), Ann (Hodgen), John, George, Virginia (deceased), Robert S. and Martha (deceased). Robert S. Montague married, in October, 1847, Miss Margaret E., daughter of Archibald C. and Sallie (Howe) Cox. To them have been born Sallie E., wife of Dr. H. D. Hubbard, of Greensburg; Virginia, who married Joseph E. Hagerman; Mary A., whose husband is H. E. Baker; Maggie, who married Charles Phillips, of the Lebanon bar, and Lelia. In his extreme youth Mr. Montague possessed good educational advantages, but was compelled, at the age of fourteen years, to go to work. He persisted nevertheless in his studies during his spare time, mainly at night, and in this way not only secured a good English education, but also made considerable progress in the higher branches. He began work (as above stated) for himself in his fifteenth year, acting for several years as a clerk, and about 1846 began the study of the law, which profession he was licensed to practice the following year, since which time he has been actively engaged in the practice with good success. He is a man of extended reading, both legal and general, and Judge Hardin says of him "I consider him the best chancery lawyer in my district." He served the people of Taylor County for six years as county clerk of that county, is a thoroughly self-made man, and in politics is a Democrat.

DR. W. C. MONTGOMERY was born in Alabama in 1821, and when but three years of age his father, Dr. W. C. Montgomery, died. Col. William Montgomery, his grandfather, brought him to Lincoln County, Ky., near Stanford, and has lived at different times in Lincoln, Madison and Garrard Counties ever since, now a citizen of Garrard. Dr. Montgomery received a liberal education, and graduated in medicine from the medical department of Transylvania University at Lexington. He represented Lincoln County in the Legislature in the session of 1855–56. He has been four times married, first to Miss M. E. Ried, a daughter of Dr. James Ried; second, to Miss Emma Swope; third, to Miss Fannie Thurman, and fourth to Miss Lou Martin.

JOHN H. MONTGOMERY was born April 16, 1823, and is a son of David and Tabitha (Holland) Montgomery, parents of five boys and four girls. David Montgomery, born in 1800, was the first man that ever ran a freight boat from Greensburg, Ky., to New Orleans. He was a farmer and slave-holder, a trader in tobacco, built the mill on the narrows of Pitman Creek, had 300 acres of land in the bend, and was also a carpenter. He died in 1876. His father, Hugh Montgomery, was born in Ireland, was a tailor for a few years, a sailor, but finally settled in Green County, and married a Kentucky lady. Mrs. Tabitha Montgomery was a native of Green County, and a daughter of Burchy Holland, whose wife was captured and scalped by the Indians, but was afterward rescued. Her father and mother, however, were killed. Her name was Mary McCaslin, born in Virginia. John H. Montgomery, a native of Green County, was reared a farmer, and at the age of twenty, in the fall of 1843, married Tamer Ann Ray, and commenced farming on his own account. The father of Mrs. Montgomery, William Ray, married Miss Isabella Abnel, and had served in the battle of New Orleans. John H. Montgomery had born to him nine children by this union: Elizabeth N. Jamerson, William David, Joshua T., Tabitha I. McCubbin, Richard M., Bob A., Narcissa Jamerson, John A. and Sallie L. Emery. Mrs. Montgomery died in 1855, aged forty years, and a member of the Cumberland Presbyterian Church, and in July, 1867, Mr. Montgomery married Mrs. Nancy A. Donan, a daughter of James and Elizabeth (Edgar) McCubbin. To this last union six children have been born: Jennie A., Mary W., Amanda Lee, George T., Laura J. and Martha H. By her former marriage Mrs. Montgomery had two children, Sophronia C. Whitlow and Thomas J. Donan. Mr. Montgomery owns the old mill and several farms; is a Democrat and Free Mason, and with his wife a member of the Methodist Episcopal Church.

JOHN B. MONTGOMERY, son of Nathan and Patsey (Winston) Montgomery, was born September 13, 1849. Nathan Montgomery, a native of Green County, was born in 1807; he was a farmer and slave-holder, was a constable, then sheriff of Adair County for nearly twenty years; was an elder in the Presbyterian Church and died April 15, 1860. His father, also named Nathan, married a Miss Lawson and came to Kentucky from Virginia with a party of surveyors, remained a while in Green County, but subsequently removed to Rushville, Ill. He married his second wife, a Miss Miller, in Adair County prior to his removal to Illinois. Mrs. Patsey Montgomery was born in Green County and was a daughter of John B. and Judah (Dudley) Winston. John B. Montgomery was born in Columbia, Adair County, and began life as a farmer and stock trader. In 1870 he went to Campbellsville and for five years was in the hotel business, and three more in the drug trade. He then returned to Columbia and served four years as deputy sheriff; in 1882 he resumed the hotel business at Campbellsville; in 1884 was elected to the Democratic National Convention, and was appointed storekeeper in 1885, when he located at New Hope, where he still resides. September 22, 1874, he married Sallie Bailey, of Taylor County, a daughter of Grief and Martha (Durham) Bailey, natives of Green County, and there has been born to him one child, Augusta. Mr. Montgomery is a Free Mason, an Odd Fellow, and, with his wife, a member of the Presbyterian Church. His first presidential vote was for Horace Greeley.

JAMES WESLEY MOORE (deceased) was born in Pickaway County, Ohio, and, while yet a young man, removed to Danville, Ky. He entered in Capt. Graves' company, Sixteenth Kentucky Infantry, in the Mexican war, and died at Camp Mier on the Rio Grande during his term of service. He was the son of William Moore, a native of Ireland, who married Elizabeth Banford. Their union was favored by the birth of John B., James W., Elizabeth (Stanley and Ellsworth), Hannah (Davis), Samuel A. and Mrs. White. In 1833 James W. married Eliza A., daughter of James and Mary (McMullen) Trumbull, of Danville, Ky. (born in 1816, died December 14, 1875), and to them were born James W. (deceased), John B. (deceased), Mary J. (Bedford), William H., Elizabeth S., Martha E. (deceased), Irvin W., Samuel F. and Nancy D. (deceased). Mary J. Redford's children are Kate (Threlkeld), Joseph F., William A. and James W. William H. Moore's children are Robert E. and James W. Irvin W. and Samuel F. are in active partnership in farming and stock dealing, having 200 acres of productive land. They are members of the Presbyterian Church, and in politics Democrats and prohibitionists. Miss Elizabeth S. Moore is a Methodist.

CHARLES D. MOORE, M. D., was born April 17, 1826, and is the third of five sons and four daughters, seven of whom lived to be grown, born to Richard L. and Elinor A. (Hilliard) Moore, who were born in Virginia. Richard L. Moore was born in June, 1796, came to Kentucky with his parents, was a soldier of 1812, and was in the battle of the Thames, under Capt. Moss Shelby. He settled first in Clark County, moved thence to Logan, thence to Barren, and finally, in 1820, to Greensburg, where he continued the trade of tailoring; later in life, he turned his attention to mercantile business, served as magistrate for many years, also as coroner for twenty years, and died in February in 1871. He was a son of James Moore, who was born in Virginia, and came to Kentucky as early as 1805. From Logan County, Ky., he moved to Charleston, Ill. He was a substantial farmer, reared a family of eighteen children (seven sons, Richard L. being the eldest of the family) and died at the age of about ninety-five years, with excellent sight, being able to read common print without glasses, to the time of his death. Mrs. Elinor A. Moore was born in Green County, and was a daughter of Bartlett and Mary (Moss) Hilliard, who migrated in an early day to Virginia. Mr. Hilliard was a substantial farmer and owner of slave property, and for thirty years was one of the board of three tobacco inspectors at Greensburg, to which place he had been appointed by the court. Dr. Charles D. Moore grew to manhood in Greensburg, where he was born and where he received a good common-school education. In 1847 he enlisted in Company A, Second Kentucky Infantry, and was in the battle of Buena Vista, serving as fourth sergeant. After his return home he commenced the study of medicine under the instruction of Dr. Hardin, of Greensburg; graduated from the University of Louisville in 1850, then went to California, where he remained twelve months, mining for a short time, and then entered into practice in San Francisco. Returning to Greensburg, he continued his practice successfully till 1861, when he entered the Thirteenth Kentucky Infantry as surgeon, but was on detached duty the greater part of the time. He was appointed chief operator of the Second Brigade, Second Division, Twenty-third Army Corps, under Gen. Schofield, at Atlanta, and was discharged at Louisville in January, 1865. He returned to Greensburg, and in November, 1866, entered the revenue service as storekeeper and gauger, which position he continued to fill till November 15, 1885. In the winter of 1868, he spent his time in the hospitals in New York and Philadelphia, in order to renew his acquaintance with the various diseases. In December, 1885, he resumed his practice, locating in the eastern part of Green County, at Camp Knox. He is unable to fill all his calls, although at his age he is one of the most active men in the county, and is, perhaps, one of the best physicians and surgeons in the State. February 1, 1853, he was united in marriage to Nannie, a daughter of William M. and Mary (Gatewood) Spencer, natives, respectively, of Virginia and Kentucky. Mr. Spencer was a carpenter and cabinet-maker, and served eight or ten years as revenue assessor. The Doctor had born to him, by this union, one child, William R. Moore. His wife died in Campbellsville in February, 1862, a member of the Methodist Episcopal Church. The Doctor married his second wife, Martha W. Lane, December 25, 1869; she was a daughter of Elisha and Nancy (Reed) Lane, respectively of Sumner County, Tenn., and Green County, Ky. By this union three children were born: Charles S., Thomas O. and Mattie. The Doctor is a member of the Masonic fraternity and G. A. R.; cast his first presidential vote for L. Cass, but since 1864 has been an active and leading Republican. He has never missed a presidential election, and is the only man now living in Green County who voted for Lincoln and Barnes in 1864. The Doctor now resides on a hill one-quarter of a mile from Camp Knox, the place where the Long hunters camped.

HENRY B. MOORE was born December 11, 1826. His paternal ancestors came from Virginia, and were of English descent. His grandfather, Jesse Moore, came to Kentucky in an early day by flatboat, and landed on the present site of Louisville, when there were but few cabins in that now flourishing city. He settled near the Chaplin River in Nelson County, was a farmer, and died a number of years before H. B. Moore's birth. John R. Moore was born in Virginia about 1785, and was brought to Kentucky in his infancy. He settled in Washington County in early manhood and engaged in farming in what is now the Glenville Precinct, where he acquired a large estate. He was a soldier in the Indian war of 1811–12, serving under Gen. Anthony Wayne, and in 1845 was elected to represent Washington County in the State Legislature; was magistrate for a number of years under the old Constitution, and died in Bloomfield, Nelson County, in 1858. His wife was Martha Bayne, daughter of Walter Bayne, who came to Kentucky before the organization of the State. He was a native of Virginia, located near the Moore settlement on Chaplin River, and there died. Mrs. Moore was born in Virginia, was brought to Kentucky, when quite young, and died in Washington County in 1854, aged sixty-five years. The children of Mr. and Mrs. Moore were the following: Jetson, W. H., Walter B., Jesse, Milton, James F., Henry B., Susan (Hill) and J. R. Moore. Henry B. Moore was born and has lived all his life in Washington County. He was reared to agricultural pursuits and received a fair English education in the country schools which he attended until twenty years of age. At the breaking out of the Mexican war he enlisted in the Fourth Kentucky Infantry with which he served from September, 1847, until July of the following year, his regiment remaining in the City of Mexico the greater part of that time. He returned to Washington County after the close of the war, and in 1852 purchased his present farm in Glenville Precinct, nine miles north of Springfield, where he has since resided. His 400 acres are all under cultivation. He engaged in the distillery business about 1852, and for twenty years thereafter did a thriving business, manufacturing the Moore and Grigsby brand, which achieved a noted reputation. Mr. Moore was married June 29, 1852, in Washington County, to Miss Jane M. Pile, daughter of Benjamin and Rhoda (Weathers) Pile, of the same county. Benjamin Pile was born in 1801, and is one of the oldest living settlers of Washington County. Mrs. Pile was the daughter of James and Margaret (Cutsinger) Weathers. She was born in Washington County, and died in 1851. Mr. and Mrs. Moore have had eight children, namely: Mary E. (deceased), Lucas, Victor C. (deceased), Luther, (deceased), Lulu B. (wife of Isaac Breeding), J. R., Mary W. and an infant (deceased). Mr. Moore is a Democrat in politics, and, with his wife, belongs to the Christian Church, with which he has been identified twenty-five years.

CAPT. SAMUEL W. MOORE was born March 28, 1828, six miles south of Greensburg, Ky., and is the son of John and Margaret (Moore) Moore, who reared five sons and four daughters. John Moore was born in 1802, south of Greensburg; when a child lost his parents, after which he was taken to Granger County, Tenn., by his grandfather; when he became of age he returned to Kentucky, where he remained during his life. He was a son of William and Nancy (Jack) Moore, both natives of Virginia, of Scotch-Irish descent, who moved to Tennessee, thence to Green County, Ky., about 1800. Mrs. Margaret Moore was a daughter of Samuel and Mary (Thomas) Moore, natives of Virginia and Pennsylvania, and early pioneers of Kentucky. Shortly after their settlement in Kentucky, Samuel Moore died, when his wife, who survived him, returned to Virginia, where she again married and came back to Kentucky. Capt. S. W. Moore grew up on a farm, received a fair English education, and remained with his mother until 1861. He enlisted in October, in Company G, Thirteenth Kentucky. In his first great battle, Shiloh, he was wounded in the left thigh; he afterward took part in the battle of Huff's Ferry, Campbell's Station, siege of Knoxville (here was promoted from sergeant to captain), was at Resaca, Ga., where he received a wound in the head, and was at Atlanta. He was discharged in July, 1864, returned to his home and resumed farm life. In 1869 he was appointed storekeeper, but in 1878 resigned, and located on a farm of 100 acres, where he now resides, less than two miles south of Greensburg, which he had purchased a few years previous. June 21, 1869, he was united in marriage to Miss Mary I., daughter of J. T. and Jane (Conn) Williams, natives of Kentucky and Virginia respectively, and to this union one child was born, Hugh H. (deceased). His wife died in August, 1870, a member of the Presbyterian Church. In May, 1875, he was married to Miss Eliza J., daughter of Charles and Mary A. (Stiles) Beeler, natives of Nelson County, Ky. Mr. and Mrs. Moore had born to them by this union five children: Marvin, S. W. (deceased), Charles B., John W. and Mary M. Mr. Moore is a member of the F. & A. M., cast his first presidential vote for Gen. Scott, but became a Republican after the war; he and wife are members of the Presbyterian Church.

WILLIAM T. MOORE, a son of William and Lucinda (Gentry) Moore, was born April 17, 1832, in Adair County. William Moore (his father) was a native of Bedford County, Va., and a son of Tandy and Sally (Bridgewaters) Moore; was born in January, 1800. He was brought to Green County when a boy, where he lived until he was thirty years of age, engaged uniformly in the occupation of farming, which was his life-long vocation. In 1830 he was united in marriage with Miss Lucinda Gentry, the eldest of three daughters born to Moses and Lucy (Yeows) Gentry, natives of the Old Dominion. After his marriage William Moore continued to oversee for others until about 1836, when he purchased 218 acres of land on which was a brick residence. This was situated on Russell Creek near Milltown, and here he lived the remainder of his life in good circumstances. The names of his children are Mary, wife of John J. Orr; William T.; Louisa, wife of Robert O. Craig; Judy, wife of Thomas Flowers, and after his death of James Browning; Jenetta, wife of Alexander Pollard; Elizabeth, wife of William Carpenter; Cary J.; James; Lucietta, who died young; and Lucinda, wife of James Kimbrew. Lucietta, James and Judy are now deceased. William Moore and wife were members of the Baptist Church, and his death occurred in 1865; hers about 1846. His second marriage occurred in Adair County, to Miss Polly Mann, daughter of Archibald Mann, but no children were born to them. Mrs. Polly Moore died in 1883. Tandy Moore was a native of Virginia, a farmer, and immigrated to Green County, Ky., early in the nineteenth century, where he bought a farm on which he lived, became a man of considerable wealth and was a slave owner. The names of his children were Schuyler, William, Thomas, Nancy (Botts), Samuel, Alexander, and Elizabeth (Botts). He died in 1825 in the fortieth year of his age. Moses Gentry was also a Virginian, who immigrated with his family to Green County, where he became a man of prominence. William T. Moore remained at home working with and for his father until twenty years old. December 25, 1852, he married Miss Sarah A. Moore, the youngest of three children, two of whom were daughters, born to George and Sally (Williams) Moore, native Kentuckians. This marriage was blessed by eight children, viz.: James D., Mary T. (wife of William Bradshaw), Sarah B. (wife of Arthur Bradshaw), Annie Meade (wife of William Simpson), George W., Charles O., John Edgar, and Lucietta, of whom Charles O. died in infancy and George W. died in Missouri after reaching maturity. Mrs. Moore was first a member of the Christian Church, and after of the Baptist, and departed this life May 30, 1878, in the fifty-first year of her age. Mr. Moore next married Mrs. Myra H. (Butler) Sharp, a daughter of Champion and Amanda (Cheatham) Butler, the former a native of Virginia, and the latter of Adair County. Champion Butler was a son of John and Nellie (Dillingham) Butler, and Amanda Cheatham was a daughter of Edmund and Millie (Norman) Cheatham, Virginians. John Butler was a Revolutionary soldier. Mr. Moore has owned three different farms in life and settled his present location in 1867. This is a beautiful farm of 200 acres, well improved and in a high state of cultivation, on which he has recently built a two-story frame residence. He turns his attention principally to farming and stock raising and owns a blooded and pedigreed stallion, which he values at $650, and a fine Jack worth $900. He is a member of the Baptist Church, and his wife of the Christian; in politics he has been a life-long Democrat. He began life with nothing, and notwithstanding misfortunes, has surrounded himself with a comfortable competency, which is the result of his own industry and economy.

GEORGE R. MORAN, a native of Barren County, was born May 25, 1833. His father, Robert P. Moran, was also a native of Barren County, and in his twenty-third year (1832) inherited a farm of 150 acres from his father's estate. During the same year he married Miss Ann Adams, the eldest of seven children born to John and Elizabeth (Gillock) Adams, both Kentuckians. The children born to this marriage are Hezekiah, G. R., John, William, Schuyler, Eliza Jane (Wilcoxson and Franklin), Elizabeth (Level), Susan M. (Powell), Elijah, Thomas and Sarah (Payton) of whom Elijah, Thomas, William and Schuyler are dead. William Moran in life wore a beard that reached to the ground. Robert P. Moran died in January, 1858, but his wife is still living, residing in

Hart County, with her son-in-law, Rev. W. T. Payton. William Moran, grandfather of George Moran, was a native of Virginia, where he was a man of wealth and prominence. He immigrated to Barren County, where he owned large tracts of land and a great many slaves, and was one of the substantial farmers of the county. He married Miss Elizabeth Blaine, and was the father of eight children—four sons and four daughters—of whom Robert P. Moran was the eldest, and three are still living: William, P. P., and Emily (Grooms). George R. Moran received little education, and in youth was trained to hard work on the farm, which has since been his fortune in life. After becoming of age, he hired to the neighboring farmers until December, 1860, when he married Miss Mary P. Carpenter, the eldest of four daughters born to Andrew and Elizabeth (Bridgewaters) Carpenter, native Kentuckians. Andrew Carpenter was a son of Andrew and Elizabeth (Kinslow) Carpenter, of Culpeper County, Va., and Elizabeth Bridgewaters was a daughter of Nathan and Polly (Page) Bridgewaters, also Virginians. This marriage has been blessed by the addition of the following children: John W., Marietta (deceased), Thomas P., James J., Robert P., Elizabeth Ann, and one son, born August 16, 1886, and died August 28, 1886. Mr. Moran's eldest son, J. W. Moran, was married February 15, 1882, to Amanda W. Stotts, of Adair County, and daughter of Elizabeth Stotts. To this union three children have been born. In 1858 Mr. Moran, with his brother, Hezekiah, bought 130 acres of land in Barren County, on which was a grist-mill, and they paid $2,000 on the place and lost it. After marriage he rented and cultivated land successfully four years, and at the end of that time he was able to purchase a farm of eighty acres, in 1865, where he lived until 1874. This farm, which he had highly improved, he sold in 1873, and purchased his present location, 226 acres in Adair County, which at that time was in a very dilapidated condition. He has enriched, improved and cleared most of the farm, erected a residence, barns and stables, and built a good fence around it, and it is now in a high state of cultivation, and one of the best farms in the section. He turns his attention to no particular line of farming, but raises tobacco and all the cereals common to the county very successfully. All that he has is the result of his own industry and good management, and besides the $2,000 lost in 1858, he was victimized to the extent of $1,050 in another business transaction. Mr. Moran is a Democrat, and a member of the Baptist Church; his wife of the Christian Church.

DR. ROBERT C. MORGAN was born in Cumberland County, June 18, 1835, and is a son of Reece and Caroline (Conover) Morgan, who reared six children, of whom the Doctor (the only son), and one sister, Lydia A. Morgan (who married Robert H. Cofer, of Adair County), are living. The Doctor is the third child in order of birth and is a twin. Reece Morgan was born in Cumberland County in 1802, moved to Adair County in 1850 and died January 12, 1882, a member of the Christian Church. He was a son of Morgan Morgan, of Virginia, who settled on Crocus Creek as early as 1795. Mrs. Caroline Morgan was a daughter of Garrard Conover and was born in Adair County. Dr. Robert C. Morgan began life as a teacher; subsequently he became a salesman, and at the age of twenty-five he began the study of dentistry; he was graduated from the Cincinnati Dental College and for three years practiced in Columbia, Ky.; then moved to Burkesville, then to Lebanon, and in 1882 settled in Lancaster. He has furnished a number of articles on dental surgery to the press, and has filled the offices of vice-president and president of the State Dental Association. He was married October 6, 1868, to Miss Mollie E., daughter of Richard W. and Rosana M. (Hurt) Wallace. Mr. Wallace is a Christian minister and was a soldier in the Mexican war. He is still living and was a son of William Wallace, who came from Virginia and settled in Adair County many years ago. Mrs. Mollie E. Morgan died in 1878, a member of the Christian Church.

JOHN W. MOUSER was born January 12, 1840; his father, John Mouser, in 1811, and now resides on the old homestead near Riley's in Marion County. His life has been spent in the pursuits of the farm, but he retired from active work in 1870. His wife, to whom he was married in 1833, was a Miss Nancy Hardgrove of Boyle County; nine children blessed this union; six of the number are living, namely: Frederick, of Dallas County, Tex.; John W., Mary E. (Sparrow) of Marion County; Edward G. of Lynn County, Mo.; Gabriel T. of Madison County, Tex., and Redford M. of Marion County. Nancy (Hardgrove) Mouser was born in the State of Kentucky, in 1812; she was reared in Boyle County, Ky., and is yet living, aged seventy-four years. Her parents were of English descent and by birth Virginians. Frederick Mouser, the father of John, was born in North Carolina, and came to Kentucky when a boy and located in Nelson (now Marion) County, he was a farmer and came from German descent, and died prior to 1850; his grandfather, a native of Germany, came to America and settled in the Virginia colony as early as 1750. John W. Mouser was born on a farm in Marion County, and at the age of nineteen visited the State of Texas, where he remained until the beginning of the civil war, when he returned to Kentucky, and soon after joined the Federal Army, enlisting in Company D, of the Tenth Kentucky Volunteer Infantry, in November, 1861; during the three years and two months that he served participated in the engagements at Mill Springs, was wounded at Chickamauga, Mission Ridge, Tunnel Hill, Resaca, Atlanta, Kenesaw, and Jonesboro, and many minor engagements. He was discharged from the service at Louisville, Ky., in November, 1864, and on the 10th of October, 1865, was united in marriage to Miss Sallie A. Brown. To this marriage have been born three sons: Otis U., Zenas A. and Edward B. Sallie (Brown) Mouser was born October 16, 1837. Her father, Alexander Brown, was descended from English ancestors; he was born in Nelson (now Marion) County, Ky.; his wife was a Miss Margaret Mouser, whose parents were of German extraction. Mr. and Mrs. John W. Mouser are members of the Methodist Episcopal Church, with which they united in 1876. Mr. Mouser's political views are Republican. He held the office of United States Internal Revenue storekeeper from May, 1880, to September, 1885; since that time he has been engaged in agricultural pursuits on the farm that he owns, lying near Riley's Station.

W. A. MULLINS, son of B. *G. and Elizabeth (Kennedy) Mullins, was born August 19, 1867. B. G. Mullins, now a farmer and shorthorn cattle breeder, served three years in the Confederate cavalry under John Morgan; was captured in Ohio and imprisoned twenty-two months. He is a son of Williamson G. and Mary Ann (Graves) Mullins, who had a family of six: John G., William Jordan (deceased), Benjamin G., Martha (deceased), Emily (deceased), and Mary L. Samuel G. Mullins, a brother of Williamson G., was president of the Madison Female Institute, and also of the Daughters Female College, at Harrodsburg. Mary A. (Graves) Mullins was a sister of William J. Graves, member of Congress, whose duel at Bladensburg, Md., with Jonathan Cilley, member of Congress, from Maine, is a matter of history. William J. Graves also ran for governor on the Whig ticket, about 1840, and was defeated by only a very small majority for his opponent. Mrs. Elizabeth Mullins is a daughter of David and Eliza (Kennedy) Kennedy, the father of David Kennedy having been a famous Indian fighter. The children born to David and Eliza were seven in number, and were named Andrew, William, Elbert, Jennie, Mary, Sarah and Bettie. W. A. Mullins was reared on a farm in his native county of Garrard, and was graduated from the Lebanon (Ohio) Normal School, in the summer of 1885, after which he taught at Independence, Ky., for a while, and then bought and became editor of the Central (Kentucky) News, now the Journal.

SQUIRE MURPHY was born February 1, 1820. His father, Robert Murphy, also a native of Nelson County, died about 1875. He was the son of Gabriel Murphy, a native of Maryland, one of the first settlers on Cox's Creek, and an Indian fighter, who, alternately with his neighbors, assisted in guarding and cutting their crops in times of Indian depredations. He was a soldier in the war of 1812, and died about 1841, aged over eighty years. His offspring were Gabriel, Abraham, Robert, Isaac, Elizabeth (Young), Polly (Sousley), Kitty (Cheser) and Sarah (Curry). Robert married Lucy Connell, who died in 1881, at the age of sixty-eight years, and from their union sprang Maria (Raymond), and our subject as above. In February, 1841, Squire Murphy was married to Miss Mary P., daughter of Joshua and Polly Shirley, of Nelson County (born in 1818, and died in 1847), and to them were born William Henry, Mary Eliza (Roby), and Sarah Margaret (Bean). Mr. Murphy was next married, in 1849, to Miss Juliet, daughter of Aquilla Hagan, of Nelson County (born in 1818), and from this union there has been no issue. Squire Murphy has served twenty-two years as magistrate and member of the court of claims of Nelson County, and was also sheriff for six years; since the organization of the Agricultural Association, he has been either president, vice-president or director. Mr. Murphy had an even start in life, but by industry, economy, and attention to business, has secured a comfortable competency. He is a farmer, trader and stock raiser, owning over 1,300 acres of land on Cox's Creek, Nelson County, where he was born, much of which is in a high state of cultivation. He also owns a half interest in a distillery, with a capacity of 250 bushels of corn per day. He lost seven slaves by the late war. In politics Mr. Murphy is a Democrat.

CAPT. DAVID A. MURPHY, of Danville, the founder and for seven years the managing editor of *The Danville* (Ky.) *Tribune*, was born on a farm near Shamrock, Adams Co., Ohio, on April 3, 1842. His father, David Whittaker Murphy, was born in Salem County, N. J., in November, 1800, and his mother, Cynthia Ann McCall, eldest daughter of David Ball, Esq., in All Saints Protestant Episcopal Church, Portsmouth, Ohio, by the rector, Rev. Erastus Burr, D. D., September 18, 1865. His wife, a regal Christian woman, is a descendant of George Washington's family. Capt. Murphy is now a member of St. John's Methodist Episcopal Church, Cincinnati, Ohio, and is one of the board of trustees. He was the superintendent of the Sunday-school connected with.

CAPT. DAVID A. MURPHY.

was born in Scioto County, Ohio, in April, 1816, and David Asbury is the first born of their seven children. His parents sold the farm in 1849 and removed to Buena Vista, Scioto Co., Ohio, a pretty village situated 100 miles above Cincinnati and on the right bank of the Ohio River. David Asbury was a close student from his childhood and in the public school he stood at the head of all the classes, and for many years was the champion of all the spelling matches in the schools. He was married to Miss Jennie M. Ball, the that church in 1875 and 1876. He removed to Danville, Ky., from Cincinnati, Ohio, January 1, 1880. "The Murphy Mansion," his palatial residence, is one of the best built houses in Danville, and the latch string is always out to his friends. In August, 1862, Mr. D. A. Murphy enlisted in Company H, Eighty-first Ohio Volunteer Infantry, Col. Thomas Morton's regiment. He was mustered into the service at Camp Lima, Ohio, and went as a private "to the tented field." He was with Grant in Mississippi, McPherson in

Tennessee, Thomas in Alabama, and Sherman in Georgia. In fifty battles, and under fire one hundred days, he was never captured or injured. He was three times stoutly recommended by the officers of his regiment for promotion, "for good conduct upon the battle-field." In January, 1865, he was granted a furlough for thirty days. On arrival at Columbus, Ohio, he presented a letter from his division commander, Gen. John M. Corse, the hero of Allatoona Pass, in Georgia, to Hon. John Brough, the governor of the Buckeye State in 1865, assuring the governor that "private D. A. Murphy would reflect credit upon any commission that might be given him." Gov. Brough immediately asked the Secretary of War to discharge private Murphy, which was done without delay, and gave him a commission as first lieutenant and adjutant of the One Hundred and Eighty-fourth Ohio Infantry Volunteers, Col. Henry S. Commager's regiment. At Bridgeport, Ala., Col. Commager received a commission as brevet brigadier general and his adjutant was assigned to duty on his staff as acting assistant adjutant general; and that is where the adjutant received his present military title of captain. During his services in the army, from sickness and frequent exposures, Capt. Murphy became quite deaf and to that extent he is crippled for life. In 1861 Capt. Murphy started and published his first newspaper, called The Kentucky and Ohio Union. It was published at Beuna Vista, Ohio, and circulated on both sides of the Ohio River. He sold this paper when it was just one year old and enlisted in the army of his country. In 1863 and 1864 he was the army correspondent of the Cincinnati Commercial and in 1865 he was special correspondent of the Cincinnati Gazette. After the war he was for many years contributor to the Sunday School Workman of New York, the Sunday School Times of Philadelphia, and the Golden Hours of Cincinnati. In December, 1879, Capt. Murphy planned in his mind the regal Danville (Ky.) Tribune, with all its novel features. It is from first to last his own brain-child, his ideal of the modern family weekly. On March 1, 1880, The Danville (Ky.) Tribune, an eight-paged paper, supplanted The Kentucky Tribune, a four-paged paper, and for seven years, "it has stood at the head of all the country weeklies in America." Gen. U. S. Grant in all his travels around the world did not find "any paper half so beautiful as the regal Danville (Ky.) Tribune!" Capt. D. A. Murphy was for fifteen years connected with the prominent contractors and builders of Cincinnati, Ohio, and, in consequence, became familiar with plans and specifications and all kinds of building material used in this country. His employers erected buildings in Cincinnati, Chicago, Cairo, Dayton, New York, Boston, and Washington. In October, 1862, under President Arthur's administration, Capt. Murphy was appointed superintendent of construction of the new United States Public Building to be erected at Frankfort, Ky. The plans were not completed until July 27, 1883, and on August 1, 1883, Capt. Murphy "broke ground" for the new public building. The plans called for a public building two and a half stories above basement, and to cost $150,000. Capt. Murphy as superintendent pushed the several contractors with the utmost vigor, so that when he was relieved on September 10, 1885, the building was within six months of completion. The United States Inspector reported every part of the work correctly and admirably done. Hon. J. Proctor Knott, the governor of Kentucky; Hon. E. H. Taylor, Jr., the mayor of Frankfort; the lawyers, the bankers, and the citizens of the State capital, united in a letter addressed to Hon. Daniel Manning, Secretary of the United States Treasury, Washington, D. C., strongly commending "Capt. D. A. Murphy as having proved himself to be a competent and courteous public official," and earnestly requesting "his retention as superintendent until the final completion of the building." The United States public building at Frankfort is practically his building and personally his monument.

DR. WILLIAM D. MURRAH was born in Adair County, Ky., January 14, 1836, where he grew to manhood and resided until 1883, when he removed to his present home in Taylor County. He was a member during the late war of the Third Kentucky Infantry, first of Company G, with which he served for eighteen months, most of the time on detailed duty as hospital steward, and thence was promoted to the lieutenancy of Company I, with which he served for about the same length of time. He was present at Murfreesboro, Chickamauga, Missionary Ridge and a large number of minor battles and skirmishes. During the first he was wounded by a shell in the left knee. His father, Joseph Murrah, was born either in Virginia or North Carolina, in probably the latter part of 1796. When eight years of age he removed with his parents to Kentucky, locating on the Walnut Flat in Russell County, of which his father was one of the pioneer settlers. Joseph Murrah was married about 1818, to Miss Mary Easley. To this union were born Sally(Jones), Emily (Perryman), Sydney, Rachel (Jones), John E., Frederick T., Carlisle H. and Dr. William D. The last named was married May 28, 1865, to Miss Eliza M., daughter of Joshua and Nancy (Barnes) Murrah. To them have been born Edward T., William D., Jr., Joseph J. and Hettie M. Dr. Murrah's early educational advantages were limited, but by close application to study he has obtained a good English education and is well versed in current topics. He began life as a farmer and early in life engaged for two years in clerking at Creelsboro, after which he taught two years and in his twenty-fifth year began the study of medicine, and after spending two years in the study of that profession at home, he continued the reading in the army and immediately on the receipt of his discharge he began the practice, in which he has since been engaged. He is a member with his family of the Cumberland Presbyterian Church, a Mason and a Republican.

DAVID G. NAVE (deceased) was born April 24, 1824, in Jessamine County, Ky. In 1862 he removed to Boyle County, where he died April 13, 1878. He was a member of the Masonic fraternity, a Baptist, a farmer and lost seven slaves by the late war. He was the son of Peter Nave, a native of Virginia, an early settler in Jessamine County, a Methodist and a farmer, who died in 1860 over ninety years of age. His children are Solomon, Jefferson, Jacob, Peter (deceased), David (deceased), Michael, David G., Sally (Grow), Polly (Lackey), Jemima (Johnson), Rachel (Dean) and Mahala (Ketran). David G. married Melinda, daughter of Alexander and Jennie (Scott) Collier, of Garrard County, born in 1820 and died January 4, 1885, and to them were born Alexander P., Robert, John, Georgia A. (Burdett), Winfield S., Mary J. (McDonald), William D. and Sallie. Alexander P., Robert, William and Sallie are engaged in partnership farming, having 273 acres of productive land in Boyle County in a high state of cultivation. In religion Miss Sallie is a Baptist. The brothers, in politics, are Democrats.

JAMES LEWIS NEAL was born December 22, 1832, in Jessamine County, and in 1866 removed to Mercer County, locating on the Harrodsburg and Munday's Landing pike, five miles north of Harrodsburg, where he has since resided. His father, David Neal, was born in 1807, in Jessamine County, and still owns the old family homestead; was formerly a farmer; lost twelve or more slaves through the late war; is a member of the Christian Church, and now resides in Lexington. He is the son of George Neal, a native of Virginia, who enlisted in the Revolutionary war at the age of thirteen years, and remained until the close of the struggle, when he immediately came to Bryant's Station, in Kentucky. He was a farmer, a Baptist, a Whig, and died about 1838. February 15, 1785, he married Elizabeth, daughter of Col. Manoah Singleton, whom he first met in the fort at Bryant's Station. It was she who blew the conch shell, to warn the men when the Indians attacked the fort, and the conch is still kept as a souvenir in the family. Their offspring were James, Elijah and George, soldiers in the war of 1812; Creath, Jesse, John, Mary (Hughes) and David. David married, in 1825, Rebecca A., daughter of James and Elizabeth Elmore, of Jessamine County, born in 1809, died May 18, 1884, and from their union sprang Mary (deceased), James L., Lenis A. (Farra) and Susan M. (Headly). June 5, 1866, James L. Neal was united in marriage with Miss Sue Helm, daughter of David W. and Sarah M. (Withers) Thompson, of Mercer County (born July 17, 1842), but from this union there has been no issue. David W. Thompson was born February 29, 1816, and died November 20, 1865. Sarah M. (Withers) Thompson was born June 2, 1820, and died November 5, 1862. James L. Neal is a farmer and stock raiser, and owns 287 acres of highly improved lands. He has acted four years as master of the State Grange of Kentucky, is an elder in the Christian Church, a member of the I. O. O. F., and in politics a Democrat.

JOHN W. NEALE, an enterprising farmer of Nelson County, was born in the city of Lexington, Ky., January 8, 1836, being the eldest in a family of four children born to Christopher and Mary (Boswell) Neale. Rodham Neale, paternal grandfather of John W. Neale, was a native of Virginia, whence he came to Fayette County, Ky., where he resided until his death. John W. Neale remained at home until he attained the age of sixteen years, up to which time he attended the schools of the vicinity at intervals, obtaining a good common education. Having natural talent for carpentering he then engaged at that trade, which he continued until October 1, 1867, when his marriage with Miss Sarah C. Humphrey was solemnized, by whom he is the father of six children, these four now living: Maggie B., Laura F., Mary K. and Nannie F. Since his marriage he has made farming his vocation, in which he has been successful, owning a fine farm of 217 acres well improved. He and wife are members of the Methodist Episcopal Church South. He belongs to the Masonic fraternity, but is now on demit. In politics he has always been a stanch Democrat.

WILLIAM NEIKIRK, a superannuated minister of the Methodist Episcopal Church South, was born in Pulaski County, Ky., October 19, 1819. Of a family of fifteen children born to John and Elizabeth (Aker) Neikirk, he was the next eldest. His father, John Neikirk, was born in Hagerstown, Md., and came to Kentucky in company with the Aker family some time prior to the year 1815. He had learned the blacksmith trade in his native State, which he continued to follow after his settlement in Pulaski County. He was an honorable and respected citizen, and died in 1859. William Neikirk, at the age of twenty-four, became a member of the Kentucky Conference of the Methodist Episcopal Church, and was ordained minister, for which he had been for several years fitting himself. He was first assigned to the Burlington Circuit, and continued in the ministerial profession, filling various charges for thirty-two years. He retired from active work in 1875, owing to impaired health. In August, 1847, he was married to Laura E., daughter of William Davison, one of her maternal ancestors having been William Hardin. To the union of Mr. and Mrs. Neikirk three children were born, of whom two are now living: Mary T. (wife of E. Y. Penick) and William F. (who married Elizabeth A. Penick). To the marriage of the latter four children have been born, three now living: Buford, Annie and George. William F. received a good education at private schools, sufficiently proficient to enable him to teach, in which profession he continued four years. Upon his marriage in 1875 he engaged in farming, which vocation he has since followed with success, and owns a fine farm of 140 acres situated on the Perryville pike. He takes an active part in politics, and is chairman of the Republican Central Committee of Washington County.

GEORGE NELL, editor of the Columbia *Herald*, was born in Adair County, September 23, 1840, the fifth of thirteen children born to James and Nancy (Thurman) Nell, the former a native of Adair and the latter of Todd County, Ky., and of Scotch and English descent, respectively. James Nell was born in 1807, was married soon after attaining his majority, and shortly after that event, entered wild land eight miles south of Columbia on the waters of Crocus Creek, in Adair County, having previously sold the farm in same county inherited from his father. Here he subsequently improved a farm upon which he resided for about fifteen years. After this he bought and sold several different farms, all in Adair County, and was engaged in agricultural pursuits until his death, April 15, 1864. He and wife were life-long members of the Methodist Episcopal Church, in which he was class leader for many years. His father, John Nell, was born in Scotland, but in early life in the latter half of the last century came to America. He served in the Continental Army during the struggle for independence, and soon after the close of the war removed to Kentucky, settling in what is now Adair County, some eight miles south of Columbia, where he was engaged in tanning (which he had learned in early life), in connection with agricultural pursuits. Mrs. Nancy (Thurman) Nell was born in 1809, and departed this life, March 10, 1869, in Henry County, Mo. George Nell (subject) received a common-school education, which he has very materially added to by his own exertions. His early life was passed on the old homestead in Adair County. In August, 1861, he enlisted in Company A, Third Kentucky Volunteer Infantry (Federal), and served with that regiment in all its marches and engagements until September, 1863, when he was discharged on account of disability. He participated in the battles of Ft. Donelson, Corinth and lesser engagements. After his return from the service he removed to Scott County, Ill., where he followed farming for three years, when he returned to Adair County, and continued to farm for several years and was also engaged during a part of the time at the house carpenter's trade, which he had learned before the war. In 1876 he was appointed United States deputy marshal, and for several years was the terror of the illicit liquor dealers and moonshiners generally. In 1881 he accepted the general agency for Hitchcock's Analysis, and for the three or three and a half years following traveled extensively through the Southern States with the same. He has at various times served as town marshal, constable and deputy sheriff of the county. In November, 1885, he bought the Columbia *Herald*, the first and only Republican paper printed in this part of the State, and although only about eight months old, has the second largest circulation of any newspaper in this congressional district, being liberally patronized in Adair and neighboring counties. Mr. Nell is an able editor, a clear and forcible writer, and the work he is doing for his party in this part of the State cannot be overestimated. He has been twice married: first, January 6, 1864, to Miss Malinda A. McGinnis, a native of Adair County, born February 10, 1841. She was a daughter of Green B. and Polley Ann (Turner) McGinnis, and departed this life, July 10, 1871. One daughter blessed this union, Cordelia. Mr. Nell was next married, March 4, 1877, to Mrs. Durinda (Simpson) Curry, also a native of Adair County, born about 1838. She was daughter of Marion and Polley (Dixon) Simpson, and her death occurred August 17, 1880. Mr. Nell is a consistent member of the Presbyterian Church, and in politics an uncompromising Republican.

DR. W. C. NELSON, a prominent physician, is of English parentage, and was brought to Mercer County by his parents when quite young, about the year 1838. His father was a prominent Baptist preacher, as was also his grandfather. His educational advantages were limited, but by his exertions he succeeded in obtaining a medium education. Dr. Nelson married Miss A. E. Furr, a daughter of Maj. M. Furr, of Woodford County, Ky. They have three children living, viz.: Bettie, Katy, and Will Edwards. Dr. Nelson is a member of the Baptist Church, his wife of the Methodist Church. In politics he is a Democrat.

GEORGE P. NEWBOLT is a Kentuckian by birth, and dates his nativity from the 29th of June, 1844. His father, William Newbolt, was born in Nelson (now Marion) County in the year 1800; he married Cecilia Penick in 1828, and they became parents of five children, of which number our subject is the only survivor. Cecilia Penick was born in 1810 and died in July, 1875; she was a daughter of Edward and Nancy (Nash) Penick, the former a native of Virginia, the latter of Mississippi, and both of English extraction. William Newbolt was a farmer, and during his last thirty-five years a ruling elder in the Presbyterian Church of Lebanon. He died at his home in 1860. His father, John Newbolt, was a native of Maryland and came to Kentucky with the Robertses and Spaldings at an early period in the history of the State. He located at a point three miles east of the present city of Lebanon, where he followed the vocation of a farmer until his death. George P. Newbolt was sixteen years of age when his father died, and from that time the superintending of the work on the home farm devolved upon him. His early school training was the best that could be obtained in the common schools of his native county. He is now the proprietor of farms aggregating

several hundred acres, 265 of which are well improved and highly cultivated. The home called "Hillendale" is one of the most beautiful locations in Marion County. Mr. Newbolt has been twice married. His first wife, to whom he was married in 1867, was a daughter of the Rev. S. W. Cheney, who is widely known in the history of the Presbyterian Church in Kentucky. To this marriage were born two sons (William and George) and three daughters (Agnes, Lizzie and Maud). Mrs. Newbolt died in January, 1881. His second marriage occurred on the 20th of December, 1882, with Miss Sue Caldwell. She was born June 17, 1853, and is a daughter of James B. and Jane (Crawford) Caldwell, who were of English parentage, and natives of Boyle County, Ky. Mr. and Mrs. Newbolt are members of the Presbyterian Church, in which Mr. Newbolt is a ruling elder. Politically he is a Republican. He has persistently refused to hold any office, though frequently importuned to do so. He patronizes the schools, and is a Master Mason in Marion Lodge, No. 136.

HENRY M. NICHOLLS was born June 30, 1864. His paternal grandfather, Henry Nicholls, was a native of Maryland, and was born in the year 1772; he came to Kentucky when a young man and located in Nelson County. In 1814 he married Catherine Harris; they reared two sons and two daughters, among whom was Henry M. Nicholls, Sr., who was born in Nelson County in November, 1829. In 1853 he was united in marriage to Miss Jeanette Sutherland, daughter of William Sutherland. He followed farming and trading, in both of which he was successful, but later in life lost quite heavily in securities. He left some property to his family, including a farm of 478 acres, well improved, 300 acres of which are still in possession of his family. His death occurred in 1870. He was the father of four children: Katie (Siscoe), Maggie (Hammond), William and Henry M. Mrs. Nicholls was born in 1829, and received her education in the Bardstown Academy, from which institution she graduated at the age of nineteen years. She is a member of the Presbyterian Church, with which she united when quite young, Henry M. Nicholls was born in Nelson County, was reared on the farm and received a common education. He is a member of the Presbyterian Church, and politically a Democrat.

STITH T. NOE is the fifth of a family of twelve children born to Alexander K. and Jane B. (Thompson) Noe. Alexander Noe was a native of Lincoln County, Ky., born in 1800. He moved to Washington

County when about sixteen or seventeen years of age, and was a resident of the same until his death in 1864. He was a farmer, and resided in what is known as the Pleasant Grove neighborhood, six miles north of Springfield. Jane E. (Thompson) Noe was born in 1807, and died in 1880. The following are the children of Mr and Mrs. Noe: Isaac, James, John, Martha, Stith T., Robert A., George A., Thomas W., Sallie Catherine, Mordecai H. and Edward H. Stith T. Noe was born in Washington County August 3; 1834. He was reared to agricultural pursuits and received a fair English education in the country schools, which he attended at intervals until his eighteenth year. He commenced life for himself at the age of twenty-one as overseer, for Hugh McElroy, with whom he remained for five years. He then effected a partnership with S. L. Sharp, they carrying on farming quite extensively for seven years. He afterward purchased a farm near Springfield, upon which he resided for one year and then purchased a second place on the Bloomfield pike, northeast of the county seat, where he resided about one year. He bought a third farm near Springfield about 1879, and one year later purchased his present beautiful home place of 470 acres in the Pleasant Grove neighborhood, where he has since resided. Mr. Noe is one of Washington County's most successful farmers and stock raisers. He is emphatically a self-made man, having begun life with no capital, and by untiring industry and skillful management accumulated a handsome competency. He was married, May 28, 1861, to Miss Mary E. Graham, daughter of John Graham, of Boyle County. Five children have been born to this marriage: Hugh M., Lizzie L., Sarah A., Arvin G. and Mary W. Mr. Noe is a member of the Baptist Church, with which he has been identified since 1856. He is a Democrat in politics, but never aspired to official position. Mrs. Noe is a member of the Methodist Church.

ANDREW OFFUTT was born November 9, 1837. He is the fifth of a family of eleven children born to Zephamiah Offutt and Elizabeth P. Brown, the former a native of Spencer and the latter of Washington County, Ky. Zephamiah was a son of Andrew Offutt, an early settler in Spencer County, and Elizabeth was the daughter of William and Catherine Brown. Zephamiah Offutt in his early manhood removed to Washington County, where he lived until his death in 1850, having served the county in various official capacities. His widow next contracted marriage with a Mr. Rease, removed to Missouri and there died in 1857. Andrew Offutt, a native of Washington County, was reared chiefly on the farm, but learned the trade of a carpenter to which he has devoted several years of his life. He returned from Missouri to Washington County, Ky., in 1860, and in October, 1861, entered the Federal Army as a member of Company A, Fifth Kentucky Cavalry. In June, 1863, he was made first lieutenant of Company K, and in December of the same year was made captain of Company B, with which commission he was mustered out in May, 1865. He shared the fortunes of his command through their entire service, and commanded a pioneer corps of 500 men on Sherman's memorable march to the seaboard. After the close of the war he located in Lebanon, his present home, where he engaged at his trade. In 1871 he established his planing-mill and lumber business, which he has successfully conducted since. Mr. Offutt married in Lebanon, in April, 1866, Lizzie A. Davis, daughter of A. P. Davis of Nelson County, Ky. Six sons have blessed their union, viz.: William V., Davis C., John R., Marshall W., Charles M., and Walter C. Offutt.

SANFORD OLDHAM was born near where he now resides, five miles south of Boonesborough, and is a son of Dawson and Caroline (Smith) Oldham, to whom four sons and five daughters were born, eight of whom lived to be grown, Sanford being the first child. Dawson Oldham was born on Otter Creek, three miles south of Boonesborough in 1817. He is a substantial and prosperous farmer and owned slave property before the war. He is the son of Nathaniel and Sadie (Spence) Oldham, who were early pioneers of Madison County. Nathaniel Oldham was born in North Carolina about 1790; was brought to Kentucky by his parents, reared a family of two sons and five daughters and was a leading farmer and slave-holder. He was a son of Jesse Oldham, who was born in Guilford County, N. C., and married a Miss Simpson of North Carolina. He reared a family of six sons and four daughters. The sons were Richard, Tyrie, Jesse, Elias, Nathaniel and John, some of whom served in the war for independence. Jesse Oldham entered land on Otter Creek, Madison County, and became a leading farmer. In religion the Oldham family were Baptists and were of Welsh extraction. Caroline (Smith) Oldham was a daughter of John and Nancy (Fowler) Smith, both natives of Madison County. John Smith was born in 1792, was a soldier in the war of 1812, and died in 1856. He was a son of Jesse Smith, who was born in Maryland, of Irish descent, and came to Madison County about 1785. Sanford Oldham was reared on a farm and received a common English education, and then attended Asbury University in 1863–64, after which he taught three months in the common schools. He married December 22, 1875, Zerelda Neal, of Lexington, a native of Madison County and a daughter of William and Zerelda (Howard) Neal. William Neal was born in Lexington about 1818; was one of the editors of the Richmond *Chronicle* and was a stanch and active Whig. After his marriage he became a farmer until 1860. In 1865 he moved to Lexington and opened a book store. His wife was born in the house which is now occupied by Sanford Oldham. She died in 1858, leaving three children. In 1864 William Neal married Carrie Goodloe, a daughter of Judge William Goodloe. The fruits of the second marriage were one son and one daughter. William L. Neal represented Madison County in the Legislature two terms; was a strong and stanch advocate of the union during the war, and served as quartermaster at Camp Nelson. He was in the revenue service about eight years. He was a son of James Neal, who came from England and whose wife was Ann Raney. Sanford Oldham and wife had born to them three bright children: Howard S., James M. and Anna Neal. Mr. and Mrs. Oldham are members of the Methodist Episcopal Church. After marriage they located where they now reside on what is known as the Ben Howard farm. Ben Howard was born on the farm in 1796 and died in 1880, and had never lived anywhere else. His father was born in 1755 and died on this same farm in 1830, and was one of the pioneers of Madison County. Mr. Oldham is the possessor of 100 acres of this Howard farm and also owns a farm in Missouri. He is a Master Mason and K. T. His first presidential vote was cast for Seymour.

JUDGE WILLIAM F. OWSLEY was born July 9, 1813. His father, Dr. Joel Owsley, was born in Lincoln County, June 28, 1790. When he was in his twentieth year he began the study of medicine under Dr. Mason, of Lancaster, Garrard County, and about 1811 attended a course of lectures at Lexington, but was never a graduate. He then moved to Cumberland County, where he began the practice of his profession. In April, 1812, he was united in marriage to Miss Mary Ann Lewis, a daughter of Joseph F. and Sarah (Whitley) Lewis. Joseph F. Lewis emigrated from London, England, to the United States, and settled in Lincoln County, where he carried on his trade of

brick masonry, building many of the court-houses and public buildings erected in early times. He died in Cumberland County about 1828. Sarah Whitley was a sister of Col. William Whitley, a Virginian and a veteran of the Revolution. He immigrated to Kentucky and was a celebrated Indian fighter in pioneer times, and a remarkably daring man, who had great influence with the Indians. He served in the campaigns against the Indians of Indiana, and it is said he killed the celebrated Indian chief, Tecumseh, and he himself was killed in the same battle. He commanded a regiment of provincial troops in the American Revolution, but served in the capacity of a scout in the Indian troubles, in which he lost his life. Whitley County is named for him. The marriage of Dr. and Mrs. Owsley was blessed by the addition of nine children: William F., Oscar, Edwards K., Amelia G. (wife of Robert Haskins), John Q., Helen M. (wife of James H. Ritchey), James H., M. H. and one who died in infancy. Dr. Owsley died May 30, 1869, worth $20,000, after having given each of his children a start in life. He was the first man in Cumberland County who joined the Christian Church, in which he was elder afterward. Mrs. Owsley, who was a member of the Christian Church, departed this life December 4, 1874, in the seventy-ninth year of her age. Dr. and Mrs. Owsley had lived in the town of Burkesville from 1811 until the time of their death. William Owsley, grandfather of Judge Owsley, was a native of Virginia, who immigrated to Lincoln County, Ky., when it was almost an unbroken wilderness. His marriage occurred in Virginia, and the maiden name of his wife was Catherine Bouldin. They were the parents of the following children: Newdigat, William, Samuel, John, Joel, Thomas, Nancy (Middleton), Obedience (Baughman), Patience and Kittie (Owsley). Hon. Wm. Owsley is a very prominent man in State politics, was for many years judge of the court of appeals, was a champion of the old court party, and in 1844 was elected governor of the State on the Whig ticket. William Owsley, grandfather of Judge Owsley, came from London, England, to the United States, settling first in Maryland, afterward in Virginia, but finally moved to Garrard County, and is buried near Lancaster. Hon. M. H. Owsley has been, during the last twelve years, judge of the circuit court of the Eighth Judicial District, and during the twelve years preceding was prosecuting attorney in the same district. He was also a prominent candidate for the Democratic nomination for

30

governor of the State in 1883. Judge William F. Owsley, a native of Cumberland County, in boyhood received a limited English education, and began the battle of life on his own account at the age of fourteen. At the age of sixteen he began selling goods in Burkesville, and with the exception of one year's residence in Frankfort, where he was in the circuit clerk's office one year, he has always lived in Cumberland County. In 1836, in partnership with his father, he began selling a line of general merchandise, which he continued six years. On February 22, 1842, he was united in marriage to Miss Ellen P. King, a daughter of Milton and Susan (Wilds) King, the former of Cumberland County, the latter of Virginia. In 1843 Judge Owsley again embarked in mercantile business on his own account with a capital of $12,000, which he continued until 1851. On July 8, 1847, Mrs. Owsley, who was a member of the Christian Church, departed this life, aged twenty-three, leaving one child, Adelaide, born July 21, 1845, and married to George F. Baker. On October 23, 1851, Judge Owsley was married to Miss Mary Agnes Bledsoe, a daughter of Joseph S. and Elizabeth Susan (Bowman) Bledsoe, natives of Cumberland County. Judge Owsley has carried on a farm many years in addition to selling goods, and besides has done a great deal of brokerage. In 1858, with F. W. Alexander, he took charge of a branch of the bank of Louisville, in Burkesville, and continued the banking business until 1865. Judge Owsley began life with nothing, and during the course of his life, has received in all, $1,500 from his father's estate. His estate now aggregates at least $100,000, all of which is the result of his own business management. The names of the children born to Judge and Mrs. Owsley are William F., born August 2, 1852; Laura Susan, born May 22, 1854, and died March 5, 1864; and Leila Ellen, born January 5, 1866, and married to Dr. Horace H. Grant, of Louisville, Ky., August 3, 1886. Mr. and Mrs. Owsley and all of their children are members of the Christian Church, and Judge Owsley, who has persistently refused political preferment and has never held office, except police judge of Burkesville, is independent in politics. He lives on his farm, three-quarters of a mile from Burkesville, valued at $25,000 and containing 800 acres. William F. Owsley, Jr., was married October 13, 1874, to Miss Sally Alexander, a daughter of F. W. and Nancy G. (King) Alexander, natives of Cumberland County. This marriage has been blessed by the addition of three children: Susan King,

William Fayette and Mary Agnes. Mr. Owsley has turned his entire attention during life to agriculture, and has a good English education. He has entire charge of his father's farm, besides owning a large quantity of land himself.

JUDGE M. H. OWSLEY was born December 10, 1834, in Burkesville, Cumberland Co., Ky., and is a son of Dr. Joel and Mary A. (Lewis) Owsley; the former a native of Lincoln County (this State) and a prominent physician, was a member of the Legislature several years, and died in 1869. He was a son of William Owsley, a Virginian and a Revolutionary soldier, and an early settler in Lincoln County. Mary A. (Lewis) Owsley was born in Lincoln County, and was a daughter of Joseph Lewis, a native of London, England. Judge Owsley, the subject of this sketch, received a liberal education and graduated in Centre College at Danville, in 1854, and at once began the study of law. He attended lectures in Lexington and Louisville, and graduated from the law department of the University of Louisville in 1856. Immediately after his admission to the bar, he located in Burkesville, and commenced the practice of his profession. He soon became a leading member of the bar of Southern Kentucky, and won a large and lucrative practice. In 1861 he entered in the Federal Army as captain of Company I, First Kentucky Cavalry. He remained with that regiment for four months and was then transferred to the Fifth Kentucky Cavalry and promoted to major. He participated in numerous engagements in Kentucky, Tennessee and Alabama. In 1862 he retired from the service to take the office of commonwealth's attorney, to which he had been elected. He was re-elected in 1868 without opposition. In 1874 he was elected judge, and in 1880 was re-elected without opposition. In 1864 he removed to Lancaster. He was married in March, 1865, to Ellen Letcher, a daughter of Dr. Joseph P. Letcher, of Lexington, and grand-niece of ex-Gov. Letcher and Chief Justice George Robertson. They have five children. Judge and Mrs. Owsley are members of the Christian Church. His first presidential vote was cast in 1860 for Bell and Everett; since the war he has affiliated with the Democrats.

MRS. VIRGINIA OWSLEY was born June 1, 1835; her grandfather, John Tucker, was a native of the Old Dominion, was a noted divine of the Methodist Church, and was one of the pioneer ministers of Kentucky, and he and wife were murdered at Fort Columbia by the Indians. His family consisted of two sons and two daughters, among whom was James H., the father of Mrs. Virginia Owsley. James H. Tucker was born January 15, 1788, and married Nancy Kennett of Marion County, and to them were born twelve children; of that number six are living—John H., Elizabeth (Avritt), Rhoda (Yowell) Dr. James H., Dr. D. C., and Mrs. Virginia Owsley. Nancy Kennett was born January 31, 1791, and died March 23, 1856. James H. Tucker during his lifetime followed the pursuits of the farm. He was a man of undoubted integrity and sterling worth, and held the esteem of all who knew him, in token of which he held the office of magistrate in his county for many years; his death occurred in 1871. Mrs. Virginia Owsley, a native of Marion County, has been twice married, first in 1854 to Leonard Taylor. This union was blessed by the birth of five sons: James H., Albert C., DeWitt C., John and Leonard. Mr. Taylor died in 1865. He was a farmer, was one of the landed proprietors of Boyle County, and left a neat fortune to his children. His father, Henly Taylor, owned a large estate in Marion County, and was one of its magistrates for many years. He reared a family of twelve children, of whom one son (John) is the only survivor. Mrs. Virginia's second marriage took place in 1871, with Lucien C. Owsley, a native of Alabama, and to this marriage is born one son, William. Mrs. Owsley is the owner of a neat farm of excellent land lying at the confluence of the north and south branches of Rolling Fork River in Marion County, where she was born. She has been a life-long member of the Methodist Church.

JOHN D. PARKES is the sixth in a family of ten children born to John W. Parkes, who was a native of Madison County, was born December 17, 1802, died July 3, 1879, and whose children were as follows: Samuel S., Margaret J. (Wilmore), Elizabeth (Smith), Jefferson W., Fannie (Smith), John B., James B., Mary (Watts), Nancy (Embry), Emma (Herndon). John B. Parkes was born January 18, 1844, in Madison County, where he lived until 1880, when he removed to Garrard County. He married, February 18, 1869, Miss Maggie Wallace, a daughter of Salem Wallace, who represented Madison County in the Legislature. Mr. and Mrs. Parkes have two children: Fannie B. and Jennie W. Mrs. Maggie Parkes died August 20, 1886, and was a Presbyterian. Mr. Parkes is a member of the same church. He owns 350 acres of land, 240 acres of it lying on the Kentucky Central Railroad. He is a Democrat in politics.

STEPHEN D. PARRISH, a young lawyer of Richmond, was born June 26, 1857, in Gonzales, Tex., and is a son of Socrates and Mary H. (Adams) Parrish, to whom eight children were born—four sons and two daughters reared. Socrates Parrish was born and reared in Madison County, Ky.; was a farmer, trader and surveyor. In 1855 he moved to Texas, and returned in 1858. He served as sheriff of Madison County for sixteen years. In 1870 he moved to Kansas, and returned in 1874, when he served as deputy sheriff a few years, and as constable of Madison County. He is at present city engineer of Richmond. He is a son of Wesley and Harriet (Hugely) Parrish, natives of Virginia, and among the early pioneers of Madison County. Wesley Parrish was an extensive farmer, served as magistrate of the county for many years; was a soldier in the war of 1812, and participated in the battle of New Orleans. He reared a family of six sons and four daughters; he was the owner of a large family of slaves; was a member of the Christian Church, and in politics was an active Whig prior to the war, but afterward a Democrat. Mrs. Mary H. Parrish was born in Madison County, and is a daughter of Thomas C. and Nancy (Goff) Adams, who were natives of Clark and Montgomery Counties, respectively. Mr. Adams was a thrifty farmer and the owner of a large family of slaves prior to 1860. He was of Scotch extraction, in religion a Methodist, and in politics a Whig. Stephen D. Parrish received a good English education, and was a salesman in Lawrence, Kas., for a short time, and assistant postmaster at LeRoy, Kas., for two years. In 1875 he returned to Kentucky, and served as deputy sheriff of Madison County two years; then spent two years in Central University, after which he taught one year and then re-entered college. In 1879-80 he attended the Louisville Law School, and in 1880 began to practice in Richmond with H. S. Douthitt. In 1883-84 he served as school commissioner of the county. He now turns his entire attention to his profession and is becoming one of the most successful lawyers of Richmond. He is not an aspirant for office, but was tendered a first clerkship in the land office in WaKeeney, Kas., which he respectfully declined, preferring to devote his time to his profession. October 7, 1886, he purchased the Richmond Herald, of which he is editor-in-chief, and Prof. P. H. Sullivan associate editor. He is a member of the I. O. O. F., also a member of the Methodist Episcopal Church North, and in politics is a Democrat.

ALEX L. PATTON, the subject of our sketch, is a great-grandson of William Patton, who moved to Madison County, Ky., from Virginia, about the year 1781, with three sons and two daughters. Alexander, the eldest, traded in stock, and on one of his trips to South Carolina met and married Sarah Simpson, and moved with her near the mouth of Brush Creek, Green County, Ky. His brothers and sisters settled in Lincoln County, Ky. He had five children. William S. Patton, the eldest, was the father of Alex L., was born April 30, 1803; he was a farmer and surveyor, and was a leading and active member of the Baptist Church. He was married to Miss Margaret Lee, July 11, 1827, and raised eleven children—two sons and nine daughters. He died February 29, 1856, aged fifty-three years. Margaret (Lee) Patton was a daughter of Joshua Lee, who was a soldier of the Revolutionary war, and moved from Virginia at an early day, and settled near the mouth of Little Barren River in Green County, Ky.; died at about eighty years of age. She died October, 1863, aged fifty-six years. Alex L. Patton was born February, 6, 1840, on Brush Creek, reared and received his early training on the farm, taught school, and in September, 1862, enlisted in Company K, Third Kentucky Confederate Cavalry, under Gen. John H. Morgan. He remained with Morgan's command constantly up to the time he started on the Ohio raid; at that time he was courier between Gen. Morgan's and Gen. Bragg's headquarters. He was not relieved from his post in time to overtake his command. He attached himself to Capt. Dorch's company and remained with it until Morgan's return from prison, when he again joined Morgan and remained with him until captured at Cynthiana, Ky., in June, 1864; he was sent to Rock Island prison, where he remained until the close of the war. January, 1865, he returned home and engaged in farming two years; in 1867 he moved to Greensburg, and clerked in a dry goods store until 1869, when he went into business for himself with A. N. Chelf as partner, and has remained in the dry goods business up to the present time. He married, February 8, 1877, Ella Durham, a daughter of John J. and Elizabeth (Henry) Durham, who were natives of Green County. Mr. Durham was an extensive farmer, and was sheriff and county judge, and died in August, 1875. Mr. and Mrs. Patton have had born to them five children: Henry Lee, Nuna, Willie C., Leslie L., and Ella A. Mr. and Mrs. Patton are members of the Baptist and Christian Churches respectively; he is a Democrat, and cast his first vote for Seymour and Blair. He is also a member of the F. & A. M.

LEWIS T. PAYNE was born November 2, 1813, in Scott County, and in 1881 moved to Mercer County, where he has since resided. His father, Asa Payne, was born March 19, 1788, also in Scott County. In 1809 his uncle, Col. Richard M. Johnson, secured to him an appointment as cadet to West Point, which he resigned in 1810 to accept from President Madison, a clerkship in the Government trading house at Fort Madison, Iowa, where he remained two years. In the war of 1812, he was *aide* to his father, Gen. John Payne, in the Northern campaign, and after the war engaged in farming in Scott County. He had given his children many slaves, and lost ten himself by the late war. He is a Democrat in politics, casting his first vote for President Madison, and now (August, 1886) in his ninety-ninth year is sprightly for one of his age, and is remarkably well preserved in body and mind, reading without glasses. He is a member of the Baptist Church, and has always been temperate, and of cheerful disposition. For fifteen of his later years he served as magistrate and a member of the court of claims of Scott County. His father, Gen. John Payne, was born near Alexandria, Va., 1763; received a good education; was in the Virginia militia, and present at the surrender of Lord Cornwallis, soon after which he settled in Kentucky; was active in the Indian wars on the frontier; a general in the war of 1812, a State senator, a farmer and large slave-holder, and died in 1837. He was a son of William Payne, born in 1670, a Virginian farmer who died in 1775, at the age of one hundred and five years. William's father was from Wales, and received a grant of land twelve miles square in Virginia. William's children were Edward (who under the law of primogeniture inherited the estate, and married Lady Conyers), William, Jr., and Sandford. At the age of ninety-five years William, Sr., married Ann Jennings and their offspring were John (Gen.) and Milly (Riley). John married Elizabeth, daughter of Col. Robert Johnson (sister of Col. Richard M. Johnson, born in 1773, died in 1847), and from their union sprang Asa, Robert, Nancy (Offutt), Sally (Thompson), John, Newton, Jefferson, Franklin, Emeline (Peak), Betsy (Sebree), and Cyrus, who was killed in the Mexican war. Asa married in 1811 Theodosia Turner (born February 26, 1788, died June 11, 1841), and their offspring are Lewis T., John F., and

Henry. Lewis T. Payne was first married in 1835, to Miss Sally, daughter of Nathan and Kittie (Hall) Payne, of Fayette County (born November 15, 1815, died July 12, 1841), and there were born John Henry, Lewis Elzay (deceased) and Sarah (deceased). October 12, 1842, he married Mrs. Martha Gaines, daughter of Capt. Willa and Lydia (Smith) Viley, of Scott County (born April 25, 1819, died November 2, 1883), and to them were born Asa, Jr. (November 15, 1852), and Lydia V. (Cogar), born April 16, 1860. Lydia V.'s child is Mattie M. Cogar. January 14, 1879, Asa, Jr., married Miss Rosa, a daughter of Andrew McCracken, of Richmond (born April 26, 1858), and their child is Mattie V. Lewis T. Payne is a farmer, having 167 acres of well improved land. He is a member of the Christian Church and a Democrat.

EUGENE H. PEARCE was born September 16, 1844, near Maysville, Ky., and is the only son of four children born to Wesley and Rachael (Woods) Pearce. Wesley Pearce was born and reared near Evansville, Va.; emigrated to Brown County, Ohio, near Maysville, Ky., about 1825, was a farmer, and died in 1877, aged seventy-four years. He was a son of Capt. Samuel Pearce of Evansville, Preston Co., W. Va., and who was one of its pioneers. The Pearce families of Virginia, Maryland and Delaware are of Scotch and Scotch-Irish nativity, the father, Samuel Pearce, immigrating to America about 1752, from Lurgan, north Ireland, whither the family had been driven by the religious persecutions in Scotland, under James II, against Protestants. Pursued by the dragoons of Claverhouse, executing the edicts of James II, the early ancestor, Mark Pearce, had only time to pause for a moment at his own door and say to his wife, "you go to Lurgan—I go to France." By that persecution, a part of the Pearce family became identified with the Huguenots of France, afterward immigrating to America, and settling in the Carolinas and Georgia. From the Huguenot branch came the Pierces of the Carolinas and Georgia, represented in the present generation by the eminent Rev. Dr. Lovick Pierce, of Georgia, and his distinguished son, Bishop Geo. F. Pierce, of the Methodist Episcopal Church South. Samuel Pearce, the paternal grandfather of Eugene H. Pearce, was captain of a cavalry company in Gen. Green's corps, during the war for independence, was wounded at the battle of Brandywine, and was at the Yorktown surrender. He married Margaret Cunningham, of Virginia, a half

sister of Zachariah Morgan, the founder of Morgantown, W. Va., and a prominent pioneer—her brother, Lieut. Cunningham, was in the fleet under Com. Perry and was killed in the battle of Lake Erie during the war of 1812. The mother of E. H. Pearce was born near Maysville, Ky., and was a daughter of Micha and Hester (Bowman) Woods, one a native of Mason, the other of Bracken County, Ky. Micha Woods was a planter and trader, a soldier of 1812; from Mason County moved to Brown County, Ohio, where he died at an advanced age. For some years Judge Woods was judge of the county court of Brown County. He was a son of Samuel Woods, who was born in Carlisle, Penn., and who was a soldier during the war for independence, 1776 to 1781. He migrated to Limestone, now Maysville, in 1782, where he lived till his death. His brother, Ezekiel Woods, migrated from Mason County, Ky., and settled in Toledo, Ohio. Hon. William B. Woods, of the supreme court of the United States, 1880–87, is a son of Ezekiel Woods. Eugene H. Pearce was reared on a farm, graduated from the National Normal University of Ohio, in August, 1865, and also received honorary degree from Kentucky Wesleyan College; studied law with Hon. T. W. Bartley, an ex-chief justice of the supreme court of Ohio, at Cincinnati, also with Hon. R. H. Stanton of Maysville, Ky.; April, 1867, was admitted to the bar, and practiced his profession till 1870, when he entered the licentiate of the ministry, acting till 1875 as assistant superintendent of the American Bible Society for western Kentucky; receiving leave of absence, was appointed by Gov. Leslie as commissioner to the Vienna International Exposition, making a general tour of Europe and Great Britain. After his resignation with the American Bible Society, he entered and completed a course of study at Drew Theological Seminary, and subsequently entered the Kentucky Conference, Methodist Episcopal Church South, and was first stationed at Covington, in September, 1876; he has since been appointed to pastorates at Paris, Versailles, Nicholasville and Danville, while at three of these places he caused handsome churches to be built—at Covington, Versailles and Nicholasville. In May, 1882, he purchased a residence in Danville—"Grace lawn," the former residence of Col. Jno. Cowan. While he was connected with the Bible Society, October, 1869, to July, 1875, he traveled 37,459 miles and delivered 630 sermons and addresses. In 1870 he invented and introduced the supply of the Scriptures to railroad coaches, whilst acting as superintendent of the American Bible Society in western Kentucky. After filling pastorates with much acceptance at Covington, Paris, Versailles, Nicholasville and also as member of the board of education of the Kentucky Conference, Mr. Pearce became pastor of the Walnut Street Methodist Church South, at Danville, in September, 1884. Under his ministry here, there was an increase of thirty per cent in the membership, from 1884 to 1886, placing the church among the first in the South, in organization and influence. In 1884 he published a "Manual of Church Work and Organization," more especially for use of his own congregation, but which through notice and commendation of the religious press and pastors elsewhere, had subsequently a circulation and sale in twenty States of the Union. As a member of the board of curators of Kentucky, Wesleyan College at Millersburg, Mr. Pearce, chiefly in 1887, advocated the relocation of the institution at Winchester, Ky., his addresses and arguments in behalf of the educational interests of the church being widely circulated and attracting much attention and commendation. Being officially appointed by the Kentucky Conference to represent its interests in Kentucky Wesleyan College, he made application and argument before the Kentucky Legislature, in the winter of 1886, for enactment of temperance legislation for Kentucky Wesleyan College and vicinity. In discharge of the duty, he became engaged in a newspaper controversy with Hon. Charles Offutt, speaker of the House and representative of the county in which the college was located (Bourbon). The result of the controversy was a very signal triumph for the interests of the conference and the welfare of the institution. In 1882 Mr. Pearce became interested in the growth and development of Florida, his influence and contributions to the press contributing in no small degree to advancement of its interests, especially on the western coast and vicinity of Tampa Bay, where he located an estate and winter residence near Bay View, one of the most picturesque and attractive localities in Florida. In 1887 he was elected president of the Kentucky Chautauqua Assembly, at its first organization in the city of Lexington, in convention composed of ministers and laymen from different denominations throughout the State. For fourteen years, 1863 to 1877, he was also a member of the State executive committee of the Young Men's Christian Association of Kentucky, assisting in organizing and promoting the work in many places. Mr. Pearce was married October 15, 1874, to Miss Annie E. Armstrong, second daughter of Charles Q. and Amanda F. Armstrong, at "Idylwild," the country and ancestral residence of the family, near Bloomfield, Nelson Co., Ky. Miss Armstrong was born and reared in Louisville, Ky., and was educated at the Nold school for young ladies, and Louisville Female College. Possessed of culture, with graces of person and an active and benevolent disposition, Mrs. Pearce's influence and usefulness has been of signal and marked character in all the walks of life. Her father, Charles Q. Armstrong, was for many years one of the most active and prosperous citizens of the city of Louisville and was most highly esteemed. Her mother, Amanda F. Allen, was a daughter of Jas. Allen, one of the pioneers of Nelson County, and a most popular and useful citizen, greatly respected by all who knew him. The Allen family was one of unusual force of character. Col. Jno. Allen, a brother of James Allen, and member of the Shelbyville bar, was a graduate of the University of Virginia and commanded the Second Kentucky Regiment at the battle of the River Raisin, in the war of 1812, where he fell at the head of his regiment. A descendant of the Allen family, also, was Rev. David Nelson of Danville, Ky., the celebrated author of "Cause and Cure of Infidelity." Gen. Thomas H. Crittenden and Gen. E. H. Murray are grandsons of Col. John Allen. Both were distinguished officers in the civil war, and subsequently became governors of Missouri and Utah. Another grandson is Logan C. Murray, president of the United States National Bank of New York City. Mr. and Mrs. Pearce have had born to them five children: Eugene Lovick, born in 1875, in Louisville; Stanley Dodd, born in 1876, at "Idylwild," Nelson County; Lilian, born in 1880, at Versailles; Allene, born in 1882, and Charles Wesley (deceased), born in 1885, at Danville, Ky.

BENJAMIN W. PENICK was born June 3, 1841, and is a son of Thomas B. and Mary (Ingram) Penick, who reared two sons and one daughter, Thomas B. Penick was born in Prince Edward County, Va., and was one of the early settlers of Green County, where he became one of the leading and substantial farmers and slave owners, and traded quite extensively in mules. He died in 1851 at the age of forty-two years, leaving an estate of 1,200 acres, and thirty slaves. He was a son of William Penick of Virginia who came to Green County in an early day with his father. Mrs. Mary Penick was born in Adair County, and is a daughter of Benjamin and Elizabeth (Irvin) Ingram, who emigrated from Virginia to Adair County, in an early day, where Mr. Ingram became an extensive and prominent farmer. B. W. Penick was born on Russell's Creek, Green County, on a farm; received the rudiments of an English education which was augmented at Columbia High School and at Greensburg, and he graduated at Georgetown College, Kentucky, in 1860. In 1861, at the death of an uncle, he went to live with his grandmother Ingram. On October 8, 1861, he married Elizabeth F. Brummal, a daughter of Josiah and Mary (Hundley) Brummal, who emigrated from Virginia to Cumberland County, Ky., where Mr. Brummal was engaged in the mercantile business. Thence he moved to Green County, which he afterward represented in the Legislature. He retained his residence in Green County, but ran a sugar plantation in Louisiana for many years. Mr. and Mrs. Penick had born to them four children: Brummal, Mary Lewis, S. Hundly (deceased) and Clifton. After marriage he located where he was born. In 1867 he moved to Greensburg, and entered the circuit clerk's office as deputy. In August, 1868, was elected circuit clerk and is now serving his fourth term. He has also run a farm all this time, and is a breeder and dealer in shorthorn cattle, one-half a mile east of the courthouse. His wife died in June, 1872, a devoted member of the Presbyterian Church. In September, 1875, he married Anna M. Hobson, a daughter of Gen. E. H. Hobson. He and wife are members of the Baptist and Presbyterian Churches, respectively, and Mr. Penick is a member of the F. and A. M. He is a Democrat in politics.

EPHRAIM PENNINGTON. Prominent among the early citizens of Lincoln County was Ephraim Pennington, who was born in Rockbridge County, Va., in 1785, and was of Scotch-Irish ancestors, who were among the first settlers of Virginia. When he was but two years old his parents removed to Kentucky and located at Crab Orchard. Here Ephraim grew to manhood and married, in 1812, Bettie Vardiman. He reared two sons and six daughters, named as follows: Polly P., T. M. Pennington, E. D. Pennington, Ibeann, Easter Louis, Betsy V., Lavisa Emily and Sabra Ellen Pennington. Ephraim Pennington was for many years a magistrate of Lincoln under the old constitution, and at that time when only the best men were honored by that office, and as an evidence of

that respect in which his memory is held, his portrait (a large oil painting) hangs in the court room of the county courthouse. He died December 11, 1861, and his wife, Betsey Pennington, died in 1846 in the fifty-fourth year of her age. E. D. Pennington, their second son, married Mary F. Welch, daughter of J. M. Welch. They have three children: Bettie V., John W. and Mary Sabry. E. D. Pennington died in Lincoln County in 1872. J. W. Pennington married Jennie M. Huffman September 7, 1879, and has two children, named Ephraim D. and Mary Paxton.

ALBERT R. PENNY, senior member of the firm of Penny & McAlister, druggists af Stanford, Ky., is a native of Hamilton County, Ohio, where he was born in 1840. His parents were W. H. Penny and Mary A. Penny. He was educated in the city of Cincinnati, Ohio, where he took a thorough course in the science of pharmacy, and where he served an apprenticeship as drug clerk. In 1860 he came to Stanford, Ky., where he formed a business partnership with J. M. Cooper, under the firm name of Cooper & Penny. Mr. Penny is one of the leading business men of his town, a member of high order in the Masonic fraternity, and in politics a Democrat. He was married, in 1861, to Miss Mary E. Boone, a daughter of George G. Boone and Patience O. Boughman, the former a native of Fayette County, Ky., and now of Lincoln County; the latter a representative of one of the early and numerous families of Lincoln County. Albert R. and Mary E. Penny have reared three children: Dr. W. B. Penny, Sarah E. (wife of Rev. R. B. Mahoney, of Richmond, Ky.), and George L. Penny. Dr. William B. Penny was educated in Stanford, Ky., and 1882 entered the Philadelphia Dental College, where he graduated in 1883, since which time he has successfully practiced his profession in Stanford, Ky. He was married, in 1885, to Miss Julia Cooper, a daughter of the late J. M. Cooper, of Stanford.

RICHARD H. PERRYMAN, M. D., was born in Russell County, Ky., December 30, 1840, and is the youngest of twelve children born to William, Jr., and Sabrina (Johnson) Perryman, natives of Maryland and North Carolina respectively, and of English descent. William Perryman, Jr., was born in 1781, and when a small boy came with his parents to Russell County, Ky. (then a part of Green County), in 1806, when the youngest child, Washington, was two years old. In that county he grew to manhood, and was married. Soon after attaining his majority he bought wild land on the waters of the Cumberland near Jamestown, and improved a farm on which he resided until his death, September 15, 1865. In early life he had learned the carpenter's trade which he continued to follow all his life in connection with farming. Both he and wife were from childhood members of the Old School Baptist Church. William Perryman, Sr., was born and educated in Maryland, and afterward one of the early pioneers of Kentucky, settling in what is now Russell County. He served as a teamster in the Continental Army during the entire struggle, and was once captured and held a prisoner of war for a time. He was also frost bitten during his service, from the effects of which he lost his hearing. He was a pensioner until his death, at the age of one hundred years, being the only centenarian in the county. He was also a life-long and devoted member of the Old School Baptist Church. His father, the great grandfather of our subject, also named William Perryman, was a native of England, but in early life came to America with the company brought out with Lord Baltimore. Mrs. Sabrina (Johnson) Perryman, was born in 1784, and died January 10, 1863. Her father, Thomas Johnson, was a native of North Carolina, and was also one of the first settlers in what is now Russell County, Ky. Dr. Richard H. Perryman received an excellent English and scientific education in youth and taught school several years, commencing at the age of sixteen. In January 1860, he commenced the study of medicine under the preceptorship of Dr. John M. Wolford, of Jamestown, Russell Co., Ky., with whom he continued until June, 1863, when he went to Hardinsburg, Washington Co., Ind., where he continued his studies under Drs. John Ellis and William Schoonover, until the following October, when he returned to Kentucky, and enlisted as a private in Company K, Thirteenth Kentucky Volunteer Cavalry (Federal). December 23, following he was promoted to hospital steward, but performed the duties of an assistant surgeon until the close of the war, when he was mustered out at Camp Nelson, Ky., January 10, 1865. He participated in the battles and skirmishes in which his regiment engaged, and usually had special charge of the field hospital after each engagement; in May, 1865, removed to Neetsville, Adair County, where he engaged in the practice of his profession. The Doctor has won for himself a place at the head of his profession, and is recognized as one of the leading and most successful

surgeons and physicians in this part of the State. In 1877 he bought a farm of 160 acres, three miles below Neetsville, on the Green River, where he now resides, and is engaged in agricultural pursuits in connection with the practice of medicine. He married October 3, 1865, Miss Margaret C. Wolford, also a native of Russell County, Ky., born May 8, 1848, and the youngest of eleven children, born to Dr. John M. and Jane (Grider) Wolford, natives of Russell and Adair Counties respectively, and of English descent. They were life-long and devoted members of the Old School Baptist Church. John M. Wolford's father, John Wolford, was one of the pioneers of south central Kentucky, where for many years he was a teacher in the select schools, and also one of the best land surveyors of that day. To Mr. and Mrs. Perryman have been born eleven children: Owen G. (deceased), Virginia E. (deceased), William C., Fannie E., George N., Luther B., Melvin R., Junius C., an infant (deceased), John F. and Elba R. Mrs. Perryman is a member of the Christian Church, and also of the order of the Eastern Star. The Doctor is not a member of any church, but is a bright member of the Masonic fraternity, and has held various official positions in his lodge. In politics he is a Republican, and although never an office seeker, is recognized as a party leader in his part of the county.

HENRY B. PETERSON, M. D., was born October 3, 1838, and is a son of William and Celia A. (Buckler) Peterson, to whom eight sons and two daughters were born, all of whom lived to be grown, except one son and one daughter. William Peterson was born in September, 1811; he was a substantial farmer and owned a number of negroes; died April 7, 1886. He was a son of Garrett Peterson, who was born in Washington County, Ky.; was a captain in the war of 1812, served under Gen. Harrison; was a farmer and slave-holder, and died of cholera in Marion County, in 1833. He had married Nancy Smock; was a son of Henry Peterson. His father also married a Miss Smock, was born in Pennsylvania, was of Holland descent, and was one of the first settlers of Marion County. Mrs. Celia A. (Buckler) Peterson was born in Marion County, and a daughter of Henry and Elizabeth (Tolbert) Buckler, who were born in Virginia and Maryland respectively, and came to Marion County, Ky., as early as 1804 and settled near Loretto. Henry Buckler died in 1854, aged seventy-five years. Dr. Henry B. Peterson was born near Chicago, Marion

Co., Ky., and received a liberal education. At the age of twenty he commenced teaching and continued till after twenty-two in the common schools. At the age of twenty-four he turned his entire attention to the study of medicine; graduated from Jefferson Medical College, Philadelphia, in the spring of 1866 and located where he now resides, in Raywick, meeting with success. He is a member of the Marion County Medical Association, and Beech Fork Association, and also a member of the board of health. He married Mary E. Beall in April, 1867. She is a daughter of Thomas J. and Sarah Jane (Stiles) Beall, natives of Marion and Nelson Counties respectively. Mr. Beall was a farmer and distiller and a large slave-holder. In 1874 he moved to Jackson County, Kas. He was a son of Washington and Mary (Carter) Beall, who came from Maryland in an early day. Washington Beall was a substantial farmer and distiller. He built and owned one of the first mills on Salt Lick Creek, and in that part of the country was a large land owner. Mr. and Mrs. Peterson have had born to them three children: Stiles T., Wesley W. and Anna B., all members of the Methodist Episcopal Church South, as are their parents. The Doctor is a member of the F. & A. M., in politics is a consistent Democrat, and cast his first vote for Douglas, in 1860.

DR. JOSEPH D. PETTUS. In the year 1807, Joseph Pettus, with his wife, Lucy (Graves) Pettus, and three children, James O., Virginia and Richard G., came from Petersburg, Va., to Kentucky, and settled on Drake's Creek, in Lincoln County, where the four younger children, Nancy, Joseph, Barbara and William H., were born, and where Joseph Pettus died in 1854, at the age of seventy-four years. Richard G., the father of our subject, was born in Petersburg, Va., in 1806, reared in Lincoln County, Ky., and married Miss Nancy Adams, daughter of Daniel and Lydia Adams, of Garrard County, Ky. Their family, consisting of four children, were William H., born in 1827; Joseph D., born in 1829; John F., born in 1832, and Margaret A., born in 1835. Dr. Joseph D. Pettus received a good English education and studied medicine at Lancaster, Ky., and is one of the oldest practitioners in Lincoln County, located at Crab Orchard. He was married in 1855 to Miss Edith, daughter of Thomas and Mary Francis, of Madison County, Ky. Their union has been blessed with seven children: Thomas R., born in 1856; Lewis A., born in 1860; Ida L., born in 1868; Maud, born in 1870; Joseph H., born

in 1872; William C., born in 1874, and Philip T., born in 1878.

THOMAS PHELPS was born April 9, 1838, two miles north of Richmond, and is a son of Samuel and Tabitha (Taylor) Phelps, to whom seven sons and four daughters were born, eight of whom reached maturity: George W. (deceased), Peter T., Samuel B., Anthony (deceased), Marcus A., Thomas, Josiah, Nancy B. (Jones), Pollie (deceased), Tabitha A. (Todd), and Isabella (deceased). Tabitha A. was first married to Col. D. Waller Chenault, who distinguished himself in the war between the States, and who fell at the battle of Green River bridge, in 1863, during the famous Morgan raid through Kentucky and Ohio. Samuel Phelps, the father, was born October 13, 1788, four miles north of Richmond; he was a prosperous farmer, and succeeded in accumulating an estate of about 2,000 acres of blue-grass land, and more than a hundred slaves. He was the first to improve the famous blue-grass of Kentucky, and was the first man in the county to handle jack stock. He was a liberal, useful, public-spirited man, a member of the Christian Church, a Democrat in politics, and died in April, 1852. His father, George Phelps, was born in Virginia and came with his father, Thomas Phelps, and family to Kentucky, as early as 1775, and were with Boone in the fort at Boonesborough during the stormy days of that period. Lucy Phelps (Brashears), daughter of Thomas Phelps, was in the fort at Boonesborough, and was afterward married in Louisville, being the first white woman who was married in that city. They all moved to Bullitt County, where George Phelps married Tabitha Simmons and then came to Madison County. The issue of this marriage was eight children: Samuel, Anthony, Sallie (Deatherage), Verlinda (Williams), Lucy (Winburn), wife of Capt. Winburn, who distinguished himself in the war of 1812. The next children were William, Edwin, and Patsie (now Simmons). Sallie Deatherage is yet living, aged ninety-three. Mrs. Tabitha (Taylor) Phelps, wife of Samuel Phelps, and mother of Thomas Phelps, subject of this sketch, belonged to an old and aristocratic family, and was the daughter of Peter W. and Nancy (Crossthwaite) Taylor. Mr. and Mrs. Taylor came to Madison County as early as 1785, and settled three miles west of Richmond. They reared a family of five sons and three daughters—the daughters all marrying prominent men, and the sons reaching distinction in the different professions. Thomas Phelps, our subject, was reared on a farm and attended the common schools until 1854, when he entered Georgetown College and graduated from that institution in 1857, at the age of nineteen, after which he engaged in farming on his own account. June 15, 1865, he was married to Miss Sallie W. Cobb, of Lincoln County, a daughter of Richard and Minerva (Park) Cobb, who were born respectively in Estill and Madison Counties. Mr. Cobb was born in March, 1818, is a prosperous and influential farmer, and he and wife are yet living in Lincoln County. Richard is the son of Jesse and Edith (Oldham) Cobb, who came from North Carolina and settled in Estill County as early as 1785, and ranked among the prominent and wealthy families of the county, Jesse Cobb representing his county in the Legislature a number of terms. Mr. Phelps is the owner of three farms containing in all about 800 acres, and is a large dealer in cattle and swine. He owns and lives on what is known as the Dreaming Creek Heights, one and a half miles north of Richmond. He is a member of the Baptist Church, a member of the F. & A. M., and in politics a Democrat. Formerly he was a Whig, and cast his first presidential vote for Bell.

LEWIS V. PHILLIPS, a resident of Lancaster, Garrard Co., Ky., was born in Amherst County, Va., June 21, 1806, and is a son of Isaac and Lucy (Goodrich) Phillips. When he was but three years old his parents removed to Kentucky and settled on Gilbert's Creek, in Garrard County, and have a large number of descendants in Garrard and adjacent counties. The grandparents of our subject were George Phillips and Sallie Mayfield, the former a preacher, and the latter a daughter of Isaac and Jane (Baxter) Mayfield, who was a native of Scotland. George Phillips was of Irish descent. He had a family of four sons and six daughters: Isaac, Jacob, John, George, Frankie, Jinny, Suky, Millie, Sally and Peggy. They all removed to Kentucky about 1809 and settled in Garrard County. Lewis V. Phillips was married in 1828 to Indiana Burnside, a daughter of John and Nancy (Smith) Burnside, both of whom have an extensive connection in Garrard County. They had a family of four sons and five daughters, the eldest of whom, Martha A., married Nathan A. Thompson of Lancaster, Garrard County. As a result of this last named union, two sons were reared, viz.: John C. and Isaac Thompson. The former has a large jewelry business in Lancaster, with a good branch house in Stanford, Ky., and the younger son is associated with his father in the grocery business in Lancaster, Ky. The Mayfield family already mentioned in this sketch were highly respectable people, and among their descendants are a number of the best families in Garrard County, viz.: Henry Marksbury, the wife of G. W. Yancey; Dr. O. P. Hill and others. Sallie (Mayfield) Phillips lived to the age of one hundred and thirteen years. Lewis V. Phillips and his wife are still living, making their home in Lancaster with the family of N. A. Thompson, the former in his eighty-first year, and the latter in her seventy-sixth year.

JOHN C. THOMPSON, the elder grandson of

Lewis V. Phillips, is a prominent business man of Lancaster, Garrard Co., Ky. He was born on the 10th of August, 1851, and is the eldest son of Nathan A. Thompson, who is a business man of Lascaster, and his mother was Martha A. Phillips, the eldest daughter of Lewis V. Phillips of Garrard County. He was well educated but early acquired a taste for a mechanical trade, and during his school days, his teacher often found his desk provided with tools not required in the analysis of a sentence, nor a solution of a problem in mathematics. He chose the trade of watchmaker and jeweler, in which he became skilled, and at which he worked for some years. In 1872 he established his present house, which then consisted of a small stock, but which is now second to none in central Kentucky. This success is due to native energy, thorough business qualifications, and honest dealing; the jewelry house of John C. Thompson has now more than a local reputation. He makes a specialty of fine diamonds, and draws a patronage from various counties of central Kentucky. On account of increasing trade Mr. Thompson has established a branch house in Stanford, Ky. His business success verifies the adage "honesty is the best policy," and also serves as an incentive to young men. He is a member of the Board of Trustees of Lancaster; director in the building and loan association; a member of the Christian Church, of the Masonic fraternity, and I. O. O. F. Being aggressive his influence is felt in the enterprise of his town. Mr. Thompson was married, in 1876, to Miss Sallie, daughter of Richard Simpson of Garrard County. They have three children: Lizzie, Mattie and May.

FELIX GRUNDY PHILLIPS (deceased) was born September 12, 1807, in what is now Marion County, Ky., but at that time was embraced in Washington County. He was the youngest of a large family, children of William and Margaret Phillips. William Phillips, in company with three elder brothers, reached Kentucky in 1779, coming from Maryland by way of Pennsylvania; they stopped about one year in Allegheny County, then came on to Kentucky, floating down the Ohio River to the falls at Louisville. After considerable delay, they settled on Hardin's Creek, and built Hardin's Creek Fort, about eighteen miles west of Sandusky's Fort, their nearest neighbors. From this place William Phillips moved in 1800 to a farm near Lebanon, where he continued to live till March 22, 1834, when he died, aged seventy-five years. F. G. Phillips received as good an education as the schools of the county there afforded, and after leaving school studied civil engineering and was for twenty years county surveyor of Marion County, at a time when that office was of great importance on account of the careless system of land warrants and entry of public lands then prevailing in this State. In this capacity he became universally known and respected throughout the county, no less for the capable execution of the duties of the office, than for his genial, peace-loving disposition. This spirit combined with that sturdy integrity of principle which ever formed the solid base of his character, enabled him to amicably adjust many serious differences arising from confusion of title and boundary lines. During his entire manhood, Mr. Phillips was a consistent member of the Methodist Episcopal Church South, faithful in the discharge of every duty imposed by that obligation; without sectarianism, abounding in genuine Christian charity. He was widely known and honored among the ministry of the Louisville Conference, possessing in an unstinted degree the affection and confidence of the acquaintance of his youth—the late Bishop H. H. Kavanaugh—between whom and Mr. Phillips there existed for long years, until broken by death, a friendship without alloy, in all its relations mutually pleasant and profitable. On the 22d of May, 1834, Mr. Phillips was married to Frances Moss Penick, daughter of Edward Penick, Sr., who had emigrated from Virginia in 1810, and at that time lived near Bradfordsville, on Lebanon road, living there until his death in 1840. Of this union there were born twelve children: Ann Eliza, who died in early youth; Mary, now Mrs. Irwin, a prominent teacher in Knoxville, Tenn.; Edward, who studied medicine, dying in 1872; J. Howard, who served through the war in the Tenth Kentucky Federal Volunteers, was severely wounded in the battle of Chickamauga, rejoined his regiment after recovery, was honorably discharged in 1865, and died in Minnesota in September, 1868; Lettie, who died in girlhood in 1862; Nannie, who died in 1876; Fannie, now Mrs. Frye, of Hustonville, Ky.; Agnes, now Mrs. Berryman, of Owensboro, Ky.; F. G., Jr., a farmer in Marion County; Buford, a merchant in Knoxville, Tenn.: Charles M., attorney at law, Lebanon, Ky.; Capitola, the youngest, who died in early womanhood in 1884. In 1841 Mr. Phillips became the owner of his father-in-law's farm, removing to it from Lebanon in the same year and continued there to live, dispensing a generous hospitality to all who came within his gates, until his death, September 12, 1875. Mrs. Phillips survived her husband nearly eight years, and died in June, 1883, loved and mourned by all who knew her.

JAMES G. PHILLIPS, JR., one of the oldest as well as most prosperous merchants of Lebanon, was born in Washington County, Ky., November 9, 1830. His parents were Thomas and Julia (Maxwell) Phillips, both of whom were born in Washington County, where they grew to maturity and married, and where they made a residence until 1832, when, with their family, they removed to Meade County, settling on a farm near Brandenburg. There they passed the remainder of their lives, the mother dying in 1841, and the father in 1846. In 1846 James G. removed to Lebanon, Marion County, becoming a member of the family of an uncle, David Phillips. In 1847 he began his mercantile career as a salesman; in 1861 he opened his first business house with a stock valued at $5,000, which in three years he had increased to $75,000. He was at first associated with T. W. Blanford; in 1864 the firm became Phillips & Bro., which partnership continued for a period of twenty years, since which the firm has been styled J. G. Phillips & Co. Besides his extensive mercantile business in Lebanon, Mr. Phillips is entire owner of the Lebanon Flouring Mills, and a senior partner of an immense mercantile house in Owensboro, Ky. Mr. Phillips was married in 1863 in Boyle County, Ky., to Miss Eusebia Q., daughter of John Burton. Their four children are, Emma, wife of E. M. Hundley; John, Thomas and Birdie Phillips. The family are members of the Methodist Episcopal Church.

REV. BURNET JOHNSON PINKERTON was born April 12, 1843, in Lexington, Ky.; in 1844 removed with his parents to Midway; in 1860 to Harrodsburg, and in 1883 he located at Harrodsburg Junction, Mercer County, where he now resides. His father, Rev. Lewis L. Pinkerton, M. D., a native of Baltimore, Md., was born January 28, 1812, and while enjoying but limited facilities, by his own efforts and untiring zeal he mastered the sciences and obtained a superior education. He attended medical lectures at Cincinnati and graduated at the Medical Department of the Transylvania University, Lexington, Ky. In 1836 he practiced his profession at Carthage, Ohio, and in 1838 commenced preaching in the Christian Church. In 1839 he removed to Brunerstown, Ky., and engaged in general evangelistic work. In 1840 he located at New Union Church, Woodford County, and in 1841 became pastor at Lexington; moved thence to Midway, in 1844, and opened a female school. In 1845 he labored for the establishment of his school, the Baconian Institute, was pastor of the church, and raised funds for the female orphan school at Midway. In 1849 he edited the *Christian Mirror*, and in 1853-54, the Kentucky department of the *Christian Age*. In 1854 he edited the *New Era*, a temperance paper published at Lexington. In 1860 he became professor of English literature, Kentucky University, Harrodsburg, and in 1862 was surgeon of the Eleventh Kentucky Cavalry. In 1865 he removed, with the University, to Lexington; in 1866 was agent of the Freedmen's Bureau, and in 1867 delivered a course of lectures at Hiram College, Ohio. In 1868-69 he published the *Independent Monthly*, and in 1873 was, by President Grant, appointed special mail agent for Kentucky. Abounding in labors, untiring in zeal, unflinching in integrity, and a patriotism that knew no wavering, this friend of humanity laid down his life at Lexington, January 28, 1875. His biography has been published in which President Garfield says of him: "In his nature was the rarest combination of independence, strength, courage, severity, gentleness, inflexible persistency, affectionate tenderness, sadness and jollity, I have ever known." He was the son of William Pinkerton, born in Chester County, Penn., 1780, a captain in the war of 1812, who died at Midway, Ky., 1857. His father was John Pinkerton, a native of North of Ireland. William married Elizabeth Littig, daughter of a sea captain (who gave a ninety-nine year lease on Fell's Point, Baltimore), and their offspring were John W., Rev. William, Rev. Lewis L., Rev. Thomas, Rev. Samuel J., Mary (Peebles), Kate (Martin), Collin M., Rebecca (Clark), Elisha Y., and Sally (Bashford). Lewis L. married March 19, 1833, Sarah, daughter of Stephen A. Ball, of Trenton, Ohio (born December 29, 1813, died in Lexington February 11, 1878), and from their union sprang Susan (deceased), Mary J. (deceased), William W. (deceased), Virginia L. (Crutcher), Burnet J., James P., Samuel D., Lewis L., and Mary B. (Price). July 17, 1867, subject married Miss Sallie, daughter of William J. and Sallie (Stone) Walker, of Richmond, born January 5, 1847, and to them have been born Mary P., Charlie W. (deceased), William W., Burnet B., Sallie S., Lewis L., and Percival P. (deceased). In 1863 subject graduated at the Kentucky University, Harrodsburg. He taught school in Jessamine and Fayette Counties, and was three years in charge of the male academy at Richmond. In 1863 he was ordained a preacher in the Christian Church, at Harrodsburg, and in 1868 was pastor at East Cleveland, Ohio, and in 1870 at New Castle, Penn. In 1871–72 he taught the male academy at Harrodsburg, and in 1873 at Richmond. In 1874 he became principal of the Female Institute at Richmond, where he remained six years, and in 1882 became pastor at Eureka, Ill. He is now engaged in farming, having 143 acres of very productive land, in a high state of cultivation. In politics Mr. Pinkerton is a Republican and a Prohibitionist.

SAM. HENRY PIRTLE was born November 23, 1834. His grandfather was born in Germany and came to Kentucky after his marriage, and settled in Washington County, where his life was spent in agricultural pursuits. He reared a family of sons and daughters, among whom was Abner, the father of Sam. Henry, and who was also a farmer. He held the office of high sheriff of Hardin County, where he resided during the latter years of his life. He was twice married. His first wife left two daughters; one of them, Cecilia A. (Matthis), is yet living. His second marriage was with Miss Martha Williams, daughter of Samuel Williams, of Washington County, Ky. She died in 1840. Her husband survived her about one year, and of their children three are living: Samuel H., William W. and Martha, widow of Jesse Embree. Samuel H. Pirtle, a native of Hardin County, was seven years of age when his father died, and from that time until he attained his eighteenth year he resided with an uncle, Mr. Nathaniel Linder; then migrated to Missouri, engaged in the livery business for awhile, and returning to Kentucky in 1856 attended school until 1860, when he took a trip to Arkansas, and in the following year joined the Confederate States Army, for two years serving under Price and Van Dorn. He participated in the siege of Corinth, and was afterward captured and held for some months a prisoner of war at Alton, Ill., after which he was exchanged and returned to his home in Kentucky, and soon after, August 23, 1864, married Sarah M. Dudgeon, of Marion County. To this marriage have been born seven children: Nannie M., John E., Margaret E. (Harmon), William H., Mattie D., Minnie L., and Laura. Mrs. Pirtle was born February 29, 1846. Her parents, John and Margaret Dudgeon, were natives of Kentucky. The latter was born in 1818 and is yet living; the former died August

30, 1873. Sam. Henry Pirtle purchased 190 acres of land in 1870, to which he has added by subsequent purchases until he is now the proprietor of 270 acres of well improved and productive land. He is not a member of the church, but holds the Methodist faith, of which church his wife is a lifelong and consistent member. His political views are Democratic.

HENRY PLUMMER, M. D., practicing physician and surgeon, was born May 14, 1837, in Fleming County, Ky. His father, Benjamin Plummer, a native of Maryland and born June 15, 1793, was a farmer and miller. He was brought by his father to what is now Mason County, Ky., when only eighteen months old, and when about ten years old to Fleming County. The early part of his life was spent in agricultural pursuits, afterward in the saw and grist-milling business; and during the war he lost most of his property, his water wheel, worth $5,000, being destroyed by fire, the work of Federal troops. On August 15, 1816, he was united in marriage to Miss Mary M. Seever, a daughter of Henry and Elizabeth (Myers) Seever, natives of Pennsylvania. By this marriage Benjamin Plummer became the father of nine children: Matilda, wife of W. B. Evans, a farmer of Fleming County, now dead; Martha, who died in Fleming County; James, who died in Holt County, Mo.; Julia A. (died in 1860 in the State of Ohio), wife of Rev. W. G. Montgomery, a minister of the Methodist Episcopal Church, who lives in Putnam County, Ohio; John, who died in Navarro County, Tex., in 1883; Amanda, wife of Thomas J. Crain, of Missouri (died in 1870); William, county judge of Fleming County and a practicing attorney (died in 1878); Henry, and Franklin, a master mechanic of the railroad shops in Springfield, Mo., of whom only Dr. Plummer and Franklin are now living. Benjamin Plummer, a member of the Methodist Episcopal Church, died January 6, 1866, and his wife, who was also a member of the Methodist Episcopal Church, died May 22, 1867. James Plummer, the grandfather of Dr. Plummer, was born in Maryland, likewise his wife, who before marriage was Miss Dorcas Cash. He immigrated to Mason County, Ky., in 1795, and his almost sole occupation was hunting. As the country became settled he moved farther away in the pursuit of his favorite sport, so he soon removed to Fleming County, where he and his wife are buried. The Plummer family are of English origin and Dr. Plummer's father, Benjamin Plummer, was a veteran of the war of 1812, serving under Gen. Wilkinson in his campaign and in Capt. Mathew's company, receiving a wound at Dayton, Ohio (which then contained but one house), which kept him confined to his bed an entire winter. Dr. Plummer re-received an ordinary school education, and in his twenty-first year began the study of medicine under Dr. R. P. Samuel, of Poplar Plains, Fleming County, and in the fall of 1859 attended his first course of lectures at the Medical College of Ohio, at Cincinnati. He graduated from that institution in the spring of 1861, and enlisted in Capt. Ben. Desha's company (Confederate Infantry). He was the medical officer of the company and remained in the hospital at Bowling Green until February, 1862, when, on retreat, he was assigned to Maj. Kelly's Arkansas battalion as assistant surgeon. He held this position until after the battle of Shiloh, when he became assistant surgeon of the Eighth Arkansas Regiment, and after the battle of Perryville was promoted to surgeon of the Twenty-third Tennessee, until the battle of Chickamauga, when he was transferred to the Thirty-second and Fifty-eighth Consolidated Alabama Regiments, remaining with them until the surrender of Gen. J. E. Johnston. He then located at Brandon, Warren Co., Miss., and practiced medicine two years. Dr. Plummer then returned to Kentucky, locating at Eldorado, Mercer County, where he practiced three years, removing to Harrodsburg. On October 3, 1867, he married Miss Elizabeth Mills, the daughter of Benjamin Mills and Jane (O'Conner) Mills, the former a native of New York, the latter of Dunda, Ireland. Maj. Mills was in command of Harper's Ferry as chief armory officer, when it was captured by the notorious John Brown. Three years after his marriage Dr. Plummer removed to Poplar Plains, in Fleming County, where he practiced three years, returning again to Harrodsburg, which since has been his home. To the marriage of Dr. and Mrs. Plummer have been born six children: William, died in infancy; Virginia Morton, died at the age of six months; Lutie Mills, died aged two years; Jennie Mac, now living in her twelfth year; Bessie Moore, in her eighth year, and Benjamin Dawson, in his sixth year. Dr. and Mrs. Plummer are members of the Southern Presbyterian Church, and Dr. Plummer is a Democrat. In 1883 he was president of the Central Kentucky Medical Association.

JOHN WILLIAM POOR was born November 20, 1822, on the bluffs of Kentucky River, three miles above the mouth of Dick's River in Garrard County, and in 1826 with his parents located near Boone's Knob, on the Garrard side, where he was reared to manhood, and has since resided. His father, William L. Poor, a native of the same place with subject, was born February 17, 1791, was a soldier in the war of 1812, a farmer, a Whig, a Methodist, and died of cholera, July 26, 1833. He was the son of John Poor, a native of Virginia, a soldier in the Revolutionary war and an early settler in Garrard County, Ky. He married Jane Legin, and their offspring were William L., Robert C., Thomas, Sally (Ford), Hopie (Wilds), Lucy (West) and Mrs. Hancock. William L. married May 25, 1820, Elizabeth, daughter of William and Elizabeth (Withers) Kemper, of Garrard County (born July 21, 1798, died May 23, 1870), and from their union sprang John W., Elizabeth, Frances A. (Ison) and James G. May 1, 1845, John W. married Miss Martha A., daughter of Murell and Hannah (Burnside) Smith, of Garrard County, born December 5, 1829, and to them have been born Hannah E. (Davis), Mary B. (Feathers), William M. (deceased) and Maggie L. (Boulden). In the commencement of his business career Mr. Poor had an even start with the world, having, literally, to rely upon his own efforts, but by diligence and careful attention to business, he is now possessed of an ample competency, although he has had to settle $40,000 in security debts. He is a farmer and trader, owning over 1,100 acres of good land, devoted largely to stock grazing. Mr. Poor is a member of the Methodist Episcopal Church South, a Mason, an Ancient Odd Fellow; was formerly an old line Whig, but is now a Democrat. He has established his children all on good farms.

DR. JOHN WEST POWELL was born August 29, 1832, in Bowling Green, Ky., and in 1840, being left an orphan, was taken to Mercer County by his uncle, Dr. T. J. Moore, with whom he grew to manhood. In 1855 he located at "Dunlora," a part of the original McAfee survey on the Louisville pike, five and one-half miles north of Harrodsburg, where he has since resided. His father, Maj. John W. Powell, Sr., a native of Virginia, removed with his parents to Adair County, Ky., lived in Danville, was a soldier in the war of 1812, and engaged in merchandising in Bowling Green, where he died in 1840. He was the son of Robert Powell, a Virginian, a major in the Revolutionary war, a relative of the Powells of Powell's Valley, and died in Adair County, Ky. His wife was a half sister to Benjamin West, the artist, and their offspring were Robert, John W., Sr., William, Susan

(Jacobs), Fanny (Kerr), Margaret (Bledsoe) and Mary (Jones). John W., Sr., married Anne St. Clair, daughter of George Moore, of Bowling Green (died in 1840), and from their union sprang Ann E. (Worthington), Mary F. (Dudley), George M., Ellen B. (Long), Patsy Bell (Kennedy), John W., Sarah A. (Kennedy), Hobson (killed at the battle of Franklin, Tenn.) and Thomas S. John W., Jr., first married, May 16, 1856, Susan, daughter of Peter R. and Mary (Buchanan) Dunn, of Mercer County (died in 1864, aged thirty-one years), and their chil-dren were Thomas M. (deceased), William D., George M. (deceased) and Annie (deceased). On January 25, 1881, he was married to Margaret, daughter of John J. Halsey (born June 29, 1853), and to them have been born Mary D. Halsey. John West and Lafon. In 1850 Jno. West Powell commenced the study of medicine with Drs. Moore & Spillman, of Harrodsburg, graduating in 1854 in the medical department of the University of Louisville, after which, by solicitation from Dr. Gross, professor of surgery, was associated with him for one year in his practice. The following year he commenced practice at McAfee, which he continued with success eleven years. In 1875–76 he was a representative in the Legislature. He is now engaged in farming and stock raising, owning 550 acres of land. Dr. Powell is an Ancient Odd Fellow; for ten years he was an elder in the Providence Presbyterian Church, and in politics he is a Democrat. He lost twelve slaves through the late war.

JOHN W. POWELL, a native of Adair County, was born December 17, 1837. His father, Kelsoe Powell, also a native of Adair County, was born in 1796, and his life-long occupation was milling. He was married first to a Miss Grider, and they were the parents of one child, Harriet, wife of Josiah Sparks. After the death of his first wife, Mr. Powell was married to Miss Oney Gilkey, a daughter of Jonathan Gilkey, a native of Adair County, and the father of a large family of children, most of whom now live in Missouri. By his second marriage Mr. Powell became the father of eight children: Polly Ann, wife of Archelaus Strange; Rosa E., wife of Robert H. Caldwell; James, John W., Jephtha T., Elizabeth M., Frances, wife of Thomas Carter, and Louis C., all of whom are living. Kelsoe Powell was owner of a mill on Powell's Creek, a branch of Crocus Creek, and besides cultivated a farm of 400 acres, most of which was in timber. His death occurred in 1875; that of his wife, August 3, 1882, in the seventy-ninth year of her

age. John Powell, grandfather of John W. Powell, was a Virginian and a farmer, who settled in Adair County while it was yet an unbroken wilderness. He cleared, cultivated and owned about 400 acres of land in the county, but was never wealthy. He was the father of six children, only two of whom remained in Adair County, the rest emigrating to other parts of Kentucky. John W. Powell in youth acquired a good business education in the county schools, and also attended the high school at Campbellsville a few months. He remained on the home farm until he reached his majority, and then taught in the common schools about three years, after which he commenced purchasing tobacco for a New York firm, which was his business for the next three years in connection with farming. Mr. Powell was married October 1, 1867, to Miss Laura T. Botts, a daughter of Thompson and Elizabeth (Moore) Botts, natives of Virginia. Mr. and Mrs. Powell have had born to them six children: Thompson, Leslie, Birdie, Lillie and Nora; Annie, who was the third child, died in infancy. Mr. Powell first purchased 160 acres of land, which was well improved; three years later he sold and purchased 170 acres, on which he remained ten years. His present farm of 275 acres, near Glenville, he settled in 1880, and this has since been his home; 200 acres are cleared and in cultivation. Mr. Powell is purchasing tobacco in the Louisville market, and he also buys and raises stock. He began life with no inheritance, but has always been a successful trader, and is at present in comfortable circumstances. Mr. and Mrs. Powell are both members of the Christian Church of Glenville.

DR. J. M. POYNTZ was born March 22, 1838, in Scott County, Ky., and is a son of John and Xantippe (Jones) Poyntz, to whom three sons were born and reared: John, James M. and Cyrus, he having two daughters by a former marriage—Annie and Carrie. Their mother was Grace Jones. John Poyntz, the father, was born in Scott County January 14, 1795; served in the war of 1812; was in Dudley's defeat; was a farmer and owner of slaves. In 1855 he moved to Cass County, Mo., and there resided until his death in 1867. He was the son of Arthur Poyntz, who with two brothers, Nathaniel and Patrick, came from Ireland at the beginning of the Revolution, settled in Pennsylvania, and there entered the war for independence. At the close of the war they came to Kentucky. One was killed by the Indians. One afterward settled in Maysville, and Arthur, who came to Kentucky with Mr. McBride, settled in Scott County; was one of the earliest pioneers of Kentucky and participated in many of the Indian troubles. Arthur Poyntz married Nancy Rayburn. (She was one of the excellent of the earth.) She came from Scotland, and they were married in Pennsylvania in 1790. She died in Indiana in 1844. Their children were Sarah, Nancy, John, Joseph, Betsey, James, Jane, Ellener, Patsey and Mary Ann. In religion the family were Presbyterians, and in politics Whigs. Mrs. Xantippe Poyntz was born in Fayette County, Ky., in 1802, and was a daughter of Richard Jones, a native of Virginia and early pioneer of Fayette County. She died in 1864. James M. Poyntz was brought up on a farm; received his early education in the common schools, afterward attended an academy until his eighteenth year, when he began the study of medicine and graduated from the University of Louisville as M. D. In the year 1861 he entered the Confederate Army, serving a while as adjutant. In January, 1862, was appointed assistant surgeon, with rank of captain, in which capacity he served to the end, after which he located at Leesburg, Harrison Co., Ky., where he continued practice for fifteen years, having taken a postgraduate course in 1872. He located in Richmond in 1882, where he is doing a successful practice, and is an active member of the State and county medical associations, also of the State Board of Health. November 15, 1870, he was united in marriage to Miss Clara Lilly, of Harrison County, Ky., a daughter of Pleasant and Priscilla (Shackelford) Lilly. Mr. Lilly was born near Leesburg, and his wife in Montgomery, Ala. The Doctor had born to him by this marriage three children: C. Edwin, Kathleen and Estelle. Their mother died May 20, 1879. In February, 1886, he took for his second wife Mrs. Bettie Gatewood, a daughter of Hon. A. J. Ewing, of Bath County, Ky. In religion he is a Presbyterian; in politics a Democrat. He is a member of F. & A. M., being a Knight Templar and Past Commander; also a member of the I. O. O. F.

W. P. PREWITT was born in Madison County, Ky., March 23, 1841, son of James Prewitt and Marilda Sebastian; married in 1839. Their offspring are three sons. James Prewitt was born in Madison County, Ky., January 8, 1815; was a successful farmer and a Free Mason. Died in 1882 at the age of sixty-seven years. His wife was born in Garrard County, Ky., in 1825, died in 1875; a daughter of Mily Sebastian and Margaret Broadus. Mr. John Prewitt, grandfather of subject, was born in Virginia; immigrated to

Kentucky at an early day with eight sons. It was supposed that five were killed by the Indians. He was a farmer and owned a large body of land; married Miss Mary Ford, born in Virginia. She was captured by the Indians at the age of seven years, and remained in their custody for several years. She gained her freedom by permission to visit her parents. Subject is first in order of birth; began business for himself at the age of twenty-five years at farming. In 1866 he opened a general store of merchandise in Spoonville, Ky.; remained there in business three years. In 1875 moved to Kirksville, Ky., and opened a large store; has since remained there as a substantial citizen and a man of large business. He is a Free Mason and a Democrat; has held the office of deputy county clerk for twelve years; married, in 1858, Miss Margaret A. Sanders, a daughter of Eliza Sanders and Jane Broadus. Mrs. Prewitt died March 9, 1886, a true Christian woman. Nine children have been born to them: Sarah E. (deceased), James E., Mirrilda Jane Finnell, Ida M., Lillie Lee, Sterling Price, Nancy U., Wade Hampton and Million F. (deceased).

THOMAS W. PRICE was born August 2, 1817, and is a son of Reason and Tabitha (Simmons) Price, to whom six sons and three daughters were born, as follows: William S., Tabitha S., Richard, Thomas W., Ed., Theresa A., Rob S., Elizabeth H. and Reason. Reason Price was born in Maryland, December 5, 1785, and his wife December 15, 1786. He was brought to Kentucky when a lad of ten years, and became an extensive farmer and slave owner in Nelson County, accumulating about 1,800 acres. He served as major of militia, and died August 5, 1832. Richard Price, his father, was born in Virginia; he married Rachael Willett, of Maryland, and came to Nelson County in 1795; he was a sailor in early life, but became a farmer and slave-holder; he also carried on a distillery in later years, and died in June, 1837, aged seventy-eight years; his widow died September 18, 1848, aged ninety-five years; they were of English and Welsh descent respectively. Mr. Price's mother was a daughter of Richard and Tabitha (Willett) Willett, natives of Maryland, who immigrated to Bullitt County, Ky., and settled near Shepherdsville in 1795; they raised a family of three sons and three daughters. Thomas W. Price was born two miles north of New Hope and was reared on a farm. He attended St. Mary's College two years, and at the age of sixteen commenced the battle of life for himself on a farm. He was married September 7, 1858, to Emily, daughter of Thomas and Ann (Head) Hutchins. Mr. Hutchins was a blacksmith and farmer, served as magistrate several terms, and was a son of John Hutchins, who married a Miss Schanks. They came from Maryland. Mr. Price's wife died in 1880, a member of the Roman Catholic Church. He married his second wife, Anna Lillis, November 13, 1883. She was a daughter of Henry and Catharine (Armstrong) Lillis, natives of Ireland, who immigrated and settled in Louisville, Ky. By this second marriage two children were born: Mary and Tabitha. Mrs. Price died April 7, 1886. Mr. Price, after his first marriage, located where he now resides, at New Hope, where he has lived since. He owns a fine farm of 300 acres—200 in a good state of cultivation—and was once owner of ten slaves. Mr. Price cast his first presidential vote for Gen. Harrison; since 1860 he has affiliated with the Democratic party.

DR. JOHN LEWIS PRICE was born April 20, 1835, in Nicholasville, Ky., and was taken in 1837, by his parents, to Clark County; in 1845 to Newcastle; in 1848 again to Clark, and in 1859 to Mercer County, where he has since resided. His father, Dr. Andrew B. Price, was born in 1802, in Richmond, Ky. He graduated at Transylvania University and enjoyed an extensive practice. He was a Democrat, lost twelve slaves by the late war, and died August 3, 1873. He was the son of Moses Price, who was born near Richmond, Va., and came to Kentucky previous to 1800; was high sheriff, held office fifty years, was a merchant, farmer and slave owner, and died about 1853, aged over ninety years. He married Sarah Broadus, and their offspring were John, Andrew B., Thomas, Arjalon, Morton, Sarah (Daniel) Mrs. Childs, Mrs. Scott, Lucy (Scott) and Amelia (Poor). These brothers were all physicians. Andrew B. married Evelyne E., daughter of Shastine and Nancy (Duncan) Watkins, of Clark County (born in 1806, now living), and from this union sprang Dr. Dillard S., Catherine (Calk), Dr. John L., Dr. Ansil D., Lucy (Smedley, deceased), and Evelyne E. (Buck). June 13, 1861, Dr. John Lewis Price married Miss Anna T., daughter of Nelson and Lucy (Vivian) Keas, of Mercer County (born in Montgomery County, June 14, 1834), and to them have been born Isaac N. K. (deceased) and John F. In 1857 the Doctor commenced the study of medicine with his uncle, Dr. John L. Price, of Independence, Mo.; attended one course of lectures at McDowell College, St. Louis, and

graduated in 1860, in the medical department of the University of Louisville, since which time he has been successfully engaged in practice. He also owns a valuable farm of 170 acres on the Lexington Turnpike. Nelson Keas was born in 1797, and died September 19, 1866. His wife, Lucy (Vivian) Keas, was born in 1803, and died March 10, 1876. Their children are Isaac, Anna T. (Price) and Albert H. Dr. Price is a Democrat and a prohibitionist.

JOHN W. PULLIAM, liveryman and county jailer, is a native of Shelby County, Ky., and the second of a family of nine children born to Archibald and Rosamond (Reddish) Pulliam. Mr. Pulliam's paternal grandfather was William Pulliam, a native of Virginia. He came to Kentucky many years ago and settled in Shelby County, where he engaged in farming, and where he died in 1851. Archibald Pulliam was born in Shelby County, Ky., in 1816. He was a farmer by occupation, resided the greater part of his life in Shelby, and died in Nelson County, April 9, 1883. John Reddish, the maternal grandfather of John W. Pulliam, was a native of Virginia and an early comer to Shelby County. He was a teacher by profession and died in the State of his adoption when subject was a small boy. Rosamond (Reddish) Pulliam was born either in Shelby or Spencer County, and is still living at Chaplin, Nelson County. John W. Pulliam was born December 5, 1842, and spent the first twenty years of his life upon the paternal homestead. He received a good English education in the country schools of his county, which he attended until sixteen years of age, and later pursued his studies at the Mt. Eden school, Mt. Eden Village, for two years, obtaining a fair knowledge of the higher branches of learning in the meantime. He commenced life for himself in the mercantile business, at the town of Harrisonville, Shelby County, where he sold goods for two and a half years, at the end of which time he discontinued the business and engaged in agricultural pursuits in Nelson County, whither he had removed in 1866. In 1872 he again engaged in the goods business, opening near the Russell schoolhouse a general store, which he operated until 1874. From 1874 until 1878 he followed farming, but in the latter year he was elected jailer of Nelson County, a position he has held by successive elections ever since. In November, 1885 he engaged in the livery business with Mr. Muir, under the firm name of Pulliam & Muir, a partnership which still continues. Mr. Pulliam married, April 17, 1872, in Anderson

County, Ky., Miss Lydia Glass, daughter of Wakefield and Rebecca Glass, of the same county and State. Five children were born to their union, only two of whom are living, namely: Lizzie and Archie Pulliam. Mr. Pulliam takes a lively interest in political affairs and votes the Democratic ticket. He has been a member of the Baptist Church since 1859, and with his wife belongs to the Bardstown congregation.

THOMAS W. PULLIAM is a native Kentuckian, born in Shelby County, February 28, 1841, the eldest of a family of nine children. His father, Achilles S. Pulliam, was a son of William Pulliam, also a native of Shelby County, of which county he always remained a resident, following the vocation of farming. He died there at the age of sixty-five, about 1849. His wife, Martha Scott, by him became the mother of five children, three of whom grew to man and womanhood, Fannie, Sarah and Achilles. The latter was born December 27, 1817. In October, 1865, he removed from his native county of Shelby to Nelson County, where he finished his days April 9, 1882. He was united in marriage February 10, 1840, to Miss Rosamond F. Reddish, daughter of John Reddish, who was a native of Culpeper County, Va., from whence he immigrated to and settled in Scott County, Ky., in the year 1808; four years later he removed to Shelby County, where he lived until his death. His wife, Nancy (Samuels) Reddish, bore him nine children: Sarah, Reuben, Elizabeth, Selene, Lucy, Catherine, Martha, John and Rosamond. By profession Mr. Reddish was a school-teacher. He died at the age of sixty-six, about 1838. To the union of Mr. and Mrs. Pulliam nine children were born: Thomas W., John W., James W., Barney S., Benjamin K., Henry M., Theodore K., Edward P. and Mary A. The last named is Mrs. John H. Thomas. Mr. Pulliam was a farmer and died possessed of quite an estate. Thomas W. Pulliam, now a resident of Nelson County, was married to Miss Mary Cook, December 20, 1860. This union has been blessed with five children: William H., Sallie F., Mary A. G., Theodore D. and James C. He has met with uniform success in his vocation of farming, and owns 332 acres of improved land in Chaplin District. He is a member of the Baptist Church and in politics a Democrat.

WILLIAM THOMPSON PURDY was born October 25, 1823. His father, John S. Purdy, was born in Nelson County in 1798. He married Lydia Kirk in 1818, and they became the parents of ten children, of whom are living Daniel H., Nancy Sherrell, William T., Presley, Mary J. (Wayne), and John W. Lydia Kirk, a daughter of Daniel Kirk, was born in 1802 and died in 1854. John S. Purdy was a carpenter and builder and plied that trade in connection with farming, and died in Marion County in 1872. He was a son of Henry Purdy, a native of Maryland, who came early to Kentucky and located in what is now Marion County. He was a farmer and followed that vocation up to the year of his death (1833). The maternal grandfather, Daniel Kirk, was a native of Maryland, and was among the early settlers of Nelson County. He was the father of one son (Henry) and one daughter (Lydia). Henry Purdy was thrice married. His first wife's name was Smith and she was a Virginian; his second wife was a Miss Scarbour Staten, and the third a Miss Hanley. To these three marriages were born twenty-one children. William Thompson Purdy was born and reared on a farm in Marion County, and educated in the common schools. At the age of nineteen he engaged in farming on his own account; this he has followed up to the present time with success, and is now the proprietor of farms aggregating 300 acres, lying on the waters of south Rolling Fork, in Marion County. In 1842 and 1843 he made two trips South with stock for markets. Those trips proved successful and in the following year, 1844, he was married on the 10th of October, to Martha McAlister, and they are the parents of seven sons and three daughters: James, Richard, Leonard, William L., Sam, George T., Harvey, Rosa, Lydia (Hocker) and Isabell. Martha McAlister was born September 27, 1825. Her parents were Cornelius and Eleanor (Brawner) McAlister, the former a native of Ireland who came to America with his parents when a child; the latter was of Scottish parentage and a native of Kentucky. Mrs. Purdy is a member of the Catholic Church; Mr. Purdy is not a member of any church. Politically he is a Democrat, but cast his first ballot for Henry Clay. He is a Royal Arch Mason, and a member of the J. P. Knott Chapter. Mr. Purdy is a stanch advocate of temperance and prides himself on the fact of his never having in all his life tasted any kind of spirituous liquor.

ROBERT E. PURYEAR was born July 28, 1849, and except the years from 1871 to 1876, has been a life-long resident of Taylor County. That period he spent at DeWitt, Ark. His father, John H. Puryear, was also a native of Taylor County, and was born April 15, 1821. In early life he taught school; afterward engaged in farming to a limited extent and in merchandising, giving his personal attention to the latter. He was a son of Hezekiah Puryear, who was born in Henrico County, Va., and who married Miss Elizabeth Harding, a sister of Hon. Aaron Harding. Hezekiah Puryear was a farmer, and a son of Jesse Puryear, and of French Huguenot descent. John H. Puryear married, September 5, 1848, Miss Mildred E., daughter of John B. and Mary A. Chandler. Her father was a large and successful merchant, an active and influential citizen, and one of the first magistrates of Taylor County. The children of John H. and Mildred Puryear were Robert E. (subject), and Ann R., wife of Capt. T. T. Fisher. Robert E. Puryear married, June 23, 1873, Miss Emily Visart, daughter of Julian J. and Emily (Kepler) Visart of DeWitt, Ark. Her parents were natives of France and located at an early day at the French trading post of Arkansas. To Mr. and Mrs. Puryear have been born Basil C. (deceased), Emmet Vance, John Visart (deceased), Anna Mildred, Julian Edwin (deceased), and Emma Lillian (deceased). Mr. Puryear began the study of law under the preceptorship of J. R. Robinson, Esq., of Campbellsville, and in 1868 was by special act of the Legislature, admitted to the practice, since which time he has given his attention to that profession, the success which has followed his labors being in a great measure due to his forensic eloquence. While a resident of Arkansas he was elected county attorney and after his return to Kentucky, city judge of Campbellsville. In 1885–86 he was a member of the State Board of Equalization of Kentucky, from the Eleventh Congressional District, and a candidate for Congress; in the latter aspiration, after a creditable contest, he was defeated. He is a member with his wife of the Baptist Church, and in politics is a Democrat. He had the advantages of good schools, having received his education at Shelbyville, Ky. He has accumulated a comfortable competency.

REV. JAMES C. RANDOLPH was born on the 7th of December, 1830, and is the fifth of three sons and six daughters born to Clarkson Edward and Phœbe Brewer (Demaree) Randolph. C. E. Randolph was born January 13, 1793, in New Jersey; was brought by his parents to Mercer County, Ky., in 1797; moved to Boyle in 1844; was a farmer, and was an active and leading member of the Presbyterian Church. In 1850 moved to Carrollton, Ill., thence to Brighton, Ill., and finally to Douglas County, Ill., where he died in October, 1865; was in politics a Whig, and strong Union man during the war. He was a son of Hezekiah Randolph of New Jersey, who was a soldier in the war for independence. He immigrated to Mercer County, Ky., purchased lands near Harrodsburg, and resided there until his death in 1836, aged about seventy-five. He was related to the Randolph family of Virginia. Mrs. Phœbe B. Randolph was born in Mercer County, Ky., September 10, 1796, and was a daughter of Cornelius Demaree, who had married his third wife. His first wife, James C.'s grandmother, gave birth to two sons and four daughters. Cornelius Demaree was a native of Pennsylvania, and migrated to Mercer County as early as 1790; he was a fine weaver by trade, was an elder and much devoted to the Presbyterian Church, and was conscientious in his dealings; he died in 1851 in his ninetieth year. James C. Randolph is a native of Mercer County, lived on a farm, and attended the common district schools till seventeen, when he entered Centre College, from which he was graduated in 1852, and from the Theological Seminary in 1856. He entered without any means, but by his indomitable energy and will, succeeded in keeping up his studies and teaching private students; he also taught in college. When he left after graduating, he had succeeded in accumulating by private instruction and teaching $3,000. After graduating he lived in Stanford three years as teacher. In 1861 he went to Nicholasville and opened a school, but on account of the war the school was broken up. In 1863 he was made United States marshal of Jessamine County, Ky.; in 1863 was made assistant assessor, and held both positions till the close of the war. In the spring of 1867 he resigned the position of assessor. He then came to Danville and accepted the chair of Greek, which he held by appointment for two years, when he was elected to the chair of mathematics, which he filled until 1876, at the same time preaching nearly every Sunday. Since he retired from college, he has devoted his time almost exclusively to the ministry at Newport, Lebanon, Lancaster, St. Louis, and other places. He has been most active in his work. He was married May 15, 1856, to Georgia B. (Mays) of Boyle County, a daughter of Nelson and Anna (Turner) Mays, who were natives of Jessamine County, Ky., and North Carolina, respectively. Nelson Mays was born in 1788, his wife in 1793; they settled in Perryville as early as 1812. He was a farmer, and served as sheriff for many years; was a son of John and Mary (Brown) Mays, who were among the first pioneers of Jessamine County from Virginia, of English descent, and members of the Methodist Episcopal Church. Mr. and Mrs. Randolph had born to them six children: Howard, Edward, Alice (all deceased), Margaret E., John N. and Mary McKee (deceased). He is a Republican and cast his first presidential vote for Lincoln. Dr. Randolph owns fine property in and near Danville.

SYLVESTER RAPIER, of New Haven, Nelson Co., Ky., was born April 25, 1847, in La Rue County, and is a son of Nicholas A. Rapier, of La Rue County, who was born Aplil 2, 1821, in Nelson County, and is now living. Charlotte Mary Boone, wife of Nicholas A., was born July 27, 1827, in La Rue County (which was then a part of Hardin County) and died September 29, 1873. The paternal grandfather of Sylvester was Charles Rapier of Nelson County, Ky., formerly of Maryland; his grandmother on the paternal side was Elizabeth Gwynn, also of Nelson County. His maternal grandfather was Charles Boone of La Rue County, formerly of Maryland, and his maternal grandmother was Susan Howard, also of La Rue County and formerly of Maryland. His uncle, Silvester Johnson, of New Haven, Ky., after whom he was named, took him in charge December 8, 1863, at the age of sixteen, where he began in the capacity of store-boy, and, by following the advice and business training of his uncle, with whom he has been connected as his private secretary and cashier for nearly a quarter of a century, he is to-day one of the foremost merchants in Nelson County, having of late years associated with him in business Francis Bowling, a nephew of Silvester Johnson, under the firm name of Rapier & Bowling. As he began business life at an early age he did not have the advantage of a college, and received only a common-school education. He being commercially engaged in the same house for over twenty-three years, has not sought any public office, but has always quietly voted the Democratic straight ticket through. He being a practical Roman Catholic has contributed liberally toward the erection of the Catholic Church in New Haven and takes a great pride and interest in the Catholic school, of which he is a trustee. He was married January 30, 1872, to Miss Alice Ross of Louisville, Ky., who lived only a short time afterward, and died at St. Joseph's Infirmary, Louisville, Ky., July 5, 1873. He next married Miss Mary Agnes Kister (November 3, 1875), who was born near Gethsemane Abbey, in Nelson County, August 30, 1857, a daughter of John S. and Cecelia

(Fritz) Kister, natives of Germany. He has five children: Cecelia Agnes, aged ten years; Nicholas Augustin, aged eight years; Alma Regina, aged six years; Marie Magdalen, aged four years and John Hugh, aged two years.

HON. ALSON RAWLINGS was born in 1822. His grandfather, Henry Rawlings, was born in Maryland, from which State he removed to Virginia and thence (in 1807) to Kentucky. He was a farmer and reared a family of three sons and two daughters, among whom was John B., the father of Alson; two sons and one daughter subsequently removed to Missouri. Henry Rawlings continued to reside in Marion County until his death. John B. was born in Pittsylvania County, Va., in October, 1779, and came to Kentucky in 1807, and located in Washington County; here he married Miss Elizabeth Hindman in 1811. This union was blessed by the birth of four sons and five daughters: James H., Alson, Henry H., John L., Melissa (Purdom, of Texas), Necy (Tharp, of Owensboro), Sophia (Glasscock) and Artemise (Hayes, of Marion County) and Polly (deceased). John B. Rawlings followed farming in Marion County, where he died in 1877. It is said of him that he was a man of strict religious principles and "after the straightest sect"—a Methodist. He was noted for his sterling integrity and uprightness in business transactions; he never held an office or engaged in politics; his advice to his sons was "the less you engage in politics the better you will succeed in life." Alson Rawlings was born in Washington, now Marion County, received a good common-school education; at the age of twenty-two was made captain of militia, and six years later (in 1850) was elected colonel of the Fourth Kentucky militia, in which capacity he served for several years; he also held the office of constable from 1846 to 1849, when he resigned. He was married in 1849 to Maria, daughter of Elijah and Margaret (Hayes) Glasscock; to this marriage were born ten children; four sons and one daughter are living, namely: Lewis C., John W., Clement H., Robert E. L. and Fannie Lee, wife of J. C. Elder. In 1856 Mr. Rawlings was elected magistrate in Marion County, which office he held through successive re-elections for seventeen years. He resigned in 1878, at which time he was elected to a seat in the Lower House of the Kentucky Legislature, in which he served one term. Mr. Rawlings' political views are Democratic. At the beginning of the civil war he was commissioned a captain in the Federal

Army, which, however, he did not enter, as his sympathies rather favored the Southern cause. He takes an active part in political campaigns, but his time is given principally to his farming operations; he is the proprietor of 300 acres of land lying in Marion County, a part of the "Cloyd Patent," settled in 1794 by his grandfather in company with the Taylors, Biggers, Crews and Thomases, of Virginia, and Thorps, of Pennsylvania. Mr. Rawlings also owns nearly 3,000 acres lying in Scurry and Floyd Counties, Tex. His life has been a busy one, and he has never failed to make a success of any enterprise in which he engaged; he has for some years held the office of president of the Lebanon & Rolling Fork Turnpike Company, and is a member and efficient worker in the Methodist Episcopal Church South; served as a grand juror in his county for many years, and is a Royal Arch Mason in J. L. Rawlings Chapter, No. 122. In his official career in the House of Representatives he stood shoulder to shoulder with such men as Burnett, Dycus, Yantes, Hindman and Connor, and his voice was always raised in support of measures that seemed to be to the best interests of the Kentucky people.

CLEMENT H. RAWLINGS. Among the enterprising young business men of Marion County we mention the gentleman whose name heads this sketch. He is a native Kentuckian, born in Marion County, on the 9th of July, 1862. His early educational training was received in the common schools of his home district; he afterward finished an academic course in 1881, and in the same year entered into a general merchandise trade with L. C. Rawlings at Riley Station, on the Louisville & Nashville Railway. In 1884 removed the business to the town of Bradfordsville. The Rawlings Bros. are energetic men of business and drive a flourishing trade. Clement H. Rawlings is a members of the Baptist Church, and is a Royal Arch Mason, Lodge No. 115. He is a Democrat and takes an active part in politics.

NICHOLAS S. RAY (deceased) was a native Kentuckian. After being well advanced in common English branches, he re ceived a collegiate education in Centre College, Danville, after which he practiced law for a few years, and was also engaged in banking business up to beginning of the late war. After the war he went to New York City where he engaged in the banking business for three years, then returned to Lebanon, Ky., where he was cashier of Marion National Bank, and was also engaged in farm-

ing and stock trading till his death, March 5, 1885, at the age of sixty-three years. He was married to Catherine Wade, as his first wife, by whom three sons were born. His second wife was Mrs. Sallie E. Estes, whom he married October 10, 1877. N. S. Ray was a son of N. and Mary (Smith) Ray. Mrs. Sallie E. Ray is a daughter of Dr. W. K. and Ann M. (Payne) Mitchell. December 27, 1867, she was united in marriage to A. C. Estes, and by this union four children were born: Taylor M., Warner, Willie and Columbus, the last three now deceased. The first named was educated at Washington and Lee University in Virginia. Mr. A. C. Estes was a captain during the late war in Gano's regiment from Texas, afterward was transferred to Morgan's command, and during the last year of the war served in Leadveter's command in Virginia; after the war he was a merchant at Raywick, Ky., also a farmer. Dr. W. K. Mitchell was born in Clark County, Ind., May 11, 1810. He graduated from a Cincinnati Medical College about 1834, and shortly after located near Raywick, Ky. Here he formed the acquaintance of and married Ann M. Payne in April, 1838; she was born October 11, 1818. The children born to this union were two sons and one daughter, the sons now deceased. One soń, William H. Mitchell, was a lieutenant in Morgan's command and was captured on the Ohio raid, but afterward escaped from Camp Douglas. Dr. W. K. Mitchell had an extensive practice, had accumulated a large fortune, was the possessor of a fine landed estate and slave property, and was one of the leading and most influential citizens of Marion County. In ante bellum days he was an active Clay Whig, but after the war affiliated with the Democrats. He was a leading member of the Methodist society, and was one of the originators and builders of the Methodist Episcopal and only Protestant church in Raywick. He died in January, 1877, leaving an estate worth $75,000. He was a son of Andrew Mitchell, who was one of the early pioneers of Clark County, Ind. Mrs. Sallie Ray is now living on a farm of 1,000 acres two miles east of Raywick, on Rolling Fork, embellished with a fine brick residence. She also owns a farm of 300 acres of her father's old homestead near Raywick. She is an estimable lady, benevolent and charitable, and is esteemed by all who form her acquaintance.

WILLIAM E. RAY was born in September, 1837, being the second in a family of seven children born to Samuel T. and Margaret (McElroy) Ray. His paternal grandfather, Nicholas Ray, of English descent, was a native of Maryland; his father, in turn, was one of three brothers who immigrated to America and the colonies; the latter was a soldier in the Revolutionary war. Nicholas Ray, the first of the family to come to Kentucky, was a contemporary of Daniel Boone, and was one of the inmates of the fort at Boonesborough; some years later he removed to and settled in Washington County, where he continued to reside until his death; he lived an active, highly respected and useful life, and left quite a competency at his death. William E. McElroy, maternal grandfather of William E. Ray, was a native of Virginia, whence he emigrated with his parents to Kentucky. He was one of the large and prosperous farmers of Marion County; reared a large family of children, some filling the highest positions in the State. He was an exemplary citizen and died at the advanced age of ninety-nine years. Samuel T. Ray, father of William E., was born in 1804, at the Ray homestead in Marion County. He was three times married, and was the father of seventeen children. Upon the death of his parents he inherited the farm, and always with success continued in the vocation of farming. He died in 1884, in the eighty-first year of his age. William E. Ray was born and reared on the home farm, receiving a collegiate education at Georgetown College. At the age of twenty- he sought the broad fields of the West, where he remained until the opening of the civil war, when he returned and enlisted in the cause of the South, joining Gen. Breckinridge's brigade. In 1863 he was taken prisoner at the battle of Shiloh and was paroled, and never again entered the service, but returned home and took charge of his father's farm. September 5, 1868, his marriage with Miss Annie Logan, daughter of Dr. M. B. Logan, was solemnized; one child was born to their union, Katie L. Mrs. Ray died in 1873, and in July, 1875, his marriage with Miss Fannie Froman, daughter of Isaac Froman, was celebrated; by this union he is the father of the following named children: Tilden and Hendricks (twins), Lucy, Margie, Annie and Robert. Mr. Ray has been a very successful farmer, and makes a special feature of raising shorthorn Durham cattle. He owns 700 acres of well improved land; is a member of the Masonic and K. of H. fraternities, and an ardent supporter of the Democratic party.

JOHN BOYLE READ was born March 29, 1835, five miles north of Danville, where he grew to manhood, but in 1859 removed to Lincoln County, remaining until 1884, when he returned to Boyle County, where he has since resided. His father, Francis S. Read, a native of Culpeper County, Va., and early a merchant at Stanford, Ky., died August 16, 1852. He was twice married; first to a sister of Chief Justice McKinley, and their offspring are Alexander P., Dr. Francis S., Sr., Elizabeth A. (Blaine), John, James W. and Mary (Camden). His second wife was Ann, daughter of Maj. Thomas T. Waggener (a veteran of the war of 1812). She died March 3, 1864. From their union sprang Thomas H., Hannah F. (Bowman), William T., Rev. Henry C., Martha, Annie M. and subject, as above. October 18, 1859, subject was married to Miss Eliza A., daughter of Samuel and Nancy (Burton) Givens, of Lincoln County, born January 6, 1840, and to them have been born Francis S., Jr., Nannie B., Elizabeth M. and Eugene D. Mr. Read is a farmer, having 218 acres of productive land in a good state of cultivation. He is a member of the Presbyterian Church, and politically affiliates with the Democratic party.

WILLIAM LOGAN REED was born May 19, 1819, in Lexington, Ky., where he was reared until 1835, when he was sent to Kelley's High School, at Harrodsburg. In 1836 he commenced to learn the tanner's trade with his brothers, and spent two and one-half years with his uncle in Danville, at the same vocation. In 1841 he entered into partnership with George C. Timberlake, of Garrard County, in the tanner's trade, at which he continued three years, when he removed to Lexington, and purchased the old Trotter farm, upon which he located. In 1850 he removed to Boyle County and engaged in farming seven years, after which he established a tannery in Lincoln County, which he operated for five years. In 1864 he located on Cane Run Turnpike, three miles east of Harrodsburg, Mercer County, where he has since resided. His father, Isaac Reed, a native of Maryland, removed to Kentucky about 1795, locating at Lexington, where he engaged extensively in the manufacture of boots and shoes, often employing from forty to sixty men on sewed work alone. He amassed a handsome property at the business, and died in 1847 at the age of seventy-two years. He married Rebecca Prall, of Lexington, and from their union sprang Henry W., John P., Emeline (Timberlake), Mary J. (Bridges), Andrew J. and William L. September 22, 1845, William L. Reed was united in marriage with Miss Josephine, daughter of John and Mary (Dunn) Hogan, of Garrard

County, born September 24, 1824, and to them have been born Emeline I., deceased; Mary R., wife of Thomas P. Embry, of Fayette County; Andrew J. (deceased), Ophelia, wife of Bedelle Chancellor of Virginia; Julia H. (deceased), Lizzie H., wife of B. C. Sandidge, of Lincoln County, and William A. J. Mr. Reed is a farmer and stock raiser, directing his attention to shorthorn cattle and trotting horses, and owns 433 acres of finely improved and productive land. He is a member of the Methodist Episcopal Church South, an Odd Fellow and a Democrat.

RIED FAMILY. About the close of the last century, Samuel Reid with his wife, Susan (Wood) Reid, and their children, came from Virginia to Kentucky, and settled in what is now Garrard County. Samuel Reid was a native of Virginia but descended from Scotch parentage; followed the pursuits of agriculture, and reared a family of three sons and one daughter, viz.: Alexander Reid, John W. Reid, Dr. James Reid, and Mary (Woods) Reid. He was a man of fair education for his day and time, and possessed of more than ordinary information; was a stanch Presbyterian, and died in that faith at an advanced age. His eldest son, Alexander, was married first to a Miss Blain, and after her death to Miss Mariah Thompson, leaving descendants as the result of each. John W. Reid was born in Virginia in 1784, was chiefly reared in Garrard County, Ky., and married Miss Jane Murrell, a native of Kentucky, and daughter of Col. James Murrell, an Indian fighter, and an early member of the Kentucky Legislature from Lincoln County. She died in 1852, leaving seven children: Dr. James M. (deceased), Amanda M. (McMurtry), Eliza J. (Lee), Sallie T. (wife of Dr. F. S. Read), John M., Samuel, and William Reid. John M. Reid, the fifth of this family, was born in Lincoln County, in the year 1823. He received the advantages of the common schools, and has given his attention to farming, in which he has been quite successful, being one of the most extensive land owners in Lincoln County. In 1854 he married Miss Bettie A. Hays, daughter of Hugh Hays and Elizabeth (Blain) Hays. To them were born five children: Dr. Hugh Reid, a prominent young physician of Stanford, Ky.; Fannie M. (Jones), James C., Mary (Foster), and Bessie Reid. Bettie A. (Hays) Reid was the seventh of a family of eleven children born to Hugh and Elizabeth Hays. She died in the year 1881, at the age of fifty-one. Dr. Hugh Reid, the eldest son, was born in Lincoln County in 1856, was reared on his father's farm, educated at Centre College, Danville, Ky., graduating in the class of 1878–79. He then performed the usual preparatory reading with Dr. L. S. McMurtry, of Danville, and in 1880 entered the medical department of the University of Virginia, taking one course; then entered the Jefferson Medical College of Philadelphia, and received the degree conferred by that institution in 1882. Since that date he has been in the practice of his profession at Stanford, Ky. He was married in 1886 to Miss Sabra Pennington.

WILLIAM H. RIKER was born February 16, 1820. His ancestors came from Holland and settled in New Jersey, which was the home of the family until about the year 1800. Charles Riker, father of William H., was born in January, 1774, was a farmer, and in his twenty-sixth year came to the region of Kentucky, in which Mercer County lies, where he began life with no means. He was married to Miss Mary Bonta, daughter of Samuel Bonta, a farmer of Mercer County. Shortly after marriage he purchased fifty acres of land in what is now Boyle County; several years later he sold out, and very early in the present century purchased a tract of between 250 and 300 acres, one and a half miles from Harrodsburg, and at his death, in 1857, left an estate of about $30,000. He was an invalid a great part of his life, suffering from white swelling, which caused him to use crutches. The names of the children born to Mr. and Mrs. Riker are, Cynthia, who died in her twenty-second year; Samuel, who was a farmer of Mercer County (deceased); Diana, wife of J. H. Sutfield, of Mercer County, who removed to Missouri in 1842; Cornelius, a farmer of Mercer County, who died of cholera in 1850, and whose children live in Indiana; Ida, wife of John VanAnglen of Mercer County, her cousin who immigrated from New Jersey; Sally, wife of William S. Vanarsdall, a farmer of Mercer County; Charles, a saddler who died in Dover, Mo.; Jane, wife of Peter Davis, a hotel-keeper of Bardstown, Ky., and afterward a farmer of Mercer County; William H. and James Harvey, twin brothers, the latter of whom is a farmer of Mercer County, living on a part of the old homestead. Of this family Mrs. Vanarsdall, Mrs. Davis, James Harvey, and William H. are now living. The mother of William H. Riker, who during life was a member of the Presbyterian Church, departed this life in 1868, in the eighty-fourth year of her age. W. H. Riker, a native of Mercer County, received only a business education in youth, and began selling goods early in life. He formed a partnership, in 1845, with Joel

P. Williams, deceased, under the firm name of Williams & Riker, and Mr. Riker began with a very limited capital. They handled a stock of dry goods, and continued their business until 1847, when Nat Lafon purchased the interest of Mr. Williams, and the business was carried on under the firm name of Riker & Lafon. In 1859 the firm erected a brick building, the one in which Mr. Riker now does business, and in 1863 Mr. Riker purchased the interest in the stock of goods and building, and continued the dry goods business with a capital of $10,000 on his own account. In 1871 he took into the business with him, his nephew, William B. Davis, and in 1875 his son, W. Letcher Riker, was also admitted into the firm, and they have continued business under the firm name of W. H. Riker & Co. Mr. Riker, on November 25, 1847, was united in marriage to Miss Martha D. Smedley, a daughter of John L. and Patsy (Letcher) Smedley, the former of Philadelphia, the latter of Mercer County. John L. Smedley was a man of considerable prominence in the history of Mercer County, whose father was an Englishman who lived to the advanced age of one hundred and five. Pasty Davis (Letcher) Smedley, his wife, who is still living, is the daughter of Stephen G. Letcher, a brother of ex-Gov. Letcher, of Kentucky. Mr. and Mrs. Riker had seven children, John (died in 1860 in his thirteenth year); Mary, wife of Camillus D. Thompson, of Harrodsburg; W. Letcher, married to Miss Fanny M. Simrall, of Covington; Patti, wife of John Lafon, of Harrodsburg; Sarah, wife of A. R. McKee, of Boyle County; Ida and Lafon. Mr. and Mrs. Riker and their children are members of the Assembly Presbyterian Church.

JOHN W. RINEHART, of the firm of Ray & Rinehart, general merchants at Lebanon, was born in Marion County in 1854. His grandparents, William and Sallie Rinehart, came to Kentucky from Maryland, settling within the limits of Marion County, where they engaged in farming. They had four sons and four daughters, among the former being Thomas C., the father of John W. Rinehart. Thos. C. was born in Marion County in the year 1819, and is still an honored citizen of that county, having followed the pursuits of agriculture as a life business. He married Miss Sarah Funk, a daughter of John and Harriet Funk, who came from Virginia. Thos. C. and Sarah Rinehart had a family of eight children, John W., Pattie and Lizzie being the only surviving ones. John W. began his mercantile life when seventeen as a salesman for P. C. W. Peterson of

Washington County. He came to Lebanon (1879) and engaged in clerical work for John B. Carlile until January, 1882, when he formed his present partnership. Both members of this substantial firm are young men of great energy and pronounced business ability. Mr. Rinehart is a member of the Masonic order and K. of H.

DR. W. H. ROACH, physician, was born in 1833, and is a son of Joseph B. Roach, born in 1779, and died in 1860. His grandfather, Littleberry Roach, came from Virginia in 1782, and was of Scotch-Irish descent. He was a soldier in the Revolutionary war. Dr. Roach, a native of Mercer County, after receiving the rudiments of a fair education, read medicine and graduated from the medical department of the University of Louisville. He commenced, and still continues practice at Salvisa, where he has won a reputation attained by few. In 1859 he was married to Miss Mary L. Conner, daughter of W. G. Conner. They have one child, a son, now a practicing lawyer in Harrodsburg. Mrs. Roach is a devoted member of the Christian Church; the Doctor is a freethinker. He is a Democrat in politics.

DR. WILLIAM OTHO ROBARDS was born August 1, 1830, in Jessamine County. In 1853 he removed to Perryville, in 1857 to Marion County, in 1859 to North Fork Station, Boyle County, in 1874 to Lebanon and in 1877 he located at "Linwood" farm, on Pleasant Hill pike, five miles north of Danville, where he has since resided. His father, Otho Robards, a native of Jessamine County, was born February 24, 1794, three miles northwest of Nicholasville. He served many years in the capacity of sheriff, was long a deacon in the Presbyterian Church, was a public-spirited and liberal man; in politics a Whig; a farmer and large slaveholder. He died February 9, 1857. He was the son of William Robards, a native of Virginia, who removed to Jessamine County, Ky., in a very early day, and was a successful business man, an extensive land owner, and died about 1820 at the age of sixty-five years. His children by his first wife were Mrs. Floyd and Mrs. Davis. His second wife was Mrs. Elizabeth Cox, nee Lewis, of Virginia, and their offspring were William, Otho, John M., Rebecca (Singleton), Kittie (Mervey), Susan and Mary (Caldwell). Otho married Mrs. Cassa Gregg, daughter of Younger and Elizabeth (Rogers) Pitts of Scott County (born November 9, 1802, now living), and from their union sprang John M., William O., Younger P., Elizabeth (deceased), Kittie (Caldwell), of

Williamsville, Ill., James H. and Lewis S. May 8, 1855, William Otho Robards married Miss Augusta C., daughter of Capt. John A. and Louisiana (Chandler) Burton, of Perryville (born September 23, 1838), and their union has been favored by the birth of Louisiana B. Huguely, Isabell B., John B., William B. (deceased), Richard B., Robert B. and Eusebia B. In 1851 Mr. Robards commenced the study of medicine with Dr. Joseph P. Letcher, of Nicholasville, and after attending three courses of lectures (two at Lexington and one at Louisville, intervening), he graduated at Transylvania University, and has met with marked success in the practice of his profession, at present only practicing to a limited extent among friends. He is engaged in farming, having 333 acres of highly improved land. His mansion, one of the best in Mercer County, was constructed for and by Abram Bowman in 1850. The farm lies in Mercer and Boyle Counties. Dr. Robards lost seventeen slaves as a result of the late war. He is a member of the Masonic fraternity, also a member of the Methodist Episcopal Church South, and in politics a Democrat.

JEFFERSON ROBARDS, Jr., was born October 6, 1848, near Bergen, Mercer Co., Ky., and in 1854, with his parents, located three miles south of Harrodsburg, where he has since resided. His father, Jefferson Robards, Sr., was born January 28, 1806, in Garrard County, where he was reared, was a farmer and slave-holder, a Whig; provost-marshal during the late war, and died September 3, 1882. He was the son of Jesse Robards, a native Virginian, an early settler in Kentucky and a soldier in the war of 1812. He married a Miss Lewis, and from their union sprang Robert, Joseph, Thomas, John, Jefferson, Sr., Ellen (Allen), Polly (Corn), Betsy (Baker), Nancy (Piper) and Frances (Anderson). Jefferson, Sr., married Eliza, daughter of Peter Farlee, of Garrard County (born in 1818, died June 22, 1878), and to them were born Louisa (Clark), Lewis (deceased), Robert and Jefferson, Jr. Jefferson, Jr., married, October 16, 1883, Miss Kate, daughter of Abram and Cynthia (Young) Terhune, of Mercer County, born in January, 1863. Mr. Robards is a farmer, having 216 acres of land in a high state of cultivation. He is a member of the Southern Presbyterian Church, and in politics a Democrat.

WILLIAM J. and GEORGE D. ROBERTSON were born respectively November 9, 1818, and February 14, 1834, in Springfield, Ky. Of a family of six children

born to Dudley and Catherine (Wright Jones) Robertson, they were the eldest and youngest. At the time of the death of the father, in 1833, of cholera, William J. for a time, as the eldest son, became the head of the family. Mrs. Robertson, a native of the Shenandoah Valley, Virginia, in 1837 became the wife of John Freeman, who reared the younger children by her marriage with Mr. Robertson. William J. commenced life for himself, at the age of fifteen years, as a clerk in the store of James H. Cunningham, with whom he continued three years. He then engaged as clerk with the firm of Davison & Smith. In 1840 he, in partnership with Geo. W. Parrott, embarked in the mercantile trade. Two years later they met with the misfortune of losing their stock by fire. In 1843 he formed a copartnership with William S. Davison and again engaged in the mercantile business, which he continued until the death of Mr. Davison in 1856. He then took charge of and operated the stage lines carrying the mail until 1862. In 1864 he went into the wholesale grocery trade at Louisville. Two years later he returned to Springfield and, as a member of the firm of Robertson, Thomas & Co., again engaged in operating the stage lines. In 1870 they dissolved, and he took charge of the Lebanon & Springfield route, which he continued until 1883. In 1880, in company with A. H. McChord, he established a dry goods store at Springfield, and in 1884 transferred his interest in the same to his son William. He had in 1869 purchased a fine farm of 170 acres, situated on the Lebanon and Springfield pike, about three miies from the latter place, to which he removed, and where he has since lived. June 27, 1848, he was united in marriage with Lucy A. H. Knott. To their union eight children have been born, of whom seven are now living: Sarah C , wife of Judge W. E. Selecman; George R.; Marion T., now Mrs. W. H. Booker; Mary, consort of E. F. Mayes; William K., Maggie and Charles D. Susan, the deceased child, died in 1865.

GEORGE D. ROBERTSON also commenced life for himself at the age of fifteen, as an apprentice at the buggy and wagon-maker's trade at Glasgow, Ky. At the age of twenty-one he entered his brother's store as clerk, on a salary of $50 and board for his first year. Two years subsequently he engaged with Young & Bro., with whom he only remained one year; then spent three years in the employ of T. Anderson & Co. and J. M. Robison & Co., at Louisville, after which he returned to Springfield and formed a partnership with Rinehart & McElroy in the mercantile trade. Four years later he retired from that firm and purchased another store, in which he has since continued, and carries the largest and most extensive stock of groceries in Springfield, and enjoys a large and profitable custom. May 12, 1863, he married Miss Lucinda Hamilton, daughter of Alexander Hamilton. By her he became the father of eleven children, six now living: Florence, Annie, Joseph B., Mattie, George and William T. Both William J. and George D. are representative, enterprising and wide-awake citizens. In politics they are Democratic, but neither has sought any political preferment.

BOYLE C. ROBERTSON was born January 31, 1855, in Springfield, Ky., and in 1858 removed with his parents to Perryville, Boyle County, where he grew to manhood, and in 1879 located at Aliceton, where he has since resided. His father, Austin M. Robertson, also a native of Springfield, Ky., was born September 8, 1823, and is engaged in the blacksmithing business. He is a member of the Methodist Episcopal Church South. He is the son of Dudley Robertson, a native of Washington County and also a blacksmith, who died of cholera in 1833. His offspring are John, James, Louisa (Dyre), William J., Mary (Freeman), Austin M., Lucy (Bates), Green and George D. Austin M. Robertson married Miss Elizabeth J., daughter of William S. and Elizabeth B. (Williams) Bottom, of Boyle County (born in 1827),and from their union sprang Dudley B., George W., James A., Boyle C. and Lemuel M. (twins). On the 24th of November, 1877, Boyle C. Robertson was united in marriage with Miss Georgia W., daughter of Philip S. and Mary J. (Graham) Board of Boyle County, and to them have been born Cassie J., Maggie L., Ada F. and Jennie K. In 1879 Mr. Robertson commenced clerking in the store of James A. Bottom, of Aliceton, and now with his brother, Lemuel M. Robertson, is engaged in conducting a general merchandise establishment, in which they are meeting with encouraging success. In politics Mr. Robertson affiliates with the Democratic party.

RICHARD M. ROBINSON was born near Ashland, in Fayette County, Ky., September 15, 1817, and was the son of Benjamin and Mary (Beattey) Robinson. His education was received at the old Bacon College, Georgetown, Ky. February 11, 1840, he married, in the county of Garrard, Miss Margaret Hoskins, a daughter of William and Elizabeth (Bright) Hoskins, and to this union

were born three children: Mary, Maggie and William. Though an excellent citizen and a man of broad and liberal charity, he was not a member of any church. He died at his home, Camp Dick Robinson, June 13, 1869, and in speaking of this event, the Frankfort (Ky.) *Commonwealth* took occasion to remark as follows: " When the events of yesterday and to-day have become a part of the facts of history, Richard M. Robinson will be read of as one of the patriotic faithful men, who unfolded the flag of his country above him when peril was in the breeze and the days were full of darkness, acknowledging no other allegiance and worshiping at no other shrine. To that spirit of heroism—that pure and exalted and holy patriotism—was due the founding on his farm, in 1861, by Gen. Nelson, of ' Camp Dick Robinson,' where the soldiery of the Union first marshaled in Kentucky and disciplined their ranks for the great contest that has ended in peace and liberty and National integrity. For years the sound of the drum and the fife broke the morning echoes in the vicinity of his home, and now they are gone and green grass grows where the bivouac fires were once lighted and the tents spread their white wings, and the sad vestiges of strife are swept away leaving peace and quietude, his soul finds a proper time to leave its frail tenement and to return to his father and its God. Buried with the honors of the Masonic brotherhood, of which he was a worthy member, and attended to the grave by the largest funeral procession ever witnessed in the county, his life journey is ended and his spirit at rest."

JAMES BENJAMIN ROBINSON was born December 8, 1834, on the waters of Dick's River, in the northwestern portion of Garrard County, Ky., where he has always resided. His father, Michael Robinson, Jr., born in 1804, was a farmer and slave owner, an elder in the Presbyterian Church, a Whig, a Union man, and died in 1861. He was the son of Michael Robinson, Sr., whose offspring were Harry, John, William, Michael, Jr., Mary (Alford), Ann (Calbfus), and Lucy (Watts). Michael, Jr., married in 1829 Margaret, daughter of Benjamin and Margaret (Hocker) Dunn (born in 1812), and their union was favored by the birth of Mary A (Spillman), Silas C., James B., Sarah J. (Smith), John, Gabrilla (Perkins), Belle (Tomlinson), Margaret, George W., Michael and Kate Leavell. March 17, 1859, James B. Robinson married Miss Mary E., daughter of Joseph and Elizabeth (Taylor) Tomlinson, of Garrard County (born May

25, 1840), and to them have been born Lizzie M., Lula, Joseph M. (deceased), Zelma (Wilds), Alice and Charles S. Mr. Robinson was reared as a farmer, and followed that vocation until 1884, when he also engaged in general merchandising at Buena Vista, at which he has met with encouraging success. He also owns a well improved and productive farm of ninety-three acres. He is a member of the Methodist Episcopal Church; also a member of the Masonic fraternity, and of the K. of H. He is postmaster of Buena Vista, was a Union man and is now a Republican and a prohibitionist.

ZACK ROBINSON was born January 10, 1838, and is a son of Uriah Robinson, who was born in Garrard County, in 1811, moved to Mercer County in 1836, and afterward settled in Washington County. The first marriage of Uriah Robinson was to a Miss Bledson, who bore him seven children, Adderson (deceased), Benjamin (deceased), John (killed by guerrillas during the late war), U. P. (deceased), Kittie Sea (deceased), Betsie Barnett, and Jane Harley (deceased). His second mariage, about 1835, was to Miss Jennie Jenkins, who also bore him seven children: J. W., Zack, George W., Sarah A. (Bell), Henry Jackson (deceased), Thomas J. (deceased), Marian F. (deceased). Zack Robinson was reared in his native county of Washington, served two years as sheriff, owned a distillery for several years, and afterward dealt in real estate. He is now located at Tom, Mercer County, engaged in mercantile pursuits, and also owns and cultivates a farm of 400 acres. He married Miss Isabel Driskell, who has borne him five children: Lizzie (Brown), Henry L., Larue, Theodore and Grover C. Mr. Robinson is a Free Mason, a Baptist and a Democrat.

JOHN S. ROBINSON was born April 23, 1849, in Garrard County, Ky., but was reared to manhood in Mercer County, where he still resides. His father, William H. Robinson, also a native of Garrard County, was born in 1818, was a farmer, slave-holder and Southern trader, was formerly an old line Whig, latterly a Democrat, but voted for Garfield, in 1880; lost twelve slaves by the late war, and died July 22, 1885. He was the son of James H. Robinson, a native Virginian, who removed when quite young with his parents to Kentucky, was sheriff of Garrard County, a farmer and slave owner, and died about 1850, very old. His wife was a Miss Alford, and their offspring were William H., John B. and Elizabeth (Moore). William H. married, in 1846, Miss Sarah, daughter of

Henry and Sally (Isaacs) Taylor, of Marion County (born in 1824, died October 8, 1883), and from their union sprang John S., James H., Fannie L. (Huguely), William T., Charles W. and Artemisia. October 23, 1878, John S. Robinson was united in marriage with Miss Jennie L., daughter of Dr. William and Mary (Forsythe) Evans, of Danville, Ky. (born July 21, 1856), and to them has been born one child, William E., November 22, 1885. Mr. Robinson traded south with mules and horses for eight years, but is now farming, and raising and trading in live stock, having 375 acres of land, 225 of which are well improved, and in a high state of cultivation. In religion he is a member of the Christian Church, and in politics a Democrat.

HUGH D. RODMAN, M. D., a prominent physician, was born May 22, 1842, and is the fourth of nine sons and two daughters born to John H. and Mary A. (Hogan) Rodman. John H. Rodman was born October 1, 1809, in Shelby County, Ky., and when a lad of about twelve years his parents moved to Dubois County, Ind., where they lived for a short time, when they moved to Washington County, Ind. At the age of eighteen years he returned to Louisville, and learned the carpenter trade; thence he went to Washington County, Ky., where he lived for some years and met and married Miss Mary A. Hogan. He then moved to Indiana, and engaged in the construction of turnpike roads for a time, then returned to Louisville, thence to Marion County, Ky., and finally in 1844 located near Knottsville, in Daviess County, Ky. After living there seven years he moved to the southwest portion of the county, near Curdsville, where he is now living at the age of seventy-seven years, and where he has been extensively engaged in farming. John H. was the eldest son of Hugh Rodman, who was born, where Louisville, Ky., now stands, in 1788 in a tent, and within four days after his birth his parents moved to Shelby County, Ky., into a fort for protection from the Indians, where he met and married Elizabeth McClain. In 1816 he moved to Indiana, where he engaged in farming until his death a good old age. His parents came from Pennsylvania, and settled in Shelby County, Ky., where they were among the first settlers, and engaged in carpentering and farming. Mrs. Mary A. Rodman is a daughter of Capt. William and Mary E. (Drury) Hogan, both of whom came from Maryland, about 1810, and settled in Nelson County, Ky., where they were married January 4, 1814. They then moved to

Washington County, Ky., where Capt. Hogan kept a hotel in Fredericksburg up to the time of his death. He was a soldier in the war of 1812. His parents came from Ireland. The Rodman family were Whigs in politics, and the Hogans Democrats. Dr. Rodman was born near St. Mary's College in Marion County, Ky., was reared on a farm in Daviess County, received his early education in the common schools, then attended Notre Dame University, Indiana, two years, after which he spent five months in teaching school. When he reached maturity he commenced life for himself on a farm, which he followed four years, then clerked in a store and taught alternately for three years, at the same time reading medicine. He attended his first course of lectures in 1868–69, graduating from the medical department of the University of Louisville in 1871. He immediately located at High Grove, Nelson Co., Ky., where he remained until February, 1878, when he moved to New Haven, where he now lives, and is successfully engaged in the practice of his profession. The Doctor is a member of the State Medical Society and District Medical Society, is a member of and State president of, the C. K. of A., is also a member of the C. T. A. U. of A. He was united in marriage January 16, 1877, to Miss Mary Josephine Fowler, of Louisville, daughter of Samuel O. Fowler and Susan (Overton) Fowler, both natives of Washington County, Ky. Samuel O. Fowler was a son of John and Mary Overton Fowler. He followed various occupations, and was a soldier in the war with Mexico. The Doctor and wife are the happy possessors of five children: Mary Frances, Paul Edward, Joseph Hugh, John Samuel and James Sylvester. The Doctor has attained a good reputation as a physician and citizen. He has been secretary of the County Board of Health ever since its creation. In politics he is a Democrat, and with his wife, a member of the Roman Catholic Church.

S. D. ROTHWELL was born October 17, 1841, at Paint Lick, Garrard County, and is the seventh in a family of six sons and two daughters, born to Fontaine and Jennie (Roberts) Rothwell, natives of Albemarle County, Va., and born in 1799 and 1802 respectively. Fontaine Rothwell, at the age of twenty, was apprenticed to Gideon Fitch, a Government surveyor; came to Kentucky at the age of twenty-two, located in Madison County, and was there married, and one year later moved to Paint Lick, became a prosperous farmer and slave owner, and died March

4, 1883, a member of the Baptist Church; his wife died in April, 1874. Fontaine was a son of Thomas Rothwell, who married Elizabeth Fitch; Thomas Rothwell was a son of Claiborn Rothwell, who came from England. Mrs. Jennie (Roberts) Rothwell was a daughter of Namon Roberts, who married Mary Rose, both of North Carolina. Namon Roberts was a soldier under Washington, lost an eye in the Revolutionary war, and was one of the first settlers in Madison County, Ky. He was of French descent and died in 1848. Samuel D. Rothwell was reared a farmer. In 1861 he entered the Federal Army as wagon-master. August 4, 1862, he enlisted in Company H, Seventh Kentucky Federal Cavalry, and served until discharged as second sergeant, at Nashville, Tenn., July 19, 1865. On his return to Kentucky he engaged in farming until August, 1882, when he was elected jailer of Garrard County on the Democratic ticket, and re-elected in 1886. He was married, January 7, 1868, to Miss Eliza, daughter of James and Martha (Nickelson) Henry, and to this union two children have been born: Martha A. (deceased), and James M. Mr. Rothwell is a Free Mason, and a member of the Presbyterian Church. Mrs. Rothwell is also a Presbyterian.

WILLIAM H. ROWAN, county court clerk and son of John and Rebecca (Carnes) Rowan, was born in Nelson County September 17, 1837. His grandfather, Hon. John Rowan, was one of Kentucky's most distinguished lawyers. Mr. Rowan's maternal ancestors were among the early residents of Maryland, his grandfather, Peter Carnes, having been for a number of years a successful business man of Baltimore. He was also a major in the United States Army; served as Indian agent in an early day, and died in his native State about the year 1848 or 1849. John Rowan, Jr., subject's father, was born in Nelson County, Ky., in 1807; was a lawyer by profession and a man of considerable prominence in the State. He was the United States minister to Naples during Polk's administration and died in Nelson County in August, 1855. His wife, Rebecca (Carnes) Rowan, was born in St. Mary's County, Md., and is still living near Bardstown. John and Rebecca Rowan reared a family of ten children, of whom the following are living: Mrs. Josephine Reid, William H., Maud A., Julia and Madge Rowan. The deceased members of the family are John, Rebecca, Lytle, Henry and Mary. William H. Rowan was reared near Bardstown and passed his youth upon a farm, attending the schools of the town in the meantime. He was with his father during the latter's residence in Italy, and while in Naples attended school in that city, where he made substantial progress in his various studies. He returned to Kentucky in 1850, and the year following attended the Mt. St. Mary's College, Maryland, where he prosecuted his studies until about the year 1852. After his father's death he began the study of law with Wm. P. Boone and Charles D. Pennebaker, of Louisville, with whom he remained for a period of eighteen months, and in 1859 was admitted to the bar, receiving his license from Judges Caleb Logan and Peter B. Muir. He did not engage in his practice, however, but instead secured the position of deputy circuit clerk of Jefferson County, in which capacity he continued until the breaking out of the civil war, when he entered the Confederate service, enlisting in Company D, First Kentucky Regiment, in which he held a lieutenant's commission and served as lieutenant until the first battle of Manassas, when, for gallant conduct, he was promoted to the captaincy of his company, a position he held until after the battle of Williamsburg, when the first regiment was disbanded. He was made captain of the regulars in 1862, and held commission until some time the following year, when he was assigned to the command of the Third Kentucky Battalion, Hodgen's brigade, in which capacity he continued until his capture at Farmington, Tenn., in October, 1863; was held a prisoner from the latter date until July, 1865, spending the interim at Johnson's Island, Old Capitol prison at Washington and Ft. Delaware, from the last of which he was paroled at the time mentioned above. During his period of service as a soldier Maj. Rowan participated in a number of bloody engagements, among which were Manassas, Dranesville, seven days' battles in front of Richmond, Chickamauga, and many others, through all of which he escaped unhurt. At the close of the war he returned to Bardstown and effected a copartnership in the law with William R. Grigsby, Esq., with whom he practiced his profession about one year. At the end of that time he disposed of his legal business and made an extensive tour of the Western States and Territories, remaining in the same for a period of ten years, following various vocations in the meantime. He returned to Bardstown in 1876, since which time he has been a resident of the city; was elected county court clerk in August, 1878; re-elected in 1882, and at the present time (1886) is candidate for re-election to the same office without opposition.

Mr. Rowan is an active politician, and votes with the Democratic party, with which he has been identified since his twenty-first year. He married, September 20, 1877, in Nelson County, Miss Nannie T. Hardin, daughter of Rowan and Eliza (Cartnell) Hardin, of Fleming County, Ky. Two children have been born to this marriage, viz.: Ben Hardin Rowan and Rebecca B. Rowan (deceased). Mrs. Rowan is a member of the Bardstown Baptist Church.

OWEN RUBEL, carriage manufacturer at Lebanon, was born in Jefferson County, Ky., in the year 1831, and reared to manhood in the city of Louisville, where, with William P. Shepherd, he learned the trade of carriage-maker to which he has since devoted his life. His father, Jesse Rubel, came from Virginia about 1820 and located at Middletown, Ky., being a tailor by trade. He married Miss Sarah, daughter of William Wallace, who came in early life from New York. Five children blessed their union, viz.: James L.; W. F. Rubel, present jailer of Louisville; Owen; Martha (Smith), and Jesse Rubel. The father died of cholera in 1833, and his widow subsequently married Mr. John F. Randolph, who is also deceased. The mother was born May 6, 1807, and is still living. In 1851 Owen Rubel removed to Bardstown, Ky., where he engaged in business until 1858, removing thence to Lebanon. He married in Bardstown (1853) Miss Mary O. Ramey, daughter of William Ramey, of Montgomery County. Their children are John, William R., Mattie (Knott), Jessie, Harry Lee and Walter Rubel. Mr. Rubel is an honored member of the Methodist Episcopal Church, Masonic fraternity and of the K. of H.

EDWARD B. RUSSEL, contractor, was born October 2, 1820, in Danville, Ky., and is the second of two sons and two daughters born to Robert and Malinda (Parrish) Russel. Robert Russel was born near Petersburg, Va., and was brought to Kentucky by his parents when a lad of eight years. His occupation was that of a brickmaker and mason. He built the Centre College Home in 1820, and built nearly all the first brick buildings erected in Danville. He was a son of Robert Russel and Jenet Robison; both were born and raised in Edinburgh, Scotland, and after their marriage emigrated and settled near Petersburg, Va. Their first child was born while at sea. Six children in all were born by this marriage—five sons and one daughter. His second wife was Susan Wheeler; the issue from this second marriage was three sons. He settled in Kentucky about 1805, first at Danville, later in Casey County, where he owned a large tract of land. He died there in 1827. Mrs. Malinda Russel was born in Goochland County, Va., and was a daughter of Nicholas Parrish, a soldier of 1812. Edward B. Russel was reared in Danville, where he has lived all his life, except one year in Macoupin County, Ill. He received a good English education, and has always followed brickmaking. When the war broke out he had twenty slaves. He has served two terms as magistrate. He was married December 14, 1843, to Mary W. Alford, of Garrard County, a daughter of Morgan and Mary W. (Robison) Alford, natives of Virginia and Garrard County, Ky., respectively. Mr. and Mrs. Russel have had born to them six children: Rob. S., Virginia (now Dillahey, of Chattanooga, Tenn.) Chas. M., Edward Y., Mary Durham and Warren A. Mr. and Mrs. Russel are members of the Christian Church. He is a Free Mason, and cast his first presidential vote for Henry Clay. Since the war he has affiliated with the Democratic party.

JUDGE WILLIAM E. RUSSELL, for many years a prominent member of the bar, and now judge of the circuit comprising the counties of Marion, Washington, Mercer, Nelson, Taylor and La Rue, was born on the 6th of October, 1830. His father, Andrew Russell, was born near the old Logan fort, in Lincoln County, in the close of the last century, and was the son of Joseph Russell, who came from Maryland. Andrew Russell married Elizabeth Echols, a descendant of a Virginia family. Andrew Russell died in 1852, and his widow in 1873. They were the parents of five children, our subject being the second, and the only one now living, except A. K. Russell, of Lebanon. Mr. Russell was educated in the schools of his native county of Adair, and when seventeen years old entered upon the study of law, performing the usual preparatory reading under the instruction of Isaac Caldwell, and was regularly admitted to the practice in 1849. He established a practice first in Adair County, but in 1867 removed to Lebanon, his present home, where he has been prominent as a lawyer and highly respected as a citizen. In 1857 he was elected to the Kentucky State Legislature and served the session of 1877–78. He was twice a candidate for judge of the court of appeals, and in August, 1886, was elected to the responsible position of circuit judge. Judge Russell was married in Lebanon, in 1854, to Miss Sue Elder, daughter of Sylvester and Elizabeth Elder, and has a family of seven children, the eldest of whom, Sylvester A.

Russell, is a brilliant young attorney of the Lebanon bar. Judge Russell is a member of the Catholic Church, and the Supreme President of the C. K. of A.

JOSEPH B. RUSSELL was born January 30, 1837, and is the ninth of six sons and seven daughters, all of whom lived to be grown, born to Charles and Julia (Buckman) Russell. Charles Russell, Jr., was born and reared in Marion County; was a farmer, and died in 1854. He was a son of Charles Russell, Sr., who came from Maryland to Kentucky in the early settlement of the State. He was a farmer and of English origin. Mrs. Julia (Buckman) Russell was born and reared on Rolling Fork, and was a daughter of Charles Buckman, who married a Miss Dunbar, and who came from Maryland with family in a very early day. J. B. Russell was born on Rolling Fork, Marion County, and he remained with and supported his mother until her death, when he commenced the battle of life for himself at farming. January 30, 1867, he was united in marriage to Mrs. Almarinda Short, a daughter of Stephen and Charlotte (Cleaver) Harding, who were natives of Taylor and Marion Counties, respectively. Mr. Harding was a substantial farmer and slave owner. He was a son of John Harding, who married a Miss Taylor, and both were among the first settlers of Kentucky, and were of Irish stock. Mr. and Mrs. Russell had born to them by this union three children: Effie E., Stephen Thomas (deceased), and Hubert B. Mr. and Mrs. Russell are members of the Roman Catholic and Baptist Churches, respectively. After their marriage they located on Rolling Fork, and in 1874 located on thirty-six (which he has increased to sixty-five) acres, of fine bottom land, in a high state of cultivation, improved with a neat cottage. He has had, however, the misfortune of losing two houses by fire. In politics he is now an active Republican, but cast his first vote for Douglas.

ANDREW K. RUSSELL, present sheriff of Marion County, is a son of Andrew and Elizabeth Russell; was born on the 17th of August, 1838, in Columbia, Adair Co., Ky. He was chiefly reared in his native county, but attended St. Mary's College, of Marion County. In 1861 he enlisted in the Confederate Army, as a member of Company F, of the Fourth Kentucky Regiment. He shared the fortunes of this regiment from the date of his enlistment until the general surrender, participating in several hard-fought battles, among which were Shiloh, Chickamauga, Atlanta, Jackson, Vicksburg, Murfreesboro, Stone River and Jonesboro. Soon after his return from the war, and in November, 1865, he married Miss Laura, daughter of John F. and Elizabeth Bridgewater, of Adair County. Their children are Bettie, Lelah, Tippie R., Corina, Nellie B. and Timoleon M. Russell. Mr. Russell is a member of the Masonic fraternity, and of the Christian Church. In 1884 he was elected to the office of sheriff of Marion County, having previously served the county as deputy sheriff.

E. M. RUSSELL, jeweler, is a son of William and Margaret (Clusker) Russell, both parents natives of Ireland. William Russell was born in the city of Dublin, where he grew to manhood and married. He in early life learned the jewelry business, became a skillful workman, and carried on a thriving business in his native city until 1832. In that year he came to the United States, and for several years thereafter worked at his trade in New York City; he afterward moved to Kentucky, and after several years spent in Lexington, removed to Richmond, where he established a thriving business which he carried on for a number of years. From Richmond he removed to Bardstown in 1844, where he carried on an extensive business until 1880, at which time he moved to Louisville, where he still resides. William and Margaret Russell are the parents of eight children whose names are as follows: Arthur, Ellen, Maria, George, Robert, Ed. M., Maggie and Joseph Russell. Ed. M. Russell was born and reared in Bardstown, and educated at St. Joseph's College, which he attended three years. He learned the jewelry business with his father, and after quitting school worked at the trade in Bardstown for several years. In 1871 he went to San Francisco, Cal., for the purpose of engaging with a large watch company, but upon his arrival in the city, found the said company had failed, hence he was compelled to seek his fortune elsewhere. From San Francisco he went to San Diego, and after a short time spent in the latter city, took his departure for Julian City, a mining town, where he remained several years, prospecting a portion of the time, and meeting with many varied experiences in that romantic part of California. He next went to Los Angeles, and later to San Bernardino, where he engaged in the hotel and restaurant business, which he carried on for two years, meeting with the most encouraging success in the meantime. From San Bernardino he went to the mining town of Darwin, Inyo County, where he bought and operated several mines but with little

success. Tiring of that kind of employment a few months later he returned to San Francisco. From the latter place he went to Salt Lake, and after spending several months there, he returned to Kentucky, after an absence of seven years. In October, 1878, he established himself in the jewelry business at Springfield where he has since resided, his store being the only one of the kind in Washington County. Mr. Russell was married May 5, 1879, to Miss Louisa Bird, daughter of R. L. and Sarah (Collier) Bird. Mrs. Russell was born in St. Johnswood, England, in the year 1862. Mr. and Mrs. Russell have three children, namely: Catherine, Margaret and Emily Russell. Mr. Russell has held the office of town marshal of Springfield; is a Democrat in politics, and with his wife, belongs to the Catholic Church, being members of the St. Dominic's congregation.

SAINT JOSEPH'S COLLEGE, a Catholic educational institution, situated in the vicinity of Bardstown, was founded by the Right Rev. Bishop Flaget, first bishop of Bardstown, in 1820, with a view of giving to Catholics a thorough literary education. The college became a corporate institution in 1824, and received the privilege of conferring degrees. Its first president was the Rev. George A. Elder, whose mild and gentle rule continued for nearly twenty years. After his death, in the year 1838, Rev. M. J. Spalding, D. D., became president. He afterward was made bishop of Louisville, and subsequently transferred to the arch-diocese of Baltimore. To him succeeded the Rev. James M. Lancaster and Rev. Abraham Mc-Mahan, when, in 1848, the management of the college was transferred to the Jesuit fathers of the province of Missouri. For nearly twenty years this institution was conducted by the secular clergy, and during this time the average number of students was not less than 200 yearly. They were not only from Kentucky, but from nearly all the States in the South. Among these may be mentioned Hon. Lazarus W. Powell, governor of Kentucky and United States senator; Hon. James Speed, Attorney-general during President Lincoln's administration; Govs. Roman and Wickliffe, of Louisiana; Judges Buckner, of Lexington, and DeHaven, of La Grange, Ky.; Hons. Rowan and Hardin, of Bardstown. Here were educated the Catholic clergy of the diocese of Louisville, many of whom were remarkable for their talents and ability—the cultivated Ignatius S. Reynolds, successor to the learned John England, in the See of Charleston, S. C.; the scholarly, logical John McGill, bishop of Richmond,

Va., author of "Our Faith the Victory." It was while teaching here that Francis P. Kenrick, D. D., afterward archbishop of Baltimore, wrote in classical Latin his "Dogmatic and Moral Theology," a work of vast learning and deep research, which has been reprinted in Europe, and is still used as a text book in many of our theological seminaries. For half a century this college has been one of the great centers of education in the Southwest, and it has well merited the confidence of Catholics and non-Catholics. It has been well patronized by the people of the Southern States. Many students from Mexico and the West Indies Islands come here to be educated. In 1848 the Jesuit fathers of the Western Province assumed the management and remained in charge of the affairs until 1861, when, in consequence of the civil war, it was closed. While in charge of the Jesuit fathers the college was highly successful, and many young men, afterward distinguished in civil life, received, at their hands, a thorough Christian and liberal education, amongst whom may be mentioned the present Attorney-general, in Cleveland's administration, Hon. Augustus Garland, of Arkansas; Hon. Zachariah Montgomery, of California. The presidents of the college during the management of the Jesuit fathers were Father Verhegen, S. J.; Father Emig, S. J., and Father I. O'Neil, S. J., during whose term of office the institution was closed. In 1869 the secular clergy, under the authority of the ordinary of the diocese, Right Rev. Dr. McCoskey, again assumed charge of the college—the Rev. P. De Fraine, president, assisted by Revs. A. Viala, J. P. Ryan, William Bourke and Charles Eggermont. This arrangement lasted until 1872, when Rev. Coghlan became president. He died in March, 1877, and Rev. E. Crane acted as president until September of the same year. Rev. W. Dunn was then appointed president. In the year 1880, Rev. W. P. Mackin, by the authority of the bishop, Rt. Rev. W. McCoskey, was appointed president. The faculty is at present made up of Rev. Civill, vice-president; Revs. John A. Barrett, William Bourke, D. Crane, Mr. A. P. Shaedler, A. M., and A. Smith, M. D. The affairs of the college are now prosperous, and at no time from its incipiency has it been more adequate to the educational needs of the youth of the country. The situation of St. Joseph's College can not be excelled. It is easy of access by the Bardstown branch of the Louisville & Nashville Railroad. The buildings are spacious, and the playgrounds all that can be desired. Under its present management it will no doubt retain its well established reputation. *Vivat* and *crescat*.

MARTIN PHILLIPS SALLEE was born March 16, 1828, in Wayne County, Ky., where he lived until 1883, when he removed to Boyle County, and located two miles east of Danville, where he now resides. His father, Capt. Moses Sallee, of Wayne County, was long a magistrate and member of the court of claims, and a representative in the Legislature. He was a Whig, a farmer and slave owner, and died in 1840 at the age of fifty-five years. He was the son of Peter Sallee, whose offspring were John, Joseph, Moses, Charity (VanWinkle) and Susan (Bruton). Moses married Mary Deering of Wayne County (died in 1858, aged about sixty years), and their union was favored by the birth of Harrison M. (Redman), Melinda (Redman), Martha (Huff), Anna (Hurt), Martin P. and Cyrina (Parmley). Martin Phillips Sallee has been twice married; first, on August 21, 1849, to Margaret A., daughter of Jefferson and Rachael (Coffey) Jones of Wayne County (born in 1830, died January 11, 1862), and from their union sprang Elizabeth (Jones), Jefferson, Amanda (Lanier) and Margaret (Lanier). On May 18, 1864, he was united in marriage with Miss Susan, daughter of Harrison and Elizabeth (Carter) Berry of Wayne County (born July 18, 1842), and to them have been born Etta V. and Edna K. (twins), William H. and Robert E. Mr. Sallee is a farmer and general trader, and owns 390 acres of highly improved land. He is a member of the Christian Church; also a member of the Masonic fraternity; was formerly an old line Whig, but now affiliates with the Democratic party. He lost twenty-eight slaves as a result of the late war.

TAYLOR W. SAMUELS was born January 9, 1821. His father, William Samuels, a native of Virginia, removed to Kentucky in an early day, was an extensive farmer and slave owner, served as high sheriff and magistrate in Nelson County for many years, and died in 1836, aged about sixty-five years. He was the son of James Samuels. William married Sarah Hogland of Nelson County, and their offspring are Robert F., Rev. Preston B. (deceased) and Taylor W. In 1844 Taylor W. was married to Miss Levina, daughter of Isaac Osburn, of Nelson County, and to them have been born William I., Thomas P., Robert B. (deceased), and Mary K. (Martin). Mr. Samuels was educated at the common schools and Bardstown College. He has always been a farmer, owning at present 3,000 acres of land in Nelson, the county of his birth, much of it in a high state of cultivation. He has also, with success, been engaged in merchandising since 1867. He commenced distilling whisky in 1844, and with the exception of a short period has been engaged in the business, having had one valuable distillery burned. He has been very successful in the venture, and his distillery has now a capacity of 215 bushels of corn per day, He served eight years as sheriff and deputy, and four years as magistrate in Nelson County. He suffered severely by the late war, losing fifteen valuable slaves and other property. He is an Ancient Odd Fellow, and in politics is a Democrat.

WILLIAM B. SAMUELS was born May 18, 1843. In 1861 he enlisted in Capt. Wickliffe's company of infantry, Col. Hunt's regiment, Breckinridge's brigade of Confederate Army, and during his two years' service was much of the time on detached duty. His father, Wilson Samuels, was born in 1814, was a farmer and merchant, served many years as magistrate and member of the court of claims of Nelson County, and died July 24, 1874. He was the son of John Samuels, a magistrate and large slave-holder. Wilson Samuels married Martha M., daughter of John and Mary (Jack) Stoner of Nelson County (born in 1822), and their offspring are John (deceased), William B., James S. (deceased), Mary R. (Pence), Alexander P., Isabell (Pence), Finetta F. (Miles). Dr. Augustus W., Enola (deceased) and Annie M. On November, 1870, Mr. Samuels was married to Miss Mary A., daughter of John and Elizabeth (Thompson) Barclay of Nelson County (born in 1850), and to them has been born Harry Mark, August 25, 1875. In 1850 Mr. Samuels commenced dealing in general merchandise, grain and produce at Samuel's Depot, near the spot where he was born in Nelson County. In 1870 he commenced distilling whisky, with a capacity of four barrels, and has increased to twenty barrels per day, securing marked success in the business. He is a non-affiliating Mason and a Democrat.

ALEXANDER SAYERS, Esq., was born March 4, 1824, near Glasgow, Scotland, and in 1838 immigrated with his two brothers to the United States, landing at New York, and proceeding to Louisville, Ky., where he remained six years, attending school, and employed in the grocery business. In 1844 he went to St. Louis, and after remaining one year, returned to Jefferson County, Ky., where he served as deputy sheriff and deputy marshal. In 1853 he located in Nelson County, where he has since resided. His father, James Sayers, a farmer in Scotland, was a brother of Peter Sayers, owner of Paisley Bleach Fields, at Nether Kirkton. James Sayers' offspring are David, William, Peter, John, James, George, Alexander and Henry. On March 4, 1852, Alexander was married to Miss Finetta, daughter of John and Rachel (Kurtz) Samuels, of Nelson County, and to them have been born Mary (deceased), Rachel, Elizabeth, John Wilson, Orietta (Samuels), Mary M., Finetta E. and James Alexander. Alexander Sayers served as county judge for a short time, has acted eight years as magistrate and member of the court of claims for Nelson County, and is in favor of the public improvements now in progress in the county. He is a farmer and trader, owning nearly 5,000 acres of land, 400 of which, constituting his homestead, are well improved and in a fine state of cultivation. In religion he is a Missionary Baptist, and in politics a Democrat.

GEORGE T. SCHOOLFIELD, a mute, was born in Foster, Bracken Co., Ky., May 4, 1841, and is a son of G. T. and Mary (Maxwell) Schoolfield, who were born respectively in Maryland and Kentucky. They had born to them three sons and six daughters. G. T., the father, was a farmer, and served as magistrate; he died in 1877, and was a son of Isaac B. Schoolfield, who came from Maryland to Kentucky in 1814, settled in Bracken County, and married Mary Atkinson. The Schoolfields came from England in 1638 and settled in Maryland. George T. Schoolfield, the younger, was reared on a farm, and was educated in Indiana until 1856, when he entered the Deaf and Dumb Institution at Danville. In 1866 he began teaching in the same institution, and has remained ever since, making a most excellent and efficient teacher. He is a man of great information. His twenty years' experience is the best evidence of his superior intellect and excellent qualities as a teacher. He married Miss Emma Beard, daughter of Stephen M. and Elizabeth (Thomas) Beard. This union is blessed with three sons: Stephen B., Allie T. and Charles B. Mr. Schoolfield and wife are both members of the Methodist Episcopal Church. In politics he is a Democrat.

WILLIAM SCOMP was born April 9, 1821, near Harrodsburg, Mercer Co., Ky.; in 1843 he removed to Boyle County where he has since resided. His father, Henry Scomp, a native of Somerset County, N. J., was born October 11, 1785, and removed to Mercer County, Ky., in 1794, where he engaged in farming, and died June 12, 1841. He was the son of George N. Scomp (or Schamp) of New Jersey, a soldier in the Revolutionary war, who died in 1844, at the age of ninety-seven years. George N. married Mary Smock, of New Jersey, and their offspring were George, John, Henry, Anna (Byers), Sally and Hannah (French). Henry married Flora, daughter of Cornelius and Mary Van Nice, of Mercer County (born in 1788, died January 1, 1862) and from their union sprang John, George, Cornelius, William, Mary (deceased), Sally (Slaughter and Vanarsdall) and Cynthia H. (deceased). October 12, 1842, William Scomp was married to Miss Sarah L., daughter of Anselm Minor, of Boyle County(born in 1805,died December 24, 1869) and to them were born Henry Anselm and Martha King (Moore). Henry Anselm Scomp is a professor of languages in Emory College, Oxford, Ga. Wm. Scomp is a farmer, having 206 acres of land, 130 of which are in a high state of cultivation. He is an elder in the Cumberland Presbyterian Church, a member of the A. F. & A. M., and in politics is identified with the Democratic party.

J. A. SEAY was born March 2, 1842, and is the eldest child of Austin L. and Rose A. (Mattingly) Seay. The father of Austin Seay was Jacob Seay, a native of Lynchburg, Va., and a soldier of the war of 1812. He came to Kentucky many years ago, and settled in Washington County, where he became a very successful business man, and died about the year 1854. Austin L. Seay was born in 1812, spent all his life in Washington County, was a farmer, and died at his home three miles west of Willisburgh in 1872. Rose A. Seay was the daughter of Philip Mattingly, an early resident of Washington County. She was born in Washington County, and died in 1883. The following are the names of the children born to Austin and Rose Seay: J. A., William, Mrs. Mary Goatley, Mrs. Ann Crow, Mrs. Hittie Smothers, Philip Stephen, Mrs. Mattie Gist and Mrs. Susan Bishop. J. A. Seay was born three miles west of Springfield, was reared on a farm, and obtained a good English education in the country schools, which he attended until nineteen years of age. When twenty years old he commenced business for himself, purchasing a farm in 1863, five miles north of Willisburgh, upon which he resided for six years; he then moved to the village of Willisburgh and engaged in the blacksmithing and undertaking business, at the same time opening a boarding-house, all of which he successfully carries on. He es-

tablished a mercantile house in 1881, and since then has been one of the most successful merchants in Washington County outside of Springfield, his stock representing a capital of $6,000, with annual sales aggregating $20,000. Mr. Seay is a member of the Christian Church of Willisburgh, with which he has been identified since 1860. He votes the Democratic ticket, and is a member of the Masonic fraternity, belonging to J. Speed Smith Lodge, No. 298. He has been twice married, the first time on the 10th of December, 1863, to Miss Sallie, daughter of James and Mary E. Mays, of Washington County, by whom he had five children, namely: William M., J. B., Stephen M. (deceased), Ezra V. and John Seay. His second marriage was solemnized in 1881, with Miss Alice Mays, sister of his former wife. This marriage has been blessed with two children, Asa and Effie Seay, both living.

DR. RICHARD A. SHADBURNE was born April 4, 1819. In 1861 he entered the Confederate Army as lieutenant of Company B, Morgan's cavalry, and remained in that service two years, voluntarily acting as surgeon of his own company, and assisting other surgeons in times of emergency. He was for a time a prisoner of war at both Camp Chase and Johnson's Island. His father, Thomas Shadburne, a native of Jefferson County, engaged in the manufacture of hand-made nails, and subsequently merchandising in Bardstown, where he died, about 1828. His wife was Rebecca Foreman, and their offspring are Matilda (Birkhead), Richard A., Joseph and Thomas. The grandfather of Dr. Shadburne was Amos Shadburne, an Englishman. Dr. Shadburne, who was born in Bardstown, Ky., was married October 28, 1856, to Miss Catherine, daughter of Benjamin and Elizabeth (Montgomery) Foreman, and to them have been born Elizabeth K. (Allen), Issa G. (Straus), Rebecca L. Beam and Matilda A. In youth the Doctor obtained a fair English education at Bardstown College, and other literary institutions, and by a course of careful reading has kept pace with the progress of the age, and the current literature of the day. In 1844 he commenced the study of medicine with Dr. Foreman of Nelson County, and afterward graduated at the Kentucky School of Medicine, of the Louisville University. He first practiced at Shepherdsville, afterward in Lincoln County, Mo., and in 1855 located in Spencer County, Ky., where he remained until 1861. Subsequently he practiced in Spencer and Bullitt Counties, and in 1866 established a drug store in Louisville, engaged in practice and acted as coroner by appointment. He practiced in Spencer County from 1871 to 1882, when he located in Nelson County, where he has since engaged in farming, and to a limited extent dispensing the benefits of his knowledge of the healing art among his old friends, free of charge. He owns and is cultivating a valuable farm of 654 acres. He is a member of the Masonic fraternity and in politics is a Democrat.

C. H. SHAUNTY, M. D. Dr. Shaunty's ancestors on his father's side were Germans, his grandfather, Henry Shaunty, immigrating to America in 1775. He settled in Virginia, and at the breaking out of the Revolutionary war enlisted in the American Army, with which he served seven years. He came to Kentucky in 1800, or perhaps a little earlier, and settled in the northwestern part of Washington County, where his death occurred about the year 1825. Subject's father, Joseph Shaunty, was born in Virginia in 1798; was brought to Kentucky when a small boy, and spent the remainder of his life in Washington County, dying near Fredericktown in 1867. His wife, Sallie (Hays) Shaunty, was a daughter of William and Eleanor (Burchman) Hays (see sketch of D. R. Hays). She was born in April, 1807, and died December 11, 1874. Mr. and Mrs. Shaunty were parents of ten children, the following of whom are now living: John, C. H., Mrs. Marietta Croake and William Shaunty. The deceased members of the family are William, Henry, Joseph, Nellie and James. Dr. Shaunty spent his youth and early manhood on a farm near Fredericktown, and obtained a good education in the country and village schools, which he attended until twenty-two years of age. He commenced reading medicine in 1859 with Dr. J. B. Mudd at Fredericktown, with whom he remained three years; entered the medical university at Louisville in 1860, remaining one session, and in 1862 commenced the practice of his profession at Manton Village, Washington County, where he continued one year; returned to the university in 1863, graduated from the same in April, 1864, and immediately thereafter engaged in the practice at Fredericktown, his present place of residence. The Doctor has won an enviable reputation as a physician and surgeon, and at the present time has a large and lucrative practice in Washington and Nelson Counties. He was married June 21, 1864, to Miss Sallie Norris, daughter of Ignatius and Drusilla (Elliott) Norris, of Washington County. The children born to this marriage are ten in number, namely:

Mary (deceased), George, Ella, James, Norris (deceased), Daisy, Katie, John, Paul and Cleveland. The Doctor and Mrs. Shaunty are both active members of the Christian Church, and belong to the Botland congregation.

WILLIAM HENRY SHEARS was born November 15, 1830, at Lexington, Ky.; in 1859 he located on the Lexington Turnpike, near Danville, Boyle County, where he has since resided. His father, William Shears, Sr., was born at Fredericksburg, Va., in 1798; removed with his uncle, William McFarlan, to Fayette County, Ky., when six years of age, and died in 1880. He was the son of Robert Shears. William, Sr., married Miss Barbara, daughter of George Shindlebower, of Lexington (died in 1872, at the age of seventy-two years), and from their union sprang Robert, Georgia A. (Gibbons), Margaret (Umbersaugh), William Henry, Barbara (Cure), Thomas J., Samuel S. (deceased) and Andrew J. August 1, 1850, William Henry Shears was united in marriage with Miss Edward A., daughter of Edward W. and Elizabeth (Bomb) Harris, of Fayette County, Ky. (born October 14, 1829), and to them have been born Mary J. (Myers), William F., Nannie (Hays), Elizabeth, Georgia (Linney), Robert, Virgil and Claude (deceased). In youth Mr. Shears learned the cabinetmaker's trade, which he followed until 1860. He is now a farmer and stock raiser, owning 100 acres of productive land. For the past twenty-five years he has, in addition to his farming, been engaged in butchering, and in winter slaughtering and packing pork, at which he has been successful. He is a member of the K. of P., and an Ancient Odd Fellow. He was and is an uncompromising Union man, a member of the Methodist Episcopal Church, and a Republican.

FINLEY SHUCK, commonwealth's attorney for the judicial district embracing Marion, Washington, Nelson, Taylor, La Rue and Mercer Counties, was born on the 10th of December, 1842. His father, John Shuck, who was one of the finest orators as well as ablest lawyers of central Kentucky, was born in Marion County in 1807. He was deprived of the advantages of collegiate education, his privileges in that respect covering a period of six months' attendance in a common school. Being possessed, however, of great native energy, by personal application he acquired a good knowledge of books, and became thoroughly versed in the current literature of the day. When eighteen years old he began the study of the law, and two years later was regularly admitted to the bar, after which he practiced successfully for a third of a century. In 1862, ten years prior to his death, he received a paralytic stroke, which compelled his retirement from the busy practice of his former life. He was married in Franklin, Ky., to Lucretia C. Finley, daughter of J. C. Finley. She was born in 1811 and is now living. Their children are Joseph, Octavia (Harrison), Susan (deceased wife of J. R. Thomas), Mollie (deceased), Fannie (Corley), Finley and Minnie M. McAfee. Finley Shuck, a native of Marion County, was admitted to the practice of law in 1863. In 1882 he was appointed to the position of attorney for the commonwealth, to fill the unexpired term of Hon. Thomas Robinson; he was elected to the same office in 1883, and re-elected in August, 1886. He was married, in 1879, to Miss Hattie H. Heffernan, of Louisville, Ky., and has two children, viz.: Marie and David Finley Shuck. The paternal grandparents of Finley Shuck were John and Mary Shuck, who came from Pennsylvania to Kentucky in 1799, the grandfather having served as a soldier in the Revolutionary war.

MARTIN SIMPSON, tenth child of a family of fourteen children born to James and Eliza (Edelin) Simpson, was born October 15, 1822. Benedict Simpson, his paternal grandfather, was born and always lived in the State of Maryland. He was twice married and raised a large family of children. James Simpson, father of our subject, was born, reared and married in Maryland. About the year 1812 he and family, for he had then six children, immigrated to Kentucky and settled in Washington County, where he lived until his death, which occurred in his ninety-second year. For several years after locating in Kentucky he followed house carpentering, but later commenced farming, in which he was engaged when he died. Martin Simpson, who was born in Washington County, after remaining at home with his parents until he reached his majority, secured employment at St. Catherine's Convent, where he remained five years. December 20, 1847, he was united in marriage with Theresa Carrico, by whom he is the father of two children: Eliza (who has taken the veil) and Sarah. Mr. Simpson was reared a farmer, and has always pursued that vocation with great success; he now owns 300 acres of improved land. He and family are members of the Catholic Church. In politics he has always been a Democrat.

GEORGE T. SIMPSON, M. D., a native of Adair County, and a son of J. C. and Alcie J. (Thomas) Simpson, was born November 11, 1852. J. Clark Simpson, also a native of Adair County and a farmer, was born October 10, 1832. His father and mother died when he was an infant, and he was reared and educated by a cousin, George Breeding, with whom he lived until he was twenty-one years of age. A little before twenty-one years of age he was united in marriage with Miss Alcie J. Thomas, a daughter of John and Ellen Thomas, Virginians, who immigrated to Warren County, Ky., where they lived near Smith's Grove, and are there buried. John Thomas was born in 1801, and died in March, 1884. J. Clark Simpson rented a year or two and then bought a small place of 140 acres, partly cleared. Here he lived until 1866, when he bought another place of 200 acres adjoining, and has since sold the 140 acres. Here he lives on the 200 acres, a fertile and highly improved tract, on which he has erected a two-story frame residence, good barns, stables, and general improvements. He is one of the successful farmers of Adair, and resides about half a mile from Breeding's. The names of his children are George T., John M., M. E., wife of James M. Patterson; Rachael E., wife of Dr. W. R. Grissom; James W.; Lucy, who is dead; Robert Y. and Minnie, who died in infancy. Clark Simpson and wife are both members of the Methodist Episcopal Church South. Robert Simpson, grandfather of Dr. Simpson, a Virginian, came to Adair County with his wife, and died suddenly in the prime of life in 1832, and was followed soon after by his wife, both of whom died of cholera. Their children are James, Milton, William, John, George W., Polly (Gibson), Ann (Blair), and J. C. who lives in Illinois, of whom James, Milton and John are dead. William Simpson was a soldier in the Federal service during the late civil war, as was also D. W. Thomas, a maternal uncle, who was a captain of a company. George T. Simpson in youth received a good English education in the common and district schools of the county. His early life until twenty-two years of age was spent at home on his father's farm, but in 1874 he began the study of medicine under Dr. Cartright. In 1875 he attended a course of lectures at the University of Louisville, and again in 1877 he attended a course, graduating in the spring of 1878. He then began the practice of his profession in the village of Breeding's, where he has since resided. Dr. Simpson married, December 17, 1878, Miss Nannie D. Breeding, a daughter of Richard P. and M. T. (Williams) Breeding, the former of Adair, the latter of Cumberland County. The home of Mr. and Mrs. Simpson has been gladdened by three children: Lida, Holland B. and an infant not named. Mrs. Simpson is a member of the Methodist Episcopal Church. Dr. Simpson has been a life-long Democrat. He owns a residence in the town of Breeding's, and a farm near of seventy acres, and besides his practice of medicine is engaged in stock raising.

THOMAS Y. SIMPSON, a prominent farmer of Nelson County, was born in Prince William County, Va., October 22, 1827, being the third in a family of seven children born to John W. and Catherine (King) Simpson. Francis Simpson, paternal grandfather of Thomas Y., was a native of Virginia. He served in the war of 1812 and remained a resident of his native State until 1838 when he came to Kentucky, his son, John W., having preceded him in 1834. By occupation he was a farmer and was moderately successful. He died a resident of the county of his adoption (Jefferson) about 1858. Subject's maternal grandfather, Basil King, was a native of Maryland, but in early manhood removed to Virginia, of which State he always remained a resident. John W. Simpson was born in 1801; his marriage to Miss Catherine King was consummated January 29, 1824, in his native State; to their union seven children were born: John F., Robert S. (deceased), Thomas Y., George R. (deceased), Howard R., William F. (deceased) and Sarah C. On removing to Kentucky John W. Simpson settled in Jefferson County, where he has since remained. In early life he obtained a good education and was engaged in teaching for about eighteen years, but since coming to Kentucky he has made farming his chief occupation. In 1873 he retired from active farm life and removed to Louisville, where he is now living at ease in his old age. He is a devout member of the Methodist Episcopal Church South, having been connected with that organization for over fifty-four years. From his childhood up the principles of the Democratic party were taught him and he has always cast his influence and suffrage in its favor. Thomas Y. Simpson received a good education, and, in 1854, he was united in marriage with Miss Mary Carrithers, by whom he is the father of three living children: Francis C., who married Eleanor Wickliffe; Anna W., and Elizabeth R. Mr. Simpson continued a resident of Jefferson County until 1868, when he purchased a farm in Nelson County, to which he removed and where he has since lived. He has been very successful and owns a fine,

well improved farm of 212 acres, located on Bardstown and Bloomfield pike. In politics he is an ardent Democrat. He belongs to the Masonic fraternity.

JOHN KEMPER SLAUGHTER was born October 19, 1823, in Garrard County, and in 1830 was taken by his parents to Mercer County, where he grew to manhood; and in 1852 he located four miles north of Harrodsburg, where he has since resided. His father, Edmund Slaughter, was born in 1788 in Culpeper County, Va., removed in childhood with his parents to Mercer County, Ky., where he was reared; was a soldier in the Northern Army in the war of 1812; contracted rheumatism in the service from which he never fully recovered; was a farmer and slave owner, a Whig and a Baptist, and died in 1859. He was the son of Robert Slaughter, a native of Virginia, a soldier in the Revolutionary war, a farmer and slave owner, who died about 1828. He married Lucy, a sister to Gov. Gabriel Slaughter, and their offspring were Charles, Edmund, Nancy (McCown and Samuel), Mildred (Curd), Susan (Munday) and Frances (Curd). Edmund Slaughter married Mildred, daughter of William and Elizabeth (Withers) Kemper, of Garrard County (born in 1798, died about 1870), and from their union sprang Elizabeth W. (Smith), John J.., Lucy (Ballard) and Frances W. (Smit'). John K. Slaughter was married, October 26, 1852, to Miss Judith A., daughter of Ephraim and Caroline (Trabue) Maxey, of Mercer County (born August 23, 1830), and to them were born John Maxey (deceased), Edmund (deceased) and Carrie Lee. Mr. Slaughter is a farmer in Harrodsburg Precinct, having 200 acres of productive and well improved land. He is a member of the Baptist Church and was formerly an old line Whig, but now affiliates with the Democratic party.

JAMES A. SLAUGHTER was born September 11, 1835, in Logan County; in 1837 he removed with his parents to Jessamine County, in 1840 to Harrodsburg and in 1846 he located on the Lancaster pike, three miles east of Danville, Boyle County, where he has since resided. His father, Gabriel Slaughter, a native of Mercer County, born in 1809, was a farmer and slave owner and a Whig; was twenty years a deacon in the Baptist Church and was accidentally killed by a log rolling upon him in 1850. He was the son of Augustin Slaughter, a native of Culpeper County, Va., a soldier in the Revolutionary war, who came to Kentucky in an early day and died in 1846, aged seventy-eight years. His brothers in Kentucky were Gabriel, Robert, Stephen and James. His children were Stephen, Gabriel, Robert, Lucinda (Majors), Susan (Hawkins), Eliza (Nelson and Bradshaw) and Mary (Burros). Gabriel married Eliza, daughter of Col. A. S. and Hannah (Prall) Drake, of Lexington (born in 1812, died in 1867), and from their union sprang Mary (Gaines), James A., Simeon and Benjamin. James A. Slaughter has been twice married; first, July 19, 1861, to Miss Mary, daughter of M. T. and M. A. (Vinson) Cooper, of Bedford County, Tenn. (born in 1838, died in 1862), to whom there was no issue. He was next married, August 1, 1865, to Miss Ada P., daughter of John and Susan (Bohanan) Stout, of Woodford County (born in 1846), and to them have been born Florence T. and Lula D. Mr. Slaughter is a farmer and stock raiser and owns 250 acres of productive and well improved land. He is a member of the Baptist Church and a prohibitionist. He is also interested in a stock ranch of 165,000 acres of land in Texas, on which are 20,000 cattle.

G. M. SLAUGHTER was born in Mercer County, July 13, 1839, and is a most enterprising business man. He is a member of the firm of Adams & Slaughter, commission merchants of the town of Oregon, who do a large and lucrative business; they handle coal, salt and grain. Mr. Slaughter was married March 7, 1867, to Miss Lizzie Derr; they have the following children: Lena, Sarah M., Thomas E., DeWitt, Henry T. and G. M. Slaughter, Jr. Mr. and Mrs. Slaughter are both members of the Presbyterian Church. He is a member of the Democratic party.

D. G. SLAUGHTER is a representative of one of the old and prominent families of Kentucky and Virginia. They settled early in 1720 in that part of Orange County, Va., which was afterward formed into Culpeper County, and were originally from Wales. Many members of the family drifted to Kentucky in the early days of the commonwealth, and filled prominent positions of honor and trust. Gabriel Slaughter was lieutenant-governor and governor of the State. The subject of this sketch is, on his mother's side a great-great-grandson of Hon. James Garrard, the second and third governor of Kentucky (served two terms) and for whom Garrard County was named. Few families have produced more distinguished members than the Slaughter family. D. G. Slaughter (the subject) was born in Owsley County, this State, July 10, 1850, is a son of James L. and Lucinda (Price) Slaughter, and is one of two children living,

the other Katy M. (McKinney), (or "Katy Did," the poetess). When quite young his father removed to London, Ky., where he lived until subject was thirteen years old, when he settled in Paint Lick, Garrard County. The subject has been in the mercantile business all his life, and may be regarded as a successful business man. He has a large store at Paint Lick and another at Muddy Creek; both of which he manages very successfully. He married Miss Mary E. Stephens, a daughter of T. J. Stephens of Madison County. They have five children, viz.: James T., Charles G., Katy M., Capitola and Daniel G. Mr. and Mrs. Slaughter belong to the Reformed Church. He is a Democrat in politics. Mr. Slaughter is the proprietor of the Dripping Springs, a famous summer resort, situated two and one-half miles from Crab Orchard, Ky. The springs furnish waters of the strongest medicinal properties, rendering them not only a pleasure but a health resort, and are annually visited by a great many of the best families of Kentucky and the South.

GREEN CLAY SMITH. Gen. Smith was born on the 2d of July, 1832. He is a native Kentuckian, his birthplace being Richmond. He is a son of John Speed Smith and Eliza Lewis (Clay) Smith, the eldest daughter of Gen. Green Clay. They came from Virginia and the Carolinas, and were among the early settlers of Kentucky; the father was a prominent lawyer and politician, and was a member of Congress from Kentucky. Green Clay Smith married Lena Duke, daughter of James K. Duke, who was a nephew of Chief Justice Marshall, United States Supreme Court. To them have been born five children: Keith Duke, Mary Buford, Lena D., Green Clay, and Eliza (now Mrs. James B. Hawkins). The career of Rev. Green Clay Smith has been somewhat remarkable. He was educated at Danville, and Transylvania University, completing his studies at the latter place after his return from the Mexican war. He afterward studied law at the same university, and after graduation practiced at home for a year or two. He then went to Covington, where he soon won an important place at the bar; was sent to the Legislature from Kenton County, and at the expiration of his term, volunteered as a private in the war, in Col. Bush Foley's Home regiment for three months' service; was afterward appointed major, colonel, then brigadier, and then brevet major-general. He was elected to Congress while in the field, and took his seat in 1863, was reelected, and President Johnson next appointed him governor of Montana; he resigned in 1869 to enter the ministry, and is now pastor of the Louisville Baptist Church, Twenty-second and Walnut Streets, which he took charge of three years ago, and which has grown rapidly since. The General is one of the leading Prohibitionists, having been their candidate for President, nominated in 1876 at the National Convention. He was chiefly instrumental in gaining a foothold for the third party. He is one of the hardest of workers in the church and the temperance cause, besides being a most successful evangelist.

JOHN E. SMITH was born October 4, 1837, and is the eldest child of H. F. and Catherine (Brown) Smith, parents of seven sons and three daughters. H. F. Smith was born in Garrard County, in 1803, and his wife in Madison County in 1818; the latter died in 1872. Edwin Smith, grandfather of John E., was born in Arlington, Va., in 1789, and was but six months old when brought to Kentucky by his parents, who settled near Bryantsville; he married Jane Ann Finley, daughter of John Finley, a companion of Daniel Boone. Henry Smith, a brother of Edwin, was governor of Texas during the Mexican war. Mrs. Catherine (Brown) Smith, was a daughter of John and Hannah (Rochester) Brown, natives of Virginia and Boyle County, Ky., respectively. John Brown was one of the early pioneers of Madison County, but went to Arkansas about 1832, and bought a cotton plantation near Little Rock. John E. Smith was reared on a farm in his native county of Garrard. At the age of eighteen he taught a term of school, and then traded in horses and mules until the war, when he enlisted in Company C, Second Kentucky Cavalry, in Gen. John H. Morgan's command; was afterward transferred to Buford's command, and then again restored to Morgan. He was in the battles of Murfreesboro and Milton (Tenn), and in the latter was wounded; he also took part in numerous other fights and skirmishes; was a prisoner at Camps Chase and Douglas; subsequently joined his command, and was at Greensboro, N. C., when the general surrender took place. After his return he engaged for two years in cotton planting in Mississippi. In 1868 he came to Danville, Ky., and was for two years in mercantile trade; in 1869, November 13, he married Josephine, daughter of Capt. John and Mary (Elliott) Neet, and to this union were born four children: Katie May, Harold, Josie and Anna Laura (the last deceased). In 1870 he

went to Bonham, Fannin Co., Tex., conducted mercantile business four years, then returned to Garrard County, Ky., and purchased his father's farm. In 1882 he moved to Danville, where he now has an interest in the Danville Rolling Mills. He is a Free Mason and an Odd Fellow, and with his wife a member of the Presbyterian Church.

ASAHEL WILKES SMITH, M. D., D. D. S., was born September 12, 1844, in Champaign County, Ohio, and is the second son of James and Mary (Lang) Smith. James Smith was born in 1817, in New York City, and when a child removed with his parents to Kentucky, where later he became a merchant. After his marriage he moved to New Albany, Ind., thence to Champaign County, Ohio. After the war he emigrated to Trenton, Ind., where he was engaged in the mercantile business until his death in 1882. The epitaph upon his tombstone that marks his grave tells the history of his life: "A kind father, a Christian gentleman." He was the son of John Smith, a native of Yorkshire, England, who came to the United States as early as 1790; settled in New York City and served in the war of 1812. He married Martha Britton, of New Jersey, and about 1818 moved to Kentucky where he was engaged as a merchant. He died at the advanced age of ninety years. Mary (Lang) Smith was born in 1819 in Martinsburg, Va., and was the daughter of Thomas and Sarah (Elliott) Lang, to whom one son and four daughters were born. Mr. Lang was an officer in the the war of 1812, and was a substantial planter. Sarah (Elliott) Lang was the daughter of Robert Elliott, who distinguished himself in the war of independence. Mrs. Mary Smith lost her parents in Virginia and immigrated to Kentucky with an uncle who was appointed her guardian. She is still living. The Smiths were Baptist in religion, and Whigs in politics; the Langs Presbyterians and Democrats. Dr. Asahel Wilkes Smith was thrown upon his own resources early in life, owing to the financial reverses occurring to his father at that time. He received his early education at a district school in his native county, but it was to his father, who was a scholarly gentleman and applied himself with earnestness and devotion to instructing his son in the higher branches, especially as to a knowledge of the English language and of history, that he is indebted for the substantial foundation for all his success in life. At the age of nineteen he began the study of medicine and dentistry in Ohio, and after becoming of age studied the languages and sciences. He began the practice of dentistry in 1870 and in 1872 graduated from the Pennsylvania College of Dental Surgery; in 1884 graduated from the Hospital College of Medicine in Louisville. He located in Richmond, Ky., in May, 1871, where he has since been successfully engaged in practice. He is a member of the Masonic fraternity and is a Past Commander of Richmond Commandery, No. 19, K. T. Dr. Smith fills the chair as professor of physiology in Central University, and is dean of the Louisville College of Dentistry. He is a member of the Kentucky State Medical Society, the American Dental Association and of the Kentucky State Dental Association, of which he has served as president. He is editor of the dental department of *Progress*, a medical journal, published at Louisville, Ky. November 8, 1881, Dr. Smith was united in marriage to Bertha Cecil O'Donnell Miller, of Louisville, a native of Virginia. She is the daughter of James and Mary (Poe) Miller, also natives of Virginia. Mr. Miller is a scientist, of English descent, and an Episcopalian in religion. The Doctor and wife have one bright boy to bless their home, Elliott Poe. They are members of the Presbyterian and Episcopal Churches respectively.

WILLIAM J. SMITH was born June 27, 1844, and is the first of five sons and one daughter born to James R. and Elizabeth (O'Bryan) Smith. James R. Smith was born July 16, 1820, in Marion County. He was an active and substantial farmer and slaveholder, and is still living. His father, Joseph Smith, married Sarah Peterson. Mrs. Elizabeth Smith was born September 20, 1822, in Marion County, and is a daughter of William and Elizabeth (Knicheloc) O'Bryan, who were born, respectively, in Maryland and Nelson County, Ky. William O'Bryan was an early settler of Marion County, and a leading and representative farmer and slave owner. William J. Smith, who was born in West Marion County, received his early training on a farm. November 9, 1861, he enlisted in Company G, Tenth Kentucky Federal Infantry, and participated in all the battles in which the regiment was engaged from Chickamauga and Missionary Ridge to Jonesboro, N. C. He was a brave and true soldier, always ready for duty when called; was wounded at Missionary Ridge and was discharged in December, 1864, at Louisville. After his return home he attended St. Mary's College, and also spent one year on the farm. In May, 1867, he entered the store of T. J. Smith as salesman, served three years, after which he became a partner. In

1876 he took entire control, while he has met with success ever since. He is the owner of two fine store rooms at Loretto, also a good farm of seventy-six acres, with a fine residence at the station; also another farm of 200 acres, immediately west of the station, which is mostly under cultivation; also runs a blacksmith shop; is a breeder of thoroughbred race horses (Hairpin, among them, sired by Kingpin), fine saddle horses, also is owner of a fine Blackhawk Jack. Mr. Smith was married August 30, 1870, to Nancy Ballard, a daughter of George L. and Letitia (Cessell) Ballard, natives of Nelson County. Mr. and Mrs. Smith are parents of the following children: James A., Willie J., Anna Bell, George P. (deceased) Mary Clara, Phillip R., Mary Jennie, Mary Terresa. Mr. Smith, formerly a Democrat, cast his first presidential vote for George B. MacClellan; after he became a Republican, his first vote was for James G. Blaine. He has served two terms as police judge, and is now a justice of the peace. With his wife he is a member of the Roman Catholic Church.

A. W. SMITH was born March 12, 1851, where he now lives, two miles southeast of Danville. He is the fifth of five sons born to Wesley D. and Permelia (Kenley) Smith, who were born respectively in Culpeper County, Va., and Lincoln County, Ky. Wesley D. Smith was brought to Oldham County, Ky., when a child, by his parents; he grew to be a leading farmer and slave owner; he was a stanch Whig till 1860 when he became a Democrat. He died November 24, 1882, aged seventy years. He was a son of Isaac Smith, who married Rebecca Downing, both of Virginia; migrated to Oldham County about 1813, where he remained till his death in 1848, aged about eighty-one; was in turn a son of Isaac Smith, who was born in Scotland. On his passage the vessel on which he sailed was disabled and sank. He secured some gold and jumped overboard and was finally saved by being picked up by a lifeboat. He settled in Virginia after landing in America. He participated as a common soldier in the war for independence. Permelia (Kenley) Smith was a daughter of Freding Kenley, who was one of the pioneers of Lincoln County, and was a soldier in 1812. A. W. Smith received his early training on the farm and received a good English education. He was married February 13, 1877, to Fannie L. Hopkins, of Christian County, Ky., a daughter of Robert G. and Ruth B. (Booton) Hopkins, natives of Cumberland and Christian Counties, respectively. He was a son of Joseph H. Hopkins, who married Martha Garnett, came from Virginia, and was of Scotch, Irish and French descent. A. W. and wife have two children to bless their union: Permelia H. and Ruth G. Mr. and Mrs. Smith are both members of the Christian Church. After their marriage they lived in Lincoln County six years. In January, 1883, he located where he now resides, on 430 acres, which is his father's first farm in Boyle County. He is a dealer and trader in cattle and fine trotting stock. In politics he is a Democrat; was a member of Grange.

BENJAMIN FRANKLIN SOPER was born January 1, 1838, in Jessamine County, Ky., where he lived until October 1, 1882, when he removed to Boyle County. His father, James Soper, a native of Maryland, born in 1792, was a farmer and mechanic, and died in 1861. He was the son of John Soper, of Maryland, who came to Kentucky about 1799. James married Elizabeth, daughter of Elijah Bibb of Jessamine County (born October 15, 1808, died August 11, 1870), and to them were born Nancy A. (Allin), William B., James R., subject, David M., John E., Oremandel T. and Amos B. On the 15th of October, 1877, Benjamin F. Soper was married to Miss Louisa W., daughter of John and Paulina (Cravens) Dickerson, of Jessamine County (born March 7, 1843), and this union has been favored by the birth of Lewis Edgar, Nora Lee, Charlie Elbert, Frank Walden and Lorris. Enjoying but limited educational advantages himself, Mr. Soper is taking a decided interest in the education of his children. For sixteen years he was engaged with some success as a manufacturer and dealer in lumber. He is now engaged in farming, owning 210 acres of productive land, which, under his careful management, is in a fine state of cultivation. In religion he is a member of the Christian Church, and in politics a Democrat.

MATHEW SPARKS, a native of Adair County, and one of its leading farmers and millers, was born January 25, 1831. His father, William Sparks, a native of South Carolina, came to Kentucky in his boyhood, in the latter part of the eighteenth century. He lived in Adair, and followed farming all his life. He was united in matrimony with Miss Elizabeth Crawhorn, a daughter of Thomas Crawhorn, a Kentucky farmer. This marriage was blessed by eleven children, of whom Mathew Sparks is the second. The names of the children are Thomas, Mathew, James Riley, Biddy Ann (wife of Franklin McKinney), Polly Ann (wife of Thomas Walker), William, Nancy Jane (wife of James Johnson), Elizabeth (wife of Frank Saters), Sally Ann (Saters), Patsy Jane (wife of John Helstead) and Susan (wife of Jno. Mitchell), of whom six are now living. William Sparks died January 25, 1878, a consistent Christian, and a member of the Cumberland Presbyterian Church. His wife died about the age of sixty, a member of no church, but a professor of religion. Mathew Sparks, grandfather of subject, was a native of Virginia, and a farmer there; emigrated to South Carolina, and thence to Adair County, Ky., and afterward to Iowa, where he died and is buried. He reared about thirteen children. His father, William Sparks, was also a Virginian, and a farmer. Thomas Crawhorn, maternal grandfather of Mr. Sparks, was one of that noble band who gained American independence. The Sparks family are of Irish and English origin. Mathew Sparks remained at home until eighteen years of age, working with and for his father, at which time he was united in matrimony to Mrs. Polly Ann (England) McNeely, a widow with three children, whose names were James M. (killed in Federal service), Betsy Jane (wife of James Jones) and Martha Ann (wife of John England). To Mr. and Mrs. Sparks was born one child, who died in infancy. Mrs. Sparks, a member of the Church of United Brethren, was called from the scene of her earthly labors in 1867, in the thirty-fifth year of her age. Her first husband, John McNeely, lived only a few years after marriage. The second marriage of Mr. Sparks occurred in March, 1868, with Miss Juliet Akin, a daughter of Joseph K. and Nancy B. (Fowler) Akin, both natives of Kentucky. To this marriage have been born five children: George Ann, Mary Ellen, Moses S., Josiah William and Victoria, all of whom are living. Mr. Sparks in 1849 bought the farm his wife had contracted for before marriage, where he lived until 1860, when he moved to Indiana. In the fall of 1862 he enlisted in Company B, Forty-ninth Indiana Infantry, Federal service, and served eighteen months, but in 1864, on account of sickness and disability, was dismissed from the service, receiving an honorable discharge, and now draws a pension. He returned home and in 1865 embarked in the milling business, owned a share in a $4,000 mill, which was bought on credit, and which was destroyed by fire just as it was beginning to be operated. He and partners then erected another mill, in which Mr. Sparks sold out his interest. He owns a fine farm of 215 acres, well improved, with good residence and out-buildings, and four other farms of 390 acres, besides a saw and grist-mill. His estate, worth $10,000, is the result of his own industry and economy, as he began without a dollar. He has traded extensively in cattle, and raises cattle to a considerable extent now, and has had eight years' experience in merchandising. Mr. and Mrs. Sparks and two of their daughters are members of the Cumberland Presbyterian Church, and in politics he is a Democrat.

MRS. MARY J. (LANCASTER) SPALDING is a native Kentuckian, born on the 25th of May, 1816. She is a direct descendant of the Lancaster family of England, and her ancestors came to America about fifteen years after the Maryland colony was planted by Lord Baltimore. At that time came John Lancaster, the great-grandfather of John L., the father of Mary J. He and two bachelor brothers settled with the Catholic colony in Charles County, Md. John married Fannie Jarnaghan, an Irish lady from near Cork. It is said that her beauty surpassed that of any other lady in the colonies at that time. To her and her husband were born five daughters and one son, all of whom lived to be married; one of the daughters was the grandmother of Chief Justice R. B. Taney; among them was a son named John, who married a Maryland lady. He left two sons and six daughters. The sons were John and Raphael; Raphael immigrated to Kentucky, married Eleanor Bradford, and with her came to Kentucky in 1785. John, the eldest son of Raphael, was born in 1766, and at the age of eighteen also came to Kentucky; his parents, Raphael and Eleanor, came one year later. John married Catherine Miles in 1789; she was a native of St. Mary's County, Md. John Lancaster was one of the prominent men of his day; he was highly educated, and a man of true moral worth and sterling integrity, and was a member of the Kentucky Legislature from the year 1800 to 1808. He accumulated a large property, and was considered one of the wealthiest citizens of Washington County. He reared a family of eight sons and four daughters. Ten of the number were living at the time of his death, which occurred in 1838. Our subject, Mary J., and Judge W. D. Lancaster, of Elizabethtown, Ky., are now the only survivors. The Lancaster family have always held the Catholic faith, and left old England by reason of the persecutions they sustained from the established church. Mary J. Lancaster, a native of Washington County, now Marion, was married in 1839, to Richard M. Spalding. They reared a family of five sons and four daughters, namely: John L., bishop of the see of Peoria; Richard C., who died at the age of twenty; Catherine, the widow of Ra-

phael Spalding; Dr. Leonard Spalding of Peoria, Ill.; Henrietta, a member of the convent of the Sacred Heart; Mary Ellen (Slevin) of Peoria, Ill.; Rev. B. J. Spalding of Peoria, Ill.; Anna E. (Putnam), and Martin John, who died at seven and one-half years of age. The archbishop of Baltimore, Most Rev. Martin John Spalding (died in 1872) was a younger brother of Richard M. Spalding.

MARY ZERELDA SPALDING was born October 19, 1828. She is a daughter of Francis Roberts and Eleanor (Hayden) Roberts, both of whom were natives of Kentucky. They were the parents of four daughters and two sons, viz.: George B., of Lincoln County, Mo.; Francis J., of Marion County, Ky.; Margaret (Shockley) and Elizabeth (Shockley), both of Lincoln County, Mo.; Eliza E. (Rapier), of Daviess County, Ky., and Mary Z. (Spalding), native and resident of Marion County. Francis Roberts was a cabinet workman, and a farmer; he died in 1880. His father, William Roberts, was a native of Delaware, came early to Kentucky and located in Scott County, but died in Marion County in 1830. His wife, Eleanor, was a daughter of Basil Hayden, who died of cholera in 1833. His ancestors were of English descent and natives of the Virginia colony. Mary Z. Roberts was united in marriage on the 21st of September, 1852, to Mr. John Spalding, a son of Thomas Spalding, of Marion County. To this marriage were born four sons—Francis B., Benedict A., John L., and George L.—and four daughters: Martha P., who married James Jans, of Washington County, Ky.; Catherine E., of Milwood, Mo., married D. H. Mudd; Ann M., and Mary J. John Spalding was born January 15, 1804. He was born a farmer, and in his vocation was very successful. He accumulated a fine property, including about 1,000 acres of valuable land, and a number of slaves, and died May 10, 1874. He was a member of the Catholic Church, was prominent as a patron of public enterprises, and noted for his sterling worth and business integrity.

JOHN SPAULDING was born September 13, 1840. His father, Henry P. Spaulding, was born in Washington County, January 13, 1802. He was one of the successful farmers of his day, and left an extensive landed estate to his children. He died in 1866. His wife was a Miss Lucy Turnham, a daughter of George Turnham, of Spencer County, Ky.; they were married in 1826, and were the parents of eleven children, viz.: George P., Nancy, Frances, Henry L., Caroline,

John, Benjamin F., Dr. James M. (deceased in 1864), Dr. W. E., Logan T., and Martin V. The mother was born in 1811, and is yet living aged seventy-five years. Capt. George Turnham was a soldier in the war of 1812 and engaged in the battle of New Orleans; he died at his home in Spencer County in 1826. Henry Spaulding, the grandfather of our subject, was a native of Nelson County, Ky.; his ancestors came from Ireland and settled in Virginia prior to the war of the Revolution. John Spaulding was born in Washington County, reared on a farm, and educated in the common schools, and finished his school days in 1864, under Dr. J. W. Wright. From that time until the present he has been engaged in farming and stockraising, in which he has been uniformly successful, and is the proprietor of 360 acres of farming lands lying in Marion and Washington Counties. He married, in 1873, Miss Mattie B. Bricken. To them were born three children: Marcus, James R., and Lucy A. Mrs. Mattie B. (Bricken) Spaulding was born April 1, 1852; she is a daughter of Alexander and Ann (Graham) Bricken, the former of German, and the latter of Irish descent, and both natives of Kentucky. Mr. Spaulding is a member of the Baptist Church, while Mrs. Spaulding holds the Presbyterian faith. Politically Mr. Spaulding is a Democrat.

GEORGE HARVEY SPEARS was born November 26, 1832, in Fayette County, Ky. In 1840 he removed with his parents to Jessamine County, and in 1850 to Boyle County; in 1852 he somewhat extensively engaged in a tannery in Marion County, in which he was successful until 1869, and in 1872 he returned to Boyle County, where he has since resided. His father, George C. Spears, was born May 16, 1797, in Fayette County, and died in Boyle County in 1864. He owned thirty slaves. He was the son of John Spears, who was a native of Rockingham County, Va., born in April, 1771, and who assisted his brother, George, as teamster in the Revolutionary war, and entered the service a short time before, and was present at the surrender of Cornwallis. John S. removed to Kentucky about 1795, engaged in Indian fights, was with Neely when killed, and was himself grazed by an Indian bullet. For many years he was an elder in the Christian Church, and died January 14, 1866. He married Margaret Chrismun, and their offspring were Hannah (Baker), George C., Charles C., Rebecca (Bonaugh), Chrismun, Lee W., John F., Margaret (Jackson) and Eliza. George C. Spears married in 1821 Miss Ann Spears, of Lincoln County (born May 28, 1800, died August 14, 1879), and the result of this union was the birth of William H., Charles C., Hugh C., George Harvey, John L. and Sidney C. George H. Spears was married May 10, 1859, to Miss Mary L., daughter of Walker Baker, of Washington County (born July 7, 1840), but from their union there has been no issue. Mr. Spears is a farmer and stock breeder, and has 160 acres of land in a good state of cultivation, on the dividing ridge between Kentucky and Salt Rivers, where his brick residence was erected in 1801. Bones of a mastodon were found in a sink on this place. The farm was entered in 1781, by John Bragsdale, and the patent now in the hands of Mr. Spears was issued by Gov. Benj. Harrison, of Virginia. Mr. Spears handles a few high grade cattle, raises high bred trotting horses, and pure Berkshire hogs. He has a granddaughter of the famous horse, Lexington. He lost six slaves by the late war. In politics Mr. Spears is a Democrat.

JAMES P. SPOONAMORE was born June 6, 1837. He is the son of John Spoonamore, a native of Lincoln County, and born in 1806. He married Elizabeth, daughter of John Miller, of Boyle County, and from their union sprang James P., John M., David C., William (deceased), Samuel M., Adam (deceased), Mary A. (Smith), Christina (deceased), Emily (Hubble), Paulina A. (Hickle), Henry M. and Andrew L. James P. Spoonamore was born and reared in Lincoln County and October 15, 1863, married Miss Sallie, daughter of Elder James E. Crow, of Garrard County (born September 11, 1842), and to them have been born John D. (deceased), Hollice, Elizabeth E., Eliza A., Margaret D., Mary C., Louanna and James A. Mr. Spoonamore is a farmer by occupation, having sixty-seven acres of productive land and in a good state of cultivation. He is a member of the Methodist Episcopal Church South, and was Southern in his sentiments during the late civil war. (See sketch of Rev. James E. Crow.)

DR. ANDREW TRIBBLE STEPHENSON was born February 23, 1821. His father, Joseph H. Stephenson, born in Orange County, Va., November 6, 1771, was a contractor, came to Madison County, Ky., prior to the year 1800, and purchased five small farms. He was married December 23, 1806, to Miss Mary Tribble, a daughter of Rev. Andrew Tribble, one of the pioneer Baptist ministers of Kentucky. To their marriage were born twelve children, ten of whom lived to be grown, Paulina, Albert G., John C. (a veteran of the Mexican war), Sarah J. (wife of Thompson Arnold), Frances (wife of Thomas Bogie), Dr. Andrew T., Mary Ann (wife of J. K. Wilson), Martha M. (wife of Charles Cosby), Peter T. and Dr. Joe Thomas, all of whom are now dead, except Andrew T. and Mary Ann. Joseph Stephenson served in three campaigns against the Indians of Indiana, but always had an aversion to political life. He owned 600 acres of land in Madison County, and a number of slaves, and departed this life in 1837. Mrs. Stephenson, who during the early part of her life was a member of the Baptist Church, and later of the Christian Church, departed this life in 1872, in the eighty-fourth year of her age. Thomas Stephenson, grandfather of Dr. Stephenson, was of English descent; he married a Miss Hawkins and acquired considerable property, consisting of land and slaves. He enlisted in the southern division of the Continental Army in the Revolutionary war, and when his term of enlistment expired, returned home, when the day afterward Col. Tarleton, during his raid in Virginia, stopped to forage on him. The Colonel soon recognized in him an American soldier, when he gave the order "put that man under guard," whereupon Thomas Stephenson was put in chains. In his old age Thomas Stephenson was removed to Madison County by his son Joseph, and is buried there. He was the father of a very large family, among whom were James, Joseph, John, Nathan, Nicholas, Thomas, Catherine (Patton, Slaven), Betsy and Nancy (Long). Joseph H. Stephenson was a third cousin to Hon. Andrew Stephenson, the Speaker of Congress, and father of Hon. John W. Stephenson, governor of Kentucky. Owing to a schoolmaster's teaching he changed the spelling of his name from "v" in Stephenson to "ph." Dr. Stephenson was educated in the common schools of his native county of Madison, and began the study of medicine in 1845. In 1846–47 he attended his first course of lectures at Transylvania University at Lexington, Ky., graduating at the Medical School of Ohio in Cincinnati in 1848, attending in 1852 the hospitals and schools in Philadelphia and New York. He formed in 1847 a partnership with Dr. Pearce in Lancaster, Ky., which they continued two years, doing a large practice; then removed to Madison County; there he continued the practice until 1860, when he retired. On April 22, 1852, he was married to Miss Elizabeth Ann Smith, daughter of Benjamin and Judith (Smith) Smith

of Madison County. Dr. and Mrs. Stephenson are the parents of five children: Mattie, Mary, William W., Julia (wife of Charles M. Kurts of New York City), and Elizabeth, all living. Dr. Stephenson, in 1860, removed to Washington County and bought 700 acres of land. By the war he lost twelve valuable slaves, and sold out in 1864 and removed to Mercer County, buying a farm of 452 acres. He has carried on agriculture and engaged part of the time in banking since, but at present is engaged only in the former. Dr. and Mrs. Stephenson and their children are members of the Christian Church; his son, W. W. Stephenson, is an attorney at the bar of Harrodsburg.

DR. E. T. STEPHENSON. In the early part of the present century Lindsey Stephenson and his wife, Annie (Vardimar) Stephenson, came from Virginia to Kentucky, and settled in Lincoln County. Their children were David M. (deceased), William T., Malinda, James A., Patsey A. (deceased), and Lindsey V. Stephenson. William T., the second of this family, is the father of Dr. E. T. Stephenson, and was born March 3, 1825. He established a tannery in Lincoln County, and in connection with this pursuit, engaged in agriculture. He married Miss Margaret McRoberts, and their children were John F., Charles M. (deceased), William L. (deceased), Alexander J., Ephraim T., Rebecca and Anna (both deceased), and George L. Stephenson. Dr. Ephraim T. was born in Lincoln County, Ky., where he grew to manhood. He early manifested a desire to pursue the study of medicine, which he did, performing the usual preparatory reading under Dr. William L. Stephenson and graduating from the university of the city of New York in 1882, since which time he has been in active and successful practice, located at Crab Orchard, Ky.

EDWARD L. STILES, born August 15, 1825, is a son of Henry and Ann (McAtee) Stiles. Henry Stiles was born in Maryland, came to Nelson County, Ky., with the earliest Catholic settlers, and was wounded in a fight with the Indians, in coming down the Ohio River. He was not a wealthy man at the start, but left an estate of 1,000 acres at his death in 1839, at the age of sixty-nine. His father, Philip Stiles, was a native of Maryland, of Scotch-Irish descent, and married a Miss O'Brian. Mrs. Ann Stiles was a daughter of George McAtee, who married a Miss Hamilton, of Maryland, and both came to Nelson County, Ky., at an early day. Edward L. Stiles was born where he still resides in Nelson County, was educated at St.

Joseph's College, Bardstown, and graduated in 1846. In May, 1848, he married Anna Bradford, daughter of David and Amanda (Davis) Bradford. David Bradford was an attorney, and for many years was superintendent of the mint at New Orleans. After his marriage, Mr. Stiles purchased a farm near Bardstown, but five years later removed to the old homestead. About 1857 he went to Louisiana and purchased an interest in a sugar plantation of 1,000 acres, and also owned about 100 negroes. At the close of the late war he sold his interest in the land, and returned to New Hope, Ky., and in the winter of 1867–68 built a distillery, starting with a capacity of 200 bushels, which had been increased in 1881 to 1,000 bushels. In 1871, however, he sold out to Tom Shirley. At present he owns 1,000 acres of farming land, and his residence is a fine brick, erected by his father over seventy years ago, but recently remodeled and enlarged. Mr. and Mrs. Stiles are members of the Church of Rome.

VAN BUREN STILES was born September 9, 1835, where he now resides, on Rolling Fork. He is the youngest of four sons and seven daughters born to Lewis and Rebecca (Willett) Stiles. Lewis Stiles was born near Morristown, N. J., in 1785; immigrated to Nelson County as early as 1809 and located on Rolling Fork. His parents came one year later. He served as magistrate and sheriff of Nelson County; was also extensively engaged in farming and was a large slaveholder; was a distiller and flatboated to New Orleans. He was drafted in 1812 and furnished a substitute. He died in November, 1858. He was a son of David Stiles, of New Jersey, of German origin. Mrs. Rebecca Stiles was born in Nelson County, and was a daughter of Griffin Willett, who came from Maryland and settled on Pottinger's Creek. Van Buren Stiles, when a lad of nine years, lost his mother. In 1866 he went to Louisville and engaged in the distilling business with George Beall. June 26, 1872, he married Anna C. Bland, of Louisville, a daughter of E. H. and Corrilla (Willett) Bland, and had born to their union six children: Bland (deceased), Joseph B., George F. (deceased), Lewis K., Elijah Van and Corrilla P. Mr. and Mrs. Stiles are members of the Baptist Church. After marriage Mr. Stiles engaged in mercantile business at Chaplin, Nelson Co., Ky., for four years, then located where he now resides, on 350 acres near New Hope, where he makes a specialty of stock. In politics he is a Democrat.

JONATHAN STILES was born December 3, 1844, where he now resides on Rolling Fork, and is a son of John and Rhoda (Edwards) Stiles, to whom thirteen children were born: James F., Eunice (now Miller), Thomas and Elizabeth (deceased), John C., Henry C., Electa (now Stark), Jacob, Joseph and David (all deceased), Demus, Jonathan and Sallie A. John Stiles was born in New Jersey in 1796; came to Nelson County with his parents in 1810, and settled in the extreme southern part of Nelson County, on Rolling Fork, where he grew to manhood, became the owner of 1,700 acres of land and a large family of slaves, and died in 1876. He was a son of David Stiles, who married Elizabeth Kitchel, natives of Vermont and New Jersey, respectively. David was a soldier in the war for independence, and died in 1839, at a ripe old age. He was a son of Jacob Stiles. Mrs. Rhoda Stiles was born in Culpeper County, Va., and was brought to Marion County, Ky., in childhood. Jonathan Stiles at the age of twenty-one commenced life on his own account. He is now the owner of 230 acres of the original homestead, 170 under cultivation. He is an active member of the Baptist Church, as were his parents before him. He cast his first presidential vote for Seymour. James Stiles, the eldest member of the family living, is spoken of as one of the best historians in all his part of the country. John C. Stiles, another brother, was married on the 31st of March, 1859, to Elizabeth Carter, daughter of Edward and Elizabeth (Shuck) Carter, natives of Marion County. Mr. and Mrs. Stiles have had born ten children, eight living: David, Edward, John, James, Bur, Charles, Chilion and Mary R.

JOHN B. STILES, an enterprising young farmer, was born September 2, 1856, and is a son of Ogden W. and Susan A. (Pile) Stiles, to whom three sons and one daughter were born. O. W. Stiles was born and reared in Nelson County and was a large farmer and slave owner. He died in 1878, aged fifty-five years, and had lived fifteen years of his life in Washington County, where John B. Stiles was born. He had married for his first wife Lizzie Phillips, a daughter of Samuel Phillips, and to this marriage two sons were born. O. W. Stiles was a son of Lewis Stiles. Susan A. Pile was born in Washington County, and is a daughter of Benjamin P. Pile, who had married his third wife. His first wife was a Miss Weathers, by whom two sons and five daughters were born, but there were no children by the two subsequent marriages. He was born in Washington County in 1800 and is still living. When Susan A. married O. W. Stiles she was the widow of a Mr. Beckham, by whom one daughter was born and reared. John B. Stiles was reared on a farm and received a common English education. At twenty-one he commenced life on his own account near Bloomfield, and was married August 31, 1882, to Sallie Beam, daughter of William and Rebecca (Milligan) Beam, of Nelson County. This union is blessed with one son, William Ogden. Mr. Stiles lived in Nelson County till 1884, when he located on Rolling Fork, three miles west of Raywick, Marion County, on 400 acres of fine land, 200 of which are in cultivation, and well improved with fine buildings. Mr. Stiles is a member of the Methodist Episcopal Church South and in politics is a Democrat. Mrs. Stiles belongs to the Presbyterian Church.

W. M. STINE was born in Boyle County, Ky., and when eight years old his parents removed to Washington County. There subject lived until he was forty-eight years old, when he removed to Mercer County. His father, Jacob Stine, was born in Virginia and was brought to Kentucky by his father—also named Jacob Stine—when but three years old. The family is of German origin. Mr. Stine, the subject of this sketch, has been twice married; first to Miss Sarah A. Curry, who has borne ten children, six of whom are living, as follows: Mary, Robert, Louisa, Catherine, Elizabeth and James H. His wife died and he afterward married Miss Catherine Williams; she has four children, viz.: Thomas B., Mark, Elma and Carl.

SMITH THOMAS STONE was born September 22, 1830, near Camp Dick Robinson, Garrard Co., Ky., where he grew to manhood and still resides. His father, Smith Stone, also a native of Garrard County, was born in 1788, near Dick's River. He furnished a substitute in the war of 1812; was an upright man, a farmer, a millwright, a Baptist and a Whig, a Union man, lost thirty slaves in the late war and died February 28, 1875. He was the son of Spencer Stone, a Virginian, a pioneer in Kentucky when the inhabitants had to seek safety in forts and stations from marauding bands of Indians. He was a Baptist and a Whig, a farmer and slave-holder, and died about 1838, aged over eighty years. He married a Miss Smith, and their offspring were John, Caleb, Elias, Silas, Smith, William, Nancy (Clemmons, Montgomery), Lucy (Gaines, Forman), Mary (Collier, Allen). Smith married Mary, daughter of Isaac and Esther Montgomery (born December 23, 1791, died April 14, 1874), and from their union sprang Matilda (Davis), Melinda (Hodges), Esther (Onstott),

Elizabeth (Barker), Ephraim M., Sally S. (Hudson), Mary (deceased), George W. (deceased), Robert S., Smith T. and Isaac (deceased). August 6, 1863, Smith T. Stone married Maggie K., daughter of Asa and Mary (Arthur) Runyon, of Knox County (born April 1, 1841), and to them have been born Mary J. (Warner), Silas S. (married Ethel Crutchfield, December 24, 1886), Lulu B. (Dailey), Minnie M., Thomas A. (deceased). Maggie B. and William B. are two grandchildren. Mr. Stone is a farmer and owns 200 acres of productive land. He is president of the Sugar Creek Turnpike Company, a member of the K. of H., a Democrat and a prohibitionist. His family are Baptists.

DAVIS H. STONE was born in Nelson County, December 31, 1847. His father, Isaac D. Stone, was also a native of the same county and was born in 1799; he married Sallie Lockart in 1846, and to their union was born one son, our subject. Sallie Lockart was a member of the Presbyterian Church, and died in that faith in 1848, at the age of twenty-four; she was the daughter of Eli and Amy (Lacy) Lockart, of Clarksville, Tenn. Four years after the death of his first wife Mr. Stone married Elizabeth Lewis, of Nelson County. Isaac D. Stone was a very successful farmer and accumulated a fine property, including 800 acres of rich farming land lying on the east fork of Simpson Creek, in Nelson County; he died in 1873; he was a son of Davis Stone, who was of English descent, a native of Virginia, and came to Kentucky with his mother, who was at that time one hundred and one years old; she died on the way and was buried on the farm now owned by Horace Stone, of Nelson County. Davis H. Stone was reared on the farm that he now owns, and which has been the residence of three generations of his ancestors; he received a good common-school education and at the age of twenty-five took charge of the home farm of 800 acres, which he now owns. The farming operations have proved uniformly successful and he makes a specialty of tobacco culture. He was married June 11, 1867, to Miss Annie Stone, and to them was born one son, Isaac D., April 11, 1870. Mrs. Annie Stone was born in November, 1846; she is a daughter of Thomas, better known as Sure Enough Tom Stone, of Spencer County. Davis H. Stone and his wife are members of the Methodist Episcopal Church. He is a R. A. Mason in Bloomfield Chapter, No. 53, and his political views are Democratic. Adjoining his farm is the site of Camp Charity, where Gen. John A. Morgan organized his force before starting South in 1861. Isaac D. Stone furnished uniforms for one company of Breckinridge's command, which company afterward took the name of the Stone Rifles.

SAMUEL HANSON STONE was born December 4, 1849, three miles northwest of Richmond, Ky., and is a son of Capt. J. C. and Matilda (Hanson) Stone, to whom three sons and one daughter were born, S. H. and J. C. only living. Capt. J. C. Stone was born in Richmond, December 17, 1822, and was an extensive farmer and banker. He raised Company H, of Colonel Humphrey Marshall's Regiment for Mexico, and was its captain. He was the first graduate of Bethany College, Virginia, and a graduate of the Philadelphia Law School, and was a member of the Richmond bar. In 1858 he removed with his family to Leavenworth, Kas., where he organized and became president of the Second National Bank of Leavenworth, and was one of the projectors of the Union Pacific Railway, now Kansas Pacific. In the dark days of 1860–61 he was a strong advocate for the Union, and was actively engaged in raising troops. He was commissioned general and commanded the Kansas militia, and assisted in raising the first eight regiments of Kansas troops. He also served in the Lower House of Kansas. He was a son of Samuel Stone, who was born at Culpeper C. H., Va., November 22, 1790, and with his parents came to Madison County, Ky., in 1798. He was one of the first merchants in Richmond, Ky., but afterward became a farmer and a large owner of slave property. He married Nancy Rodes, of Madison County, daughter of Judge Robert Rodes, who was one of the first settlers of Madison County. He was a captain in the struggle for independence, and was present at the surrender at Yorktown. He reared two sons, J. C. and Robert R.; the latter resides in Lexington, Ky. Samuel Stone died May 5, 1880, in Kansas, to which State he moved in 1862. He was a son of Josiah and Mary Stone, who were born in Virginia and immigrated to Kentucky in 1798. He was an active and prosperous farmer and reared twelve children. His sons were John, Samuel, William, James, Thomas, Caleb and Francis, all of whom lived in Madison County and reared families. Josiah Stone died at the age of ninety years. His children all lived to a ripe age. The Stones came originally from England; three brothers landed at Massachusetts, two of whom settled in the South. Mrs. Matilda Stone was born in Winchester, Ky., daughter of Samuel Hanson, who married a Miss Hickman, and reared a family of six sons and five daughters, only one of whom is now living. Samuel Hanson was an attorney at Winchester and served in the Legislature. He was born in Washington, D. C. Our subject's great-grandmother, the wife of Gen. Hickman, was one of the girls stolen by the Indians, at the time Daniel Boone's daughter was carried off, but all were recaptured next day. The Hansons spring from the Swedes that originally settled in England and subsequently came to America. Samuel H. Stone lived in Kansas until 1864 when he entered Lee High School in western Massachusetts. In 1866 he went to Europe and studied in Leipsic and Heidelburg. In 1870 he returned to Kansas and was assistant cashier of the Second National Bank of Leavenworth. In 1874 he moved back to Kentucky and settled in Madison County, where he has turned his attention to farming and trading in stock. In 1876 he located near Fort Estill Station on 700 acres, where he is engaged in breeding fine shorthorn cattle, also race horses and Southdown sheep, and is the second largest tobacco raiser in the county. June 10, 1872, he was united in marriage with Pattie, daughter of Hon. John D. Harris. To this union four children were born: Nannie (deceased), William H., James Clifton and John H. Mrs. Stone is a member of the Christian Church and Mr. Stone is a member of the F. & A. M. He is G. W. of the Grand Commandery K. T. of the State. He is one of the leading Republicans of Kentucky and cast his first presidential vote for Gen. Grant.

WILLIAM L. STOTTS, the fifth of six sons and four daughters born to Benjamin S. and Martha (Stotts) Stotts, is a native of Adair County, and was born November 5, 1852. Benjamin Stotts, born July 17, 1815, was also a native of Adair County and during life followed farming. He married, March 10, 1842, Miss Martha Stotts (a cousin) the ninth of fourteen children, eight of whom were daughters, born to Thomas and Patsy (Gilmore) Stotts, natives of Kentucky. The names of these fourteen children are Elizabeth (Montgomery), James, Pamelia (Paxton), Esther (Taylor), Ursula (Wilson), Mary J. (Young), Alexander, Oliver, Martha (Stotts), Pauline (Paxton), John, William C., Rebecca (Blair) and Thomas, of whom John, William, Alexander, Martha and Pauline are now living. Thomas Stotts was a farmer and the son of Solomon and Ursula (Vaughan) Stotts, natives of Virginia.

William Stotts, grandfather of William L., was also a son of Solomon and Ursula Stotts, and during life followed agricultural pursuits, owning his farm. He married Miss Polly Burns, a Virginian, and they were the parents of eight children: John, Pauline (Fletcher), Benjamin S., William, Green C., Betsy (Stone), George W. and Mary (Hovious). Benjamin Stotts, father of William L. Stotts, settled the present place occupied by his son in 1874, but his whole life was spent in the neighborhood. He was a successful farmer, but never became wealthy, owning at the time of his death a farm of 345 acres. The names of the children born to Benjamin and Martha Stotts are Samuel B., who died in 1873; George Dallas, deceased; Thomas M., deceased; Robert M., deceased; Mollie E., deceased; William L., Suela (Moore), Andrew J., Hattie C. and Victoria, who is dead, Mr. Stotts was one of the respected citizens of Adair County, and departed this life in 1874, on the 14th of November. He was an industrious and energetic farmer and a life-long Democrat, who never held any office, except that of coroner, and never sought one. Mrs. Stotts is a member of the Cumberland Presbyterian Church, and is still living with her children, in the sixty-fourth year of her age. William L. Stotts in youth received a common-school education in the neighborhood schools. His occupation during life has been farming which he was trained to in boyhood's days by his father. He has traveled considerably in the West, but with this exception has always resided in Adair County. He and brother, Andrew J. Stotts, cultivate the farm originally owned by their father, 140 acres of rich, productive land, on which are erected a good residence and out-buildings. They have the farm in a high state of cultivation, and raise all the cereals common to this climate. Andrew J. Stotts was united in matrimony with Miss Mollie L. Traylor, a daughter of J. L. and Bettie H. (Cox) Traylor, natives of Adair County, and they have one child, Hattie Lee Stotts. The Stotts brothers are both among the highly respected citizens of Adair County, and have been life-long Democrats. A. J. Stotts is a member of the Christian Church.

DR. S. W. STRANGE, a native of Adair County, Ky., was born December 8, 1842. He is the fourth of a family of ten children born to Archelaus A. and Celia (Miller) Strange, both of whom were natives of Adair. Archelaus Strange, a farmer and a man of wealth and influence, was born in February, 1812. He received a small patri-

mony to begin life on, and notwithstanding he was victimized by his friends in the way of paying security, became wealthy. He was married to Miss Celia Miller, the fifth of nine children born to Adam and Patience Whitson, natives of Virginia, who had removed from there to North Carolina and emigrated from there to Kentucky. The names of the children born to Mr. and Mrs. Strange are Isaac Hardin; James Logan; Amanda C.; Shelby W.; Elizabeth, wife of La Fayette Lloyd; Ann Maria, wife of 'Squire Elliott; Eliza; Louvina; Commodore, and Victoria, wife of William Isham, of Boyle County; of whom only Isaac H. is dead. Adam Miller was married three times; first to Patience Whitson, by whom he had nine children: Jacob, Bonaparte, Hardin, John, Celia, Commodore, Eliza (Higginbottom), James P. and Patience; the second marriage was to Miss Vina Solomon, and they were the parents of three children: Willomine, Solomon and Sydney; the third marriage was to Miss Jane Mason, by whom he had two sons: David and George A. Archelaus Strange was from boyhood a member of the Christian Church, and was always in politics a Democrat. During the last twenty-four years of his life he lived within five miles of Burkesville, and at the time of his death, May 26, 1884, left an estate of $15,000. Celia Strange has always been a member of the Christian Church, and is still living on the old home place in Cumberland County, in the sixty-eighth year of her age. Archelaus A. Strange, Sr., the grandfather of Dr. Strange, was a native of Virginia, was a farmer, owned a great many slaves and a large plantation, and was the father of eleven children: John C.; Louis; William; Archelaus; Abram; Elizabeth, wife of Wm. Walkup; Polly, wife of Jno. Thomas; Levi; Larkin; Winston A., and Ellen. These were born to Archelaus A. and Elizabeth (Coffey) Strange, and there are now three living— Elder John C. Strange, Winston A. and Mrs. Elizabeth Walkup. Dr. Strange received a good English education in the common schools of Cumberland County and a neighboring high school, together with a term of one year in Burkesville College. In his twentieth year he began the study of medicine under the preceptorship of Dr. W. G. Hunter, and in 1868 attended a ten-months' term at Bellevue Medical College of New York. One month before the termination of the second course of lectures, his health failing, he was compelled to return home. The first year Dr. Strange practiced medicine with his old preceptor, Dr. Hunter, in Burkesville, after which he removed to the village of Breeding's, where he practiced by himself two years. In 1870 he moved to Glenville, where he has since resided, and has a practice averaging $2,500 per annum. March 23, 1869, he married Miss Mary J., a daughter of George and Mary (Ewing) Bird, native Kentuckians. This marriage was blessed with two children: Walter and Charles, both living. Mrs. Strange, a member of the Methodist Episcopal Church South, died August 18, 1871, in the twenty-eighth year of her age. His second marriage, on March 27, 1873, was to Miss Rosaline Grant, the youngest of eight children—four sons and four daughters—born to Eli and Frances (Cartwright) Grant, natives of Adair and Russell Counties, respectively. The names of the children of Eli and Frances Grant are Mary J., wife of O. A. Strange; Joseph M.; Huldah, wife of Dr. A. C. Strange; Sally M., wife of H. K. Walkup; Jno. Milton (deceased); Albert F.; Eli, and Rosaline. To Dr. and Mrs. Strange have been born five children: Mary, who died in childhood, Victoria, Finis, Sally and Eli. Dr. and Mrs. Strange are members of the Christian Church, and Dr. Strange is a member of the Masonic order, and in politics is a Democrat.

SAMUEL A. STRANGE, a farmer and a native of the county of Adair, was born January 21, 1850. His father, Larkin A. Strange, was also a native of Adair County and a farmer, and was born May 9, 1819. He began life with a small patrimony, the gift of his father, Archelaus A. Strange. He was married, in 1843, to Miss Mary A. Simpson, the eldest of six daughters and three sons born to Samuel and Sally (Davis) Simpson, the former a native of Ireland. The children born to Larkin and Mary Strange are named Shelby N., Sarah E. (wife of M. C. Elliott), Samuel A., Joseph H., Larkin C., Asa P., Benjamin F., Mollie B. and James Austin, all of whom are living, and all in Texas except Mollie B. and Samuel A. Samuel Simpson was brought to America during the Irish rebellion by his father, Josiah Simpson, who settled in Lincoln County in 1798, and shortly afterward removed to Adair. Josiah Simpson married Ann McCauley, who was also born in Ireland, and they were the parents of seven children, five of whom were sons. One of them, John Simpson, was a veteran of the war of 1812, and in Jackson's army, participating in his celebrated victory at New Orleans. Josiah Simpson was a farmer, and departed this life in 1826 at a ripe old age. Samuel Simpson,

his son, also a farmer in Adair County, died there, in the seventy-sixth year of his age, in 1874. His wife departed this life in 1870 in the sixty-seventh year of her age. Both Samuel Simpson and his wife were first Baptists of the most rigid Calvinistic type, and Samuel was a Baptist minister of considerable ability, though not a finished scholar, but during the late reformation he became convinced that his "theology" was not Scriptural, and both he and his wife became members of the Christian Church, of which he was also a minister. Larkin A. Strange was a member of the Christian Church. He purchased the old home place of 270 acres where he was born, and where he died in August, 1884, leaving a wife who still survives him (in the sixty-second year of her age), and nine children. Samuel A. Strange in boyhood received an ordinary English education in the common schools of Adair County, together with a ten-months' term at Burkesville High School. He remained at home with his father, working for him until twenty-five years of age, when he was united in marriage to Miss Dorinda, daughter of James T. and Dorinda A. (Kirkpatrick) Rowe, the former of Virginia, the latter of Tennessee. Two children, Lennie P. and an infant who died unnamed (twins), were born to Mr. and Mrs. Strange. Mrs. Strange, a member of the Christian Church, died April 21, 1876. The second marriage of Mr. Strange, January 1, 1885, was to Miss Melrose, daughter of James and Hannah F. (Barger) Lesemby, the former of Tennessee, the latter of Kentucky. Mr. Strange is farming on the original home tract, only 150 acres of which are in cultivation, and he raises all the cereals common to the climate with tobacco and cattle for the markets. He and his wife are both members of the Christian Church.

GEORGE W. SULLIVAN was born July 7, 1820, in Hardin County. He is the only child of Daniel and Elizabeth (Rogers) Sullivan, natives of Virginia and New Jersey respectively, who came to Kentucky with their parents in an early day. Daniel Sullivan was a farmer and son of Daniel and Jane (Settle) Sullivan, of Virginia, who were early pioneers of Green County, but soon after settled in Hardin County. The father was a farmer and soldier of 1812, and of Irish parents. George W. Sullivan was reared on a farm and received a common English education. At the age of eight years he commenced to hire out at $3 and $4 per month; at sixteen commenced working in timber, building flatboats; also made several trips on flatboats to New Orleans at $10 per month, and at the age of twenty-five commenced on a farm as superintendent. In 1852 he was married to Elizabeth Bault, of Adair County, a daughter of William and Margaret (Baker) Bault, who came from Germany and settled in Tennessee, thence moved to Adair County, Ky. Mr. Sullivan is a member of the F. & A. M. In 1861 he enlisted in Company G, Thirteenth Kentucky Volunteers, and served as wagoner. He had his leg broken by a mule falling on him, and was sent to the hospital at Madison, Ind., from which he was discharged in 1863, since which time he has followed a farm life. He located where he now resides, eight miles south of Greensburg, in 1866 on 270 acres of fine land, 100 under cultivation. Mr. Sullivan started in life without a penny, and by his economy and indomitable perseverance has succeeded in securing a fine home. His first presidential vote was for Henry Clay, but since the war he has been a Republican.

CHARLES BLOUNT SULLIVAN was born July 23, 1851, at Elkton, Ky., where he was reared until 1866, when he was appointed a cadet to the United States Naval Academy at Annapolis, Md., which position he resigned at the end of six months, and attended the Agricultural and Mechanical College at Lexington two and a half years. In 1870 he lived at Henderson; in 1871 at Louisville; in 1873 he removed to Woodford County, where he engaged in farming two years, and December, 1874, he located on the old John Taylor farm, two miles south of Pleasant Hill, Mercer County, where he has since resided. His father, John P. Sullivan, a native of Woodford County, was born in 1813, and removed to Elkton about 1830, where he engaged in merchandising and hotel-keeping. He is the son of Lewis Sullivan, a native of Virginia, a farmer, who died about 1820. He had married Miss Collins, and their offspring were Silas H., Robert, John P., James, Obadiah, Luther and U. T. Benjamin. John P. married Sarah B., daughter of Fielding and Adelaide (Halliard) Bush, of Clark County (died April 11, 1865, aged thirty-six years), and from their union sprang Fielding L., John B., Silas H. and Charles B. John P.'s second wife is Mrs. Mollie S. Garnett (nee Arnold), of Woodford County. January 14, 1874, C. B. Sullivan was united in marriage to Miss Leah M., daughter of John W., and Catherine E. (Garnett) Arnold, of Woodford County (born February 10, 1852), and to them have been born Katie Grooms, Sarah Baker (deceased), Charles B., Jr., Garnett

Arnold and Ethel (deceased). Mr. Sullivan is a farmer and trader, and owns 225 acres of good land. He deals largely in mules, and raises registered shorthorn cattle. He is also employed, at an annual salary, by Meguire, Helm & Co., Louisville, as agent in soliciting consignments, and making advances on tobacco in Mercer and adjoining counties. Mr. Sullivan is a member of the Christian Church, and is identified with the Democratic party.

HON. JOSEPH KINKEAD SUMRALL was born November 16, 1835, in Mason County, Ky., where he grew to manhood. In 1853 he entered Centre College at Danville, and graduated with second honors in the famous class of 1857, many of whom became noted in after years, especially Senator Blackburn and Gov. McCreary. In 1858 he commenced reading law in St. Louis, Mo., with Hon. Ed. A. Hannegan; received license as attorney from Judge Lackland in 1859, and practiced in that city with success until the commencement of the late war. By some fatality he was present and was captured with the forces at Camp Jackson, at St. Louis, and was paroled by Gen. Lyon but never exchanged. In 1862, refusing to take the unconstitutional oath required of attorneys to further practice law in St. Louis, he located at Maysville, Ky., where he was eminently successful in the practice of his profession, amid one of the strong bars of the commonwealth. During his stay in Maysville he served eight years as county judge, and was also attorney for the Maysville & Lexington Railroad. His health becoming impaired from arduous professional work, in 1875 he purchased and located in Blithewood, the old family homestead of Mr. Collins C. Moore, three and one-half miles northwest of Danville, Boyle County, on the Harrodsburg pike, where he has since resided. His father, Joseph K. Sumrall, was born in Scotland, removed with his parents in childhood to America, located at Pittsburgh, where he was reared, engaged in merchandising at Philadelphia, and was early a merchant at Maysville, Ky. He was a zealous Presbyterian, a prominent Democrat, and died in 1844 at the age of sixty-three years. He married Susan, daughter of Benjamin S. Clark of May's Lick, Ky. (died August 19, 1884, at Fulton, Mo., aged ninety years), and from their union sprang Mary K., Benjamin C., John T., William A., Daniel C., Julia P. (all deceased), Mrs. Elizabeth V. (wife of Maj. Dobyus, of Fulton, Mo.), Sarah J. and Joseph K., subject of this memoir. February 14, 1866, Judge Sumrall married Miss

Bettie B., daughter of Collins C. and Mary E. (Robertson) Moore, of Boyle County (born January 11, 1842), and their union has been blessed by the birth of William Lawson, Collins Moore, and Lilian C. Judge Sumrall still practices law to some extent, and is at present attorney for the Mercer National Bank of Harrodsburg, of which he is a stockholder. He is now living in the retirement of his farm, having 400 acres of finely improved and very productive land, on which he raises corn, hemp, wheat, and blue-grass for grazing. This is a portion of the original Harrod tract of land, on which there still remain evidences of the location of Harrod's Station, and also his famous spring of pure water. The Judge has been deacon in the Presbyterian Church South, for nearly twenty years. He is an Ancient Odd Fellow, and in politics is a Democrat. Judge Sumrall also during his arduous work at the bar was the author and compiler of a large digest of general and statutory law, used by him in his professional work as a hand and brief book, which would cover, if published, 1,500 pages of closely printed law matter, but he has never yet given it to the profession by publication. He did not do the work for publication but for his own use in his professional labors, and thereby much abridged and simplified it. He was also the originator of the system, as far as can be learned, in Kentucky, and compiler and draughtsman of the laws regulating the almshouse system of his native county, Mason. These laws were enacted by the Kentucky Legislature, and will be found in the acts of Assembly, 1870–71. It would be creditable to the whole State if this Mason County plan of almshouse should hereafter be adopted instead of the present poor law and poorhouse system. It is no crime to be poor, unable to maintain oneself or family, as one might conclude after perusal of the general laws in Kentucky on reference to the poor and poorhouses as designated by statute.

MISS MARY A. SURVANT was born April 15, 1834, in Boyle County, where she was reared to womanhood, and on March 26, 1857, was united in marriage with Mr. Caleb B. Overstreet, and in 1859, with her husband, located on the Lebanon pike, near the east line of Marion County, where she has since resided. Her father, William Survant, Jr., a native of Kentucky, a farmer, lost seven slaves by the late war, was thrown from his horse and died March 7, 1873, at the age of eighty-five years. He was the son of William Survant, Sr. William, Jr., first married Leah Hope,

and their child was Richard. He was next married, on June 22, 1826, to Miss Jane, daughter of James and Jane (Cairns) Guthrie, of Boyle County (born October 12, 1802, died July 15, 1874), and their offspring are James, John B., William H., Mary A. (Overstreet), Joseph, Elizabeth (Wade), Levi and Marion W. Caleb B. Overstreet was born December 14, 1823, and died March 5, 1885. He was a soldier in the Mexican war, an elder in the Cumberland Presbyterian Church, a member of the Masonic fraternity and a Democrat. In token of the esteem in which he was held, the T. W. Wash Lodge of A. F. & A. M., in full lodge assembled, "resolved, first, that in the death of Brother C. B. Overstreet this lodge feels the weight of an irreparable loss; that his personal service in the cause of the truth, his pure and noble character, affording an example to his survivors, and the now broken ties that long connected many of us in personal relationship with him, make this a heavy yoke of death which this lodge has been called on to bear; second, that we, the brethren of the T. W. Wash Lodge, No. 430, extend to the bereaved family of the deceased our heart-felt sympathy in this their sad hour of bereavement; and that, in token of which, we will wear the usual badge of mourning for thirty days. [Signed] B. F. Calhoun, D. C. May, J. R. Breeding, Committee." Elizabeth J. Overstreet, the daughter of Caleb B. and wife, was born September 30, 1860; married to Elias A. Harmon October 21, 1880. Mrs. Overstreet is farming, having over 100 acres of well improved and productive land in a good state of cultivation. Roy O. Harmon, grandson of C. B. and M. A. Overstreet, was born November 5, 1882. Mrs. Mary A. Overstreet was married November 30, 1886, to William A. Powers, of Washington County. W. A. Powers was born January 4, 1822. He is a member of the Baptist Church and belongs to the Masonic fraternity.

HENRY SUTHERLAND, farmer and distiller, was born July 17, 1826. His parents, William and Eliza (Read) Sutherland, were married about 1817. Their family consisted of five boys: John, Henry, William, Isaac W. and Archibald C; and four girls: Nancy C., Helen R., Mary E. and Jeanette W. The father was a native Kentuckian, born in 1795; a successful farmer, and magistrate for several years. In January, 1862, he was the victim of a most foul assassination, committed by a soldier of the Federal Army, who enticed him from his home and shot him. His murderer was subsequently tried, convicted and hanged at Bardstown. John Sutherland, his father, was a native of Scotland, whence he came to the United States when a young man. Anterior to his coming, he married a Miss Cameron. They came immediately to Kentucky, and settled on Beech Fork, Nelson County, where he died at an advanced age. Henry Sutherland has never left the homestead farm in Nelson County. He received a collegiate education at St. Joseph College, Bardstown, and in June, 1865, his marriage with Miss Josie Miles, daughter of John Miles, was solemnized. To their union seven children have been born: Eliza, Anna, Josie, William H., Jeanette, John D. and Archibald C. Mr. Sutherland has always followed agricultural pursuits, in which he has been very successful. He also owns and operates a distillery. In politics he has always been an ardent Democrat.

WILLIAM H. SWEENEY, attorney at law, was born October 22, 1858, in Lebanon, Ky., and is the son of Harvey and Mary Sweeney, both parents natives of the same State. Daniel Sweeney, subject's grandfather, was a native of Virginia and a soldier in the war of 1812. He came to Kentucky many years ago and was among the early settlers of Mackville, Washington County, where he resided until 1848, at which time he removed to Missouri, where his death occurred in 1855. Harvey Sweeney was born about the year 1809 and is still living in the city of Lebanon. He is a mechanic by occupation. Subject's maternal grandfather was Wilson Edmondson, a native of Essex County, Va. He was an early pioneer of Marion County and resided near Lebanon until his death in 1883, at the advanced age of ninety-two years. He was a farmer by occupation and was also one of the veterans of the war of 1812. Mary Sweeney was born in Washington County in 1812 and died in 1884. Two children were born to Harvey and Mary Sweeney, namely: William H., whose name heads this sketch, and Fannie, wife of A. C. Van Cleve. William H. Sweeney was reared on a farm near Lebanon, and received a good education in the schools of that city, attending the same until his eighteenth year. He then entered the Forrest Academy at Anchorage, in Jefferson County, where he pursued his studies for one year. After leaving school he commenced the study of law with Messrs. Russell & Avritt, of Lebanon, with whom he remained one year, receiving license to practice in the courts of Marion County in 1880. He began the practice of his profession before

attaining his majority. He came to Springfield in February, 1881, and since that time has been an active member of the Washington County bar. In 1885 he purchased the Washington *Leader*, the only newspaper in Washington County, and for one year edited the same and placed it upon a substantial footing. He received the nomination for the office of county judge at the Democratic primary election of November, 1885, a compliment to his ability and popularity. Mr. Sweeney resides two miles and a half from Springfield upon a beautiful farm which he successfully operates in connection with his profession. He was married February 28, 1882, to Miss Mary A. Leachman, daughter of Thomas and Emeline (Thompson) Leachman, of Washington County. One child has been born to this marriage, Ella Sweeney. Mr. Sweeney is an active business man and an ardent supporter of the principles advocated by the Democratic party. In September, 1886, he was appointed master commissioner and receiver of the Washington Circuit Court.

PRIOR SWIGGETT was born on the 21st of March, 1850. In early life he received such education as was afforded in the common schools of his native county, supplemented in a great measure by the practical and useful kind which is acquired through contact with the affairs of life. He remained with his parents, working on the home farm in his native county of Casey, until he attained his majority, at which time he engaged in farming on his own account. This he continued until the year 1877, when he went into the saw-milling business and lumber trade; this he has continued until the present time. He was united in marriage on the 30th of January, 1877, to Miss Maggie Coppage, youngest daughter of Uriah Coppage. To this union is born one son, Walter, born July 10, 1880. Mrs. Swiggett is a member of the Christian Church. Mr. Swiggett, though not a member of the church, bases his religious views on justice and fair dealing. His political views are Democratic.

B. C. SYMPSON, M. D., was born October 1, 1827, and is a son of James C. and Mary (Gaddie) Sympson, to whom five sons and one daughter were born. J. C. Sympson was born in Green County in 1792; he was an active farmer, served as clerk of the bank of Winchester, also the bank of Greensburg, Ky.; he represented Green County two terms in the Legislature, also served as constable and sheriff of the county; served in the war of 1812 and was one of the leading and most popular men of the county; during the civil war was a stanch and uncompromising Union man, and died in 1878. He was a son of William Sympson, who married Peggie Donahoo, both natives of Virginia, who settled in Green County, Ky., as early as 1785. He was one of the heroes under Gen. Marion during the war for independence; was a farmer and slave-holder, served as justice and sheriff, was a prominent and active citizen of his county, and died about 1847, over eighty years of age. His father, Michael Sympson, came from Ireland. Mrs. Mary Sympson was born in Green County, a daughter of Benjamin Gaddie, of Scotch and Welsh origin, and one of the early pioneers of Green County. (Dr. Sympson is a native of Green, now Taylor County; received his early training on the farm, and a good common English education, sufficient to enable him to teach, which he commenced at twenty-five and followed three years. In the meantime he commenced the study of medicine with Dr. James Lively, of Taylor County, graduated from the Kentucky School of Medicine in 1860, and located in the southern part of Nelson County. After his wife's death he spent five years in Taylor County. In the fall of 1880 he located at New Hope, where he has practiced with good success ever since. In January, 1855, he married Sarah F. Edwards, of Green County, a daughter of Thomas C. and Jane (Mitchell) Edwards. The issue of this marriage was four children: Mary J. West, who died in Kansas; Rosa E. Hobbs, of La Rue County, Ky.; Seaton E.; Richard B. The Doctor's wife died in 1878, and was a conscientious and consistent member of the Baptist Church. The Doctor is a member of the Methodist Episcopal Church South and of the Masonic fraternity. He is independent in politics, and his first presidential vote was for Taylor in 1848.

HON. ALBERT GALLATIN TALBOTT was born April 4, 1808, near Paris, Bourbon Co., Ky., but in 1813 removed with his parents to Clark County, and in 1818 to Jessamine County. He received a classical education at Forest Hill Academy under the tuition of Prof. Samuel Wilson, author of the Latin ode to Gen. LaFayette, and studied law with Hon. Samuel H. Woodson. In 1831 he commenced farming and general trading, directing his especial attention to dealing in real estate, and as the result of careful investments and judicious sales, within a few years he amassed quite a large fortune for that day. In 1838 he removed to Mercer County, where he successfully prosecuted his business as a real estate dealer until 1846, when he located in Boyle County, on the Harrodsburg pike, three miles from Danville, in which vicinity he has since resided. In 1849 he was chosen from Boyle County a member of the Constitutional Convention of Kentucky, and the following year was elected to the Legislature without opposition. In 1855 he was elected a representative to Congress in opposition to Know-nothingism, which had then assumed huge proportions, and in 1857 was returned to that honorable body. In 1859 he was elected State senator for a term of four years, and in 1883 was chosen a representative in the Legislature from Boyle County by about 800 majority. While a member of the Legislature in 1851, foreseeing and fully recognizing the inevitable consequences of the irrepressible conflict on slavery, Mr. Talbott introduced a resolution which was favored by about twenty-five members of the General Assembly, urging the surrender of the slaves of the South to the United States upon the basis of fair compensation by the General Government. This resolution, which attracted wide-spread attention at the time, was presented in order to avert war and preserve the Union intact. Col. Talbott lost about sixty slaves (in addition to other property) as a result of the late war. He is a son of Presley Talbott, who was born near Winchester, Va.; removed to Kentucky at an early day, locating in Bourbon County, was an extensive farmer and slave-holder, and died in Jessamine County from the effects of cholera in 1835 at the age of fifty-seven years. His grandfather, Demoval Talbott, a native of Virginia, a wealthy farmer in Bourbon County, died at the age of ninety-seven years. Col. A. G. Talbott has been thrice married, first to Miss Elizabeth, daughter of Capt. William Caldwell of Jessamine County; to this union were born Mary A. (Tomlinson), William P. and Albert Gallatin, Jr. His second wife was Mrs. Maria E. Talbott, daughter of Gov. William Owsley, and this union was favored by the birth of Mrs. Emma T. Cecil. On June 2, 1886, Col. Talbott was united in marriage with Miss Caroline, daughter of Mr. Peter Watson of Philadelphia. He has long been a member of the Masonic fraternity, also a member of the Christian Church, and in politics is a Democrat.

GEORGE W. TARKINGTON was born October 9, 1845, in Boyle County, where he has always resided. His father, William L. Tarkington, was born in 1811, in Giles County, Tenn., where he was reared; removed to Marion County, Ky., in 1835; located in Boyle County in 1844, where he now resides; is a farmer, and lost twenty slaves by the late war. He is the son of Joshua Tarkington,

Jr., a native of North Carolina, a pioneer in Tennessee, where he traded a gun and a pony for 1,000 acres of land at Nashville; resided in Williamson and Giles Counties; was a soldier in the battle of New Orleans in 1815, and died in 1850 at the age of seventy-three years. He was the son of Joshua Tarkington, Sr., a native of England, an American soldier, who was killed in battle in the Revolutionary war. His wife was Mary Spruel (died in 1846, aged one hundred and three years), and their offspring were Capt. Joseph (lost at sea), Joshua, Jr., Priscilla (Tarkington), Keziah (Ezell), Mary (Tarkington), mother of Rev. Joseph Tarkington, of Indiana, Nancy (Oliver), Esther (Brown) and Deborah (Swanson). Joshua, Jr., married Mary Barry, of Kentucky (died in 1822, aged forty-three years), and their children were Hugh B., Jefferson O., James W., William L., George W., Sr., Amelia (Wilsford), Mary P. (Morris), Frances (Raines), Julia H. (Raines) and Martha (Durham). William L. married Julietta, daughter of Joseph and Eunice (Stiles) Maxwell, of Marion County (born in 1822), and from their union sprang Joseph M., Mary (Edelen), George W., Julia H. (McMillen) and Martha (Shuttleworth). January 28, 1876, Geo. W. Tarkington was married to Miss Elizabeth E., daughter of David and Martha (Maxwell) Knox, of Boyle County (born January 26, 1857), and to them have been born David K. T., Hugh and George W., Jr. The subject of this sketch was favored with good educational advantages, and was thirteen years engaged as civil engineer on the Knoxville branch of the Louisville & Nashville: Erie & Pittsburgh; N. & S. A.; Houston & Great Northern, and Cincinnati Southern Railroads. He is now engaged in farming and stock trading, having 220 acres of land in a fine state of cultivation. He is turning especial attention to the breeding of jacks and jennets, having some of the best stock in Kentucky. David Knox, the son of Abner Knox, was born January 6, 1804. On May 6, 1856, he espoused in marriage Miss Martha, daughter of Joseph and Eunice (Stiles) Maxwell, of Marion County, Ky. (born December 31, 1828), and their union resulted in the birth of Elizabeth E. (Tarkington), Joseph A., Robert W., David S. (deceased) and Maria W. (For ancestors, see sketch of Mrs. Fannie Knox.)

SAMUEL TAYLOR, a Virginian, removed to Mercer County, Ky., about 1780, erected the stone mansion in 1790 now occupied by Mr. W. B. Vivian, on which he placed his motto: "Look to your laws rather than your progenitors for your inheritance." He was a member of several constitutional conventions of Kentucky, a representative in the Legislature, a farmer and slave owner, and died about 1812. His wife was Elizabeth Hughs, and their offspring were John, Samuel, William H., Mary (Wilson), Sophia (Bledsoe) and Fanny Glover, the mother of Hon. Samuel Glover of Missouri.

SIMON P. TAYLOR, a native of the county of Adair, and one of its leading farmers, was born March 20, 1822. He is the son of Rev. George W. and Frances T. (Jones) Taylor. In youth Simon P. Taylor availed himself of every opportunity to gain an education, but owing to the pioneer school system of Kentucky, was only able to obtain a moderate English education, but in his eighteenth year he attended a neighboring school, and perfected his education in the English branches. Since arriving at years of maturity he has been a considerable reader, and is well versed in the current topics of the times. In boyhood days Mr. Taylor commenced farming, which has since been his life-long occupation. He remained at home, working with and for his father, until twenty years of age. He then taught a six months' session at Canton, Ky., where he married, in 1844, Miss Sarah M. McClain, a daughter of Joseph and Susan (Hurt) McClain, both natives of Adair County, and members of prominent families. Joseph McClain died about fifty years ago in the prime of life, leaving a family of three children. His widow married James Vigus and died in Missouri in 1885. By her last marriage Susan Vigus became the mother of seven children, all of whom live in the West, and one of whom, William E. Vigus, is a man of prominence in Chicago, the author of a very fine political map of the United States, and for years superintendent of the Western Union Telegraph system. After his marriage Mr. Taylor returned to his native county, and purchased a farm of forty-five acres adjoining a sixty-acre tract belonging to his wife, which was partially improved. This tract he cultivated, built on, improved and added to by various purchases, until he owned the entire tract of 150 acres. Besides this tract he at present owns four other tracts of land, in all 427 acres, and in the course of his life has built three different residences; all of them, except the first, were frame. He also was a trader in tobacco and stock, and sold a line of general merchandise two years in Columbia, where, in 1863, he was robbed of $6,000 in goods by guerrillas. He was also a merchant at Montpelier and Glenn's Fork two years and carried stocks, during his mercantile career, of from $5,000 to $10,000. Mrs. Taylor, a consistent Christian, and a member of the Methodist Episcopal Church South, departed this life in 1856 in the twenty-eighth year of her age, leaving six children, viz.: Joseph E., Eliza F., wife of John Strange; Laura S., wife of M. Morris; George C.; Mary E., wife of J. F. Strange, and James Thomas, of whom Eliza and Laura are dead. Mr. Taylor, in 1857, was married to Miss Mary J. Harris, the second of the twelve children of Josiah Harris. Josiah Harris was one of the prominent merchants in Columbia, and was twice married; first to Miss Mary J. Selby, daughter of Hon. Benj. Selby, auditor of the State of Kentucky; by this marriage he had two children: George L. and Mary J. His second marriage was to Miss Sally King, a daughter of Milton King and a sister of Hon. J. Q. A. King, well known in Kentucky politics of twenty years ago. By this last marriage Josiah Harris became the father of the following named children: Hon. Josiah Harris of Paducah; Milton, John V., Alfred L., Edward, Elwood, Richard H., Paul J., Maud Ellen, wife of Joseph Harris, and Overton. Only three are dead—George, John and Edward. By his second marriage Mr. Taylor has seven living children: Henry W., William L., Sarah E., wife of Clay Conner; Mattie C., Emma L., Annie M. and Samuel R. One child, and the eldest, Matilda Prentiss, died in infancy. Mr. Taylor is a member of the Methodist Episcopal Church, a Democrat in politics and a prohibitionist in sentiment, while Mrs. Taylor, though not a church member, believes in the doctrines of the Christian Church. Mr. Taylor began the battle of life without a dollar, and his estate of $5,000 is the result of his own industry, economy and management.

GEORGE M. TAYLOR, a son of Rev. George W. Taylor, is a native of Adair County, and a farmer. He was born October 13, 1824; in youth received a moderate English education in the neighborhood schools, which he attended three months each year for several years. He worked with and for his father until twenty years of age. When still remaining at home, he began on his own account the battle of life. In 1850 he was united in marriage with Miss Mary J. McClain, the oldest of Robert McClain's children. Mr. McClain was twice married; first to Miss Kitty Hayden, a daughter of Richard Hayden, of Cumberland County, and by this marriage he became the father of two children: Mary J. and Oliver. His second marriage was to Miss Nancy Noel, a native of

Washington County, Ky., and by this marriage six children were born: Joseph; Sarah, wife of Parker Naylor; Ellen, wife of Charles D. Willis; James; Margeret Ann, wife of Otho Miller, and Finis, all of whom are living. He lost two children in infancy. His life-long vocation was farming, in which he was successful, and owned a great many slaves before the war. Mr. and Mrs. Taylor are the parents of nine children: James R.; Benjamin F.; Zachariah T.; Kitty F., wife of Henry B. Garnett; Mary McClellan; William S.; George B.; Richard I. and Lena, of whom James R., Mary and Richard I. are now dead. Mr. Taylor, about 1849, bought the farm of 140 acres, originally cleared by his grandfather, George Taylor. This was well improved, and on it was erected good buildings, and here he lived until the close of the late war, when he purchased a farm of 147 acres on the Crocus road about two and a half miles from Columbia. He remained there eight years, then moved to his present location, one mile northwest of Glenville, and settled on a farm of 80 acres. Here he has since lived engaged in agricultural pursuits, raising all the cereals common to Kentucky climate, and also stock. Mr. and Mrs. Taylor are both members of the Methodist Episcopal Church, and Mr. Taylor in politics is a Republican, though in ante bellum days an old line Whig. James R. Taylor died in the twenty-third year of his age, and had attended one course of medical lectures in the University of Louisville, and was practicing his profession at the time of his death on April 3, 1874. Benjamin F. Taylor is a physician and druggist at Bridgeport, Metcalfe County, and also carries on a farm. Zachariah Taylor is a farmer in Adair County. William S. Taylor is a physician and practicing with Dr. Benjamin Taylor. George B. is a farmer and still lives with his father. All of Mr. Taylor's sons have grown up to be sober, industrious and respected citizens, and men of intelligence—members mostly of the Methodist Episcopal Church.

URIAH L. TAYLOR, M. D., was born in Adair County April 21, 1833. George Taylor, his grandfather, was of English origin, and a native of North Carolina. He came to Adair County, Ky., in 1800, bringing with him a family of eight children—four sons and four daughters. He bought wild lands. which he subsequently improved; was a man in moderate circumstances, a prominent member of the Methodist Episcopal Church, of which he was a class leader. He and most of his sons immigrated to Illinois, about 1830, where he died in Pike County. Rev.

George W. Taylor (born in 1790), the father of Dr. Taylor, began the work of the ministry in the Methodist Episcopal Church at about the age of twenty-one, and for fifty-five years had the care of about twenty churches. About 1811 he married Miss Fanny Jones, a daughter of Charles Jones, who, with his family, had come from Bedford County, Va., to Adair County, Ky. This union was blessed by ten children: Dr. James G., Rev. Zachariah M., Chesley J., Caroline M. (Garnett), Simon P., George M., Charles B., Thomas C., Benjamin F. and Uriah L., of whom Zachariah, Thomas and Benjamin are now dead. Rev. George W. Taylor was presiding elder thirty years, was a member of the Louisville Conference, and at one time a delegate to the general conference of Philadelphia. He died in February, 1866, in the seventy-sixth year of his age; his wife's death occurred in 1857. A short time before his death he had contracted a second marriage to Mrs. Mary (Bridgewater) Jones, the widow of Charles Jones, and her demise occurred about 1876. Dr. Uriah L. Taylor, until seventeen years of age, lived on the farm owned by his father. He next engaged selling goods in a store of general merchandise in Columbia until twenty years of age. He next went back to farming, which was his occupation until 1858, when he began the study of medicine under his brother, Dr. James G. Taylor, of Columbia. In the winter of 1858–59 he attended the Kentucky School of Medicine, and on returning home, in 1859, began the practice of his profession. This he continued until the session of 1875, when he graduated at the University of Louisville. He has always enjoyed a large and lucrative practice. December 20, 1857, he married Miss Mary J. Patterson, the third of James and Ann Elizabeth (Epperson) Patterson's two sons and three daughters. James Patterson, a native of Adair County, was the second of William and Elizebeth (Glenn) Patterson's four sons and two daughters. William Patterson and wife were both Virginians. Elizabeth Ann Epperson was the fifth of William and Elizabeth (Montgomery) Epperson's six sons and two daughters. William Epperson and wife were also Virginians, and the two families, Eppersons and Pattersons, were families of wealth and prominence. Dr. Taylor and wife have been blessed by four children: James G., died in infancy; Dellie, who died December 16, 1883, in her twenty-first year, and in life was a teacher of music in Columbia College, as well as a graduate of that institution; Fanny, wife of Elder John W. McGarvey, Jr., and

Mattie. Dr. Taylor has given each of his children, who have lived to maturity, a thorough education in the college at Columbia, of which he is president of the board of trustees. The Columbia College was founded in 1873 by Elder W. K. Azbill. This college began with a faculty of five teachers, with Elder W. K. Azbill as president, and has continued a forty-week session each year, and very successfully, with an attendance of from 100 to 150, until within the last two years, the attendance has diminished to about 100, with three teachers, and Prof. M. F. Harmon as the principal. There are twelve members of the board of trustees: Dr. U. L. Taylor, president; F. C. Shearer, vice-president; James T. Page, secretary; G. M. Caldwell, W. N. Robinson, Tim Bradshaw, W. J. Callison, Junius Hancock, J. K. A. Strange, R. H. Hopper and W. K. Azbell. The college has a theological department in connection with it, besides a full and complete course of study, all of which is under the superintendency of the Christian Church. Dr. Taylor was in early life a member of the Methodist Episcopal Church, but, about twelve years ago, became a member of the Christian Church, in which he has since been a zealous worker, at present being one of two elders, which position he has held about twelve years. He is a Republican in politics.

MATTHEW TAYLOR, the superintendent of the Adair County public schools, is a native of the county, and was born May 24, 1838. He is a son of Jeremiah and Ann (Ewing) Taylor, the former a native of Norfolk, Va., the latter of Kentucky. Jeremiah Taylor, born in August, 1801, has been, during life, a tiller of the soil, owning a farm of about 111 acres. He has been an industrious and successful farmer, and at present lives in Glenville Precinct, about twelve miles from Columbia. He was married, in 1836, to Miss Ann Ewing, the fourth of a family of six children (two of whom were sons) born to Andrew and Mary (Patterson) Ewing, the former of whom was of Scotch-Irish origin. By this marriage Jeremiah Taylor became the father of five children: Matthew, Mary (wife of James A. Powell), Martha (wife of Wilson Lewis), Celestia (the second wife of Wilson Lewis) and James, of whom Matthew and Mary alone are living. Mrs. Taylor in life was a member of the Presbyterian Church, and died in April, 1877, in the seventy-sixth year of her age. Jeremiah Taylor is still living, one of the oldest and most highly respected citizens of Adair County, and has resided here since 1836. Andrew Ewing, maternal grandfather of

Matthew Taylor, was one of the early settlers of Adair County, and a veteran of the Indian wars under Gen. Wayne. Thirty years he held the office of magistrate in Adair County, and twice held the office of sheriff under the old constitution. He died at the ripe old age of eighty-eight years, in 1855. Robert Patterson, the brother of Mary (Patterson) Ewing, was a veteran of the American Revolution, and held the office of major in the Colonial Army. Matthew Taylor received a poor education in youth, and at the age of twenty could scarcely write his name. After this he attended the common or district schools about fifteen months, and the seminary at Campbellsville about five months, which time was scattered over four years. The money necessary to pay for books and tuition was earned on the farm, and a part of the time by hiring out to do farm labor. About the age of twenty-five he began teaching in the free schools of Adair County, which has been his life-long profession. The term of his life as a professional teacher extends over a period of seventeen years, and he has taught in the common schools of Adair, Cumberland and Metcalfe Counties. In 1868 he was elected by the board of magistrates of Adair County as commissioner of common schools, and superintended fifty schools during the ensuing two years. Again, in 1884, he was elected, on the Democratic ticket, as superintendent of the county schools, under the new law, and has supervision over eighty-four district schools, with an enumeration of 4,000 pupils. He attends specially to institute work, and every year the county teachers' institute is conducted on the normal plan, under the management of an institute expert. January 21, 1862, Mr. Taylor was united in matrimony to Miss Mary J. Loye, the daughter of Martin and Mary (Brown) Loye, North Carolinians. The home of Mr. and Mrs. Taylor has been brightened by the addition of nine children: Annie B. (wife of John S. Page), Mary Louisa, James G., Fanny, Catherine, Herschel, William C., Clemmie E., Virginia and Ethel—all living. Mr. Taylor is a member of the Masonic order, and in politics is a life-long Democrat. He has also been deputy surveyor of the county for eight years, has a farm of 140 acres, and has, in addition to teaching, followed the occupation of farming.

REV. B. F. TAYLOR was born in Anderson County, Tenn., October 4, 1843, and is a son of Robert S. and Eliza (Cobb) Taylor, who reared a family of five children: John T., Margaret E., Benjamin F., Jennie L. and Anna C. The father, Robert S., was also born in Anderson County, Tenn., was a teacher in early life, later a farmer and slave-holder, and about 1874 moved to Lyon County, Kas., where he died November 12, 1877. His wife died in Mercer County, Ky., in 1867, aged about fifty-five. His father, John Taylor, came from Virginia, settled at Stanford, Ky., but afterward moved to Anderson County, Tenn., where he died. His wife was Eliza Slemons, who bore him one child. Mrs. Eliza (Cobb) Taylor born in North Carolina, was a daughter of Benjamin Cobb, who settled in Tennessee about 1820, but was born in New Jersey, and for a time resided in North Carolina. Rev. B. F. Taylor, at the age of sixteen, entered Ewing and Jefferson Colleges. When the war broke out he enlisted in August, 1861, in Company K, First Kentucky Volunteers, and was by degrees promoted from private to major. He took part in all the engagements from Stone River to Atlanta, and was mustered out in 1864 at the expiration of his term of enlistment. He then came to Mercer County, Ky., engaged in farming, and January 17, 1867, married Mollie J., daughter of Rev. Strather and Lucy M. (Jenkins) Cook, natives of Boyle and Garrard Counties respectively. Two children have been the result of this union: Cordie A. and John C. Rev. S. Cook was a minister of the Baptist Church for fifty years, and was a son of George Cook, a native of Virginia, but of German descent. After his marriage B. F. Taylor continued farming until 1871, when he was converted, became a preacher in the Baptist Church in November, 1872, and was ordained July 17, 1874, by Elders T. M. Vaughn, W. P. Harvey, J. W. Smith, W. T. Wood, S. Cook and T. C. Bell. Since then he has been actively engaged in the ministry in Washington, Mercer, Garrard, Lincoln and Boyle Counties, and is now moderator of the South District Baptist Association of Kentucky. He is a Free Mason and an Odd Fellow, and in 1864 cast his first presidential vote for Lincoln.

SQUIRE ELIJAH JACKSON TERRILL was born December 23, 1814, in Garrard County, Ky.; in 1830 removed with his parents to Marion County, Mo.; in 1842 to Jessamine County, Ky., and in 1843 he located on Kentucky River, in the northwest portion of Garrard County, where he has since resided. His father, Robert Terrill, a native of Culpeper County, Va., removed in childhood, with his parents, to near Lancaster, Ky., where he was reared; he was a farmer, a Baptist and a Whig, and died in 1859, aged eighty-four years. He was the son of Henry Terrill, of Virginia, a very early settler in Garrard County, Ky., a farmer and slave-holder, who died in 1823, aged about seventy years. His offspring were Robert, Thomas, Mary (Ford) and Henry. By his second wife: John, Overton, James, Sydona (Underwood) and Patsey. Robert married Mary, daughter of James and Ann (Shackelford) Beazley, of Garrard County (died in 1852, aged sixty-five years), and from their union sprang Elizabeth (Dinwiddie), Winnie F. (Allen), James (dead), William H., Elijah J., Josephus Henry, Hiram K., Robert, Alma (Proctor), Almanda (Barbee), George A., Eliza A. (Yater) and John R. Oct. 7, 1841, Elijah J. married Miss Susan B., daughter of Phillip G. and Mary (Berry) Smith, of Jessamine County (born May 17, 1819), and to them have been born Mary O. (deceased), William A., Elizabeth S. (Saddler), Rev. Robert J., John A., Patrick H., Phillip S., Paralee, Rev. Elijah J., Susan M. and Thomas Johnson (deceased). While a young man Mr. Terrill engaged in clerking in a store in Philadelphia, Mo., three years, and also officiated as constable and deputy sheriff, of Marion County, Mo. He held the position of magistrate and member of the court of claims of Garrard County four years, and taught school twenty-seven years. He was formerly an old line Whig, is now a prohibitionist, and his wife is an acceptable member of the Baptist Church.

HON. W. T. TEVIS was born September 15, 1840, and is a son of Cyrus C. and Elizabeth (Stone) Tevis, parents of the following children: John (deceased), Mary (now Mrs. Cosby), Sallie Chrisman, Robert C. (deceased), Napoleon, Elizabeth Dinwiddie, Benjamin F., Squire T., Charles C. and W. T. Capt. Cyrus C. Tevis was born in Madison County, was a farmer, an extensive trader and a slave-holder· In politics he was a Whig, and in religion a Methodist, and died in 1849, aged about fifty years. His father, Robert Tevis, came from Virginia and settled in the northern part of Madison County; he began life a poor man but succeeded in accumulating a considerable fortune. Mrs. Elizabeth Tevis was born on the banks of the Potomac River, in Virginia, and was a daughter of John Stone, a surveyor and farmer. The Hon. W. T. Tevis was reared on a farm in his native county of Madison, near Kirksville. At fourteen he entered a store at Nicholasville, where he clerked for a term and then passed a year in Independence, Mo. On his return to Kentucky, he entered Company B, Eighth Cavalry, Morgan's command, and in 1862 was wounded in a fight on Red River and

taken prisoner by Col. Walker, but was paroled in 1863. He had also participated in the battles of Hartsville, Tenn., Munfordsville and Perryville. After being released from his parole he went to Canada, and placed himself under the command of the Confederate authorities there, and engaged in all their efforts for the release of Confederate prisoners, and other acts of hostility on the frontier. After the surrender of Lee he went to Europe, returned to Canada in 1886, remained until he had secured a pardon, and in the fall of that year returned to Madison County. In April, 1867, he married Lucy W. McKenny, of Lexington, a daughter of William and Sallie E. (Furguson) McKenny, natives respectively of Virginia and Clark County, Ky., and to this union have been born Arthur C., Harry D., Sallie Mc., Cyrus and Maggie. After marriage Mr. Tevis engaged in farming and stock trading. In 1876 he moved to Richmond and engaged in the furniture business and banking, but quit business and resumed farming in 1884, and in 1885 was elected to the State Legislature. Mrs. Tevis died in April, 1884, and in June, 1886, Mr. Tevis married Miss Lella, daughter of Judge Robert Y. Bush, of Hawesville, who married Anna M. Stone. Judge Bush is a son of Christopher Bush, a native of Virginia, but who came to Kentucky when quite young. Mr. and Mrs. Tevis are members of the Presbyterian Church, and Mr. Tevis was once master of the grange. He cast his first presidental vote for Greeley in 1872.

BUTLER R. THOMAS was born in the vicinity of where he now lives, June 23, 1818. Benjamin Thomas, his paternal grandfather, was born in Virginia about 1762. He was united in marriage in his native State to Miss Margaret Grigsby, by whom he was the father of twelve children who grew to manhood and womanhood. In the year 1806 he immigrated to Kentucky, coming immediately to Nelson County, of which he remained a resident until his death, July 23, 1833. He opened a farm in the county of his adoption and became, for his day, one of its most prosperous and extensive farmers. Jacob Ramey, maternal grandfather of our subject, was also a native of Virginia, whence he immigrated to Kentucky in the early history of the State. His wife, Susanna Grigsby, was born in 1751. To their union three children were born. She died at the advanced age of ninety-four years. By a former marriage Mr. Ramey was the father of eight children. Redman G. Thomas, father of our subject, was born in Prince William

County, Va., February 22, 1788, making him almost a man grown upon the occasion of his parents' settlement in Kentucky. Three years later, March 15, 1809, he married Mrs. Nancy (Ramey) King. To their union these four children were born: Elizabeth (now Mrs. Alfred Connelly), Cordelia (deceased), Butler R. and Benjamin H. Mrs. Thomas was born November 20, 1782. Mr. Thomas followed agricultural pursuits all his life, meeting with good success. Butler R. Thomas, a native of Nelson County, remained with his parents until he was twenty-three years of age, receiving a common English education. He, like his ancestors, has always followed the vocation of farming, in which he has met with uniform success. He is the proprietor of a well improved farm of 240 acres. which is a model of neatness and of itself displays the systematic manner in which Mr. Thomas handles it. June 3, 1841, Miss Louisa P. Porter became his wife. To their union ten children were born, of whom these nine are now living: Alfred P., Benjamin H., John H., Martha and Mary (twins), Charles B., Redman G., Sallie B. and Luella. Mrs. Thomas was born January 20, 1821. She died March 18, 1879.

J. W. THOMAS was born in Marion County, Ky., March 10, 1827. His paternal ancestors were natives of Maryland; his grandfather, William Thomas, emigrating from that State to Kentucky many years ago and settling near the present site of Frederickton Village, Washington County, where he opened a farm and died at an early day. J. W. Thomas, Sr., father of subject, was born near Fredericksburg, Washington County. He was a farmer and departed this life in 1826, a few months before the birth of our subject. His wife was Susannah (Davis) Thomas. She was the daughter of one of the earliest pioneers of Nelson County, who settled near the village of New Haven when the county was in possession of the Indians. Mr. Davis assisted in the construction of the old fort at Goodin Station, participating in a number of bloody engagements with the savages and died many years ago. Mrs. Thomas was born in Nelson County in 1794, and died in February, 1870. Her first husband was William Peak, by whom she had two children: John D. Peak and Mrs. Lucy Ann Wilber, both still living. By her second husband, J. W. Thomas, Sr., she became the mother of four children: Mrs. Elizabeth C. Vize, Mrs. Martha A. Coy, Mary E. and J. W. Thomas, all living at this time (1886). J. W. Thomas grew to manhood in Marion County, and was reared to agricultural pursuits; was educated in the country schools, which he attended until his twenty-fifth year, making substantial progress in the various studies in the meantime. He began reading law in 1852 with George Roberts, of Elizabethtown, under whose instructions he continued one year, and at the end of that time returned to his native county, where he acted in the capacity of deputy circuit clerk for one year; was admitted to the bar in 1854, obtaining license from Judges Bridges and Kincheloe, and immediately thereafter began the practice at Lebanon, where he remained until 1857, doing a lucrative business in the meantime. In the latter year he moved to the town of Washington, Hempstead Co., Ark., where he resided until 1862, at which time he entered the Confederate service, enlisting in the Eighth Arkansas Regiment, with which he served until the fall of the same year, when he was discharged on account of disability. Upon leaving the army he returned to Arkansas, and in 1863 moved back to Lebanon, where he resided until 1865, refraining from practicing his profession in the meantime, owing to impaired health. In June, 1865, he moved to Bardstown, where, with the exception of a short time spent in Louisville, he has since resided, practicing his profession in the courts of Nelson and adjoining counties, and in the supreme court of Kentucky and the federal court of Louisville. Mr. Thomas is an active business man, and has met with well merited success in his profession. He is one of the oldest attorneys of the Nelson County bar, and has numerous friends wherever he goes. He was originally a Whig in politics, but at the dissolution of that party he identified himself with the Democracy, of which he has since been a stanch supporter. He was married December 25, 1880, in Crothersville, Ind., to Miss Ella Applegate, daughter of Dr. Moses and Elizabeth Applegate, of Jackson County of the above State. Three children have been born to this union: Susannah E., Ella M., who lived only about thirty hours, and William R. Thomas.

HON. JOHN R. THOMAS was born February 5, 1828, and is a son of Owen D. Thomas and Emily (Lindsey) Thomas, the father born in what is now Marion County, in 1789, and the mother born in 1794, in Kenton County, Ky. The grandfather of our subject, Lewis Thomas, was a captain in the Revolution, and soon after that struggle, came from Culpeper County, Va., to Kentucky. His wife was a Miss Mary Davis, and they had four children, of whom Owen D. was the youngest. The latter married Emily Lindsey, and reared four sons: Lewis H., Marcus L., John R. and Owen D. Thomas; the father died in 1853, and the mother in 1864. John R. Thomas, a native of Marion County, received a good English education at St. Mary's College, and in 1852 entered the law office of John Shuck as a student, and came to the bar in 1855, but did not enter upon an active practice until later in life, having engaged chiefly in agriculture until 1861, when he was elected to the Lower House of the Kentucky Legislature, where he served until 1867, with credit, being regarded as one of the ablest members of that body, and peculiarly noted for his ardent support of the administration through that most perilous period. In January, 1871, he became the attorney for the commonwealth in his district, serving for one term. In 1858 he married Miss Susan Shuck, who was a bride but a few brief hours, meeting an accidental death from fire on her wedding day. His present wife was Miss Maria L., daughter of Thomas N. Lindsey of Frankfort, Ky. They have been blessed with the following-named children: Thomas (deceased), Owen D., Emily, Lucy B., John R. and Daniel D. Thomas.

DANIEL T. THOMPSON was born October 14, 1845, and is a son of Daniel B. and Malinda (Mattingly) Thompson, to whom seven sons and five daughters were born. D. B. Thompson was reared on Rolling Fork and was a farmer and slave-holder before the war. He is now sixty-seven years old. His father, Richard Thompson, was a native of St. Mary's County, Md., born about 1766. In 1803 he migrated and located near Raywick, Ky. In 1801 he married Elizabeth Kirk of Maryland, the issue being three sons and seven daughters. Richard Thompson went to sea when a lad of ten years, afterward became captain of a ship, and after became an extensive farmer. He was a son of Joseph Thompson of Maryland, of English descent and Roman Catholic faith. Mrs. Malinda Thompson was a daughter of John and Mary (Daley) Matting, who reared a family of four sons and one daughter, all members of the Roman Catholic Church. David T. Thompson was born in Marion County, and received his education in the common schools and St. Mary's College. March 15, 1870, he was united in marriage to Isabella, a daughter of Joseph and Catherine (Mudd) Russell, both natives of Marion County. Mr. Russell is a well-to-do farmer; was a slave-holder. Mr. and Mrs. Thompson have had born to them five children: Sallie Catherine, Joseph Russell,

Susan B., John Lynn and Mary Isabella. They are all members of the Roman Catholic Church. After marriage Mr. Thompson located in Washington County, but finally settled about two miles west of Lebanon, on 300 acres of fine land, and has given considerable time to stock raising and trading, shipping mostly mules to the South. In September, 1875, he was appointed Government storekeeper. In politics he is an active Democrat.

WILLIAM L. THOMSON is a native of Inverness, Scotland, and was born February 24, 1843. His parents, James and Agnes J. (Jackson) Thomson, had six children, of whom William L. was the fourth. He remained at home until he reached the age of seventeen years, receiving an academical education in the Royal Academy at Inverness. In 1860 he was bound as an apprentice to learn civil engineering; after the expiration of his term, which lasted five years, he was made assistant engineer on the Caledonia Railway, in which capacity he acted four years. He then, in company with Charles MacRitchie, now of the firm of MacRitchie & Nichols of Chicago, came to the United States and almost immediately secured the position of assistant engineer on the Milwaukee & St. Paul Railroad. In 1871 he removed to the State of Texas, and assisted in the construction of its first railways, at which he was engaged about nine years. During that time he was united in marriage with Miss Sarah Carter, daughter of Joseph Carter of Danville, Ky. She died about two years subsequent to their marriage. In 1880 Mr. Thomson came to Kentucky, and his marriage with Ellis Green, daughter of Wilson Green, was solemnized, and to their union two children have been born: Lillie and Robert. After his marriage he returned to Texas, and engaged in the construction of the Lorado & Corpus Christi Railroad, thence went to the City of Mexico, where he resided two years; he then returned to Kentucky and purchased a farm in Washington County, on which he has since lived. Mr. Thomson belongs to the Masonic fraternity, and holds his membership in Edinburgh, Scotland. Since becoming a citizen of the United States he has been identified in politics with the Democratic party.

THOMAS THORPE was born November 27, 1834, in the eastern part of Madison County, Ky., and is a son of Thomas and Emma (Hume) Thorpe, to whom four sons and four daughters were born and reared, Thomas being the fifth in the order of birth. Thomas, the father, was born in Madison

County, July 17, 1800; was an extensive farmer and slave-holder; was a Whig politically up to 1860, and then a Democrat. In religion he was what is called a Particular Baptist, and died April 17, 1885. He was a son of Zachariah Thorpe, who was born near the Peaks of Otter, on the James River, Virginia, and who came to Kentucky with his parents as early as 1795. They settled in what is known as Union Precinct, Madison County, and there he met and married Moning Harris, a daughter of Rev. Christopher Harris, a Baptist minister, who reared a family of four sons and three daughters, all of whom moved to Missouri, except Thomas. Zachariah Thorpe left Kentucky with his family and located in Platte County, Mo., in 1832. The grandfather of our subject was also a Thomas Thorpe, who married in Virginia, and lost his wife in Kentucky. He was a soldier in the war for independence, became a leading and substantial farmer and was also engaged in the nursery business. He started and owned the first nursery in Madison County. The Thorpes are of English descent. Mrs. Emma (Hume) Thorpe was born in 1803, in Madison County, Va., and is a daughter of George Hume, who married Susan Crigler, a German lady, and reared a family of three sons and six daughters. He was a son of Reuben Hume, a native of Scotland, and in religion a Baptist. Thomas Thorpe, whose name heads this sketch, was reared on a farm, and at the age of twenty-one commenced farming on his own account. In August, 1862, he enlisted in Company E, Eleventh Confederate Regiment, although the company was organized in East Tennessee. He became first lieutenant of his company and when it was on its march to Kentucky to join its regiment, was captured in Pine Mountain, Tenn. Mr. Thorpe was sent to Johnson's Island and was also imprisoned at Lexington, Camp Chase, Fort McHenry and Fort Norfolk, and was exchanged after a prison life of six months, in October, 1863. He was sent on exchange to Tennessee, and assigned to the Second Battalion, Grigsby's brigade. He participated in the battle of Sweetwater, and in October, 1863, was wounded in the knee and head at Unitia, Tenn. After an hospital experience of six weeks he joined his command and was in the battle of Dug Gap and Resaca, Ga. He was in all the engagements from Resaca to Atlanta, and was under fire forty-three days. From Atlanta he went with a force in pursuit of Gen. Stoneman, who was captured with 1,000 men. With the army he pursued the second regiment to

northern Georgia, where 300 more men were captured with 1,000 horses and mules. After this he was on a raid through East and Middle Tennessee; then joined the army in Virginia and participated in the battles of Saltsville, Bull's Gap and Marion, W. Va. In one engagement he had his horse shot from under him, pierced with seven balls in one volley. He was on the march to re-enforce Gen. Lee when the news came of his surrender. The regiment then marched to North Carolina to join Gen. Johnston and surrendered at Washington, Ga. He was at the last council of war of the Southern Confederacy at Abbeville, S. C. He returned to his home in Kentucky, on horseback and immediately resumed the quiet occupations of farm life. In 1870 he was elected assessor of Madison County, in 1882 was elected county clerk and in 1886 re-elected. He married, February 17, 1885, Florence Shearer of Madison County, daughter of Summers and Amanda (Fowler) Shearer. Mr. and Mrs. Thorpe are members of the United Baptist and Christian Churches respectively. Mr. Thorpe is a member of the F. & A. M., and was a member of the Grange. He cast his first presidential vote for Fillmore, but has since been a Democrat.

R. H. TOMLINSON was born May 22, 1852, in Garrard County, and is a son of Joseph and Elizabeth (Jones) Tomlinson to whom four sons and five daughters were born, all reared with the exception of two sons— R. H. being the third. Joseph Tomlinson was born in 1817, in New Berne, N. C., and with his parents moved to Hendricks County, Ind., about 1824, and settled near Plainfield; at the age of twenty-two located in Garrard County, Ky., where he followed his trade, that of cabinet-maker; after his marriage engaged at farming, which he followed extensively; was reared a Quaker, but after his marriage joined the Methodist Episcopal Church; was a Whig before the war; was a strong advocate for the Union and in politics was a Republican; was a son of William and Kaziale (Bland) Tomlinson, who were raised in North Carolina; they were plain Quakers; emigrated to Hendricks County, Ind., where he died in 1825; he was a farmer; his father came from Ireland. Elizabeth (Jones) Tomlinson was born in Garrard County, only child and daughter of Hugh L. and Judith (Moss) Jones. Hugh L. Jones was born and reared in Georgia. He was teacher and steamboatman; he lived about six years in Kentucky. His wife had married for her first husband A. Taylor, by whom four sons and two daughters were born. R. H. Tomlinson was reared on a farm and received a good education; graduated at Asbury University, Green Castle, Ind., in 1872, and at the law school at Lexington, in 1873; in the following year located in Lancaster, where he was admitted to the bar and has met with success; served as city attorney and police judge of Lancaster; he has been nominated three times by the Democrats of his county to represent them in the Legislature, but has each time declined to accept; was also appointed a delegate to the National Democratic Convention in 1884, but not desiring political honors did not attend. He has been chairman of the County Democratic Committee for seven years; is the attorney for Kansas City Railway Company, also for the Cincinnati Southern Railway; he is the attorney and a director of the Building & Loan Association, also a member of the board of trustees of Garrard Female College, the charter of which was procured in the winter of 1862–63; he is a leading member of the I. O. O. F. and K. of H.; was married September 19, 1877, to Lula M. Marrs, a daughter of Stephen and Margaret (Roberson) Marrs, natives of Kentucky. This union of Mr. Tomlinson has been blessed with two children: Maggie M. and Harry D. Mr. Tomlinson and wife are members of the Methodist Episcopal and Presbyterian Churches. His first presidential vote was for Tilden in 1876. He is a strong advocate of temperance.

JUDGE DAVID T. TOWLES was born January 6, 1830. He is the youngest of six sons and two daughters, all of whom lived to be grown except one boy and one girl, born to George W. and Fanny (Mason) Towles, who were born in Culpeper County, Va., respectively in 1790 and 1800. They immigrated to Green County in 1825, and located where David T. Towles was born, near Summersville. George W. Towles was an attorney, and was elected to represent Green County in the Legislature of 1846 and 1848. He was a son of Joseph Towles, who married Elizabeth Wetherall; both were born in Virginia, and came to Green County about 1825. Judge D. T. Towles was reared in Summersville and attended the common schools and laid the foundation for a good education which he finished at St. Mary's College, Marion County. At the age of twenty-one he commenced the study of law, and was admitted to the bar in 1854. In September, 1850, he was united in marriage to Martha A., a daughter of David and Tabitha (Holland) Montgomery, natives of Kentucky and

North Carolina respectively. Mr. Montgomery was a farmer and miller. Mr. and Mrs. Towles had born to them eight children: Bettie, Sallie, Lucy, Bennie (all deceased), George W., David M. Lena L. and Willie (deceased). Mr. and Mrs. Towles are members of the Methodist Episcopal Church. After marriage they located on the south side of Green River. In September, 1861, Mr. Towles raised Company A, Thirteenth Kentucky, was made its captain, and was in the battle of Shiloh. In April, 1862, he resigned, returned home and was elected clerk of Green County, which place he held for twelve years. In 1882 he was elected county judge and had been elected assessor in 1857. In 1846 he enlisted in Company B, Second Kentucky, to serve in the Mexican war, and was in the battle of Buena Vista. In 1874 he was defeated for commonwealth attorney. He is a member of the F. & A. M., and in politics is a Democrat. His wife's grandmother was captured by the Indians while on the way from North Carolina to Kentucky, with a large party of immigrants. The party were all killed by the Indians. She was scalped and left for dead, but survived, and another party picked her up and brought her to Kentucky, and settled in Green County, where she lived to be a very old lady.

MICHAEL L. TROUTMAN was born January 9, 1842, and is the third of three sons and five daughters born to Peter and Elizabeth (Shawler) Troutman. Peter Troutman was born in Laurens District, South Carolina, in 1807. When he arrived at maturity he immigrated to Bullitt County, Ky.; was a tanner by trade and a farmer; served several terms as constable and died March 10, 1861. He was a son of Michael L. Troutman, of German origin, who married a Miss Beard—both natives of Pennsylvania. In an early day he came to where Louisville now stands and entered 160 acres of land. It at that time being a sickly place, he abandoned the land and moved to South Carolina, where he remained till his death. Some of his children still hold lands at Louisville. Mrs. Elizabeth Troutman was born in Bullitt County, Ky., and was a daughter of Jacob Shawler and Mary Beard, both natives of Maryland, and among the early pioneers of Bullitt County, Ky. Michael L. Troutman was born and raised on a farm in Bullitt County and received a common education. After his father's death he remained with his mother till he was twenty-eight years old. April 6, 1871, he was united in marriage to Sarah A. Howlett, of Bullitt County, a daughter of Luke and Elizabeth (Lee) Howlett. After marriage he located on a farm of his own. His wife died in 1872. His second wife was Mrs. Mary E. Mobley, of Bullitt County, a native of Washington County, and daughter of Thomas and Katie (Lockhart) Shehan. The issue from this second marriage was one child, Ora Kate. He and wife are respectively members of the Baptist and Methodist Episcopal Churches. In the spring of 1882 he located at Nelsonville and entered the mercantile business; he also served as county assessor of Bullitt County one term. Since August, 1885, he has been agent for the Louisville & Nashville Railroad at Nelsonville. He is the owner of 800 acres of land in Bullitt County, where he has started a large orchard, with the intention of turning his attention to its cultivation. In politics he is a Democrat.

DR. DE WITT C. TUCKER was born near Lebanon, Ky., October 3, 1832, and is the eleventh child of four sons and eight daughters (eleven of whom lived to be grown) born to James H. and Nancy (Kennett) Tucker. James H. was born in Virginia in 1787, and was brought to Kentucky about 1790 by his parents; he located in Marion County; was an extensive farmer, and soldier of 1812, and died in 1870. He was a son of Rev. John Tucker, a Methodist Episcopal minister who was born in Virginia, and immigrated to Adair County, Ky., about 1790 and settled on Green River, northeast of Columbia in a fort. While the boys were out hunting, Mr. and Mrs. Tucker took a stroll around the fort and were both killed by the Indians. A negro, Stepny, who came with them, took the children and remained out in the cane till the next day; one of them, an infant, seemed to know by instinct its situation and kept perfectly quiet during the night. The six children—Matthew, Edmond, James Hall, Clarinda, Polly and Frances—were taken and reared by different parties. Edmond when grown moved to Mississippi; Matthew and Clarinda after marriage moved to Missouri. DeWitt C.'s mother was born in Maryland, and died about 1856 at the age of sixty-four years. She was a daughter of John and Ann (Crownover) Kennett. They came from Maryland, and were the earliest settlers of Rolling Fork; the father was said to have been the best Indian trailer known in that country, and was of German extraction. The Doctor was reared on a farm, and received his education at St. Mary's College; at the age of twenty commenced the study of physic under his brother, James H. In 1864 located at Danville, and has succeeded in building a large and extensive practice.

At the age of twenty-four graduated at the Kentucky School of Medicine; in 1865 at Louisville University; in 1866 at Bellevue, New York; in 1867 attended Louisville Medical College. He is a member of the County Medical Association, also of the State and American Medical Association, of Central Kentucky Medical Association, also a member of Boyle County Board of Health; owns three farms southeast of Rolling Fork, in Marion County, containing 800 acres of productive land, and an elegant residence in Danville, Ky., and is largely interested in real estate in the Northwest. He married Miss Annie Magoffin, a daughter of ex-Gov. Beriah Magoffin, January 10, 1872, and their offspring are Anna Imogene, De Witt Clinton, Virginia Gertrude, and Bariah Magoffin. His wife is a member of the Presbyterian Church; he is a Mason and Knight Templar. He is a Democrat and his first presidential vote was for the Democratic ticket.

ROBERT M. TUCKER was born in Green County, Ky., July 21, 1833, and is the fourth of nine children born to William and Melinda (Sherrill) Tucker, both natives of Green County and of Irish descent. William Tucker was born November 17, 1806, and was left an orphan at the age of eight or ten years, after which he was bound out to learn the shoemaker's trade. After his marriage he acquired a very fair practical business education by diligent study and the assistance of his wife, who taught him his letters. He was married November 18, 1828, and for several years followed his trade. About 1841 he moved to Taylor County, Ky., and bought a farm about three miles east of Campbellsville, where he was successfully engaged in agricultural pursuits until 1855, when he sold the farm and returned to Greensburg, Green County, and resumed his trade. In 1861 or 1862 he was elected jailer of Green County; was re-elected, served several years, and was also appointed sheriff of the county by the court. He was first a member of the old Whig party, and a great admirer of Henry Clay, and during the civil war was uncompromising in his devotion to the Union and the old flag, two of his sons serving through the entire struggle. His death occurred June 2, 1877. He and Mrs. Tucker were members of the United Baptist Church in which he officiated as deacon for many years, and also held other official positions. His father, Paschal Tucker, was a native of North Carolina, but when a young man, in the latter part of the last century, came to Green County, Ky. He was a veteran of the Revolution. Mrs. Melinda (Sherrill) Tucker was born July 30, 1808. She is yet living and resides at Greensburg, Green County. Her father, William Sherrill, was born in Scotland, but at an early age came to the colony of Virginia, where he afterward married Mildred Botts and soon after removed to Green County, Ky., where he bought wild land some five or six miles south of Greensburg, where he followed the shoemaker's trade in connection with farming; afterward he left the farm and went to Greensburg, where he followed shoemaking until his death in 1839. He was appointed jailer of Green County by the court, under the old constitution, and held that office for several terms. Robert M. Tucker at the age of seventeen began the blacksmith's trade in Taylor County, serving three years. After completing his trade he opened a shop at Greensburg, and still later at Haskinsville, where he continued until 1857, when he moved to Adair County, and opened a shop on Casey Creek, where he followed his trade exclusively until 1880. He then bought a farm in the same neighborhood, and farmed for two years. Since 1882 he has followed his trade in connection with agricultural pursuits. He has given considerable attention to breeding blooded horses, cattle, hogs and sheep, and has engaged in buying and selling cattle, hogs and sheep. His farm of 200 acres is now well improved. Mr. Tucker has been twice married; first, March 3, 1854, to Miss Nancy E. Knifley, a native of Adair County, Ky., born March 3, 1835. Eleven children have blessed their union, all of whom are yet living: Eliza G. (now Mrs. C. V. McWhorter), Ann A. (widow of Fielding H. Chelf), John H., Sallie M. (now Mrs. C. M. Chelf), Ellen Mc. (now Mrs. Peroy Stayton), Mary E., William O. J., Eveline D., Hardin H., Robert B. and Carrie Nora. Mrs. Nancy E. Tucker departed this life April 23, 1883. From her girlhood she was a member of the Christian Church, and died within ten feet of where she confessed her Savior. Mr. Tucker was next married February 20, 1884, to Mrs. Mary J. (Currey) Galloway, a native of Green County, Ky., a daughter of John D. and Nancy (Lemmons) Currey, natives of Green and Barren Counties, and of Irish and German descent, respectively. John D. Currey's father, William Currey, was born in Virginia, but when only a lad, in the latter part of the last century, came with his parents to Green County, Ky. Mrs. Tucker's maternal grandfather, Reuben Lemmons, was a native of North Carolina. He also removed with his parents to Barren County, Ky., when he was but a small boy. He was

a veteran of the war of 1812 and served under Jackson at the battle of New Orleans. Mr. Tucker was formerly a member of the United Baptist, but now of the Christian Church. Mrs. Tucker still belongs to the United Baptist Church. Mr. Tucker is and has been for many years clerk of his church. He is also a member of the Masonic fraternity, and has held numerous official positions in his lodge. In politics he is a Democrat.

WILLIAM CRAWFORD TURK was born July 7, 1828, in Adair County, Ky. His father, Hiram K. Turk, a native of Virginia, born October 15, 1803, was a son of Thomas and Margaret (Cleaves) Turk, also Virginians. He was a tanner by trade, and in connection with his trade carried on a farm. He was united in marriage March 23, 1823, in Adair County, with Miss Nancy Moore, a daughter of Charles Moore, also a Virginian. She was born in 1800, and is the fourth of eight children. Hiram Turk began life with no inheritance, and by his own industry acquired an estate worth about $8,000 or $10,000, which he left his widow and children. The names of the children born to Hiram and Nancy Turk are Elizabeth, wife of F. A. W. Robertson; Margaret M., wife of Robert Allen; W. C.; Hiram K.; James G.; Christopher C., George and Samuel B., all of whom are living except George. Hiram K. Turk was a member of the Cumberland Presbyterian Church and a life-long Democrat. He conducted a tannery on his farm until a short time before his death, which occurred February 16, 1880. Mrs. Turk has been a life-long member of the Cumberland Presbyterian Church and still resides with her children. Thomas Turk was a first lieutenant in the American Army in the war of 1812, and a native of Virginia; immigrated first to one of the counties of the blue-grass region and later to the county of Adair, where he spent the remainder of his life. The names of his children were Hiram K.; Noah G.; Thomas J.; Amanda, wife of Robert Allen; Eliza, wife of John Crawford; William H.; Caleb P. and Almira. William C. Turk in youth received a fair English education in the common schools of the neighborhood. His early life, until his nineteenth year, was spent on a farm, and his vocation was that of farming and tanning. In October, 1847, he enlisted in Company B, under command of Capt. Squires, of the Fourteenth Kentucky Infantry, which was under the command of Gen. John S. Williams. He served about a year and was a sergeant of his company when they were mustered out of service in July, 1848. October 26, 1848, he was united in marriage with Miss Jane Gilmer, the third of eight children, three of whom are daughters, born to Robert and Sarah (Allen) Gilmer, the former a native of Adair County, and the latter of Cumberland County. Robert Gilmer, a farmer in comfortable circumstances, and one of the oldest in the county, is still living. The union of Mr. and Mrs. Turk has been blessed by the birth of four children: Sarah A., wife of H. C. Walker; William Luther, a physician of Gallion, Hale Co., Ala.; Robert K. (deceased), and Mollie, died in early infancy. Mr. Turk began the world by buying a small tanyard on credit, and carried on the tanning business seven years. In this time, by his industry and economy, he was enabled to buy and pay for a farm of seventy-six acres. That was in 1855, since which time he has devoted his entire attention to farming, stock raising and trading. He has been trading in mules in the South during the past fifteen years, which is the principal line of trade he is engaged in. In 1865 Mr. Turk bought another tract of land adjoining the first, making the home farm of 130 acres, besides which he owns 250 acres of timber land. Mr. and Mrs. Turk are members of the Cumberland Presbyterian Church, and in politics he is a Democrat. Mr. Turk has been a successful farmer and trader, and is one of the leading farmers and among the substantial and respected citizens of Adair County. Dr. James G. Turk was second surgeon of Col. Bramlette's regiment, Federal service, in the late war. Samuel B. Turk was a private in Capt. John Adair's company, Gen. Joe Lewis' regiment, Confederate service.

GEORGE PARSON TURNER was born April 3, 1833, in Mercer County, Ky.; in 1855 removed to Missouri, where he was successfully engaged in the mercantile business until the breaking out of the war; he then returned to Kentucky, and in the year 1865 he removed to Tennessee, where he was again engaged in the mercantile business and cotton planting but was not successful in that enterprise and in 1869 returned to Boyle County, Ky., where he now resides; on November 13, 1884, he united in marriage with Mrs. Lizzie H. Newcomb (nee Miss Mason) of Natchez, Miss. Mr. Turner is a farmer, stock raiser and trader and owner of 292 acres of well improved Boyle County bluegrass land; in politics he affiliates with the Democratic party.

JOSEPH ALLEN TURNER, a native of Adair County, and a merchant, was born March 7, 1841. His father, Joseph Turner, was born near Richmond, Ky., and was brought to Adair County by his parents, Thomas and Hannah (Myers) Turner, while he was yet an infant. He was a farmer and miller and became comparatively wealthy. He married, in January, 1826, while he was in his twenty-fourth year, Miss Susan, daughter of James and Susan (Holly) McGlasson, natives of Bedford County, Va. James McGlasson was a farmer, a very strenuous Democrat and the father of a large family of children, which he reared in Adair County, Ky., to which he immigrated and where he died. Joseph Turner, by his marriage, became the father of eleven children: Francis, Israel, James Marion, William, Martha (wife of O. G. Walkup), Macy Jane (who died in childhood), Mary Susan (wife of Washington Bloyd), David B., J. Allen, Thomas M. and Samuel J. Only three of the family are now living: Mary, Joseph and Thomas M. Joseph Turner began life without a dollar, never held any office except captain and major in the State militia, and by his own industry and management, amassed a fortune of $7,000, most of which was in land to the extent of 1,500 acres. His death occurred in 1876, and forty years of his life he was a consistent Christian, and a deacon in the church at Republican, where he worshiped. Mrs. Turner, also a member of the Christian Church, is still living, in the eighty-second year of her age. Thomas Turner, grandfather of Joseph A., was a native of Bedford County, Va.; was a farmer and miller, and immigrated to Russell County about 1805, and to Adair in 1809. He and wife were both members of the Christian Church and his death occurred in 1855. Joseph Allen Turner began life with a farm worth $1,000. He received a good common-school education in Adair County, and taught a three months' school when he was in his twenty-second year. June 5, 1867, he married Miss Martha J., daughter of Abraham and Rebecca (Morrison) Strange, natives of Adair County, Ky. Four children have been born to him: Zorah B., Luther V., Myrtie Moss and Melvin Holly, who died in infancy. Mr. Turner's farm originally was 145 acres, but is now 300 acres. This he has improved with good buildings, and has it well cultivated. In 1881 he began selling a line of general merchandise at Inroad postoffice, on Crocus Creek, consisting of hardware, groceries, dry goods, clothing, boots, shoes, hats and a line of staple drugs, and does a business of $5,000 per annum, and also buys and rehandles tobacco. Mr. and Mrs. Turner are members of the Christian Church, of which Mr. Turner is a deacon.

THE TUTT FAMILY. Thomas H. Tutt
was born in Scottsville, Allen Co., Ky.,
April 8, 1825, and is the eldest of six children, only three of whom are now living,
born to Richard and Sallie (Hicks) Tutt,
the former a native of Culpeper County, Va.,
and the latter of Green County, Ky., and
both of English descent. Richard Tutt was
born in 1801, and when only five or six years
old was taken by his parents to Nelson
County, Ky., and was left an orphan soon
after coming to this State. When about
fifteen or sixteen years old he went to Greensburg, Green County, where he learned the
saddler's trade with William Hobson, serving an apprenticeship of three years. He
married after completing his apprenticeship,
and soon afterward removed to Scottsville,
where he followed his trade for about eight
or ten years. He then moved to Adair
County, where he was mainly engaged in
farming, but in connection therewith also
followed his trade to some extent until 1858,
when he removed to Johnson County, Mo.
During the war he returned to Kentucky, remaining until the fall of 1869, when he removed to Grayson County, Tex., where he
died February 17, 1870. He was a life-long
member of the Methodist Episcopal Church.
His father, Thomas Tutt, was a native of
Virginia, and served as a captain in the Virginia militia in the Revolutionary war. Sallie L. (Hicks) Tutt was born April 6, 1802,
and died September 21, 1875, also a devoted
member of the Methodist Episcopal Church.
Her father, Thomas Hicks, was also a native
of Virginia, and one of the early pioneers of
Green County, Ky. Thomas H. Tutt at the
age of nineteen commenced to learn the
blacksmith's trade at Danville, Ky., serving
an apprenticeship of one year, after which
he opened a shop of his own at Columbia,
Adair Co., Ky., where he remained two
years. In 1851 he moved to Milltown, same
county, where he has since resided, and
where he followed his trade for some thirty
years. He also owns a good farm near the
village and is exclusively engaged in agricultural pursuits. He was married January 11,
1846, to Miss Susan A. Mercer, a native of
Adair County, born February 28, 1823.
She is a daughter of Peter and Catherine
(Euing) Mercer, natives of Culpeper County,
Va., and Adair County, Ky. To Mr. and
Mrs. Tutt have been born three children:
James R., April 12, 1847; Sarah C., April
7, 1849 (now the wife of W. E. Johnson),
and Nathaniel M., born August 27, 1851.
Mr. and Mrs. Tutt were formerly members of
the Christian Church. He is a Democrat,
politically, and a member of the Masonic
fraternity. James R. Tutt at the age of
fifteen commenced to learn the blacksmith's
trade with his father, and followed the same
for some fifteen years, the last five on his
own account. He was then employed as a
salesman in a general store at Knob Lick,
Metcalfe County, for about one year, and in
a store at Milltown, Adair County, for another year. He then conducted a grocery
store at the same place on his own account
for one year, but for the last six years has
been engaged in general merchandising at
Milltown, where he is doing a thriving business. He carried a well selected stock of
about $5,000, his annual sales amounting to
from $10,000 to $15,000, and he also owns
a valuable farm near his home; for the past
fifteen years he has been postmaster at Milltown. He married, September 25, 1881,
Miss Hettie P. Caldwell, a native of Adair
County, born February 23, 1859. She was
a daughter of Jerry D. and Jennie M.
(Tresenriter) Caldwell, both natives of Adair
County, and of English and Scotch descent,
respectively. To Mr. and Mrs. James R.
Tutt was born one daughter, Hettie P., July
5, 1882. Mrs. Tutt died October 30 of the
same year, a member of the Baptist Church.
Mr. Tutt belongs to no church, but is a
member of the Masonic fraternity, and has
held numerous official positions in his lodge,
and represented the grand lodge of the State
several times. In politics he is a Democrat.
Nathaniel M. Tutt received an excellent
English and scientific education at the common schools and Columbia Christian College,
and after leaving the latter, taught in the
common schools of the county for some four
years. In April, 1881, he opened a grocery
store at Milltown, to which he soon afterward added drugs, and has since been doing
a flourishing business. He carries a well
selected stock in his line, valued at about
$1,200 or $1,500, his annual sales amounting to some $5,000. For the last four years
he has held a commission as notary public,
and for two years prior to that was deputy
county clerk. Although a young man, Mr.
Tutt is a party leader in his part of the
county, and in 1886 was nominated by the
Democratic convention for circuit court clerk
and was elected.

GEORGE W. VANARSDALL was born
April 29, 1827. His father, Cornelius B.
Vanarsdall, a native of New Jersey, removed
in early childhood with his parents to Mercer County, Ky., and located on Salt River.
He was a farmer, a Methodist, a Union man,
and died in 1862, at the age of sixty-six

years. He was the son of Cornelius O. Vanarsdall of New Jersey, a farmer, and carpenter, great framer, church and barn builder, Methodist and Democrat, who died about 1839, aged over eighty years. He married Betsey Vanarsdall, and their offspring were John, Cornelius B., Abram, Jacob, Polly (Harris), Jane (Boice), Peter, Alexander, Lucy (Adkins) and Isaac. Cornelius B. married Polly, daughter of Jacob Smock, of Mercer County (died in 1865, aged over sixty years), and from their union sprang Ann (Brown), Elizabeth (McGrath), James M., Harriet (Mitchell), George W., John W., Nannie (deceased) and Edward M. George W. Vanarsdall married, December 18, 1849, Miss Elizabeth, daughter of John and Elizabeth (Sharp) Adams of Mercer County (born in 1830), and to them have been born Charles, Emma C., Willia A. T., J. Wesley, U. S. Grant, Mary N. and Benjamin F. In youth Mr. Vanarsdall, a native of Mercer County, learned the carpenter trade, which he followed with fair success for thirty years. Being cast upon his own resources he struggled against adverse circumstances until by industry and frugality his labors have been crowned with an ample competency. He is now engaged in farming and stock raising, having 245 acres of land in a high state of cultivation. He is a member of the Christian Church, and in politics is a Republican.

JOHN WESLEY VANARSDALL was born October 4, 1829. In 1867 he located on the Danville pike, three miles southeast of Harrodsburg, where he has since resided. His father, Cornelius B. Vanarsdall, a native of New Jersey, removed in childhood with his parents to Mercer County, Ky., and located on the waters of Salt River; he was a farmer, a Methodist, a Union man, and died in 1862 at the age of sixty-nine years. He was the son of Cornelius O. Vanarsdall, a farmer, a Methodist, a Democrat, who died about 1839, aged over eighty years. He married Betsey Vanarsdall, and their offspring were John, Cornelius B., Abram, Jacob, Polly (Harris), Jane (Boice), Peter, Alexander, Lucy (Adkins) and Isaac. Cornelius B. espoused in marriage Polly B., daughter of Jacob Smock, of Mercer County (died in 1865, aged sixty-seven years), and their union was favored by the birth of Ann (Brown), Elizabeth (McGrath), James M., Harriett (Mitchell), George W., John W., Nannie (deceased) and Edward M. November 1, 1860, John W. married Miss Anna M., daughter of Isaac S. and Eudocia (Rupard) Miller, of Mercer County, born January 16, 1842, and to them have been born Mary Cornelia, Joseph Atwood, George Boone, Katie Clifford, Stanley Miller and Wesley Willard. Mr. Vanarsdall is a native of Mercer County, and engaged in the business of carpenter and builder for fifteen years, constructing many of the best buildings in Mercer County. He is now a farmer, owning 230 acres of well improved land. He is a member of the Christian Church, and in politics is identified with the Democratic party. Isaac S. Miller was born in Clark County November 12, 1813. His father, Joseph Miller, a Virginian by birth, died about 1831. Eudocia (Rupard) Miller was born November 18, 1822, was married to Isaac S. Miller November 19, 1840, and their children are Anna M. (Vanarsdall), Joseph W., Isaac S., George W., Sue R. (Hedges), Mattie H. (Berry) and Katie (Berry).

JAMES W. VANARSDALL was born January 31, 1849, at Parksville, Boyle Co., Ky. In 1878 he located at Shelby City, and in 1883 at Junction City, where he has since resided. His father, Isaac Vanarsdall, was born in 1818, near Parksville, where he is now living. He was formerly an old line Whig, and is a member of the Cumberland Presbyterian Church. He is the son of Brooks Vanarsdall, of Mercer (now Boyle) County, a farmer and slave-holder, who died in 1868, at the age of eighty-seven years. His offspring are Sterling, Bernetta (May), of Missouri, and Isaac. Isaac first married Catherine Gibson, of Lincoln County (died in 1853, aged forty-two years) and from their union sprang Lizzie (White), John B. and James W. His second wife was Narcisse Edwards, and their children are Lee, Charley and Bernetta. In September, 1878, James W. Vanarsdall was married to Miss Mollie W., daughter of William D. and Mary E. (Ridgeway) Latimer, of Parksville (born in 1861), and to them have been born Lulie Dell, Earnest and Mary. Mr. Vanarsdall clerked nine months for L. B. Baker, of Parksville, and in 1874 commenced the drug business there on his own account, which he enlarged into general merchandise, which he carried to Shelby City, and finally to his present location, where he is now successfully engaged in business. By industry, economy, and close attention to business, he is securing a comfortable competency. He is a member of the K. of H. and in politics is a Democrat.

JACKSON VANARSDELL was born September 30, 1831, and is a son of C. C. Vanarsdell, a native of New Jersey, where he was born in 1780. C. C. came to this State in an early day and settled in Mercer County. His father was also C. C. Vanarsdell. Jackson Vanarsdell was brought up on the home farm, in his native county of Mercer, receiving a common-school education. He has accumulated considerable property, owning a good farm of 354 acres of land, also a distillery which he operates six months of the year. His distillery has a capacity of 400 gallons per day, and is valued at $30,000. Mr. Vanarsdell was married to Miss Jane P. Brewer, by whom he has five children. She died and he afterward married Mrs. M. E. Bush. He and his family are members of the Presbyterian Church.

WILLIAM ALFRED VANARSDELL was born February 5, 1834, on the waters of Salt River, Mercer County, Ky., where he grew to manhood, and in 1866 he located in the pleasant village of McAfee, where he has since resided. In 1861 he enlisted in Company F, Nineteenth Kentucky Infantry, colonel, Landram, and remained in the service for about four years. His father, John J. Vanarsdell, a native of Mercer County, was a soldier in the war of 1812, was a farmer, and died in 1867 at the age of seventy-two years. He was the son of James Vanarsdell, a native of New Jersey, who removed to Kentucky in 1778, and with others, in times of danger, occupied the fort at Stanford. He married Betsey Bean, and their offspring were Isaac, William, John J., James P. and Bettie (Rice). John J. married Mary, daughter of Peter Cozine, of Mercer County (died in 1884 at the age of seventy-one years), and from their union sprang William A., James, John, Isaac, Sarah (Hawkins) and Lucy (Cozine). September 7, 1854, William A. was united in marriage to Miss Margaret, daughter of James and Diana (Dean) Thompson, of Mercer County, born May 4, 1836, and to them have been born John, Mattie (Sorrel), Susan, Annie, Addie, William R. and Minnie L. Since the year 1851, with the exception of the period of his army life, Mr. Vanarsdell has been engaged in blacksmithing with fair success. Without assistance in the beginning of his business career, he has had to rely upon his own efforts, and by a strict adherence to business has secured a comfortable competency. He is a member in good standing in the I. O. O. F. and also in the A. F. & A. M. In his religious profession he is a Baptist, and in politics is identified with the Republican party.

J. B. VAN CLEAVE was born November 24, 1836, and is a son of C. A. Van Cleave, who was twice married, first to Sarah Beam, who bore five sons and three daughters, and next to Paulina Beall, who bore seven sons and one daughter. C. A. Van Cleave was born and reared near Loretto, Marion County, and was a leading and substantial farmer and slave owner; served several terms as magistrate, and died in 1863, aged sixty-three years. His father, Aaron Van Cleave, was one of the earliest and most substantial pioneer farmers in Marion County. Mrs. Paulina Van Cleave was born in Nelson County, and was a daughter of Jacob Beall, who was one of the pioneer farmers of that part of Kentucky, and who was a Democrat in politics. J. B. Van Cleave, born ten miles west of Lebanon, received a liberal education, and September 14, 1858, was married to Lucy Knott. To this union seven children were born, five living: Fannie, Hattie (Parrott), Thomas W., Benjamin L. and Mary M. Mrs. Hattie Parrott has one child, Edward M. Parrott. After marriage, Mr. Van Cleave migrated to Lewis County, Mo., and after a residence of fourteen months, returned to Marion County, Ky. In 1870 he located where he now resides, on Prather's Creek, on a farm of 300 acres, which he has improved with substantial buildings and a fine young orchard. About 240 acres of this farm are cleared and in a good state of cultivation, all of which he has accumulated by his own industry and perseverance. Mr. Van Cleave is well informed in current literature of the day, and takes great interest in educating his children. He and wife and all his children, except the youngest, are devoted and active members of the Methodist Episcopal Church. His wife is a daughter of Thomas P. and Fannie (Payne) Knott, who were born in Virginia and Maryland, respectively. Thomas P. Knott was a farmer and surveyor, and an uncle of Gov. Knott. Mr. Van Cleave is an active member of the Masonic fraternity, and in politics is a Democrat.

DAVID W. VANDEVEER. Among the very early settlers in Casey County, Ky., was the family of George Vandeveer and his wife, Elizabeth, whose maiden name was Logan. George Vandeveer was a native of Pennsylvania, from which State he removed to North Carolina, coming thence to Kentucky, as above stated. He was a soldier in the Revolutionary war, and was present at the surrender of Cornwallis, at Yorktown. He had a family of eight children, the eldest of whom was John L. Vandeveer, the father of David W., of Stanford, Ky. John L. was born in North Carolina, and was a mere lad when the parents settled in Kentucky. He married Sallie Jones, a native of Virginia, and daughter of David Jones, one of the pioneers of Casey County, Ky. They spent their subsequent life in their adopted county, rearing, meantime, a family of fourteen children, of whom David W. is the eldest, and of whom but five are now living. David W. Vandeveer was born in the year 1820, in Casey County; received a common-school education; served his native county as sheriff under the old constitution, and in 1849 declined to accept the nomination for representative from that county. Though he takes a lively interest in the advancement of the principles of Democracy, he prefers to devote himself to merchandising, which has been his life business, and in the pursuit of which he removed to Stanford, Ky., in 1855. His first wife, to whom he was married in 1855, was Sallie Coffey, daughter of C. R. Coffey, now of Owensboro, Ky. She died in 1856, after which he married Miss Martha Lunsford, which union was blest with three children, viz.: Sallie, Mattie and Nannie Vandeveer. Mr. Vandeveer is an honored member of the Masonic fraternity and of the Christian Church.

JOHN MILTON VAN METER was born June 21, 1842, in Clark County, Ky., and in 1862 enlisted in Company E, Eighth Kentucky Confederate Regiment, Morgan's command; was captured on the Ohio raid, and remained a prisoner of war at Camps Chase and Douglas until the close of the war. His father, Isaac Van Meter, a native of Hardy County, Va., removed to Clark County, Ky., when a young man, where he engaged in farming and stock breeding, and was among the first to introduce shorthorn cattle into the State. He was for many years a deacon in the Presbyterian Church, an old line Whig, and died about 1855, at the age of sixty-four years. He married Rebecca, daughter of Capt. Isaac and Sarah (Harness) Cunningham, of Clark County (born in 1800, died in 1864) and their union resulted in the birth of Solomon, Isaac C., Jacob, Susan (Allen), Sarah A. (Hall), Rebecca (deceased), Eliza C. (deceased), Amanda E. (deceased), Benjamin F., Thomas C., William (deceased), Abram, Lewis M.· and John M. On March 29, 1866, John M. Van Meter was married to Miss Alice, daughter of Rev. Stephen and Amanda (Lovell) Yerkes, of Boyle County (born in Maryland, August 19, 1843), and to them have been born Ama Y., Susan A., Adie L. (deceased), John M. (deceased), Lizzie S. and Alice Y. In 1862 Mr. Van Meter graduated at Centre College, Danville, and in 1868 in the law department of the Kentucky University at Lexington, and practiced law two years in partnership with Judge Morton of Lexington. In 1870 he located on a farm in Woodford County, where he remained until 1883, when he sold the farm for $120 per acre, and purchased 437 acres of land in Boyle County, three miles south of Danville, where he now resides. His farm is in good condition, well improved, and in a fine state of cultivation. He has a nice herd of shorthorn cattle on the place; considerable space has been devoted to fruit culture, and he has one of the most extensive and thrifty vineyards in the vicinity. For sixteen years Mr. Van Meter has been an elder in the Southern Presbyterian Church. In politics he is a Democrat. His grandfather, Capt. Isaac Cunningham, was a soldier in the war of 1812, and represented Clark County in the Legislature. Isaac Cunningham has entertained Henry Clay and Daniel Webster at his house.

SANFORD D. VAN PELT was born October 15, 1836, in Lexington, Ky., and is the third of three sons and three daughters born to Sanford B. and Lucinda I. (Young) VanPelt, who were born in Fayette and Woodford Counties, respectively. He was born in 1808, and she in 1809. Sanford B. VanPelt was a combmaker by trade, at which he worked in his young days, afterward became a shoe merchant at Lexington. He was a zealous and uncompromising Union man during the war; was the owner of slave property, was serving as constable at the time of his death in 1872. He was a son of William VanPelt, Sr., who was born in Culpeper County, Va. William VanPelt, Sr., married Anna M. Boyer, of Frederick, Md.; they came to Kentucky as early as 1795, and located in Fayette County. He cast his first vote for Gov. Shelby, was drafted in the war of 1812, but hired a substitute; was a combmaker by trade, served as market master at Lexington for many years, also a farmer for a short time near Lexington. He served on city council for many years, was a zealous Whig, one of the first settlers of Lexington, and died in 1871, at the age of eighty-nine years. His ancestors came from Holland, and settled in New York, under Gov. Stuyvesant. Lucinda I. (Young) VanPelt was the daughter of David and Nancy Young; they were pioneers of Woodford County, and slave owners. Sanford D. VanPelt was reared in Lexington, and received a good English education; spent several years in Transylvania University, and one year at Kentucky University, Harrodsburg, and then spent a short time teaching; at eighteen he commenced a trade. During the war, being a zealous Union man, he left the community in which he was living and went to Louisville, where he enlisted in the Union Army; in September, 1862, he enlisted in Company F, Eleventh Kentucky Cavalry, under Capt. B. C. Blincoe, participated in all the engagements in which the regiment took any part; was mustered in as first sergeant, September, 1862; was detailed as clerk in brigade quartermaster's department, where he remained until May, 1863, when he was promoted to first lieutenant, Company A, Seventh Kentucky Cavalry, by order of Gen. Rosecrans, then commanding the Army of the Cumberland. With this regiment he served to the close of the war, acting as regimental quartermaster a portion of the time, but was in command of his company in all active service. He was mustered out July 10, 1865, at Edgefield, Tenn., then returned to Harrodsburg, and November, 1865, located permanently in Danville, from which town he entered the army in 1862. Since his return he has resumed his trade (marble cutter), which he has followed ever since. He was married July, 1866, to Florence P. Taylor, daughter of William R. and Eliza J. (Jackson) Taylor, natives respectively of Lancaster and New York, and of Irish and German extraction. This union has been blessed with eight children: Cora W., Hiram P., Hallie Y., John W. (deceased), Whelan C., Milton D., Florence (deceased) and Nina C. Mr. and Mrs. VanPelt are members of the Christian Church. He is a member of the F. & A. M., in good standing, also of the G. A. R. In politics he is an active Republican, and cast his first presidential vote for Bell and Everett; he is also an active temperance man and prohibitionist.

SAMUEL ALLEN VAN SICKLE was born December 23, 1842, in Marion County, Ky., and in 1866 located on Salt River, six miles west of Danville, Boyle County, where he has since retained his residence. His father, Samuel Van Sickle, a native of Pennsylvania, was born August 28, 1794, removed to Kentucky in youth, was a farmer and slave-holder, and died November 12, 1863. He was the son of Anthony Van Sickle, an immigrant to Pennsylvania, whose offspring beside Samuel were Jesse, Eli, Joseph, Patsey (Pritchett), and a son who went west whose name is not remembered. Samuel married Rachael Swan, of Pennsylvania, and from their union sprang Elizabeth (Adams), Martha (Askren and Means), Rebecca (Paddocks), Sarah (Thomure), Mary (deceased), Maria J. (Kimble) and Samuel A. His second marriage was to Mrs. Elnora Sutton (nee Root), and their children are

Jesse G. and Mary L. (Aldrich). January 1, 1868, Samuel A. Van Sickle was united in marriage with Miss Maria O., daughter of Osborn and Eliza (Lobb) Clemmons, of Boyle County (born December 2, 1846), and to them have been born Minnie and Emma C. Osborn Clemmons was born near St. Mary's, Marion Co., Ky., was a merchant at Perryville, and died in 1847. His children are Mary E. (Hardin) and Maria O. (Van Sickle). After the death of her husband Mrs. Clemmons married Jehu Harlan, and their one child was Minerva (deceased). Mr. Van Sickle was educated at the common schools of the country, and has improved his opportunities by reading standard works and current literature. He is a successful farmer, and is a member of the Methodist Episcopal Church South, also a member of the Masonic fraternity, and is a Democrat.

JOHN S. VAN WINKLE was born March 8, 1829, in Wayne County, Ky. He is the eighth and youngest son of six sons and four daughters (all of whom lived to be grown except one son) born to Micajah and Mary (Phillips) Van Winkle, natives of North Carolina. Micajah Van Winkle was born on Adkin River in 1792, and in 1798 was brought to Lincoln County, Ky.; was an active and influential citizen of Wayne County, to which he had moved with his parents; served as magistrate and sheriff of Wayne for many years; in 1853, with his family, located in Jasper County, Iowa, where he carried on farming until his death. He was a son of Abraham Van Winkle, a native of Maryland, who with his parents went to Virginia and thence to North Carolina, where he married a Miss Charity Sallee; thence moved to Lincoln County, Ky., in 1798, and thence to Wayne County, where he filled the office of justice and sheriff for a number of years; had a brother in the battle of King's Mountain. In 1837 he located in Morgan County, Ill., where many of his descendants still live. Some of his children were emancipationists. He died about 1845, at the age of eighty-five years. His ancestors came from Holland with Peter Stuyvesant. Mrs. Mary (Phillips) Van Winkle was a daughter of Cornelius Phillips, who married a Miss Shores, both of North Carolina. They settled in Wayne County about 1800. Cornelius Phillips was an influential farmer and slave owner, served as magistrate and sheriff of Wayne County, and was of English origin. John S. Van Winkle was raised on a farm, and received an academic education at Monticello. At eighteen years he entered a store as a salesman and served four years. In 1852 he began the study of law with his brother, Hon. E. L. Van Winkle; graduated in the law department of the University of Louisville, and was licensed and admitted to the bar in 1854; opened an office and practiced in his native county. In 1861 he was elected to represent his county in the Legislature; in 1863 located in Danville; in 1866 was appointed secretary of State by Gov. Thos. E. Bramlette, and at the expiration of his term resumed the practice of law at Danville. He has been engaged considerably in stock ranching and lumbering; has had considerable to do with developing the coal fields of Kentucky, in which he has an interest. For a short time he was paymaster for Kentucky troops. He was married January 21, 1858, to Mary Buster, of Wayne County, a daughter of Gen. Joshua Buster, of Monticello, Ky., who married Miss Chrisman, and who served as an officer in the war of 1812. Mr. Van Winkle's wife died in December, 1859, and he was next married January 24, 1867, to Louise Dillon, daughter of Frank Dillon, who married a Miss Julian. They were natives of Virginia and settled in Franklin County about 1810, and were of Irish and French descent, respectively. Mr. and Mrs. Van Winkle had born to them seven children: Frank D., John S., Edwin L., Julian P., Arthur C., Ernest Alfred and Mary Louise. Mr. and Mrs. Van Winkle affiliate with the Methodist Episcopal Church South. He is a member of the F. & A. M.; cast his first presidential vote for Gen. Scott; since 1860 he has been conservative rather than radical in his political views, yet decidedly national and liberal in his sympathies and convictions.

WILLIAM N. VAUGHAN was born April 18, 1823, and is the third of three sons and seven daughters born to John and Margaret (Edrington) Vaughan. John Vaughan was born in Amelia County, Va., in 1794, near the place where Lee surrendered, and was the youngest of thirteen children. After his parents' death he was brought to Kentucky by Stephen Board, who settled in Breckinridge County, from which he moved to Green County. He had raised two crops in Green County, when he enlisted in the war of 1812; was at the battle of the Thames, in Canada; was captain of a light-horse company of militia; was a good farmer and died in 1837. He was a son of Nicholas Vaughan, of Welsh extraction, who married Elizabeth Williams and who was a large owner of slaves in Amelia County, Va. Mrs. Margaret Vaughan was born in South Carolina and was a daughter of William Edrington, who was born in the same county (Westmoreland, Va.) that Gen. Washington was. He was at the siege of Yorktown. He was married to Sallie Major; moved to Green County, Ky., in 1802, and died in 1852, aged about eighty years. He was of a long-lived race and had an uncle who lived to be over one hundred years old— of Welsh descent. William N. Vaughan was born three miles south of Campbellsville, Green Co., Ky.; was reared but three months' schooling, which was after he was grown. In 1844 he moved to Greensburg and worked by the month at carpentering; also flatboated to New Orleans. In 1847 he borrowed $500, giving ten per cent interest; paid $300 of a debt and invested $200 in groceries and continued to sell groceries till 1861, when he worked into dry goods exclusively; has had the best of success; has always been able to pay 100 cents on the dollar, but made one bad venture and lost about $7,000 in an oil speculation. During the war he was an uncompromising Union man and lost all his goods by guerrillas led by Champ Ferguson. Mr. Vaughan was appointed magistrate by Gov. Morehead, and was one of the directors in the Bank of Kentucky; was united in marriage April 18, 1850, to Miss Amanda S. Moore, a daughter of Richard L. and Eleanor (Hilliard) Moore, natives of Georgetown, Ky. Richard Moore was one of the soldiers of 1812, and was at the battle of the Thames. He was the eldest of seventeen children: moved to Logan County, Ky., where he farmed for a short period, when he learned the tailor's trade in Russellville, and afterward located in Greensburg, where he passed the rest of his days; he was a magistrate for many years, became quite wealthy and was a member of the Methodist Episcopal Church. He was a son of James Moore, who was a soldier of the Revolution, and who married a Miss Lucas. Both were of Virginia, and early settlers of Green County, Ky. Mr. and Mrs. Vaughan had born to them nine children: Margaret (deceased), Margaret Elizabeth, Elenor F., John R., Sallie C., William N., Charles B. (deceased), James Thomas and Clarence Edward. Mr. and Mrs. Vaughan are members of the Cumberland Presbyterian and Methodist Episcopal Churches respectively. He is a member of the Masonic fraternity. He cast his first presidential vote for Henry Clay, but since the war has been a Republican.

WILLIAM BUSH VIVIAN was born August 1, 1801, three miles from Boonesborough, in Clark County, Ky., where he remained until 1836, when he located on the Samuel

Taylor place, two miles south of Pleasant Hill, Mercer County, where he has since resided. His father, Thomas Vivian, a native of Culpeper County, Va., was born in 1776, removed with his parents in 1787 to Clark County, Ky., furnished a substitute in the war of 1812; was a farmer and slave-holder, a Whig, at first a Baptist but went with Alexander Campbell in his reformation, was a conscientious, upright man, and died in 1860. He was the son of John Vivian, of Virginia, who died in Kentucky about 1790. John married Martha Gholson, and their offspring were John, Frankie (Bush), Smith, Milton, Lucy (Pemberton), Sally (Crosswait), Thomas, Harvey and Flavel. Thomas first married Nancy, daughter of Francis and Lucy (Davis) Bush of Clark County (born December 5, 1781, died in 1816) and from this union sprang Miranda (Combs), William B., Lucy (Keas), Martin, Sarah A. (Buckner), Thomas J., Albert G. His second wife was Ann Davis, and their children were Mary A. (Emmerson), Willis D., Lucinda A. (Sparrow), Dr. John E., Benjamin T., Martha F. (Spencer) and James H. September 23, 1823, William B. Vivian married Miss Elizabeth, daughter of Ambrose and Mary (Bush) Christy, of Clark County (born July 4, 1805, died August 19, 1860) and to them were born Newton (deceased), Thomas, Lucy M. (Lowe), John W., Simeon C., Augustus M., James H., Ann E. and Benjamin R. Mrs. Lucy M. Lowe was born December 20, 1829, and July 29, 1857, was united in marriage with Mr. James Ralph Lowe, of Clark County (born August 22, 1822, died April 10, 1863), and to them were born two children: William B., August 1, 1858, and Elizabeth C., July 25, 1860 (deceased August 18, 1881). William Vivian is a farmer having 328 acres of land in a good state of cultivation He has given about 300 acres to his children. He was many years an elder in Cane Run Christian Church, was a Union man and lost twelve slaves by the late war. His stone mansion was built in 1790 by Samuel Taylor, whose motto "Look to your laws rather than your progenitors, for inheritance," remains intact on a circular stone in the wall.

DR. GEORGE W. WADDLE was born in Hart County, Ky., August 4, 1844, and is the second child in a family of nine children born to John B. and Martha J. (Reynolds) Waddle, the former a native of the Old Dominion and the latter of Shawneetown, Ill. Both were of English descent. John B. Waddle was born in 1823, and about 1827 was brought by his parents to Hart County, Ky., where he grew to manhood and was

married, receiving such an education in youth as the primitive common schools of Kentucky afforded at that time. In early life he learned the cabinet-maker's trade, which, with farming, has been his chief occupation. For some six or seven years he was deputy sheriff of Hart County, and for the past eight years has served as magistrate, or justice of the peace, of Munfordville District, where he now resides. He belongs to no church or secret order. Mrs. Martha J. Waddle departed this life in the fall of 1854. She was a life-long and devoted member of the Methodist Episcopal Church. George W. Waddle received a good common-school and academic education in youth. At the age of twelve or thirteen years he was employed as a salesman in a drug store in Munfordville, where he remained until the fall of 1861, when he enlisted in Company I, Second Kentucky Volunteer Cavalry (Federal service). He was soon after detailed as assistant hospital steward, and served till the fall of 1863 when he was discharged on account of disability. Notwithstanding he was serving in the medical department, he yet participated in the battles of Shiloh and Corinth, being severely wounded in the left arm in the latter engagement. In the spring of 1864 he re-enlisted in the Thirtieth Kentucky State Guards, who were afterward mustered into the United States service in order to draw their pay. With this regiment he remained until the close of the war, when he came to Campbellsville, Taylor Co., Ky., where he has since been engaged in the practice of medicine. The Doctor was married March 15, 1865, to Miss Martha J. Willock, a native of Taylor County, born November 10, 1845. She is a daughter of David and Phebe T. (Burge) Willock. Six children have blessed their union, viz.: Hattie Lee, Sneed T., William P., David E., Mary E. and George W., Jr. Mrs. Waddle is, and has been from early life, a devoted and consistent member of the Methodist Episcopal Church. The Doctor belongs to no church or secret order. In politics he is a Republican and is one of the successful physicians of the county.

ATTERSON LEWIS WALDEN was born September 26, 1803, in Caroline County, Va.; removed with his parents in 1805 to Lincoln County, Ky., in 1808 to Garrard County, and in 1833 to Mercer County, locating on Cane Run pike, two and one-half miles east of Harrodsburg, where he has since resided. His father, John Walden, a native of Virginia, enlisted at the age of eighteen years in the Continental Army, and remained until the close of the war. He was a farmer and slave-holder, and died aged eighty-five years. He was the son of Lewis Walden, and married Elizabeth Pitts, of Virginia (died in 1854, aged seventy-six years), and from their union sprang Sophia (Douglas), Atterson L., Willis, Melinda (Simpson), Permelia, Payton, John, Elizabeth (Samson) and Angelina (Adams). Atterson Lewis Walden was first married in 1825, to Miss Elizabeth, daughter of Thomas McGinnis, of Mercer County (born in 1802, died in 1877), and to them were born Elizabeth (Lander), Mary (Thompkins), Frances (Prather), Angeline (Garnett) and Theresa I. In 1859 he was married to Mrs. Maria S. Meglone, daughter of William W. and Frances (Sebree) Sharp, of Lexington (born May 15, 1820). Montgomery and Maria S. Meglone's children are Whitney and Mary (Hutchinson). A. L. Walden has been president of the Mercer County Agricultural Association for twenty years. He is a farmer, having 220 acres of productive land, but lost forty-two slaves as a result of the late war. Thomas McGinnis, from the fort at Harrodsburg, pre-empted and settled this place. There is now living, but on the decline, on this farm, a seedling apple tree of his planting, fully one hundred years old, nearly twelve feet in circumference, which has never failed to bear an annual crop since it came into bearing. In politics Mr. Walden is Democrat.

JOHN H. WALKER. Among the early residents of this commonwealth deserving especial mention was William Walker, whose arrival antedates its organization as a State. He emigrated from Virginia several years prior to 1790 and settled in what is now Washington County, where he became an extensive land owner and an active business man. He served in the Revolutionary war, and died in the county of his adoption some time prior to the year 1819. His son, David C. Walker, father of John H., was born six miles northwest of Springfield, June 5, 1797. He was a farmer, became the possessor of a large tract of real estate and was one of the wealthiest men of the county. His wife, Martha S. (Grundy) Walker, was born in Washington County April 22, 1802, and is still living. Her father, Samuel Grundy, son of George Grundy, was a native of Virginia, came to Washington County several years before its organization, and settled on Cartwright's Creek. He became a large land owner and at one time operated four distilleries. He was a brother of the celebrated Judge Felix Grundy, member of Congress and Attorney-general of the United States under President Van Buren. He represented

Washington County in the Legislature, and died a number of years ago. David C. and Martha S. Walker were the parents of fifteen children, only four of whom are now living: Dr. T. R. Walker, John H., E. O. and Lewis D. Walker. John H. Walker, seventh son and eleventh child, was born August 8, 1839. He attended the country schools until his eighteenth year and then entered St. Joseph's College, where he remained one year. Quitting college he went to Mississippi, where he began reading medicine under the instruction of his brother, Dr. S. G. Walker, with whom he remained a little over two years. In 1861 he entered the Confederate service, enlisting in Charles Thompson's company, First Mississippi Infantry, under command of Col. Percy, with which he served a part of one year and then joined Col. Wirt Adams' cavalry, remaining with the same until the close of the war. These regiments formed part of the army of the Mississippi and took part in a number of bloody engagements, among which were Iuka, Corinth, Champion Hill, Vicksburg, Jackson, Raymond and others, through all of which Mr. Walker escaped unhurt. He was discharged in April, 1865, and, after receiving his parole and subscribing to the oath of allegiance, returned to Kentucky, where he has since resided engaged in farming in Washington County, and at the present time owns a beautiful farm of 230 acres, four miles from Springfield. He is a successful stock raiser and one of the active business men of the community. Mr. Walker has never married. He takes considerable interest in political matters and votes the Democratic ticket.

W. S. WALKER was born April 11, 1841, and is a son of John W. Walker, a native of Madison County, Ky., who died in Garrard County in 1885 at the age of eighty-four years. W. S. Walker was brought up on a farm and has followed the business to the present time. He owns 400 acres of excellent land lying near the Richmond and Lancaster pike. Mr. Walker, who is a native of Garrard County, married Miss Denny, a daughter of A. F. Denny. She bore him two children, Lizzie and Belle, and then died. He next married a daughter of H. T. Terrill, who has had six children, viz.: John W., Edwin H., Towles T., Archibald K., Margaret W. and Robert J. Mr. and Mrs. Walker belong to the Presbyterian Church; he votes the Democratic ticket.

JUDGE WILLIAM E. WALKER was born in Richmond, Ky., March 3, 1842, and is a son of Dr. Chas. J. and Nancy (Embry) Walker, who were the parents of ten children, of whom they reared six sons and three daughters. Chas. J. Walker was born in June, 1799, in Madison County, and was graduated from the Lexington School of Medicine; he also attended lectures in St. Louis and for a time was in practice there, and afterward for more than fifty years practiced in Richmond, Ky. He served in both branches of the Kentucky Legislature, and died in 1878. He was a son of James Walker, also a native of Madison County, who married a Miss Estill, of the same place, and reared two sons and three daughters. James was a son of Asaph, of Virginia. Mrs. Nancy (Embry) Walker was born about 1810 in Madison County and was a daughter of Talton Embry, who came from Virginia, was of Scotch descent, and died near Muddy Creek at the age of about ninety-three. William E. Walker was reared on a farm, attended the common schools, then for two years the university at Harrodsburg, and, when the war broke out, he and his brother-in-law, Green Clay, were gone for three years. He then went to Cincinnati and was for two years in the wholesale dry goods business as salesman; then returned to Richmond and engaged in farming. In May, 1872, he married Dorcas M. Leavell, of Garrard County, a daughter of Louis T. and Martha (Lackey) Leavell—the former born in February, 1828 (died in July, 1870), and the latter born in 1830. To William E. Walker and wife have been born five children, viz.: Lewis L., Charles J.. Mattie A., William E. and Green Clay. Soon after his marriage Mr. Walker located where he now resides on thirty acres of land in Lancaster, and he also owns a farm of 512 acres, five miles north of the town. In 1882 he was elected county judge and, in 1886, re-elected. He is a member of the I. O. O. F., and, with his wife, of the Presbyterian Church. In politics he is a Democrat and cast his first presidential vote for George B. MacClellan.

LEWIS D. WALKER, farmer and stock raiser, and fourteenth child of D. C. and Martha S. Walker, was born in Washington County February 26, 1846. He remained with his parents until reaching his majority, and was educated in the common schools, and the Covington Institute at Springfield, which institution he attended several years. He was reared to agricultural pursuits, and commenced farming for himself about the year 1868, taking charge of a part of the paternal homestead, which he now owns. His farm is one of the best improved in the Springfield Precinct, and as a farmer and successful stock raiser he is ranked among the best in the county. In 1878 Mr. Walker was elected magistrate of the Springfield Precinct, which position he still holds. He takes an active part in the deliberations of the county court, and is one of the most careful and methodical business men of the body. He is a Democrat in politics, but not in the strict sense of the term a partisan. Like his brother, J. H. Walker, he has never married, and the two live together upon the beautiful farm of the latter, four miles northwest of Springfield.

J. STONE WALKER, banker and speculator, was born September 15, 1848, in Madison County, and is a son of Owen W. and Carlile D. (Stone) Walker, to whom eight sons and three daughters were born, nine of whom were reared. Owen W. Walker was born April 8, 1801, on Silver Creek, Madison County. He entered mercantile business at the age of eighteen, drifting into banking, which he continued till his death in 1872. He was an active and public-spirited man, and one of the best business men of his county. He was a son of William W. Walker, who was born in Greenbrier County, W. Va., and who, when a boy, was brought to Madison County, and settled near Boonesborough. He became a leading citizen and farmer, and served as magistrate of the county for many years. He married a Miss Bates, who lost her life by a fall at the ripe age of ninety-seven years. He had preceded her some years, and at an advanced age. He was a son of Joel Walker, who in turn was a son of Felix Walker, who had written an interesting narrative of Boone's adventures. He, with seven others (in the winter of 1774-75) from Rutherford County, N. C., set out to explore a country called Leowvisay, containing the best quality of land known, and abounding in wild game. This choice and beautiful country is now known as the blue-grass section of Kentucky. Mrs. Carlile D. Walker was a daughter of James Stone, who was a wealthy and prominent farmer and banker. His wife was a Miss Harris. J. Stone Walker, who ranks as one of the leading and wealthiest citizens of Madison County, was reared in the city of Richmond, where he was partially educated, continuing his studies at Ann Arbor, Mich., and Greencastle, Ind., and graduating from the Kentucky University. In 1868 he entered a bank as clerk. In 1874 he, with his brother and W. M. Irvin, opened a private bank. In 1878 they changed to the Second National Bank, with a capital of $150,000, when he became cashier. In January, 1886, he became the president. He also owns and operates a farm of 545 acres two miles north of Richmond, where he handles all kinds of stock, especially fine jacks. October 10, 1876, he was united in marriage with Ella Moos, of Louisville, Ky., a daughter of Henry S. and Mary (Trigg) Moos. The issue by this union of Mr. and Mrs. Stone is two bright children: Laura and Carlile. Mr. Stone and wife are members of the Episcopal Church. Mr. Stone is one of the leading and active members of the Democratic party, having acted as chairman of the County Democratic Committee for years.

FRANCIS M. WARE was born December 25, 1846, in Pulaski County, Ky., and is a son of Henry G. and Eliza J. (Thompson) Ware. Quite early in the settlement of Pulaski County Rice Ware, the grandfather of Francis M., came from Virginia, locating in that county, where he afterward became an extensive land owner and an influential citizen. He was a member of the church known as the Regular Baptists, and one of the founders of that society in Pulaski County. He married Martha Van Hook about 1818, and reared a family, the second of whom was Henry G. Ware. He was born in Pulaski County, where he was reared to manhood, and in February, 1844, married Eliza J. Thompson, whose parents came from Virginia to Rockcastle County, Ky., where they acquired an extensive estate in lands. Francis M. Ware is the first son born to Henry G. and Eliza J. Ware. He was reared in his native county, and in January, 1863, he enlisted in the Thirty-second Kentucky Infantry as a private of Company H, from which he was honorably discharged at the expiration of his term of enlistment. He was married in December, 1876, to Miss Martha, daughter of Joel Hubble, of Pulaski County, and has been blessed with three children: Alma (deceased), Eugenia and Samantha. Francis M. is now the leading merchant of McKinney, Ky., carrying a large stock of general merchandise. He is also engaged in agriculture and general trading, owning one of the finest farms and residences in the county.

JOHN B. WATHEN, JR., was born on March 24, 1856, and is a son of William W. Wathen, present postmaster of Lebanon, Ky. He is a representative of one of the oldest and most highly respected families of Marion County; was educated in the schools of his native town of Lebanon, St. Mary's College of Marion County and the Cecilian College of Hardin County. Since his school days he has devoted himself chiefly to mercantile pursuits, and after serving several years as a salesman in Lebanon, he became a traveling salesman for Louisville, Cincinnati and New York merchants, resigning the latter position in 1885 to accept an appointment under President Cleveland, as Indian agent for the Territory of Dakota, the duties of which he performed until compelled to resign in November, 1885, in consequence of failing health, due to climatic causes. He returned to Lebanon and formed a business partnership with his father, under the firm name of W. W. Wathen & Son. Mr. Wathen is an affable enterprising young man, and was a member of Gov. Blackburn's staff, from which he derives the title of colonel. He was married October 24, 1883, to Miss Fannie, daughter of Judge William E. Russell.

W. C. WEAREN was born in Garrard County, Ky., July 7, 1831, and is of Scotch-Irish origin. He is a son of Drury and Hettie A. (Hardin) Wearen, married in 1830, and who had born to them eight children—five sons and three daughters. He was first married to Miss Sallie Locker, of Garrard County, and they had born to them one son and four daughters. Drury Wearen was born in Lincoln County, Ky., in 1799. Jacob Wearen, grandfather of W. C., was born in Virginia, immigrated to Kentucky, located at Hall's Gap in Lincoln County, upon a farm; remaining there four years he moved to Garrard County, and died in 1812, leaving a family of eight children. W. C. Wearen at the age of nineteen embarked in the furniture and undertaking business, and has followed it through life with good success. He was married in 1861 to Miss Nannie T. Denton, a daughter of Thompson and Josephine (Harris) Denton. Mr. and Mrs. Wearen had born to them three children: Annie (James), William H. and Thompson. He and wife are both members of the Baptist Church.

WILLIAM C. WEBB, M. D., was born in Clark County, Ky., July 21, 1854, and is a son of Richard M. and Jane A. (Carl) Webb. Richard M. Webb was born and reared in Clark County, received a classical education at Bethany College, West Virginia, studied medicine and graduated from the Lexington Transylvania Medical College, but chose agriculture as his life's pursuit; he was married in 1850, and became the father of two sons and two daughters; his father, Dr. William Webb, was a native of Virginia, and studied medicine under the famous Dr. Benjamin Rush, of Philadelphia; he took up his practice in Clark County, Ky., acquired a handsome fortune, and married Susan Quinn Morton, daughter of Richard Morton, whose seven sons were all renowned preachers; he became the father of two sons and six daughters, and died at the age òf seventy-seven years, a member of the Masonic fraternity. Dr. William C. Webb was graduated from the medical department of the Louisville University, and also from Bellevue, New York City; then settled in Bryantsville, Garrard County, Ky., in 1878, and since then has been engaged in a lucrative and active practice. The Doctor is a member of the State Medical Society, is president of the Kentucky Central Medical Association, and also is a member of the Christian Church. In politics he is a Democrat.

JAMES L. WHARTON, clerk of the Washington County Circuit Court, and son of John R. and Sarah (Caldwell) Wharton, born on the 17th of February, 1843. The Whartons were of English lineage, and several members of the family were among the early residents of Virginia. John R. Wharton was born in Virginia in 1801 and came to Kentucky about 1810, and settled in Lincoln County, but afterward moved to Danville, where Mr. Wharton followed merchandising for a number of years. He moved to Washington County in 1821, and for a number of years sold goods in Springfield. In after life he became a farmer, and died December 4, 1880. His wife, Sarah Slaughter Wharton, was the daughter of Mr. James Caldwell, who lived near Danville, Ky. He was a native of Kentucky, and a grandson of James Caldwell, D. D., one of the founders of Princeton College, New Jersey, and a distinguished clergyman of the Presbyterian Church, and who died in his native State. Mrs. Wharton died near Springfield, Washington Co., Ky., in 1855. The following are the names of the children born to John R. and Sarah S. Wharton: Mrs. Susan Loving; G. C.; Phœbe (deceased), James L. and John C. By a previous marriage with a Miss Ray, Mr. Wharton had one child, Lloyd R. Wharton (deceased). James L. Wharton grew to manhood in Washington County, and was educated in the Covington Institute, of Springfield, and Columbia College, which latter he attended for two years. At the breaking out of the war he entered Company A, Fifth Kentucky Union Cavalry, as first lieutenant, served until the latter part of 1862, when he was promoted to the captaincy, and in the spring of 1863 was promoted major, holding that position until 1864. His regiment formed part of the Army of the Cumberland, commanded by Gens. D. C. Buell and Rosecrans, with Boyle,

Negley, Smith, Mitchell and others as division commanders. Mr. Wharton participated in a number of bloody engagements, among which were Gallatin, Perryville, Chickamauga and Okolomo, in the last of which he was severely wounded (February 22, 1864), and was compelled to remain off active duty for more than six months, when he was given a military commission at Louisville, in which capacity he served until his resignation, March 18, 1865. Mr. Wharton then returned to Washington County, and engaged in agricultural pursuits until 1869, at which time he was appointed United States gauger for the county, a position he held until 1874. He was then elected clerk of the Washington County Circuit Court, which office he still holds. Mr. Wharton was elected upon the Republican ticket, a fact which speaks much for his personal popularity, the county always having been decidedly Democratic. He owns a beautiful farm a few miles from Springfield, and in addition to his official duties, gives considerable attention to farming and stock raising. He was married June 29, 1865, to Miss Lydia G. Fetter, daughter of George C. and Catherine (Gray) Fetter of Louisville. Seven children have been born to Mr. and Mrs. Wharton: J. Rutledge; Katie; G. C.; George L.; W. H.; James L. and Ormsby. Mr. Wharton is a member of the Springfield Presbyterian Church, and belongs to the Masonic fraternity. His wife is a member of the Episcopal Church.

THOMAS P. WHERRITT was born January 12, 1839, in Richmond, Madison Co., Ky. He is the seventh of five sons and seven daughters, ten of whom were reared, born to Samuel and Mary Jane (Peacock) Wherritt. Samuel Wherritt was born in Scott County, Ky., May 17, 1799; he was a silversmith by trade, which he learned in Danville and Lexington, Ky. About 1820 he located in Richmond, Ky., where he worked at his trade until his death in 1877; he never held but one office, that of constable; he was strongly opposed to slavery, although he owned many as servants; was a devout and active member in the Presbyterian Church. He was a son of William Wherritt, who was born in St. Mary's County, Md., and who had been twice married; by his first wife five children were reared; his second wife was a Miss King, to whom five sons and two daughters were born. William Wherritt migrated and located in Scott County, Ky., in 1796; in 1800 in Jessamine County, Ky., and purchased 1,500 acres of land where Camp Nelson is now situated. He purchased of speculators, the title proved to be worthless, and he lost the lands; remained in Jessamine until his death. His ancestors came from Wales to America, and settled in Maryland during Lord Baltimore's time, and as far as known, all of the same name spring from this first Maryland family. Mary Jane (Peacock) Wherritt was born in Versailles, Woodford Co., Ky., October 23, 1811. She was a daughter of William and Jane (Bean) Peacock, natives of Harrisburg, Penn., and Woodford County, Ky., respectively. William Peacock was an early pioneer of Madison County; tailor by trade, and a soldier in the war of 1812, and was captured at River Raisin; Jane Bean was a granddaughter of Gen. Warren of Revolutionary fame. Thomas P. Wherritt received a good English education; at the age of seventeen entered the county clerk's office in Richmond, under Thomas H. Barns; March, 1859, located in Lancaster, and entered the clerk's office as deputy; in August, 1861, enlisted in Company G, First Kentucky Cavalry, mustered as first sergeant. Three months later he was detailed by Gen. Thomas to take charge of quartermaster stores at Nicholasville; remained with Gen. Thomas until after the battle of Murfreesboro, when he was discharged and returned home. Remaining home but a short time, he went with Capt. George H. Dobyns to Little Rock, Ark., and remained in service two years; returned to Lancaster and entered county clerk's office as deputy, under his brother William. In 1882 he was elected to the office of clerk, re-elected in 1886. He was married August, 1868, to Sallie Miller, daughter of William S. Miller. To this union three children were born: Victor, Claude and Bessie. Mr. and Mrs. Wherritt are members of the Presbyterian Church. He is a leading member of the F. & A. M.; in politics is Democratic; his first presidential vote was for Bell and Everett.

HON. RICHARD J. WHITE was born December 15, 1827, in Silver Creek, Madison County, and is a son of Valentine M. and Jane H. (Gentry) White, to whom were born three sons and one daughter. Valentine M. was born on same farm in 1801, and was engaged all his life as a farmer and trader, and died in 1834. He was a son of Durett White, who came from Culpeper County, Va., and settled on Silver Creek as early as 1780-85, first stopping at Fort Paint Lick. Prior to his coming he had served three years in the Continental Army as lieutenant under Gen. Washington. After coming to Kentucky he also participated in many of the struggles with the Indians. He finally settled on Silver Creek, ten miles south of Richmond, on about 1,000 acres of the best land in the county; afterward added considerable to this and became one of the most substantial farmers in the county. He married a widow by the name of Lucy Clark, by whom one child was born. She had several children by her former husband. Durett White was a Baptist in religion, and died at the age of eighty-six years. He was a son of Henry White, of Virginia, whose father was also a Virginian, and was related to the Jefferson and Crawford families, and of Scotch-Irish origin tinctured with French. Mrs. Jane H. (Gentry) White was born six miles south of Richmond, on Silver Creek, and was a daughter of Richard Gentry, who married a Miss Martin. Mr. Gentry had served in the war for independence, received a land warrant, and immediately came to Kentucky and located lands. He first occupied the fort at Boonesborough, and took part in many of the struggles with the Indians. He married his second wife and reared a large family, and at the time of his death was about eighty-seven years old. Richard J. White was reared on a farm and received his education at Bethany College, West Virginia. He was united in marriage in September, 1846, to Lucy A., only daughter of Creed and Elizabeth (Duncan) Taylor, natives of Madison County, but of Virginia families of English descent. Mr. White and wife raised six children to bless their home: Valentine (deceased), William, Richard, Elizabeth, John and Martin B. Mr. and Mrs. White are active and devoted members of the Christian Church. After his marriage Mr. White located on the old homestead of his grandfather. In 1849 he removed to where he now resides, on 640 acres four miles southeast of Richmond. He now owns 340 acres; his wife and daughter own about 500 acres in their own names. Mr. White has devoted much of his time to live stock breeding and trading. Mr. White was colonel of militia in early days, has served as magistrate eight years, and in 1876 was elected to represent his county in the Senate. He is a member of the F. & A. M., and was identified with the Grange movement.

JOSEPH WHITEHOUSE was born September 2, 1844. His grandfather, Benjamin Whitehouse, was a native of Virginia, and of Irish lineage. He was one of the first settlers of Boyle County, where he followed farming, and where he died October 4, 1865. His wife, Mary Sparrow, was first cousin to Abraham Lincoln; she died October 4, 1861, leaving seven sons and seven daughters, all of whom lived to be grown and married.

The second son, Henry, who is the father of Joseph, was born December 16, 1815, and is yet residing in his native county, and has throughout his life been a farmer. In his younger days he contemplated entering the ministry of the Presbyterian Church, but subsequently abandoned the idea of preaching; he has been a life-long member and worker in the church, in which he is a ruling elder. In January, 1842, he married Miss Melissa Condor, whose parents, Peter and Lucinda, were Kentuckians. The former was of German origin, the latter of Irish parentage. To Henry Whitehouse and his wife Melissa were born two sons: Joseph (the subject) and James V., and one daughter, Mariah F., who married C. P. Miner, of Casey County, Ky. Joseph Whitehouse, a native of Boyle County, remained with his father and was engaged in the labors incident to farm life until the beginning of the civil war. July 15, 1862, he joined the Federal Army as a private in Company K, Sixth Kentucky Volunteer Cavalry, under the command of Col. Halisey, and with his company he participated in many engagements, most notably those of Nashville, Tenn., and at Tipp's River, near Tuscaloosa, Ala.; at the latter place he received two gun-shot wounds, from the effects of which he was disabled, and in consideration he now receives a small pension from the United States Government. Since the time of his discharge from the army Mr. Whitehouse has been engaged in superintending the working of a small farm that he owns. He was married, October 20, 1870, to Martha E. Hourigan, and to this union have been born two sons: Henry C., born February 13, 1875, deceased, and James R., born May 16, 1877, and five daughters: Nancy M., born September 17, 1872; Grace F., born March 23, 1879; Celeste, born April 28, 1881; Myrtle M., born February 1, 1883, and Ethel, born September 15, 1885. Mr. and Mrs. Whitehouse are consistent members of the Baptist faith, in which church Mr. Whitehouse holds the office of clerk. He is a Democrat and a worker in his party. Rufus Hourigan, father of Mrs. Martha E. Whitehouse, was born November 18, 1823, and was married to Nancy Pipes, September 20, 1843, and to this union were born three children: Martha E., wife of Joseph Whitehouse, born April 6, 1850; James P., August 30, 1852, and Rufus, March 22, 1857.

JOHN W. WILKINSON was born April 2, 1827. His father, Samuel F. Wilkinson, Sr., was of English descent. His father, in turn, was George Wilkinson, who was reared by Lord Palmore, of England, and came to this country some time prior to the Revolutionary war; settled in Fauquier County, Va., where he lived till 1792, when he immigrated to Kentucky; while en route Samuel F. was born at Morgantown, Va., October 26, 1792. They settled for a short time near Louisville, later removed to Bourbon County, and then permanently located on the head waters of Simpson's Creek, in Nelson County, near the site of the present village of Fairfield, where he lived until his death, about the year 1833, at the advanced age of ninety-five years. Samuel F. Wilkinson, Sr., grew to manhood in his native county, where, January 1, 1824, he married Miss Nancy, daughter of William and Sallie Bland, who were also natives of Virginia, and among the early settlers of Nelson County. To Samuel and Nancy Wilkinson were born ten children, eight of whom grew to manhood and womanhood: John W., William B., Christopher C., Samuel F., Jane (Froman), Mary C. (Dotson), Nancy J. (Hobbs) and Emma (Hall). Mrs. Wilkinson died in 1858, aged fifty-four years. Samuel Wilkinson, during early life, followed the profession of teaching; from the date of his marriage he made farming his occupation, dying August 4, 1883, the proprietor of 1,400 acres of good land. He was an active member of and leader in the Methodist Episcopal Church for nearly sixty years. John W. Wilkinson, also a native of Nelson County, remained with his parents until twenty-five years of age, when, March 18, 1852, he was united in marriage with Miss Elizabeth Briggs; four sons and four daughters have blessed this union: Nannie (deceased), Beatrice (deceased); Thomas C., Andrew F., Wiley S., Katie M. (wife of Dr. Nichols), Willie, Myrtle and John W. Elizabeth (Briggs) Wilkinson was born May 31, 1834; she is a daughter of Andrew and Nancy (Robertson) Briggs, the former a Scot by birth, and the latter of English descent. Mr. Wilkinson has always made farming his vocation, and now owns about 400 acres of well improved land. Mrs. Wilkinson belongs to the Methodist Episcopal Church. In politics he is a Democrat.

JOHN WESLEY WILLIAMS, circuit clerk, is a native of Cumberland County, and was born December 10, 1827. His father, John O. Williams, a native of Henry County, Va., was born March 4, 1801. He was a slave owner and farmer, and was worth at his death about $16,000. He was married in his twenty-fifth year to Miss Eliza Wathall, the daughter of Richard and Sally (Hix) Wathall of Appomattox County, Va., and this marriage was blessed by twelve children: John W., James O., Henry E., Milton R., Amanda (wife of Josiah P. Frank), Sarah A. (married first to George W. Baker, and after his death to J. J. Mc-Gee), Daniel B., Victoria (wife of John Cloyd), Julia (wife of M. O. Allen), Marshall C., Foster M. and Leslie C. (of whom Foster and Leslie are now deceased). Marshall C. Williams enlisted in the Confederate Cavalry service in 1862, and served two years. In 1805 John O. Williams was brought to Kentucky by his father, from whom he received several slaves, estimated to be worth $4,000, as a beginning in life. He owned a large tract of about 800 acres of land, only about 150 acres of which was in cultivation. His death occurred in October, 1856, and in life he was a member of the Presbyterian Church. His wife died in August, 1858, in the fifty-fourth year of her age, and in life she was a member of the Methodist Episcopal Church. Osbourn Williams, grandfather of John W. Williams, a soldier of the Revolution, was a native of Henry County, Va. He was married to Miss Sarah Wade, and immigrated in 1805 to Cumberland County, where they reared a family of nine children, five of whom were daughters, of which family of children, John O. was the second. Osbourn and Sarah Williams began life in very moderate circumstances on a farm, but accumulated valuable property, being worth at the death of Osbourn Williams, in 1853, about $35,000. Garrett Williams, of English origin, was brought from South Wales to Henry County, where he lived most of his life, but died in Cumberland County, Ky. He was a veteran of the American Revolution, serving through the entire seven years of the struggle as a company officer. John Wesley Williams remained at home on his father's farm, when not at school, until twenty-one years of age, when he attended school in Burkesville fifteen months. He followed agriculture until 1858, owning at first 40 acres, and afterward 320 acres of land three miles from Burkesville on the Columbia road. In 1858 Mr. Williams was elected on the Whig ticket, as county surveyor, which position he held until 1867. In 1868, without opposition, he was elected circuit court clerk, which position as a Democrat, he still holds, having been re-elected twice since. On December 23, 1853, he was united in marriage to Miss Elizabeth Nunn, a daughter of George W. and Caroline (Alexander) Nunn, natives of Cumberland County. To this marriage were born four children, John Elmo, Irving, Ethel (who died in childhood)

and Stewart (who also died in childhood). Mrs. Williams was a zealous member of the Presbyterian Church, but was called from the scene of her earthly labors December 8, 1873, in the thirty-third year of her age. On December 22, 1874, Mr. Williams was married to Miss Sarah E. Cheatham, a daughter of Owen and Sarah A. (Baker) Cheatham, natives of Cumberland County, and to this marriage have been born two children: Hattie M. and Hooker, both living. Mr. and Mrs. Williams, who own property and live in Burkesville, are both members of the Presbyterian Church, besides which Mr. Williams is a member of the Masonic order. He owns a farm but turns his entire attention to the duties of his office.

JAMES B. WILLIAMS was born January 6, 1840. His ancestors were English; his grandfather, Thomas Williams, was a Virginian by birth; he came to Kentucky when a young man and located on Casey Creek, in Taylor County, and afterward married Miss Eve Dryeduch. They reared a family of three daughters and two sons, one of whom was Barnett Williams, the father of James B. Thomas Williams was a farmer and died in 1856. His son Barnett was twice married, first in 1830 to Mrs. Phœbe (Calvert) Hope, of Marion County. She died in 1849, leaving six children, all of whom lived to be grown: Frances A. (Taylor), Catherine E. (Stine), Phœbe J. (Curtsinger), John Y., William H. and James B. The second wife of Barnett Williams was Nancy O. Nichols, daughter of John Nichols of Washington County; to this marriage were born three children: Robert G., Mary and George M.; the last died in infancy. Mrs. Williams is yet living. Barnett Williams died in 1884, aged eighty-six years; his principal business was that of farmer, though he was for some years engaged in freighting goods to points not accessible by railroad. He was for more than fifty years a member of the Baptist Church. James B. Williams was born near the farm on which he now resides in Marion County, and educated in the common schools; at the age of twenty-one he entered the Federal Army, and from September 27, 1861, to March 24, 1865, served as quartermaster sergeant in the Fifth Kentucky Volunteer Cavalry. He was with Kilpatrick through Georgia in 1864, and afterward served with Maj. Chamblis in the cavalry department of the Tennessee. After the war our subject returned to his home in Marion County, leased some land and engaged in farming, which he has continued with uniform success up to the present time.

He now resides on a farm of 140 acres, which he owns. He was married October 28, 1868, to Miss Susan M. Lannum. They are the parents of seven children, all of whom are living: Ada B., William E., John B., Bernetta L., Olelia D., James E. and Ethel H. Mrs. Susan Lannum Williams was born August 21, 1849. She is a daughter of Mordecai and Bernetta (Clark) Lannum, both natives of Marion County, Ky., married January 10, 1848; the former died July 20, 1853, the latter July 22, 1854. Mr. and Mrs. Williams are members of the Baptist Church, with which they united in 1867. He is a Master Mason, and a member of T. W. Wash Lodge, No. 430. His political views are Democratic, and he takes an interest in political issues in behalf of his party, and is a patron of schools and public enterprises.

ZACHARIAH T. WILLIAMS, merchant, was born February 22, 1849, in Russell County. His father, Preston G. Williams, a native of Burke County, N. C., was born October 1, 1805, and was married October 27, 1831, to Miss Prudence A., daughter of Zachariah and Nancy (Montgomery) Taylor, the former of Kentucky, the latter of Virginia. This marriage occurred in Adair County, where Mr. Williams had lived since 1808, and has been blessed by eight children: Nancy J., wife of Benjamin P. Rowe, and the mother of three children, one of whom is a son, Isaac N., who married Miss Helen Bradshaw, and is the father of eight children, three of whom are sons; Albert N., who died August 31, 1854, in his sixteenth year; Lucy A., married first to Arthur Bradshaw, by whom she had two children, a son and a daughter, and married second to James M. Carter, and has by him four children—two sons; Mary Louvena, wife of William Conover, and the mother of ten children—four sons; Leslie A., married to Miss Martha S. Bryan, and the father of three daughters; Zachariah T., and Eliza F., wife of Samuel B. Conover, and the mother of three children, one a daughter. All of this family are living except one. Mr. Williams received an estate from his father, and in 1831 settled at his present location, a farm at that time of 400 acres. He has, besides farming, carried on a wagon-shop, and in *ante bellum* days owned between thirty and forty slaves. Mr. and Mrs. Williams have been members of the Christian Church since May, 1834, and a part of this time he has held the office of deacon. His politics since the war have been Democratic, before which event he was an old time Whig. Mrs. Williams is in the seventy-third year of her age (1886). Aaron

Williams, grandfather of Zachariah T. Williams, was a native of Rockingham County, N. C., and born in 1773. He was a hatter by trade, and afterward turned his entire attention to farming, carrying on a water mill at Reynolds' Creek, Adair County, in addition. He was married about his twenty-second year to Miss Lucy, daughter of John and Lucy (Williams) Wall, natives of the Old Dominion, and they were the parents of nine children: Polly (Bradshaw), Maria (died in infancy), Preston G., Eliza (Montgomery), Lucinda (Bradshaw), Parmelia (Turner), Alvan, Clarissa (Taylor), Aaron and Drewry. Aaron Williams died in his fiftieth year. Drewry Williams, great-grandfather of Zachariah T. Williams, was a native of the Old Dominion, a veteran of the American Revolution and was married to Miss Martha Guinn, a daughter of Albern Guinn, of Virginia. He had three children by this marriage: Aaron, Charlotte (Bradshaw) and John. His second marriage was to Miss Phyllis Hayes, by whom he had six children: Andrew, Abner, Drewry, Elijah, Westley and Milton. He died in his sixty-fourth year, in 1810. Aaron Williams, great-great-grandfather of Z. T. Williams, emigrated from Wales to the United States and settled in Virginia. Preston G. Williams eleven years ago fell from a wagon and has since been a cripple unable to walk without crutches, and seven years ago he lost his sight, and yet he bears his two great afflictions with Christian fortitude. In boyhood Z. T. Williams received a business education in the schools of Russell and Adair Counties, which he attended every winter —three months—until eighteen years of age, after which he taught two terms in the common schools of Russell County. He remained at home, working with and for his father, until twenty-one years of age, at which time, February 24, 1870, he was united in marriage to Miss Clemmie J., daughter of Cyrus and Sarah (Murrah) Wheat, the former native of Adair County, the latter of Tennessee. He began the battle of life with no estate, and embarked in the general merchandise business in 1871, at Montpelier, Adair County, with Mr. Cyrus Wheat, which he has since continued. In addition to this Mr. Williams, in partnership with Mr. Wheat, carries on a farm of 400 acres. Messrs. Wheat & Williams carry a stock of general merchandise and drugs worth $3,000, and have a fine trade. In 1883 Mr. Williams was elected on the Democratic ticket to the Lower House of the Kentucky Legislature; he is a notary public, but has never sought political preferment. To Mr. and Mrs. Williams have been born six children: Luther, Lawrence, Loren, Lillie May, Sallie P. and Joseph A., all living. Mr. Williams is a member of the Christian Church, of which he is an elder. Mrs. Williams is also a member of the Christian Church.

JAMES B. WILLIAMS was born February 22, 1856, and is a son of Daniel M. and Elizabeth C. (Smith) Williams. Daniel Williams is one of the largest and most substantial farmers and tobacco growers of Green County, and was the possessor of about sixty slaves when the war broke out. In 1885 he was elected to represent his county and Taylor in the Lower House of the Legislature. He is a son of Daniel M. Williams, of Scotch descent, who was born in Virginia, and was one of the first settlers of, and erected the first house in Green County, seven miles northwest of Greensburg; he was a substantial farmer and large slave owner. Mrs. Elizabeth C. Williams was a daughter of John Smith, of English descent, an early settler of Green County, and an extensive slave owner; he was in the Mexican war, and died shortly after his return. James B. Williams, also a native of Green County, was reared on a farm, and received a good English education in the common schools and Science Hill Academy. He spent five years as a teacher in the common schools, and at twenty-four years of age engaged in the mercantile business on Dry Fork, La Rue County. In 1883 he located in Raywick, where he has continued the mercantile business with uniform success. January 15, 1886, he was appointed justice. He is the owner of 514 acres on Dry Fork, Marion County, seventy-five of which are improved and mostly bottom lands, all of which he secured for $1,200. He married Ella G. Scott, May 21, 1885, a daughter of James and Mactillus (Bickett) Scott, of Raywick. Mrs. Williams is a member of the Roman Catholic Church, while he was reared under Baptist schooling. Mr. Williams is an active Democrat, and cast his first presidential vote for Tilden in 1876.

WILLIS—McGEE. Henry Clinton Willis was born February 20, 1831, in Mercer County, Ky., where he grew to manhood, and has always resided. His father, Joseph Willis, a native of Mercer County, was a farmer and slave-holder, a reformer, a Whig, and died in 1854, aged about sixty-six years. He first married a Miss Lillard, and their children were James, William, Joseph, Elizabeth (Boice) and Mary (Garrett). His second wife was Margaret Walker, and

their offspring are Henry C. and Samuel. Henry C. married December 31, 1868, Mrs. Amanda H., widow of John J. McGee, and daughter of James B. and Lucretia (Starns) Irvin of Mercer County (born May 14, 1834), and from their union sprang Dora E. and Benna L. John J. McGee, was born March 17, 1816, and died August 7, 1864. He was a farmer and hotel-keeper, and lost twenty-five slaves as a result of the late war. He was the son of Joseph McGee, born in 1778, reared in Mercer County, and died in 1853. His father was John McGee a real pioneer in Mercer County. In 1800 Joseph married Nancy Lyen, and their children were Harvey, James, David (deceased), Thely (Beadles) and John J. November 2, 1854, John J. married Miss Amanda H. Irvin, and to them were born Joseph I., December 18, 1858 (died in 1862). William Henry, September 12, 1862, and John J., December 14, 1864. James B. Irvin was born July 2, 1802, in Madison County, Ky. He married Lucretia Starns, and their children were Mary J. (Turpen), Eliza A. (Smith), Amanda H. (McGee and Willis), James F., Henry C. (died in the army), Sallie E. (Finnell), Manta D. (Allen), Samuel W. and Benjamin B.

HERSCHEL P. WILLIS, farmer, was born January 17, 1840, in Adair County. His father, Edmund T. Willis, also a native of Adair and a farmer, was born March 24, 1808. He owned in all about 400 acres of land, and lost twenty-two slaves by the war. He was married, first, before he was of age, to Miss Ellen, daughter of Oliver Garnett, who had married a Miss Wetheral, of Cumberland County, and who was, himself, a native of Cumberland. By his first marriage Mr. Willis became the father of two children: Adeline (who died in infancy) and Sarah B. (wife of Stephen Barger). Mrs. Willis, a member of the Baptist Church, died young—May 29, 1834, and Edmund T. Willis, about 1835, was married to Miss Nancy B., daughter of Anthony G. and Harriet (Bowmar) Willis, both natives of Adair County. Anthony G. Willis was a farmer, who died in the prime of life, leaving a family of five young children, two of whom died in youth, and two of whom, Nancy B. and Benjamin R., are still living. By his second marriage Edmund T. Willis became the father of ten children: Anthony G., Harriet F., Herschel P., Joseph P., Mary V. J. (wife of William Garnett), Martha Caroline (wife of William F. Jeffries), William T. (died September 17, 1885), Nancy J. (wife of William Kertley), Benjamin F., and an infant who died unnamed. Edmund T. Willis before the war was worth about $30,000. He was a Democrat in politics, was magistrate of his precinct eight years, and judge of Adair County Court three terms. He was a member of the Baptist Church, and died November 5, 1866, in the fifty-eighth year of his age, leaving an estate of $5,000. His widow, also a member of the Baptist Church, is in the seventy-fourth year of her age. Edmund Willis, grandfather of Herschel P. Willis, was a native of old Virginia. He owned a large plantation near Columbia, which he cultivated with slave labor. By his marriage to Miss Frances Towles he became the father of the following children: Virginia (Spencer), Polly (Kertley), Sally (Squires), Nancy (Dohany), William T. (killed at Buena Vista, in the Mexican war), Joseph, Bird, Merry, America (Weatherhead) and Edmund T. The Willis family are of English origin. Herschel P. Willis remained at home working on his father's farm until twenty-seven years of age. November 28, 1866, he was united in marriage to Miss Mary E., daughter of Thomas P. and Mary A. (Nelson) Jeffries, the former of Washington County, and the latter of Russell. A small estate of about $300 was given him as a start in life, and this was immediately invested in a farm, which he cultivated about six years, living in the meantime on a rented farm. In 1871 he purchased 110 acres, seven miles from Columbia, fifty acres of which were open, and on which was a two-room log building, where he lived eleven years. He has since increased his tract to 167 acres, 100 of which are in cultivation. He has also erected a neat frame cottage residence. The home of Mr. and Mrs. Willis has been gladdened by four children: Charles Elmer, Ethel, Estelle and Elrie—all living. The parents are both members of the Zion Baptist Church, and Mr. Willis has been a life-long Democrat in politics.

JOSIAH B. WILLIS was born December 6, 1848, five miles west of Richmond, and is a son of John and Susan (Baker) Willis, to whom seven sons and four daughters were reared, and all living except one daughter. John Willis was born in 1794 in Madison County. He became a prosperous farmer and owner of a considerable slave property; was member of the Christian Church, and in politics a Whig, till the war broke out, then became a Democrat; he died in 1872. He was a son of Drury Willis, who was born in Virginia, and was of English descent; immigrated to Madison County, Ky., in 1785, and married for his first wife a Miss Phelps, a native of Madison County. The issue from this marriage was seven sons and three daughters.

His second wife was a Sherley; the issue by the second marriage was three sons and one daughter. In religion he was a Baptist and in politics a Whig. Mrs. Susan (Baker) Willis was born in Madison County in 1804 and died in March, the night prior to her husband's death, and was buried in the same grave. She was a daughter of Michael Baker, a native of North Carolina, and an early pioneer of Madison County, Ky. He married Nancy Philps. He was a Baptist in religion and died in Missouri, to which State he had moved. He was a son of David Baker, of North Carolina, a Hardshell Baptist minister, whose wife was a Gentry. He was of English descent. Josiah B. Willis received his early training on a farm, received a common English education, and was united in marriage September 30, 1869, to Pattie De Jarnett of Clark County, but a native of Madison County, and daughter of George and Sarah (Williams) De Jarnett, also natives of Madison County. Mr. De Jarnett was a farmer, served as deputy sheriff for several terms and died in 1885, aged sixty-nine; was a son of James De Jarnett, who married a Simmons. He was a farmer, served as a common soldier in 1812, and while in the service was captured by the Indians. He being a Mason, gave the Indians Masonic signs, which were recognized, and he was released. He was of French descent. He reared a family of seventeen children, was one of the pioneers of Madison County and was a member of the Christian Church. Mr. and Mrs. Willis had born to bless their happy union six children: T. C., Maud (deceased), Nannie De Jarnett, G. D. and J. D. (twins) and Cleveland. After his marriage he engaged in farming until 1877, when he commenced riding as deputy sheriff, which position he filled till 1881 when he was elected sheriff of Madison and re-elected in 1883, served until January, 1886, and then engaged in the hotel business in Richmond. He and wife are members of the Christian Church, and he of the F. & A. M. In politics he is a consistent and active Democrat and cast his first presidential vote for H. Greeley.

CAPT. JAMES HARVEY WILSON was born November 20, 1834, near Barboursville, Knox County, and in 1872 located on the Danville & Lexington pike, on the bluffs of Dick's River in Boyle County, where he has since resided. In 1861 he enlisted in Company H, Twenty-fourth Kentucky Infantry; was elected second lieutenant and afterward promoted to the position of first lieutenant. Upon the reorganization of the regiment as veterans, he was promoted to the captaincy, which position he retained until after the final surrender. His father, Peter G. Wilson, was born November 13, 1792, in Wythe County, Va.; served as a soldier in the war of 1812, and soon after his discharge removed to Knox County, Ky., where he died March 5, 1879. He was a farmer, a slaveholder, a Whig, a Union man and a member of the Christian Church. He married Dicy Dorton, of Knox County, who died in 1867 at the age of sixty-three years, and their offspring are Nancy (Sparks), Emily (Duggins), Franklin, Jordan, Lucretia (Mershon), Olivia (Slatton), Capt. James H., Jesse T. Wilson and Elizabeth (Beddow). On November 16, 1875, Capt. Wilson espoused Miss Amelia H., daughter of Thomas D. and Lucy (Bingamin) Hill, of Lincoln County (born January 10, 1851), and to them have been born Lucy, Bettie, Jesse, and James Harvey, Jr. Capt. Wilson was ten years engaged in distilling, at which he was successful. He is now a farmer, owning 2,500 acres of land, 350 of which, the home place, is well improved and productive. He is a member of the Christian Church, of the A. F. & A. M., and in politics is a Republican.

JOHN H. WILSON, a native of Adair County, and a son of David and Fanny (Coats) Wilson, was born August 20, 1841. David Wilson, born December 1, 1797, was a farmer, owning his own farm and stock. He married Miss Fanny Coats in 1826, a daughter of Alex and Lucy Coats, natives of the Old Dominion. By this marriage he became the father of six children: Minerva J. (wife of E. Grissom), Sally M., Clove Ann and Dicie Norticia (who are dead), Mellisa F. (deceased wife of William Rowe) and J. H. David Wilson was a member of the Methodist Episcopal Church South, and departed this life December 31, 1872. His widow, also a consistent member of the Methodist Episcopal Church, died in the eighty-first year of her age, in December, 1879. John Wilson, the grandfather of John H., was a native of the Old Dominion, lived near Richmond, and was born about 1762. He was a tiller of the soil during his life, and immigrated to the "dark and bloody ground," where in the midst of the forest of Adair County, he entered a tract of land, and built a cabin. Here he lived and cultivated about 200 acres. His marriage to Miss Sarah Miller occurred in Virginia and they were the parents of eight children: Samuel, David, Andrew, Miller, Washington, Charles, Dicie (Van Zant) and Milton, all dead. The death of John Wilson occurred in 1843, that of his wife, prior to that time. The Wilson family

are of English-Irish origin. John H. Wilson in youth acquired only a limited education in the common schools of the county. His early life, until twenty years of age, was spent in farming at home with his father, but in September, 1861, he enlisted in Company D, Thirteenth Kentucky Volunteer Infantry, Federal service. He served three years, participating in many of the principal battles, and received two slight wounds during that time. He was a non-commissioned officer, and served mostly in the commissary department. He was mustered out of the service and received an honorable discharge in 1864, and will receive a pension for injuries received in a runaway while in the army. Mr. Wilson, after returning home, began life with no property, but immediately bought a place of 244 acres in the woods. This he has added to and sold off from at different times, until it now contains 150 acres. Here he has built a good residence, stables and barns, and placed his farm in a high state of cultivation. Mr. Wilson was married in March, 1865, to Miss Lucy M. Blair, a daughter of John and Betsy (Royse) Blair, native Kentuckians. John Blair was a son of Wm. and Lucy (Hopkins) Blair, natives of South Carolina, and Betsy Royse was a daughter of William and Mary (Stone) Royse, the former a Kentuckian, the latter a Virginian. William Royse was a son of Solomon Royse, one of the first settlers of Kentucky. Mr. and Mrs. Wilson are the parents of eight children: Norticia, Alice, Roofic, Ora, Ada, Annie (deceased), Altie and another deceased. Mr. and Mrs. Wilson are both members of the Methodist Episcopal Church, and in politics Mr. Wilson is a member of the Republican party.

HUGH W. WILSON was born March 2, 1842, and is the third of six sons and five daughters, three sons and three daughters yet living, born to Samuel M. and Mary M. (Stearman) Wilson, who were united in marriage in December, 1836. Samuel M. Wilson was born June 5, 1811, near where Hugh W. now resides; he was a farmer and died December 20, 1883. He was a son of Hugh Wilson, who came from Ireland when a young man, settled in Virginia and married a Mrs. Moore, of Rockbridge County. He was a weaver by trade, but after settling in Kentucky became a farmer. Mrs. Mary M. Wilson was a daughter of William and Ann (Rafity) Stearman, natives of Green County, Ky. Mr. Stearman was a moderate farmer and son of Thomas Stearman, and was one of the early pioneers of Kentucky. Hugh W. Wilson, a native of Green County, was brought up on a farm and received a common-school education. He enlisted in defense of the Union, in September, 1861, in Company G, Thirteenth Kentucky Volunteers. During the first two years he was detailed to do hospital duty; was with the regiment in Tennessee during the Knoxville siege, through Georgia and around Atlanta, and was honorably discharged. Since his return he has been engaged on the farm. In February, 1861, he was united in marriage to Lucy D. Craddock, a daughter of Creed and Elizabeth (Sandridge) Craddock. The issue from this happy union was eleven children: James L., William R., Mary (deceased), Sarah S., Lucy C., Maggie J., Ella A., Samuel H., Eddie S., Mattie A. and John C. (deceased). Mr. and Mrs. Wilson are consistent and active members of the Presbyterian Church. After marriage Mr. Wilson located five miles east of Greensburg, on 138 acres; in 1882 he located on the forty acres where he now resides. In politics he is a Democrat, was a member of the Grange and an active worker in the temperance cause. His son, James Wilson, was born in December, 1861, and received a common-school education. At the age of nineteen he entered school at Greensburg, remaining two years, and then attended Columbia College two years. At twenty he commenced teaching in common schools, and taught at Columbia during the last year, still pursuing his regular studies. The past year he taught an excellent school at Gresham Postoffice. At the August election he was elected county superintendent of common schools in Green County, for a term of four years; in politics he is Democratic. Hugh W. Wilson's second son, his only married child, William R. Wilson, was united in marriage to Miss Cettie Reynolds, of Hart County, in October, 1882.

FRANK R. WINFREY, a native of that part of Cumberland County which is now a part of Russell County, was born January 12, 1843. He is the son of Frank H. and Catherine (Graves) Winfrey, both natives of Culpeper County, Va. Hon. Frank H. Winfrey was born in 1798, and in childhood (about 1804) was brought to Cumberland County by his parents. He was a man of good education and of large general information. He early in life espoused the cause of the Whig party, advocating the principles set forth by Clay, and held office under his chosen party about thirty-two years. He was elected sheriff of Cumberland County under the old constitution, and soon after was elected to represent his county in the Legislature. Every two years he was re-elected until he had held

the honorable position twenty successive years, and was contemporary with the celebrated John J. Crittenden. He was a clear, forcible speaker, of great ability as a statesman, and was in his time the most popular man in his region, often being elected when his party was in the minority. He was elected in 1843 to represent the counties of Cumberland, Clinton, Wayne and Russell in the Senate of Kentucky, when the Whig party was in the senatorial district 600 in the minority, and was re-elected at the close of his first term. Williams, when the Whig party was in the He was married to Miss Catherine Graves, a daughter of Capt. Thomas Graves, one of the noble band who aided in gaining American independence. He served seven years, enlisting when but a mere boy as a private, but securing a promotion to the position of captain of a company. He was present and took part in the closing conflict at Yorktown and in the ceremonies of the surrender. He was a very wealthy man, a resident of Russell County, where he had emigrated from Virginia, and lived to a ripe old age, dying in 1845. By his marriage Frank H. Winfrey became the father of twelve children: Polly, wife of T. W. M. Bledsoe; Matilda, wife of George W. Ross; Israel C.; Thomas C.; Fanny, wife of George W. Barger; Susan E., wife of John R. McClure; F. R.; Belle, wife of Dr. L. G. Hays; William Joseph (deceased); Kate P. (deceased), and two who died in infancy. Hon. Frank H. Winfrey died in 1855 in the fifty-seventh year of his age, his widow in 1883 in the seventy-ninth year of her age. Frank R. Winfrey in youth received an ordinary English education. While he was attending the high school of Burkesville the war began, and in September, 1861, he enlisted in Company C, of the Twelfth Kentucky Volunteer Federal Infantry. He took part in many of the bloodiest battles of the war, and in May, 1863, was promoted to the office of first lieutenant, and afterward to captain, but not mustered in as such for want of sufficient number of men, and in February, 1865, was mustered out of the service, received an honorable discharge, and came home. The first year was spent in farming, and in October, 1865, he began the study of law under Maj. T. C. Winfrey, his brother. During the winter of 1866 and 1867 he attended the Louisville University of Law, where he graduated in 1867. He remained with Maj. Winfrey, and about three years after graduation formed a partnership with him. From 1868 to 1874 he served the county of Adair as county attorney, elected on the Democratic ticket. The firm of Winfrey & Winfrey is one of the most prominent law firms of Adair County, and has always done a large and flourishing law practice in the circuit courts and court of appeals. Mr. Winfrey was married in 1874 to Miss Izora W. Saufley, the daughter of Harvey Saufley, a Virginian. There have been born to him two children: Mike C. and Iva Jane, who is dead. He and wife are members of the Methodist Episcopal Church of Columbia, and he is a member both of the Masonic order and of the I. O. O. F. In politics Mr. Winfrey espouses the cause of the national Republican party.

JAMES WOOD is a son of James and Elizabeth (Harris) Wood, and was born February 14, 1823. The father was born in Culpeper County, Va., and at the age of eight years came to Kentucky with his parents, who settled on a farm in Mercer County. The mother was born in Maryland, and was brought by her parents to Mercer County, Ky., in 1808. They were married in 1813, and had born to them three boys and seven girls, all of whom lived to be married. James Wood, the subject of this sketch, is a native of Mercer County. At the age of seventeen he left his parents and hired out as a farm hand, and has worked his way up to the ownership of 112 acres of well improved land. He married Miss Martha Coovert, who died in 1871, leaving the following named children: Elizabeth (Norris), Thomas, Nannie (deceased), Garrett, Clara (White), Mattie (deceased), William and Eliza. Mr. Wood is an Odd Fellow and a Prohibitionist.

JOHN J. WOOD was born January 6, 1839. His grandfather, William Wood, came from Virginia in the close of the eighteenth century, and settled in what was known as the Blue Spring country, in what is now Green County, where he became an extensive land owner and prominent farmer. He reared a large family, among whom was Buford Wood, the father of John J. He was born in 1808, in Green County, and in early life located in Hart County, where he served several years as sheriff. He married Frances Grant, the daughter of William Grant, and a native of Kenton County, born in 1807. She now resides in Adair County. Buford Wood died in 1854 in Barren County, Ky., where he has spent a great portion of his life as a farmer. The issue of Buford and Frances Wood, besides the subject of this sketch, were Bettie (Barrett), deceased; William T., of Boyle County; Mary (Garnett) of Adair County; Jennie (deceased) and Dr. Buford T. Wood, superintendent of a feeble-minded institute in California. John J.

Wood, born in Barren County, was chiefly educated in Columbia, Adair County, and removed to Lebanon in 1864, as bookkeeper for the old Commercial Bank, but soon after engaged in farming in Lebanon Precinct, which has since occupied his attention. Mr. Wood enjoys the universal esteem of all who know him; is a member of the Masonic fraternity and a prominent Democrat, having served as chairman of the Central Committee of Marion County. He was first married in 1866, to Miss Annie, daughter of John and Sallie (Gibbs) Young. She died in 1871, leaving two children, Bettie and Jennie, both of whom are now deceased. His second marriage was to Miss Bettie Carlile, of Green County. Their children are John, May and Annie Wood. Mr. Wood is an elder in the Second Presbyterian Church.

JAMES M. WOOD was born April 10, 1845, in Green County, Ky., where he grew up on a farm. His father, John Wood, was born January 25, 1804, near Bull Run, Va. When about one year old he was brought by his parents to Kentucky, locating in Green County, where he resided until about two years after the creation of Taylor County, when he located therein. He was a farmer and of Irish descent. John Wood married in June, 1842, Miss Harriet P., daughter of Pascal and Mildred (Pentacost) Tucker. From this union sprang Sarah F. (Phelps), George T., James M., Isham (deceased), Bettie M. (deceased), Susan M. (Brown), Jessie E. and Henry. James M. Wood married April 24, 1877, Miss Annie, daughter of Robert and Parmelia (Case) Colvin, who was educated in that illustrious school conducted by Julia A. Tevis, Shelbyville, Ky. Robert Colvin served in the Kentucky Legislature in 1838. To Mr. and Mrs. James M. Wood have been born Henry A. and Alice. Mr. Wood's early advantages were meager, but by study he has secured a good English education, and has made some progress in the study of the higher branches. He began as a teacher, and in 1870 began the study of law under a persimmon tree on Brush Creek; in 1871 he began reading in the office of J. R. Robinson, and after teaching and reading, one year thereafter was licensed to practice, since which time he has been engaged in the profession with good success, making criminal practice a specialty. In 1874 he was elected county attorney, which position he held for eight years, and is now a prominent candidate for Congress from his district. He is a member with his wife of the Baptist Church; in politics he is a Democrat, and was a member of the Legislature in 1883-84, and was three times elected school superintendent of his county.

GREEN B. WOODCOCK was born March 22, 1827, near Somerset, Ky., and is a son of Stephen and Sarah (Zachary) Woodcock, to whom seven children were born, namely: Robert, December 16, 1820; Willis, September 28, 1819; William H., October 28, 1822; Nancy, February 21, 1825; Green B., Galien Ellett, March 10, 1832, and Sarah M., January 28, 1830. Stephen Woodcock was born June 16, 1797, in Pulaski County, Ky.; was a farmer all his life, was an owner of slave property and died in 1834. He was a son of Robert Woodcock, who married a Miss Hale, both natives of Culpeper County, Va. They came to Kentucky as early as 1785 or 1790. They reared three sons and two daughters, of whom one son, Henry, was a soldier in the war of 1812, and in the battle of New Orleans, and died soon after reaching home. Robert Woodcock, of English descent, died about 1830, aged about seventy years. Mrs. Sarah Woodcock was born July 10, 1799, a daughter of William Zachary, of Virginia. William Zachary came to Kentucky with the Woodcock family, who first settled in Bourbon County, but afterward moved to Pulaski. Green B. Woodcock was reared on a farm and received but a common school education, principally after he became of age. In 1857 he moved to Boyle County and located on 250 acres, and owned upward of forty slaves in 1861. He went South at the close of the war, but returned to Pulaski County and engaged in the coal and lumber trade for nine years, when he again located in Boyle and purchased a farm north of Danville; he also owns a small farm immediately south of Danville, and a fine residence in the city limits. He was married, May 17, 1877, to Jennie, daughter of Adam Pence, of Lincoln County. He lost his wife in September, 1878, and in December, 1884, married Nannie Jet, of Marion County. The issue from this union is one son, N. B. Mr. Woodcock, before the war, was a strong advocate of Whig principles; since, he has affiliated with the Democrats.

CHARLES W. WRIGHT, one of the widely known and highly respected members of the Campbellsville bar, was born about eight miles east of Campbellsville, Ky., December 21, 1847. His father, Charles Wright, was born in King and Queen County, Va., in 1804. He was a farmer and a son of John B. Wright, who was also a native of Virginia, removing thence about 1810 to Green County, of which he was one of the pioneer settlers. He was a farmer, and de-scended from the North Carolina branch of the family. Charles Wright, Sr., was married about 1836 to Mrs. Louella (Spurling) Penn, widow of Sanford Penn and daughter of William Spurling, of Taylor County. To them six children were born: Mary J. (Gilmore), Catherine H. (Spurling), John W., Thomas R., Elizabeth (Roots) and Charles W. Charles W. married, November 10, 1870, Miss Ann M., daughter of Dr. Robert Hodgen, of Taylor County. He began life for himself as a deputy county and circuit court clerk of his county, and after serving four years served twelve years as county clerk alone, since which time he has been receiver of taxes of his county. In April, 1880, he received license to practice law, in which he has since engaged as well as in his official capacity. He is a member of the Methodist and his wife of the Presbyterian Church, and in politics is a Democrat. He is a thoroughly self-made man, having by industry and frugality secured a comfortable competency for his family.

RICHARD W. WRIGHT was born November 5. 1862, and is a son of Richard W. and Angeline E. (Moore) Wright, to whom four sons and one daughter were born, and who were natives of Washington County. R. W. Wright, Sr., was a leading and substantial farmer and slave owner, served as magistrate several years, and had quite a reputation also as administrator of estates, in which he was engaged until, in 1881, he moved to northeast Missouri. He was a son of Charles M. and Matilda (Batsell) Wright, who were born and reared in Virginia, and came to Washington County, Ky., about 1809. They were members of the Baptist Church and of Irish origin. Mrs. Angelina E. Wright is a daughter of John Moore, who married a Miss Wallace, both natives of Virginia, who came to Kentucky about 1809; they were of Irish descent and were of the Baptist faith. Richard W. Wright was born in Washington County, and was reared on a farm and educated at Lebanon and Buffalo. When he arrived at maturity he commenced life as a salesman at Loretto with Davis and Peterson. Early in 1884 he united in business with Davis in general merchandising, and in November, 1884, became sole proprietor of the establishment. Mr. Wright, by his good business qualifications and energy, has made life a success. In politics he is a Democrat.

JOHN M. WYCOFF, junior member of the firm of J. A. Wycoff & Bro., merchants at Mackville, was born in Mercer County in December, 1824, being the youngest of a family of three children born to John and Elizabeth (McGohon) Wycoff. His paternal grandfather, Nicholas Wycoff, was a native of New Jersey, where he was reared to manhood, but was one of the early immigrants to Kentucky, settling in Mercer County, where he continued to live until he became advanced in years; those of his children who were living had removed to Indiana, where he went and remained with them until his death. Mark McGohon, maternal grandfather, was a native of Ireland, and immigrated to America and the colonies when a young man. He enlisted and served in the Continental Army during the Revolutionary war, participating in a number of the important engagements of that struggle. A few years subsequent he immigrated to Kentucky, and settled in Mercer County. He died in his ninety-ninth year at the home of his daughter, Mrs. Margaret McKittric, in Washington County. John Wycoff, father of John M., was born and reared in Mercer County, and was a comparatively young man at the time of his death in August, 1824. John M. Wycoff was reared by his grandparents, the McGohons. He received a common education, and in the year 1849 he and his brother established themselves in the mercantile business at Mackville, where they have since continued. They carry quite a large stock of general merchandise, and do an extensive business. May 8, 1851, Mr. Wycoff was united in marriage to Miss Malvina Graves, by whom he is the father of four children: John, who married Miss Foley; Margaret, wife of W. J. Raybourn; Joseph and Madison, the last two in Missouri. In 1863 Mr. Wycoff suffered the bereavement of losing his beloved wife. He is a member of the Presbyterian Church, and in politics has always been a Democrat.

SQUIRE JOHN JAMESON YEISER was born October 3, 1837, one mile north of Danville, and has always been a resident of Boyle County. His father, Dr. Daniel Yeiser, a native of Baltimore, Md., was born in March, 1789, and removed in childhood with his parents to Danville, where he was reared. He graduated as a physician at the Philadelphia Medical College, and settled in 1809 in Alexandria, La., where he practiced his profession with great success for thirteen years, and then returned to the neighborhood of Danville, where he engaged in practice and farming until his death in 1878. He was one of the chief projectors of the Lexington & Danville Turnpike; was a copartner in practice with Dr. Ephraim McDowell, and was long a Royal Arch Mason. By the late

war he lost fifty-two slaves. He was the son of Phillip E. Yeiser, a native of Wittenburg, Germany, who died of cholera at Danville in 1833. Dr. Daniel Yeiser married Miss Catherine Faunt Le Roy Samuels, of Orange County, Va. (born in May, 1802, died in 1874), and from their union sprang George (deceased), Sarah J. (Borden), Catherine (Adams), Henry, Sr., Rosa M. (deceased), John J., Samuel (died from cold contracted while a prisoner of war at Camp Douglas), Fountain M., Affie G. (Jackson), Mary D. (Walworth) and Benjamin B. Our subject married Miss Ann'Maria, daughter of Abram I. and Ann M. (McDowell) Caldwell, of Boyle County (born Semptember 21, 1839), and from this union there has been no issue, but they have raised an orphan child, now Mrs. Sallie (Graham) Spears. January 1, 1886, Mr. Yeiser was by Gov. Knott appointed magistrate and member of the court of claims of Boyle County, which position he now retains. He is a farmer, having 176 acres of land in a fine state of cultivation, generally inclosed with substantial stone fences, and otherwise improved to correspond. On the place is a natural spring cave, in which the temperature scarcely varies during the year, but it is not certainly known by whom this place was first improved, nor when or by whom the stone dwelling was constructed. Squire Yeiser has been Eminent Commander of the Ryan Commandery, No. 17, of Danville; is a stanch Presbyterian, and in politics a Democrat.

JOHN W. YERKES was born April 1, 1854, in Lexington, Ky., and is the youngest of three sons and two daughters, all living, born to Rev. Dr. Stephen and Amanda (Lovell) Yerkes. Dr. Stephen Yerkes was born June 27, 1817, in Hatborough, Penn. At the age of fifteen he entered Yale College, from which he graduated in the class of 1837, after which he located in Baltimore where he was engaged in teaching, and was active in building up the schools of the city. In 1851 he located in Lexington, where he was connected with Transylvania University. In 1857 he located in Danville, and was elected to the chair of Hebrew and oriental languages in the Presbyterian Theological Seminary; has been continuously connected with the institution ever since, and is now its president. He was a son of John W. Yerkes, a native of Pennsylvania, who was one of the active movers in suppressing the Whisky Rebellion in Pennsylvania during the Washington administration. His parents came from Saxony, and were deeded lands by William Penn. He was a Presbyterian and married a Miss Wadron. The mother of John W. was born in Baltimore, and was a daughter of Thomas Lovell, a native of Maryland. His business was that of a merchant and he was of English parents. John W. Yerkes, our subject, received his education in Centre College, graduating in the class of 1873; begun the study of law and graduated from the law school at Ann Arbor, Mich. He located in Danville, where he has established a fine record as a lawyer, and is spoken of by those of his profession who know him as one of the most brilliant and best informed lawyers of his age in the State. In October, 1879, he was united in marriage to Elizabeth O. Anderson, of Boyle County, a daughter of Hon. W. C. and Amelia (Rhodes) Anderson, who were natives of Garrard County. The issue of this marriage was two children: Lovell S. and Amelia R. Mr. and Mrs. Yerkes are members of the Presbyterian Church. He is an active and leading Republican of Kentucky.

MORGAN R. YEWELL, farmer and stock raiser, was born September 26, 1825. James Yewell, his paternal grandfather, was a native of Culpeper County, Va., from whence he immigrated to Kentucky in an early day; his wife was a Miss Shirley. Martin Yewell, their son and father of Morgan R. Yewell, was born in the Old Dominion in 1787, and was quite young when his parents came to the wilds of Kentucky. In 1809 Martin married Miss Nancy Foreman, daughter of Joseph Foreman, who was a native of Maryland, and came to Kentucky in an early time. To the union of Mr. Martin Yewell and Mrs. Yewell ten children were born: Lavina (widow of Edward Nall), Harrison (deceased), Nancy (wife of Rev. James H. Brown), Elizabeth (now Mrs. James F. McGeehee), Joseph (deceased), Rebecca (deceased), Morgan R., Vardaman, Bemis and Isabel (deceased). Mr. Yewell died at the

advanced age of seventy-three years, in February, 1860, a true and devout Christian, a believer in the Baptist faith. Morgan R. Yewell was born on the farm where he yet lives in Botland Precinct, Nelson County, and assisted his parents until he attained the age of twenty-three years, receiving a common education in the common schools of the vicinity. January 11, 1849, his marriage with Susan C. Bell, daughter of John M. Bell, was solemnized, and to their union nine children have been born, of whom six are now living: A. Judson, John M., Belle, Margaret (Mrs. George Beam), Eliza and Morgan. Mr. Yewell has always made farming his occupation, devoting especial attention to the breeding of fine horses of Hambletonian and Lexington stock; he also raises the variety of jacks known as the Mammoths, and is the proprietor of 540 acres of improved land. In politics he is an ardent Democrat.

H. T. YOUNG was born December 5, 1846, and devoted the first part of his business life for several years to tanning, but at present is farming with success. His father, Franklin Young, was born in Mercer County about 1807, received a classical education in the county, and devoted the principal part of his life in merchandising in Harrodsburg and Cornishville. His first marriage was to Miss Jane Springer, who bore two children: David and William. His second marriage was to Miss Amanda Wheeler, who became the mother of H. T. Young, who was born in Cornishville, Mercer County, and who was married in 1872 to Miss Jennie E. Linney, a daughter of Hon. G. W. Linney. To this union were born five children: Flora A., George (deceased), Emma (deceased), Cecil, Charlie, Annie. Mr. Young is a member of the Presbyterian Church, a Democrat, and an honorary member of the I. O. O. F.

INDEX.

INDEX.

COUNTY SKETCHES.

INDEX.

1

ALLIN
  Mary A. (Reichenberg) 777
  Mary B. (Thompson) 778
  Mary Boswell 777
  Nancy A. (Soper) 1001
  Nancy A. (Woodson) 777
  Naomi F. (Pendleton) 778
  Philip T. 777ff
  Polly J. (Grant) 777
  Rebecca (Berkele) 789
  Saml. W. 777
  Susan J. 777ff
  Susan Hart (Warren) 777
  Thos. 777ff
  Wm. B. 777
  Wm. H. 777
  Wm. Poteet 778
ALMHOUSE LAWS 1011
ALVERSON, Jane (Forsythe) 858
AMMELLMAN, Kinelus 858
  Lulie (Forsythe) 858
ANDERSON, Alfred M. 778
  Alta 779
  Amelia (Owsley) 779
  Amelia (Rhodes) 779, 1048
  Ann Mary 778
  Bettie (Coppage) 779
  Betty (Herndon) 887
  (Boyle) 744
  Clarence 768
  Clifton R. 779
  Eliza C. 778
  Eliz.(Riffe) 898
  Eliz. O. (Yerkes) 1048
  Eveline (Fish) 855
  Frances (Robards) 985
  Franklin 779
  Garland 778
  Giles 873
  Guy W. 778
  Jemima (Mozee) 873
  Jno. 859
  Letitia (Edrington) 779
  Lizzie 779
  Lucie (Herndon) 887
  Lucinda (Coppage) 779
  Marg. (Fulton) 859
  Martha (Blair) 791
  Mary Frances (Spilman) 768
  Mary J. (Wilcher) 779
  Mary Ruth (Wilson) 778
  Millie (McCain) 779
  Millie (Weatherford) 779
  (Minor) 778
  Murder of 752
  Nancy (Hert) 778
  Paralee (Dyre) 779
  Pauline (Beeler) 779
  Robt. 791
  Sally (Trabue) 778
  Sallie A. (Miller) 778
  Sallie E. (Parrott) 778
  Simeon 744, 779
  T. 985
  Thos. J. 778
  W. C. 799, 1048
  Walter W. 799, 1048
  Wm. C. 744, 779
  Wm. Lee 778
  (Winston) 778
ANDREWS, Sarah Pitman (Hamner) 873
ANN, ST. - 2nd Roman Cath. Ch. in Ky. 817
APPLEGATE, Eliz. 1019
  Ella (Thomas) 1019
  Moses Dr. 1019
ARGO, (Kavanaugh) 779
  Martha M. (Hobbs) 779
  Robt. M. 779

ARGO
  Wm. K. 779
ARMSTRONG, Amanda F. (Allen) 776, 966
  Andrew Hogue 780
  Ann (Aid) 780
  Ann (Cruft) 780
  Ann (Hogue) 780
  Ann (Irvin, Lyle) 780
  Anna E. (Pearce) 776, 966
  Cath. (Lillis) 977
  Cath. Jane (Campbell) 780
  Chas. Q. 776, 966
  Chas. Thos. 780
  DeWitt Clinton 780
  Eliza (Williams) 780
  Eliz. (Graham) 865
  Ella 780
  Emeline (Browning) 780
  Hugh 780
  Jas. W. 780
  Jane (Cavin) 780
  Jane (Taylor) 780
  Jennie (Jelf) 780
  Jennie (Moore) 776
  Jno. A., Dr. 776, 780, 924
  Josephine 780
  Kate (Leathers) 776
  LaFayette 780
  Lilly (Offutt) 776, 780
  Lizzie 780
  Lucy (Huston) 780
  Ludic 780
  Mary (Williams) 780
  Mattie (Wilkinson) 776
  Nancy (Lillard) 919
  Nannie L. 780
  Paulina (Harlan) 879
  Priscilla (adams) 923
  Priscilla (McAfee) 924
  Prudence (Lillard) 919
  Rebecca (Rule) 780
  Rose 780
  Sally 780
  Sarah J. 780
  Sybelle (Dunn) 780
  Talitha W. (Green) 780
  Thos. Cavin, Dr. 780
  Wm. G.,Capt. 780
ARNOLD, Cath. E. (Garnett) 1010
  Jno. W. 1010
  Leah M. (Sullivan) 1010
  Mollie S. (Garnett, Sullivan) 1010
  Sarah J. (Stephenson) 1004
  Thompson 1004
ARTHUR, Mary (Runyon) 1006
  President 798, 918, 956
  Tabitha (Gooch) 783
ASBURY UNIV. 961
ASHBY, Jno., Capt. 765
  M.Q., Dr. 765
  Mary (McKee) 765
  Nathaniel,Capt. 765
  Turner, Gen. 765
ASHBY'S GAP 765
ASHFORD,Barilla(Hawkins) 882
  Nancy (Hawkins) 882
  Thos. 882
ASKREN, Martha (Van Sickle, Means) 1030
ASSASSINATION, By Federals 1011
ATCHINSON, Hamilton 884
  Melinda (Headly) 884
ATHERTON, Eliz. (Whitehead) 781
  Jas. B. 781
  Jno. S. 781
  Maria (Beeler) 781

ATHERTON
  Peter 781
ATKINSON, Allan 781
  Alma 781
  Chas. T. 781
  Florine 781
  Jane (Hill) 890
  Jno. (Rev.) 781, 869
  Jos. 781
  Lucinda (Ela) 781
  Mary (Schoolfield) 993
  (Newcomb) 781
  Odessa (Robertson) 781
  Sarah (Winans) 781
  Thos. 781
  Timothy 781
ATWOOD, Ann (Medley) 890
AULBY, Eliz. (Corley) 830
  Perry 830
AUSTIN, Jno. 901
AVERY, Mary (Hutchinson) 805
AVRITT 1012
  Eliz. (Owsley) 963
  Eliz. M. (Tucker) 781
  Geo. C. 782
  Jno. 781
  Laura E. 782
  (Vaughn) 781
  Mary (Phi-lips) 782
  Saml. 781
AZBILL, W. D., Rev. 1016
BABBITT, Alex. 808
  Sallie (Buster) 808
  Sophronia (Oatts) 808
BACK, Eliza (Hudson) 894
BACON COLLEGE 770, 778
BADIN, Stephen Theodore, Rev. 815, 817
BAILEY, America (Patton) 844
  Baswell E. 782
  Benj. W. 782
  Carroll 844
  Clarence 782
  Eliz. (Hancock) 873
  Elijah 844
  Ellen N. (Edwards) 782
  Grief 782, 949
  Jennie P. 782
  Jno.,Rev. 844
  Martha P. (Durham) 782, 949
  Robt. 782
  Sallie (Montgomery) 949
  Sarah (Dunlap) 844
  Sarah (Jackman) 844
  Tandy 873
  Willie Wood 782
BAIRD, Saml. K. 907
BAKER 748
  Adelaide (Owsley) 962
  Albert T. 782
  Amanda (Emmons) 782
  Ann Clark (Alexander) 773
  Bettie (Grissom) 782
  Betsy (Robards) 985
  Caroline (Wells) 782
  (Combs, Evans) 850
  Cora Lee (Cunningham) 783
  David 1042
  Eliz. (Edwards) 782
  Eliz. (Robinson) 782
  Feminine 782
  (Gentry) 1042
  Geo. F. 782, 962
  Geo. W. 1039
  H. E. 948
  Hannah (Spears) 1003
  Henrietta A. (Bronston) 802
  Henry 886

BAKER
Jas. A. 782
Jas. M. 782
Jos. Harrell 783
L. B. 1027
Louisa (Binns) 782
Lu y Ann (Mitchell) 782
Marg. (Bault) 1010
Marg. Steger (Bosley) 797
Maria (Henson) 886
Martha B. (Alexander) 773
Martin, Rev. 773
Mary A. (Montague) 948
Mary A. (Vaughan) 782
Mary B. (Phoebyhouse) 886
Mary L. (Spears) 1003
Michael 1042
Nancy (Philps) 1042
Nannie (Elliott) 782
Robt. Arthur 783, 800
Robt. F. 782
Saml. K. 782
Sarah A. (Cheatham) 1039
Sarah A. (Williams, McGee)
  932, 1039
Sarah Ann (Breeding) 800
Sarah Martin (Alexander) 773
Susan (Willis) 1042
Susanna (Grigsby) 782
Thos. 782
Walker 1003
BALD, Wm. 816
BALDWIN, Eliz. (Lewis) 917
Jno. H., Dr. 756
BALE, Bennie P. 783
Chas.S. 783
Diana (Dimey, Lewis) 783,
  824, 866
Edward L. 783
Eliz. (Close) 824
Eliz. F. (Shields) 783
Emily C. 783
Harriet (Weldon) 783
Holland 783
Jacob 783
Jas. L. 783
Jno., Rev. 783, 824, 866
Katie H. Young 783
Leona Leota Kann 783
Lou 783
Lura M.(Shields) 783
Mary E. (McDonald) 783
Minnie J. 783
Nancy (Graham) 866
Ossian T. 783
Saml. W. 783
Tabitha 783
Wallace 783
Wilshire 783
Wm. J. 783
BALEY, Eliza (Adams) 906
Hezekiah 821
Rhoda A. (Chelf) 820ff
BALL, Anna (Webb) 821
Barrilla (Chewning) 821
David 955
Jennie M. (Murphy) 955
Jos. K., Capt. 907
Maria (Davison) 803
Maria (McDowell) 942
Mary E. (McMurtry) 934
Mattie L. (Kelley) 907
Parmelia (Fenton) 853
Robt., Col. 821ff
Sarah (Pinkerton) 972
Stephen A. 972
BALLARD, Cath. (Dant) 836
Ellen (Clark) 788
(Ford, Tucker) 836
Geo. L. 1000

BALLARD
Letitia (Cessell) 1000
Lucy (Slaughter) 997
Mary (Greenwell) 836
Mary (Stives) 938
Nancy (Smith) 1000
Wm. P. 836
BALLINGER (Jennings) 900
BALTIMORE, Lord 819, 968,
  1002, 1037
BANE, Katie (McMakin) 801
BANFORD, Eliz. (Moore) 950
BANK, Mercer Nat. 940ff
U.S. Charter 861
BANKS, Rebecca (Davis) 836
BANTA, Mary A. (Clarke) 935
BAPTIST RECORDER 751
BAPTISTS, Regular 1035
BARBAROSSA 745
BARBEE, Almanda (Terrill) 1018
  Col. 860
  (Fisher) 856
BARBOUR, Endotia B. (Bosley)
  797
Jas. P. 924
Jno. F., Dr. 756
L. G. 755
Lucetta (Debo) 839
BARCLAY, Eliz. (Thompson) 993
Jno. 993
Mary A. (Samuels) 993
Tavern 867
BARGER, Abigail (Vaughan) 782
Fanny (Winfrey) 1044
Geo. W. 1044
Hannah F. (Lesemby) 1009
Sarah B. (Willis) 1041
Stephen 1041
BARKER, Eliz. (Stone) 1006
Va. (Conn) 828
BARKLEY, Eliz. (Campbell) 811
BARLOW, Anastasia C. (Thompson)
  740
Betsey (Bell) 739
Carrie 740
Eliz. (Kimbrough) 739
Florence 740
Harrison 739
Jas. 739
Jno. 739
Keziah (West) 739
Marg. 740
Milton V. 739ff
Robt. E. Lee 740
Rich. A. 740
Saml. 739
Sarah (Bell) 739
Thos. H. 739
Va. 740
Wm. Henry Harris 739
BARNES 748, 950
Nancy (Murrah) 957
S. M., Col. 887
BARNETT, Eliz. (Miller) 944
Jas., Col. 944
Martha (Patterson) 800
BARNS, Thos. H. 1037
BARR, Anna (Johnson) 784
Anna (Mitchell) 784
Bridget 784
Jno. 784
Jos. 784
Marietta (Mitchell) 784
Mary (McCreary) 926
Mary A. 784
Thos. J. 784
BARRETT, Bettie (Wood) 1045
Jno. A., Rev. 992
BARRIERES, M., Rev. 815
BARRY, Anna Parolee (Hagan)
  871

BARRY
Frances Felicia (Jesse)
  871, 884
Jno. J., Dr. 871, 884
Julia G. (Healy) 884ff
Mary (Tarkington) 1014
BARTLEY, Jno. 850
Sallie (evans) 850
T. W. 965
BARTON, Ann (Faulconer) 852
BASCOMB 873
BASHFORD, Sally (Pinkerton)
  972
BATES, Ellen V. (Gibson) 863
Euphemia (Booker) 796
Lucy (Robertson) 986
S. W., Dr. 863
Sarah (Hogan) 863
Thos. 796
(Walker) 1034
BATSELL, Kizzie (Drye) 841,
  854
Kizzie (Nall) 841
Matilda (Wright) 1046
Rebecca (Beard) 786
Thos. 841
BAUGHMAN, Hamilton 764
Henry 784
Jacob 784
Joel T. 784
Jno. T. 784
Maria I. (Harlan) 879
Nancy (Dunn) 784
Nancy (Gilbreath) 784
Nudiget O. 784
Obedience (Owsley) 961
Patience (Owsley) 784
Polly (McGill) 784
Rebecca (Shanks) 784
Sallie (Dunn) 784
Saml. O. 784
Ticia (Duncan) 784
Wm. O. 784
BAULT, Eliz. (Sullivan) 1010
Marg. (Baker) 1010
Wm. 1010
BAXTER, Edward Briscoe 784ff
Eliz. (Briscoe) 784
Ellen (Gregory) 785
Geo. 785
Jas. H. 784
Jane (Mayfield) 970
Lafayette 784
Lucebra 784
Mary (walker) 784
Milo 752
Sarah (David) 837
Susan (Davis) 837
Walker 785
Wm. A. 784
Zerelda (talbott) 752
BAYNE, Cath. (McMakin) 883
Martha (Moore) 951
Walter 951
BEADLES, Thely (McGee) 1041
BEALE, Nancy (Cunningham) 800
BEALL, Geo. W. 785, 1005
Jacob 1026
Lizzie Laura 785
Mary (Carter) 785, 969
Mary E. (Peterson) 969
Mattie 785
Minerva F. (Stiles) 785
Nathan 785
Paulina (Van Cleave 1028
Sarah Jane (Stiles) 785, 969
Thos. J. 969
Washington 785, 969
BEALMEAR, Saml. C. 785ff
Sarah E. (Summers) 785ff

3

BEAM, Geo. 1048
  Marg. (Yewell) 1048
  Rebecca (Milligan) 1006
  Sarah (Van Cleave) 1028
  Sallie (Stiles) 1006
  Wm. 1006
BEAN, Betsey (Van Arsdell)
    1028
  Jane (Peacock) 1037
  Sarah Marg. (Murphy) 954
  Station 864
  Creek 751
BEARD, Anna (Hatcher) 786
  Creed T. 787
  Diodema(Demia) (Mann) 786
  Elijah 786
  Eliz. (Thomas) 993
  Eliz. M. (McWhorter) 787
  Emma (Schoolfield) 993
  Eugene 787
  Fannie (ogle) 786, 857
  Florence R. 787
  Frances (Sharp) 786
  Herschell 787
  Isaiah 786
  J. C., Dr. 786
  Jas. O. 787
  Jas. W. 786ff
  Jno. J., Dr. 786ff, 857
  Jno. M. 787
  Jos. 786
  Josiah 786ff
  Mary (Shawler) 1022
  Mary E. (Evans) 850
  Mary N. (McWhorter) 786
  Mollie E. (Hendrickson) 787
  Moses 786, 850
  Rebecca (Batsell) 786
  Robt. 786
  Sallie B. 787
  Saml. 786ff
  Shelton C. 787
  Stephen M. 993
  Susan (Simpson) 850
  (Troutman) 1022
  Virgil 787
  Wm. H. 787
BEATTEY, mary (Robinson) 996
BEATTIE 740
BEATTY, Adam 741
  Cornelius 741
  Eliz. (Fullinwider) 933ff
  Hattie (McMillan) 933
  Lewis 933
  Marg. (Hansford) 875
  Mary Dorathea (Grosh) 740
  Ormond 740
  Otho 741
  Sally (Green) 741
  Sophia (Rochester) 741
  Wm. 740
  Wm. Rochester 742
BEATY, Clarinda (Clevland) 824
  Jennie (Gillmore) 851
  Jos. 851
  Keziah (Crawford, Evans) 851
  Mary A. (Clevland) 824
  Sarah (Logan) 921
BEAUCHAMP, Eliz. (Brown) 802,
    842
  Jesse 802
BEAUFORD, Abe Gen. 740
BEAVEN, Cecily (Luckett) 787ff
  Chas. Col. 787ff, 816
  Edward 788, 816
  Eliz. E. 788
  Ella C. 788
  Ellen (Green) 788
  Francis D. 787ff
  Geo. B. 788

BEAVEN
  Mary J. (Clark, Smith) 788
  Susan M. (Mattingly) 788
  Teresa (Abell) 772
BEAZLEY, (Adams, Logan) 921
  Ann (Shackelford) 1018
  Jas. 1018
  Mary (Terrill) 1018
BECKHAM 1006
  Susan A. (Pile, Stiles) 1005
BECKWITH, Verlinda (Summers)
    786
BEDDOW, Eliz. (Wilson) 1043
BEDFORD, Capt. 862
  Mary J. (Moore) 950
BEELER, Adkin 903
  Adkinson H. 867
  Chas. 952
  Christopher 781
  Dorsey 903
  Eliz. (Weaver) 781
  Eliz. S. (Grant) 867
  Eliza J. (Moore) 952
  Ellen (Hill) 903
  Ellen (Johnson) 903
  Emma (Johnson) 903
  Finetta (Miller) 867
  Jno. 781
  Marg. (Ross) 903
  Maria (Atherton) 781
  Mary A. (Stiles) 952
  Pauline (Anderson) 779
BEES, Patriotic 793
BELL 759, 794, 806, 922, 962,
    970, 1030, 1037
  (Allen) 777
  Betsey (Barlow) 739
  Cath. (Hawkins, Blaine) 898
  David 898
  Dr. 780, 928
  Fannie (Lee) 915
  Henry 923
  Hosea 739
  Jane (Burrus) 923
  Jno. M. 834, 1048
  Joshua F. 743, 777,898, 915
  Lawson 739
  Lucy (Lee) 915
  Mary M. (Helm) 915
  Nancy (Holmes, Tathan) 898
  Nellie Ann (Hunn) 898
  Sarah (Barlow) 739
  Sarah A. (Robinson) 987
  Susan C. (Yewell) 1048
  Susan F. (Lyen) 923
  T. C. 1017
  Wm. 898
BELLES, Eliz. (Floyd) 856
  Peter 856
  Sarah (Davis) 856
BENEDICT, Lydia (Humphrey) 897
BENNETT, Chas. H. 788
  Eliz. (Painter) 789
  Endora 789
  Farris 792
  Jno. 789
  Lyman 789
  Marg. T. (Blevins) 792
  Rachel(Brown) 788
  Sarah C. (Watkins) 789
  Timothy S. 788
  Wesley 789
BENTLEY, Mary (Harlan, Neal)
    879
BERGIN, Murder of 752
BERKELE, Barbara (Shumaker)
    789
  Chas. 789
  Daisey 789
  Eugene 789

BERKELE
  Henry 789
  Jno. 789
  Josephine (Klose) 789
  Loisa Wilhelmina (Rushstien)
    789
  Louisa 789
  Louis H. 789
  Marg. (Heinz) 789
  Mary (Mairer) 789
  Mary (Mullins, Campbell) 789
  Michael 789
  Nettie M. (Jean) 789
  Rebecca (Alling) 789
  Wm. A. 789
BERRY, Ann (Hagan) 789
  Edward C. 789
  Eliz. (Carter) 992
  Eliz (Hagan) 789
  Eliz (Harris) 881
  Fannie (McIlvoy) 789
  Harrison 992
  Jemima (Hudson) 894
  Jeremiah 789
  Jno. H. 789
  Josephine (Boucher) 789
  Katie (Van Arsdall) 1027
  Maggie C. (Booker) 790, 796
  Mary (Buckler) 789
  Mary (Smith) 1018
  Mattie H. (Van Arsdall) 1027
  Nannie H. (Phillips) 789
  Nicholas T. 789ff
  Robt. M. 789
  Saml. B. 789, 790, 796
  Susan (Sallee) 992
  Wm. L. 789
BERRYMAN, Agnes (Phillips) 971
  Susan (Walker) 744
BETHANY COLLEGE, 1st. grad.
    1007
BEVILL, Mary (Mourning, Lisle)
    920
BIBB, Elijah 1001
  Eliz. (Soper) 1001
  F. J., Dr. 790
  Jas. 790
  Nancy (Walker) 790
  Patsey (Durrett) 790
  Robt. 790
  Sarah (Durrett) 790
BIBLES, Introduced on R.R.'s
    966
BICKERS, Joel 923
  Nancy (Lyen) 923
BICKETT, Mactillus (Scott) 1041
BIGGERS 981
BILBO, Rebecca (Hamner) 873
BILLINGS, (Douglas) 802
BINGAMIN, Lucy (Hill) 1043
BINNS, Louisa (Baker) 782
  Wm. M. 782
BIRD, Geo. 1009
  Levinia (Breeding) 800
  Louisa (Russell) 991
  Mary (Ewing) 1009
  Mary J. (Strange) 1009
  R. L. 991
  Sarah (Collier) 991
BIRDWHISTLE, Almira (Lyen) 923
BIRKHEAD, Matilda (Shadburne)
    994
BIRNEY, Jas. 895
BISHOP, Bettie (Fisher) 856
  Jacob K. 856
  Lucretia (Fenton) 853
  Mary J. (Garnett) 856
  Susan (Seay) 994
  Wm. 853
BLACK, Ann (Noland) 838

BLACK
Clarissa (Harlan) 879
Sally (Breeding) 800
BLACKBURN, Gideon 767
Gov. & Sen. 1010, 1035
BLACK HORSE CAVALRY 765
BLACKKETTER, Frances E.
(Hamner) 873
BLACKMORE, Rebecca (Evans)
849
BLACKWOOD, Sallie (Forsythe)
858
BLAIN, Eliz. (Hays) 983
(Cooper) 829
Major 778
(Reid) 983
BLAINE, Cath. (Hawkins, Bell)
898
Eliz. (Moran) 953
Eliz. A. (Read) 982
Jas. G. 823, 909, 1000
Nancy (Purdy) 909
Rachel E. (Kirk) 909ff
Rob 898
BLAIR, 791, 964
Albert 791
Aletha M. 791
Alex. 790
Amanda C. 791
Ann (Simpson) 996
Arminta (Wilson) 791
Belva E. 791
Betsy (Royse) 1043
Burton 791
Dicy Jane (Helm) 790
Eldridge 791
Eliz. 790
Eliz. (Breeding) 790, 800
Eliz. (Helm) 790
Eliz. (Lovelace) 791
Eliz. (Rippetoe) 791
Eliz. Ellen (Rosenbaum) 790
Emeline (Leach) 791
Frosia E. 791
Geo. Paschall 790
Geo. W. 790
Harrison 791
Jas. B. 790ff
Jas. T. 791
Jesse K. Polk 790
Jno. 790, 1043
Laura A. 791
Lawrence C. 791
Lucy (Hopkins) 790, 1043
Lucy Ellen 790
Lucy Jane (Blair) 790
Lucy Lillian 791
Lucy M. (Wilson) 1043
Martha (Anderson) 791
Martha E. (Wheat, Grider,
Smith) 790
Mary Frances 790
Mary Miranda (Scott) 790
Melvin E. 791
Minnie 791
Nancy (Day) 791
Nancy (Lawless) 791
R. A. 790
Rebecca (Stotts) 1007
Robt. J. 790
Semantha (Lawless) 791
Sarah A. (McKinley) 791
Sarah Jane (Crider) 791
Ursula J. 791
Viantha 791
Wm. Dr. 790ff, 1043
Wm. A., Rev. 790
BLAND, Anna(ie) C. (Stiles)
792, 1005

BLAND
Bell (Rush) 792
Corilla (Willett) 792, 1005
Elijah H. 791, 1005
Eliza. J. (Knifley, Jones)
910
Geo. G. 792
Jno. 792
Jos E., Dr. 792
Kaziale (Tomlinson) 1021
Mattie M. (Farmsworth) 792
Nancy (Wilkinson) 1038
Osborn 791
(Osburn) 792
Sallie 1038
Sarah (Peak) 791ff
Stiles P. 792
Wm. M. 791ff, 1038
BLANDFORD 810
BLANFORD, Susan (Thompson) 872
T. W. 972
BLANTON, David 743
Edgar 744
Harry 744
Irvine 744
Jos. 744
Katie 744
Lindsay Hughes, Rev.743, 755
Lizzie M. (Irvine) 744
Lucy (Jones) 743
Mary (Dickson) 744
Rutherford 744
Susan (Walker) 743ff
BLEDSOE, Eliz. Susan (Bowman)
962
Frances (Vernon) 939
Jos. S. 962
Marg. (Powell) 975
Mary Agnes (Owsley) 962
Polly (Winfrey) 1044
Sophia (Taylor) 1014
T. W. M. 1044
BLEDSON, (Robinson) 987
BLEVINS, Chas. 792
Gabriel 792
Marg. T. (Bennett) 792
Mary E. (Mears, Underwood)
792
Sarah (Roark) 792
(Skaggs) 792
Thos. J. 792
Wm. 792
BLINCOE, B.C., Capt. 1030
BLOID, Lethe (Close) 824
Nancy (McCubbins) 824
Stephen 824
BLOYD, Mary Susan (Turner)
1025
Washington 1025
BLUE GRASS, First Improver of
969
BLUE LICKS, Battle of 908
BLYTHE, Jane (Gentry, White)
881
Jas. 881
BOARD, Georgia W. (Robertson)
986
Mary J. (Graham) 986
Philip S. 986
Stephen 1031
BOARMAN, Anna B. (Spalding) 793
Edward H. 793
Felix 793
F ancis N. 793
Geo. W. 793
Jas. A., Capt. 793
Jno. O. 793
Jos. Lee 793
Leonard E. 793

BOARMAN
Mary A. 793
Mary J. (Hughes) 793
(McAtee) 793
Nancy (Clements) 793
Nancy E. 793
Percilla (Bullock) 793
Roswell 793
Saml. E. 793
Susan E. 793
BOAT, Freight-1st. from Greens-
burg to New Orleans
949
BOGGS, Benj. 793
Bettie 793
Edgar C. 794
Edward C. 793
Eliz. (Plow) 793
Eliz. J. (Woods) 793ff
Hannah (Turley) 793
Jas. 749, 794
Jas. H. 793ff
Jas. T. 793
Jno. 793
Jos. S. 793
Lillie M. 794
Marg. (Robinson) 793
Mary E. (Turley) 793
Mary M. (Gilisbie) 793
Mollie C. (Pigg) 794
Moses 793
Nannie M. 794
Otis T. 794
Phoeba (Cornelison) 794
Robt. 793
Rollie B. 794
Sarah (Houston) 908
Wm. 793
Willie H. 794
BOGIE, Frances (Stephenson)
1004
Thos. 1004
BOHANAN, Susan (Stout) 998
Davis 795
Eliz. H. (Hudson) 794
Geo. 794
H. C. 794, 876
Hanly 795
Irene (Saunders) 795
J. T., Dr. 794
J. W. 795
Jack (Jno.) 795
Lizzie (Hudson) 894
Lucy (Williams) 795
M. M. 795
Martha (Fennell) 795
Martha (Lightfoot) 795
Mattie B. (Peacock) 794
Mildred (McAfee, Hudson) 795
Minnie 795
R. H. 795
Rane S. 795
Reuben M. 795
V. A. (Hutchinson) 794
W. J. 794
Wm. Fry 794ff, 894
BOHONTOWN, Origin of 795
BOICE, Eliz. (Willis) 1041
Jane (Van Arsdall) 1027
BOLDRICK, Carrie (Spalding) 795
Chas. 795
Geo. D. 795
Jas. P. 795
Jno. 795
Kate (Tobin) 795
Lucy (Cundiff) 795
Mary (Doneghy) 795
Mary (Mitchell) 795
Ralph 795

5

BOLDRICK
 Saml. 795
 Sarah (Gundiff) 795
BOLLING, Dread 795
 Eliz. (Greenwood) 795
 Geo. 795
 Glover 795
 Howell 795
 Jeremiah 795
 Jno. Brisco Dr. 795ff
 Knight 795
 Lucy J. (CLeaver) 795
 Mary (Davis) 795
 Mary E. (Dorsey) 795
 Mary (Kimberlain) 795
 Mary (White) 795
 Mary (Wilson) 795
 Nancy (CUrry) 795
 Rachel(Bottom) 795
 Sarah (Gray) 867
 Silas 795
 Susan (Crane) 795
 Thos. M. 795
 Wm. H. Dr. 756, 795
BOMB, Eliz. (Harris) 995
BOMER, Julia (Cravens) 873ff
BONAUGH, Rebecca (Spears) 1003
BONDURANT, Fanny (Taylor) 892
 Ida (Greenwell) 869
BONER, Edgar S. 796
 Eliz. (Cavins) 796
 Geo. Welsh 796
 Georgie Ann (Raines) 796
 Jas. Alfred 796
 Jno. C. B. 796
 Jno. Quincy 796
 Jos. C. 796
 Marg. E. 796
 Mary (Kemper) 796
 Mary F. 796
 Oliver P. Morton 796
 Speed Fry 796
 T. K. 796
 Thos. Cavins 796
 Wm. B. 796
BONTA, Mary (Riker) 983
 Saml. 983
BOOKER, Eliza 796
 Euphemia (Bates) 796
 Harriet 796
 Henrietta Louisa 796
 Horace 796
 Lizzie 796
 Louisa (Nantz) 796
 Maggie C. (Berry) 790, 796
 Marion T. (Robertson) 985
 Martha 796
 Mary (Philips) 796
 Paul 796
 Saml. 796, 803
 Thos. J. Dr. 796
 W. F. 790, 796
 W. H. 985
 Wm. B. 796
BOONE 969, 1034
 Charlotte Mary (Rapier) 980
 Chas. 764, 980
 Geo. G. 967
 Harry 818
 Mary (Caldwell) 805
 Mary E. (Penny) 967
 Mildred (Johnson) 764
 Patience O. (Boughman) 967
 Sarah (Cecil) 818
 Susan (Howard) 764, 980
 Washington 816
 Wm. P. 989
BOONE'S CREEK 907
BOONE'S KNOB 974

BOONE'S STATION 833
BOONESBORO 854ff, 914, 969,
 982
 & Founder (Danl.) 793, 826,
 828, 831, 854, 899,908,
 914, 936, 982, 999,1007
BOOTON, Ruth B. (Hopkins) 1000
BORDEN, Sarah J. (Yeiser) 1047
BORDER'S HOTEL 901
BOSLEY, A. L. (Bosley) 797
 Chas. F. 796ff, 860
 (Cole) 797
 Eliz. (Fleece) 796ff
 Endotia B. (Barbour) 797
 Gideon 796ff, 860
 Harriet (Funk) 860
 Harry P. 797
 Henry P. Dr. 797
 J. S. 797
 Josephine (Lytle) 797
 Lillie 797
 Lizzie 797
 Marg. Steger (Baker) 797
 Sallie (Denny, Walker) 797
BOSWELL, Judith (Warren) 777
 Mary (Neale) 957
BOTTOM, Eliza (Edwards) 847
 Eliz. B. (Williams) 986
 Eliz. J. (Robertson) 986
 Jas. A. 986
 Jestine (Cull, Graves) 867
 Rachel (Bolling) 795
 Wm. S. 986
BOTTS, Eliz. (Moore) 952, 975
 Laura T. (Powell) 975
 Mildred (Sherrill) 1024
 Nancy (Moore) 952
 Thompson 975
BOUCHER, Josephine (Berry) 789
BOUGHMAN, Patience O. (Boone)
 967
BOUGHN, Jos. 857
 Martha (Overstreet) 857
 Sarah H. (Ford) 857
BOULDIN,Ann C. (Alexander) 773
 Cath. (Owsley) 961
 Lucy 776
 Maggie L. (Poor) 974
 Sarah (Alexander) 773
 Thos. 773
BOURKE, Wm. Rev. 992
BOWER, Mary (Cozatt) 833
BOWLES, Ignatius 816
 Jno. 816
 Mary (Ford) 857
 Wm. 816
BOWLIN, Thos. 816
BOWLING, Francis 980
BOWMAN 944
 Abram 985
 Ellen E. (Cox) 832
 Eliz. Susan (Bledsoe) 962
 Emma (Ray) 810
 Hannah F. (Read) 982
 Hester (Woods) 965
 Jno. 810
 Maggie (Caldwell) 810
 Mary 832
 Mary (McGee) 932
 Nannie (Cooke) 828
 Sarah (Perkins) 811
 Wilson 832
BOWMAR, Harriett (Willis) 1041
BOYD, Lydia (Jones) 904
 Mary (Mitchell) 947
 R. L. Capt. 775
BOYER, Anna M. (Van Pelt) 1029
BOYLE (Anderson) 744
 Jeremiah Tilford Gen. 744,
 799, 916

BOYLE
 Jno. Ch. Just. 744, 765
 (Tilford) 744
 Wm. O. Col. 744, 1036
BRADDOCK'S DEFEAT 765, 907
BRADFORD, Amanda (Davis) 943,
 1005
 Anna (Miles) 943
 Anna (Stiles) 1005
 David 943, 1005
 Eleanor (Lancaster) 1002
BRADLEY
 Rev. S. 797
 Christine 798
 Ellen (Totten) 797
 Geo. R. 798
 Isaac 797
 Marg. (O'Connell) 797
 Marg. Robertson (Duncan)
 798
 Robt. M. 797
 Wm. O. 823, 797
BRADSHAW, Ann (Bradshaw) 798
 Ann (Lowe) 798
 Ann L. (White) 798
 Arthur 952, 1040
 Benj. 811
 Betty C. 799
 Casandra (Jones) 798
 Cath. (Campbell) 811
 Charlotte (Williams) 1040
 Charlotte (White) 798
 Charlotta W. 798
 Effie T. 799
 Elijah 798
 Eliza (Slaughter, Nelson)
 998
 Helen (Rowe) 1040
 Isaac 798
 Isaiah 798
 Jane (Campbell) 811
 Lucinda (Williams) 1040
 Lucy A. (Williams, Carter)
 1040
 Mary (Wilson) 798
 Mary G. 799
 Mary T. (Moore) 952
 Millie (Miller) 798
 Millie E. (Montgomery) 798
 Octavia (McClure) 798
 Patsey (Todd) 941
 Polly (Williams) 1040
 Sally (Wilson) 798
 Sarah B. (Moore) 952
 Sarah G. (White) 798
 Seath 798
 Tarleton T. 798
 Timoleon 798, 1016
 Wm. E. 798ff, 952
BRADY, Emily J. (Cummins) 834
 Jno. 834
 Mary (Simpson) 834
BRAGG, 762, 853, 866, 926,964
BRAGSDALE, Jno. 1003
 Martha (Ripperdam) 855
BRAMLETTE, Col. 1025
 Thos. E. Gov. 752, 1031
BRAND, Cath. (Link) 843
 Jas. 848
 Keziah (Pipes) 847ff
 Rich. Dr. 848
BRANHAM, Cinthey (Hedges) 863
 Frances V. (Gaitskill) 863
 Webb Maj. 863
BRASFIELD, Ida M. (Moberley)
 948
 Jas. E. 948
 Letitia (Ross) 948
 Tabitha (Moberley) 948

6

BRASFIELD
Wiley R. 916, 948
BRASHEAR, Camilla (Parker) 898
Lucy (Phelps) 969
BRAWNER, Eleanor (McAlister)
  978
Jno. 813
Mary (Carlile) 813
Sophia (Page) 826
BREATH, Jas. Capt. 770
Mary (Welsh) 770
BRECK, Danl. 749ff
R. L. Rev. 754ff
BRECKINRIDGE 759, 1007
Brigade 993
Jno. 799
Jno. C. Gen. 744, 779, 782,
  799, 862, 882, 921,926,
  941, 982
Kate (Morrison) 800
Mary (Cabell) 799
Morrison 800
(Preston) 799
R. J. 925
Robt. J. (Rev.) 799ff
Sophonisba (Preston) 799
Wm. C. P. 742, 876
BREEDING, David C. 800
Eliz. (Blair) 790, 800
Eliz. B. (Patterson) 800
Francis M. 800
Geo. W. 800, 814, 996
Hulda J. (Cartwright) 814
Isaac 951
J. R. 1011
Jackson E. Dr. 800
Jas. Rev. 800
Jas. A. Dr. 800
Jane C. (Nunn) 800
Jno. C. 800, 836
Levinia (Bird) 800
Lulu B. (Moore) 951
M. T. (Williams) 996
Marg. (Cloyd) 800
Marg. Susan (Williams) 800
Mary Eliz. 800
Nannie D. (Simpson) 996
Parthenia L. (Carter, Turk)
  800
Peter 800
Polly (Davis) 836
Rachael (Cassiday) 800
Rachel Jane (Priestly) 800
Rich. P. 800, 996
Sallie (Nell) 814
Sally (Black) 800
Sally (Young) 800
Sarah Ann (Baker) 800
Saml. K. Rev. 800
BREEN, Mary (Hagan) 962
BREWER, J. B. 922
Jane P. (Van Arsdell) 1028
Wm. 816
BRICKEN, Alex. 801, 1003
Ann (Graham) 1003
Blanche 801
Eliz. V. (Johnson) 801
Ellen (Cunningham, Corley)
  800, 830
Felix J. 801
Geo. A. 800ff
(Hardwick) 801
Mahala (Wilkinson) 801
Maria (Spraggins) 801
Martha (Johnson) 801
Mattie B. (Spaulding) 1003
Rosella 801
Saml. B. 800
(Terrell) 801

BRICKEN
Wm. G. 801
Wm. M. 800, 830
BRICK HOUSE, First in Nelson
  Co. 945
BRIDGEFORD 740
BRIDGES, Eliz. (Jones) 904
Judge 1019
Mary J. (Reed) 982
BRIDGEWATER, Eliz. 991
Jno. F. 991
Laura (Russell) 991
Mary (Jones, Taylor) 1016
BRIDGEWATERS, Eliz. (Carpenter)
  953
Nathan 953
Polly (Page) 953
Sally (Moore) 952
BRIGADE, Orphan 799
BRIGGS 801
Alex. 801
Andrew 801, 1038
Eliz. (McMakin) 801
Eliz. (Muir) 801
Eliz. (Wilkinson) 1038
Elmo 801
Jno. 801
Katie 801
Mary (Ferguson) 801
Nancy (Robinson or Robertson)
  801, 1038
Peyton 801
Sarah (Humphrey) 897
Thos. H. 801
BRIGHT, Betsy (Eliz.)(Hoskins)
  810, 986
Eliz. (Morrison) 919
Eliz. J. (Grimes) 802
Geo. Robt. 801ff
Jas. 801
Jno. R. 901ff, 918
Marg. (Garvin) 801ff
Marg. (Smith) 801
Martha (Smith) 801
Martha E. (Saunders) 802
Mary (Williams, Lillard) 918
Mary H. (Robinson) 802
Sarah E. (Harlan) 878
Sophia (Rochester) 801
Thos. H. 801ff
Wm. H. 801ff
BRINTON, Sallie F. (Mann) 935
BRISCOE, Edward 784
Eliz. (Baxter) 784
Marg. (Harbison) 784
BRITTON, Martha (Smith) 999
BROADERSON, Annie (Kelley) 907
C. 907
BROADUS, Jane (Sanders) 976
Marg. (Sebastian) 976
Sarah (Price) 977
BROADDUS, Ann E. (Ferguson)
  937
Marg. (Noland) 838
Sarah L. (Matheny) 937
Thos. 937
BRONSTON, Cath. B. (Douglas)
  802
Henrietta A. (Baker) 802
Jos. S. 802
Thos. S. 802
BROUGH, Jno. Gov. 956
BROWN 815
Abe J. 803
Alex. 942, 954
Ann (Van Arsdall) 1027
B. H. 868
Benj. F. 802
Bettie (Dolling) 803

BROWN
Beverly 802
Cath. (Dugan) 802, 842, 960
Cath. (Oldham) 946
Cath. (Smith) 999
Chas. W. 803
Elias B. 802
Eliz. (Beauchamp) 802, 842
Eliz. (Milburn) 942
Eliz. P. (Offutt, Rease) 960
Emma 803
Esther (Tarkington) 1014
Geo. W. 802
Georgia 803
H. Clay 832
Hannah (Rochester) 999
Holland 788
Jas. 741
Jas. B. 802
Jas. H. (Rev.) 803, 1048
Jas. T. 802
Jane D. (Ewing) 802
Jeremiah 816
Jewett 802
Jno. 974, 999
Jno. Young 876
Jonathan 802ff, 842
Lizzie (Robinson) 987
Lucy (Monday) 802, 931
Mary 802
Mary (Huston) 780
Mary (Loye) 1017
Marg. (Mouser) 942, 954
Mary (Mays) 979
Mary D. (Cox) 832
Mary E. (Crume) 802, 913
Mary E. (Thompson) 802
Mary E. (Tichener) 803
Nancy (McKenzie) 803
Nancy (Yewell) 1048
Nannie (McCLosky) 802
R. J. 917, 924
Rachel (Bennett) 788
Ruth (McFerran) 931
Sallie 878
Sallie A. (Mouser) 954
Scott 931
Stephen C. 802, 913,(See
  Browne)
Sue D. (Leachman) 913 (See
  Browne)
Susan M. (Wood) 1045
Veola 802
Wm. R. 802, 960
Zerelda (Jennings) 803
BROWNE, Ardie (Myer) 804
Beverly B. 803
Elias B. 803
Eliz. (Cook) 803
Eliz. (Nichols) 803
Irvin M. 804
Jno. H. 803
Lizzie C. 804
Lucy (Rogers) 803
Mary E. 803
Mary E. (Rogers) 804
Mary Eleanor (Davison) 803
Mary R. (Martin) 804
Sarah J. (Thompson) 803
Stephen C. 803
Stephen E. 803
Susan (Leachman) 803
Thos. R. 803ff
Wm. D. 803
BROWNING, Eliza (Caldwell) 746
Emeline (Armstrong) 780
Jas. A. 810, 952
Judy (Moore, Flower) 952
Marg. (Callison) 810
Nancy (Davis) 836ff

7

BROWNING
O. H. 746
Polly (Callison) 810
BROWNLEE, Chas. Capt. 886
Eliz. (Allen) 886
Marg. (Henry) 885ff
Wm. Gen. 886
BRUCE, Annie (Ross) 804
Anslem 804
Caroline R. 804
Carrie M. (Harlan) 879
Christopher L. 804
Frederick 804
Jas. 804
Jno. G. Rev. 804
Julia C. (Morgan) 804
Mary (Eads) 804
Mary C. (Harlan) 879
Mary W. (Winters) 804
Susan (Edelen) 845ff
Tabitha (Musteen) 804
Thos. J. 804
Ward 804
Wm. E. 804, 846
Wm. L. 804
BRUMFIELD, Annie 805
Caldwell 805
Ella 805
Ellen (Crumbaugh) 804ff
Jas. 804ff
Joie 805
Lucy 805
Maria J. (Irvine) 805
Nancy (Crow) 804
Obadiah 804ff
Phoebe A. (Caldwell) 805
Rachael (Yeager) 804
Rich. 804
Robt. 804
Ruan C. (Sherrill) 805
Saml. 804ff
Sue 805
Wm. 804ff
BRUMMAL, Eliz. F. (Penick) 967
Josiah 967
Mary (Hundley) 967
BRUTON, Susan (Sallee) 992
BRYAN, Eliz. (Harlan) 879
Francis 816
Mary Priscilla (Epperson)
848
Martha S. (Williams) 1040
Nancy T. (Thomas) 879
Robt. 879
W. H. 848
BRYANT, Allie(Spalding) 884
Ben S. 884
(Fisher) 856
Mary E. (Head) 884
Wm. 884
BRYANT'S STATION 957
BRYANTSVILLE 845
BUCHANAN 835
Alex. 805
Alice V. (Hagan) 805
Carl A. 805
Corae H. 806
E. F. Dr. 806
Emma S. 806
Geo. 806
Geo. H. 805ff
Gracie A. 805
H. P. 805
Hattie A. 806
J. A. (Smoot) 806
J. Hubert 806
Jas. 800, 824, 871
Jane (Gants) 806
Jan(i)e (Caldwell) 805ff

BUCHANAN
Jessie F. 805
Jno. 806
Laura J. 806
Lester S. 805
Louisa C. (Sherrill) 805
Marg. (McAfee) 806
Mary (Dunn) 975
Mary (Lewis) 917
Mary A. (Hagan) 805
Mary W. 806
Mattie E. 806
Melvin A. 805
Monta P. 805
Nancy (Mitchen) 805
Robt. B. 805
Robt C. 806
Sallie (Moore) 805
Sallie (Shively) 806
Sallie G. 806
Samantha A. (Elder) 805
Susan R. (Hutchinson) 805
Thos. G. 805ff
Virgene B. 805
BUCK, Evelyne E. (Price) 977
BUCKLER, Celia A. (Peterson)
968
Eliz. (Tolbert) 968
Henry 968
Mary (Berry) 789
BUCKMAN, Chas. 990
Clem. N. 863
Clement 816
(Dunbar) 990
Ignatius 816
Julia (Russell) 990
Martha (Gardiner) 863
Plagia (Leak) 863
BUCKNER, Judge 991
Mary (Lewis) 918
Rich. A. 861, 908
Robt. W. 918
S. B. Gen. 744, 762, 900
Sarah (Hazelwood) 918
Sarah A. (Vivian) 1032
BUELL, D. C. 846, 1036
BUFFINGTON ISLAND 762, 875
BUFORD 999
Julia (Forsythe) 858
BUKEY, Ellen B. (Coleman) 827
Julius 827
BULL, Capt. 812
BULLOCK 815
Percilla (Boarman) 793
Thos. S. Dr. 756
BURBRIDGE, Gen. 763
BURCH, Walter 816
BURCHUM, David 883
Eleanor (Hays) 883, 995
BURDETT, America Letcher
(Samuel) 806
Belle (Walton) 807
Benj. M. 806
Frederick 806
Georgia A. (Nave) 957
Joshua 806
Nelson 806
BURDETTE 845, 906
BURGE, Phebe T. (Willock) 1032
BURGIN, Mary W. (Gaitskill) 863
Nancy (Tevis) 825
Narcissa (Smith, Jones) 904
Temple 904
BURKE, Judia (Chelf) 819ff
Wm. 820
BURNAM, Curtis F. 750, 753ff
Edmund H. Rev. 753
Martha (Davis) 837
BURNETT 981

BURNETT
Eliz. A. (Campbell, Eastland,
Funk) 859
Ella (Hoover) 859
Jas. 859, 865
Permelia (Shepherd) 865
Sallie (Graham) 865
BURNS, Alvin 807
Amanda (McClure) 807
Amelia 807
Benj. E. 807
Chas. H. Col. 807
Ella J. 807
Jas. 818
Mary (McLane) 925
Polly (Stotts) 1008
Sallie J. (Edmonds) 807
Sarah E. (Cecil) 818
Thos. E. 807
BURNSIDE, Belle (Dunn) 845
Eliz. (Thomas) 811
Gen. 762ff, 789
Hannah (Smith) 974
Jno. 970
Mary (Landram) 912
Nancy (Smith) 970
Nannie D. (Campbell) 811
Wm. 811, 845
BURNSIDES, Eliz. (Kinnaird) 909
Indiana (Phillips) 970
BURR, Erastus Rev. 955
BURROS, Mary (Slaughter) 807,
998
BURRUS, Edmund 807
F. P. 807
J. G. 807
Jane (Bell) 923
Lizzie (Miller) 807
Lucy A. (Miller) 807
M. L. 807
Mary (Slaughter) 807
Mary (Threlkeld) 807
Nathaniel 807
BURTON, Archibald 829
Augusta C. (Robards) 808,985
Eusebia Q. (Phillips) 808, 972
Isabella M. (Irven) 808
Jno. A. Capt. 808, 972, 985
Louisiana (Chandler) 808, 985
Marg. (Lowry) 808
Marion C. 808
Martha (Cooper) 829
Mary A. 808
Nancy (Givens) 982
Rich. C. Col. 808
Robt. A. 808
Robt. Lee 808
Susan F. (Cooper) 829
BUSH, Adelaide (Halliard) 870,
1010
Anna M. (Stone) 1018
Christopher 1018
Fielding 870, 1010
Francis 1032
Frankie (Vivian) 1032
Lella (Trevis) 1018
Lucy (Davis) 1032
M. E. (Van Aradell) 1028
Mary (Christy) 1032
Nancy (Vivian) 1032
Robt. Y. 1018
Sarah B. (Sullivan) 1010
Va. A. (Grooms) 870
BUSINESS, Close Attention to 840
BUSTER, Chas. H. 808
(Chrisman) 1031
Emerine (Ingram) 808
Emma T. 808
Everett 808

8

BUSTER
Jno. S. 808
Joshua Gen. 808, 819, 1031
Mary (Van Winkle) 1031
Nimrod I. 809
Sallie (Babbitt) 808
Sarah Ann (Cecil) 818ff
Sophronia 808
BUTLER, Abigail (Nuckols) 941
Amanda S. (Cheatham) 808, 952
Annie V. (Callison) 810
Champion 952
Champness 808
(Hamilton) 872
Jas. 810
Jemima (Martin) 910
Jno. 808, 952
Jonietta (Gaitshill) 862
Lucinda (Harmon) 879
Mary Tildon 809
Myra H. (Sharp, Moore) 952
Myra S. (Smith) 809
Nathan C. 809
Nathan G. Lt. 808
Nellis (Dillingham) 952
Rev. 817
Susan (Conover) 809
Wm. R. 809
BUTLER'S CREEK 836
BUTNER, Mary (Hubbard, Fish)
855
BYARS, Harriet (Dunn) 845
BYERS, Anna (Scomp) 994
Ellen A. (Mock) 948
Harriet (Dunn) 948
Jno. 948
Mary J. (Floyd) 856
BYRNE, Ignatius 816
Robt. Rev. 817
Wm. Rev. 817, 889

CABELL, Bettie (Penick) 809
Carrie 809
Chas. R. 809
Frederick 809
Jno. F. 809
(Jordan) 809
L. H. 809
Mary (Breckenridge) 799
Mary D. (Owsley) 809
Oliver 809
Paulina E. (Sprowl) 809
Saml. J. 809
Sophronia H. (Lewis) 809
Susan J. 809
Susanah (Ewing) 809
Thos. H. 809
Wm. Dr. 809
CAIRNS, Jane (Gutherie) 1011
CALBFUS, Ann (Robinson) 986
CALDWELL, Abraham I. (Abram)
810, 1047
Alex. 745
Amelia C. (Starkey) 810
Andrew 745
Ann M. (McDowell) 1047
Ann Maria (Yeiser) 1047
Annie Belle (Fox) 747, 759
Bessie 810
Betsey (Caldwell) 834
Beverly 746
Cary A. 834
Chas. G. 745ff, 810
Chas. Wickliffe 747
County (Origin of name) 746
Daniel 745
David 745ff, 834, 923
Dicey (Mann) 746
Dicey (Curry, McAfee) 834,
923

CALDWELL
Eliza (Browning) 746
Eliza Hunton 747
Eliz. (Clemens) 746
Eliz. (Talbott) 1013
Ella (Palmer) 748, 810
Ellen B. (crumbaugh) 747
Fontaine Fox 747
Francis 834
G. M. 1016
Gabriel I. 810
Gabriel S. 805
Geo. Robertson 810
Hettie P. (Tutt) 1026
Isaac 990
Isabella (Knox) 834
Jas. 805ff, 834, 1036
Jas. Bowman 747, 810, 959
Jas. Rev. 746
Jas. L. 810
Jane (Crawford) 959
Jane (Fox) 758
Janie (Buchanan) 805ff
Jennie M. (Tresenriter) 1026
Jeremiah Clemens 746, 759
Jerry D. 1026
Jno. 746, 834
Jno. Dr. 758
Jno. T. 805
Jos. W. 745, 810
Josiah 834
Kittie (Robards) 984ff
Logan W. 810
Lucinda (Grinstead) 805
Lucinda (Moss) 805
Lucy A. (Wharton) 805
Lucy E. (Irvine) 748, 809ff
Lydia (McCord) 746, 924ff
Maggie (Bowman) 810
Marg. (Cozatt) 833
Marg. (Wilson) 746
Marg. (Phillips) 746
Maria 748
Martha (Calhoun) 746
Mary (Boone) 805
Mary (Harlan) 879
Mary (Knox) 834
Mary (Logan) 746
Mary (Palmer) 746
Mary (Robards) 984
Mary (Slaughter) 747
Nannie C. 747
Obadiah B. 748
Oliver 745
Parmelia (Smith) 805
Phebe J. (Starkey) 810
Phoeba A. (Brumfield) 805
Phoebe (ADams) 834
Phoebe (Caldwell) 747
Phoebe E. (Crowder) 834
Phoebe (Henderson) 746ff, 885
Phoebe (Mann) 834
Polly (Henderson) 746, 885
Rachel A. (Harberson) 809
Robt. 746ff
Robt. C. Dr. 747, 810
Robt. Crumbaugh 810
Robt. Henderson Rev. 809,
747, 975
Robt. T. 810
Rosa E. (Powell) 975
Sallie (Kirk) 805
Sally 834
Saml. Maj. Gen. 746, 834
Sarah Slaughter (Wharton)
1036
Settlement 746
Station 746
Sue (Newbolt) 959

CALDWELL
Susan (Fleece) 805
Thos. 746, 834
(Wickliffe) 746
Wm. Capt. 746, 834, 924,1013
Wm. Logan 746ff, 180, 834
CALHOUN, B. F. 1011
Jno. Caldwell 746
Martha (Caldwell) 746
CALIFORNIA, Trip to & Mission
work 756ff, 847
CALK, Cath. (Price) 977
CALLAGAN 795
CALLENDAR, Sallie (Harding) 877
CALLISON, Annie V. (Butler) 810
Bruce M. 810
Carry Lee 810
Charity (Smith) 809ff
Chas. 810
Dawson 810
(Dawson) 810
Eliz. (Miller) 810
Eliz. R. 810
Geo. L. 810
Gilmer 810
Jas. Robinson 810
Jos. 810
Josiah 810
Laura E.(Robinson) 810
Louisa (Miller) 810
Lula Belle 810
Marg. (Browning) 810
Martha (Mourning) 810
Mary L. (Miller) 810
Mattie B. (Tupman) 810
Montie S. 810
Patsy (Davis) 836
Phoebe 810
Polly (Browning) 810
Robt. 810
Susan (Stark) 810
Wm. J. 810, 1016
CALVERT, Phoebe (Hope, Williams)
1039
CAMBRON, Baptist 811
Chas. 811
Christopher C. 811
(Harberson) 811
Harry 811
Henry 816
Jas. R. 811
Marg. (Montgomery) 811
Marg. I. 811
Marry C. (WRINN) 811
Martha A. (McGill) 811
Nicholas L. 811
Stephen H. 811
Wm. C. 811
CAMDEN, Mary (Read) 982
CAMERON (Sutherland) 1012
CAMP Boone 799
Charity 1007
Chase 875, 871, 994, 999
Douglas 875, 921, 945, 981,
9-9
Knox 950ff
Mier 950
Morton 945
Nelson 968
Dick Robinson 877ff
CAMPBELL, Adam 859
Alex. Rev. 750, 811, 1032
Andrew 859
Ann P. (Key) 811
Arthur B. 812
Benj. B. 811
Ben. P. 811
Bessie 812
(Carlton) 811

9

CLEAVER
  Paul C.   823ff
  Robt. A.   824
  Rose   824
  Stephen Gray   824
  Wm. Wells Dr.   823, 931,937
  Wm. G.   824
CLEAVES, Marg. (Turk)   1024
CLELAND, (Fales)   851
  Jemima (May)   833
  Kittie (McElroy)   930
  Thos. H. Rev.   851, 935
  W. G.   755
CLELLAN, Thos. Rev. Dr.   827
CLEMENS, Eliz. (Caldwell) 746
  Jeremiah   746
CLEMENTS, Jno.   793
  Polly (Hocker)   793
CLEMMONS, Eliza (Lobb, Harlan)
    1030
  Maria O. (Van Sickle)   1030
  Mary E. (Hardin)   1030
  Nancy (Stone, Montgomery)1006
  Osborn   1030
CLEMONS, Fanny (Hood)   892
  Francis   892
  Jane (Mason)   892
CLEVELAND   790, 1035
CLEVLAND, Adin   824
  Clarinda (Beaty)   824
  Delitha (Temple)   824
  Eli   824
  Eliz. (Hand)   824
  Eliz. (Yates)   824
  Geo.   824
  Jas.   824
  Jno.   824
  Mary A. (Beaty)   824
  Morris   824
  Nancy (Ramsey)   824
  Sarah   824
  Wm.   824
  Zatthue   824
CLIFTON, Sally (King)   774
CLOSE, C. L.   824
  Eliz. (Bale)   824
  Grayson   824
  Jas. T.   824
  Jno. G.   824
  Laura L.   824
  Lethe (Bloid)   824
  R. T.   824
CLOYD, Jas.   800
  Jane (Lapsley)   800
  Jno.   1039
  Marg. (Breeding)   800
  Patent   981
  Victoria (Williams)   1039
CLUSKER, Marg. (Russell)   991
COAKLEY, Ada   825
  Bettie J.   825
  Cassander F.   824
  Eliza Ann   824
  Eliz. C. (Hazelwood)   824
  Emma C. (Williams)   824
  Florence E.   824
  Geo. H.   824ff
  Lee W.   824
  Marg. (Carter)   824
  Martha J. (Durham)   825
  Mary E.   824
  Mattie S.   824
  Nancy V. (Ingram)   825
  Saml. D. Dr.   825, 911
  Sarah M. (Webster)   824
  Thos. E.   824ff
  Walter G.   825
  Wm. Col.   824
  Willie J.   824
COATS, Alex.   1043

COATS
  Fanny (Wilson)   1043
  Lucy   1043
  Mary (Moss)   882
COBB, Amanda Terry   825
  Benj.   1017
  Brutus W.   825
  Durrett W.   825
  Edith (Oldham)   970
  Eliz. (Taylor)   825, 1017
  Frances   825
  Harvey   825
  Jesse   825, 970
  Jno.   825
  Matilda   825
  Minerva (Park)   970
  Nancy (Peyton)   825
  Parker   825
  Provy (Tevis)   825
  Rich.   970
  Rosalinda (Ross)   804
  S. T.   825
  Sallie (Phelps)   970
  Saml.   825
  Zena G.   825
  Zerilda Mitchell   825
COBERT   825
  David   825
  Eliz. (Woods)   825
  Garrett   825
  Mary (Morgan)   825
COCK, Eliz. (Browne)   803
COCKRELL, Anna E. (Mann)   935
  Gen.   935
COE, Jas. R.   842
  Nancy M. (Dulworth)   842
COFER, Lydia A. (Morgan)   953
  Robt. H.   953
COFFEY, C. R.   1029
  Eliz. (Strange)   1008
  Geo.   826
  Henry R.   826
  Jane (Graves)   825
  Jno. B.   826
  Jos.   825ff
  Mary E. (Warden)   826
  Rachel (Jones)   992
  Robt. G.   826
  Sallie (Vandeveer)   1029
  Sophia   826
  Va. R. (Page)   826
  Wm. A.   826
COFFY, Eliz. (Riffe)   898
COGAR, Amanda T. (Edgerton)940
  D. N.   940
  Eliz. (Robb)   940
  Jesse E.   940
  Jno. S.   940
  Lucy A. (Newton)   940
  Lydia V. (Payne)   965
  M. H.   940
  Mary C.   940
  Mattie M.   965
  Ruth (Ewing)   940
  T. M.   940
  Thos.   940
COGHLAN, Rev.   992
COHEN, Dixie (Coleman)   828
  Henry   828
COLE, (Bosley)   797
  Polly (Hamner)   873
COLEMAN, Anna E.   826
  Basil W.   826
  Bozell W.   827
  Burr H.   827
  Bushrod   826
  Cath. (Robinson)   826
  Clara (Rosser)   828
  Dixie (Cohen)   828
  Elinda L. (Conrad)   827

COLEMAN
  Ellen B. (Bukey)   827
  Ferris   826
  Foster   826
  Geo. D.   826ff
  Henry   827
  Jas. Henry   826ff
  Jas. M. Rev.   827
  Jane Amanda (Sorrell)   826ff
  Jennie   827
  Jno. L.   826ff
  (Jordan)   827
  Laura L.   826
  Linda   827
  Linsfield   826ff
  Littleton   826
  Maggie (Hughes)   812
  Mamie (Moberly)   828
  Marg. A. (Hughes)   827
  Maria (Dedman)   826ff
  Martha A. (Lewis)   827
  Mary (Dannell)   826
  Mary (Penny)   826ff
  Mary B.   826
  Mary R. (Daniel)   827
  Meredith R.   826ff
  Patsy   826
  (Prather)   827
  R. E.   812
  Robt. E.   826ff
  Roberta   828
  Rosser   828
  Sallie Ann   826ff
  Sarah C.   826
  Sarah M. (Hahn)   826
  Simeon Burton   827
  Stevana(IA) A. (Cardwell)
    812, 828
  Susan D.   826
  Susan Eliz. (Simpson)   827
  Thos. C.   826ff
  Thos. H. Rev.   827ff
  Wm. L.   826
  Willis L.   826
COLLEGE, Alexander   933
  Daughters   770
COLLIER, Alexander   957
  Jennie (Scott)   957
  Mary (Stone, Allen)   1006
  Melinda (Nave)   957
  Sarah (Bird)   991
COLLINGSWORTH, Susan (Cotton)
    831
COLLINS, Christopher   766
  D. C.   755
  Hist. of Ky.   814ff
  Louisa (Wood)   890
  (Sullivan)   1010
COLUMBIA COLLEGE   1016
COLVIN, Annie (Wood)   1045
  Parmelia (Case)   1045
  Robt.   1045
COMBS, Asa   769
  (Baker, Evans)   850
  Cordelia H. (Ford)   857
  Miranda (Vivian)   1032
  Nancy (Welsh, Stewart)   769
COMINGORE, Henry   833
  Marg. (Cozatt)   833
COMMAGER, Henry S. Gen.   956
COMPTON, Patsey (Durham)   782
CONCH SHELL, Used Bryant's St.
    957
CONDER, Cynthia (Penn)   903
CONDOR, Lucinda   1038
  Melissa (Whitehouse)   1038
  Peter   1038
CONFEDERATES   794, 875, 921,
    1018, 1021
CONGRESS, Price of land   924

CONN, Eliz. (Faulkiner) 828
J. P. 828
J. T. 828
Jane (Williams) 951
Jno. Fields 828
Lillie Price 828
Lillie W. 828
Lizzie (Yakey) 828
Mary 828
Mike Owsley 828
Penelope Pocahontas
(Barker) 828
Va. (Barker) 828
Wm. H. 828
Wm. W. 828
CONNELL, Lucy (Murphy) 954
CONNELLY, Alfred 1019
Eliz. (Thomas) 1019
CONNER, Clay 1015
Mary L. (Roach) 984
Sarah E. (Taylor) 1015
W. G. 984
CONNOR 981
CONOVER, Caroline (Morgan) 953
Cornelia Minor (Johnston)
904
Eliza F. (Williams) 1040
Garrard 953
Joann (Rucker) 809
Mary Louvena (Williams) 1040
Peter T. 809
Robt. 904
Saml. B. 1040
Susan (Butler) 809
Wm. 1040
CONRAD, Elinda (Coleman) 827
Jas. E. 827
CONWAY, Ann (Goodwin) 933
CONYER, Betsy (Lyen) 923
CONYERS, Lady (Payne) 964
COOK, Amanda W. (Cooper) 829
Eliza A. (Dunn) 845
Geo. 1017
Jas. M. 829
Kate (Huffman) 895
Lucy B. 829
Lucy M. (Jenkins) 1017
Mary (Pulliam) 978
Mollie J. (Taylor) 1017
Moses 895
Sallie (Robison) 895
Strather Rev. 1017
COOKE, Anna (Parker) 828
Anna L. 828
Grant 828
Nannie (Bowman) 828
Nellie 828
Rebecca 828
Sarah A. (Grant) 828
Wm. A. 828
Wm. Grant 828
Wm. H. D. 828
COOMES, Wm. 814ff
COOPER, Amanda W. (Cook) 829
Annie 829
Archie 829
Basil P. 828
Benj. J. 829
Bettie 829
(Blain) 829
Cath. (Hamilton) 829
Cordelia (Smith) 828ff
Eliz. E. (Spalding) 829
Geo. B. 829
Geo. E. 829
Hugh P. 828ff
J. M. 967
Jennie 829
Jno. M. 829
Jos. 829

COOPER
Josie E. (Kindred) 829
Julia (Penny) 967
Leenett 829
Levi 943
Lucille 829
M. A. (Vinson) 998
M. T. 998
Malachi Rev. 943
Martha (Burton) 829
Mary (Quinley) 829ff
Mary (Slaughter) 998
Mary E. (Craycroft) 829
Mittie 829
Nellie 829
Philip B. 828ff
Rosa 829
Saml. P. 829
Saml. S. 829
Sarah (Ware) 943
Susan (Spalding) 829
Susan F. (Burton) 829
Thos. J. 829
Walter H. 829
COOVERT 829ff
David 829
Eliz. (Woods) 830
Garret 829
Martha (Wood) 1045
Mary (Morgan) 829
COPPAGE 787
Amanda (Coppage) 830
Bettie (anderson) 779
Eliz. 830
Ellen 830
Fielden 779
Hardin 830
Jas. 830
Jos. 830
Killis 830
Lucinda 830
Lucinda (anderson) 779
Maggie (Swiggett) 1012, 830
Marg. (Mann) 830
Mollie 830
Moses 830
Oscar 830
Nancy (O'Bannon) 830
Rhoda (Tapscott) 830
Sarah (Kemper) 779
Sarah (Steele) 830
Stephen 830
Uriah 830, 1012
Wm. 830
Willis 830
CORLEY, America 830
Anderson 830
Cassella 831
Eliz. (Aulby) 830
Ellen (Cunningham, Bricken)
830
Fannie (Shuck) 996
Jas. 830
Jno. 830
Nancy (Tyrrell) 830
Sallie 830
Wm. 830
CORN CROP, 1st.Cent. Ky. 854
CORN, Polly (Robards) 985
CORNELISON, Edward 794
PHOEBA (Boggs) 794
CORNWALLIS, Lord 765, 793, 796, 964,
1003, 1028
CORSE, Jno. M. Gen. 956
CORWIN, Thos. 907
COSBY, Chas. 1004
Martha M. (Stephenson) 1004
Mary (Tevis) 1018
(Nantz) 895

COSSON, Mercie (Alexander)831
COTTON, Almede 831
Belle I. 831
David 831
(Fintch) 831
Geo. 831
Harry 831
Jno. Templeman 831
(Jones) 831
Lou W. 831
Lucy (Wilson) 831
Mary (Oldham) 831
Mary P. (Cowherd) 831
Minnie 831
Robt. 831
Saml. Wilson 831
Stella Lee 831
Susan (Collingsworth) 831
Susan (Gess) 831
Susan (Hudson) 831
Thos. Gess 831
COUN, Amelia E. (Mitchell)947
COURTS, 831
Braxton E. 831ff
Clarissa (Winn) 831
(Douglass) 831
Eliza J. (Durham) 831ff
Jas. J. 831ff
Jesse W. 831
Jno. 831
Jno. W. 831
Mary J. (Price) 831
Mercie C. (Alexander) 831
Mary J. 831
Wm. E. 831
COUSINS, Phoebe J. (Haselwood)
882
COVENANTERS 924
COVINGTON INSTITUTE 1034
COWAN, Jno. Col. 965
COWHERD, Alice Bell (Kirk) 910
Frank 910
Jas. Major 831ff
Judith F. (Cox) 910
Martha (Mitchell) 822
Mary P. (Cotton) 831
Nancy (Haselwood) 881
Origin of 882
Sally (Richardson) 822
Sarah Ann (Chewning) 822
Simeon L. 822
COWLING, R. O. 898, 926
COX, A. K. Dr. 832
Anna B. (Price) 832
ARchibald C. 948
Bettie H. (Traylor) 1008
David 832, 932
Delia M. (Tingle) 832
Eliz. (Lewis, Robards) 984
Ella B. 833
Ellen E. (Bowman) 832
Eliz. (McGee) 932
Emma (Groves) 832
Emma M. 833
Gabriel E. Dr. 832
Geo. 832
Harvey P. 832
Ida (Wells) 832
Isaac S. 832
Jas. Gen. 832
Jas. A. 832
Jonathan 832
Judith F. (Cowherd) 910
Kate (Martin) 832
Marg. E. (Montague) 948
Mary D. (Brown) 832
Martha A. (Jeter) 902
Obie (Wycoff) 833

13

COX
  Polly (McGee) 932
  Sallie (Howe) 948
  Sarah (Tutt) 832
  Sarah T. 832
  Shelby 832
  T. C. 902
  Wm. T. 832
COX'S CREEK 954
COY, Martha A. (Thomas) 1019
COZATT, Abraham 833
  Albert 833
  Ann (Davis) 833
  Charlotte L. 833
  Daniel 833
  David 833
  Elisha 833
  Emily (May) 833
  Francis 833
  Henry C. 833
  Jacob Rev. 833
  Jacob C. 833
  Jemima (Sinkhorn) 833
  Jno. A. 833
  Marg. (Caldwell) 833
  Marg. (Comingore) 833
  Mary (Bower) 833
  Mary (Randolph) 833
  Peter 833
  Rachael (Terhune) 833
  Susan 833
  Wm. T. 833
COZINE, Lucy (Van Arsdell) 1028
  Mary (Vanarsdell) 1028
  Peter 1028
CRAB CIDER 867
CRABTREE, Naomi (Spears) 842
CRADDOCK, Chas. W. 834
CREED H. 833, 1044
  Edward L. 834
  Eliza G. (Sandridge) 833
  Eliz. (Sandridge) 1044
  Emma F. (Gooch) 833
  Lizzie (Moore) 805
  Lucy D. (Wilson) 1044
  Nancy J. (Perry, Whitlock) 834
  Robt. 901
  Robt. F. 833ff
  Susan S. (Jeter) 901
CRADLEBAUCH, Proctor 750
CRAIG, Cyrena M. 784
  Louisa (Moore) 952
  Robt. O. 952
CRAIN, Amanda (Plummer) 973
  Thos. J. 973
CRANE, D. Rev. 992
  E. Rev. 992
  Jane 795
  Nelson Dr. 795
  Susan (Bolling) 795
CRAVENS, Celestia B. (Hancock) 874
  Elijah 873ff
  Eliz. (Hancock) 873
  Julia (Bomer) 873ff
  Nancy (Ferrill) 912
  Paulina (Dickerson) 1001
CRAWFORD 1037
  Cath. 947
  Eliz (Turk) 1024
  Harriet (Mahan) 935
  Jas. 947
  Jane (Caldwell) 959
  Jno. 935, 1024
  Keziah(Evans, Beaty) 851
  Mrs. 928ff
  Nancy (McCreary) 926
  Rachel (Mitchell) 947
  Sallie 935

CRAWFORD, Eliz. (Sparks) 1001
  Thos. R. S. 1001
CRAYCROFT, Mary E. (Cooper) 829
CREAGOR, Eliz. (Link) 848
CREATH, Jacob 750
CREGOR, Thos. 860
CREWS 981
  Frances P. (Spires) 913
CRIDER, Jno. 791
  Sarah Jane (Blair) 791
CRIGLER, Susan (Hume) 1021
CRITTENDEN, Thos. H. Gen. 966
  Jno. J. 759, 1044
CROAKE, Marietta (Shaunty) 995
CROCKETT, Lucy (Forsythe) 858
CROMWELL, Oliver 745, 924
CROOKS, C. G. 755
  Mary (Graham) 865
CROSS HOLY-1st R.C. Ch. in Ky. 814ff
CROSSTHWAITE, Nancy (Taylor) 969
CROSSWAIT, Sally (Vivian) 1032
CROTHWAIT, Ann P. (Herndon) 887
CROW, Ann (Seay) 994
  Cyrus 834
  Delitha 834
  Eleanor (Robinson) 834
  Geo. 834
  Jalila (Scott) 834
  Jas. E. Rev. 834, 1003
  Jas. T. 834
  Jno. T. 834
  Nancy (Brumfield) 804
  Polly (Larrimore) 834
  Polly (Pascal) 834
  Rebecca (Mantz) 834
  Robt. R. 834
  Saml. 834
  Sarah (Sally, Spoonamore) 834, 1003
  Susan (Dickerson) 834
  Thos. D. 834
  Wm. 834
CROWDER, David K. 834
  Geo. L. 834
  Hamilton 834
  Isabella D. (Durham) 834
  Jas. A. 834
  Jno. 834
  Jos. 834
  Martha A. (Thompson) 834
  Mary J. (Lyons) 834
  Phoebe E. (Caldwell) 834
  Phoebe E. (Crowder) 834
  Saml. K. N. 834
  Thos. J. 834
  Wm. A. 834
CROWNOVER, Ann (Kennett) 1023
CROXTON 841
CRUES, Susan (Gaddie) 860
CRUFT, Ann (Armstrong) 780
CRUMBAUGH, Eli 747
  Ellen (Brumfield) 804ff
  Ellen B. (Caldwell) 747
CRUME, Mary E. (Brown) 802
  W. J. 802
CRUMES, Griffin 853
  Lutitia (Montgomery) 853
  Mary J. (Fenton) 853
CRUTCHER, Eliz. (Long) 922
  Jas. 922
  Va.L. (Pinkerton) 972
CRUTCHFIELD, Ethel (Stone) 1006
CULL, Jestine (Bottom, Graves) 867
CUMMINGS, Caroline C. (McCord, Grant) 866
  "Doc" 835

CUMMINGS
  Mary F. (Curry) 835
CUMMINS, Anna(a) M. 834
  Arthur 834
  Cath. W. 834
  Eliz. J. 834
  Ellen (Whallen) 834
  Emily J. (Brady) 834
  Jas. P. 834
  Jno. A. 834
  Jno. R. 834
  M. A. 834
  Mary A. 834
  Mary E. 834
  Rich. D. 834
CUNDIFF, Emma (Hancock) 873
  Lucy (Boldrick) 795
  Rich. 873
  Sarah (Boldrick) 795
CUNNINGHAM, Artemisia (Curry) 835
  Chas. 758
  Cora Lee (Baker) 783
  Ellen (Bricken, Corley) 800, 830
  Isaac Capt. 1029
  Jas. B. 783
  Jas. H. 985
  Jenny (Parks) 785
  Lt. 965
  Marg. (Pearce) 965
  Nancy (Beale) 800
  Nancy (Drake) 898
  Robt. 800
  Rebecca (Van Meter) 1029
  Sarah (Harness) 1029
CURD, Eliz. L. (Frazer) 835
  Frances (Slaughter) 997
  Jas. H. 835
  Mattie (Moses) 835
  Mildred (Slaughter) 997
  Thos. H. Dr. 835
CURDSVILLE 987
CURE, Barbara (Shears) 995
CURL, Jane A. (Webb) 1035
CURREY, Jno. D. 1024
  Mary J. (Galloway, Tucker) 1025
  Nancy (Lemmons) 1024
  Wm. 1024
CURRY, Artemisia (Cunningham) 835
  Artemisia (Hill) 835
  Cath. (Stagg) 836
  Dicey (Caldwell, McAfee) 923
  Durinda (Simpson, Nell) 959
  Edward 835
  Eliz. (Lewis) 836
  Geo. Ann 835
  Hannah (Whittinghill) 835
  Icylinda (Philips, Salle) 835
  Isaac 835
  Jas. 836
  Jas. A. 835ff
  Jane (Forsythe) 858
  Jane (Yeast) 835
  Jno. 835
  Martha 835
  Mary (Wilham) 835
  Mary A. (Mayes) 939
  Mary F. (Cummings) 835
  Nancy (Bolling) 795
  Mary I. (Matheny) 937
  Robt. B. 835
  Saml. L. 835ff
  Sarah (Murphy) 954
  Sarah A. (Stine(s) 835, 1006
  Sarah (Thomas) 835
  Sarah E. 835

14

CURRY
  Thos 835
  W. T. 876
  Wm. 835
CURTSINGER, Civilla (Milburn)
  942
  Phoebe J. (Williams) 1029
CUSTIS 757
CUTSINGER, Marg. (Weathers)
  951

DABNEY, Mary (Harris 881
  Saml. G. Dr. 756
DAILEY, Lulu B. (Stone) 1006
DALEY, Mary (Mattin(gl)y) 1020
DAMRON, Eliz. V. (Watson) 874
  Geo. W. 874
  Mollie J. (Hancock) 874
DANDRIDGE 864
DANIEL, Louisa (Gaitskill,
  Suddeth) 863
  Mary R. (Coleman) 827
  Sarah (Price) 977
  Wm. R. 826
DANNELL, Mary (Coleman) 826
DANT, Anna C. 836
  Cath. (Ballard) 836
  Ellen S. 836
  Francis L. 836
  Geo. W. 836
  J. W. 836
  Jas. R. 816, 836
  John Baptist 816, 836
  Jno. P. 836
  Jos. 816, 836
  Jos. Bernard 836
  Malinda (Shirkles) 836
  Mary J. (Smith) 836
  Thos. S. 836
  Wm. W. 836
DARBY (Welsh) 769
DARTMORE Prison 875
DAUGHTERS' COLLEGE 770
DAVENPORT, Eliz. (Williams)
  896
  Eunice F. (Hughes) 896
  Major 896
DAVIDSON 748
  Susanna (Hughes) 895
DAVIESS 775
  Hannah (McAfee) 923
  Jos. Hamilton Col. 765, 775
  (McKee) 765
DAVIS, A. P. 960
  Amanda (Bradford) 943, 1005
  Ann (Cozatt) 833
  Ann (Vivian) 1032
  Asael 837, 931
  Ashley McKee 837
  Barbara (Hawkins) 837
  Benj. 837
  Brothers 906
  Diana (Montague) 948
  Edmund 837
  Eliz. (Allen) 837
  Eliz. (Grant) 867
  Eliz. (Holman) 837
  Eliz. (Page) 836
  Eliz. (Schuyler) 836
  Eliz. James 837
  Frances (Green) 885
  Frances Henry (edrington) 837
  Garrett 907
  Geo. R. 837
  Hannah (Moore) 950
  Hannah E. (Poor) 837, 974
  (Henderson) 837
  Hester A. (Green) 885
  Jas. 911
  Jas. H. 837, 931

DAVIS
  Jas. N. 836ff
  Jane (McClure) 837
  Jane (Riker) 983
  Jefferson 850, 921
  Jenny (Snead) 836
  Jno. 836ff
  Jno. Allen 837
  Jno. M. 837
  Jno. W. 857
  Joshua 837
  Judith (Walker) 836
  Lizzie A. (Offutt) 960
  Lucy (Bush) 1032
  Lucy (Lage) 836
  Marg. (Street) 837
  Martha (Burnam) 837
  Martha (Elliz) 885
  Martha (Pierce) 837
  Mary (Bolling) 795
  Mary (Fogle) 857
  Mary (Iving) 837
  Mary (Knox) 911
  Mary (Thomas) 1019
  Mary (Walker, Henderson)
  885
  Matilda(Stone) 1006
  Matilda J. (Ellis) 885
  Mattie (Alexander) 931
  Mattie (McFerran) 931
  Mr. 1019
  Nancy (Browning) 836ff
  Nannie C. (McAfee) 923
  Patsy (Callison 836
  Peter 836, 983
  Peterson 1046
  Place 863
  Polly (Breeding) 836
  Rebecca (Banks) 836
  (Robards) 984
  Robt. L. 837
  Sally (Mann) 935
  Sally (Simpson) 1009
  Sarah (Baxter) 837
  Sarah (Belles) 856
  Sarah (Tucker) 931
  Sarah Balenger (Tucker) 837
  Solomon 837
  (Sprowl) 809
  Susan (Baxter) 837
  Susan (Mitchell) 885
  Susannah (Peak, Thomas) 1019
  Thos. 795, 885
  Wm. 837
  Wm. B. 984
  Wm. Barnes 837
  Wm. Flemming 837
DAVISON 985
  Abner 772
  Elias 803
  Eliz. (Adams) 772
  Laura E. (Neikirck) 958
  Maria (Ball) 803
  Martha (Grashaw) 772
  Mary Eleanor (Browne) 803
  Wm. 958
DAWSON, Ben Capt. 903
  (Callison) 810
  Eliz. (Ice) 837
  Ignatius 837
  Jas. Lee 837
  Jennie (Wilson) 837
  Jno. 837ff
  Mehala (Lyon) 903
  Mary E. Russell 837
  Nannie 837
  Sally (Johnston) 903
  Sally (Logan) 921
  Wm. 903
DAY, Jno. 873
  Nancy (Blair) 791

DAY
  Nancy (Hamner) 873
  Rebecca (Hamner) 873
DAYTON, Ohio-1 house in 974
DEACON, Emma F. (Fenton) 853
  Minnie 853
  Nathaniel W. 853
  Orvill Woods 853
DEAN, Diana (Thompson) 1028
  Rachel (Have) 957
DEARING 836
DEATHERAGE, Amos 838
  Baird 838
  Mary A. (Oldham) 838
  Mary E. (Noland) 838
  Nathan B. 838
  Sallie (Phelps) 838, 969
  Susan G. (Lipscomb) 838
DEBAUN, Ellen (Philips) 838
  Ida 838
  Jno. W. 838
  Jos. 838
  Kate (Mays) 838
  Pleasant M. 838
  Saml. P. 838
DEBO, Bettie B. 839
  Eliz. (Porter) 838
  Henry 838
  Horatio 838ff
  Jno. Dr. 838ff
  Lucetta (Barbour) 839
DECKER, Sarah (Hamner) 873
DEDMAN, Annie M. (Duke) 839
  Eliz. (Timberlake) 839
  Jas. O. 839
  Maria (Coleman) 826ff
  Phil T. Dr. 839
  Robt. 839
  Saml. L. 839
  Wm. D. 839
DEERING, Mary (Sallee) 992
DE FRAINE, P. Rev. 992
DE GRAFFENREID, Cecily (McCaw)
  776
DE HAVEN, Judge 991
DE JARNETT, Geo. 1042
  Jas. 1042
  Pattie (Willis) 1042
  Sarah (Williams) 1042
DELANEY, Jane (Miller) 943
  Wm. Leroy 876
DEMAREE, Annie B. 839
  Cornelius 979
  Frances (Leathers) 839
  Jno. D. 839
  Louisa (Forsten) 839
  Maggie L. 839
  Mary L. 839
  Peter 839
  Phoebe Brewer (Randolph)979
  Racie L. (Smith) 839
  Rosella 839
  Saml. 839
DENNY, A. F. 1033
  Alex. 839
  Ameliz J. (Kavanaugh) 797
  Eliz. (Faulkner) 840
  Geo. 839
  Jas. G. 797
  Marg. (Miller) 839
  Mary D. (Dunlap) 844
  Sallie (Walker, Bosley) 797
  Sally (Graham) 839ff
  (Walker) 1033
DENT, Eliz. (Edwards) 847
DENTON, Josephine (Harris) 1035
  Nannie T. (Wearen) 1035
  Thompson 1035
DEPEW, Bartholomew 876
DE ROHAN, Wm. Rev. 814, 816

15

17

18

FAUNTERLOY 837
FAUNT LE ROY, Harrod 780
FEARS, Joyce (Hudson) 893
FEASE, Geo. A. 843
  Martha (Dulsworth) 843
FEATHERS, Mary B. (Poor) 974
FECHHEIMER, M. 922
FEE, Jno. B. 821
FEICHHEIMER, L. S. 922
FELAND, Albert 852
  Armstead M. 852
  F. R. 852
  Isabella (Hay) 852
  Isabella (Robison) 852
  Jas. 852
  Jno. Morgan Dr. 852
  Sallie (Milner) 852
  Thos. 852
  Wm. B. 852
FELL'S POINT LEASE 972
FENNELL, Martha (Bohon) 795
FENNESSY, Cath. (Ryan) 852
  David Rev. 852ff
  Jno. 852
FENTON, Abigail (Smith) 853
  Andrew 853
  Chas F. 853
  David 853
  Emma F. (Deacon) 853
  Frederick 853
  Geo. W. 853
  Jas. 853
  Jno. 853
  Lucretia (Bishop) 853
  Lucretia (Truce) 853
  Mary A. (Ringgold) 853
  Mary A. (Hulfish) 853
  Mary J. (Crumes) 853
  Parmelia (Ball) 853
  Peter 853
  Philip C. 853
  Robt. 853
FENWICK, Edward Rev. 817
  (Mattingly) 938
FERGUSON, America (Dodson) 878
  Ann E. (Broaddus) 937
  Champ 1031
  Ed. V. 858
  Mary (Briggs) 801
  Mary E. (Harding) 878
  Wayne 878
  Willette (Forsythe) 858
FERRILL, Joel 912
  Mary (Killen) 912
  Melissa J. (Laha) 911ff
  Nancy (Cravens) 912
  Wm. 912
FERTILIZER, 1882 sale of 810
FETTER, Cath. (Gray) 1036
  Geo. C. 1036
  Lydia G. (Wharton) 1036
FEVER, Remedy 861
  Yellow 844
FIDLER, Jas. M. Capt. 853
  Jesse P. 853ff
  Jno. F. 853
  Lou (Drve) 841, 854
  Minerva (Lawrence) 853
  Mollie F. 853
  Nannie E. (Johnston) 853
  Napoleon F. 853
  Saml. 853
  Susan (Fidler, Richeson) 853
  Wm. H. Maj. 853ff
FIELD, C. J. Col. 750
  Patsie I. (Miller) 944
  Saml. B. Dr. 862
FIELDS, Alice 854
  Ann (Thorn) 854
  Anna F. 854

FIELDS
  Carrie B. 854
  (Childs) 855
  Danl. 854ff
  Eliza A. 854
  Eliz. D. (Joffrian) 854
  Everiste 854
  Frederick R. 854
  Henry R. 854
  Jas. 854ff
  Jefferson 855
  Jemima 855
  Jeremiah 855
  Jno. 854
  Joshua M. 855
  L. B. 854ff
  Liberty B. 854
  Mary (Miller, Wright) 854
  Ralph 854
  Sarah (Ripperdam) 855
  Sarah C. 854
  Smith M. 854
  Susan (Ripperdam) 854ff
  Susan R. (Joffrian) 854
  Theodore T. 854
  Wm. 854ff
  Wm. M. 854ff
  (Wright) 855
FIGHT, Indian 923
FILMORE 790, 825, 930, 1021
FILSON, Map mentioned 746
FINCK, T. D. Dr. 756
FINLEY, J. C. 996
  Jane Ann (Smith) 999
  Jno. 999
  Lucretia C. (Shuck) 996
FINNELL, Chas. H. 855
  J. W. 855
  Leonta Dudley 855
  Lida Pearl 855
  Lula H. 855
  Mirrilda Jane (Prewitt) 976
  Sallie E. (Irvin) 855, 1041
  W. D. 855
FINTCH, Capt. 831
  (Cotton) 831
FISH, Addie 855
  Albert T. 855
  Eveline (anderson) 855
  (Givins) 855
  Grover C. 855
  Jennie (Galloway) 855
  Jesse 855
  Mary (Hubbard, Butner) 855
  Samantha (Haley) 855
  Thos. 855
FISHER, Albert 856
  Ann E. (Shanks) 856
  Ann R. (Puryear) 979
  Ann (Read) 856
  (Barbee) 856
  Barnett 948
  Bettie (Bishop) 856
  (Bryant) 856
  Caroline 856
  Franklin 856
  Garnett P. 856
  (Harlan) 856
  Issachar P. 855
  Maria (Pope) 856
  Mary G. 856
  Rich. McKenney 855ff
  Sallie (Doores) 840
  Sallie (Mock) 948
  Sarah (Taylor) 856
  Stephen 856
  Susan (Harding) 878
  Susan (McKinney) 856
  T. T. Capt. 979

FISHER
  Va. A. (McKenney) 856
  Va. M. 856
  Wm. 856
FITCH, Eliz. (Rothwell) 988
  Gideon 988
FITZPATRICK, Eliz. (Fox) 758
  Jno. 758
FITCHPORT 941
FLAGET, Benedict Jos. Rev.
  817, 922ff, 991
FLEECE, Eliz. (Bosley) 796ff
  Jno. 797
  Jno. Dr. 766, 797
  Mary (Harlan) 879
  Sally (Logan) 904
  Susan (Caldwell) 805
  (Withers) 797
FLETCHER, Pauline (Stotts)
  1008
FLOOR, 1st tongue groove in
  Lex. 818
FLORIDA, Investments in 966
FLOWERS, Judy (Moore, Browning)
  952
  Thos. 952
FLOYD, Christopher 856
  Davis 856
  Eliz. (Belles) 856
  Fannie E. 856
  Henry 856
  Hope (Fogle) 857
  Jas. B. 856
  Jno. B. 856
  Marion 856
  Mary J. (Byers) 856
  Mary J. (Swope) 858
  Nicy (Herring) 887
  Rebecca (Lyons) 910
  (Robards) 984
  Robt. 856
  Sarah (Singleton) 856
  Thos. D. 856
  Wm. H. 856
FOGLE, Adam 856ff
  Betty P. (Allen) 857
  Cath. (Glazebrook) 857
  Ebenezer A. 856
  Eliz. 857
  Fannie (Beard) Beard 857
  Hope (Floyd) 857
  Jas. M. 857
  Jno. D. 857
  Jno. N. 856
  Jos. McD. 856
  Maria C. 856
  Martha B. (Grundy) 857
  Mary D. 856ff
  Mary (Davis) 857
  Mary A. (Penick) 857
  Maud (Jennings) 857
  Melissa (Lawrence) 857
  Nancy J. 857
  Rachael (Helm) 857
  Rachael (Shuttlesworth) 856
  Robt. H. 856ff
  Sallie (Newbolt) 856
  Sallie A. 856
  Sallie F. (Withrow) 857
  Wm. P. 857
FOLEY, Bush Col. 998
  Jane (Nordyke) 866
  (Wycoff) 1047
FORD, Benj. B. 857
  Betsy W. (Webber) 857
  Cordelia H. (Combs) 857
  Danl. 857ff
  E. S. 845
  Edward S. 857

19

FORD
Eliza (Ryan) 857
Eliz 857
Eliz. (Harris) 882
Emily J. (Thurman) 882
Fanny B. (Smith) 857
Francis 915
Jno. B. 857
Josephine L. (Jennings) 857
Keziah (Evans) 849ff
Lewis T. 857
Luella S. (Haselwood) 882
Mary (Bowles) 857
Mary (Prewitt) 976
Mary (Terrill) 1018
Orville 755
Polly (Hughs) 857
Polly W. (England, Reynolds) 857
Reuben Rev. 857
Sallie (Jewell) 857
Sally (Poor) 974
Sally G. (Henly, Mobley) 857
Sarah H. (Boughn) 857
Susan (Hayden, Lee) 915
Susan B. 857
Timothy 857
Thos. J. 882
(Tucker, Ballard) 836
Wm. 882
Wm. A. 857
Wm. W. 857
Zachariah 850
FOREE, E. D. Dr. 754ff
FOREMAN, Benj. 994
Cath. (Shadburne) 994
Dr. 994
Eliz. (Montgomery) 994
Jos. 1048
Nancy (Yewell) 1048
Rebecca (Shadburne) 994
FORMAN, Eliz. (Hanna) 870
Lucy (Stone, Gaines) 1006
Melissa (Evans) 849
FORREST 921ff
Academy 758, 1012
FORSTEN, Louisa (Demaree) 839
FORSYTHE, Andrew (Dunbar) 849, 858ff
Annie (Mayes) 858
Belle (Ralston) 858
Cardwell 858
Cozzie (Cardwell) 858
Edgar 858
Eliz. (Griffin) 859
Fred 858
Geo. M. 858
Given 858
Howard 858
Jas. M. 858, 941
Jane (Alverson) 858
Jane (Curry) 858
Jane (McAfee) 858
Jno. L. 858
Jos. 858
Julia (Buford) 858
Katie (Alexander) 858
Levinia Bush 859
Lillie 858
Lizzie (Mullins) 858
Lizzie M. (Washbourn) 858
Louise Tweed 859
Lucy (Crockett) 858
Lulie (Ammellman) 858
Mary 858
Mary (Irvin) 858
Mary (Lawrence) 853
Mary (McAfee) 858
Mary J. Lee (Evans) 849, 858, 987

FORSYTHE
Matt. 858
M. Leander Dr. 858
N. W. (McAfee) 858
Nannie 858
Naomi 858
Narcissa (McAfee) 849
Pattie (Trible) 858
Robt. B. 858
Russell 858
Sallie (Blackwood) 858
Sallie (Given) 858
Sallie (Woods) 858
Saml. 858
Walter 858
Willette (Ferguson) 858ff
Wm. S. 858
FORT, Columbia 962
Donelson 922
Estill Station 1007
Hardinn's Creek 971
Meigs 899
Paint Lick 914
Sandusky 971
FORTRESS, Monroe 851
FORX, Lizzie (Joseph) 906
FOSTER, Jane (Mahan) 935
Mary (Reid) 983
Mary S. (Messinger, Moore) 766
Nancy (McClure) 837
Sarah L. (Greer) 869
FOSTES, Martha (Emery) 885
FOURNIER, M. Rev. 815
FOWLER, Amanda (Shearer) 1021
Frances (Hill) 890
Jno. 9-8
Mary (Overton) 988
Mary Josephine (Rodman) 988
Nancy (Shearer) 890
Nancy (Smith) 960
Nancy B. (Akin) 1001
Saml. O. 988
Susan (Overton) 988
FOX, Amanda (Goggin) 758
Annie Belle (Caldwell) 747, 759
Bettie W. (Smith) 922
Cassandra (Embry) 848
Chas. C. 759
Eliza Jane (Hunton) 759
Eliz. (Fitzpatrick) 758
Eliz. (Hockaday) 772, 890
F. T. 917
Felix G. 759
Fontaine Talbot 747, 757, 759
Jane (Caldwell) 758
Jno. O. 759
Peter C. 759
Rhoda (Pickering) 758
Saml. 758
Saml. I. Dr. 759
Sophie (Irvine) 758
Sophie (Kindrick) 758
Sophie Irvine (Sea) 759
Thos. H. 759
Wm. McKee 758ff
FOYLE, Frances (Beard) 786
Jno. D. 786
FRANCIS 745
Edith (Pettus) 969
Mary 969
Thos. 969
FRANK, Amanda (Williams) 1039
Josiah P. 1039
FRANKLIN, Eliza Jane (Moran, Wilcoxson) 952
FRASER, Mary (Hogarty) 891
FRAZEE, L. J. Dr. 888

FRAZEE
Susan J. (Walton) 807
FRAZER, Eliz. L. (Curd) 835
FREEMAN, Cath. (Wright, Jones, Robertson) 985
Jno. 985
Mary (Robertson) 986
FRENCH, Annie (Talbott) 752
Ark. Trading Post 979
Hannah (Scomp) 994
Ignatius 816
Robt. Dr. 752
FRITZ, Cecelia (Kister) 980
FROMAN, Fannie (Ray) 982
Isaac 982
Jane (Wilkinson) 1038
FROST, Jno. N. 896
Sallie S. (Hughes) 896
FRY, Cynthia A. (Hope) 759
Eliz. Julia (Smith) 759
Frank W. 760
Joshua 759
Mildred S. (Turner) 759
Mildred T. (Smith) 759
Patsey A. (Summers) 786
Peachy (Walker) 759
S. S. Capt. 879
Speed S. Gen. 759ff
Thos. J. 760
Thos. Walker 742, 759
FRYE, Fannie (Phillips) 971
FULLINWIDER, Eliz. (Beatty) 933ff
(Winter) 933ff
FULTON, Eugene A. 859
Geo. S. 859
J. A. 859
Kate R. (Adams) 859
Marg. (Anderson) 859
Mary (McClaskey) 859
Saml. S. 859
Stephen G. 859
W. A. 859
FUNK, Chas. P. 860
Eliz. A. (Campbell, Eastland, Burnett) 859
Emma L. 860
Enna 860
Harriet (Bosley) 860
Harriet M. 860, 984
Hattie B. 860
Jacob 859
Jas. F. 860
Jane B. 860
Jno. H. 860, 984
Jno. W. 860
Jos. 860
Madison B. 860
Martha W. 860
Sarah (Rinehart) 984
Sarah E. 860
Wm. H. 860
Willie A. (Sharpe) 860
FURGUSON, Sallie E. (McKenny) 1018
FURNACE, Red River 739
FURR, A. E. (Nelson) 959
M. Major 959

GABBARD, David 760
Nancy (Hill) 760
GADDIE, Bartholomew S. 860
Benj. 860, 1013
Chas. B. 860
Cris A. (Stiles) 860
Geo. T. 860
Ira C. 860
Jno. L. 860
Jno. R. 860
Jos. H. 860

GADDIE
Lewis F. 860
Mary (Sympson) 1012
Robt. D. 860
Robt. P. 860
Sarah A. (Handley) 860
Susan (Crues) 860
GAINES, Bettie (Dunn) 845
General 740
Lucy (Stone, Forman) 1006
Martha (Viley, Payne) 965
Mary (Slaughter) 998
Sarah (Dunn) 845
GAITHER, Edgar B. Capt. 862
Edgar H. 862
Edward Dr. 860
Emily R. (Hutchinson) 862
Geo. B. 862
Kate 862
Marg. 862
Marg. (Watkins) 860
Martha (Morrison) 861
Mattie 862
Nat 862
Nathan Dr. 860ff
Nicholas 860
W. N. Dr. 862
GAITSKILL, Chas. Webb 862ff
Edward 863
Fannie 863
Frances V. (Branham) 863
Henry 862
Jas. E. 863
Jno. W. 862ff
Jonietta (Butler) 862
Jonietta (Rodgers) 863
Jos. 862
Katie 863
Louisa (Suddeth, Daniel) 863
Lula (Willis) 863
Marietta (Prewitt) 863
Martha (Hedges)
Mary W. (Burgin) 863
Nancy (Thompson) 863
Nannie (Jones) 863
Nannie W. 863
Silas H. 862ff
Strother S. 863
Sue F. (White) 863
GALE, Susanna (Hughes) 896
GALLOWAY, Arminta (Kerly) 855
Frank 855
Jennie (Fish) 855
Mary J. (Currey, Tucker)1024
GANIHL, Anthony Rev. 815
GANO 921, 981
GANTS, Jane (Buchanan) 806
Mary (McAfee) 806
Thos. R. 806
GARDINER, Arabella 863
Christina (Heady) 863
Clement 863
Eliza A. 863
Eliz. 863
Eliz. (Rapier) 863
Francis B. 863
Harry T. 863
Ida L. (Head) 863
Jno. I. 863
Jos. E. 863
Louisa (Walker) 863
Martha (Buckman) 863
Matilda (O'Bryant) 863
Mattie B. 863
Nancy Mills 863
Plagia 863
Rich. 863
Rosella (Adams) 863
Theodore 863
Wm. G. 863

GARDINER
Wm. H. 863
GARDNER, Lucy (Welden) 783
Lydia C. (Gooch) 833
(Stiles) 785
GARFIELD 763, 893, 926, 972,
987
GARLAND, Augustus 992
GARNETT, Angeline (Walden)1033
Caroline M. (Taylor) 1016
Cath. E. (Arnold) 1010
Ellen (Willis) 1041
Henry B. 1015
Jas. 946
Kitty F. (Taylor) 1015
Martha (Hopkins) 1000ff
Mary (Wood) 1045
Mary J. (Bishop) 856
Mary V. J. (Willis) 1041
Mollie S. (Arnold, Sullivan)
1010
Oliver 1041
(Wetheral) 1041
Wm. 1041
GARRARD, Femal College 757
James Gov. 998
GARRET 926
Benj. 926
Jno. Capt. 841
Mary (Willis) 1041
Martha (McClure) 926
Sarah 926
GARTIN, Adelia (Speed) 820
Delilah H. (Chelf) 820
Nathan H. 820
GARVIN, Marg. (Bright) 801
GATEWOOD, Bettie (Ewing,
Poyntz) 976
Mary (Spencer) 950
GENTRY (Baker) 1042
(Harding) 877
Jas. H. 877ff
Jane H. (White, Blythe)
881, 1037
Jno. 948
Lucinda (Moore) 952
Lucy (Yeows) 952
(Martin) 1037
Moses 952
Nancy (Lipscomb) 838, 948
Rich. 1037
GEORGE, II 746, 773
III 775
Cath. (Jesse) 885
Martha (Landram) 912
GERHART, Obedience (Alexander)
773
GESS, Susan (Cotton) 831
GHOLSON, Martha (Vivian) 1032
GIBBONS, Georgia A. (Shears)
995
GIBBS, Sallie (Young) 1045
GIBSON, Ann 863
Cath. (Van Arsdall) 1027
Eliz. (Peach) 897
Ellen V. (Bates) 863
Jno. 863
Polly (Simpson) 996
Stephen 863
Wm. 863
GILBERT, G. G. 907
Creek 765
GILBREATH, Nancy (Baughman)
784
GILISBIE, Mary M. (Boggs) 793
Philip 793
Susan (Mullins) 793
GILKESON, J. R. 846
Sallie (Edelen) 846
GILKEY, Jonathan 975

GILKEY
Oney (Powell) 975
GILL, Marg. R. (Kinnaird) 909
W. E. 941
GILLMORE, Ellen (Evans) 851
Jennie (Beaty) 851
GILLOCK, Eliz. (Adams) 952
GILMER, Jane (Turk) 1025
Robt. 1025
Sarah (Allen) 1025
GILMORE, Mary J. (Wright) 1046
Patsy (Stotts) 1007
Susan (Farris) 851
GILTNER, Col. 862
GIST, Mattie (Seay) 994
GIVEN, S. W. 858
Rachel B. (Alcorn) 772
Sallie (Forsythe) 858
GIVENS, Annie K. (Alcorn) 772
Eliza A. (Read) 982
Nancy (Burton) 982
Rebecca (Kenny) 907
Sally (Harberson) 809
Saml. 982
GIVINS, (Fish) 855
GLASS, Lydia (Pulliam) 978
Rebecca 978
Wakefield 978
GLASSCOCK, Elijah 980
Marg. (Hayes) 980
Maria (Rawlings) 980
Sophia (Rawlings) 980
GLAZEBROOK, Cath. (Fogle) 857
GLENN, Eliz. (Patterson) 1016
GLENN'S FORK 790, 1014
GLENVILLE 975
GLOVER, Fanny (Taylor) 1014
Jane (Kyle) 911
Jno. 911
Judith (Irvin) 898
Saml. Taylor 811, 1014
GOATLEY, Mary (Seay) 994
GOFF, Nancy (Adams) 963
GOGGIN, Amanda (Fox) 758
Bourne 758
GOOCH, A. E. 833ff
Emma F. (Craddock) 833
Lydia C. (Gardner) 833ff
Tabitha (Arthur) 783
Tabitha (McDonald) 783
Thos. 783
GOODE 864
Alfred Col. 864
Clarie 865
Deroy 864
Edmond Capt. 863, 886
Elgeline E. (Christeson) 864
Emmit E. 864
Fleming 864
Franklin 863
Jerome 865
Jno. 864
Louisa (Caskey) 863ff
Marg. B. 865
Mary (Ward) 864
Mary E. 865
Nannie (Wethington) 864
Nannie J. 865
Silas F. 865
Susan A. 865
Thos. J. 864ff
Thos. McClosky 865
GOODIN Station 1019
GOODLOE, A. W. 752
Carrie (Neal) 961
D. S. Gen. 750
Emily (Duncan) 881
Maria (Estill) 752
Wm. 750, 961
Wm. C. 881

21

GOODRICH, Lucy (Phillips) 970
GOODWIN, Ann (Conway) 933
  Bettie (McKenna) 933
  Patrick 933
GORDAN, Lucy B. (Munday) 819
GORDON, Priscilla (Henderson)
  885
GORE, Andrew 865
  (Casey) 865
  Cath. (Haines) 865
  CHristian 865
  Eliz. (Weston) 865
  George 865
  Jacob 865
  Jas. 865
  Jno. 865
  Michael 865
  Philip 865
  Saml. 865
  Sarah 865
  Thos. Weston 865
CORTHORP, Anna (Thorn) 854
GOUL, Eliz. (Grooms) 870
GRABLE, Mary (Duvall) 845
GRAHAM, Alberta 866
  Alice (Farris) 852, 865
  Ann (Bricken) 1003
  Ann (Spillman) 865
  Anna E. (Risk) 865
  Belle (McEwen) 865
  Benj. Major 866
  Bess 865
  Burnett 865
  Chas. Peyton 865
  Chas. S. 865
  E. J. Dr. 865ff
  Edward Y. 866
  Eliz. (Armstrong) 865
  Eliz. (Nichols) 865
  Eliz. (Sutherland) 866
  Eliz. (Young) 865
  Emily P. (Grant) 866
  Geo. W. 865
  Jas. H. 866
  Jas. S. 865
  Jno. 960
  Jno. J. 865
  Jno. R. 866
  Josephine (Evans) 850
  Jane (Shaw) 865
  Loutie 865
  Mary (Crooks) 865
  Mary (Robinson) 865
  Mary E. (Noe) 960
  Mary J. (Board) 986
  Minnie (McAfee) 865
  Nancy (Bale) 866
  Nancy (Price) 866
  Peyton R. 865
  Polly (Hamilton) 865
  R. W. 850
  Robt. 865
  Robt. G. 852
  Rutha C. 866
  Sallie (Burnett) 865
  Sally (Denny) 839
  Sallie (Spears) 1047
  Saml. M. 865
  Sarah (Williamson) 865
  Susan A. (Owsley) 850, 852
  Wm. M. 866
  Wm. S. 865
GRANT 763, 823
  Albert F. 1009
  Caroline C. (McCord,
    Cummings) 866
  Don Carlos Dixon 777
  Drummond B. 867
  Eli 1009
  Eliz. (Davis) 867

GRANT
  Eliz. D. 867
  Eliz. S. (Beeler) 867
  Emily P. (Graham) 866
  Frances (Cartwright) 814,
    1009
  Frances (Wood) 1045
  Geo. 867
  Horace H. Dr. 962
  Hugh McKee 866ff
  Huldah (Strange) 1009
  Ida May 867
  Jas. W. Dr. 866ff
  Janet (McGinnis) 866
  Jno. 866
  Jno. Milton 1009
  Jos. M. 1009
  Leila Ellen (Owsley) 962
  Lilla Dale Price 867
  Lucy Jennings 867
  Marg. A. (Thurman) 867
  Mary M. 867
  Matilda (Nordyke) 866
  Nancy L. (Mosby) 828
  Nannie 867
  Nellie 867
  Polly J. (Allin) 777
  Posey B. 867
  Posey D. 867
  Rosalie (Strange) 1009
  Rosaline 1009
  Sally M.(Walkup) 1009
  Sarah A. (Cooke) 828
  Sophia (Thurman) 867
  Sophia M. (Price) 866
  Squire 828
  U. S. Pres. 744, 798, 822,
    911, 918, 955, 972,
    1007
  Vaughan 867
  Will H. 867
  Wm. 867, 1045
GRASHAW, Martha (Davison) 772
GRAVES, Adaline 867
  Andrew J. 867
  Capt. 950
  Caroline 867
  Cath. (Winfrey) 1044
  Jane (Coffey) 825
  Jestine (Bottom, Cull) 867
  Jno. 938
  Louisa 867
  Lucy (Pettus) 969
  Mary Ann (Mullins) 954
  Malvina (Wycoff) 1047
  Nancy 867
  Sarah (Lawson) 867
  Susan 867
  Susan (Mattingly) 938
  Susan (Noble) 938
  Thos. Capt. 826, 867, 1044
  Wm. 867
  Wm. J. 954
GRAY, Archie 867
  Cath. (Fetter) 1036
  Chas. 867
  Eliz. (Gray) 867
  Isaac M. 868
  Jas. 867
  Jane (Pipes, Harmon) 879
  Jane (Sandifer) 867
  Jno. 867
  Lucy (Jones) 867
  Lucy (Kelsie) 867
  Lucy (Webster) 867
  Martha A. (Montgomery) 868
  Mary (Richeson) 867
  Nancy (Holland) 867
  Nancy (Pipes) 867
  Nancy E. (Harmon) 868

GRAY
  Patsey (Kinley) 867
  Polly (Huberry) 867
  Robt. 867
  Sallie K. (Wade) 868
  Sarah (Bolling) 867
  Wm. 867
GREELEY, Horace 823, 903,
    949, 1018, 1042
GREEN, Ellen (Beaven) 788
  Chas. 910
  Clifton 868
  Co. 1st house in 1041
  Ellis (Thomson) 1020
  F. M. 868
  Frances (Davis) 885
  Gen. 740, 965
  Grace (Kirk) 910
  Hester A. (Davis) 885
  Irvine T. 868
  Jas. 780, 868
  Jno. Capt. 741
  Kate (Kimberlin) 868
  Lilly 868
  Lina (Moore) 868
  Mamie 868
  Mary (Taylor) 780, 868
  Mary L. (Mayes) 939
  Nancy (Phelps) 868
  Polly (Huguely) 897
  Rachel (Huguely) 897
  Sally (Beatty) 741
  Sidney 868
  Talitha W. (Armstrong) 780
  Wm. 868
  Wilson 1020
GREENE, Annie (Shader) 869
  Chas. 868
  Frank 868
  G. W. 868ff
  Gen. 777, 920
  Jno. 868
  Julia (McIntire) 868
GREENLEAF, Emma (Kauffman) 906
  Ida V. (Jennings) 900
GREENUP, Col. 777
GREENWAY, Jno. 770
  Mary Louise (Welsh) 770
GREENWELL, Basil M. 869
  Chas. L. 869
  Hilroy J. 869
  Ida (Bondurant) 869
  Jno. W. 869
  Mary (Ballard) 836
  Mary (Greenwell) 869
  Wilton R. 869
GREENWOOD, Eliz. (Bolling) 795
  Mines 919
GREER, Anna D. 869
  Bertha 869
  Bessie C. 870
  Cornelia A. 869
  Eliz. (Milton) 869ff
  Harriet H. (Wigington) 869
  Jas. F. 869ff
  Kate W. (Watts) 870
  Marg. F. 869
  Mattie W. 870
  Milton 869
  Minnie L. 870
  Rebecca (Howard) 869
  Rich. J. 869ff
  Saml. H. 869
  Sarah L. (Foster) 869
  Thos. N. 869
  Va. (Lee) 869
  Walter 869
  Wm. B. 869
GREGG, Cassa (Pitts, Robards)
    984

GREGORY, Ellen (Baxter) 785
  Maria (Eastland) 859
  Mary (Durham) 785
  Mary (Litsey) 920
  Olivia (Duncan) 881
  Rich. 920
  Walter 785
GRIDER, Frederick 790
  Jane (Wolford) 968
  Martha E. (Wheat, Blair,
    Smith) 790
  (Powell) 975
  Rachel(McKinley) 791
GRIFFING, Eliz. (Forsythe) 859
  Eliz. (Pearson) 859
  J. D. 859
GRIGSBY 951
  Col. 850, 921, 1021
  Marg. (Thomas) 1018
  Susanna (Baker) 782
  Susanna (Ramey) 1018
  Wm. R. 781, 989
GRIMES, Eliz. J. (Bright) 802
GRINSTEAD, Lucinda (Caldwell)
    805
GRISSOM, Bettie (Baker) 782
  E. 1043
  E. O. 782
  Minerva J. (Wilson) 1043
  Rachel E. (Simpson) 996
  T. M. 783
  W. R. Dr. 996
GRIST Mill, 1st in Adair 787
GROOMS, Chas. 870
  Eliz. (Goul) 870
  Emily (Moran) 953
  Forrest B. 870
  Hiram Butler Dr. 870
  Horatio Col. 870
  Horace Bass 870
  Nancy (Hanna) 870
  Stephen Hanna Dr. 870
  Stephen Madison 870
  Thornton 870
  Va. A. (Bush) 870
  Walter Bush 870
GROSH, Adam 741
  Cath. (Hunt) 741
  Eleanor (Hart) 741
  Jno. Conrad 740
  Mary (Charlton) 741
  Mary Dorathea (Beatty) 740
  Peter 741
  Sophia (Clay) 741
GROSS, Saml. D. Dr. 849, 888,
    929, 975
GROVES, Emma (Cox) 832
  (Lewis) 917
GROW, Sally (Nave) 957
GRUNDY, Andrew January 870
  Bessie R. 871
  Eliz. 870
  Felix B. 823, 870, 1033
  Frank 870
  Geo. 1033
  Hannah M. (Camfield) 870
  Hattie C. 871
  Jas. 870
  Joanna (Cleaver) 823
  Jno. A. 871
  (Kemper) 870
  Martha B. (Fogle) 857
  Martha S. (Walker) 1033
  Mary L. 871
  Nellie 870
  R. C. Rev. 870
  Robt. 870
  Saml. 870, 1033
  Sarah A. (January) 870
  Sarah J. 870ff

GRUNDY
  Wm. 870
  Willie J. (McElroy) 871
GUARDS, HOME 760
GUFFEY, Anna (Peyton) 825
GUILFORD COURT HOUSE BATTLE
    919
GUINN, Albern 1040
  Martha (Williams) 1040
GUM, Eliza (Vaughan) 893
GUNTER, (Harmon) 880
GUNTERMANN, Peter Dr. 756
GUTHRIE, Jas. 1011
  Jane (Cairns) 1011
  Jane (Survant) 1011
  (Welsh) 769
GWYNN, Eliz. (Rapier) 980
  Thos. 816
GYNECOLOGY 928ff

HAGAN, Alice V. (Buchanan)805
  Ann (Berry) 789
  Anna Parolee (Barry) 871
  Aquilla 954
  Augustine Bradford 871
  Clem 871
  Ed C. 871
  Eliz. (Berry) 789
  Frank Miles 871
  H. T. 872
  Ignatius 816
  Jno. 932
  Jno. Sidney 871
  Jos. S. 871
  Juliet (Murphy) 954
  Mary (Breen) 932
  Mary A. (Buchanan) 805
  Mary Jane (Smith) 872
  Millie (Miles) 871
  Monica 816
  Nancy (Hammett, Cecil) 871
  Nancy E. (Hamilton) 872
  Randall 816
  Rosana (McGarvey) 932
  Sidney 871
HAGEN, (Mattingly) 938
  Polly (Mattingly) 937ff
HAGERMAN, Jos. E. 948
  Va. (Montague) 948
HAHN, Sarah M. (Coleman) 826
HAILEY, Cath. (Laha) 911
HAINES, Cath. (Gore) 865
  Michael 865
HALE, (Woodcock) 1046
HALEY, Jno. 855
  Matilda (Lankford) 855
  Samantha (Fish) 855
  Susan (Maupin) 938
HALISEY, Col. 1038
HALL 940
  Emma (Wilkinson) 1038
  (Evans) 756
  Kitty (Payne) 965
  Sarah A. (Van Meter) 1029
HALL"S GAP 1035
HALLECK, Fitz-Greene 927
HALLIARD, Adelaide (Bush) 870,
    1010
HALSEY, Jno. J. 975
  Marg. (Powell) 975
HAM, Mourney (Philips) 835
HAMILTON, Aletha (Edelen) 846
  A. Rich. 872
  Alex. 871, 986
  Ann Marg. (Mayes) 872
  Anna (McAfee) 858
  Benj. Dr. 786
  Benj. A. 872
  (Butler) 872
  Cath. (Cooper) 829

HAMILTON
  Cordelia (Smith) 828
  Dorothy (Smith) 829
  Eda (Mears) 792
  Edward 872
  Eliza (Nichols) 923
  Eliz. (Luckett) 788
  Eliz. (Price) 872
  Ellen (McAtee) 829
  Gilford Etrick 873
  Harriet (Edelen) 871
  Jas. L. 872
  Jno. 872
  Lela G. 872
  Leonard 872, 889
  Lucinda (Robertson) 986
  Lucy (Edelen) 846
  Martha (Chaudoin) 872
  Mary (Hill) 889
  Mary S. 872
  (McAfee) 943
  (McAtee) 1004
  Melissa F. (Kinnaird) 872
  Nancy E. (Hagan) 872
  Polly (Graham) 865
  Rich. 871ff
  S. Thos. 872
  Sallie J. (Thompson,
    Thompson) 872
  Susan (Marrs) 872
  Theo K. (Woodward) 873
  Thos. 889
  Thos. G. 871
  Ulysses Grant 872
  Walter 829
  Wm. 829
  Wm. H. 872ff
HAMMETT, Jas. 871
  Nancy (Cecil, Hagan) 871
  Susan 871
HAMMIT, Frances (Cecil) 818
HAMMOND, Maggie (Nicholls) 959
HAMPTON, "Uncle" (Slave) 827
HAMNER, Edmund D. 873
  Eliz. (Minor) 873
  Frances E. (Blackketter) 873
  Henry L. Rev. 873
  Jas. B. 873
  Jesse 873
  Jno. W. 873
  Lucy (Clarkston) 873
  Martha J. (Owsley) 873
  Nancy (Day) 873
  Polly (Cole) 873
  Rachel Ann 873
  Rebecca (Bilbo) 873
  Rebecca (Day) 873
  Sarah (Decker) 873
  Sarah (Mitchell) 873
  Sarah A. (Hopkins) 873
  Sarah Frances 873
  Sarah Pitman (Andrews) 873
  Wm. M. 873
HANCOCK 896, 912
  Alsie (Settles) 874
  Benj. C. 873
  Bettie D. 874
  Celestia B. (Cravens) 874
  Edward F. 874
  Eliz. (Bailey) 873
  Eliz. (Cheatham) 874
  Eliz. (Cravens) 873
  Elijah P. 874
  Emma (Cundiff) 873
  Geo. W. 873
  Hannah J. 873
  House (Hotel) 865
  J. P. 873ff
  Jno. 874
  Julia E. 874

HANCOCK
Junius 874, 1016
Martha J. (Miller) 874
Mary (Emerson) 874
Mary E. (Stone) 873
Mason W. 874
Mollie J. (Damron) 874
Nancy Bell 873ff
O. H. 874
Oliver P. 873
(Poor) 974
Rich. 873
Sally F. 873ff
Saml. N. 874
Simon 874
T. T. 873
Theodore T. 874
Wm. 874
Wm. E. 873ff
Wm. F. 874
HAND, Eliz. (Clevland) 824
HANDLEY, Jane (McColgan) 860
Sarah A. (Gaddie) 860
Wm. 860
HANDY, Amelia (McGaughey) 875
Benj. W. 875
Geo. Nuckols 875
Georgie 875
Jn. G. 874ff
Martha J. 875
Mary (Watkins) 875
Mary E. (McElroy) 875
Mary H. (McGaughey) 875
Walter 875
Wm. A. 875
HANES, Mrs. 837
HANLEY, (Purdy) 978
HANNA, Eliz. (Forman) 870
Nancy (Grooms) 870
Stephen, Sr. 870
HANNEGAN, Ed. A. 1010
HANSFORD, Cornelia (Oldham)
876
Eliz. A. (Wilson) 875
Emma (Middleton) 875
Emma Bird 876
Harriet (Farris) 875
Hattie May 876
Jno. S. 875
Lucinda (Stevenson) 875
Marg. (Beatty) 875
Marg. (Stevenson) 875
Maurice Farris 876
Smith 875
Susan M. (Swift, Lyne) 875
Thos. Rev. 875
W. T. 875
HANSON 740
(Hickman) 1007
Matilda (Stone) 1007
Minerva (Mason, Jones) 904
Saml. 1007
HARBERSON, (Cambron) 811
Jas. 809
Rachel A. (Caldwell) 809
Sally (Givens) 809
HARBISON, Eliz. (Mahan) 935
Marg. (Briscoe) 784
HARDEE 762
HARDGROVE, Nancy (Mouser) 953
HARDIN 759, 991
Aaron 920
B. L. 812
Ben 908
Caroline (Watkins) 876
Chas. A. 876
Dr. 950
E. M. 876
Eliza (Cartnell) 989
Hettie A. (Wearen) 1035

HARDIN
Jennie (Magoffin) 976
Judge 949
Mary E. (Clemmons) 1030
McKee 766
Mordecai 877
Nannie T. (Rowan) 989
P. W. 876
Parker C. 876
Rowan 857, 989
Sue (Cardwell) 812
Wm. 958
HARDIN'S CREEK FORT 971
HARDIN'S Creek, Rom. Cath.
Settlement 816
HARDING 876
Almarinda (Russell, Short)
990
Aaron 876ff, 979
Charlotte (Cleaver) 878,990
David 878
Eliz. (Puryear) 979
(Gentry) 877
Jno. 877, 990
Jno. C. 878
Maggie B. (Robinson) 877ff
Marg. (Campbell) 877
Mary E. (Ferguson) 878
Mattie 877
(McDonald) 877
Robt. 877ff
Rowan Capt. 845
Sallie (Callendar) 877ff
Saml. 877
Stephen 878, 990
Susan (Fisher) 878
(Taylor) 990
HARDWICK, (Bricken) 801
HARDY, Jane B. (Evans) 849
HARGIS, Maria (Lillard) 918
HARLAN, Almira 878
Annie S. (Harlan) 879
Atlanta B. (Harlan) 879
Benj. 879
Carrie M. (Bruce) 879
Cath. (Carter) 879
Cath. (Pope) 879
Chas. M. 879
Clarissa (Black) 879
Clarissa (Dunn) 879
Elijah Sgt. 766, 879
Eliza 878
Eliza (Lobb, Clemmons) 1030
Eliz. (Bryan) 879
Eliz. (Street) 879
Eunice (McCord) 879
(Fisher) 856
Geo. Wellington 878ff
Henry Miller 878ff
Hugh Lee 879
Jacob 878ff
Jas. L. "Big Jim" 879, 908
Jas. P. 879
Jane (Evans, Henderson) 885
Jehu Wellington 878ff, 1030
Jennie M. 879
Jeremiah 879
Jno. M. 879
Jos. M. 879
Julia (Starks) 879
Lettie (Maxwell) 879
Louisa T. (Center, Roberts)
879
Maria I. (Baughman) 879
Martha (Hutchings) 878
Martha (Simpson) 879
Mary (Bentley, Neal) 879
Mary (Caldwell) 879
Mary (Fleece) 879
Mary A. 878

HARLAN
Mary C. (Bruce) 879
MInerva 1030
Paulina (Armstrong) 879
Rhoda 878
Robt. J. 878ff
Sally (Moore) 766, 879
Saml. 878
Sarah E. (Bright) 878
Sarah E. (Middleton) 878
Silas Maj. 879
Station 879
Susan (McGee) 879
Susie Lee 879
Thos. J. 878
Walter Scott 879
Wm. Baughman 878ff
HARLIN, Jno. M. Gen. 927
HARMON, Abigail (Pipes) 879
Archibald 880
Barbara (Roberson) 879
Benj. N. 880
C. W. 880
Cassander (White) 880
Cath. (Montgomery) 879
Cath. J. (Montgomery) 879ff
Creed W. 880
Elias A. 880
Eliz. J. (Overstreet) 1011
Geo. D. 880
(Gunter) 880
Ida E. 880
Jacob 879
Jane (Pipes, Gray) 879
Jno. Bradford 879ff
Jno. C. B. 880
Katie (Henry) 879
Lena Burkley 880
Louisa (Smith) 880
Lucinda (Butler) 879
M. F. 1016
Marg. (Pipes) 879
Marg. (Trump) 879
Marg. E. (Pirtle) 973
Marion F. Rev. 880
Mary L. 880
Mary S. (Squires) 880
Martha S. 880
Michael 879
Minerva J. (Russell) 879
Montie C. 880
Nancy A. (Williams) 880
Nancy E. (Gray) 868
Nancy M. 880
Nathaniel 879
Peter 879
Rice 879
Rollie 880
Roy O. 1011
Saml. 879
Sarah C. (Montgomery) 880
Sophronia 880
Thos. J. 879
Ulysses S. 880
Wm. D. 879
Wm. T. 880
HARMONIA COLLEGE 847
HARNED, Cassie E. (Allen) 890
Charlotte (Johnson) 913
Ella (Johnson) 903
Henry 913
(Holsclaw, Hill) 890
Jno. D. 890, 903
Kate (Lee) 903
N. A. 890
HARNEDD, Ann (Rubell) 842
HARNESS, Sarah (Cunningham)
1029
HARPER'S Ferry 937, 974
HARRIS 751

24

HARRIS
Alfred L. 1015
Barney 881
Benj. 881
Betsey (Woods) 881
Cath. (Nicholls) 959
Christopher, Rev. 881, 946,
    1021
Dabney 881
Edward 1015
Edward A. (Shears) 995
Edward W. 995
Eliz. (Berry) 881
Eliz. (Bomb) 995
Eliz. (Ford) 882
Eliz. (Wood) 1045
Elwood 1015
Frances M. (Miller) 945
Geo. L. 1015
Isabel 881
Jas. 881
Jane (Ellison) 881
Jno. D. 880ff, 946, 1007
Jno. M. 881
Jno. V. 1015
Jos. 1015
Josephine (Denton) 1035
Josiah 774, 1015
Malinda (Duncan) 880ff
Marg. (Maupin) 880ff, 946
Martha (King) 774
Mary (Dabney) 881
Mary J. (Selby) 1015
Mary J. (Taylor) 1015
Mary P. 881
Maud Ellen (Harris) 1015
    (McCord) 946
Milton 1015
Minerva (Harris) 881
Minerva J. (Nichols, McAfee)
    923
Moning (Thorpe) 1021
Mourning 881
Nancy (McCord) 881
Nancy (White) 881
Overton 881, 1015
Pattie (Stone) 881, 1007
Paul 1015
Polly (Van Arsdall) 1027
Polly (Woods) 881
Rich. H. 1015
Robt. 881
Sallie 881
Sallie (Wallace) 946
Sally Wiles (King) 774, 1015
Sarah (Wallace) 881
Station 772
    (Stone) 1034
Susanna W. (Duncan) 881
Talitha (Chenault) 851
Talitha (Miller) 945ff
Tyre 881
Wm. V. 880ff
HARRISON 748
Benj. Gov. 1003
Chas. B. 925
Eliza L. 925
General 761, 822, 854, 891,
    900, 926, 938, 968, 977
Judith (Moore) 766
Lizzie L. (McChord) 925
Octavia (Shuck) 996
Wm. H. 793
HARROD, Capt. 855
Jas. 837
Landing 865
Station 814, 837, 852, 1011
HART, Eleanor (Grosh) 741
Geo. Dr. 814
Lou Ann (Duncan) 881

HART
Thos. 741
HARTSUFF, Gen. 762
HARVEY, Capt. 922
W. P. Rev. 812, 1017
HASKINS, Amelia G. (Owsley)
    961
Bettie B. (Jeter) 902
Creed 902
Robt. 961
HATCHER, Anna (Beard) 786
Sallie (Miller) 778
Selden 786
HATHAWAY, Mary L. (Williams)
    771
Philip 771
HAWKINS, Allen 882
Barbara (Davis) 837
Barilla (Ashford) 882
Benj. 778
Carey A. 900
Cath. (Bell, Baline) 898
Celia (Walker) 900
Chas. M. 882ff
Eliza (Smith) 998
Eliz. (Leavell) 914
Emily (Watkins) 882
Geo. 882
Hannah (Smith) 882
J. E. Dr. 883
J. W. Col. 883
Jas. Capt. 882
Jas. B. 998
Jas. Elgin 882ff
Jas. Weathers 882
Jno. T. 882ff
Katie (singleton) 882
Lena 883
Lucy (Allin) 778
Lucy (Jennings) 900
Martha (McDowell) 929ff
Matilda A. (nooe) 882
Nancy (Ashford) 882
Nancy (Talbott) 882
Nancy A. (Robinson) 900
Nicholas 900, 930
Patsy (Overstreet) 882
Polly (Reed) 882
Sallie Bell (Reed 882ff
Sally (Haydon) 882
Sarah (Vanarsdell) 1028
Sarah E. (Elgin) 882ff
Senate A. 882
(Stephenson) 1004
Susan (Slaughter) 998
Thos. 882
(Weathers) 882
Wm. H. 882ff
HAY, Isabella (Feland) 852
W. M. 852
HAYDEN 815
Basil 815ff, 1002
Eleanor (Roberts) 1002
Kitty (McClain) 1015
Rich. 1015
Susan (Lee, Ford) 915
HAYDON, Sally (Hawkins) 882
HAYES, 823
Artemise (Rawlings) 980
Marg. (Glasscock) 980
Phyllis (Williams) 1040
HAYS, Alfred B. 883
Belle (Winfrey) 1044
Bettie A. (Reid) 983
Cath. E. (Litsey) 883
Cyrus W. 883
D. R. 883, 920, 995
Eleanor (Burchum, Burchman)
    883, 995
Eliz. (Blain) 983

HAYS
Ellen 883
Hercules 883
Hugh 983
Jas. B. 883
Jno. J. 883
Kate (Litsey) 920
L. G. Dr. 1044
Mary (Lewis) 883
Mary (McMakin) 883, 920
Mary E. 883
Nancy (Ray) 883
Nannie (Shears) 995
Rebecca (Short) 883
Sallie (Shaunty) 883, 995
Teneriffe 883
Wm. 883, 995
Wm. H. 883
Wm. P. 883
HAYSVILLE 942
HASELWOOD, Alfred H. 882
Clifford 881ff
Emma J. (Rickets) 882
Emma McAfee 882
Geo. M. 882
Geo. W. 882
Jane H. (Haselwood) 882
Lowelace 882
Luella S. (Ford) 882
Mary E. 882
Nancy (Cowherd) 881
Phoebe J. (Cousins) 882
R. W. Dr. 881ff
Rich. M. 881ff
Susan L. 882
Thos. P. 882
(Towler) 881
Wm. H. 882
HAZLEWOOD, Cassander W. (Moss)
    824, 882
Eliz. C. (Coakley) 824
Henry C. 824, 882
Priscilla (Jeter) 901
Sarah (Buckner) 918
HEAD, Ann (Hutchins) 977
Ann C. (Medley) 883
Caroline (Humphrey) 944
Francis M. 883
Frank Paul 884
Ida L. (Gardiner) 863
Jos. Mary 884
Jos. Regmon 884
Marion Jos. 884
Mary E. (Bryant) 884
Mary Lizzie 884
Mary Regina 884
Rich. 863
Robt. Vincent 884
Rosalie (Spandling) 884
Victor E. 884
(Willett) 883
Wm. 884
HEADLY, Alex. 884
Eliz. (Elmore) 884
Eliz. (Patterson) 884
Francis 884
Geo. A. 884
Hamilton Atchison 884
Jas. Hamilton 884
Jno. 884
Marshall 884
Melinda (Atchinson) 884
Nancy (Farra) 884
Polly (shivry) 884
Rebecca (Dunn) 884
Sallie A. (Farra) 884
Susan M. (Neal) 957
Saml. 884
Wm. 884
HEADY, Christina (Gardiner) 863

25

HEALY, Jas. 884
  Jno. Dr. 884
  Julia G. (Barry) 884ff
  Winifred (O'Brian) 884
HEATH, (Chapel) 885
  Flora H. 885
  J. J. 885
  M. C. Dr. 885
  Mary (Emery) 885
  Mary (Morrow) 885
  Moses C. 885
  Nannie C. 885
HEDGES, Cinthey (Branham) 863
  Martha (Gaitskill) 863
  Sue R. (Van Arsdall) 1027
HEFFERNAN, Hattie H. (Shuck)
  996
HEINZ, Marg. (Berkele) 789
HELM 1010
  Amanda C. (Fales) 851
  Ben Hardin Col. 905
  Dicy Jane (Blair) 790
  Eliz. (Blair) 790
  Jos. 851
  Mary M. (Bell) 915
  Matilda (Hocker) 891
  Rachael (Fogle) 857
  Sydney 790
  Wm. H. 790
HELSTEAD, Jno. 1001
  Patsy Jane (Sparks) 1001
HENDERSON 839
  Albert E. 885
  Ann (Rice) 885
  (Davis) 837
  Dycie (Johnson) 885
  Eliz. 747
  Eliz. (Mann) 885
  Eliz. (Pritchett) 885
  Emeline (Drake, Irvin) 898
  Esther (Duncan) 885
  Jas. 885
  Jane (evans, Harlan) 885
  Jno. 747, 885
  Louisa 885
  Mary (Walker, Davis) 885
  Nancy (Magill) 885
  Peggy (Robinson) 885
  Phoebe (Caldwell) 747, 885
  Polly (Caldwell) 885
  Priscilla (Gordon) 885
  Sarah (Parkes) 885
  Sophia (Merriman) 903
  Thos. C. 898
  Wm. Dr. 898
  Wm. Walker 885
HENDRICKS 790, 857, 896
HENDRICKSON, Felix 821
  Louisa (Chelf) 821
  Mary A. (Monday) 821
  Mollie E. (Beard) 787
  Wm. B. 787
HENLY, Sally G. (Ford, Mobley)
  857
HENRY, A. 755
  Bellfield 886
  C. M. Gen. 886
  Claudia M. 886
  Eliza (Rothwell) 988
  Eliz. (Durham) 964
  Eliz. (Kirtley) 886
  Jas. L. 885ff, 988
  Jeff 885ff
  Josie L. (Tery) 886
  Katie (Harmon) 879
  Marg. (Brownlee) 886
  Martha (Nickelson) 988
HENSON, Amanda (Evans) 886
  Anna 886
  Cath. (Holliday) 886

HENSON
  Chas. L. 886
  David 886
  Elisha 886
  Eliz. (Evans) 886
  Eliz. (Meeks) 886
  Ellen M. 886
  Geo. 886
  H. C. 886
  Henry J. 886
  Jas. H. 886
  Jemima (Evans) 886
  Jno. T. 886
  Jno. W. 886
  Jos. S. 886
  Maria (Baker) 886
  Mary (Evans) 886
  Mary (Tupman) 886
  Mattie OCilla 886
  Melinda (Murphy, Malson,
    Newman) 886
  Nancy (Vest) 886
  Nanny (Pitts) 886
  Polly (Raborn) 886
  Retta F. 886
  Robt. 886
  Rosa L. 886
  Saml. T. 886
  Serilda (Rexrhod) 886
  Truman K. 886
  Wm. J. 886
HERNDON, A. G. 887
  Ann P. (Crothwait) 887
  Annie C. 887
  Ben D. 887
  Betty (Anderson) 887
  Cath. (Winn) 887
  Elijah 887
  Eliz. (Zachery) 887
  Emma (Parkes) 963
  Geo. 887
  Helen (Kinn(i)ard) 887, 909
  Horace K. 887
  Lewis 887
  Lucie (Anderson) 887
  Nancy B. (Pollard) 887
  Nancy Jane 887
  Wm. L . 887
HERRING, Lee 887
  Maggie 887
  Nancy (Pollard) 887
  Nicy (Floyd) 887
  Patty 887
  Sallie 887
  Terrell 887
  Thos. J. 887
HERT, Nancy (Anderson 778
HEVENHILL 840
HEWEY, Sarah E. (Mock) 948
HICKEY, Mary J. (Martin) 932
HICKLE, Paulina A. (Spoonamore)
  1003
HICKMAN, Gen. 1007
  Wm. Dr. 850
Hicks, Sallie (Tutt) 1026
  Thos. 1026
HIESTAN, Araminta 888
  Etsel 888
  Evy (Lainhart) 888
  Evy (Landis) 887
  Maria J. (Mercer) 888
  Morgan 888
  Oliver P. Dr. 887ff
  Perry 888
  Thornton 888
HIESTAND, Jacob 887ff
HIGGINBOTTOM, Eliza (Miller)
  1008
HIGHT, Rebecca (Lainhart) 910
HILL, Alathair (Spalding) 889

HILL
  Amelia H. (Wilson) 1043
  Ann Mary 889
  Artemisia (Curry) 835
  Blanche 890
  Clement J. 889
  Clement S. 888ff
  Eliz. (Mann) 830
  Eliz. (Medley) 890
  Eliz. (Young) 760
  Ella E. 890
  Ellen (Beeler) 903
  Frances (Fowler) 890
  Frank A. 890
  Geo. 760
  Golden 773
  Harry 816, 889
  Henrietta (Johnson) 763
  Henry V. 890
  (Holsclaw, Harned) 890
  Hopy (Campbell) 811
  Ida G. 890
  Isaac 760
  Jas. A. Dr. 890
  Jane (Atkinson) 890
  Jane (campbell) 811
  Jane (Martin) 760
  Jno. B. 760, 763, 889
  Jos. 890
  Julia F. (Potter) 852
  Louisa (Magruder) 890
  Louisa (Peyton) 889
  Lucy (Bingamin) 1043
  Malinda (Pollard) 760
  Maria A. (Peyton) 890
  Martha (Woods) 760
  Mary (Hamilton) 889
  Mary (Sullivan) 760
  Mary V. 890
  Nancy (Gabbard) 760
  Nancy (Mayfield) 760
  Oliver Perry Dr. 760, 970
  Rebecca (Miles) 888
  Susan (Moore) 951
  Susan (Rives) 889
  Thos. 760, 888ff
  Thos. D. 1043
  Thos. P. 889ff
  Wm. 760
  Wm. S. B. 890
  Wm. W. 742
HILLIARD, Bartlett 950
  Elinor A. (Moore) 950, 1031
  Mary (Moss) 950
HILLS 816
HINCKSTON CREEK 904
HINDMAN 981
  Eliz. (Rawlings) 980
HINDS, Hannah (McGee) 932
  Saml. 932
HINES, Thos. H. 744
HITCHCOCK'S ANALYSIS 958
HITE, Nancy (Evans) 849
HIX, Sally (Wathall) 1038
HOARD, Wm. Major 766
HOBBS, Annie P. (Nuckols) 941
  G. Helm 941
  Jno. 779
  Martha M. (Argo) 779
  Nancy (White) 779
  Nancy J. (Wilkinson) 1038
  Rosa E. (Sympson) 1013
  S. M. Dr. 839
HOBSON, Agnes, (Edwards) 782
  Anna M. (Penick) 763, 967
  Atwood M. 763
  Bettie K. 763
  Edward H. Gen. 761, 967
  Edwena 763
  Jno. A. 763

HOBSON
 Katie (Adair) 763
 Lucy A. (Kertly) 761
 Mattie (Hodges) 891
 (Patteson) 761
 Wm. A. 761, 763, 1026
HOCKADAY, Eliz. (Fox) 772, 890
 Eliz. (Irvine) 899
 Jas. S. 772, 890
 Lawson S. 890
 Louisa D. (Wood) 890
 Mary V. 890
 Nancy (Adams) 772
 Sumyra-Sumira (Shearer) 772, 890
 Walter 890
 Wm. L. Dr. 890
HOCKER, Ann 891
 Chas. R. 891
 Eliza 891
 Frances 891
 Jesse 891
 Lizzie (Fair) 891
 Lucinda (Carter) 891
 Lucinda (McKinney) 891
 Lydia (Purdy) 978
 Marg. (Dunn) 986
 Mary C. (Settle) 891
 Mary F. 891
 Mary J. (Miller) 943
 Matilda (Helm) 891
 Nicholas Col. 943
 Polly (Hocker) 891
 Polly (Clements) 793
 Rich. P. 891
 Saml. G. Dr. 891
 Tilman 891
 Wm. R. 891
HODGEN, Ann (Montague) 948
 Ann M. (Wright) 1046
 Lucy (Montague) 948
 Robt. Dr. 1046
HODGEN'S Brigade 989
HODGES, Cath. (Carter) 891
 Jas. C. 891
 Mattie (Hobson) 891
 Melinda (Stone) 1006
 Thos. P. Dr. 866, 891
HOFFMAN, Eliz. E. (Kirk) 909
HOGAN, Jno. 982
 Josephine (Reed) 982
 Mary (Dunn) 982
 Mary A. (Rodman) 987
 Mary E. (Drury) 987
 Sarah (Bates) 863
 Wm. Capt. 987ff
HOGARTY, Alex. 891
 Jos. A. Rev. 891ff
 Martin 891
 Mary (Fraser) 891
 Michael 891
 Wm. 891
HOGLAND, Sarah (Samuels) 992
HOGUE, Ann (Armstrong) 780
HOLDERMAN, (Peak) 792
HOLLAND, Burchy 949
 Mary (McCaslin) 949
 Nancy (Gray) 867
 Tabitha (Montgomery) 949,1022
HOLLIDAY, Cath. (Henson) 886
 Mary (Reynolds) 886
 Wm. 886
HOLLOWAY, Wm. Col. 749
HOLLY, Dr. 742
 Susan (McGalsson) 1025
HOLMAN, Eliz. (Davis) 837
 Frances 837
 Jno. 837, 923
 Priscilla A. (Sharp) 892
 Sallie 923

HOLMAN
 Sue N. (Lyen) 923
 W. A. 892
HOLMES, Mary (Estill) 752
 Mary (Kauffman) 906
 Mary (Faulker) 906
 Nancy (Tathan, Bell) 898
 Saml. 906
HOLSCLAW, Eliza (Johnson) 890
 (Harned, Hill) 890
 Jas. 890
HOOD, Allie M. 892
 Ann (Chandler) 899
 Betty (Irvine) 899
 Creed 892
 Dollie 892
 Eliphalet 892
 Eliz. (Young) 892
 Fanny (Clemons) 892
 Gooy 899
 (Jarvis) 892
 Jesse 892
 Joel 892
 Jno. 892
 Jos. 892
 Kalista (Taylor) 892
 Louellen 892
 Martha (Sharp) 892
 Melvin 892
 Myrtie Valeria 892
 Napoleon 892
 Patsy (Murray) 892
 Robt. 892
 Sarah Ann (Kelly) 892
 Theresa (Hunn) 898
 Thos. 892
 Walter A. 892
 Wm. 892
HOOKER, Anna M. (Phelps) 775
HOOTON, Frances (Johnson) 903
HOOVER, Ella (Burnett) 859
HOPE, Cynthia A. (Fry) 759
 Leah (Survant) 1011
 Phoebe (Calvert, Williams) 1039
HOPKINS, Fannie L. (Smith)
 Gen. 855, 920
 Jos. H. 1000
 Lucy (Blair) 790, 1043
 Martha (Garnett) 1000ff
 Robt. G. 1000
 Ruth B. (Booton) 1000
 Sarah A. (Hamner) 873
 Wm. 790
HOPPER 845, 906
 Annie L. 893
 Isabella (Johnson) 893
 Jas. W. 892
 Jno. 893
 Lee M. 893
 Lucy A. (Campbell) 893
 R. H. 1016
HORACE 756
HORINE, Polly (Jones) 905
 Mill 856
HORSE, Site of Louisville once priced for 824
 Price of 828
HORSEMANSHIP, Superior 796
HOSKINS, Betsy (Bright) 801, 986
 Jas. 941
 Marg. (Robinson) 986
 Nancy (Kirk) 909
 Nancy (Merritt) 941
 Rudolph 909
 Wm. 986
HOSPITALITY, Ky. 902
HOURIGAN, Jas. P. 1038
 Martha E. (Whitehouse) 1038

HOURIGAN
 Nancy (Pipes) 1038
 Rufus 1038
HOUSE, First in Green Co. Ky. 1041
 Richmond, Ky. 944
HOUSTON, Eliz.)Kenney) 908
 Ephemia (McDowell) 908
 Hester 908
 Jane 908
 Jno. 908
 Marg. (McCreary) 908
 Patience (Kerr) 908
 Phoebe (Kenney) 908
 Robt. C. 908
 Sarah (Boggs) 908
 Sarah (January) 870
HOVIOUS, Mary (Stotts) 1008
HOWARD 815, 836
 Artitia (Moorman) 947
 Ben 961
 (Embry) 848
 Rebecca (Greer) 869
 Susan (Boone) 764, 980
 Zerelda (Neal) 961
HOWE, Jas. Lewis Dr. 755ff
 Jos. 816
 Sallie (Cox) 948
HOWLETT, Eliz. (Lee) 1022
 Luke 1022
 Sarah A. (Troutman) 1022
HUBBARD, H. D. Dr. 948
 Keturah J. (McElroy) 930
 Mary (Butner, Fish) 855
 Sallie E. (Montague) 948
HUBBLE, Emily (Spoonamore) 1003
 Joel 1035
 Martha (Ware) 1035
HUDBERRY, Polly (Gray) 867
HUDGIN, Daisey 893
 Eliz. (Sweeney) 893
 Emery B. 893
 Ethel 893
 Hugh 893
 Jno. 893
 Martha (Vaughan) 893
 Maud 893
 Payton 893
 Susan A. (Rogers) 893
 Thos. 893
HUDSON, Abraham L. 894
 Banks 894
 Benj. R. S. 894
 Betsy 894
 Bettie H. (McAfee) 923
 Bettie J. (Vaughan) 893
 David 894
 Drury 893
 Eliza (Back) 894
 Eliza (Rithcie) 894
 Eliza (Schooler) 894
 Eliz. 894
 Eliz. H. (Bohan) 794
 Fannie 894
 Fielding L. 894
 Florence (Knight) 894
 Francis 894
 Helen (Sandidge) 894
 Horace G. 894
 Jas. S. 894
 Jemima (Berry) 894
 Jeriah (Downing) 894
 Jesse Berry 894
 John P. 893ff
 Joshua 894
 Joyce (Fears) 893
 L. B. Dr. 894
 L. W. 794, 894
 Lizzie (Bohon) 894
 Lynn W. 894

27

28

IRVIN
Harry B. 898
Henry C. 1041
Jas. B. 1041
Jas. F. 1041
Jno. Glover 898
Judith (Glover) 898
Lela 898
Lucretia (Starns) 1041
Manta D. (Allen) 1041
Mary (Forsythe) 858
Mary (Praither) 898
Mary J. (Turpen) 1041
Robt. O. 898
Sallie E. (Finnell) 855, 1041
Saml. W. 1041
Sarah M. (Lyle) 898
W. M. 1034
Wm. Drake 898
Wm. P. 898
IRVINE, Abraham D. 744, 809ff
Adam 899
Albert 899
Amelia T. (Moss) 810, 899
Betty, (Hood) 899
Christopher 899
David Col. 749ff, 898ff
Edmond 899
Eliza (Mann) 935
Eliz. 896
Eliz. (Hockady) 899
Family, long Col. Clk.record
899
Isaac Shelby 898ff
Lizzie M. (Blanton) 744
Lucy E. (Caldwell) 809
Maria J. (Brumfield) 805
Mary P. (Irvine) 744
Patsie 899
Sallie (McDowell) 930
Sarah 898
Sophia (Fox) 758
Susan (McDowell) 898ff
Wm.Col. 899
IRVING, Mary (Davis) 837
IRWIN, Mary (Phillips) 971
ISAACA, Martha J. (Lankford)
913
Sally (Taylor) 987
ISHAM, Artimissia 899
Ersley (McDonald) 899
Gordon 899
Henrietta 899
Henry 899
Maggie 899
Marg. (McKittrick) 899
Mary 899
Orin J. 899
Tolitha (Reid) 899
Victoria (Strange) 1008
Wm. 899, 1008
ISLAND, JOHNSON'S 799
ISON, Frances A. (Poor) 974

JACK, Mary (Stoner) 993
Nancy (Moore) 951
Stock, 1st in Madison Co.969
JACKMAN, Eliz. (Huffman) 894
Jno. 895
Sarah (Bailey) 844
JACKSON 918
Conf. S. 853
Affie G. (Yeiser) 1047
Agnes J. (Thomson) 1020
Andrew Gen. 748ff, 800, 843,
861, 908, 937, 1009,1024
Camp 1010
Eliza J. (Taylor) 1030
Jno. D. Dr. 929, 934
Marg. (Spears) 1003

JACKSON
Rebecca (Myers) 942
T. W. Dr. 878
JACOBS, Susan (Powell) 974ff
JAMERSON, Narcissa (Montgomery)
949
JAMES I 745
II 965
Annie (Wearen) 1035
Martha T. (Lyen) 923
Mattie (Evans) 851
JAMESON, Lucinda (Pottinger)
944
JANS, Jas. 1002
Martha P. (Spalding) 1002
JANUARY, Andrew McConnell 870
Sarah A. (Grundy) 870
Sarah (Houston) 870
JARVIS, (Hood) 892
J. L. 899
W. L. 899ff
JARNAGHAN, Fannie (Lancaster)
1002
JAY 748
JEAN, Nettie M. (Berkele) 789
JEFFERSON 799, 823, 1017,1037
JEFFRIES, Martha Caroline
(Willis) 1041
Mary A. (Nelson) 1042
Mary E. (Willis) 1042
Thos. P. 1042
Wm. F. 1041
JELF, Jennie (Armstrong) 780
JENKINS, Jennie (Robinson) 987
Jonathan 894
JENKINS, Lucy M. (Cook) 1017
JENNER 860
JENNINGS, 840
Ann (Payne) 964
(Ballinger) 900
Carey H. 900
Dr. 857
Eliz. May (Love) 900
Gen. 760
Humphrey 866
Ida V. (Greenleaf) 900
Jas. L. 900
Jno. M. 844, 900
Josephine L. (Ford) 857
Lucy (Hawkins) 900
Lucy (Price) 866
(Marksberry) 900
Maud (Fogle) 857
Nancy E. 900
Nancy E. (Dunlap) 844
Nickoleena H. (Chenault) 900
Rosana (McDonald) 803
Saml. 803
Wm. 844, 900
Wm. Dr. 900
Wm. Gen. 900
Zerelda (Brown) 803
JESSE, Cath. (George) 885
Frances Felicia (Barry) 871,
884
Saml. Rev. 871, 885
JAMERSON, Eliz. N. (Montgomery)
949
JESUITS 991
JET, Nannie (Woodcock) 1046
JETER, Anderson Major 900ff
Bettie B. (Haskins) 902
Danl. 901
Geo. R. 901
Geo. W. 900ff
Jno. J. 902
Lucy H. 901
Maggie A. (Shipp) 901
Martha A. (Chaudoin) 902
Martha A. (Cox) 902

JETER
Mary S. (Durham) 901
Priscilla (Hazelwood) 901
Robt. H. 901
Rodophil Col. 901
Rodophil E. Capt. 901ff
Sorrow S. (Allen) 900ff
Susan S. (Craddock) 901
Thos. R. 902
JETT, Jemimah (Doores) 840
JEWELL, Sallie (Ford) 857
JOFFRIAN, Eliz. D. (Fields)
854
Susan R. (Fields) 854
JOHNS, Lucy (Blanton) 743
JOHNSON 761, 823, 947
Absalom 903
Alex. 902ff
Andrew Camp 762
Ann (Smith) 902
Anna (Barr) 784
Annie (McAlister) 924
Cath. 763
Chas. 763
Charlotte (Harned) 913
Dick 852
Dorothy (Miles) 763
Dycie (Henderson) 885
Eliza (Holsclaw) 890
Eliz. V. (Bricken) 763, 801
Eliz. (Johnson) 903
Eliz. (Payne) 963
Eliz. (Russell) 902
Ella (Harned) 903
Ellen 763
Emme (Beeler) 903
Felix 801
Frances (Hooton) 903
Gen. 763
Hannah (Wilford) 902
Hazard 903
Henrietta (Hill) 763
Hillery 763
Isabella (Hopper) 893
Jacob 902
Jas. 1001
Jas. B. 903
Jas. L. 932
Jemima(Nave) 957
Jno. J. 763, 902
Jos. E. 903
Leonard 816
Lucy Lee 902
M. C. 776
Maggie J. (Merriman) 903
Major 903
Mary L. (Langsford) 763, 913
Martha (Bricken) 801
Mildred (Boone) 764
Nancy (McGee) 763, 932
Nancy Jane (Sparks) 1001
Oliver H. P. 903
P. B. 903
Perry 902
Phoebe A. (Penn) 902ff
Pres. 912, 998
Priscilla 763
Rich. M. Col. 862, 964
Robt. Col. 964
Rosetta (Medley) 801
Sabrina (Perryman) 967ff
Sally 763
Sarah C. (Tutt) 1026
Silvester 763, 980
Thos. M. 763, 902, 968
W. E. 1026
(Wilson) 932
Wm. B. 763, 902ff
Wm. Ru 902

29

JOHNSON'S ISLAND 785, 921,
  994, 1021
JOHNSTON, Agnes (Waller)903ff
Agnes A. (Wilson) 798
Annie Maria 904
Cornelia Minor (Conover)904
Diana (Logan) 904
Dollie Eliz. 904
Gen. 850, 974, 1021
Henry 903
Jas. L. 903ff
Jno. Waller 904
Mary Agnes (Hunter) 904
Mattie Sally (Robertson)
  904
Nannie E. (Fidler) 853
S. D. 904
Sally (Dawson) 903
Stephen 903ff
Thos. B. 903ff
Wm. H. 904
JOHNSTONE, Jane (Rule) 780
JONES, Amanda (Owsley) 905
Anna M. 905
Augustus 937
Benj. 904
Beriah M. 905
Betsy Jane (McNeely) 1001
Bryant Owsley 905
Bryant R. 905
Casandra (Bradshaw) 798
Cath. (Wright, Robertson,
  Freeman) 985
Chas. 1016
Chas. F. 798
Chas. H. 910
Christopher L. 905
(Cotton) 831
Danl. R. 904
Danl. W. 863
David 905, 1029
David L. 904
David M. 905
Dr. 778
Eliza F. 906
Eliza J. (Knifley, Bland)
  910
Eliz. 905
Eliz. (Bridges) 904
Eliz. (Sallee) 992
Eliz. (Sutherland) 866
Eliz. (Tomlinson) 1021
Eliz. C. (Jones) 905
Eliz. E. 904
Eliz. H. (Woods, Mitchell)
  904
Eliz. V. (Humphries) 905ff
Fanny (Taylor) 1016
Frances T. (Taylor) 1014
Geo. G. 906
Geo. W. 905
Fannie M. (Reid) 983
Franklin 904
Hannah (Renfrew) 904
Hannah L. (Wilson) 904
Hezekiah B. 906
Hugh L. 1021
J. W. 778
Jas. P. 906, 1001
Jas. R. 904
Jas. W. 905ff
Jas. Milton 904
Jefferson 992
Jennie (Chenault) 905
Jesse 904ff
Jno. 904ff
Jno. R. 904
Jno. Sanford 904
Jno. W. 906
Jonathan 905

JONES
Jos. 904ff
Judith (Moss, Taylor) 1021
Landy 932
Lizzie C. (Jones) 905
Lockie (Squires) 880
Lucy (Farrow) 932
Lucy (Gray) 867
Lydia (Boyd) 904
Lydia (Ralls) 904
Maggie (Allin) 778
Marg. A. (Nelson) 904
Marg. A. (Sallee) 992
Marg. P. (Woods) 904
Mary (Bridgewater, Taylor)
  1016
Mary (Owsley) 905
Mary (Powell) 975
Mary E. (Morgan) 905
Meriwether Rev. 932
Minerva (Mason, Hanson) 904
Nancy B. (Phelps) 905, 969
Nancy E. 906
Nannie B. (Gaitskill) 863,
  905
Naomi (Fair) 891
Narcissa (Burgin, Smith) 904
(Parks) 905
Patsy (Shy) 905
Paulina M. (Renfrew) 904
Pearl A. 905
Philip A. 905ff
Polly (Horine) 904ff
Rachel (Coffey) 992
Rachel (Murrah) 957
Rebecca R. (Dunlap) 863, 905
Rich. 905, 976
Robt. 905
(Robinson) 905
Sallie (Newland) 904ff
Sallie (Vandeveer) 1028
Sally (Murrah) 957
Saml. H. 905
Saml. M. 905
Sarah (McGee) 932
Sarah C. 905
Sarah E. 906
Susan (Lillard) 905, 919
Susan A. (Adams) 906
Susan M. 906
Tabitah 905
Thos. T. 904, 906
Waller 905
Welch H. 905
Wilkes M. 905
Wm. C. 905
Wm. M. 905
Xantippe (Poyntz) 975
JOPLIN, Josiah Dr. 900
JORDAN, Abraham 827
(Cabell) 809
(Coleman) 827
Col. 827
JOSEPH, Abraham 906
Jacob 906
Lizzie (Forx) 906
Marg. Marie 906
Sarah E. (Abraham) 906
JOSEPH'S CHAPEL 919
JOUETT, Jno. 777
Mary (Allin) 777
Mourning 777
JUDA, Gen. 762ff
JUDD, Lucy (Cartwright) 814
JULIAN, (Dillon) 1031

KALFUS, Sarah (Mock) 948
KAUFFMAN, Alice L. 906ff
Emma (Greenleaf) 906
Frances 907

KAUFFMAN
Francis S. 906
H. Clay 906
Louisa 906
Mary (Holmes) 906
Minnie 906
KAVANAUGH 751
Amelia J. (Denny) 797
(Argo) 779
H. H. Bishop 840, 971
Pollie (Oldham 946
KAVENAUGH, Jane (Faulkner,
  Walker) 840
KEAN, Sallie (McClure) 946
KEAS, Albert H. 977
Anna T. (Price 977
Isaac 977
Lucy (Vivian) 977, 1032
Nelson 977
KELLEY, Anna B. 907
Annie (Broaderson) 907
Dailey 907
Jno. 907
Mattie L. (Ball) 907
Sabina (Woodsmall) 907
Saml. Major 907
KELLEY'S HIGH SCHOOL 982
KELLY, Jno. J. 907
Major 974
Sarah Ann (Hood) 892
KELSEY, E. B. Dr. 946
Louvenia (Miller) 946
Mary (Allen) 775
KELSIE, Lucy (Gray) 867
KEMPER Eliz. (Poor) 974
Eliz. (Withers) 974, 997
(Grundy) 870
Mary (Boner) 796
Mildred (Slaughter) 997
Sarah (Coppage) 779
Wm. 974, 997
KENLYE, Freding 1000
Permelia (Smith) 1000
KENNEDY, Andrew 954
Annie (Lyen) 923
Bettie 954
David 954
Elbert 954
Eliza (Kennedy) 954
Eliz. (Mullins) 954
(Embry) 848
Jennie 954
Mary 954
Patsy Bell (Powell) 975
Sarah A. (Powell) 954, 975
Wm. 954
KENNETT, Ann (Crownover) 1023
Jno. 1023
Nancy (Tucker) 963, 1023
KENNEY, Agnes (Lyle) 907
Alex. Dr. 907
Eliz. (Houston) 908
Eliz. (Montgomery) 907
Jas. 907
Jane (Smith) 907
Jno. Smith 907ff
Jos.S. 908
Marg. 907
Mary 907
Matt. 907
Phoebe (Houston) 908
REbecca (Givens) 907
Robt. P. 907
(Robinson) 907
Sarah F. (Campbell) 907ff
Silas P. 907
Va. (Sherer) 908
Wm. Mc. 907
Wm. R. 908

30

33

34

MATHENY
Eliz. (Lowry) 937
F. A. 937
F. G. 937
Henry Eugene 937
J. H. 937
Jos. Stiles 937
L. T. 937
Mary E. (McCoun) 937
Mary I. (Curry) 937
Michael M. 937
Nannie 937
Rachel (Ruby) 937
Sarah L. (Broaddus) 937
W. M. 937
MATHEWS, Capt. 974
MATTHIS, Cecilia A. (Pirtle)
  973
MATTINGLY, Agnes 938
Alathaise-Alethis (Spalding)
  788, 937
Anna Mary 938
Basil 937
Benedict 938
Benj. 938
Benj. F. 938
Bernard 938
E. H. 788
Edward H. 937
(Fenwick) 938
Francis X. 938
Gertrude 938
(Hagen) 938
Imelda 938
Jno. 938, 1020
Kate (Willett) 938
Leonard 816, 937ff
Lucas 816
Malinda (Thompson) 1020
Marg. 938
Mary (Daley) 1020
Mary Jane (Spalding) 937ff
Paul 938
Philip 816, 994
Polly (Hagen) 937ff
Rose A. (Seay) 994
Susan (Graves) 938
Susan M. (Beavens) 788
Teresa 938
Veronica 938
Wm. E. Dr. 816, 937
MAUPIN, David 938
Fannie (Stives) 938
Geo. W. 938ff
Horace 939
Jas. McCreary 939
Jennings W. 939
Jessamine P. 939
Marg. (Harris) 880ff
Marg. (McWilliams) 938
Marg. (Miller) 946
Mary (Walker) 938
Mary P. 939
Peggy (Miller) 946
Susan (Haley) 938
Wm. 939
MAXEY, Attie (Miller) 939
Caroline (Trabue) 997
David W. 939
Ephraim 997
Eugenia Mattie 939
Jas. W. 939
Jane (Whitman) 997
Sue Hite 939
MAXWELL, Eliz. (Phillips) 840
Eunice (Stiles) 879, 1014
Jos. 879, 1014
Julia (Phillips) 972
Julietta (Tarkington) 846,
  1014

MAXWELL
Lettie (Harlan) 879
Martha (Knox) 1014
Mary (Schoolfield) 993
MAY, Bernetta (Van Arsdall)
  1027
D. C. 1011
Eliz. (Fair) 891
Emily (Cozatt) 833
Henry 833
Jemima (Cleland) 833
Mary W. (McLane) 926
Mary (Murphy) 840
MAYES, Ann Marg. (Hamilton)
  872
Annie 939
Annie (Forsythe) 858
Archibald S. 939
E. F. 985
Eusebius S. 939
Harriet P. (McElroy) 939
Jas. 872
Kate 939
Marg. (McClanahan) 939
Mary 939
Mary (Robertson) 986
Mary A. (Curry) 939
Mary L. (Green) 939
Mat 939
Paulina 939
Robt. 939
Wm. 858
MAYFIELD, Isaac 970
Jane (Baxter) 970
Nancy (Hill) 760
Sallie (Phillips) 970
MAYS, Alice (Seay) 994
Anna (Turner) 979
Dr. 909
Georgia B. (Randolph) 979
Jas. 994
Jno. 979
Kate (Debaun) 838
Mary (Brown) 979
Mary E. 994
Nelson 979
Sallie (Seay) 994
McAFEE, Anna (Hamilton) 858
Bettie H. (Hudson) 923
C. F. 795
Caldwell 923
Cynthia (Allen) 923
Dicey (Caldwell, Curry) 834,
  923
Eliz. (Lillard) 919, 923
Eliz. J. (Adams) 923
Eliz. M. (Rickets) 882
Francis M. 923
Geo. 858, 923
Hannah (Daviess) 923
Jas. J. 923
Jane (Forsythe) 858
Jane (Macgoffin) 923
Joel P. 923
Jno. Col. 923ff, 937
Jno. Armstrong 924
Jos. 923ff
Marg. (Buchanan) 806
Mary (Forsythe) 858
Mary (Gants) 806
Mary (Moore) 923
Mary A. (Singleton, Williams,
  King) 923
(McCama) 923
(McCousic) 923
Mildred (Bohon, Hudson) 795
Minerva J. (Nichols, Harris)
  923
Minnie (Graham) 865
Monroe Harris 923

McAFEE
N. W. (Forsythe) 858
Nannie C. (Davis) 923
Narcissa (Forsythe) 849
Phoebe E. (Thompson) 923
Priscilla (Armstrong) 924
Robt. 858, 923
Robt. Gen. 858
Robt. Rev. 766
Saml. 923ff
Sarah A. (Edelen) 845ff
Station 827, 923
Survey 974
Wm. 923ff
McAHAN, Emma (Green) 869
McALISTER 967
Annie (Johnson) 924
Cornelius 978
Eleanor (Brawner) 978
Ellen (Evans) 851, 924
Geo. 924
Jas. W. 924
Jennie (Hundley) 924
Jno. 924
Jos. H. 851, 924
Martha (Owsley) 851, 924
Martha (Purdy) 978
Mattie 924
Rachel (McKenzie) 924
Robt. Rev. 924
McATEE, Ann (Miles) 943
Ann (Stiles) 1004
(Boarman) 793
Cath. (Spalding) 829
Ellen (Hamilton) 829
George 943, 1004
(Hamilton 943, 1004
Henry 816
McBEATH, Antoinette (Cleaver)
  824
Dorinda (Price) 824
Geo. W. 824
McBRAYER 940
Dr. 849
Henrietta (Moore) 767
Wm. H. 755, 767
McBRIDE 975
McCAIN, Millie (Anderson) 779
McCALEB, Jas. F. 766
Sophia (Moore) 766
McCALL, Cynthia Ann (Murphy)
  955
McCAME, (McAfee) 923
McCARLEY, Nannie (Faulconer)
  852
McCASLIN, Mary (Holland) 949
McCAULEY, Ann (Simpson) 1009
McCAW, (Allen) 776
Cecily (De Graffenreid) 776
Jno. 776
McChord, A. H. 924, 985
Annie L. 925
Chas. C. 924ff
Chas. M. 925
Eliz. 924
Jno. 924ff
Laura (Hynes) 924ff
Lizzie L. (Harrison) 925
Lydia (Caldwell) 924ff
Mary 924
Nannie (McElroy) 925
Robt. C. Dr. 924ff
Wm. C. 924ff
McCalin, Eliz. (Rodman) 987
Ellen (Willis) 1015
Finis 1015
Gen. 763
Jas. 1015
Jos. 1014ff
Kitty (Hayden) 1015

35

McCLAIN
Marg. Ann (Miller) 1015
Mary J. (Taylor) 1015
Nancy (Noel) 1015
Oliver 1015
Robt. 1015
Sarah (Naylor) 1015
Sarah M. (Taylor) 1014
Susan (Hurt, Vigus) 1014
McCLANAHAN, Marg. (Mayes) 939
McCLASKEY, Mary (Fulton) 859
McCLELLAN, Geo. B. Gen. 784,
794, 806, 829, 939
McCLINTOCK, Jno. 755
McCLOSKY, Nannie (Brown) 802
Newell 802
McCLUER'S FORK 864
McCLUNG, Sarah (McDowell) 928,
930
McClure, Aaron 798
Alex. 837
Amanda (Burns) 807
Jane (Davis) 837
Jno. R. 1044
Lue (Chapman) 926
Martha (Garrett) 926
Nancy (Foster) 837
Nathan 946
Octavia (Bradshaw) 798
Sallie (Kean) 946
Sarah A. (Miller) 946
Strather 926
Susan E. (Winfrey) 1044
Wm. B. 926
McCOLGAN, Jane (Handley) 860
McCONNELL, Rebecca E. (Parker)
828
McCORD 746
Caroline C. (Cummings, Grant)
866
Eunice (Harlan) 879
(Harris) 946
Lydia (Caldwell) 746
Nancy (Harris) 881
McCORMICK, Andrew 945
Nancy (Oliphant) 849
Priscilla 845
Rebecca (Duvall) 845
McCOSKEY, W. Bishop 992
McCOUN, Jno. 937
Jos. 937
Marg. 937
Mary E. (Matheny) 937
Nancy (Tilford) 937
Saml. Major 937
Nancy (Slaughter, Samuel)
997
McCRACKEN, Andrew 965
Rosa (Payne) 965
McCREARY, Chas. Dr. 926
E. R. Dr. 926
Jas. 926
Jas. Bennett Gov. 802, 876,
926ff, 1010
Jno. Col. 908, 926
Katie (Hughes) 927
Marg. (Houston) 907ff
Mary (Barr) 926
Nancy (Crawford) 926
Robt. H. 927
Sabrina (Bennett) 926
McCROCKLIN, Annie (Marshall)
936
McCUBBIN, Eliz. (Edgar) 949
Jas. 949
Nancy A. (Donan, Montgomery)
949
Tabitha I. (Montgomery) 949
McCUBBINS, Nancy (Bloid) 824

McCULLOCK, Ben Gen. (Capt.)
776
McDONALD, Ersley (Isham) 899
(Harding) 877
Jno. 783
Mary E. (Bale) 783
Mary J. (Nave) 957
Matt. 783
Rev. 877
Tabitha (Gooch) 783
McDOWELL, Abram Irvin 930
Andrew 930
Ann M. (Caldwell) 1047
Annie 930
Bessie 930
Caleb 930
Chas. 929
Ephemia (Houston) 908
Ephraim Dr. 899, 927ff,
930, 1047
Irwin Gen. 930
Jas. Dr. 929ff
Jno. 930
Jos. Col. 929ff
Lizzie (McElroy) 930
Marg. 930
Magdaline (Wood) 930
Maria (Ball) 942
Martha (Hawkins) 929ff
Mary 930
Mary R. (Myer) 942
Nicholas 929ff
Sallie (Irvine) 930
Saml. 928ff, 930, 942
Sarah (McClung) 928, 930
Sarah (Shelby) 899, 929
Square 929
Sue 930
Susan (Irvine) 898ff
Wm. 929ff
McDOWELLS 744
McDUFFIE, Geo. 861
McELROY 847, 986
Abram 931
Ada (Lisle) 920
Anna G. (Rice) 930
Anthony 930
Cecil F. 930
Chas. R. 925
Clarence U. 931
Dr. 937
Eliza K. 930
Eliza N. (Skiles) 931
Geo. W. 931
Grundy 931
Harriet P. (Mayes) 930, 939
Hiram 931
Hugh 960
Jas. F. Dr. 930
Jennie F. 931
Jno. 871
Keturah J. (Hubbard) 930
Kittie (Cleland) 930
Lizzie (McDowell) 930
Lucy (Cleaver) 931
Lucy (Ray) 930
Lucy A. (Lee) 914
Marg. I. 930
Marg. (Ray) 981ff
Maria J. 930
Mary (Kirk) 930
Mary (Shuck) 925
Mary E. (Handy) 875
Mary L. 931
Mary R. (Hughes) 895
Nannie (McChord) 925
Paul Irvin 930ff
Phillip E. 930
Proctor K. 931
Robt. L. 930

McELROY
Saml. 930
Saml. R. 930
Sarah 930
Susan (McElroy) 931
Wm. C. 931
Wm. E. 930, 982
Wm. T. 930
Willie J. (Grundy) 871
McEWEN, Belle (Graham) 865
McFARLAN, Wm. 995
McFARLNAD, Addie (Landram)
912ff
McFERRAN, Eliz. (Young) 931
Jas. B. 931
Jas. M. 931
Jno. 931
Martin 931
Mattie (Davis) 931
Ruth (Brown) 931
McGARV(V)EY, Bridget (Shearon)
932
Eliza 932
Ellen (O'Harran) 932
Fanny (Taylor) 1016
Francis 932
Hugh 932
Jas. 931ff
Jno. W. 932, 1016
Lena 932
Mary (Sweery) 932
Mary (True) 932
Peter 932
Rosana (Hagan) 932
Stephen 931ff
Susan (SHarry) 932
McGARY, Hugh Major 865
McGAUGHEY, Amelia (Handy) 875
David S. Dr. 875
Mary H. (Handy) 875
McGEE, Amanda H. (Irvin,
Willis) 1041
Chas. 932
Curtis 932
David 1041
Effie 932
Eliz. (Cox) 932
Ellen (Martin) 932
Elva 932
Frank 932
Granville B. 932
Hannah (Hinds) 932
Harvey 1041
Hattie 932
J. J. 1039
Jacob 932
Jas. L. 932, 1041
Jane (Lawhon) 932
Jane(Martin) 932
Jno. 932
Jno. J. 1041
Jno. Q. 932
Jos. I. 1041
Julia Ann (Eaton) 932
Leslie 932
Marg. (Dixon) 932
Mary (Bowman) 93
Mary T. (Alexander) 932
Nancy (Johnson) 932
Nancy (Lyen) 1041
Polly (Cox) 932
Rachel (Moss) 932
Robt. 932
Saml. 932
Sarah (Jones) 932
Sarah (Williams, Baker) 932,
1039
Susan (Harlan) 879
Thely (Beadles) 1041
Wm. 932

METCALF, Camillus W. 770
Eliz. (Welsh) 770
MEYER, A. D. 804
Alice (Mann) 935
MIDDLETON, Eliza O. (Harlan)
  878
Emma (Hansford) 875
H. P. 875
Mary (Porter) 878
Nancy (Owsley) 961
Saml. O. 878
Sarah E. (Harlan) 878
MILBURN, Celesta F. (Ware) 943
Civilla (Curtsinger) 942
Eliz. (Brown) 942
Frederick 942
Henry 942
Hobart 942
Israel 942
Jno. H. 942
Marg. (Thurman, Inman) 942
Minnie 942
Myrtie M. 943
Rich. C. 942
Robt. Rev. 942
Sallie (Ware) 942
Thos. C. 942
Wm. B. 942ff
Wm. R. R. 943
MILES 944
Ann (McAtee) 943
Anna (Bradford) 943
Cath. (Lancaster) 1002
Dorothy (Johnson) 763
Edward L. 943
Finetta F. (Samuels) 993
Harry 816
Henry 943
Jno. 1012
Jos. 816
Josie (Sutherland) 1012
Millie (Hagan) 871
(O'Brian) 943
Philip 760, 816, 888ff, 943
Rebecca (Hill) 760, 888
MILLER 751, 890
Adam 946, 1008
Al Dr. 944
Albert 946
Alice (Humphrey) 944
Amanda (Shaw) 944
Anna (Lyons) 910, 944
Anna M. (Van Arsdall) 1027
Attie (Maxey) 939, 945
Benj. Hardin 944ff
Bertha Cecil O'Donnell
  (Smith) 1000
Bessie 944
Birdie 945
Bonaparte 1008
Bryan S. 946
Caroline 944
Casandra (Magruder) 939
Cath. (Oldham) 946
Cath. (Fortman) 945
Celia (Strange) 1008
Christopher I. 943, 945ff
Col. 826
Commodore 1008
Danl. 914, 943, 945ff
David 1008
Edward 946
Eliza (Higginbottom) 1008
Eliz. 943, 946
Eliz. D. 807
Eliz. F. 945ff
Eliz. (Barnett) 944
Eliz. (Callison) 810
Eliz. (Lee) 915
Eliz. (Masterson) 944

MILLER
Eliz. (Miller) 944
Eliz. (Spoonamore) 1003
Ellen Kate (Winifrey) 946
Eudocia (Ruppard) 1027
Eunice (Stiles) 1005
Finetta (Beeler) 867
Frances M. (Harris) 881, 945
Geo. A. 946, 1008
Hardin 1008
Harrison J. (Harry J.) 944
Iron Works 907
Isaac S. 1027
Isabella (Leavell) 914
Jacob 939, 944, 1008
Jas. 881, 943, 945ff, 1000
Jas. C. 945
Jas. O. 946
Jas. P. 946, 1008
Jane (Delaney) 943
Jane (Mason) 1008
Jno. 943, 1003, 1008
Jno, Capt. 944
Jno. Gen. 946
Jno. T. 945
Jos. 1027
Julia (Pottinger) 944
Laura A. (Carry) 813
Lizzie (Burrus) 807
Louvenia (Kelsey) 946
Louvenia (Lester) 946
Lucy A. (Burrus) 807
Madison 807
Malinda 946
Malinda (Shackelford) 943
Marg. (Denny) 839, 946
Marg. (Shackelford) 943
Marg. Ann (McClain) 1015
Martha J. (Hancock) 874
Mary 943
Mary (Poe) 1000
Mary (Wright,Fields) 854
Mary E. 945
Mary J. (Hocker) 943
Mary L. (Callison) 810
Mary P. 946
Mary Willie 944
McKay 944
Millie (Bradshaw) 798
(Montgomery) 949
Nancy (Magruder) 890
Nancy (Yancy) 839, 914
Naomi 945
Nathan 810, 874
Nathan Braxton 946
Otho 1015
Patience (Whitson) 946, 1008
Patience I. (Field) 944
Pattie F. 944
Peggy (Maupin) 946
Polly 946
Rachael (Vannoy) 810, 874
Ramey 945
Robt. Col. 914, 943ff, 946
Robt. D. 945
S. Malinda (Owsley) 943
Salome 944
Sallie (Estill) 943ff
Sallie (Hatcher) 778
Sallie (Murrell) 914ff
Sallie (Wherritt) 1037
Sallie A. (Anderson) 778
Sallie E. 944, 946
Sally (Wilson) 791
Saml. 791
Saml. P. Dr. 946
Sarah (Wilson) 1043
Sarah A. (McClure) 946
Sarah W. 945
Solomon 1008

MILLER
Solomon 1008
Susan (Hume) 943
Susan (Woods) 943, 945ff
Susan B. (Vernon) 939
Susan J. (Lee) 914
Susan W. 945
Susannah 946
Sydney 1008
Talitha (Harris) 945ff
Thos. H. 778, 939
Thos. J. 944
Thos. W. 943, 946
Vienna 945
Vina (Solomon) 1008
W. C. 868
Wm. 839, 914, 939
Wm. H. 945ff
Wm. S. 1037
Willomine 1008
MILLERSBURG, Female college
  757
MILLIGAN, Rebecca (Beam) 1006
MILLS, Benj. Major 974
Eliz. (Plummer) 974
Jane (O'Connor) 974
MILNER, Armstead 852
Sallie (Feland) 852
MILTON 947
Caroline (Watkins) 882
Eliz. (Greer) 869ff
Rich. 869
MINER, C. P. 1038
Mariah F. (Whitehouse) 1038
MINOR, (Anderson) 778
Anselm 994
Eliz. (Hamner) 873
Sarah L. (Scomp) 994
MINTER, Jane (Watkins) 875
MITCHELL 1036
Andrew 821, 981
Amelia E. (Coun) 947
Ann M. (Payne) 981
Anna (Barr) 784
Dr. 944
Eliz. C. 947
Eliz. H. (Woods, Jones) 904
Emily (Chenault) 821, 897
Florence C. 947
Geo. 784
Harriett (Van Arsdall) 1027
Hugh 782
Jane (Edwards) 782, 1013
Jno. A. 947, 1001
Lee 795
Lucy Ann (Baker) 782
Marg. (Porter) 947
Marietta (Barr) 784
Mary 947
Mary (Boldrick) 795
Mary (Boyd) 947
Mary J. 947
Martha (Cowherd) 822
(Moorman, Hitchinson) 947
Nellie 947
Rachel (Crawford) 947
Sallie E. (Estes, Ray) 981
Sarah (Hamber) 873
Susan (Davis) 885
Susan (Sparks) 1001
Thos. R. 947
Thos. W. 947
Wm. H. Lt. 981
W. K. Dr. 981
MITCHEM, Little Berren 805
Nancy (Buchanan) 805
Rachael (WHalen) 805
MIZE, Nancy (Pigg) 794
MOBERLEY, Genevieve Eliz. 948
Ida M. (Brasfield) 948

38

MOBERLEY
Jas. H.   828
Jno. M.   828
Mamie (Coleman)   828
Nancy (Lipscomb)   947ff
Rich. Rev.   948
Shelton Nevilla   948
Tabitha (Brasfield)   948
Thos. Shelton   751, 947ff
MOBLEY, Mary E.   (Shehan,
    Troutman)   1023
Sally G. (Ford, Henly)   857
MOCK, Amanda (Offutt)   948
Ann E. (Vanarsdall)   948
Eliza (Saunders)   948
Ellen A. (Byers)   948
Ezek. F.   948
Harriet A. (Nichols)   948
Henry C.   948
Jarrett T.   948
Jno. J.   948
Jno. L.   948
Joshua D.   948
Lewis M.   948
Mary E. (Rice)   948
(Miller)   949
Randolph   948
Robt. A.   948
Rosa (McKay)   948
Sallie (Fisher)   948
Sarah (Kalfus)   948
Sarah E. (Hewey)   948
Wm. Randolph   948
MOLLIHORNE, Jas.   816
MONTAGUE, Ann (Hodgen)   948
Diana (Davis)   948
Eliz. (Edmonson)   948
Geo.   948
Jas.   948
Jno.   948
Lelia   948
Lucy (Hodgen)   948
Maggie (Phillips)   948
Marg. E. (Cox)   948
Martha   948
Mary A. (Baker)   948
Robt. S.   948
Sallie E. (Hubbard)   948
Saml.   948
Va. (Hagerman)   948
Warner R.   948
MONDAY, Lucy (Brown)   931
Mary A. (Hendrickson)   821
MONK, Colored Man   750
MONROE, Benj.   918
Eliz. (Adair)   763
Katie (Adair)   918
Pres.   765, 870
Thos. B.   862, 918
MONTGOMERY, Amanda Lee   949
Augusta   949
Basil   811
Benj.   880
Bob A.   949
Cath. J. (Harmon)   879ff
David   949, 1022
Eliza. (Williams)   1040
Eliz. (Chumley)   822
Eliz. (Epperson)   848, 1016
Eliz. (Foreman)   994
Eliz. (Kenney)   907
Eliz. (Stotts)   1007
Eliz. (Jamerson   949
Emma (Swope)   949
Esther   1006
Fannie (Thurman)   949
Francis   848
Geo. T.   949
Hugh   949
Isaac   868, 880, 1006

MONTGOMERY
Jennie A.   949
Jno.   742
Jno. A.   949
Jno. B.   949
Jno. H.   949
Joshua T.   949
Julia A. (Plummer)   973
Junius B.   848
Laura J.   949
(Lawson)   949
Lou (Martin)   949
Lutitia (Crumes)   853
M. E. (Ried)   949
Marg. (Cambron)   811
Martha A. (Gray)   868
Martha A. (Towles)   1022
Martha H.   949
Mary (Stone)   1006
Mary W.   949
Millie E. (Bradshaw)   798
Nancy (Stone, Clemmons)
    868, 880, 1006
Nancy (Taylor)   1040
Nancy A. (McCubbin, Donan)
    949
Narcissa (Jamerson)   949
Nathan   949
Parmelia (Lee)   915
Patsey (Winston)   949
Rich. M.   949
Sallie (Bailey)   949
Sallie L. (Emery)   949
Sally M. (Squires)   880
Sarah C. (Harmon)   880
Sarah Eliz. (Epperson)   848
Settlement   914
T. W.   798
Tabitha (Holland)   949, 1022
Tabitha I. (McCubbin)   949
Tamer Ann (Ray)   949
Thos. B.   908
W. C. D.   949
W. G. Rev.   973
Wm. Col.   822, 949
Wm. David   949
Zach.   992
MOORE, Alex.   952
Amanda S. (Vaughan)   1031
Angeline E. (Wright)   1046
Anne St. Clair (Powell)   975
Annie Meade (Simpson)   952
Artemisia (Sloan)   766
Bacon Rochester   767
Betsy Lawson (Moore)   766
Bettie B. (Sumrall)   1011
Cary J.   952
Chas.   1024
Chas. B.   952
Chas. D. Dr.   950
Chas. O.   766, 952
Chas. S.   950
Chas. W.   907
Christopher Collins   766,
    1010ff
Danl. Lawson   767
Dr.   975
Eleanor (Hilliard)   1031
Elijah   766
Elinor A. (Hilliard)   950
Eliza A. (Trumble)   950
Eliza J. (Beeler)   952
Eliz. (Banford)   950
Eliz. (Botts)   952, 975
Eliz. (Carpenter)   952
Eliz. (Peyton)   825
Eliz. (Robinson)   987
Eliz. (Rochester)   766
Eliz. (Stanley, Ellsworth)
    950

MOORE
Eliz. (Sublett)   814
Eliz. S.   950
Geo. Rev.   766, 952, 975
Hannah (Davis)   950
Henrietta (McBrayer)   767
Henry B.   951
Irvin W.   950
J. H.   940ff
Jas.   766, 950, 952, 1031
Jas. D.   952
Jas. F.   951
Jas. Harrison   765, 767
Jas. Wesley   949ff
Jane(McKee)   766
Jane (Rochester)   879
Jane M. (Pile)   951
Jane Murray (Rochester)   766
Jenetta (Pollard)   952
Jennie (Armstrong)   776
Jesse   951
Jetson   951
Jno.   1046
Jno. B.   950
Jno. R.   951
Jno. W.   952
Jno. Edgar   952
Jno. Rochester Dr.   766
Jos. Lapsley   766
Judith (Harrison)   766
Judy (Flowers, Browning)   952
Lawson   766, 879
Lina (Green)   868
Lizzie (Craddock)   805
Louisa (Craig)   952
Lucas   951
(Lucas)   1031
Lucietta   952
Lucinda (Gentry)   952
Lucinda (Kimbrew)   952
LUlu B. (Breeding)   951
Luther   951
Marg. (Moore)   951
Martha (Bayne)   951
Martha E.   950
Martha King (Scomp)   994
Martha W. (Lane)   950
Marvin   952
Mary (McAfee)   923
Mary (Orr)   952
Mary (Thomas)   951
Mary E.   951
Mary E. (Robertson)   1011
Mary I. (Willimason)   951
Mary J. (Bedford)   950
Mary J. (Redford)   950
Mary M.   952
Mary S. (Messe(i)nger,
    Foster)   766ff
Mary T. (Bradshaw)   952
Mary W.   951
Mattie   950
May   767
McBrayer   767
Milton   951
Myra H. (Butler, Sharp)   952
Nancy (Botts)   952
Nancy (Jack)   951
Nancy (Mahan, Penny)   935
Nancy (Turk)   1024
Nancy D.   950
Nancy Jordan (Yell)   766
Nannie (Spencer)   950
Polly (Mann)   952
Rich. L.   950, 1031
Robt. E.   950
Sallie (Buchanan)   805
Sallie (Hardin)   879
Sally (Bridgewater)   952
Sally (Harlan)   766

39

MOORE
Sally (Williams) 952
Saml. 868, 951ff
Saml. A. 950
Saml. F. 950
Saml. W. Capt. 951ff
Sarah (Lawson) 766
Sarah (Lillard) 919
Sarah A. (Moore) 952
Sarah B. (Bradshaw) 952
Schuyler 952
Sophia (McCaleb) 766
Suela (Stotts) 1008
Susan (Hill) 951
T. J. Dr. 974
Tandy 952
Thos. 765ff, 805, 952
Thos. O. 950
Thos. Rochester 766
Victor C. 951
Vincent 766
Wallace 767
(Wallace) 1046
Walter B. 951
(White) 950
Wm. Gen. 766, 950ff
Wm. H. 950ff
Wm. R. 950
Wm. T. 952
(Wilson) 1043
MOORE'S BLUFF 766
MOORMAN, Artitia (Howard) 947
Chas. R. 947
(Hutchinson, Mitchell) 947
MOOS, Ella (Walker) 1035
Henry S. 1035
Mary (Trigg) 1035
MORAN, Amanda W. (Stotts) 953
Ann (Adams) 952
Elijah 952
Eliz. Ann 953
Eliza Jane (Wilcoxson,
    Franklin) 952
Eliz. (Blaine) 953
Eliz. (Level) 952
Emily (Grooms) 953
Geo. R. 952ff
Hez. 952ff
Jas. J. 953
Jno. W. 952ff
Marietta 953
Mary P. (Carpenter) 953
P. P. 953
Robt. P. 952ff
Sarah (Payton) 952
Schuyler 952
Susan M. (Powell) 952
Thos. P. 952ff
Wm. 952ff
MOREHEAD, Gov. 1031
MORGAN 785
Caroline (Conover) 953
Cavalry 827, 994
Gen. 765
Jas. Hines 756
Jno. A. Gen. 850, 1007
Jno. Hunt Gen. 740, 762ff,
    777, 794, 862, 864,
    874ff, 882, 892, 900,
    914, 921, 926, 945,954,
    964, 969, 981, 999, 1018,
    1029
Julia C. (Bruce) 804
Lydia A. (Cofer) 953
Martha (Farris) 905
Mary (Cobert) 825
Mary (Coovert) 829
Mary E. (Jones) 905
Mollie E. (Wallace) 953
Morgan 953

MORGAN
Philip Lt. 825, 829
Reece 953
Robt. C. Dr. 953
Wilkes 905
Zach. 965
MORRIS, Eliz. (Epperson) 848
Laura S. (Taylor) 1015
M. 1015
Mary (Pipes) 847
Mary P. (Tarkington) 1014
Nancy (Lillard) 918
Saml. 848
Sarah (Hurt) 848
MORRISON 861
Eliz. (Bright) 918
Kate (Breckinridge) 800
Kate (Taylor) 800
M. B. 800
Martha (Gaither) 861
Rebecca (Strange) 1025
MORROW, Mary (Heath) 885
Station 933
MORTON, Jno. P. 869
Judge 1029
Rich. 1035
Susan Quinn (Webb) 1035
Thos. Col. 955
MOSBY, Nancy L. (Grant) 828
MOSES, Mattie (Curd) 835
Wm. 835
MOSS, Amelia T. (Irvine) 810
Cassander W. (Hazlewood)
    824, 882
Cath. (Price) 882
David 882
Fred 882
Jno. 932
Judith (Jones, Taylor) 1021
Lucinda (Caldwell) 805
Mary (Coats) 882
Mary (Hilliard) 950
Rachel (McGee) 932
Sarah (Campbell) 859
MOURING, Mary (Bevill, Lisle)
    920
MOURNING, Jno. D. 810
Martha (Callison) 810
Roger 910
Sarah (Knifley) 910
Wm. B. Dr. 806
MOUSER, Edward B. 954
Edward G. 953
Fred. 953ff
Gabriel T. 953
Jno. W. 953ff
Marg. (Brown) 942, 954
Mary E. (Sparrow) 953
Nancy (Haregrove) 953
Otis U. 954
Redford M. 953
Sallie A. (Brown) 954
Sarah E. (Lankford) 913
Zenas A. 954
MOZEE, Jemima (Andrews) 873
MUDD, Cath. (Russell) 1020
Cath. E. (Spalding) 1002
D. H. 1002
J. B. Dr. 995
Raphael R. 816
Thos. 816
MUIR 977
Eliz. (Briggs) 801
Peter B. 989
MULDROW'S HILLS 935
MULLINS, B. G. 954
Benj. G. 954
Benj. Dr. 789
Eliz. (Kennedy) 954
Emily 954

MULLINS
Jno. G. 954
Lizzie (Forsythe) 858
Martha 954
Mary (Campbell, Berkele) 789
Mary Ann (Graves) 954
Mary L. 954
Prof. 776
Saml. G. 954
Susan (Gillisbie) 793
W. A. 954
Wm. Jordan 954
Williamson G. 954
MUNDAY, Geo. 819
Lucy B. (Gordan) 819
Sarah (Champion) 819
Susan (Slaughter) 997
MUNDY'S LANDING 882, 957
MURPHY, Abraham 954
Cynthia Ann (McCall) 955
David Asbury Capt. 955ff
David Whittaker 955
Eliz. (Young) 954
F. D. 840
Gabriel 954
Isaac 954
Jennie M. (Ball) 955
Juliet (Hagan) 954
Kitty (Cheser) 954
Lucy (Connell) 954
Maria (Raymond) 954
Mary (May) 840
Mary Eliza (Roby) 954
Mary P. (Shirley) 954
Melinda (Henson, Malson,
    Newman) 886
Mollie (Doom) 840
Polly (Sousley) 954
Robt. 954
Sarah (Curry) 954
Sarah Marg. (Bean 954
Squire 954
Wm. Henry 954
MURRAH, Carlisle H. 957
Edward T. 957
Eliza M. (Murrah) 957
Emily (Perryman) 957
Fred. T. 957
Hettie M. 957
Jno. E. 957
Jos. J. 956ff
Joshua 957
Mary (Easley) 957
Nancy (Barnes) 957
Rachel (Jones) 957
Sally (Jones) 957
Sarah (Wheat) 1040
Sydney 957
Wm. D. Dr. 956ff
MURRAY 836
E. H. Gen. 966
Logan C. 966
Patsy (Hood) 892
Susan M. (Kirk) 909
MURRELL, Jas. Col. 983
Jane (Reid) 983
Sallie (Miller) 914ff
MUSTEEN, Tabitha (Bruce) 804
MYER, Anselm D. 942
Ardie (Browne) 804
Caroline 942
David 942
Davis 942
Eliz. 804
Eliz. (Marshall) 942
Florence 942
Jas. J. 942
Jno. M. 942
Jonathan 942
Jos. 942

MYER
Maria Bell (McGoodwin) 942
Martha (Stallings) 942
Mary (Lyne) 942
Mary (Mann) 935 -
Mary R. (McDowell) 942
Michael 942
Oscar 942
Rebecca (Jackson) 942
Rebecca (Love) 942
Thornwell 942
MYERS, Hannah (Turner) 1025
Mary J. (Shears) 995

NALL, Kizzie (Batsell) 841
Lavina (Yewell) 1048
NALLY, Bernard 816
NANTZ, (Cosby) 895
Fred 796, 895
Harriet (Watkins) 895
Henry 808
Louisa (Booker) 796
Maria (Chandler) 808
Martha H. (Hughes) 895
NASH, Nancy (Penick) 959
NASHVILLE, TENN., Land Deal
    for Gun 1014
NAVAL BATTLE 861
NAVE, Alex. P. 957
David G. 957
Georgia A. (Burdett) 957
Jacob 957
Jeff. 957
Jemima (Johnson) 957
Jno. 957
Mahala (Ketran) 957
Mary J. (McKonald) 957
Melinda (Collier) 957
Michael 957
Peter 957
Polly (Lackey) 957
Rachel (Dean) 957
Robt. 957
Sallie 957
Sally (Grow) 957
Solomon 957
Wm. D. 957
Winfield S. 957
NAYLOR, Parker 1015
Sarah (McClain) 1015
NEAL, Anna 961
Ann (Raney) 961
Carrie (Goodloe) 961
Creath 957
David 957
Elijah 957
Emily (Tichenor) 803
Geo. 957
Eliz. (Singleton) 957
Geo. 957
Jas. Lewis 957, 961
Jesse 957
Jno. 957
Lenis A. (Farra) 957
Mary (Harlan, Bentley) 879
Mary (Hughes) 957
Michael 803
Rebecca A. (Elmore) 957
Sarah (Champion) 819
Sue Helm (Thompson) 957
Susan M. (Headly) 957
Wm. L. 961
Zerelda (Howard) 961
Zerelda (Oldham) 961
NEALE, Christopher 957
Jno. W. 957
Laura F. 957
Maggie B. 957
Mary (Boswell) 957
Mary K. 957

NEALE
Nannie F. 957
Rodham 957
Sarah C. (Humphrey) 957
NEELY 1003
Eliz. (Dixon) 932
NEET, Josephine (Smith) 999
Jno. Capt. 999
Mary (Elliott) 999
Sallie (Farra) 884
NEETSVILLE 843, 880, 968
NEGLEY 1036
NEGRO WOMAN, Traded for land
    879
NEIKIRK, Annie 958
Buford 958
Eliz. (Aker) 958
Eliz. A. (Penick) 958
Geo. 958
Jno. 958
Laura E. (Davison) 958
Mary T. (Penick) 958
Wm. F. Rev. 958
NELL, Cordelia 959
Durinda (Simpson, Curry)959
Jas. 958
Geo. 958
Jno. 958
Malinda A. (McGinnis) 959
Nancy (Thurman) 958
Sallie (Bredding) 814
NELSON, A. E. (Furr) 959
Bettie 959
Camp 762, 1036
David Rev. 966
Eliza (Slaughter, Bradshaw)
    998
Gen. 760, 762, 877, 986
Katy 959
Marg. A. (Jones) 904
Mary A. (Jeffries) 1042
W. C. Dr. 959
Will Edwards 959
NERINCKX, Chas. Rev. 815ff
NEWBOLT, Agnes -59
Cecelia (Penick) 959
(Cheney) 959
Geo. P. 959
Jno. 865, 959
Lizzie 959
Maud 959
Sallie (Fogle) 856
Sue (Caldwell) 959
Wm. 959
NEWCOMB 785
(Atkinson) 781
E. B. 781
Lizzie H. (Mason, Turner)
    1025
NEWLAND, Abraham 905
Sallie (Jones) 904
NEWMAN, Jno. E. 917
Melinda (Henson, Malson,
    Murphy) 886
NEWSPAPERS 868ff, 956
NEWTON, Draper 940
Lucy A. (Cogar) 940
NICHOLS 1020
Dr. 1038
Eliza (Hamilton) 923
Eliz. (Brown) 803
Eliz. (Graham) 865
Eliz. (Welsh) 769
Harriet A. (Mock) 948
Jas. 769
Jno. 1039
Jonathan 865, 923
Jos. W. 769
Julia (Faulconer) 852
Katie M. (Wilkinson) 1038

NICHOLS
Minerva J. (Harris, McAfee)
    923
Nancy O. (Williams) 1039
Sarah F. (Langsford) 913
NICHOLLS, Cath. (Harris) 959
Henry M. 959
Jeanette (Sutherland) 959
Katie (Siscoe) 959
Maggie (Hammond) 959
Wm. 959
NICKELS, Rachel (Watkins) 789
NICKELSON, Martha (Henry) 988
NOBLE, Susan (Graves) 938
NOE, Alex. K. 959ff
Arvin G. 960
Edward H. 960
Geo. A. 960
Hugh M. 960
Isaac 960
Jas. 960
Jane B. (Thompson) 959ff
Jno. 960
Lizzie L. 960
Martha 960
Mary E. (Graham) 960
Mary W. 960
Mordecai H. 960
Robt. A. 960
Sallie Cath. 960
Sarah A. 960
Stith T. 959ff
Thos. W. 960
NOEL Nancy (McCalin) 1015
NOLAND, Ann (Black) 838
Jno. Col. 838
Marg. (Broaddus) 838
Mary E. (Deatherage) 838
Nathan 838
Sidney (Oldham) 821
Sydonia (Oldham) 838
(White) 838
NOLD, School for Young Ladies
    966
NOOE, Matilda A. (Hawkins) 882
NORDYKE, Bennajah 866
Jane (Foley) 866
Matilda (Grant) 866
NORMAN, Millie (CHeatham) 952
NORRIS, Drusilla (Elliott) 995
Eliz. (Wood) 1045
Henry 816
Ignatius 995
Rodolphus 816
Sallie (Shaunty) 995
NOURSE, Rebecca (Kyle) 911
NUCKOLS, Abigail (Butler) 941
Annie P. (Hobbs) 941
Chas. 941
Geo. W. Dr. 941
Jackson Cecil 941
Lydia S. (Viley) 941
Mary Louise 941
Robt. G. 940ff
(Thustin) 941
NUNN, Caroline (Alexander)1039
Eliz. (Williams) 1039
Geo. W. 1039
Jane C. (Breeding) 800
Jno. M. 800

OATTS, Sophronia (Babbitt) 808
O'BANNON, Nancy (Coppage) 830
OBESITY & HEART TROUBLE 902
O'BRIAN, (Miles) 943
(Stiles) 1004
Winifred (Healy) 884
O'BRYAN, Eliz. (Knicheloc)1000
Eliz. (Smith) 1000
Rev. 817

41

O'BRYAN
 Wm. 1000
O'BRYANT, Matilda (Gardiner)
  863
O'CONNELL, Danl. 797
 Marg. (Bradley) 797
O'CONNER, Jane (Mills) 974
OFFUTT, Amanda (Mock) 948
 Andrew 960
 Chas. M. 960, 966
 Davis C. 960
 Eliz. P. (Brown, Rease) 960
 Frank 776
 Jno. R. 960
 Lillie (Armstrong) 776
 Lizzie A. (Davis) 960
 Marshall W. 960
 Nancy (Payne) 984
 Susan (Faulconer) 852
 Walter C. 960
 Wm. V. 960
 Zeph. 960
O'HARA, Theodore Col. 862
O'HARRAN, Ellen (McGarvey) 932
OHIO RIVER, Indians 888
OLDHAM, Caroline (Smith) 960
 Cath. (Brown) 946
 Cath. (Miller) 946
 Cornelia (Hansford) 876
 Dawson 960
 Edith (Cobb) 970
 Elias 960
 Elinor B. (Chenault) 821
 Hez. 946
 Howard S. 961
 Jas. M. 961
 Jesse 960
 Jno. Dr. 756, 960
 Mary (Cotton) 831
 Mary A. (Deatherage) 838
 Nathaniel 960
 Otheniel 821, 838
 Pollie (Kavanaugh) 946
 Rich. 960
 Sadie (Spence) 960
 Sanford 960ff
 Sidney (Noland) 821
 (Simpson) 960
 Six Bros. 960
 Sydonia (Noland) 838
 Tyrie 960
 Wm. K. 946
 Zerelda (Neal) 961
OLIPHANT, Andrew 849
 Nancy (McCormick) 849
 Sarah L. (Evans) 849
OLIVER, Nancy (Tarkington) 1014
O'NEIL, I. Rev. 992
ONSTOTT, Esther (Stone) 1006
ORANGE, Wm. of 924
ORR, David 933
 Jno. J. 933, 952
 Jos. 933
 Linn 933
 Marg. Ann (McMillan) 933
 Martha Eliz. (McMillan) 933
 Mary (Moore) 952
 Mary Jane (McMillan) 933
OSBORNE, Marg. (Thurman) 867
OSBURN, (Bland) 792
 Isaac 992
 Levina (Samuels) 992
OVERALL, Louisana (Duvall) 845
 V. 936
OVERSTREET, Betsy (Hawkins)
  882
 Caleb B. 1011
 Eliz. J. (Harmon) 1011
 Martha (Boughn) 857
 Mary A. (Survant, Powers)1011

OVERSTREET
 Patsy (Hawkins) 882
OVERTON, Dr. 860
 Mary (Fowler) 988
 Susan (Fowler) 988
OWENS, Emily (Wilson) 778
OWSLEY, Adelaide (Baker) 962
 Amanda (Jones) 905
 Amanda (Rhodes) 779
 Amelia (Anderson) 779
 Amelia G. (Haskins) 961
 Anna 905
 Cath. (Boudin) 961
 Edwards D. 961
 Eliz. (Avritt) 963
 Ellen (Letcher) 962
 Ellen Hopkins (King) 774
 Ellen P. (King) 962
 Gov. 779, 875, 1013
 Helen M. (Ritchey) 961
 Jas. H. 961
 Jennie (SHanks) 851
 Joel Dr. 961ff
 Jno. 851, 924
 Jno. Q. 961
 Kittie (Owsley) 961
 Laura Susan 962
 Leila Ellen (Grant) 962
 Lucian C. 963
 M. H. 961ff
 Maria E. (Talbott) 1013
 Mary (Evans) 851
 Mary (Jones) 905
 Mary Ann (Lewis) 961ff
 Mary Agnes (Bledsoe) 962
 Mary D. (Cabell) 809
 Martha (McAlister) 851, 924
 Martha Bain (Farris) 875
 Martha J. (Hamner) 873
 Mason H. 905
 Nancy (Middleton) 961
 Newdigat 961
 Obedienc (Baughman) 961
 Oscar 961
 Patience (Baughman) 784, 961
 S. Malinda (Miller) 943
 Sally A. (Alexander) 775,
  962
 Saml. 961
 Susan A. (Graham) 50
 Susan Ann (Farris) 851
 Susan King 962
 Thos. 961
 Va. (Tucker, Taylor) 962ff
 Wm. Fayette 774, 784, 905,
  961ff

PADDOCKS, Rebecca (Van Sickle)
  1030
PAGE, Annie B. (Taylor) 1017
 Eliz. (Davis) 836
 Jas. T. 1016
 Jno. S. 1017
 Polly (Bridgewaters) 953
 Robin 836
 Sophia (Brawner) 826
 Va. R. (Coffey) 826
 W. W. 826
PAINTER, Eliz. (Bennett) 789
 Jane 789
 Jno. 789
PAISLEY B LEACH FIELDS (Place)
  993
PALMER, Ella (Caldwell) 748,
  810
 Mary (Caldwell) 746
 R. C. Dr. 746, 748
PALMORE, Lord 1038
PARISH, Jno. 749
 Westly 749

PARK, Minerva (Cobb) 970
PARKER, Andrew 898
 Anna (Cooke) 828
 Camilla (Brashear) 898
 Corrilla (Irvin) 898
 Mary (Todd) 898
 Rebecca E. (McConnell) 828
 Warren O. 828
PARKES, Eliz. (Smith) 963
 Emma (Herndon) 963
 Fannie (Smith) 963
 Fannie B. 963
 Jas. B. 963
 Jeff. W. 963
 Jennie W. 963
 Jno. D. 963
 Maggie (Wallace) 963
 Marg. J. (Wilmore) 963
 Mary (Watts) 963
 Nancy (Embry) 963
 Saml. S. 963
 Sarah (Henderson) 885
PARKS, Jenny (Cunningham) 783
 Jno. W. 749
 (Jones) 905
PARMLEY, Cyrina (Sallee) 992
PARRISH, Harriet (hugely) 963
 Malinda (Russel) 989
 Mary H. (Adams) 963
 Nich. 990
 Socrates 963
 Stephen D. 963
 Wesley 963
PARROLT, Geo. W. 985
PARROTT, Ed. M. 1028
 Hattie (Van Cleave) 1028
 Sallie E. (Anderson) 778
PASCAL, Polly (Crow) 834
PATTERSON, Ann Eliz. (Epperson)
  1016
 Cath. (Lillard) 918
 Eliz. (Glenn) 1016
 Eliz. (Headly) 884
 Eliz. B. (Breeding) 800
 Isaphena (Kinnaird) 872
 Jas. M. 996, 1016
 M. E. (Simpson) 996
 Mary (Ewing) 1016ff
 Mary J. (Taylor) 1016
 Martha (Barnett) 800
 Rich. 800
 Robt. 1017
 Wm. 1016
PATTESON, (Hobson) 761
 Jonathan 761
PATTON, Alex. L. 964
 America (Bailey) 844
 Cath. (Stephenson, Slaven)
  1004
 Ella A. (Durham) 964, 1004
 Henry Lee 964
 Leslie L. 964
 Marg. (Lee) 964
 Maria (Lewis) 916ff
 Nuna 964
 Sallie A. (Dunn) 780
 Sarah (Simpson) 964
 Thos. 917
 Wm. S. 964
 Willie C. 964
PAWLING, Wm. Dr. 760
PAXTON, Pamelia (Stotts) 1007
 Pauline (Stotts) 1007
PAYNE, Ann (Jennings) 964
 Ann M. (Mitchell) 981
 Anna (Lane) 776
 Asa 964ff
 Betsy (Sebree) 964
 Chas. 816
 Cyrus 964

42

43

PHELPS
Thos. 969ff
Verlinda (Williams) 969
Wm. 969
(Willis) 1042
PHILANTHROPY, Johnson's 764
PHILIPS, & Co. 924
Eliz. (Lewis) 918
Ellen (Debaun) 838
Icylinda (Salle, Curry) 835
Jas. G. 835, 918
Laura (Castleman) 918
Mournen (Ham) 835
PHILLIPS, Agnes (Berryman) 971
Ann Eliza 971
Birdie 972
Buford 971
Capitola 971
Chas. M. 948, 971
Cornelius 1030
David 840, 972
Edward 971
Eliz. (Maxwell) 840
Emma (Hundley) 972
Eusebia Q. (Burton) 808, 972
Fannie (Frye) 971
Felix Grundy 971ff
Frances Moss (Penick) 971ff
Frankie 970
Geo. Rev. 970
Indiana (Burnside) 970
Isaac 970
J. G. 782, 808
Jacob 970
Jas. G. 972
Jinny 970
Jno. 970, 972
Jno. F. 743, 876
J. Howard 971
Julia (Maxwell) 972
Lettie 971
Lewis V. 970ff
Lizzie (Stiles) 1005
Lucy (Goodrich) 970
Maggie (Montague) 948
Marg. 971
Marg. (Caldwell) 746
Martha A. (Thompson) 970ff
Mary (Avritt) 782
Mary (Irwin) 971
Mary (Van Winkle) 1030
Millie 970
Nannie 971
Nannie H. (Berry) 789
Peggy 970
Sallie(y) (Mayfield) 970
Saml. 1005
Sarah E. (Doom) 840
(Shores) 1030
Suky 970
Thos. 972
Wm. 971
PHILPS, Nancy (Baker) 1042
PHOEBYHOUSE, Mary B. (Baker)
886
PHYSIC, Dr. 860
PICKERING, Lucy 758
Rhoda (Fox) 758
Rich. 758
PIERCE 748
Franklin 803, 825
Geo. F. Bishop 965
Lovick Rev. Dr. 965
Martha (Davis) 837
PIGG, Anderson 794
Johnson 794
Mollie C. (Boggs) 794
Nancy (Mize) 794
Polly (Perry) 794
PILE, Benj. P. 951, 1005

PILE
Jane M. (Moore) 951
Rhoda (Weathers) 951
Susan A. (Beckham, Stiles)
1005
(Weathers) 1005
PILLOW, Gen. 841, 853ff
PINKARD, Marg. St. Clair
(Cecil) 819
PINKERTON, Burnet B. 972
Burnet Johnson Rev. 972
Charlie W. 972
Collin M. 972
Elisha Y. 972
Eliz. (Littig) 972
Jas. P. 972
Jno. W. 972
Kate (Martin) 972
Lewis L. Dr. Rev. 972
Mary (Peebles) 972
Mary B. (Price) 972
Mary J. 972
Mary P. 972
Percival P. 972
Rebecca (Clark) 972
Sallie S. (Walker) 972
Sally (Bashford) 972
Saml. D. 972
Saml. J. Rev. 972
Sarah (Ball) 972
Susan 972
Thos. Rev. 972
Va. L. (Cruther) 972
Wm. Capt. 972
Wm. W. 972
PINKSTAFF, Francis M. 913
Mary E. (Lankford) 913
PIPER, Nancy (Robards) 985
PIPES, Abigail (Harmon) 879
Fannie L. (Edwards) 847
Jane (Gray, Harmon) 879
Jno. 847
Keziah (Brank) 847ff
Marg. (Harmon) 879
Mary (Morris) 847
Nancy (Gray) 867
Nancy (Hourigan) 1038
Nathan W. 847
Nathaniel 847
PIRTLE, Abner 973
Cecilia A. (Matthis) 973
Jno. E. 973
Laura 973
Marg. E. (Harmon) 973
Martha (Embree) 973
Martha (Williams) 973
Mattie D. 973
Minnie L. 973
Nannie M. 973
Sam. Henry 973
Sarah M. (Dudgeon) 973
Wm. H. 973
Wm. W. 973
PITTS, Cassa (Greeg, Robards)
984
Eliz. (Rogers) 984
Eliz. (Walden) 1033
Nanny (Henson) 886
R. 886
Younger 984
PLANETARIUM 739ff
PLOW, Eliz. (Boggs) 793
PLUMMER, Amanda (Crain) 973
Benj. Dawson 973ff
Bessie Moore 974
Dorcas (Cash) 973
Eliz. (Mills) 974
Franklin 973
Henry D. Dr. 973ff
Jas. 973

PLUMMER
Jennie Mae 974
Jno. 973
Julia A. (Montgomery) 973
Lutie Mills 974
Martha 973
Mary M. (Seever) 973
Matilda (Evans) 973
Va. Morton 974
Wm. 973ff
PLYMOUTH ROCK (Gardiner) 863
POE, Mary (Miller) 1000
POLIN, Dr. 895
POLK, Jas. K. 783, 803, 836,
861, 894
POLLARD, Absalom 760
Alex. 952
Jenatta (Moore) 952
Malinda (Hill) 760
Nancy (Herring) 887
Nancy B. (Herndon) 887
POLLY'S Bend 824
POOR, Amelia (Price) 977
Eliz. (Kemper) 974
Frances A. (Ison) 974
(Hancock) 974
Hannah (Davis) 837, 974
Hopie (Wilds) 974
Jas. G. 974
Jane (Legin) 974
Jno. 974
Jno. Wm. 837, 974
Lucy (West) 974
Maggie L. (Boulden) 974
Martha A. (Smith) 837, 974
Mary B. (Feathers) 974
Robt. C. 974
Sally (Ford) 974
Thos. 974
Wm. L. 974
Wm. M. 974
POPE 947
Cath. (Harlan) 879
Maria (Fisher) 856
PORTER, Eliz. (Debo 838
Louisa P. (Thomas) 1019
Marg. (Mitchell) 947
Mary (Middleton) 878
Rich. 838ff
Susan (Alexander) 773
PORTMAN, Cath. (Miller) 945
M. C. 945
PORTRAIT, Pennington (Lincoln
Co. Ct. H) 967
POTEET, W. J. 937
POTTER, Dr. 888
Effie C. (Faulconer) 852
Julia F. (Hill) 852
Pleasant J. 852
POTTINGER, Ann (Lancaster) 912
Creek (Rom, Cath. Settlement)
816
Julia (Miller) 944
Lucinda (Jameson) 944
Saml. 944ff
Thos. J. 844ff
Vienna (Ramey) 944
POTTS, Eugenia (Dunlap) 844
Rich. Dr. 845
POWDER MILL, 1st in Hart Co.
831
POWELL, Ann E. (Worthington)
975
Anne St. Clair (Moore) 975
Annie 975
Annie D. (Matheny) 937
Birdie 975
Eliz. M. 975
Ellen B. (Long) 975
Fanny (Kerr) 975

44

45

46

RICHARDS, Jemima (Mail,
    Kinnaird) 909
  Mr. 909
RICHARDSON, Sally (Cowherd)
    822
RICHESON, Mary (Gray) 867
  Susan (Fidler, Fidler) 853
  Wm. 853
RICKETS, Eliz. M. (McAfee) 882
  Emma J. (Haselwood) 882
  Moses 882
RICKETTS, Caleb H. 904
RIDGEWAY, Mary E. (Latimer)
    1027
RIED, Jas. Dr. 949
  M. E. (Montgomery) 949
RIFFE, Christopher Gen. 898
  Eliz. (Anderson) 898
  Eliz. (Coffy) 898
  Emma C. (Hunn) 898
  Geo. C. 898
  Mary (Spears) 898
RIFLE CANNON 739
RIKER, Chas. 983
  Cornelius 983
  Cynthia 983
  Diana (Sutfield) 983
  Fanny M. (Simrall) 984
  Ida (Van Anglen) 983ff
  Jas. Harvey 983
  Jane (Davis) 983
  Jno. 984
  Lafon 984
  Martha D. (Smedley) 984
  Mary (Bonta) 983
  Mary (Thompson) 984
  Pattie (Lafon) 984
  Sally (Vanarsdall) 983
  Saml. 983
  Sarah (McKee) 984
  W. Letcher 984
  Wm. H. 983ff
RILEY, Lucy R. (Edelen) 846
  Milly (Payne) 964
  Station 954, 981
RINEHART 986
  Jno. W. 984
  Lizzie 984
  Pattie 984
  Sallie 984
  Sarah (Funk) 984
  Thos. C. 984
  Wm. 984
RINEY, Roselle (Cecil) 818
RINGGOLD, Mary A. (Fenton) 853
RIPPERDAM, Abram 855
  Cath. (Shaw) 855
  Esther (Wingate) 855
  Frederick 854ff
  Jno. 855
  Martha (Bragsdale) 855
  Mary (Wigham) 855
  Sarah (Chiticks) 854
  Sarah (Fields) 855
  Susan (Fields) 854ff
RIPPETOE, Eliz. (Blair) 791
  Eliz. (Vincent) 791
  Wm. 791
RISK, Anna E. (Graham) 865
RITCHEY, Helen M. (Owsley) 961
  Jas. H. 961
  Jno. H. 775
  Nancy A. (Alexander) 775
RITCHIE, Eliza (Hudson) 894
RIVES, H. W. 889
  Susan (Hill) 889
ROACH, Jane (Snively) 806
  Jos. B. 984
  Littleberry 984
  Mary L. (Conner) 984

ROACH
  Ville 806
  W. H. Dr. 984
ROADS, Early Ky. 750
ROAN'S Knob 938
ROARK, Sarah (Blevins) 792
ROBARDS, Augusta C. (Burton)
    808, 985
  Betsy (Baker) 985
  Cassa (Pitts, Gregg) 984
  (Davis) 984
  Eliza (Farlee) 985
  Eliz. (Lewis, Cox) 984
  Ellen (Allen) 985
  Eusebia B. 985
  (Floyd) 984
  Frances (Anderson) 985
  Isabell B. 985
  Jas. H. 985
  Jeff. 985
  Jesse 985
  Jno. B. 985
  Jno. M. 984
  Jos. 985
  Kate (Terhune) 985
  Kittie (Caldwell) 984ff
  Kittie (Mervey) 984
  (Lewis) 985
  Lewis S. 985
  Louisa (Clark) 985
  Louisiana B. (Huguely 985
  Mary (Caldwell) 984
  Nancy (Piper) 985
  Otho 984
  Polly (Corn) 985
  Rebecca (Singleton) 984
  Rich. B. 985
  Robt. B. 985
  Susan 984
  Thos. 985
  Wm. B. 984ff
  William Otho Dr. 808, 984ff
  Yonger P. 984
ROBB, Eliz. (Cogar) 940
ROBERSON, Barbara (Harmon) 879
  Marg. (Marrs) 1022
ROBERTS 959
  Eleanor (Hayden) 1002
  Eliza. E. (Rapier) 1002
  Eliz (Shockley) 1002
  Francis J. 1002
  Geo. B. 1002, 1019
  Jennie (Rothwell) 988
  Louisa T. (Center, Harlan)
    879
  Marg. (Shockley) 1002
  Mary (Rose) 988
  Mary Zerelda (Spalding) 1002
  Namon 988
  Wm. 1002
ROBERTSON, Ada F. 986
  Alex. 765
  Annie 986
  Austin M. 986
  Boyle C. 986
  Cassie J. 986
  Cath. (Wright, Jones,
    Freeman) 985
  Chas. D. 985
  Dudley B. 985ff
  Eliz. (Turk) 1024
  Eliz. J. (Bottom) 986
  Ellen (Letcher) 915
  F. A. W. 1024
  Florence 986
  G. W. Rev. 781, 986
  Geo. Ch. Justice 765, 798,
    908, 915ff, 962
  Geo. D. 985ff
  Geo. R. 985

ROBERTSON
  Georgia W. (Board) 986
  Green 986
  H. K. 904
  Jas. A. 986
  Jennie K. 986
  Jno. 986
  Jos. B. 986
  Lemuel M. 986
  (Letcher) 765, 916
  Louisa (Drye) 986
  Lucinda (Hamilton) 986
  Lucy A. H. (Knott) 985
  Lucy (Bates) 986
  Maggie L. 985ff
  Marion T. (Booker) 985
  Martha (McKee) 765
  Mary (Freeman) 986
  Mary (Mayes) 985
  Mary E. (Moore) 1011
  Mattie Sally (johnston) 904,
    986
  Nancy (Brigg) 1038
  Odessa (Atkinson) 781
  Rebecca (Dunlap) 844
  Sarah C. (Selecman) 985
  Sarah M. 781
  Susan 985
  Wm. J. 985ff
  Wm. K. 985
  Wm. T. 986
ROBINSON, Adderson 987
  (Alford) 987
  Alice 987
  Ann (Calbfus) 986
  Artemisia 987
  Belle (Tomlinson) 986
  Ben 793, 986ff
  Betsie Barnett 987
  (Bledson) 987
  Cath. (Coleman) 826
  Chas. S. 987
  Chas. W. 987
  Ch. Justice 907
  Creek 787
  Dick Camp 760, 912, 986
  Duncan 759
  Eleanor (Crow) 834
  Eliz. (Baker) 782
  Eliz. (Moore) 987
  Fannie (Huguely) 897, 987
  Fannie (Lillard) 918
  Gabrilla (Perkins) 986
  Geo. W. 907, 986ff
  Grover C. 987
  Harry 986
  Henry Jackson 987
  Henry L. 987
  Isabel (Driskell) 987
  J. M. 985
  J. R. 979, 1045
  J. W. 987
  Jas. Benj. 986
  Jas. H. 987
  Jane Harley 987
  Jennie (Jenkins) 987
  Jennie Lee (evans) 849, 987
  Jno. B. 986ff
  Jno. S. 849, 987
  (Jones) 905
  Jos. M. 987
  Kate Leavell 986
  (Kenney) 907
  Kittie Sea 987
  Laura E. (Callison) 810
  Larue 987
  Lizzie (Brown) 987
  Lizzie M. 787
  Lucy (Watts) 986
  Lula 987

47

48

49

51

SPALDING
Frances B. 1002
Geo. L. 1002
Henrietta (Rom. Cath. Nun)
  1002
Jane (Abell) 912
Jno. L. Bishop (Rom.Cath.)
  816, 1002
Jos. 816, 889
Leonard Dr. 1002
Martha P. (Jans) 1002
Martin Jno. Rev. (Rom. Cath.
  Archbishop) 818, 889,
  991, 1002
Mary Ellen (Slevin) 1002
Mary J. (Lancaster) 1002
Mary Jane (Mattingly) 937
Mary Zeralda (Roberts) 1002
Raphael 1002
Rich. 818, 1002
Rich. M. 1002
Rosalie (Head) 884
Susan (Abell) 937
Susan (Cooper) 829
Thos. 829, 937, 1002
Wm. 829
SPARKS, Biddy Ann (McKinney)
  1001
Eliz. (Crawhorn) 1001
Eliz. (Saters) 1001
Geo. Ann 1001
Harriet (Powell) 975
Jas. Riley 1001
Josiah Wm. 975, 1001
Juliet (Akin) 1001
Mary Ellen 1001
Mathew 1001ff
Moses S. 1001
Nancy (Wilson) 1043
Nancy Jane (Johnson) 1001
Patsy Jane (Helstead) 1001
Polly Ann (England, McNeely)
  1001
Polly Ann (Walker) 1001
Sally Ann (Saters) 1001
Susan (Mitchell) 1001
Thos. 1001
Wm. 1001
Victoria 1001
SPARROW, Lucinda A. (Vivian)
  1032
Mary (Whitehouse) Lincoln's
  1st cousin 1037
Mary E. (Mouser) 953
SPAULDING, Benj. F. 1003
Caroline 1002
Frances 1002
Geo. P. 1002
Henry L. 1002
Henry P. 1002
Jas. M. Dr. 1003
Jno. 1002ff
Logan T. 1003
Lucy (Turnham) 1002
Martin V. 1003
Mattie B. (Bricken) 1003
Nancy 1002
W. E. Dr. 1003
SPEAKS, Urban 816
SPEARS, Ann (Spears) 1003
Benj. 842
Chas. C. 1003
Chrismun 1003
Eliza 1003
Eliz. (Williams) 842
Eliz. Gwinn (Dulworth) 842
Geo. 1003
Geo. C. 1003
Geo. Harvey 1003
Hannah (Baker) 1003

SPEARS
Hugh C. 1003
Jno. 842, 1003
Jno. F. 1003
Jno. L. 1003
Lee W. 1003
Marg. (Chrismun) 1003
Marg. (Jackson) 1003
Mary (Faulconer) 852
Mary (Riffe) 898
Mary L. (Baker) 1003
Maomi (Crabtree) 842
Rachel (Campbell) 859
Rebecca (Bonaugh) 1003
Sallie (Graham) 1047
Sidney C. 1003
Wm. H. 1003
SPEED, Adelia (Gartin) 820
Jas. 991
  (Smith) 759
SPELMANNUS, Henricus 767
SPENCE, Sadie (Oldham) 960
SPENCER, Martha F. (Vivian)
  1032
Mary (Gatewood) 950
Nannie (Mopre) 950
Va. (Willis) 1042
Wm. M. 950
SPILMAN, Abraham T. 768
Benj. 767ff
Chas. Harvey 767
Eliz. A. (Alexander) 768
Jno. T. 768
Mary Duryea (Skillman) 767ff
Mary Frances (Anderson) 768
Nancy R. (Rice) 767
SPILLMAN, Ann (Graham) 865
Dr. 975
Mary A. (Roninson) 986
SPIRES, Frances P. (Crews) 913
Joel 913
Rachael E. (Lankford) 913
SPOONAMORE, Adam 1003
Andrew L. 1003
Christian 1003
David C. 1003
Eliza A. 1003
Eliz. (Miller) 1003
Eliz. E. 1003
Emily (Hubble) 1003
Henry M. 1003
Hollice 1003
Jas. A. 1003
Jas. P. 1003
Jno. D. 1003
Jno. M. 1003
Louanna 1003
Marg. D. 1003
Mary A. (Smith) 1003
Mary C. 1003
Pauline A. (Hickle) 1003
Sallie (Crow) 834, 1003
Saml. M. 1003
Sarah (Crow) 834, 1003
Wm. 1003
SPOONVILLE 976
SPRAGGINS, Maria (Bricken)
  801
SPRINGER, Jane (Young) 1048
SPROWL, (Davis) 809
Oliver 809
Paulina E. (Cabell) 809
SPRUAL, Mary (Tarkington) 1014
SPURLING, Cath. H. (Wright)
  1046
Louella (Penn, Wright) 1046
Wm. 1046
SQUIRES, Capt. 1024
Jno. 880
Lockie (Jones) 880

SQUIRES
Mary S. (Harmon) 880
Sally (Willis) 1042
Sally M. (Montgomery) 880
Winfield 880
STAGG, Cath. (Curry) 836
STAKE, McCoun burned at by
  Indians 937
STALLARD, David 913
Eliz. (Stone) 913
Rebecca (Langsford) 913
STALLINGS, Martha (Myer) 942
STANLEY, Eliz. (Moore,
  Ellsworth) 950
STANTON, R. H. 965
STARK, Electa (Stiles) 1005
Susan (Callison) 810
STARKEY, Amelia C. (Caldwell)
  810
Phebe J. (Caldwell) 810
STARKS, Julia (Harlan) 879
STARNS, Lucretia (Irvin) 1041
STATION (Pioneer) Bryant's 957
Carpenter's 787
Goodin 1019
Goodwin's 815
McAfee's 923
STATEN, Scarbour (Purdy) 978
STAYTON, Ellen Mc. (Tucker)
  1024
Peroy 1024
STEARMAN, Ann (Rafity) 1043
Mary M. (Wilson) 1043
Thos. 1043
Wm. 1043
STEELE 947
Sarah (Coppage) 830
STEPHENS, Mary E. (Slaughter)
  998
Susan (Christeson) 864
T. J. 998
STEPHENSON, Changed from
  Stevenson 1004
Albert G. 1004
Alex. J. 1004
Andrew Tribble Dr. 1003ff
Anna 1004
Annie (Vardimar) 1004
Betsy 1004
Cath. (Patton, Salven) 1004
Chas. M. 1004
David M. 1004
E. T. Dr. 1004
Eliz. 1004
Eliz. Ann (Smith) 1004
Ephraim T. 1004
Frances (Bogie) 1004
Geo. L. 1004
(Hawkins) 1004
Jas. A. 1004
Joe Thos. Dr. 1004
Jno. C. 1004
Jno. F. 1004
Jno. W. Gov. 1004
Jos. H. 1003ff
Julia (Kurts) 1004
Lindsey V. 1004
Malinda 1004
Marg. (McRoberts) 1004
Martha M. (Cosby) 1004
Mary 1004
Mary (Tribble) 1003
Mary Ann (Wilson) 1004
Mattie 1004
Nancy (Long) 1004
Nathan 1004
Nicholas 1004
Patsey A. 1004
Paulina 1004
Peter T. 1004

52

STEPHENSON
Rebecca 1004
Sarah J. (Arnold) 1004
Thos. 1004
Wm. L. Dr. 1004
Wm. T. 1004
Wm. W. 1004
STEPNY 1023
STEVENS, Jas. 816
STEVENSON, Change in spelling
873, 1004
Andrew 861
Lucinda (Hansford) 875
Marg. (Hansord) 875
STEWART, Female College 933
Nancy (Welsh, Combs) 769
Wm. 769
STILES, Ann (McAtee) 1004
Ann (Willett) 860
Anna (Bradford) 1005
Anna(ie) C. (Bland) 792,
1005
Boland 1005
Bur 1005
Chas. 860, 1005
Chilion 1005
Corrilla P. 1005
Cris A. (Gaddie) 860
David 785, 1005
Demus 1005
Edward L. 1004ff
Electa (Stark) 1005
Elijah Van 1005
Eliz. 1005
Eliz. (Carter) 1005
Eliz. (Kitchell) 785, 1005
Eunice (Maxwell) 879, 1014
Eunice (Miller) 1005
(Gardner) 785
Geo. F. 1005
Henry C. 1004ff
Jacob 1005
Jas. F. 1005
Jno. B. 1005
Jno. C. 1005
Jonathan 1005
Jos. B. 785, 1005
Lewis K. 785, 1005
Lizzie (Phillips) 1005
Mary A. (Beeler) 952
Mary R. 1005
Minerva F. (Beall) 785
(O'Brian) 1004
Ogden W. 1005
Philip 1004
Rebecca (Willett) 785, 1005
Rhoda (Edwards) 1005
Rhoda (Willett) 792
Sallie (Beam) 1006
Sallie A. 1005
Sarah Jane (Beall) 969
Susan A. (Pile, Beckham)
1005
Thos. 1005
Van Buren 1005
Wm. Ogden 1006
STILL, First in Wash. Co. 818
STINE, Carl 1006
Cath. E. (Williams) 1006,
1039
Eliz. 1006
Elma 1006
Jacob 1006
Jas. H. 1006
Louisa 1006
Mark 1006
Mary 1006
Robt. 1006
Thos. B. 1006
W. M. 1006

STINES, Sarah A. (Curry) 835,
1006
STIVES, Fannie (Maupin) 938
Jno. W. 938
Mary (ballard) 938
STONE, 839
Anna M. (Bush) 1018
Annie (stone) 1006
Barton W. Rev. 833, 875
Bernard 909
Betsy (Stotts) 909, 1008
Caleb 1006ff
Carlile D. (Walker) 1034ff
Davis H. 1006
Elias 1006
Eliz. (Barker) 1006
Eliz. (stallard) 913
Eliz. (Tevis) 1018
Ephraim M. 1006
Esther (Onstott) 1006
Ethel (Crutchfield) 1006
Francis 1007
Geo. W. 1006
(Harris) 1034
Horace 1006
Isaac D. 1006ff
J. C. Capt. (Gen.) 1007
Jas. Clifton 1007, 1034
Jno. 1006ff, 1018
Josiah 1007
Laura 1035
Lucy (Gaines, Forman) 1006
Lulu B. (Dailey) 1006
Maggie B. 1006
Maggie K. (Runyon) 1006
Mary (Collier, Allen) 1006ff
Mary (Montgomery) 1006
Mary (Royse) 1043
Mary E. (Hancock) 873
Mary J. (Warner) 1006
Matilda (Davis) 1006
Matilda (hanson) 1007
Melinda (Hodges) 1006
Minnie M. 1006
Nancy (Clemmons, Montgomery)
868, 880, 1006
Nancy (King) 909
Nancy (Rodes) 1007
Nannie 1007
Pattie (Harris) 881, 1007
Rifles 1007
Robt. S. 1006
Sallie (Lockart) 1006
Sallie (Walker) 972
Sallie C. (Robinson) 810
Sally S. (Hudson) 1006
Saml. Hanson 1007
Silas 1006
(Smith) 1006
Smith Thos. 1006
Spencer 1006
Susan (Ralls) 904
Thos. N. ("Sure Enough" Tom)
1006ff
Wm. B. 1006ff
Wm. H. 1007
STONEMAN, Gen. 1021
Raid 864
STONER, Anna (Langsford) 913
Jno. 993
Martha M. (Samuels) 993
Mary (Jack) 993
STOTTS, Alex. 1007
Amanda W. (Moran) 953
Andrew J. 1008
Benj. S. 1007ff
Betsy (Stone) 1008
Eliz. (Montgomery) 953, 1007
Esther (Taylor) 1007
Geo. W. 1008

STOTTS
Geo. Dallas 1008
Green C. 1008
Hattie C. 1008
Hattie Lee 1008
Jas. 1007
Jno. 1007ff
Martha (Stotts) 1007ff
Mary (Hoviqus) 1008
Mary J. (Young) 1007
Mollie E. 1008
Mollie L. (Traylor) 1008
Oliver 1007
Pamelia (Paxton) 1007
Patsy (Gilmore) 1007
Pauline (Fletcher) 1008
Pauline (Paxton) 1007
Polly (Burns) 1008
Rebecca (Blair) 1007
Robt. M. 1008
Saml. B. 1008
Suela (moore) 1008
Solomon 1007ff
Thos. M. 1007ff
Ursula (Vaughan) 1007ff
Ursula (Wilson) 791, 1007ff
Victoria 1008
Wm. C. 1007
Wm. L. 1007ff
STOUT, Ada P. (Slaughter) 998
Jno. B. 919, 998
Lula (Lillard) 919
Susan (Bohanan) 998
STRANGE, A. C. Dr. 1009
Abram(ham) 1008, 1025
Amanda C. 1008
Ann Maria (Elliott) 1008
Archelaus A. 975, 1008ff
Asa P. 1009
Benj. F. 1009
Celia (miller) 1008
Chas. 1009
Commodore 1008
Dorinda (Rowe) 1009
Eli 1009
Eliza 1008
Eliza F. (Taylor) 1015
Eliz. (Coffey) 1008
Eliz. (Lloyd) 1008
Eliz. (Walkup) 1008
Ellen 1008
Finis 1009
Huldah (grant) 1009
Isaac Hardin 1008
J. F. 1015
J. K. A. 1016
Jas. Austin 1009
Jas. Logan 1008
Jno. C. Rev. 1008, 1015
Jos. H. 1009
Larkin A. 1008ff
Larkin C. 1009
Lennie P. 1009
Levi 1008
Louis 1008
Louvina 1008
Martha J. (Turner) 1025
Mary A. (Simpson) 1009
Mary E. (Taylor) 1015
Mary J. (Bird) 1009
Melrose (Lesemby) 1009
Mollie B. 1009
O. A. 1009
Polly (thomas) 1008
Polly Ann (Powell) 975
Rebecca (Morrison) 1025
Rosalie (Grant) 1009
S. W. Dr. 1008ff
Sally 1009
Saml.A. 1009

53

STRANGE
  Sarah E. (Elliott) 1009
  Shelby N. 1009
  Shelby W. 1008
  Victoria (Isham) 1008ff
  Walter 1009
  Wm. 1008
  Winston A. 1008
STRAUS, Issa G. (Shadburne)
  994
STREET, Marg. (Davis) 837
STREIT, Eliz. (Harlan) 879
  Susan (Harlan) 879
STRINGTOWN 936
STUART 867
STUCKY, T. Hunt 756
STUYVESANT, Peter Gov. 1029ff
SUBLETT, Eliz. (Moore) 814
  Jas. A. 814
  Martha E. (Carter) 814
SUDDETH, Louisa (Gaitskill,
  Daniel) 863
SULLIVAN, Chas. Blount 1010
  (Collins) 1010
  Danl. 1009
  Eliz. (Bault) 1010
  Eliz. (Rogers) 1009
  Ethel 1010
  Fielding L. 1010
  Garnett Arnold 1010
  Geo W. 1009ff
  Jas. 1010
  Jane (Settle) 1009
  Jno. 760
  Jno. B. 1010
  Jno. P. 1010
  Katie Grooms 1010
  Leah M. (Arnold) 1010
  Lewis 1010
  Luther 1010
  Mary (Hill) 760
  Mollie S. (Arnold, Garnett)
    1010
  Obadiah 1010
  P. H. 963
  Robt. 1010
  Sarah B. (Bush) 1010
  Sarah Baker 1010
  Silas H. 1010
  U. T. Benj. 1010
SULTANA DISASTER 854
SUMMERS, Benj. F. 785ff
  Beverly B. 786
  Geo. W. 786
  Jno. B. 786
  Martha 786
  Mary V. (Williams) 786
  Patsey A. (Fry) 786
  Rufus K. 786
  Sarah E. (Bealmear) 785ff
  Susan W. (Sanders) 786
  Theresa (Wilson) 786
  Verlinda (Beckwith) 786
SUMRALL, Benj. C. 1010
  Bettie B. (Moore) 1011
  Collins Moore 1011
  Danl. C. 1010
  Eliz. V. (Dobyns) 1010
  Jno. T. 1010
  Jos. Kinkead 940ff, 1010ff
  Judge 837
  Julia P. 1010
  Lilian C. 1011
  Mary D. 1010
  Sarah J. 1010
  Susan (Clark) 1010
  Wm. A. 1010
  Wm. Lawson 1011
SUMTER, Ft. 762
SURVANT, Eliz. (Wade) 1011

SURVANT
  Jas. 1011
  Jane (Guthrie) 1011
  Jno. B. 1011
  Jos. 1011
  Leah (Hope) 1011
  Levi 1011
  Marion W. 1011
  Mary A. (Overstreet, Powers)
    1011
  Rich. 1011
  Wm. H. 1011
SUTFIELD, Diana (Riker) 983
  J. H. 983
SUTHERLAND, Anna 1012
  Archibald C. 1011ff
  (Cameron) 1012
  Eliza (Read) 1011ff
  Eliz. (Graham) 866
  Eliz. (Jones) 866
  Helen R. 1011
  Henry 1011ff
  Isaac W. 1011
  Jeanette (Nicholls) 959
  Jeanette W. 1011ff
  Jno. D. 1011ff
  Josie (Miles) 1012
  Mary E. 1011
  Nancy C. 1011
  Stewart 866
  Wm. H. 959, 1011ff
SUTTON, Elnora (Root, Van
  Sickle) 1030
  Jno. 835
  Selena (Salle) 835
SWAN, Rachel (Van Sickle) 1030
SWANSON, Deborah (Tarkington)
  1014
SWEENEY, Danl. 1012
  Eliz. (Hudgin) 893
  Ella 1012
  Fannie (Van Cleve) 1012
  Harvey 1012
  Jno. W. Rev. 880
  Mary (Edmondson) 1012
  Mary A. (Leachman) 1012
  Wm. H. 1012
  Dr. 885
  Mary (McGarvey) 932
SWEET, Louis 774
  Susan Victoria (King) 774
SWIFT, Rich. Rev. 875
  Susan M. (Hansford, Lyne)
    875
SWIGGETT, Maggie (Coppage)
  830, 1012
  Prior 1012
  Walter 1012
SWOPE, Eliz. (Dunn) 845
  Emma (Montgomery) 949
  Fanny (Rorerty) 856
  Jno. 856
  Mary J. (Floyd) 856
SYMPSON, B. C. Dr. 1012ff
  Jas. C. 1012
  Mary (Gaddie) 1012
  Mary J. (West) 1013
  Michael 1013
  Peggy (Donahoo) 1013
  Rich. B. 1013
  Rosa E. (Hobbs) 1013
  Sarah F. (Edwards) 1013
  Seaton E. 1013
  Wm. 1013
SYNOD, Civ. War Differences
  754

TABLER, DR. 939
TAGART, Eliz. (Knox) 911

TALBOTT, Albert Gallatin Col.
  752, 819, 1013
  Annie (French) 752
  Caroline (Watson) 1013
  Clyde 752
  Demoval 1013
  Eliz. (Caldwell) 1013
  Emma (Cecil) 819, 1013
  Leonidas (Lee) B. 752
  Marie E. (Owsley, Talbott)
    1013
  Mary A. (Tomlinson) 1013
  Mary P. (Carpenter) 752
  Nancy (Hawkins) 882
  Presley 1013
  Wm. C. 742ff
  Wm. P. 1013
  Zerelda (Baxter) 752
TALLIAFERRO, Dr. 888
TANEY, R. B. Ch. Justice 1002
TANYARD, First in Ky. 840
TAPSCOTT, Rhoda (Coppage) 830
  Stewart 830
TARKINGTON, Amelia (Wilsford)
  1014
  Deborah (Swanson) 1014
  David K. T. 1014
  David S. 1014
  Eliz. E. (Knox) 1014
  Eliz. E. (Tarkington) 1014
  Esther (Brown) 1014
  Frances (Raines) 1014
  Geo. W. 1013ff
  Hugh B. 1014
  Jas. W. 1014
  Jeff. O. 1014
  Jos. Rev. Capt. 1014
  Jos. A. 1014
  Jos. M. 1014
  Joshua 1013ff
  Julia H. (McMillen) 1014
  Julia H. (Raines) 1014
  Julietta (Maxwell) 846, 1014
  Keziah (Ezell) 1014
  Maria W. 1014
  Martha (Durham) 1014
  Martha (Shuttleworth) 1014
  Mary (Barry) 1014
  Mary E. (Edelen) 846, 1014
  Mary P. (Morris) 1014
  Mary (Spruel) 1014
  Mary (Tarkington) 1014
  Nancy (Oliver) 1014
  Priscilla (Tarkington) 1014
  Robt. W. 1014
  Wm. L. 846, 1013ff
TARLETON, Col. 1004
TATE, Capt. 919
  Nanny J. C. (Lisle) 919
TATHAN, Nancy (Holmes, Bell)
  898
TAYLOR, 981, 1013
  A. 1021
  Albert R. 963
  Ann (Ewing) 1016
  Anna C. 1017
  Annie B. (Page) 1017
  Annie M. 1015
  Benj. F. Rev. Dr. 1015
  Caroline M. (Garnett) 1016
  Cath. 1017
  Celestia (Lewis) 1016
  Chas. B. 1016
  Chesley J. 1016
  Clarissa (Williams) 1040
  Clemmie E. 1017
  Cordie A. 1017
  Creed 1037
  Dellie 1016
  Delray 799

54

TAYLOR
De Witt C. 963
E. H. 956
Eliz. (Slemons) 1017
Eliza F. (Strange) 1015
Eliza J. (Jackson) 1030
Eliz. (Cobb) 825, 1017
Eliz. (Duncan) 881, 1037
Eliz. (Hughs) 1014
Eliz. (McLane) 925
Eliz. (Tomlinson) 986
Emma L. 1015
Esther (Stotts) 1007
Ethel 1017
F. T. DR. 856
Fanny (Bondurant) 892
Fanny (Glover) 1014
Fanny (Jones) 1016
Fanny (McGarvey) 1016ff
Florence P.(Van Pelt) 1030
Fork (Place Name) 914
Frances A. (Williams) 1039
Frances T. (Jones) 1014
Geo. B. 1015
Geo. C. 1015
Geo. M. 1015ff
Geo. W. Rev. 1014ff
(Harding) 990
Henly 963
Henry 987, 1015
Herschel 1017
Jas. G. Dr. 1016ff
Jas. H. 963
Jas. R. 1015ff
Jas. Thos. 1015
Jane (Armstrong) 780
Jennie L. 1017
Jer. 1016
Jno. 812, 963, 1010, 1014,
1017
Jno. C. 1017
Jno. T. 1017
Jos. E. 892, 1015
Judith (Moss, Jones) 1021
Kalista (Hood) 892
Kate (Morrison) 800
Kitty F. (Garnett) 1015
Laura S. (Morris) 1015
Lena 1015
Leonard 868, 963
Lucy A. (White) 1037
Marg. (Faulconer) 852
Marg. E. 1017
Martha (Lewis) 1016
Mary (Bridgewater, Jones)
1016
Mary (Green) 780, 868
Mary (Powell) 1016
Mary (Wilson) 1014
Mary E. (Strange) 1015
Mary J. (Harris) 1015
Mary J. (Loye) 1017
Mary J. (McClain) 1015
Mary J. (Patterson) 1016
Mary Louisa 1017
Mary McClellan 1015
Matilda Prentiss 1015
Matt. 1016ff
Mattie C. 1015ff
Mollie J. (Cook) 1017
Nancy (Crossthwaite) 969
Nancy (Lewis) 812
Nancy (Montgomery) 1040
Peter W. 969
Pres. (Gen.) ---
Prudence A. (Williams) 1040
Rich. I. 1015
Robt. S. 1017
Sally (Isaacs) 987
Saml. R. 1014ff, 1032

TAYLOR
Sarah (Fisher) 856
Sarah (Robinson) 897, 987
Sarah E. (Conner) 1015
Sarah M. (McClain) 1014
Simon P. 1014, 1016
Sophia (Bledsoe) 1014
Sophia Bledsoe (Cardwell)
812
Tabitha (Phelps) 905, 969
Thos. C. 1016
Uriah L. Dr. 814, 1015ff
Va. (Tucker, Owsley) 962ff,
1017
Wm. C. 1017
Wm. H. 1014
Wm. L. 1015
Wm. R. 1030
Wm. S. Dr. 1015
Zach. M. Rev. 1016, 1040
TEACHERS, State Assoc. 771
TEA PARTY, Boston 895
TEBBS, Bend (Place Name) 762
Sarah (Tery) 886
TECUMSEH 822, 961
TEMPLE. Delitha (Clevland) 824
TEMPLEMAN, Mary (Wilson) 831
TERHUNE, Abram 985
Cynthia (Young) 985
Garrett 935
Kate (Robards) 985
Mary (Mann) 935
Rachel (Cozatt) 833
Rachel (Rynerson) 935
TERRELL, E. R. 801
(Bricken) 801
TERRILL, Alma (Proctor) 1018
Almanda (Barbee) 1018
Capt. 938
Eliza A. (Yater) 1018
Eliz. (Dinwiddle) 1018
Eliz. S. (Saddler) 1018
Elijah Jackson 1017ff
Geo. A. 1018
H. T. 1033
Henry 1017ff
Hiram K. 1018
Jas. 1018
Jno. A. 1018
Jno. R. 1018
Josephina Henry 1018
Mary (Beazley) 1018
Mary (Ford) 1018
Mary O. 1018
Overton 1018
Paralee 1018
Patrick H. 1018
Patsey 1018
Phillip S. 1018
Robt. J. Rev. 1017ff
Susan B. (Smith) 1018
Susan M. 1018
Sydona (Underwood) 1018
Thos. Johnson 1018
(Walker) 1033
Wm. A. 1018
Wm. H. 1018
Winnie F. (Allen) 1018
TERY, Jos. 886
Josie L. (Henry) 886
Sarah (Tebbs) 886
TEVIS, Arthur C. 1018
Benj. F. 1018
Chas. C. 1018
Cyrus C. 1018
Eliz. (Stone) 1018
Eliz. Dinwiddie 1018
Harry D. 1018
Jno. 1018
Julia A. 1045

TEVIS
Lella (Bush) 1018
Lucy W. (McKenny) 1018
Maggie 1018
Mary (Cosby) 1018
Nancy (Burgin) 825
Napoleon 1018
Nathaniel 825
Provy (Cobb) 825
Robt. C. 1018
Sallie Chrisman 1018
Sallie Mc. 1018
Squire T. 1018
W. T. 1018
THARP, Necy (Rawlings) 980
THAWLES, Isaac 816
THOMAS, Alcie J. (Simpson) 996
Alfred P. 1019
Benj. H. 1018ff
Butler R. 1018
Chas. B. 1019
Cordelia 1019
D. W. Capt. 996
Danl. D. 1020
Eliz. (Beard) 993
Eliz. (Burnside) 811
Eliz. (Connelly) 1019
Eliz. C. (Vize) 1019
Ella (Applegate) 1019
Ella M. 1019
Ellen 996
Emily 1020
Emily (Lindsey) 1019
Enoch 835
Frances 835
Geo. H. Gen. 760, 762, 902,
916, 1037
J. R. 996
J. W. 1019
Joanna (Masterson) 841
Jno. 996, 1008
Jno. H. 978, 1019
Jno. R. 1019ff
Lewis Capt. 1019
Lewis H. 1020
Louisa P. (Porter) 1019
Lucy B. 1020
Luella 1019
Marcus L. 1020
Maria L. (Lindsey) 1020
Mary (Davis) 1019
Mary (Moore) 951
Mary (Wilson) 778
Mary A. (Doores) 841
Mary A. (Pulliam) 978
Nancy T. (Bryan) 879
Owen D. 1019ff
Polly (Strange) 1008
Redman G. 1018ff
Sallie B. 1019
sarah (Curry) 835
Susan (Shuck) 996, 1020
Susannah (Davis, Peak) 1019
Susannah E. 1019
Thos. 841, 1020
Un. Sldr. 956, 981, 985
Wm. R. 1019
THOMPKINS, Mary (Walden) 1033
THOMPSON 815
Alex. 872
Anastasia C. (Barlow) 740
Andrew 915
Anna (Allin) 778
Camillus D. 984
(Carr) 914
Cath. (McIlvoy) 872
Chas. 1033
Col. 827
Danl. B. 1020
Danl. M. 872

55

THOMPSON
Danl. T. 1020
David W. 957
Diana (Dean) 1028
Eliza J. (Ware) 1035
Eliz. (Barclay) 993
Eliz. (Kirk) 1020
Emeline (Leachman) 1012
Emily (Kerr) 915
Geo. 818
Geo. Major 778
Isaac 970
Isabella (Russell) 1020
Jas. 802, 1028
Jane B. (Noe) 959ff
Jno. 872
Jno. B. 939
Jno. C. 872, 970ff
Jno. Lynn 1020
Jno. M. 872
Jos. 1020
Jos. Russell 1020
Lewis A. 740
Lizzie 971
Lucy (Lee) 914ff
Maggie (Thompson) 872
Malinda (Mattingly) 1020
Marg. (Grigsby) 1018
Marg. (Vanarsdell) 1028
Mariah (Reid) 983
Martha A. (Coy) 1019
Martha A. (Crowder) 834
Martha A. (Phillip) 970ff
Mary (Riker) 984
Mary B. (Allin) 778
Mary E. (Brown) 802, 1019
Mary F. (Cecil) 818
Mary Isabella 1020
Mattie 971
May 971
Nancy (Gaitskill) 863
Nancy (Litsey) 802
Nancy (Ramey, King) 1019
Nathan A. 970ff
Nelson A. 914
Peter J. 872
Phil. B. 767
Phoebe E. (McAfee) 923
Polly (Carpenter) 751
Robt. 1020
Rosa 872
Rich. 1020
S. B. 778
Sallie (Simpson) 971
Sallie Cath. 1020
Sallie J. (Hamilton) 872
Sallie J. (Thompson) 872
Sally (Payne) 964
Sarah J. (Browne) 803
Sarah M. (WIthers) 957
Simeon A. 872
Stith 872
Sue Helm (Neal) 957
Susan (Blanford) 872
Susan B. 1020
Thos. 872
Wm. R. 872
THOMSON, Agnes J. (Jackson) 1020
Ellis (Green) 1020
Jas. 1020
Lillie 1020
Phil B. Capt. 875
Sarah (Carter) 1020
Wm. L. 1020
THOMURE, Sarah (Van Sickle) 1030
THORN, Ann (Fields) 854
Anna (Gorthorp) 854
Wm. 854

THORP 981
THORPE, Emma (Hume) 1020ff
Florence (Shearer) 1021
Moning (Harris) 1021
Thos. 1020ff
Zach. 1021
THRELKELD, Kate (Redford) 950
Mary (Burrus) 807
THORNTON, Lucy (Slaughter) 807
THURMAN, Allen G. 773
Baz 867
Emily J. (Ford) 882
Fannie (Montgomery) 949
Marg. (Milburn, Inman) 942
Marg. (Osborne) 867
Marg. A. (Grant) 867
Martha R. (Alexander) 773
Nancy (Nell) 958
Sophia (Grant) 867
Wm. 773
THUSTIN (Nuckols) 941
TICHENOR, Emily (Neal) 803
Mary E. (Brown) 802
Timothy 803
TILDEN 792, 857, 886, 907, 1022
TILESTON, H. B. Dr. 756
TILFORD, (Boyle) 744
Jno. Major 937
Nancy (McCoun) 937
TIMBERLAKE, Eliz. (Dedman) 839
Emeline (Reed) 982
Geo. 982
TINGLE, Delia M. (Cox) 832
TOBIN, Kate (Boldrick) 795
Lawrence 795
TODD, Jenny (Yates) 941
Mary (Parker) 898
Nancy T. (Merritt) 941
Patsey (Bradshaw) 941ff
Robt. S. 898, 941
Tabitha A. (Phelps, Chenault) 969
Wm. N. 742, 941ff
TOLBERT, Eliz. (Buckler) 968
TOMLINSON, Belle (Robinson) 986
Eliz. (Jones) 1021
Eliz. (Taylor) 986
Harry D. 1022
Jas. A. 939
Jos. 986, 1021
Kaziale (Bland) 1021
Lula M. (Marrs) 1022
Maggie M. 1022
Mary A. (Talbott) 1013
Mary E. (Robinson) 986
R. H. 1021ff
Wm. 1021
TOTTEN, Ellen (Bradley) 797
Jos. H. 797
RS 797
TOWLER (Haselwood) 881
TOWLES, Bennie 1022
Bettie 1022
David M. 1022
David T. 1022
Eliz. (Wetherall) 1022
Fanny (Mason) 1022
Frances (Willis) 1042
Geo. W. 1022
Jos. 1022
Lena L. 1022
Lucy 1022
Martha A. (Montgomery) 1022
Sallie 1022
Willie 1022
TRABUE, Caroline (Maxey) 997
Sally (Anderson) 778
TRAPUALE 940

TRAYLOR, Bettie H. (Cox) 1008
J. L. 1008
Mollie L. (Stotts) 1008
TRESENITER, Jennie M. (Caldwell) 1026
TRIBBLE 876
Andrew REv. 821, 1003
Mary (Stephenson) 1003
Nancy (Chenault) 821
TRIGG, Mary (Moos) 1035
TRIMBLE, Gov. 907
TRIP, Pioneer-Va. to Ky. 826ff
TRIPLETS (Jones) 905
TROTTER FARM 982
TROUTMAN, (Beard) 1022
Eliz. (Shawler) 1022
Mary E. (Shehan, Mobley) 1023
Michael L. 1022
Ora Kate 1023
Peter 1022
Sarah A. (Howlett) 1022
TRUCE, Lucretai (Fenton) 853
TRUE, Mary (McGarvey) 932
TRUMBLE, Eliza A. (Moore) 950
Jas. 950
Mary (McMullen) 950
TRUMP, Marg. (Harmon) 879
TUCKER, Alice (Humphrey) 897
Ann A. (Chelf) 1024
Anna Imogene 1023
Annie (Magoffin) 1023
Bariah Magoffin 1023
Carrie Nora 1024
Clarinda 1023
D. C. Dr. 963
DeWitt Clinton Dr. 1023
Edmond 1023
Eliza G. (McWhorter) 935, 1024
Eliz. M. (Avritt) 781
Ellen Mc(Stayton) 1024
Eveline D. 1024
(Ford, Ballard) 836
Fort 781
Frances 1023
Hardin H. 1024
Harriet P. (Wood) 1045
Jas. H. Dr. 963
Jas. Hall 1023
Jno. Rev. 962, 1023
Jno. H. Rev. 781, 963, 1023ff
Lydia E. (Humphrey) 897
Matt. 1023
Mary E. 1024
Mary J. (Currey, Galloway) 1025
Melinda (Sherrill) 1023
Mildred (Pentacost) 1045
Nancy (Kennett) 963, 1023
Nancy E. (Knifley) 910, 935, 1024
Paschal 1023, 1045
Phoebe 837
Polly 1023
R. M. 910
Rhoda (Yowell) 963
Robt. 837
Robt. B. 1024
Robt. M. 935, 1023
Sallie M. (Chelf) 1024
Sarah (Davis) 931
Sarah Balenger (Davis) 837
Va. (Owsley, Taylor) 962ff
Va. Gertrude 1023
Wm. 1023
Wm. O. J. 1024
TUITE, Rev. 817
TUPMAN, Jno. 886

56

TUPMAN
Martha (Reynolds) 886
Mary (Henson) 886
Mattie B. (Callison) 810
T. T. 810
TURK, Amanda (Allen) 1024
ALMIRE 1024
Caleb P. 1024
Christopher C. 1024
Eliza (Crawford) 1024
Eliz. (Robertson) 1024
Geo. 1024
Hiram K. 1024
Jas. G. Dr. 1024ff
Jane (Gilmer) 1025
Marg. (Cleaves) 1024
Marg. M. (Allen) 1024
Mollie 1025
Nancy (Moore) 1024
Noah G. 1024
Parthenia L. (Carter
Breeding) 800
Robt. K. 1025
Saml. B. 1024ff
Sarah A. (Walker) 1025
Thos. Lt. 1024
Thos. J. 1024
Wm. Crawford 1024
Wm. H. 1024
Wm. Luther Dr. 1025
TURLEY, Jas. N. 793
Mary E. (Boggs) 793
TURPEN, Mary J. (Irvin) 1041
TURNER, Anna (Mays) 979
David B. 1025
Francis 1025
Geo. Parson 1025
Hannah (Myers) 1025
Israiel 1025
Jas. Marion 1025
Jos. 1025
Jos. Allen 1025
Lizzie H. (Mason, Newcomb)
1025
Luther V. 1025
Macy Jane 1025
Martha (Walkup) 1025
Martha J. (Strange) 1025
Mary Susan (Bloyd) 1025
Melvin Holly 1025
Mildred S. (Fry) 759
Myrtie Moss 1025
Parmelia (Williams) 1040
Polley Ann (McGinnis) 959
Rebecca (Campbell) 859
Saml. J. 1025
Squire Major 750, 908, 945
Susan (McGlasson) 1025
Theodosia (Payne) 964
Thos. M. 1025
Wm. 1025
Zorah B. 1025
TURNERSVILLE 891
TURNHAM, Geo. Capt. 1002ff
Lucy (Spaulding) 1002
TUTT, Hettie P. (Caldwell)
1026
Jas. R. 1026
Nathaniel M. 1026
Rich. 1026
Sallie (Hicks) 1026
Sarah (Cox) 832
Sarah C. (Johnson) 1026
Susan A. (Mercer) 1026
Thos. 1026
Thos. H. 1026
Wm. 832
TYLER, Maria (Lewis) 917
TRYRELL, Nancy (Corley) 830

UMBERSAUGH, Marg. (Shears) 995
UNDERWOOD, Garrett 792
Mary E. (Mears, Blevins) 792
Sydona (Terrill) 1018
UNION, First Camp South of
Ohio 877
URANIA COLLEGE 775
VAN ANGLEN, Ida (Riker) 983
Jno. 983
VAN ARSDALL, Abram 1027
Alex. 1027
Ann (Brown) 1027
Ann E. (Mock) 948
Anna M. (Miller) 1027
Anna M. (Van Arsdall) 1027
Benj. F. 1027
Bernetta (May) 1027
Betsy (Van Arsdall) 1027
Brooks 1027
Cath. (Gibson) 1027
Charley 1027
Cornelius B. 1026ff
Cornelius O. 1027
Earnest 1027
Edward M. 1027
Eliz. (Adams) 1027
Eliz. (McGrath) 1027
Emma C. 1027
Geo. Boone 1027
Geo. W. o026ff
Harriett (Mitchell) 1027
Isaac S. 1027
Jacob 1027
Jas. M. 1027
Jas. W. 1027
Jane (Boice) 1027
Jno. B. 1027
Jno. Wesley 1027
Jos. Atwood 1027
Jos. W. 1027
Katie (Berry) 1027
Katie Clifford 1027
Lee 1027
Lizzie (White) 1027
Lucy (Adkins) 1027
Lulie Dell 1027
Mary 1027
Mary Cornelia 1027
Mary N. 1027
Mattie H. (Berry) 1027
Mollie W. (Latimer) 1027
Nannie 1027
Narcisse (edwards) 1027
Peter 1027
Polly (Harris) 1027
Polly (Smock) 1027
Sally (Riker) 983
Sally (Scomp, Slaughter) 994
Stanley Miller 1027
Sterling 1027
Sue R. (Hedges) 1027
U. S. Grant 1027
Wesley Willard 1027
Willia A. T. 1027
Wm. S. 983
VAN ARSDELL, Addie 1028
Annie 1028
Betsey (Bean) 1028
Bettie (Rice) 1028
(Bush, M. E.) 1028
C. C. 1027ff
Isaac 1028
Jackson 1027ff
Jas. P. 1028
Jane P. (Brewer) 1028
Jno. J. 1028
Lucy (Cozine) 1028
Marg. (Thompson) 1028
Mary (Cozine) 1028

VAN ARSDELL
Mattie (Sorrel) 1028
Minnie L. 1028
Sarah (Hawkins) 1028
Susan 1028
Wm. Alfred 1028
Wm. R. 1028
VAN BUREN 761, 1033
VANCE, Fanny (Wooldridge) 893
Marg. (Hudson) 893
Wm. 893
VAN CLEAVE, Aaron 1028
Benj. L. 1028
C. A. 1028
Fannie 1028
Hattie (Parrott) 1028
J. B. 1028
Lucy (Knott) 1028
Mary M. 1028
Paulina (Beall) 1028
Sarah (Beam) 1028
Thos. W. 1028
VAN CLEVE, A. C. 1012
Fannie (Sweeney) 1012
Mary J. (Campbell) 859
VAN DALSEM 739
VANDEVEER, David W. 1028ff
Eliz. (Logan) 1028
Geo. 1028
Jno. L. 1028
Martha (Lunsford) 1029
Mattie 1029
Nannie 1029
Sallie (Coffey) 1029
Sallie (Jones) 1028
VAN DORN 973
VAN HOOK, Martha (Ware) 1035
VAN METER, Abram 1029
Adie L. 1029
Alice (Yerkes) 1029
Alice Y. 1029
Ama Y. 1029
Amanda E. 1029
Benj. F. 1029
Eliza C. 1029
Isaac C. 1029
Jacob 1029
Jno. Milton 1029
Lewis M. 1029
Lizzie S. 1029
Orphah (Campbell) 811
Rebecca (Cunningham) 1029
Sarah A. (Hall) 1029
Solomon 1029
Susan (Allen) 1029
Susan A. 1029
Thos. C. 1029
Wm. 1029
VAN NICE, Cornelius 994
Flora (Scomp) 994
Mary 994
VANNOY, Rachael (Miller) 810,
874
VAN PELT, Anna M. (Boyer) 1029
Cora W. 1030
Florence 1030
Florence P. (Taylor) 1030
Hallie Y. 1030
Hiram P. 1030
Jno. W. 1030
Lucinda I. (Young) 1029
Milton D. 1030
Nina C. 1030
Sanford B. 1029
Sanford D. 1029
Whelan C. 1030
Wm. 1029
VAN ZANT, Dicie (Wilson) 1043
VARDIMAN, Bettie (Pennington)
967

57

WALLACE
(Moore) 1046
Rich. W. Rev. 953
Rosana M. (Hurt) 953
Salem 963
Sallie (Harris) 881, 946
Sarah (Rubel, Randolph) 989
Wm. 953, 989
WALLER, Agnes (Johnston) 903ff
Edmund Rev. 904
Geo. REv. 904
Jno. Rev. 816, 904
WALTER, David 941
Levi 812
Lulu (Cardwell, Reid) 812
WALTERS, Anna W. 755
Hattie (Letcher) 916
Minerva (Kidendall) 916
S. P. 754
Sarah E.(Logan) 921
Singleton P. 916
WALSTON, Martha (Edwards) 847
WALTON, Belle (Burdett) 807
Jno. H. 807
Matt. 796
Susan J. (Frazee) 807
WALWORTH, Mary D. (Yeiser) 1047
WARD, Mary (Goode) 864
Thos. 864
WARDEN, Eliz. (Lankford) 826
Jas. V. 826
Mary E. (Coffey) 826
WARE, Alma 1035
Celesta F. (Milburn) 943
Eliza J. (Thompson) 1035
Eugenia 1035
Francis M. 1035
Henry G. 1035
Jno. 942
Martha (Hubble) 1035
Martha (Van Hook) 1035
Rice 943, 1035
Sallie (Milburn) 942
Samantha 1035
Sarah (Cooper) 943
WARFIELD, Elisha Dr. 823
Mary J. (Clay) 823
WARNER, Mary J. (Stone) 1006
WARREN, Gen. 1037
Jno. 777
Judith (Boswell) 777
Susan Hart (Allin) 777
WASH, T. W. (Lodge) 1011
WASHBOURN, Judge 858
Lizzie M. (Forsythe) 858
WASHINGTON, Geo. Gen. 741,
744, 765, 793, 836,
908, 911, 944, 955, 988,
1031, 1037
WATHALL, Eliza (Williams) 1038
Rich. 1038
Sally (Hix) 1038
WATHEN, Fannie (Russell) 1035
Jer. 816
Jno. B. 1035
Wm. W. 1035
WATKINS, Benj. 875
Caroline (Hardin) 876
Caroline (Milton) 882
Emily (Hawkins) 882
Ephraim 789
Evelyne E. (Price) 977
Harriet (Nanta) 895
Hays 841
Jane (Minter) 875
Jno. 882
Marg. (Gaither) 860
Mary (Handy) 875
Mary (Knuckols) 926
Nancy (Duncan) 977

WATKINS
Rachel (nickels) 789
Sarah C. (Bennett) 789
Shastine 977
WATSON, Caroline (Talbott)
1013
Eliz. V. (Damron) 874
P. S. G. Rev. 807
Peter 1013
WATTS, Kate W. (Greer) 870
Lucy (Robinson) 986
Mary (Parkes) 963
WAY, Gen. 1017
WAYNE, Anthony Gen. 781, 791,
951
Mary J. (Purdy) 978
WEAREN, Annie (James) 1035
Drury 1035
Hettie A. (Hardin) 1035
Jacob 1035
Nannie T. (Denton) 1035
Sallie (Locker) 1035
Thompson 1035
W. C. 1035
Wm. H. 1035
WEATHERFORD, Geo. 779
Millie (anderson) 779
WEATHERHEAD, America (Willis)
1042
WEATHERS, (Hawkins) 882
Jas. 951
Marg. (Cutsinger) 951
Rhoda (Pile) 951, 1005
WEAVER, Eliz. (Beeler) 781
Katie (Chelf) 820
WEBB, Anna (Ball) 821
Ben J. 814ff, 818
Jane A. (Curl) 1035
Nehemiah 816
Rich. M. 1035
Susan Quinn (Morton) 1035
Wm. C. Dr. 1035ff
WEBBER, Betsy W. (Ford) 857
Philip 909
Polly (King) 909
Wm. Rev. 857
WEBSTER, A. C. 824
Danl. 1029
Lucy (Gray) 867
Sarah (Coakley) 824
WEISIGER, Jos. Dr. 766
Jos. Mrs. 908
(kincaid) 908
Mary A. (Kinnaird) 909
WELCH, J. M. 967
Mary F. (Penningnton) 967
WELDEN, Harriet (Bale) 783
Isaac 783
Lucy (Gardner) 783
WELLS, Caroline (Baker) 782
Chas. 782
Eliz. (King) 909
Ida (Cox) 832
Sarah A. (King) 909
WELSH, Adeline (Wiseman) 770
Andrew 769
(Darby) 769
(Douglass) 768
Edward 769
Eliz. (Metcalf) 770
Eliz. (Nichols) 769
Emily (Lee) 915
Geo. Winston 768ff
(Guthrie) 769
Jas. B. 768ff
Jno. Edward 770
Jos. 769
Mary (Breath) 770
Mary Louise (Greenway) 770
Nancy (Stewart, Combs) 769

WELSH
Pamelia (Lee) 769
Sarah (Merrifield) 769
Sarah (Withers) 769
Thos. 769
Wm. L. 769ff
WESLEY, Jno. 780
WESLEYAN COLLEGE, Relocation
966
WEST, Benj. 974
Keziah (Barlow) 739
Lucy (Poor) 974
Mary J. (Sympson) 1013
WESTON, Eliz. (Gore) 865
WETHERAL(L), (Garnett) 1041
Eliz. (Towles) 1022
WETHINGTON, Mary A. (Carico)
864ff
Nannie (Goode) 864
Wm. 864
WHAL(L)EN, Rachael (Mitchem)
805
Ellen (Cummins) 834
WHARTON, G. C. 1036
Geo. L. 1036
Jas. L. 1036
Jno. C. 1036
J. Rutledge 1036
Jno. R. 1036
Katie 1036
Lloyd R. 1036
Lucy A. (Caldwell) 805
Lydia G. (Fetter) 1036
Ormsby 1036
Phoebe 1036
(Ray) 1036
Sarah Slaughter (Caldwell)
1036
Susan (Loving) 1036
W. H. 1036
WHEAT, Clemmie J. (Williams)
1040
Cyrus 1040
Eli 936
Eliz. (Allen) 936
Martha (Grider, Blair, Smith)
790
Sarah (Murrah) 1040
Sophia S. (Martin) 936
WHEELER, Amanda (Young) 1048
Gen. 850, 853, 922
Susan (Russell) 989
WHELAN, M. Rev. 814
WHERRITT, Bessie 1037
Claude 1037
(King) 1036
Mary Jane (Peacock) 1036ff
Sallie (Miller) 1037
Saml. 1036
Thos. P. 1036ff
Victor 1037
Wm. 1036ff
WHISKY, "Old Mock" 948
WHITE, Ann L. (Bradshaw) 798
Ann M. (Letcher) 916
Cassander (Harmon) 880
Charlotte (Bradshaw) 798
Clara (Wood) 1045
Durett Lt. 1037
Eliz. 1037
Hall (Place Name) 851
Henry 1037
Hugh Gen. 916
Hugh L. 795
Isabella (Knox) 911
J. G. 798
Jane (Gentry, Blythe) 881,
1037
Jer. 863
Jno. 1037

59

WHITE
  Lizzie (Van Arsdall) 1027
  Lucy (Clark) 1037
  Lucy (Duncan) 881
  Lucy A. (Taylor) 1037
  Martin B. 1037
  Mary (Bolling) 795
  Mary (Cartwright) 814
  (Moore) 950
  Nanny (Abrell) 798
  Nancy (Harris) 881
  Nancy (Hobbs) 779
  Nancy (Preston) 863
  (Noland) 838
  Rich. J. 1037
  Sarah G. (Bradshaw) 798
  Sue F. (Gaitskill) 863
  Thos. 798
  Valentine M. 881, 1037
  Wm. 1037
WHITEHEAD, Eliz. (Atherton)
  781
WHITEHOUSE, Benj. 1037
  Celeste 1038
  Ethel 1038
  Grace F. 1038
  Henry C. 1038
  Jas. R. 1038
  Jas. V. 1038
  Jos. 1037ff
  Mariah F. (Miner) 1038
  Martha E. (Hourigan) 1038
  Mary (Sparrow-Lincoln's kin)
  1037
  Melissa (Condor) 1038
  Myrtle M. 1038
  Nancy M. 1038
WHITIEY, Sarah (Lewis) 961
  Wm. Col. 961
WHITLOCK, Nancy J. (Perry,
  Craddock) 834
WHITLOW, Sophronia C. (Donan)
  949
WHITMAN, Jane (Maxey) 939
WHITSON, Patience (Miller)
  946, 1008
WHITTINGHILL, Hannah (Curry)
  835
WICKLIFFE, (Caldwell) 746
  Capt. 993
  Chas. A. 908
  Eleanor (Simpson) 997
  Gov. 746, 991
  Robt. 908
WIGHAM, Mary (Ripperdam) 855
WIGINGTON, Harriet H. (Greer)
  869
  Hezekiah 869
WILBER, Lucy Ann (Peak) 1019
WILCHER, Mary J. (Anderson)
  779
WILCOXSON, Eliza Jane (Moran,
  Franklin) 952
WILDS, Hopie (Poor) 974
  Susan (King) 962
  Zelma (Robinson) 987
WILES, Susan (King) 774
WILHAM, Mary (Curry) 835
WILKES, Harry 916
WILKINSON, Andrew F. 1038
  Beatrice 1038
  Christopher C. 1038
  Eliz. (Briggs) 1038
  Emma (Hall) 1038
  Geo. 1038
  Gen. 974
  Jane (Froman) 1038
  Jno. W. 1038
  Katie M. (Nichols) 1038
  Mahala (Bricken) 801

WILKINSON
  Mary (Evans) 849
  Mary C. (Dotson) 1038
  Mattie (armstrong) 776
  Myrtle 1038
  Nancy (Bland) 1038
  Nancy J. (Hobbs) 1038
  Nannie 1038
  S. F. 776
  Saml. F. 1038
  Thos. C. 1038
  Wm. B. 1038
  Wiley S. 1038
  Willie 1038
  Zach. 849
WILLETT, Ann (Stiles) 860
  Cath. (Miles) 938
  Corilla(Bland) 792, 1005
  Geo. 792, 938
  Griffin 1005
  Griffith 792
  (head) 883
  Kate (Mattingly) 938
  Rachael (Price) 976
  Rebecca (Stiles) 785, 1005
  Rhoda (Stiles) 792
  Rich. 976
  Tabitha (Willett) 976
WILLIAMS, Aaron 1040
  Abner 1040
  Ada B. 1040
  Albert N. 1040
  Alvan 1040
  Amanda (Frank) 1039
  Andrew 1040
  Arabella (Dodge) 770
  Aug. E. 771
  Barnett 1039
  Bernetta L. 1040
  Bowman Guy 771
  C. W. Dr. 800
  Cath. (Stine) 1006, 1039
  Charlotte (Bradshaw) 1040
  Chas. E. Dr. 770
  Clarissa (Taylor) 1040
  Clemmie J. (Wheat) 1040
  Danl. B. 1039
  Danl. M. 824, 1041
  Dr. 888
  Drewry 1040
  Eliza (Armstrong) 780
  Eliza (Montgomery) 1040
  Eliza (Wathall) 1038
  Eliza F. (Conover) 1040
  Eliz (Davenport) 896
  Eliz. (Nunn) 1039
  Eliz. (Spear) 842
  Eliz. (Vaughan) 1031
  Eliz. B. (Bottom) 986
  Eliz. C. (Smith) 1041
  Elijah 1040
  Ella G. (Scott) 1041
  Elmo 1039
  Emma C. (Coakley) 824
  Ethel H. 1039ff
  Eve (Dryeduch) 1039
  Foster M. 1039
  Frances A. (Taylor) 1039
  Garrett 1039
  Geo. M. 1039
  H. C. 941
  Hattie M. 1039
  Henry E. 1039
  Hooker 1039
  Ibby (Dulworth) 842
  Irving 1039
  J. T. 951
  Jas. B. 1039, 1041
  Jas. E. 1040
  Jas. O. 1039

WILLIAMS
  Jane (Conn) 951
  Joel P. 983ff
  Jno. 780
  Jno. Augustus 770
  Jno. B. 1040
  Jno. O. 1038ff
  Jno. S. Gen. 1024
  Jno. Wesley 1038ff
  Jno. Y. 1039
  Jos. A. 1041
  Julia (Allen) 1039
  Lawrence 1041
  Lee Price 771
  Leslie A. 1040
  Leslie C. 1039
  Lillie May 1041
  Loren 1041
  Lucinda (Bradshaw) 1040
  Lucy (Bohon) 795
  Lucy (Wall) 1040
  Lucy A. (Bradshaw, Carter)
  1040
  Luther 1041
  M. T. (Breeding) 996
  Marg. Susan (Breeding) 800
  Maria 1040
  Marshall C. 1039
  Martha (Guinn) 1040
  Martha (Pirtle) 973
  Martha S. (Bryan) 1040
  Mary 1039
  Mary (Armstrong) 780
  Mary (Bright, Lillard) 918
  Mary A. (McAfee, Singleton,
  King) 923
  Mary Cath. (Edelen) 845ff
  Mary I. (Moore) 951
  Mary L. (Hathaway) 771
  Mary Louvena (Conover) 1040
  Mary V. (Summers) 786
  Milton R. 1039ff
  Nancy A. (Harmon) 880
  Nancy J. (Rowe) 1040
  Nancy O. (Nichols) 1039
  Olelia D. 1040
  Osbourn 1039
  Parmelia (Turner) 1040
  Phoebe (Calvert, Hope) 1039
  Phoebe J. (Curtsinger) 1039
  Phyllis (Hayes) 1040
  Polly (Bradshaw) 1040
  Preston G. 1040
  Prudence A. (Taylor) 1040
  R. D. 863
  Raleigh 770
  Rich. 842
  Robt. G. 1039
  Sallie P. 1041
  Sally (Moore) 952
  Saml. 780, 973
  Sarah (Baker, McGee) 932
  Sarah (De Jarnett) 1042
  Sarah (Wade) 1039
  Sarah A. (Baker, McGee) 1039
  Sarah E. (Cheatham) 1039
  Sherod A. 1044
  Stewart 1039
  Susan M. (Lannum) 1040
  Thos. 1039
  Verlinda (Phelps) 969
  Victoria (Cloyd) 1039
  Westley 1040
  Wm. E. 1040
  Wm.H. 1039
  Zach. T. 1040
WILLIAMSON, Co. Tenn.
  Migration to 751
  Sarah (Graham) 865
WILLIS, Adeline 1041

WILLIS
Amanda H. (Irwin, McGee)
  1041
America (Weatherhead) 1042
Anthony G. 1040
Benj. F. 1041
Benj. R. 1041
Benna L. 1041
Bird 1042
Burrell 843
Chas. 843
Chas. D. 1015
Charles Elmer 1042
Cleveland 1042
Dora E. 1041
Drury 1042
Edmund T. 1041ff
Eliz. (Boice) 1041
Ellen (Garnett) 1041
Ellen (McClain) 1015
Elrie 1042
Estelle 1042
Ethel 1042
Frances (Towles) 1042
G. D. 1042
Hannah (Dulworth) 843
Harriett(Bowmar) 1041
Harriett F. 1041
Henry Clinton 1041
Herschel P. 1041ff
J. D. 1042
Jas. 1041
Jane (Smith) 843
Jno. 843, 1042
Jos. P. 1041ff
Josiah B. 1042
(Lillard) 1041
Lula (Gaitskill) 863
Marg. (Walker) 1041
Martha Caroline (Jeffires)
  1041
Mary (Garrett) 1041
Mary V. J. (Garnett) 1041
Mary E. (Jeffries) 1042
Maud 1042
Merry 1042
Nancy (Dohany) 1042
Nancy B. (Willis) 1041
Nancy J. (Kertley) 1041
Nannie De Jarnett 1042
Pattie (De Jarnett) 1042
(Phelps) 1042
Polly (Kertley) 1042
Sally (Squires) 1042
Saml. 1041
Sarah B. (Barger) 1041
(Sherley) 1042
Susan (Baker) 1042
T. C. 1042
Va. (Spencer) 1042
Wm. T. 877, 1041ff
WILLISBURGH 994
WILLOCK, David 1032
Martha J. (Waddle) 1032
Phebe T. (Burge) 1032
WILLSON, W. M. Prof. 755
WILMORE, Marg. J. (Parkes) 963
WILSFORD, Amelia (Tarkington)
  1014
WILSON, Ada 1043
AgnesA. (Johnston) 798
Alice 1043
Altie 1043
Amelia H. (Hill) 1043
Andrew J. 778, 791, 1043
Annie 1043
Arminta (Blair) 791
Bettie 1043
C. J. Major 837
Cettie (Reynolds) 1044

WILSON
Chas. 1043
Clove Ann 1043
Clyde G. 778
D. N. 777
David 1043
Dicie Norticia (Van Zant)
  1043
Dicy (Dorton) 1043
Eddie S. 1044
Eliz. (Beddow) 1043
Eliz. A. (Hansford) 875
Ella A. 1044
Emily (Duggins) 1043
Emily(Owens) 778
Emma O. 778
Fanny (Coats) 1043
Frank C. Dr. 756
Franklin 1043
Gen. 823
Hannah L. (Jones) 904
Hugh W. 778, 798, 1043
Jas. C. 875
Jas. Harvey Capt. 1042
Jas. L. 1044
Jennie (Dawson) 837
Jesse T. 1043
Jno. 778, 791, 875, 1043
Jno. C. 1044
Jno. H. 939, 1043
Jno. K. 875, 1004
(Johnson) 932
Jordan 1043
Lucretia (Mershon) 1043
Lucy C. 1044
Lucy (Cotton) 831
Lucy D. (Craddock) 1044
Lucy M. (Blair) 1043
Maggie J. 1044
Marg. (Caldwell) 746
Maria (Knox) 911
Maria C. (Allin) 777
Mary 1044
Mary (Bradshaw) 798
Mary (Bolling) 795
Mary (Taylor) 1014
Mary (Templeman) 831
Mary (Thomas) 778
Mary Ann (Stephenson) 1004
Mary M. (Stearman) 1043
Mary Ruth (Anderson) 778
Mattie A. 1044
Mellisa F. (Rowe) 1043
Miller 1043
Milton 1043
Minerva J. (Grissom) 1043
(Moore) 1043
Nancy (Sparks) 1043
Norticia 1043
Olivia (Slatton) 1043
Ora 1043
Peter G. 1043
Rev. 817
RS 798, 831, 853
Roofic 1043
Sally (Bradshaw) 798
Sally (Miller) 791
Sally M. 1043
Saml. 758, 831, 1013, 1043
Saml. H. 1044
Saml. M. 1043
Sarah (Miller) 1043
Sarah S. 1044
Susan (Caperton) 751
Theresa (Summers) 786
Ursula (Stotts) 791, 1007
Wallace 751
Wash. 1043
Wm. R. 1044
WINANS, Sarah (Atkinson) 781

WINBURN, Capt. 969
Lucy (Phelps) 969
WINCHESTER, Boyd 777, 876
Gen. 904
WINDOWS, Glass-1st in Ky. 898
WINFREY, Belle (Hays) 1044
Cath. (Graves) 1044
Ellen Kate (Miller) 946
Fanny (Barger) 1044
Frank H. 1044
Frank R. 1044
Israel C. 1044
Iva Jane 1045
Izora W. (Saufley) 1045
Kate P. 1044
Matilda (Ross) 1044
Mike C. 1045
Polly (Bledsoe) 1044
Susan E. (McClure) 1044
Thos. C. Major 874, 946,
  1044
Wm. Jos. 1044
WINGATE, Esther (Ripperdam)
  855
WINN, Cath. (Herndon) 887
Clarissa (Courts) 831
WINSTON, (Anderson) 778
Jno. B. 949
Judah (Dudley) 949
Patsey (Montgomery) 949
WINTER, (Fullinwider) 934
WINTERS, Mary W. (Bruce) 804
WISE, (Hunn) 897
WISEMAN, Adeline (Welsh) 770
G. E. 770
WITCHER, (Hudson) 893
WITHERS, Eliz. (Kemper) 974,
  997
(Fleece) 797
Sarah (Welsh) 769
Sarah M. (Thompson) 957
Wm. 769
WITHROW, Nancy 857
Sallie F. (Fogle) 857
Wm. 857
WOLFORD, Col. 762, 841
G. W. 902
Gen. 913
Hannah (Johnson) 902
Jane (Grider) 968
Jno. M. Dr. 791, 968
Marg. C. (Perryman) 968
WOOD, Alice 1045
Annie 1045
Annie (Colvin) 1045
Annie (Young) 1045
Bettie (Barrett) 1045
Bettie (Carlile) 1045
Bettie M. 1045
Buford T. Dr. 1045
Clara (White) 1045
Effie H. (Cartwright) 814
Eliza 1045
Eliz. (Harris) 1045
Eliz. (Norris) 1045
Frances (Grant) 1045
Garrett 1045
Geo. T. 1045
Harriet P. (Tucker) 1045
Henry A. 1045
Isham 1045
Jas. M. 1045
January 870
Jennie 1045
Jessie E. 1045
Jno. J. 1045
Louisa (Collins) 890
Louisa D. (Hockaday) 890
Magdaline (McDowell) 930
Martha (Coovert) 1045

WOOD
　Martha (Lyons)　910
　Mary (Garnett)　1045
　Mattie　1045
　May　1045
　Nannie　1045
　Sarah F. (Phelps)　1045
　Starling　890
　Susan (Reid)　983
　Susan M. (Brown)　1045
　Thos.　1045
　Wm. T.　1017, 1045
WOODCOCK, Galien Ellett　1046
　Green B.　1046
　Henry　1046
　Jennie (Pence)　1046
　N. B.　1046
　Nannie (Jet)　1046
　(Hale)　1046
　Nancy　1046
　Robt.　1046
　Sarah (Zachary)　1046
　Sarah M.　1046
　Stephen　1046
　Wm. H.　1046
　Willis　1046
WOODS　751
　Adam　794
　Anderson　881
　Andrew　751, 794
　Archibald　748ff, 751, 760
　Betsey (Harris)　881
　Eliz. (Cobert)　825
　Eliz. (Coovert)　830
　Eliz. H. (Mitchell, Jones)
　　904
　Eliz. J. (Boggs)　793ff
　Ezekiel　965
　Hannah (Wallace)　974
　Harvey　904
　Hester (Bowman)　965
　Huldah (Carperton)　751
　Jno.　794, 904
　Lucy (Caperton)　751
　Marg. P. (Jones)　904
　Martha (Hill)　760
　Mary (Reid)　983
　Micha　965
　Michael　794
　Nancy　904
　Polly (Harris)　881
　Rachel (Pearce)　965
　Sallie (Forsythe)　858
　Saml.　965
　Sarah　904
　Susan (Miller)　943, 945ff
　Wm. B.　794, 965
WOODSIDE, Saml.　941
WOODSMALL, Jno.　907
　Sabina (Kelley)　907
WOODSON, Nancy H. (Allin)　777
　Saml. H.　742, 777, 1013
WOODWARD, Julius　873
　Mary J. (Marrs)　873
　Theo. K. (Hamilton)　873
WOODRIDGE, Fanny (Vance)　893
WOOLY, Cyrena (Dunn)　784
WORTHINGTON, Ann E. (Powell)
　　975
　C. T.　849
　Mary R. (Evans)　849
WRIGHT, Angeline E. (Moore)
　　1046
　Ann M. (Hodgen)　1046
　Cath. (Jones, Robertson,
　　Freeman)　985
　Cath. H. (Spurling)　1046
　Chas. M.　1046
　Chas. W.　1046
　Eliz. (Roots)　1046

WRIGHT
　Elmira (King)　909
　(Fields)　855
　J. W. Dr.　1003
　Jno. B.　1046
　Jno. W.　1046
　Louella (Spurlding, Penn)
　　1046
　Mary (Miller, Fields)　854
　Mary J. (Gilmore)　1046
　Matilda (Batsell)　1046
　Rachel (Estill)　944
　Rich. W.　1046
　Thos. R.　1046
WRINN, Julia A.　811
　Marry C. (Cambron)　811
　Patrick　811
WROTEN, G. W. Dr.　926
WYCOFF, Eliz. (McGohon)　1047
　(Foley)　1047
　Jno. M.　1046ff
　Jos.　1047
　Madison　1047
　Malvina (Graves)　1047
　Marg. (Raybourn)　1047
　Nich.　1047
　Obie (Cox)　833

YANCY, Nancy (Miller)　839,914
YANCEY, G. W.　970
YAKEY, Lizzie (Conn)　828
YANTES　981
YANTIS, Arethusa (Lewis)　836
YATER, Eliza A. (Terrill)　1018
YATES, Eliz. (Cleveland)　824
　Jenny (Todd)　941
YEAGER, Rachael (Brumfield)　804
YEAST, Jane (Curry)　835
YEISER, Adam　814
　Affie G. (Jackson)　1047
　Ann Maria (Caldwell)　1047
　Benj. B.　1047
　Cath. (Adams)　1047
　Cath. (Cartwright)　814
　Cath. Fauntleroy (Samuels)
　　1047
　Danl. Dr.　1047
　Fountain M.　1047
　Geo.　1047
　Henry Sr.　1047
　Jno. Jameson　1047
　Mary D. (Walworth)　1047
　Phillip E.　1047
　Rosa M.　1047
　Saml.　1047
　Sarah J. (Borden)　1047
　Susan (Walker)　814
YELL, Archibald Gov.　766
　Nancy Jordan (Moore)　766
YEOWS, Lucy (Gentry)　952
YERKES, Alice (Van Meter)　1029
　Amanda (Lovell)　1029, 1047
　Amelia R.　1048
　Eliz. O. (Anderson)　1048
　Jno. W.　1047ff
　Lovell S.　1048
　Stephen Rev.　1029, 1047
　(Wadron)　1048
YEWELL, A. Judson　1048
　Belle　1048
　Bemis　1048
　Eliza　1048
　Eliz. (McGeehee)　1048
　Harrison　1048
　Isabel　1048
　Jas.　1048
　Jno. M.　1048
　Jos.　1048
　Lavina (Nall)　1048
　Marg. (Beam)　1048

YEWELL
　Martin　1048
　Morgan R.　1048
　Nancy (Brown)　1048
　Nancy (Foreman)　1048
　Rebecca　1048
　(Shirley)　1048
　Susan C. (Bell)　1048
　Vardaman　1048
YOUNG　985
　Amanda (Wheeler)　1048
　Annie　1048
　Annie (Wood)　1045
　Bennett H.　755
　Camilla (Irvin)　898
　Cecil　1048
　Charlie　1048
　Cynthia (Terhune)　985
　David　1029, 1048
　Dominie Rev.　817
　Eliz. (Graham)　865
　Eliz. (Hill)　760
　Eliz. (Hood)　892
　Eliz. (McFerran)　931
　Eliz. (Murphy)　954
　Emma　1048
　Flora A.　1048
　Franklin　1048
　Geo.　1048
　H. T.　1048
　Jane (Springer)　1048
　Jennie E. (LInney)　1048
　Jno.　1045
　Jno. C. Rev.　742
　Lucinda I. (Van Pelt)　1029
　Mary J. (Stotts)　1007
　Matilda (Martin)　936
　Nancy　1029
　Patrick　936
　Sallie (Gibbs)　1045
　Sallie (Huffman)　895
　Sally (Breeding)　800
　Wm.　760, 1048
YOUNGER, Helen Lee (Evans)　757
YOWELL, Rhoda (Tucker)　963

ZACHARY, Sarah (Woodcock)　1046
　Wm.　1046
ZACHERY, Eliz. (Herndon)　887

62